THE WG&L HANDBOOK OF

FINANCIAL MARKETS

EDITOR

DENNIS E. LOGUE

AMOS TUCK SCHOOL OF BUSINESS ADMINISTRATION
DARTMOUTH COLLEGE

WARREN, GORHAM & LAMONT

COLLEGE DIVISION South-Western Publishing Co.

Cincinnati Ohio

Acquisitions Editor: Christopher Will
Production Editors: Sharon Smith and Sue Ellen Brown
Marketing Manager: Denise Carlson
Cover Designer: Lotus Wittkopf

FI62AA
Copyright © 1995
by
South-Western College Publishing
Cincinnati, Ohio
and Warren Gorham Lamont

1 2 3 4 5 6 MA 9 8 7 6 5 4

Printed in the United States of America

Library of Congress Cataloging-in-Publication Data

The WG&L handbook of financial markets / editor, Dennis E. Logue.
    p. cm.
   Includes bibliographical references and index.
   ISBN 0-538-84250-4
   1. Finance. 2. Financial services industry. 3. Investment
banking. 4. Money market. 5. Business mathematics. 6. Securities.
7. Options (Finance) 8. Financial futures. 9. Auctions.
I. Logue, Dennis E.
HG173.W47 1995
332.1—dc20   94-20612
                                          CIP

 I(T)P

International Thomson Publishing

South-Western College Publishing is an ITP Company. The ITP trademark is used under license.

 This book is printed on acid-free paper that meets Environmental Protection Agency standards for recycled paper.

Preface

As the editor for the W, G, & L *Handbook of Modern Finance, Third Edition,* I am happy to note that South-Western Publishing Company is publishing this series of five "break-out" readings books for use in your classroom:

The W, G, & L *Handbook of International Finance*
The W, G, & L *Handbook of Financial Markets*
The W, G, & L *Handbook of Securities and Investment Management*
The W, G, & L *Handbook of Financial Policy*
The W, G, & L *Handbook of Short-Term and Long-Term Financial Management.*

These readers make a unique contribution to the classroom in that they are written primarily from the practitioner's point of view; showing students how the principles they are learning in class can be applied to real-world financial problems.

Thus they are ideally suited to supplement courses in Corporate Finance, Investments, Capital Markets, Financial Institutions, and International Finance both at the undergraduate and MBA level. They are also ideally suited for use in an executive education program.

These readers cover virtually every major technical, analytical, and theoretical financial question likely to be raised by active, inquisitive corporate financial and business executives, strategic planners, accountants (public and private), attorneys, security analysts, and bankers. They provide your students with insights for solving day-to-day business problems as well as provide guidance in long-term planning. Institutional arrangements are explained; relevant economic and financial theory and its application are presented and described. In addition, sophisticated quantitative analyses are presented in the context of real-world examples, numerous figures illustrate textual explanations, and end-of-chapter readings direct interested readers to additional technical literature in the field. The intent has been to produce a series of readings books that will help students understand the practical applications of the theory presented in their textbooks, thus helping them become better-prepared business professionals.

The W, G, & L *Handbook of Financial Markets* deals with financial institutions and markets. Not only does it explain how the markets currently operate, but it draws inferences regarding how the markets might evolve. Furthermore, valuation concepts and ways in which these markets (e.g., options and futures) might be used by practitioners are thoroughly explored. Contributors include:

John P. Colligan
Senior Vice-President, Emerging Markets, Kidder, Peabody & Co., Inc.

Thomas E. Copeland
Consultant, McKinsey & Company

Robert Hanson
Professor, Amos Tuck School of Business Administration, Dartmouth College

Alan G. Jirkovsky
Vice-President, Continental Illinois National Bank

Timothy W. Koch
S.C. Bankers Association Chair of Banking, College of Business Administration, University of South Carolina

Richard W. McEnally
Meade H. Willis Senior Professor of Investment Banking, Kenan-Flagler Business School, University of North Carolina at Chapel Hill

George G. C. Parker
Senior Lecturer in Management and Director of Executive Education, Graduate School of Business, Stanford University

Andrew Rudd
Managing Director, BARRA

Thomas Schneeweis
Professor of Finance, School of Management, University of Massachusetts

Hans R. Stoll
Anne Marie and Thomas B. Walker, Jr. Professor of Finance, Owen Graduate School of Management, Vanderbilt University

T. Craig Tapley
Assistant Dean and Director of Undergraduate Programs, College of Business Administration, University of Florida

J. Peter Williamson
Professor, Amos Tuck School of Business Administration, Dartmouth College

Jot Yau
Assistant Professor of Finance, George Mason University

The editor wants to thank all of the authors who have worked so hard to produce highly focused chapters with a strong managerial slant. All are to be thanked and congratulated.

In addition to the authors, thanks must also go to Audrey Hanlon, who helped organize the work done by Tuck; Beverly Salbin of Warren Gorman Lamont, who brought so much to the party that she deserves much more recognition than this; and to Leora Harris and Vibert Gale, also of WGL, whose skills contributed so much to the final product.

Finally, I want to thank South-Western Publishing Company for bringing these readers to the college market.

DENNIS E. LOGUE

Hanover, New Hampshire
November 1993

Contents

CONTENTS

THE WG&L HANDBOOK OF

FINANCIAL MARKETS

Chapter 1

The Financial Services Industry

JOHN P. COLLIGAN

1.01 INTRODUCTION

In a world of expanding free markets and capitalism, the financial services industry continues to evolve, shaping and redefining the 24-hour global marketplace at breakneck speed.

Banks, nonbank financial institutions, and investment banks make up the financial services industry. The competition is intense and increasing, information is needed instantaneously, and market actions do not wait for board meetings or strategic planning sessions. The evolution of the financial services industry demands that institutions have the ability to anticipate changes in the markets in which they compete.

Four major forces are driving the changes in the financial services industry: globalization, technology, securitization,[1] and deregulation. This chapter explores the impact of these forces on different sectors of the financial services industry, and highlights the immediate trends using specific examples for banks, nonbanks, and investment banks from the perspective of an active participant in the international capital markets.

1.02 MAJOR ISSUES CONFRONTING THE GLOBAL BANKING SYSTEM

Banking is a complex, 24-hour global business that processes market information and moves money around the world rapidly. As the speed of banking has increased, so have the systematic risks. In October 1992, Alan Greenspan, Chairman of the Federal Reserve Board (Fed), warned that global financial transactions may be too fast and too complex for senior bank managers to understand, and he called on governments to step up their supervision of international banks. Greenspan emphasized that "the transition from manual, paper-based banking to split-second electronic systems may not have been managed by those sufficiently sensitive to credit and risk exposure." Today, money moves faster and in larger volume. The United States' Fedwire and Clearing House Interbank Payment System (CHIPS)[2] handle the equivalent of the gross domestic product (GDP) every 2.5 days. Japan's counterpart, the BOJ-Net, turns over an amount equal to the GDP every 3 days, and the United Kingdom's system turns over an amount equal to the GDP every 4 days. More than 90 percent of this volume is from financial market transactions. The global banking system has been slow to adapt to new technology, new competition, and customer needs and, as a result, is colliding with the nonbanks in the financial services market.

The nonbank financial institutions are forcing the banking system to reexamine and redefine its historical role of collecting deposits and making loans. In the United States, the banking system continues to aggressively push for expanded powers and Glass-Steagall[3] reform. The Glass-Steagall framework, now 60 years old, has put banks at a major disadvantage in the intensely competitive financial services industry. In Figure

---

[1] Securitization involves the repackaging of illiquid loans such as home mortgages, car loans, and credit card receivables into liquid, tradable fixed-income securities.

[2] CHIPS enables banks to make and receive payments from other banks by using accounts held at the central bank.

[3] The Glass-Steagall Banking Act of 1933 was enacted to prevent banks from competing with each other and with other financial institutions. It also separated investment banking from commercial banking, prohibited payment of interest on demand deposits, and gave the Fed the power to set maximum interest rates on bank time deposits (Regulation Q).

1-1, the major trend toward capital markets and securitization and away from banks and bank deposits is evident. In 1980, deposits represented 24 percent of U.S. household financial assets, while money market funds and mutual funds represented just 2 percent. Ten years later, bank deposits slipped to 19 percent, while money market and mutual fund shares have jumped to 7 percent. The banks are losing business to the nonbanks and investment banks.

In Europe, the banking system is bracing for a bigger, more competitive market. In 1993, 12 European nations will open up their borders to create one market. This in turn will allow members of one country to open bank accounts and borrow from financial institutions in the other European Community (EC) countries. Figure 1-2 shows the high concentration of the European banking industry. On average, the top 5 banks control more than 50 percent of the total deposits in a country. This deposit concentration and the deregulation of savings has intensified the competitive pressures among EC financial institutions. European banks and insurance companies have recognized a global demographic shift toward decreased borrowing and increased saving. This trend has led to a new European financial conglomerate. Banks and insurance companies are combining through mergers or joint ventures because investment and insurance products are more profitable than banking products and services. Figure 1-3 highlights some of these European bank-insurance combinations. This selling of financial services to an aging and sophisticated population is called *bancassurance* in France, and *allfinanz* in Germany.

Since 1990, the Japanese have been forced to turn their focus internally. The painful process of real estate and stock price deflation and the bursting of the speculative "bubble" from the 1980s expansion will continue to require careful attention. Despite this deflationary contraction, the Japanese still dominate world banking, in contrast to a decade earlier, when the U.K. and U.S. banks were dominant. Figure 1-4 shows that the 4 largest and 6 of the 10 largest banks in the world are Japanese. Figure 1-5 defines the size and distribution of financial assets in the Japanese banking system.

[1] Capital Adequacy

One of the most important issues in global banking is capital adequacy. Over the past four years, global bank regulators, in an attempt to minimize both specific and systematic financial crisis, have sought to define and enforce new guidelines for capital adequacy in the world's banking system.

Capital is crucial in the financing of fixed assets and feeding of new investments. In banking, capital also underpins lending and protects depositors. Bank managements seek to maximize risk-adjusted returns, while bank regulators try to minimize risk and bank shareholders target maximum returns. "The capital level of a bank is thus subject to conflicting requirements of bank managements, regulators and investors," concludes a 1992 Salomon Brothers research report entitled *Capital Adequacy: Are Regulators and Investors on a Collision Course? What Capital Level Does the World's Banking System Need?*

In 1988, the Basel Committee on Banking Regulations and Supervisory Practices, consisting of central bankers and supervisory authorities from Belgium, Canada, France, Germany, Italy, Japan, the Netherlands, Sweden, the United Kingdom, and the United States, signed an accord that made capital a top global banking priority. The accord had two basic objectives: first, to protect depositors by establishing a minimum capital base for the global banking system, and second, to level the interna-

FIGURE 1-1
U.S. Household Financial Assets

Source: Federal Reserve Board; First Boston Equity Research

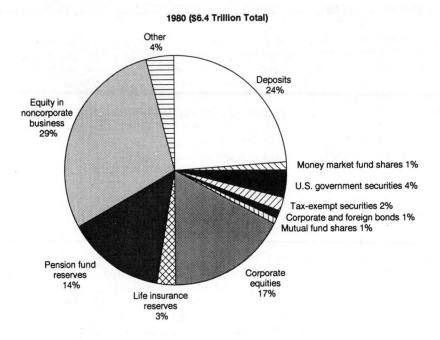

1980 ($6.4 Trillion Total)

- Other 4%
- Deposits 24%
- Money market fund shares 1%
- U.S. government securities 4%
- Tax-exempt securities 2%
- Corporate and foreign bonds 1%
- Mutual fund shares 1%
- Corporate equities 17%
- Life insurance reserves 3%
- Pension fund reserves 14%
- Equity in noncorporate business 29%

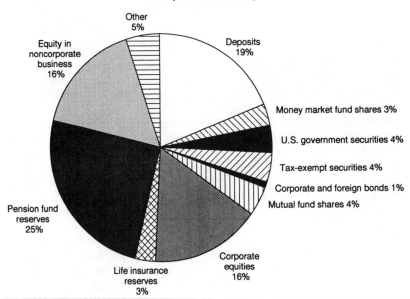

1991 ($15.2 Trillion Total)

- Other 5%
- Deposits 19%
- Money market fund shares 3%
- U.S. government securities 4%
- Tax-exempt securities 4%
- Corporate and foreign bonds 1%
- Mutual fund shares 4%
- Corporate equities 16%
- Life insurance reserves 3%
- Pension fund reserves 25%
- Equity in noncorporate business 16%

FIGURE 1-2

Market Concentration (1989)

Source: McKinsey; "A Survey of World Banking," The Economist *(May 1992)*

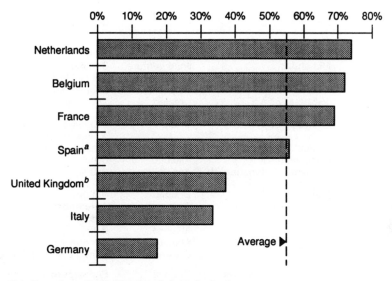

Note: Percentage of total client deposits in top five banks.
a 1990.
b Excludes all overseas deposits.

tional playing field. The banking system had until the end of 1992 to meet the capital conditions under the new accord.

The Basel ratios, also referred to as the (Bank for International Settlements) BIS ratios, required that banks hold $8 of capital for every $100 of lending. A minimum of half of the capital must be equity or near equity called tier 1 capital. The remainder may consist of subordinated debt, provisions against unexpected loan losses, and other elements of riskier tier 2 capital. For example, commercial loans required $8 of capital; home mortgages, $4; and government loans or bonds, zero capital.

Since 1988, banks have boosted capital ratios. The stronger banks have issued debt and equity in the capital markets, investing in lower risk-weighted assets and executing off-balance sheet transactions such as derivatives.[4] The weaker banks were priced out of the capital markets and were forced to sell loans, cut back on new lending, and invest in lower-risk-weighted assets or off-balance sheet products. In 1989 and 1990,

---

[4] Derivatives include futures, warrants, swaps, swaptions, collars, floors, caps, circuses, and others. Derivatives are recently developed tools for managing financial risk. Under the Basel accord, derivatives received very favorable risk weightings. According to the BIS, outstanding derivatives have exploded from $1 trillion in 1986 to almost $8 trillion at the end of 1991. This new market has also become an increasing concern of global regulators.

FIGURE 1-3

European Banks and Insurance

Source: The Boston Consulting Group; "A Survey of World Banking," The Economist *(May 1992)*

	Purchaser	Result	Company Purchased
United Kingdom	Barclays	Created	Barclays Life[a]
	National Westminster	Joint venture	Clerical Medical[a]
	Midland	Joint venture	Commercial Union[a]
	Lloyds	Acquisition	Abbey Life[a]
	Abbey National	Acquisition	Scottish Mutual[a]
	TSB	Created	TSB Trust[a]
Germany	Deutsche Bank	Created	Lebensversicherungs AG der Deutschen Bank[a]
	Allianz[a]	Alliance	Dresdner Bank
	Commerzbank	Alliance	DBV[a]
	Aachener & Münchener[a]	Acquisition	BfG
France	BNP	Created	Natiovie[a]
	Crédit Lyonnais	Created	Assurances Fédérales Vie[a]
	Crédit Agricole	Created	Predica[a]
	UAP[a]	Alliance	BNP
	UAP[a]	Acquisition	Banque Worms
	AGF[a]	Created	Banque Générale de Crédit
Spain	Banco Bilbao Vizcaya	Created	Euroseguros;[a] Aurora Polar[a]
	Mapfre[a]	Created	Banco Mapfre

[a] Insurance company.

FIGURE 1-4

Ten Largest Banks by Capital

Source: The Banker; *"A Survey of World Banking,"* The Economist *(May 1992)*

1980	Capital	1990	Capital
Crédit Agricole	$6.2	Sumitomo	$15.7
National Westminster	5.1	Dai-Ichi Kangyo	14.8
Barclays	4.8	Fuji	13.8
Bank America	3.9	Sanwa	13.4
Citicorp	3.9	Union Bank of Switzerland	13.2
Banco do Brasil	3.6	Crédit Agricole	13.2
Lloyds	3.3	Mitsui Taiyo Kobe	12.2
Midland	3.2	Barclays	11.9
Paribas	3.0	Mitsubishi	11.9
Algemene Spaar-en Lijfrenteras	3.0	National Westminster	10.7

Note: Dollars in billions.

FIGURE 1-5

Japanese Financial Assets by Institution (January 1992)

Source: Bank of Japan; "A Survey of World Banking," The Economist (May 1992)

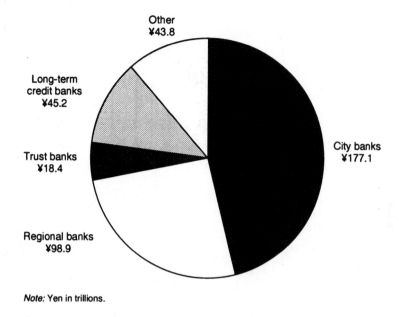

Other
¥43.8

Long-term
credit banks
¥45.2

Trust banks
¥18.4

City banks
¥177.1

Regional banks
¥98.9

Note: Yen in trillions.

most major banking groups achieved the Basel 8 percent capital guideline. Figure 1-6 shows the world's major banks ranked by the ratio of capital to risk-weighted assets, and Figure 1-7 shows the average capital ratios by country.

Despite compliance with the capital guidelines, the evidence suggests that the international playing field remains uneven. When the guidelines were negotiated, individual interests resulted in watered-down, multiple definitions for tier 2 capital. Unfortunately, there are almost as many different definitions of "tier 2 capital" as countries on the Basel Committee. National regulators monitoring undercapitalized banks in weak economies have taken advantage of this deficiency in the tier 2 definition. Though not alone, Japanese banks have been the most aggressive, counting 45 percent of unrealized gains on their securities holdings as tier 2 capital. This gives them a major advantage over their international competitors. However, it also creates risk, because the capital ratios are vulnerable to stock market drops. For example, in 1992, the Japanese stock market index (Nikkei) fell 22 percent to close at 16,924. Many large commercial banks are not in compliance with the Basel capital guidelines when the Nikkei is below 20,000. These commercial banks were forced to find a solution to this before March 31, 1993, the end of the Japanese fiscal year.

In addition to increasing the level of capital, the new framework of the Basel accord encourages governments to supervise and become proactive with the banking community. It also promotes a shift away from the 1980s mania for asset growth, to a more

FIGURE 1-6
Today's Capital

Source: IBCA; "A Survey of World Banking," The Economist (May 1992)

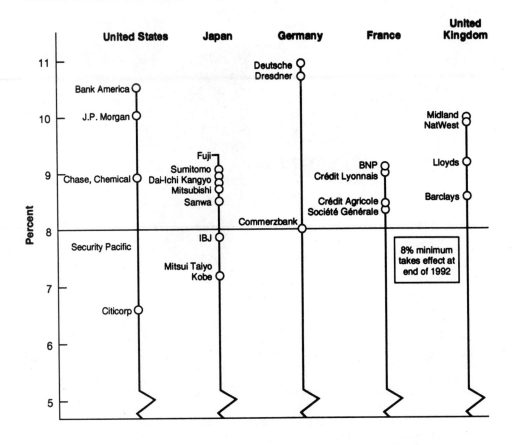

disciplined pursuit of profitability. In a 1991 report, *Bank Asset Quality: A Global Profile,* Salomon Brothers' "overwhelming conclusion is that management, not external conditions, is the key determinant for asset quality." It also stated that "the single best predictor of future asset quality problems is the rate of loan growth. Virtually all of the recent major asset quality problems stem from previous 20% plus annual growth rates."

U.S. banks have led the market shift, emphasizing the quality, not just the quantity, of bank lending. Bankers Trust's new tool for asset quality control, risk-adjusted return on capital (RAROC), systematically measures the expected return on an investment of capital adjusted for risk. Ironically, this new, more disciplined focus on how to

FIGURE 1-7

Average Capital Ratios by Country (1989–1990)

Source: IBCA; J. Leonard, D. Glossman, and J. Naschek, Capital Adequacy (New York: Salomon Brothers Inc., Jan. 1992)

	1989			1990		
	Tier 1	Tier 2	Total	Tier 1	Tier 2	Total
Australia	5.9%	3.8%	9.7%	5.5%	3.8%	9.3%
Canada	5.0	2.5	7.5	5.3	2.6	7.9
France	5.0	3.1	8.1	5.1	3.3	8.4
Germany	5.0	5.0	10.0	NA	NA	NA
Japan	4.2	3.8	8.0	4.4	4.1	8.5
Spain	7.7	2.3	10.0	9.2	2.3	11.5
United Kingdom	5.2	3.7	8.9	5.4	3.5	8.9
United States[a]	5.6	4.1	9.7	5.6	4.0	9.6

Note: Fiscal year ended closest to December 31 of respective year.

[a] Money centers.

price risk and allocate capital also reinforces the global shift from lending toward securitization. When a risk can be priced systematically, it can be traded like a security. Investment banks and nonbanks are more efficient at trading and distribution than the banks. The stronger, better-performing banks understand this and are accelerating the investment of people and capital toward achieving the trading and distribution elements.

The experience since the Basel accord highlights the difficulty in the deregulation-regulation balancing act in the international banking system. In the Salomon Brothers capital adequacy study, the authors emphasized that "in our view, banks succeed or fail in the marketplace not only because of capital ratios, but also because of their ability to generate sustained superior earnings, to minimize the level of problem loans and to enjoy sufficient liquidity through a substantial retail franchise or adept asset/liability management."

1.03 SUCCESS AND FAILURE IN U.S. BANKING

J.P. Morgan and Bankers Trust are two examples of U.S. money center banks that are succeeding in the market. They are strongly capitalized and generate sustained earnings relative to global banking competitors. In 1990, the Fed recognized the strength of both and rewarded the institutions by allowing them to expand into some activities that Glass-Steagall prevented. After two years, their strong performances have continued to be compelling forces behind the banking industry's push to break down Glass-Steagall.

The keys to J.P. Morgan's success were reviewed by Chairman Dennis Weatherstone in the February 1992 letter to shareholders: "Accelerating changes in global markets led to a program of expansion and diversification." This program began 10 years ago, and Weatherstone credited these new or expanded capabilities for 1991's strong performance. "J.P. Morgan's strategy has three major thrusts. First, growth through focused diversification, specifically, underwriting and dealing in corporate securities; trading developing country debt; commodities and a host of derivative instruments; also providing merger and acquisition advice in Europe and Asia. The second area is to emphasize client relationship development. Finally, the third area is to balance investment, people and technology with cost control." Analyzing J.P. Morgan's revenues highlights the powerful impact of trading on this financial institution. In 1991, $1.297 billion, or 32 percent of total revenue, was generated by trading. The trading revenue was 48 percent from swaps and derivatives and 36 percent from debt instruments.

Bankers Trust credited broad-based capital markets, global trading, and fiduciary and funds management businesses with providing record 1991 results. Record trading revenue of $1.2 billion represented about 37 percent of total revenue. Trading revenues were principally generated from foreign exchange, interest rate, currency, equity and commodity derivatives, and developing country debt. Bankers Trust highlighted rigorous cost control and technology. Technology continues to play a critical role both as an information processing and communication tool and as an analytical tool for managing risk in Bankers Trust's drive for global leadership. Furthermore, it cited the strength of its capital position and the enhancement achieved through RAROC. Bankers Trust believes that quality earnings are diversified and sustainable through its five principal business functions: client finance, client advisory, client financial risk management, client transaction processing, and trading and positioning risks. Underscoring the global nature of the firm, 60 percent of Bankers Trust's earnings are derived from activities outside of the United States.

Both J.P. Morgan and Bankers Trust are thriving and competing head to head with the big investment banks in most activities. In fact, both institutions are more like investment banks than commercial banks. While J.P. Morgan and Bankers Trust are not the only examples of success, they are among the market leaders. In addition, they are both far ahead of other banks in the financial services market with the integration of trading, distribution, and risk management.

In contrast to J.P. Morgan and Bankers Trust, the Bank of New England is an example of failure in the U.S. banking system. In 1989, the Bank of New England was the United States' fifteenth largest bank, with assets of $32 billion. It was viewed as a prototype superregional. Leading an aggressive 1980s charge into lending, the bank extended credit at a rapid clip. Property developers and commercial and industrial borrowers all leveraged themselves with the help of the Bank of New England to ride the New England construction wave. The wave passed, and, by the end of 1990, 20 percent, or $3.2 billion, of the Bank of New England loan portfolio was nonperforming. On January 6, 1991, the Bank of New England collapsed under that weight and became the United States' third-biggest bank failure in history. The Federal Deposit Insurance Corporation (FDIC) took control as a quasi receiver and, to avert panic, guaranteed 100 percent of depositors' money ($16 billion in deposits) even for deposits above the $100,000 single-account ceiling. In addition to angering depositors in smaller banks that had failed previously, the FDIC's deposit insurance fund was overwhelmed and rapidly approached insolvency. In April 1992, the FDIC reported that the deposit insurance fund had a deficit of approximately $8 billion whereas a year earlier it had a $4 billion surplus. The collapse of the so-called safety net continues to be at the center of debate over the crisis in the U.S. banking system.

FIGURE 1-8

U.S. Bank Failures by Assets

Source: Federal Deposit Insurance Corporation; "A Survey of World Banking," The Economist *(May 1992)*

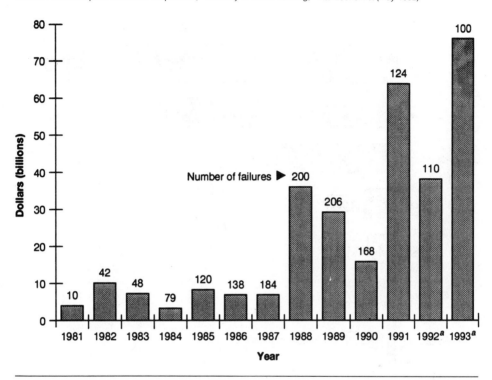

1.04 CONSOLIDATION IN U.S. BANKING

The Bank of New England story illustrates many of the challenges facing the U.S. banking system today. This case included mismanagement, excessive lending growth rates that resulted in asset quality deterioration, lack of diversification, eventual insolvency, and an FDIC deposit insurance fund crisis. Figure 1-8 highlights the rising tide of U.S. bank failures. This has heightened the anxiety and the awareness of the fundamental need for banking reform. As this is written, there are approximately 12,000 federally insured commercial banks in the United States. The consensus is that there are still too many banks chasing less business at ever-decreasing margins. Thus, the trend toward fewer U.S. banks will continue. Figure 1-9 measures the dimensions of the capacity glut in the U.S. banking system. Relative to the major international banking competitors, the United States has more banks banking fewer assets. For example, the United States has almost 18 times as many banks yet only 3 percent of the average assets per bank as Japan.

Figure 1-10 shows the foreign banks operating in the United States. Japanese institutions are also dominant in this category, accounting for 60 percent of commercial and

FIGURE 1-9

Average Assets per Bank (Year-End 1990)

Source: Bank of America; "A Survey of World Banking," The Economist *(May 1992)*

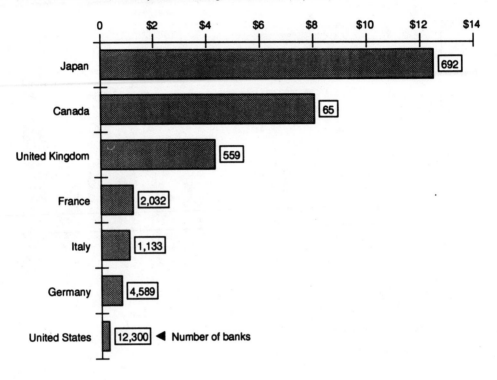

industrial loans, 50 percent of deposits, and 54 percent of assets. In this overcrowded market, more banks will fail while others will be acquired or merge. It has been estimated that by the year 2000, only 3,000 to 9,000 banks will survive. For example, in 1991–1992, the 300 largest banks acquired 409 banks with total deposits of $236 billion. Most of the acquisitions were made by the superregionals. NationsBank and Banc One have been among the most aggressive acquirors. Their acquisition strategies have become a model for growth and have propelled them into the top 10 of the biggest banks in the United States.

The most visible examples of the U.S. banking consolidation trend are the megamergers. The Fed and regulators have encouraged these consolidation strategies. For example, Bank of America and Security Pacific merged, creating an institution with $194 billion in assets, the second-largest U.S. bank after Citicorp. Chemical New York and Manufacturers Hanover, also staying within the same regional market, formed the third-largest U.S. bank, with $135 billion in assets. Through mergers, banks are

FIGURE 1-10

Foreign Banks in the United States: Market Position (June 30, 1990)

Source: American Banker *(Mar. 22, 1991)*; T. Hanley et al., Bank Asset Quality: A Global Profile *(New York: Salomon Brothers Inc., Oct. 1991)*

Country	Number of Banks	Offices[a]	Commercial and Industrial		Deposits		Assets	
			Amount	Percentage of Total	Amount	Percentage of Total	Amount	Percentage of Total
Japan	45	137	$113.9	60.0	$189.0	50.1	$408.9	54.0
United Kingdom	11	42	12.3	6.5	28.8	7.6	38.6	5.1
Italy	13	27	10.3	5.4	14.3	3.8	46.6	6.2
Canada	6	49	9.8	5.2	19.4	5.1	42.8	5.7
Hong Kong	10	30	5.6	2.9	19.7	5.2	25.9	3.4
France	15	37	5.3	2.8	15.9	4.2	33.2	4.4
Netherlands	4	27	4.7	2.5	9.0	2.4	15.7	2.1
Israel	4	23	3.3	1.7	10.9	2.9	12.5	1.7
Switzerland	6	17	3.0	1.6	12.1	3.2	22.4	3.0
Spain	8	27	2.9	1.5	9.2	2.4	13.2	1.7
Others	166	302	18.8	9.9	49.3	13.1	97.6	12.9
Total	288	718	$189.9	100.0	$377.6	100.0	$757.4	100.0

Note: Dollars in billions.
[a] Excludes branches of subsidiary banks.

trying to cut costs, generate capital, and shrink competition, which ultimately should improve future bank profitability.

Figure 1-11 shows changes in the past decade, the emergence of the superregionals (NationsBank and Banc One), and the decline and consolidation of the U.S. money center banks. After the consolidation trend, the key question is, Will the survivors be stronger and more profitable or larger, unfocused, and endangered?

1.05 DEPOSIT INSURANCE REFORM FALLS SHORT

In November 1991, Congress passed the Federal Deposit Insurance Corporation Improvement Act (FDICIA). What started out as a bold, meaningful plan to overhaul the U.S. financial system ended as a deposit insurance fund bailout, with tighter regulatory constraints.

The 1991 attempt at reform began on track, only to be derailed by a gridlocking, special-interest-driven political system. The original bill package included deposit insurance reform, an attempt to improve on the "too big to fail" doctrine and alleviate the stress this created in the banking system. It also included regulatory reform, proposing one superregulator instead of three for the Office of the Comptroller of the Currency, which regulates nationally chartered banks; the Office of Thrift and Supervision, which regulates savings and loan associations (S&Ls), and the Fed, which regu-

FIGURE 1-11

Ten Largest U.S. Banks by Assets

Source: American Banker; *"A Survey of World Banking,"* The Economist *(May 1992)*

End 1981[a]	Location	Assets	June 1991	Location	Assets
BankAmerica	San Francisco	$181.4	Citicorp	New York	$217.4
Citicorp	New York	178.4	BankAmerica[b]	San Francisco	193.6
Chase Manhattan	New York	115.0	Chemical Bank[b]	New York	135.4
Manufacturers Hanover	New York	88.5	NationsBank[b]	Charlotte, North Carolina	118.2
J.P. Morgan	New York	80.1	Chase Manhattan	New York	98.5
Continental Illinois	Chicago	70.4	J.P. Morgan	New York	96.9
Chemical New York	New York	67.2	Bankers Trust	New York	58.9
First Interstate Bancorp	Los Angeles	55.4	Wells Fargo	San Francisco	54.4
Bankers Trust	New York	51.2	First Interstate Bancorp	Los Angeles	50.3
First Chicago	Chicago	50.3	Banc One[c]	Columbus, Ohio	49.3

Note: Dollars in billions.

[a] 1981 prices inflated by U.S. consumer prices.

[b] Assuming completion of proposed mergers (Bank America and Security Pacific; Chemical and Manufacturers Hanover, NCNB and C&S Sovran).

[c] Assuming consolidation of Texas operations and three minor mergers.

lates bank holding companies. The original bill also focused on the critical structural reform, including repeal of the Glass-Steagall Act of 1933, which separates commercial from investment banking; the McFadden Act of 1927, which prevents banks from doing business across state borders; and the Bank Holding Company Act, which limits the nonbanking activities of banks. The Bank Holding Company Act prevents universal banking,[5] which has been effective in other countries. In addition, the original bill would have allowed nonfinancial companies to own commercial banks. This would strengthen the financial system by attracting capital from outside of the industry. Indeed, companies such as General Electric (GE), Ford Motor, and Sears already own big, sophisticated financial subsidiaries that are part of the nonbank financial sector of the financial services industry.

Unfortunately, deposit insurance, regulatory, and structural reforms did not happen; the FDICIA did. The FDICIA's main objective was to reduce banking risk through tougher enforcement of capital requirements. Critics charge that it ignores the impact of technological changes in financial services. Today, more traditional banking is being done by nonbanks, and more banks are nontraditional. For example, as Figure 1-12

---

[5] In countries where investment banking and commercial banking are combined, a single financial institution may take deposits, make loans, purchase securities for investment or resale, and engage in all types of financial transactions for corporate and individual customers.

shows, banks are holding more U.S. government bonds. Instead of traditional commercial and industrial credit-risk lending, banks are pouring billions into U.S. Treasury bonds, in effect lending to the risk-free credit of the U.S. government. The explosion in U.S. Treasury purchases by banks was a result of both weak loan demand (during the 1990–1991 recession) and tighter capital regulations from the Basel accord. The last time commercial banks held more government bonds than commercial and industrial loans was in 1965. However, with this trade-off, bank portfolios have increased their interest rate risk. As Figure 1-12 illustrates, this shift away from loans into securities has been dramatic. According to the FDIC, in 1991 banks added $56 billion in U.S. Treasury notes and bonds, accounting for most of the portfolio growth. The portfolios are weighted towards one-to-five-year maturities yielding 4 percent to 6 percent at year-end 1992, which compares very favorably with interest rates of 3 percent or less on passbook savings accounts. However, the volatility of interest rates and yield curves could eliminate this attractive spread at any moment with little or no warning. The risk of an interest rate mismatch between assets and liabilities could cause large losses in bank portfolios, like the U.S. thrift debacle, which will ultimately cost taxpayers at least $200 billion to clean up.

This trend of converting bank deposits into government securities is another example of the threat to the banks' declining role as intermediaries between borrowers and lenders. Are the securities markets more efficient? Will yesterday's bank loan officer become a security portfolio manager tomorrow? As the customers and even the providers of financial services go directly to the capital markets, securitization will accelerate and the banking industry will continue to consolidate.

1.06 NONBANK FINANCIAL INSTITUTIONS

Nonbank financial institutions can be categorized as thrift institutions, such as S&Ls, mutual savings banks, and credit unions; contractual institutions such as life insurance and property insurance underwriters and private and public pension funds; investment institutions such as money market funds, mutual funds, security dealers and brokers; and other nonbank financial institutions such as finance companies, mortgage companies, and real estate investment trusts. The primary objective of these nonbank financial institutions is to maximize shareholder, depositor, policyholder, and beneficiary wealth through the delivery of superior financial products and services demanded by savers and borrowers in the international capital markets.

There are also nonbank financial institutions whose primary mission is public policy, e.g., the Fed, the Social Security Administration and other federal and state government pension funds, federal lending agencies such as the Federal National Mortgage Association (FNMA or Fannie Mae), Government National Mortgage Association (GNMA or Ginnie Mae), Federal Home Loan Mortgage Corporation (FHLMC or Freddie Mac), Student Loan Marketing Association (SLMA or Sallie Mae), Federal Home Loan Banks, Federal Land banks, Federal Farm Credit System, Export-Import Bank, Commodity Credit Corporation, and Rural Electrification Administration.

[1] Government-Sponsored Enterprises

The government-sponsored federal lending agencies, the FNMA, FHLMC and SLMA, are hybrid government-private companies, established to finance the public policy

FIGURE 1-12

Commercial Banks' Holdings of Commercial and Industrial Loans and U.S. Government Securities

Source: Federal Reserve Board: "What Are Banks for?" The Economist (July 11, 1992)

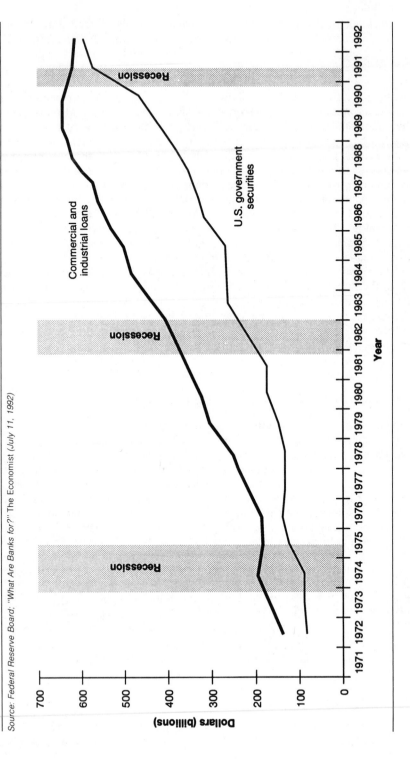

goals of making home ownership and college education available to more Americans. For example, the two largest government-sponsored enterprises (GSEs), FNMA and FHLMC, buy mortgages from primary lenders such as banks, mortgage banks, and S&Ls. They then bring Wall Street's investment banks into the process and repackage the mortgages into securities. Finally, with assistance from the investment banks, they sell and distribute the new securities to end investors in the international capital markets. The end investors, such as banks, S&Ls, insurance companies, mutual funds, and pension funds, are attracted to mortgage-backed securities (MBSs) because they pay interest rates almost one percent higher than comparable government bonds and are equal in credit risk. Their unique hybrid ownership structure has enabled GSE debt issues to carry a government guarantee, which provides virtually unlimited access to capital in the international capital markets. Figure 1-13 illustrates this mortgage chain in detail and highlights the close integration of the GSEs with many of the players in the financial services industry.

The GSEs have been among the most powerful forces in the securitization boom; in essence, they are securitization. Their borrowing has exploded from $37 billion in 1970 to more than $1 trillion today. The magnitude of the mortgage-backed securitization trend is illustrated in Figure 1-14. The first MBS was issued in 1970, and, owing to the real estate, debt, and securitization explosion of the 1980s, MBSs totaled $1.2 trillion by the end of 1991.

[2] Resolution Trust Corporation

In 1989, Congress passed the Financial Institutions Reform, Recovery, and Enforcement Act (FIRREA), which set up the Resolution Trust Corporation (RTC) to execute the huge bailout of the U.S. government's S&L insurance program. The legislation authorized funds to shut down and liquidate insolvent thrifts, more than 500 of them immediately. Some of the funding came from increasing S&L insurance premiums, but most of the funding came from debt issued directly and indirectly by the U.S. government through the RTC. As a result, the RTC became a frequent borrower in the international bond markets. The final cost of the operation, including interest on the debt issued, is expected to exceed $300 billion. Thus, the RTC, almost overnight, became a large, important player in the nonbank financial institutions market.

The growth of the MBS market is expected to continue, perhaps at a slower rate. As Figure 1-14 shows, less than 50 percent of total residential mortgages have been securitized. In addition, there are many examples of distressed commercial real estate holdings that will look to the capital markets to find liquidity and free up capital. For example, the RTC and many U.S. insurance portfolios are actively looking to use securitization strategies to exit previously illiquid commercial and residential real estate holdings. Figure 1-15 reviews the RTC activities through September 30, 1992 and demonstrates that the ability to securitize mortgages causes a faster disposition and greater recovery value. This strategy has allowed federal regulators an effective exit from the assets of failed banks and S&Ls. Figure 1-16 illustrates the importance of insurance companies' identifying strategies to manage their real estate portfolio crisis. In 1990, the largest U.S. insurance portfolios were struggling to stop the bleeding. Nonperforming mortgages averaged more than 50 percent of their capital and surplus. Asset quality deterioration forced the U.S. insurance industry, as well as the global banking and U.S. thrift industries, to search aggressively for ways to increase capital. Life insurance companies were also the biggest purchasers of junk bonds. Whereas

FIGURE 1-13

Mortgage Chain

Source: Company reports; B. Harting and D. Dusenbury, Equity Investment Opportunities Along the "Mortgage Food Chain" (New York: Salomon Brothers Inc., Sept. 23, 1992)

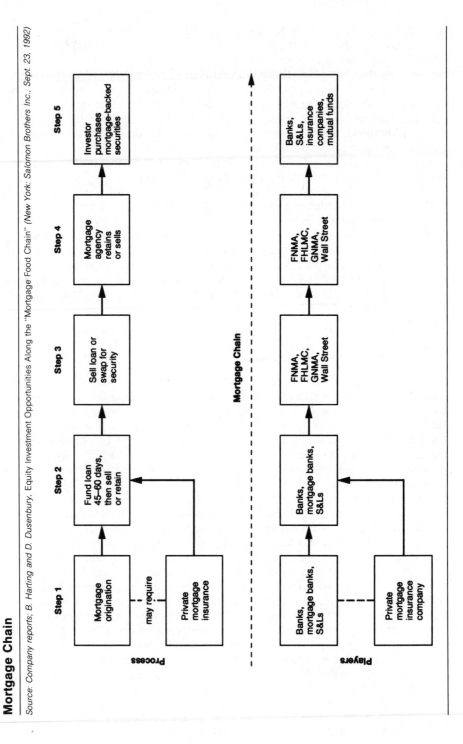

FIGURE 1-14

New Issues of Agency Mortgage-Backed Securities

Source: Salomon Brothers Inc.; " Paper Houses." The Economist (Aug. 15. 1992)

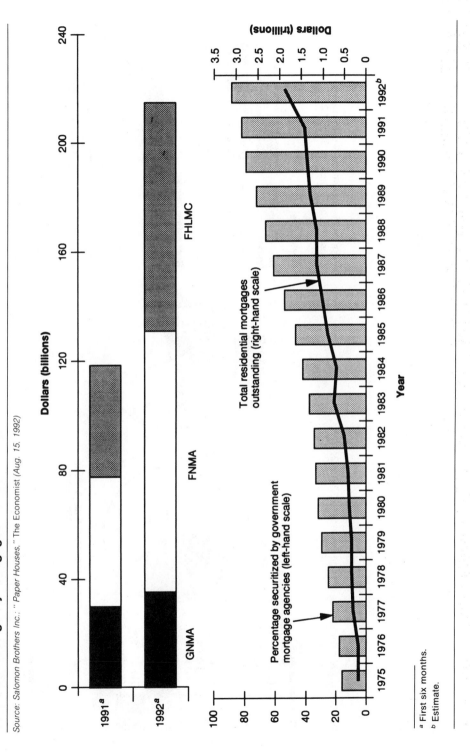

FIGURE 1-15

RTC Activities

Source: Resolution Trust Corporation; The New York Times (1993)

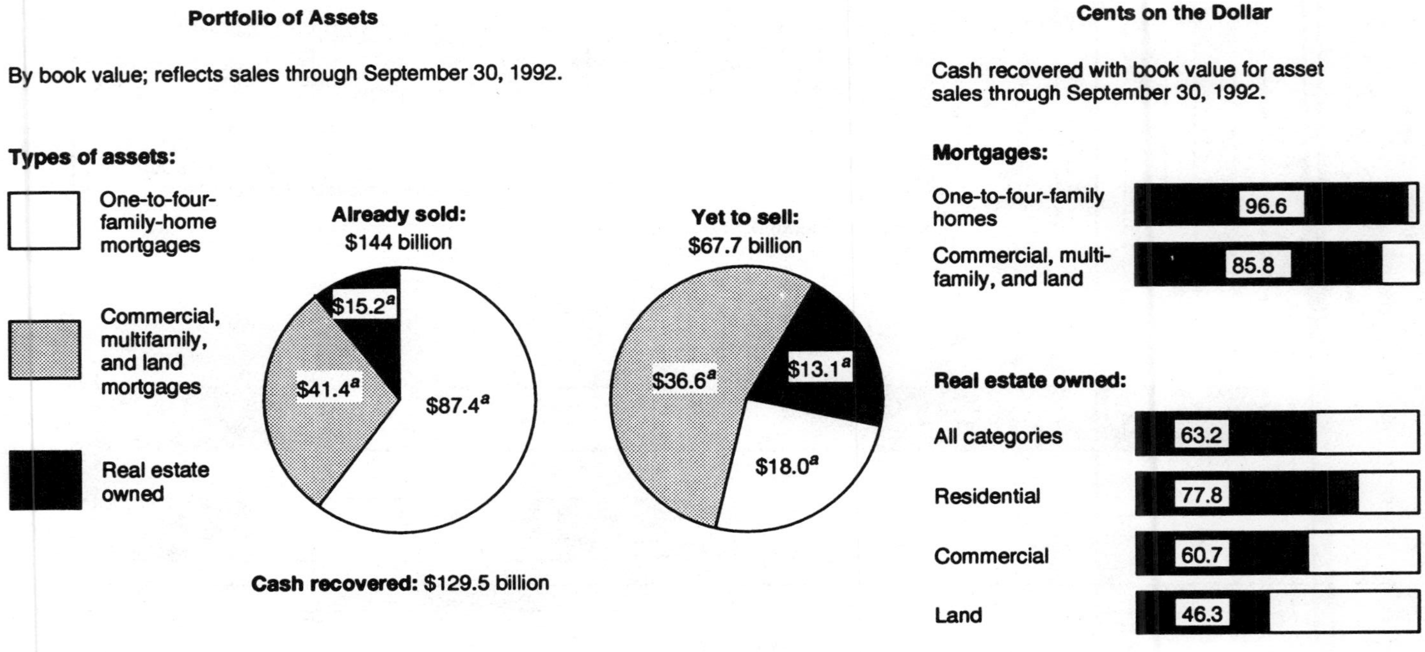

Portfolio of Assets

By book value; reflects sales through September 30, 1992.

Types of assets:

☐ One-to-four-family-home mortgages

▨ Commercial, multifamily, and land mortgages

■ Real estate owned

Already sold:
$144 billion

$15.2[a]

$41.4[a]

$87.4[a]

Cash recovered: $129.5 billion

Yet to sell:
$67.7 billion

$13.1[a]

$36.6[a]

$18.0[a]

Cents on the Dollar

Cash recovered with book value for asset sales through September 30, 1992.

Mortgages:

One-to-four-family homes — 96.6

Commercial, multi-family, and land — 85.8

Real estate owned:

All categories — 63.2

Residential — 77.8

Commercial — 60.7

Land — 46.3

[a]Dollars in billions.

FIGURE 1-16

Nonperforming Mortgages (Percentage of Capital and Surplus)[a]

Source: Weiss Research; "Small Earthquake," The Economist (Aug. 3, 1991)

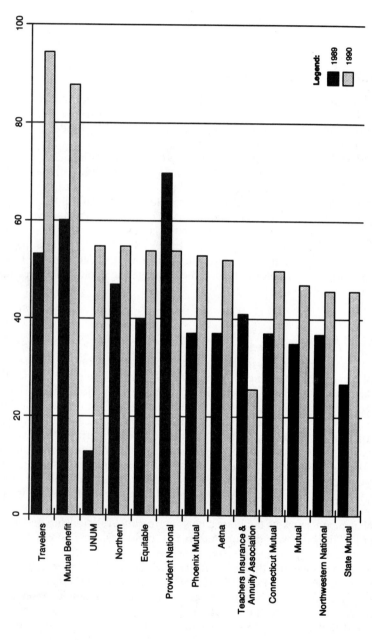

[a]Residential and commercial mortgages 90 days overdue, in the process of foreclosure, or foreclosed during the year. Life and health insurers with $2 billion or more in admitted assets.

junk bonds accounted for only 8 percent of assets, 22 percent of total assets were invested in real estate. In contrast, the banks had 29 percent of total assets in real estate lending. Like the United States' banks, insurers are focused on managing nonperforming assets, rebuilding capital, cutting costs, and expanding profits instead of assets and market share.

[3] Multilateral Development Banks

The multilateral development banks (MDBs) are another important part of the public policy, nonbank financial institutions market. Figure 1-17 lists the MDBs with selected information. The MDBs serve as conduits for channeling funds from conservative investors to borrowers in less developed, higher-risk regions of the world. They are sophisticated financial institutions with very conservative financial policies. In addition, they have the explicit political and financial support of the world's most developed countries. As a result, MDBs have enjoyed unlimited access to capital. Member countries support the MDBs financially as shareholders, through full faith and credit subscription capital, and as ultimate guarantors. They use the capital markets for almost all of their funding. In fact, they are among the largest bond issuers in the international capital markets. In 1990, bond issuance by MDBs was $33.14 billion, bringing the total to $202 billion outstanding at year-end. The MDBs will continue to exert world leadership, providing capital to feed and encourage the evolution of free markets and capitalism.

[4] Mutual Funds

The investment institutions in the nonbank sector are a powerful force in the global financial services market. These institutions continue to capitalize on the macro forces of globalization, technology, securitization, and deregulation. Figure 1-18 illustrates a long, recently accelerating trend of the diminishing role of the banks as intermediary between borrowers and savers. Securitization is the major reason for this trend. Owing to securitization and the creation of a secondary trading market, the buyers and sellers of financial services can avoid paying a banker to analyze credits and hold them in a loan portfolio. The investment institutions move information faster and further with telecommunications, facsimile machines, and computers. Financial service customers use funds such as Fidelity and Vanguard to store cash and invest savings, while GE Financial Services and Ford Motor are examples of sophisticated nonbank lenders. The global capital markets facilitate a new, more direct relationship between the saver-investor and the borrower-debtor. As a result, credit is dominated by financial institutions outside of the banking system, as shown in Figure 1-19.

Figure 1-20 shows the flow of funds in U.S. household financial assets from 1980 through the second quarter of 1992. The mutual funds market's share growth is impressive. With the continuation of the great bull markets in financial assets, people have been pouring money into the mutual funds, giving up on low-yielding certificates of deposit and bank deposits. As of year-end 1992, the flow of new money into the mutual funds was $1 billion a day, bringing the total to $1.6 trillion in industry net assets. This is in dramatic contrast to the situation 15 years ago, when people were pulling more money out of funds, the number of funds was declining, and the mutual funds industry was endangered. Figure 1-21 highlights the amazing growth of the mutual

FIGURE 1-17

Multilateral Development Banks

Source: D. Damrau, J. Change, J.F.H. Purcell, M. Fall, J. Camins, and A. Goldman, The Multilateral Development Banks
(New York: Salomon Brothers Inc., June 1991)

Membership

Bank	Number of Members	Nature of Membership Countries
African Development Bank	76	51 African (not including South Africa) and 25 nonregional (including the United States)
Asian Development Bank	51	36 Asian/Pacific and 15 nonregional (including the United States)
European Bank for Reconstruction and Development[a]	42	23 nonborrowing European members; 7 Central and Eastern European members and 10 nonregional members; 2 European institutions, the European Investment Bank and the EC, also hold shares
European Investment Bank	12	12 members of the EC
Inter-American Development Bank	44	26 North American (including Canada and the United States) and 18 nonregional members
International Finance Corporation	135	135 from all regions, including 24 industrialized countries
Nordic Investment Bank	5	Sweden, Denmark, Norway, Finland, Iceland
World Bank	155	155 from all regions, including 24 industrialized countries

Selected Information (December 31, 1990)

	Total Assets	Loans Disbursed and Outstanding	Credit Ratings: Moody's/ Standard & Poor's
African Development Bank	$ 8.66	$ 4.71	Aaa/AAA (senior)
Asian Development Bank	15.09	9.39	Aaa/AAA
European Investment Bank	86.51	74.52	Aaa/AAA
Inter-American Development Bank	24.58	17.73	Aaa/AAA
International Finance Corporation	6.45	3.50	Aaa/AAA
Nordic Investment Bank	7.44	4.71	Aaa/AAA
World Bank	130.67	96.75	Aaa/AAA
European Bank for Reconstruction and Development[a]			Aaa/AAA

Note: U.S. dollars in billions.

[a] Established in 1991, the world's newest MDB, aimed at supporting economic development in the new democracies in Central and Eastern Europe.

FIGURE 1-18

Financial Assets Held by Depository Institutions as Percentage of Total Financial Sector Assets (1900 to date)

Source: First Boston Corporation; GRANT's Interest Rate Observer (New York: 1991)

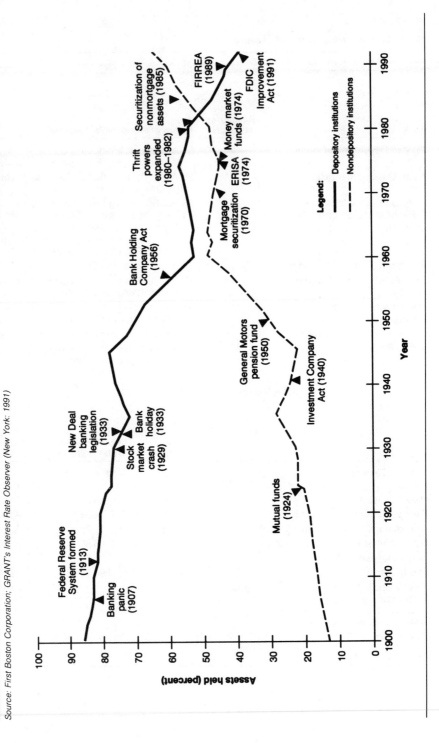

FIGURE 1-19

Credit Created Inside and Outside of Banking System

Source: E.S. Hyman and N. Lazar (New York: ISI Group, 1993)

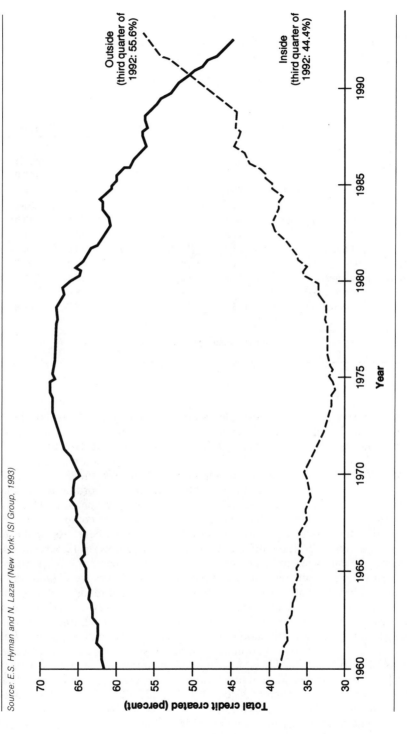

FIGURE 1-20

U.S. Household Financial Assets: Flow of Funds
(1980–Second Quarter of 1992)

Source: Federal Reserve Board; First Boston Equity Research

	1980	1981	1982	1983	1984	1985
Net acquisition of financial assets	$253.4	$269.4	$295.1	$378.7	$432.1	$469.5
Deposits	152.8	186.3	173.1	176.2	266.0	138.0
U.S. government securities	29.4	19.1	34.1	46.6	77.6	46.6
Tax-exempt securities	0.7	19.8	31.8	38.9	31.6	79.2
Corporate and foreign bonds	(10.6)	3.1	(4.0)	(9.0)	(3.6)	0.9
Mortgages	17.9	10.9	9.7	0.7	1.5	3.4
Open-market paper	3.8	(10.2)	(15.9)	18.3	6.0	60.5
Mutual fund shares	1.7	6.4	7.6	26.1	21.9	73.5
Corporate equities	(12.3)	(43.5)	(23.2)	(30.1)	(71.3)	(126.5)
Life insurance reserves	9.7	9.2	7.2	8.0	5.2	10.7
Pension fund reserves	108.8	108.7	146.3	172.7	177.8	207.2

Note: Dollars in billions.

[a] Figures for 1992 are quarterly flows at annual rates.

funds industry, whose assets, some estimate, could exceed $4 trillion by the end of the decade. The mutual funds giants, such as Fidelity Investments, Merrill Lynch Asset Management, The Vanguard Group, Dreyfus, and The Franklin/Templeton Group, lead the industry. Figure 1-22 shows the largest fund managers in the United States. These companies have become household names, moving capital around the international markets in ways that the banks cannot. According to the Fed, mutual funds' share of total U.S. financial assets in 1975 was only 2 percent, whereas commercial banks had 38 percent, S&Ls had 19 percent, insurance companies had 18 percent, pension funds had 14 percent, and all others had 9 percent. As of the end of the second quarter of 1992, the mutual funds share had jumped to 12 percent. Meanwhile, commercial banks fell to 27 percent, S&Ls fell to 10 percent, and pension funds increased to 21 percent. Insurance companies and all others were about the same.

Mutual funds are attractive for many reasons. Mutual funds pool investors' money and buy stocks, bonds, or money market securities. They are simple, and business can be done by telephone, mail, or electronic funds transfer. Large and small investors can get immediate diversification, a menu of many alternatives, professional money management, lower costs, and more favorable risk-adjusted returns. In addition, the funds offer superior liquidity and very low maintenance compared with individual portfolios of securities. Mutual funds have also lowered the cost of capital for industry and government. For example, since 1989, mutual funds have invested more than $300 billion in stocks. In 1992, corporations sold a record $846 billion of securities in the U.S. public markets. Of this amount, $744 billion were bonds and $101 billion were stocks. Mutual funds drove much of the new issue equity market, representing 7 of

1986	1987	1988	1989	1990	1991	1992 (First Quarter)[a]	1992 (Second Quarter)[a]
$525.8	$386.4	$453.4	$528.0	$474.3	$388.1	$528.3	$398.4
232.4	148.9	168.2	200.9	87.6	17.6	201.6	(117.8)
(35.1)	62.1	123.3	103.5	101.7	(75.2)	138.3	72.6
0.4	93.1	54.5	62.4	30.3	21.9	25.2	(8.9)
50.2	2.5	(35.6)	(5.8)	6.5	42.9	(64.4)	(62.7)
18.6	21.0	25.2	19.5	21.3	18.7	62.0	6.8
13.6	2.0	31.6	(0.1)	12.4	(22.5)	(67.5)	54.1
141.5	71.8	2.3	41.9	50.7	129.2	176.8	208.2
(136.3)	(103.9)	(122.0)	(139.1)	(27.2)	(68.7)	16.2	(12.2)
17.5	26.0	25.3	28.8	25.7	22.0	21.2	24.6
231.5	104.5	193.6	221.4	186.8	268.1	112.7	225.5

the 10 top buyers on most deals. Even more impressive, in the first half of 1992, the mutual funds provided 96 percent of the total money that went into all stocks, compared with 80 percent in 1991. In addition to changing the way Americans save and invest, the giant mutual fund industry has had an impact on the entire global economy. Mutual funds are channeling capital everywhere, including both developed and emerging countries; federal, state and municipal governments; and corporations, from biotechnology start-ups to the largest, mature conglomerates.

As money market mutual funds provided higher yields to investors and lower interest expense to borrowers, the banks were the big losers. Through the expansion of the commercial paper (CP) market, it is estimated that the funds saved corporations $100 billion in interest expense over the past 15 years. At the same time the banks were losing deposits, the CP market became cost effective and convenient and ultimately lured the biggest and most creditworthy borrowers away from the banks. Banks are now aggressively trying to enter the business of selling investment products and services. However, it will be difficult for them to recapture many of these customers. For example, in the mutual funds industry, one low-cost provider is Vanguard, which recently introduced a series of U.S. government securities funds with a maximum expense ratio of $.015 per $100 invested. In contrast, the banks now must pay $0.23 per $100 deposits for the federal deposit insurance alone. Clearly, the banks cannot succeed in the fund business competing on price alone, and as long as investors and savers seek to increase their total return on financial assets, the nonbank investment institutions and the banks will continue to compete in the mutual funds market.

FIGURE 1-21
Mutual Funds: Total Industry Net Assets

Source: ICI; First Boston Equity Research

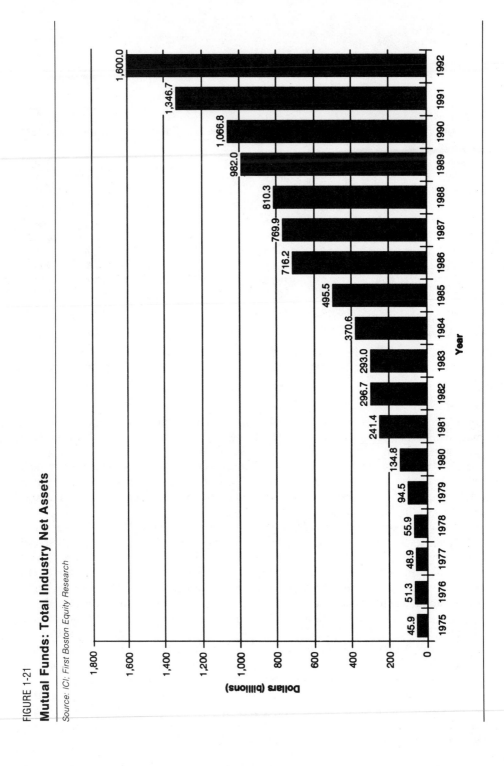

FIGURE 1-22

Largest Fund Managers

Source: Strategic Insight; *"The Power of Mutual Funds,"* Business Week *(Jan. 18, 1993)*

Management Company	Assets[a]	Mutual Share[a]
Fidelity	$164.3	10.2%
Merrill Lynch	107.6	6.0
Vanguard	92.6	5.8
Dreyfus	75.8	4.7
Franklin[b]	64.6	4.0
Capital Research	62.1	3.9
Dean Witter	52.9	3.3
Kemper	45.4	2.8
Federated	45.2	2.8
Shearson	45.1	2.8
Putnam	41.4	2.6
Prudential	34.2	2.1
IDS	27.9	1.7
Scudder	26.2	1.6
Nuveen	25.8	1.6
T. Rowe Price	25.3	1.6
Provident Institutional	24.3	1.5
MFS	23.2	1.5
Goldman, Sachs & Co.	23.0	1.4
Alliance Capital	20.9	1.3
PaineWebber Inc.	20.5	1.3
Oppenheimer	19.8	1.2
AIM	18.7	1.2
20th Century	17.3	1.1
American Capital	13.8	0.9

Note: Dollars in billions.

[a] Includes mutual funds and closed-end funds as of September 1992.

[b] Has since acquired Templeton Funds, which brings Franklin's total to $76.9 billion with a 4.8 percent share of the market.

[5] Finance Companies

Finance companies typically originate loans to two major customer groups: individuals through consumer lending and industries through commercial lending operations. Consumer lending includes secured residential real estate such as home equity loans and second mortgages, consumer installment loans (credit cards), and other secured and unsecured consumer installment loans. Commercial lending includes secured commercial real estate such as construction and building loans, inventories and receivables financing, equipment leasing, and other commercial loans, including highly leveraged transactions (HLTs). Commercial lending activities are typically secured by the assets financed. Finance companies tend to be more conservatively leveraged than other lending institutions. They use tighter credit standards and prefer lending on a cash flow basis rather than an asset value basis. In addition, finance companies are more conservative because they carry a higher allowance for credit losses. Liability management strategies, including interest rate and currency swap transactions, have helped to reduce the credit quality risks associated with spread banking. In the 1980s, the ability to package and sell nearly all types of cash flows in securitizations significantly increased the liquidity of the finance companies' receivables. Also, finance company receivables tend to be more geographically diverse and less concentrated by type of business compared with those of other lending institutions. Figure 1-23 shows selected finance companies with earnings and market data. The key variables driving this industry are asset growth, spreads, and credit quality concerns. Recent Fed and U.S. Department of Commerce data suggest that the consumer is deleveraging. With the exception of credit card receivables, there is a trend toward lower personal debt. According to Salomon Brothers, the long-term annual growth in total consumer receivables for the major finance companies has been around 10 percent. In contrast, net consumer debt growth during the 1991–1992 period may not exceed 5 percent.

Historically, the credit card market was one of the most profitable activities for the banks. For example, the average credit card interest rate is 17.5 percent, with a range of 7 percent to 21 percent. Between 1985 and 1992, credit card debt grew by at least 10 percent annually. In June 1992, the total debt outstanding was $247 billion. For banks, 80 percent of the money they make on credit cards is from interest charged to unpaid balances. The remaining 20 percent is split between commissions from merchants and annual fees from card holders.

Asset-backed securities (ABSs) is one type of securitization that has also contributed to the significant growth of the credit card business. The ABS market was created through the securitization of consumer credit card receivables. Figure 1-24 shows the dramatic growth of the ABS market, which began in 1985 and grew to a record $51 billion in 1992. These securities are mostly rated triple-A credits. The issue is credit enhanced by overcollateralization, letters of credit, and subordination of a portion of the cash flows to cushion against any losses on the underlying receivables. Investment banks, nonbanks, and banks are all active players in the ABS markets as underwriters, dealers, issuers, servicers, and investors.

The credit card business is under a massive competitive attack from the nonbanks. Companies such as AT&T, Sears, GE, General Motors Co., and Ford Motor Co. are going head to head with the American Express Company and the many bank credit cards. With amazing speed and apparent ease, in only two years AT&T has become the largest general-purpose credit card issuer after Citicorp. AT&T reported an 18 percent increase in net income for 1992 and highlighted a big profit increase from its new Universal credit card, which now has 16 million cards in circulation. Recognizing this profitable market, nonbank credit cards have risen from 5 percent of the industry total in 1986 to 24 percent in 1993. Some estimate that they could be 50 percent of the market by 1995. Nonbank issuers are less regulated and have enjoyed access to lower-cost funds. Also, the nonbanks are competing on price, with lower interest rates, lower or no fees, and financial equivalents like money-back coupons. This competitive battle between the banks and the nonbanks will continue to intensify as banks leave the credit card business, and as the credit card industry continues to consolidate, it will inevitably become much less profitable.

FIGURE 1-23

Selected Finance Companies: Earnings and Market Data as of July 1992 (1991–1993)[a]

Source: S. Liss, Finance Companies—All Dressed Up, but Where's the Party? (New York: Salomon Brothers Inc., July 17, 1992)

	Price	Range	Market Capital	Earnings per Share			Price/Earnings Ratio			Yield	Price/ Book Value
				1993	1992[a]	1991	1993[a]	1992[a]	1991		
American Express	$24	$28–$18	$11,280	$2.40	$2.00	$1.59	10.0	12.0	15.1	4.2%	1.6
Beneficial Corporation	60	67–53	1,512	7.00	6.30	5.80	8.6	9.6	10.4	4.3	1.4
Comdisco	17	24–12	668	1.80	0.50	2.13	9.5	34.8	8.0	1.6	1.1
Household International	52	63–41	2,100	5.50	4.10	3.10	9.6	12.8	16.9	4.3	1.4
Kemper Corporation	26	46–23	1,230	3.25	3.00	4.20	7.9	8.5	6.1	3.6	0.7
MBNA Corporation	43	44–28	2,138	4.10	3.50	3.00	10.4	1.22	14.2	4.1	3.5
Primerica	40	43–28	4,477	5.00	5.00[b]	4.27	7.9	8.2	9.3	2.0	1.2
Sears, Roebuck & Co.	39	48–33	13,537	4.90	4.30	3.71	8.0	9.1	10.6	5.1	1.0
Transamerica	45	47–31	3,422	4.50	4.00	1.14	9.9	11.1	39.1	4.5	1.2

Note: Dollars in millions except per-share amounts.
[a] Salomon Brothers Inc. estimate.
[b] Before anticipated capital gains.

FIGURE 1-24

Asset-Backed Securities

Source: Merrill Lynch Asset Backed Securities Group; "All the World's a Security," The Economist (Aug. 29, 1992)

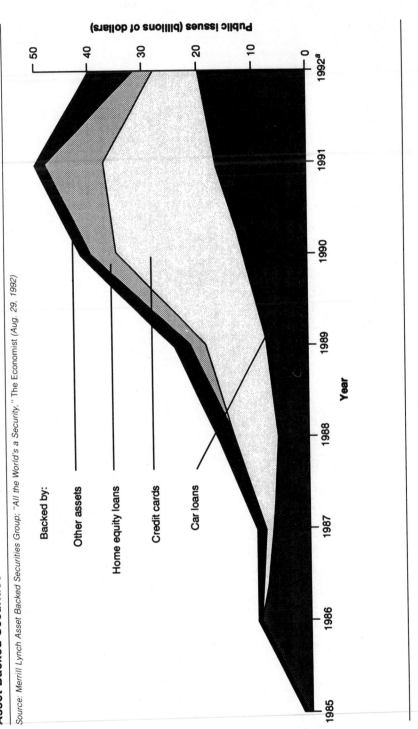

[6] Financial Subsidiaries

GE's finance subsidiary, GE Financial Services (GEFS), is one example of a nonbank financial institution that contributes significant value to its parent company. GEFS conducts its business through three principal affiliates, GE Capital, Employers Reinsurance Corporation, and Kidder, Peabody & Co., which operate in the financing, insurance, and securities broker-dealer segments of financial services.

GEFS had $8 billion in capital, $16 billion in revenues, and a 17 percent return on equity as of year-end 1991, the tenth consecutive year achieving returns in this range. This compares with GE's capital of $22 billion, revenues of $60 billion and a 1991 return on equity of 12 percent.

These large, diversified, strongly capitalized finance companies, many with triple-A credit ratings, have not been constrained by banking regulations. They aggressively compete with banks, investment banks, and nonbanks and have achieved great success in many areas of the financial services industry. The financial subsidiaries are often able to anticipate changes in the markets in which they compete.

These nonbank financial institutions have aggressively entered the financial services arena, participating in acquisitions, issuing credit cards, and marketing mutual funds and insurance products.

Anticipating the globalization trend, many financial subsidiaries now have strong investment positions in Canada, Europe, and Asia. If the crowded financial services industry continues to produce highly competitive conditions, these nonbanks will find ample opportunity for asset and activity growth.

1.07 INVESTMENT BANKING

Investment banks perform many financial services and activities, including underwriting and distribution of debt, equity, and derivative securities; arbitrage, trading, and market making in securities, currencies, commodities, and derivative products for clients and the firm's own proprietary accounts; fixed-income and equity market research; individual and institutional asset management; principal investments; portfolio support services, including custody and securities lending and borrowing; and advisory services for mergers and acquisitions, financial restructurings, and capital-raising activities. (See Chapter 2.)

Since the enactment of the Glass-Steagall Act, commercial banking and investment banking in the United States have operated as separate industries. In an attempt to protect the financial system from collapse in the event of future market dislocations such as the stock market crash of 1929, the act prohibited commercial banks from underwriting and dealing in private debt and equity securities. There were also concerns at the time that the powerful universal banks or investment houses, particularly J.P. Morgan, were controlling both the lending and investment business of the country's largest corporations.

Competition in investment banking continues to increase. Many securities firms, both U.S.-based and non-U.S.-based, have significantly increased their capital through mergers or acquisitions or through public offerings or private placements of their securities. In addition, competition has increased from other financial service players, such as commercial banks (led by J.P. Morgan and Bankers Trust), insurance companies, and major corporations that have entered securities and related businesses. While the financial performance in the investment banking industry is often volatile and mixed, it appears that the trend toward more competition will continue, as securitization keeps the pressure on banking regulators. Even if Glass-Steagall is not repealed, market forces will continue to modify its impact, because securitization has become a more dominant form of financial intermediation.

There are several types of investment banks, including international full service, national full service, boutiques, and specialty firms. Figure 1-25 shows the structure of a typical investment bank, and Figure 1-26 shows the major investment banks, by type, ownership, and business orientation. Ten years ago, investment banks were driven by the vision of functioning in the future as financial supermarkets. Several large institutions, including American Express, Sears, and Prudential, aggressively pursued the financial supermarket concept and reshaped their companies to provide one-stop shopping of financial services and products. Despite several years of record Wall Street profitability, the now-abandoned financial supermarket concept succeeded only in generating major operating losses so large that they eventually put strain on the giant parents, particularly American Express.

The investment banks have experienced two consecutive record years: 1991 and 1992. Figures 1-27, 1-28, and 1-29 show the 1992 underwriting rankings. The rankings continue to show industry concentration; in 1992, the top six firms accounted for 55 percent of global underwriting, down from 75 percent in 1986. One significant trend of 1992 was how easily the capital markets absorbed huge new issues. Figure 1-30 highlights 1992 capital-raising activities. The fact that there were more than 25 debt and equity issues that each raised more than $1 billion in United States markets illustrates the impressive breadth and depth of the capital markets. The globalization and securitization of the markets allow the investment banks to raise more money faster, at a lower cost, and from more different borrowers than any bank or syndicate of banks. This fact will continue to drive banks and nonbanks to seek ways of moving into the investment banking businesses.

As the size of both primary and secondary markets continue to grow, capital will be a critical determinant for institutions that hope to compete in the investment banking business. Capital requirements are a function of both asset liquidity and asset levels. Asset levels and financial leverage are typically much greater for firms that trade securities and other financial instruments than for nonfinancial companies. For institutions to excel in investment banking, they need to analyze and manage working capital requirements carefully. Like the banks and nonbanks, investment banks need to define capital in terms of how much, the costs, and how to allocate it for maximum returns.

One recent example of a strategy to lower the cost of capital is the lucrative and fast-growing derivatives business. (See Chapters 9 and 10 for discussion of related issues.) Financial service customers using derivatives strategies that protect portfolios from undesired moves or capture profits from expected moves in interest rates, foreign currencies, and other financial markets have grown increasingly credit sensitive. In response, several investment banks, including Merrill Lynch & Co., Goldman, Sachs & Co., and Salomon Brothers Inc., have created special-purpose subsidiaries with triple-A credit ratings (compared with the single-A overall brokerage company rating) to handle derivatives business. This new triple-A rating significantly enhances the ability to compete in the derivatives market.

In addition to searching for strategies to lower the cost of capital, investment banks have invested billions of dollars and a decade of hiring computer experts to determine how much and where to allocate capital to maximize returns. For example, in 1991, Salomon Brothers alone spent $425 million on new computer systems, advanced com-

FIGURE 1-25

Typical Structure of Investment Bank

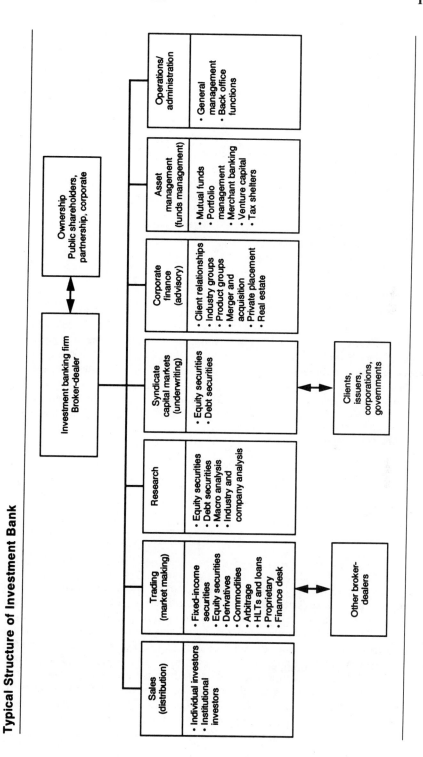

FIGURE 1-26

Major Investment Banks

Type of Firm	Ownership	Distribution Orientation
International Full Service		
First Boston Corp.	Credit Suisse	
Goldman, Sachs & Co.	Private	Institutional
Morgan Stanley	Public	Institutional
Salomon Brothers Inc.	Public	Institutional
Bankers Trust Securities	Bankers Trust	Individual and institutional
Bear, Stearns & Co.	Public	
J.P. Morgan Securities	J.P. Morgan	Individual and institutional
Kidder, Peabody & Co.	General Electric	Individual and institutional
Lehman Brothers	American Express	Individual and institutional
Merrill Lynch & Co.	Public	Individual and institutional
PaineWebber Inc.	Public	Individual and Institutional
National Full Service		
Alex. Brown & Sons	Public	Individual and institutional
Dean Witter Reynolds	Sears	Individual and institutional
Dillon Read & Co.	Travelers	Institutional
A.G. Edwards & Sons	Public	Individual
Donaldson, Lufkin & Jenrette	Equitable	Individual and institutional
Oppenheimer & Co.	Private	Individual and institutional
Prudential Securities Inc.	Prudential	Individual and institutional
Smith Barney	Primerica	Individual and institutional
Boutiques and Specialty		
Kohlberg, Kravis (leveraged buyouts)	Private	Institutional
Lazard Freres & Co. (mergers and acquisitions)	Private	Institutional
Wasserstein Perella (mergers and acquisitions)	Private	Institutional

munications networks, and upgrades to its corporate data base to achieve technological superiority and improve its competitive position in the industry. This investment in high-technology trading has produced an important shift in the investment banking business. Figure 1-31 highlights trading's increasing contribution to investment banking performance. The increased volatility of financial markets has led to an expansion in so-called proprietary trading, in which a firm takes a position for its own account, sometimes over a long period. Proprietary trading usually involves some form of arbitrage (trying to profit from price differences between similar securities that may trade in separate markets). In short, Wall Street investment banks are risking more of their own capital on market bets. Since proprietary trading represents an increasing source of investment banking revenues, capital and risk management strategies are more important than ever.

FIGURE 1-27

Global Rankings: Debt Issuance (1992)

Source: Securities Data Company

Manager	Jan. 1, 1992–Dec. 31, 1992			Jan. 1, 1991–Dec. 31, 1991	
	Amount	Percentage	Issues	Amount	Rank
Merrill Lynch & Co.	$ 124,176.9	11.9	686	$ 96,810.4	1
Goldman, Sachs & Co.	100,856.0	9.7	485	70,517.1	3
First Boston/CSFB/CS	94,602.9	9.1	407	71,596.2	2
Lehman Brothers	94,186.6	9.0	434	64,916.4	4
Kidder, Peabody & Co.	79,345.4	7.6	279	49,980.3	5
Salomon Brothers Inc.	77,978.9	7.5	277	44,926.1	7
Morgan Stanley	59,792.7	5.7	314	48,147.5	6
Bear, Stearns & Co.	52,090.2	5.0	169	32,825.1	8
J.P. Morgan & Co. Inc.	29,073.6	2.8	121	17,214.3	12
Nomura Securities Co. Ltd.	28,263.9	2.7	117	28,218.6	9
Prudential Securities Inc.	25,710.0	2.5	89	15,742.8	13
Deutsche Bank A.G.	22,135.9	2.1	74	18,305.7	11
Donaldson, Lufkin & Jenrette	17,825.7	1.7	89	10,092.0	19
Daiwa Securities	17,745.5	1.7	95	21,676.8	10
PaineWebber Inc.	15,902.8	1.5	62	9,170.3	20
Industry totals	$1,041,862.4	100.0	5,492	$781,108.0	

Note: Full credit to lead manager. Dollars in millions.

FIGURE 1-28

Mortgage-Backed Debt (1992)

Source: Securities Data Company

Manager	Jan. 1, 1992–Dec. 31, 1992			Jan. 1, 1991–Dec. 31, 1991	
	Amount	Percentage	Issues	Amount	Rank
Kidder, Peabody & Co.	$ 68,305.8	18.1	153	$ 43,267.1	1
Lehman Brothers	42,829.7	11.3	118	31,107.3	2
Bear, Stearns & Co.	41,888.7	11.1	93	29,736.4	3
Salomon Brothers Inc.	36,181.3	9.6	72	17,468.4	7
Goldman, Sachs & Co.	33,590.2	8.9	75	17,472.8	6
First Boston	30,096.3	8.0	96	19,997.4	5
Merrill Lynch & Co.	28,099.1	7.4	98	21,011.2	4
Prudential Securities Inc.	22,214.6	5.9	65	14,631.2	8
Morgan Stanley	18,220.1	4.8	41	12,039.7	9
PaineWebber Inc.	13,641.2	3.6	35	6,927.1	11
Donaldson, Lufkin & Jenrette	12,093.4	3.2	47	8,118.7	10
Nomura Securities Co. Ltd.	7,490.5	2.0	19	5,596.9	12
J.P. Morgan & Co. Inc.	7,307.6	1.9	21	3,794.7	16
Citicorp	4,708.0	1.2	17	4,068.9	15
Greenwich Capital Markets	3,330.0	0.9	11	5,159.3	13
Industry totals	$377,714.6	100.0	997	$250,161.6	

Note: Full credit to lead manager. Dollars in millions.

FIGURE 1-29

Eurobonds and Foreign Bonds (1992)

Source: Securities Data Company

Manager	Jan. 1, 1992–Dec. 31, 1992			Jan. 1, 1991–Dec. 31, 1991	
	Amount	Percentage	Issues	Amount	Rank
Deutsche Bank A.G.	$ 22,135.9	7.6	74	$ 18,306.7	2
Nomura Securities Co. Ltd.	19,761.2	6.8	93	22,621.7	1
Credit Suisse First Boston/CS	18,487.9	6.3	81	17,448.6	3
Daiwa Securities	14,361.9	4.9	84	16,907.0	4
UBS Philips & Drew/UBS	13,465.4	4.6	67	9,373.5	12
Banque Paribas	12,907.1	4.4	59	11,371.7	6
J.P. Morgan & Co. Inc.	12,462.8	4.3	41	7,162.3	13
Goldman, Sachs & Co.	12,021.2	4.1	58	11,776.1	5
Yamaichi Securities Company	10,981.2	3.8	64	10,448.4	7
Merrill Lynch & Co.	9,073.1	3.1	56	9,487.0	10
Nikko Securities	8,934.3	3.1	56	9,987.1	9
Swiss Bank	7,964.4	2.7	52	10,170.9	8
Industry totals	$291,768.2	100.0	1,681	$267,395.6	

Note: Full credit to lead manager. Dollars in millions.

1.08 CONCLUSION

The financial services industry is an information business that has an impact on the constant global movement of money (capital and credit). Technology has accelerated the speed and scope of information processing and therefore the flow of money. Securitization and the global capital markets are changing the nature of money from paper to an electronic medium. Deregulation has provided financial service companies with great market opportunities and, at the same time, exposed financial accidents caused by the mismanagement of market, credit, operational, and institutional risks.

Banks, nonbanks, and investment banks have experienced varying degrees of success and failure as globalization, technology, securitization, and deregulation change the financial services industry. The financial supermarket concept of financial intermediation has been more successful with the giant mutual funds, such as Fidelity and Vanguard, than with the large nonfinancial firms such as Sears or other financial firms such as American Express, many of which are in the process of modifying their strategy or withdrawing from financial service businesses. For these companies, providing a wide variety of financial products and services to meet most of the financial needs of individuals and businesses has not developed into a winning strategy.

Financial service institutions that are strongly capitalized will continue to have a competitive advantage. The investment banking activities of J.P. Morgan and Bankers Trust have increased the chances that the Glass-Steagall Act will eventually be modified. As more banks move into nonbank and investment banking businesses, competition will increase and the distinction of financial service institutions by product, service, and geography will continue to break down. Finally, financial markets and

FIGURE 1-30

Capital-Raising Activities (1992)

Source: Securities Data Company; The New York Times

Largest Corporate Issues

Five largest common stock offerings.

Date	Equity Issuer	Total	Lead Manager
June 20	General Motors	$1,560	Morgan Stanley
Aug. 20	Blackrock 2001 Term Trust	1,300	Prudential Securities Inc.
Jan. 21	Chemical Banking	1,226	Goldman, Sachs & Co.
July 27	Wellcome Group (advanced determination rulings)	1,068	Morgan Stanley
Sept. 16	GTE	789	PaineWebber Inc.

Five largest corporate debt offerings.

Date	Debt Issuer	Total	Lead Manager
Aug. 14	FHLMC (medium-term notes)	$1,047	Prudential Securities Inc.
Aug. 5	FNMA (step-up medium-term notes)	1,000	Merrill Lynch & Co.
Jan. 16	Hydro-Quebec (debentures)	1,000	First Boston
June 16	SLMA (floating-rate notes)	1,000	Merrill Lynch & Co.
Jan., Aug., Dec.	Tennessee Valley Authority ($1 billion power bond issues) (3 deals)	1,000	Lehman Brothers (2 deals) First Boston (1 deal)

[a] Dollars in millions.
[b] Dollars in billions.

Types of Securities[b]

Sources of all U.S. domestic corporate financing. Total: $846 billion, up 45 percent from 1991.

Equity		Change From 1991
Initial public offerings	$39	57%
Secondary offerings	33	7
Preferred stock	29	47

Debt		Change From 1991
Mortgage debt	$377	51%
Investment-grade debt	271	42
Asset-backed debt	51	2
Junk bonds	38	280
Convertible debt	7	(7)

FIGURE 1-31

Trading Revenue as Share of Total Revenue

Source: Salomon Brothers Inc.; Business Week

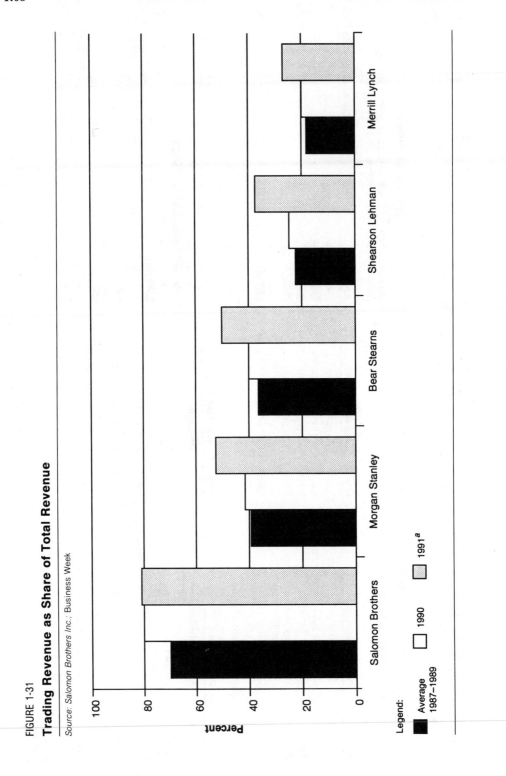

Legend:

Average
1987–1989

1990

1991[a]

therefore financial services form the foundation for capitalist, free market economies. As more regions of the world such as Latin America, Eastern Europe, and even Russia seek to stabilize and make successful transitions that embrace the free market model, the global financial services industry will play a vital role in steering capital flows between the developed and developing country economies.

Suggested Reading

Bryan, Lowell L. *Bankrupt: Restoring the Health and Profitability of Our Banking System*. New York: Harper Business, 1991.

Grant, James. *Money of the Mind: Borrowing and Lending in America From the Civil War to Michael Milken*. New York: Farrar Straus Giroux, 1992.

Miller, Richard B. *American Banking in Crisis: Views From Leading Financial Service CEOs*. Homewood, Ill: Dow Jones-Irwin, 1990.

O'Barr, William M., and Conley, John M. *Fortune & Folly: The Wealth and Power of Institutional Investing*. Homewood, Ill: Dow Jones-Irwin, 1992.

Pierce, James L. *The Future of Banking*. Binghamton, N.Y.: Yale University Press, 1991.

Rogers, David. *The Future of American Banking: Managing for Change*. New York: McGraw-Hill, Inc., 1993.

Chapter 2

Investment Banking

GEORGE G.C. PARKER

2.01 FACTORS IN THE EMERGENCE OF INVESTMENT BANKING

The investment banking industry in the United States is unique compared with that of most other countries. This uniqueness stems from the Glass-Steagall Act passed by the U.S. Congress in 1933. Under the act, the investment banking industry and the commercial banking industry were completely separated. In most other countries, the deposit-gathering and lending functions of commercial banks and the securities-underwriting and distribution functions of investment banks are conducted within a single banking company. This type of banking is often referred to as universal banking, and no distinction is made between commercial and investment banking.

Unlike commercial banks, which tend to specialize in loans to businesses and individuals, investment banks finance corporations through long-term debt and equity securities. Investment banks also derive considerable income through the trading of the securities after they have been issued. Trading in all securities, other than government bonds, is prohibited for commercial banks in the United States, thus further separating the functions of the two institutions.

There are two areas where investment banks and commercial banks compete directly. The first is in the area of government bonds, which are specifically exempted by the Glass-Steagall Act. The second is in short-term financing to corporations through commercial paper, a form of direct corporate borrowing, which is generally arranged by investment banks and which competes directly with bank loans.

While the specific reasons for the passage of the Glass-Steagall Act were not described by Congress, at least four separate reasons for its passage may be suggested: risk, conflicts of interest, concentration of power, and specialization.

[1] Risk

It is perhaps understandable that the separation of investment banking from commercial banking occurred in the United States after the collapse of the securities markets in 1929. Between 1929 and 1933, nearly 10,000 commercial banks—approximately 40 percent of all banks in the United States—failed. Many of the failed banks were active broker-dealers and underwriters for securities.

Investment banking is a risky business. Debt and equity markets are inherently subject to large fluctuations in prices, with such price risk borne by securities underwriters and dealers, at least to the extent of their inventory. The Glass-Steagall Act was an attempt to insulate commercial banks from that risk by simply prohibiting them from dealing, underwriting, or investing in private debt and equity securities.

[2] Conflicts of Interest

It was widely believed at the time of the passage of Glass-Steagall that the quality of the loan portfolios of banks was adversely affected by the relationships that many banks had as equity investors or as underwriters of the securities of their borrowing clients. To minimize such potential conflicts of interest, it was deemed only prudent to separate the deposit-taking, lending, and securities businesses.

FIGURE 2-1

Number of Investment Banking Firms

Source: Securities Industry Association

	NYSE		NASD[a]
	Total	Firms Dealing With Public	Total
1981	604	390	3,265
1982	617	387	3,697
1983	639	412	4,885
1984	628	393	5,726
1985	599	381	6,307
1986	611	417	6,658
1987	596	392	6,722
1988	555	363	6,432
1989	535	353	6,148
1990	516	327	5,827

[a] National Association of Securities Dealers.

[3] Concentration of Power

Some observers have noted that the Glass-Steagall Act was passed in part to break up the large and powerful universal banks or investment houses of New York City, especially J.P. Morgan & Company. Those banks were thought to control an excessively large portion of both the lending and investment business of the nation.

[4] Specialization

Finally, there was a desire on the part of Congress to revitalize the securities markets in the early 1930s by creating a new, independent industry that would specialize in the origination (underwriting) and distribution (selling) of securities to the public. The result was a highly specialized financial institution that had as its only means of survival the promotion of the securities markets. Investment banks simply had no other way to prosper than to sell securities aggressively to institutions and the public. One result of this specialization is that some 60 years after the passage of the act, nearly 15 percent of the U.S. population are direct owners of equity securities. This is a far higher proportion than is found in virtually any other country except Japan.

Regardless of the reasons for the passage of the Glass-Steagall Act, the financial system in the United States today is largely an outgrowth of the effects of the act. The modern investment banking industry that Glass-Steagall created is at the center of U.S. capitalism and employs thousands of people who are engaged in the financing of U.S. business and government. (See Figures 2-1, 2-2, and 2-3 for data on the size of the industry.)

FIGURE 2-2

Initial Public Offerings of Equity in the United States

Source: Investment Dealers' Digest

	1991	1990	1989	1988	1987	1986
Share value	$24,301.3	$10,130.3	$13,826.6	$23,748.6	$24,188.3	$22,388.1
Number of issues	393	214	247	279	550	717

Note: Dollars in millions.

2.02 PRIMARY SERVICES OF AN INVESTMENT BANK

The major activities of an investment bank may be divided into the categories and subcategories described in the following sections. Figure 2-4 illustrates the organization of an investment bank in diagrammatic form.

[1] Underwriting

Underwriting is among the most basic activities of investment banks, although it is highly cyclical and does not always account for the largest proportion of profits during all phases of the business cycle. For example, firms tend to issue more new securities when prices are historically high than when they have recently fallen. This results in a highly uneven flow of business for the underwriting departments of many investment banks. When underwriting is active, it may be the largest profit center within the firm; when markets are inactive, investment banks must substitute other forms of revenue and profits for the underwriting activities.

When an investment bank underwrites a new security issue, it actually buys the security—either debt or equity—from the entity needing funds (a corporation, government, or large shareholder) and then resells it to the public. The investment bank assumes the risk that the securities can be sold for at least their cost. In that respect, the investment bank operates much like any other dealer that purchases an inventory and resells it at a higher price to subsequent buyers.

Compensation for underwriting comes from the spread between the buying price and the selling price. The maximum spread permitted by the Securities and Exchange Commission (SEC) in the United States is 10 percent of the price to the buyer (that is, when the investment bank buys the securities for resale, it must pay the seller at least 90 percent of the price at which it offers them for resale). Notwithstanding the 10 percent maximum spread, investment banks usually underwrite the securities of well-known issuers for a spread of much less than 10 percent. Typical spreads on equity underwritings are between 4 percent and 8 percent of the sales price, whereas the spread on debt issues is between 0.5 percent and 2.5 percent, depending on the size and quality of the issue. The spread compensates the investment bank for the risk of resale as well as the cost of selling through a commissioned sales force.

The underwriting function is generally performed by the corporate finance department or the buying department of the investment bank. When the underwriting involves the purchase of newly issued securities, the issue is referred to as a primary offering.

FIGURE 2-3

Securities Industry Average Pretax Return on Equity

Source: Securities Industry DataBank

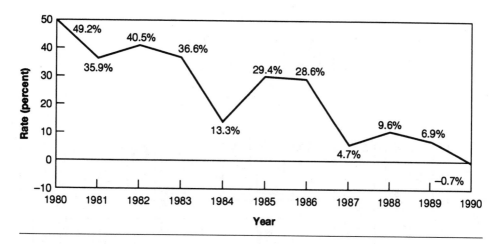

When it involves the purchase of a large block of securities that are already owned by a large shareowner, the underwriting is referred to as a secondary offering. It is not uncommon in an initial public offering for the issue to be a combination of a primary and secondary offering, meaning that part of the issue represents new capital for the company and part is the sale of stock by existing shareholders that wish to liquidate all or some of their holdings. Often, the selling shareholders are founders of the firm that wish to diversify or possibly a venture capital firm that wishes to take its profit and redeploy its funds. Figure 2-5 shows total U.S. underwritings for the five-year period ending in 1990.

[2] Negotiated Versus Competitive Deals

Most underwriting for industrial corporations in the United States is handled through negotiated deals. In a negotiated underwriting, after a preliminary search process, the issuer works exclusively with a single investment banking firm. That firm assists in the design, timing, and formation of a syndicate to purchase and sell the issue. Competition between firms in a negotiated deal happens at the time the firm is chosen to handle the issue, rather than at the time of the issuance itself.

An alternative to the negotiated deal is the competitive deal. In a competitive bid, the issuing company or governmental agency invites bids at the time of the final pricing from a number of investment banks. Competitive bidding is common with regulated public utilities and municipal governments. Indeed, many publicly regulated companies are required by law to have open competitive bidding for the purchase of their securities. Corporate issuers, however, tend to use negotiated offerings, because corporate securities are less homogeneous, and a negotiated underwriting allows the investment bank to expend more effort in preparing the market for the issue. Notwithstanding

FIGURE 2-4
Organization of a Typical Investment Bank

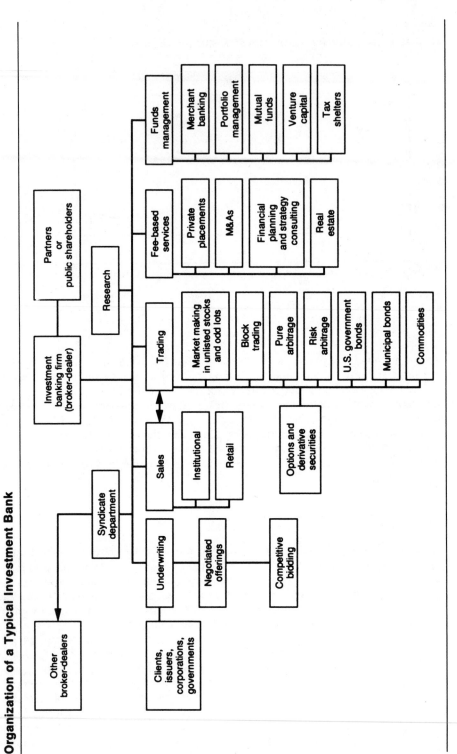

FIGURE 2-5

Total U.S. Underwritings (1986–1990)

Source: Securities Data Company, Inc.

	1986	1987	1988	1989	1990
Corporate issues					
Bonds	$227.7	$219.4	$236.8	$274.3	$290.3
Preferred stock	13.9	11.4	7.4	7.7	4.6
Common stock	43.2	41.5	29.8	22.9	19.2
All issues	$284.8	$272.3	$274.0	$304.9	$314.1
Municipal issues					
Negotiated issues	$115.2	$ 78.5	$ 90.8	$ 92.9	$ 95.5
Competitive issues	33.1	23.4	26.8	29.9	30.3
All issues	$148.3	$101.9	$117.6	$122.9	$125.8

Note: Dollars in billions.

the preference of most corporate issuers for negotiated underwritings, competitive bidding has made some inroads into the corporate world. The corporate form of competitive bidding is through Rule 415 of the SEC.

Negotiated underwritings usually involve a single investment bank as manager of the deal. Occasionally, however, two or more firms may jointly enter into the management of the underwriting. In such cases, the issue is said to be comanaged. Smaller issues tend to have a single firm as manager, unless the client firm insists on comanagers because of a desire to maintain close relationships with more than one investment bank. In some large issues, it is not uncommon for as many as five firms to be involved in comanaging a single underwriting. In those instances, one firm, called the lead comanager, handles most of the contact with the issuer.

To share the underwriting risk, the manager or comanagers generally invite other firms into the offering. The process of risk sharing with other firms is called syndication and may include as few as 5 or as many as 250 firms, although most underwritings involve a syndicate of between 10 and 40 firms. Compensation is paid to the members of the underwriting syndicate according to the size of their underwriting (buying) commitment. Firms are invited to participate as members of the syndicate on the basis of (1) reciprocity (i.e., the amount of business they have shared with the managing firm on other occasions); (2) distribution (selling) capabilities; (3) capital capacity to purchase and hold the securities during the offering period; and (4) client preferences. Traditional groupings of firms may also contribute to the structure of the syndicate, since it is traditional for certain firms that have a long history of cooperation to work together.[1]

---

[1] See infra section 2.05 for a detailed discussion of syndicates.

[a] **Registration With the SEC.** In all publicly underwritten securities offerings, approval for the underwriting syndicate to sell the securities must be obtained from the SEC. The approval procedure requires the investment banking firm to submit a written offering document (prospectus) containing a full description of the company, its competitors, risks that it faces, and its financial history, which is reviewed by the SEC. When the SEC gives final approval to the prospectus, the issue is given a final price by the managing underwriter and is sold to the public. The SEC approves only the information in the prospectus; it does not approve the price at which the securities are sold. The SEC has no opinion about value; its opinion is strictly about full disclosure. If investors wish to make poor investment decisions, they are free to do so. The SEC insists only that there be complete and adequate information available for a rational investment decision.

[b] **Rule 415.** SEC Rule 415 is an exception to the traditional registration of securities through a prospectus. The original reason for Rule 415 was that there are numerous companies in the United States that are already well known to investors, and the additional detailed information in a prospectus is not new information. These are companies that report their full financial performance to the SEC quarterly. Rule 415 allows those companies simply to announce that they plan to issue securities some time during the next two years, and, after a cursory review, the SEC gives approval in a form that is called a shelf registration. This description means that the company has securities "on the shelf," ready to issue at any time that it deems appropriate. Because the securities are effectively preregistered, the actual issuance can be quite speedy.

In many ways, Rule 415 has been viewed as increasing competition within the industry. The effect of Rule 415 has been to turn what was a previously negotiated underwriting into a modified competitive bidding process whereby the investment banking firm or syndicate that offers the most for the securities will win the business. In a negotiated underwriting, the pricing happens after a managing investment bank has been selected.

Some observers have been critical of shelf registrations because the investment banks do not have adequate time to present the securities to the market for resale. In a negotiated underwriting, one of the services the investment bank performs is advising clients on the timing and form of the issue. It also "takes the client on the road" in advance of the issue to presell it to the market. With a Rule 415 offering, no real preselling can be done, so the competing investment banking firms must price the issue as well as they can simply on the basis of current market conditions. The result is that Rule 415 issues are much more common with debt securities, which trade much more like a commodity, than they are with equity securities. With equity securities, an individual company story accompanies the sale of the shares, and that story is difficult to tell given the speed of a Rule 415 equity issue.

[c] **Best-Efforts Offering.** Occasionally, firms issue securities without the guarantee of a formal underwriting. In those instances the investment bank enters into an agency (as opposed to a principal) agreement with the issuer to sell the securities on a "best-efforts" basis. There is no assurance of sale to the issuer. Best-efforts offerings are relatively rare and tend to be used only by smaller companies that are so unknown that no investment bank is willing to accept the risk of an underwriting.

[3] Sales and Distribution

When securities are purchased by an investment banking syndicate, they are then resold to investors. The sales function in most major investment banks is divided into institutional sales and retail sales. Firms that specialize in retail sales are sometimes referred to as wire houses, a term dating back to the days when the retail offices of such firms were connected to the trading floor of the New York Stock Exchange (NYSE) by wire telegraph. Although modern communications have long surpassed primitive wire systems, the term "wire house" endures to describe firms that are active in retail securities sales. These firms often have their offices at street level to encourage walk-in business by retail customers. Among the major national wire houses are Merrill Lynch, Dean Witter, and Prudential-Bache Securities. Most smaller, regional firms are also primarily retail in their market focus.

Institutional sales involve selling large blocks of stock to institutional buyers, including pension funds, endowment trusts, insurance companies, mutual funds, and other professionally managed portfolios. Some firms specialize in institutional sales and do not sell directly to the public. While such firms are often quite large in terms of capital and revenues, they tend to have far fewer offices and far fewer sales personnel than retail firms. Included among the well-known institutional firms are First Boston, Goldman Sachs, Morgan Stanley, and Salomon Brothers Inc.

Many investment banks have both institutional and retail sales forces. The employees who sell securities are referred to as producers. (The number of producers who work in the industry is shown in Figure 2-6.) At the end of 1988, 83,000 people were classified as producers in the U.S. investment banking industry; most were in retail sales.

[4] Research

Large research departments often supplement the sales and trading operations of investment banks. Research departments are usually not profit centers in the firm, but rather are cost centers with the value of their services being captured in the sales, trading, and underwriting profits of the firm.

Research departments prepare reports and opinions about securities for customers. Major full-service broker-dealers often compete based on the quality of their research reports, which are usually passed on free to customers that make trades with them. Occasionally, research is sold to customers or to other firms on a fee basis. In those instances, research can generate direct profits for the firm.

It is common for investment banks active in underwriting to prepare favorable research reports on the companies that are their underwriting clients and in which they make a market. These reports are expected to be objective assessments of the stocks and bonds being traded, but they generally reflect favorably on the client. For that reason, research reports from investment banks are often referred to as sell-side research, meaning that they are prepared by the broker-dealer, not the ultimate purchaser of the securities.

Investment banks often maintain research opinions on the securities in which they make a market. The end of industrywide fixed commissions on May 1, 1975 significantly changed the research function at many investment banks. Prior to 1975, the commission rates in the brokerage business were nonnegotiable and high enough that elaborate research reports were a primary means of nonprice competition within the

FIGURE 2-6

Shrinking Employment in the Investment Banking Industry: Producers Versus Others

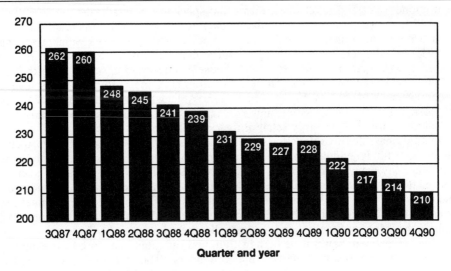

Quarter and year

```
Producers      97  92  90  89  88  88  86  84  82  81  78  77  75  74
Nonproducers  165 168 158 156 153 151 146 146 145 147 144 140 139 136
```

Note: NYSE firms' employment in thousands.

industry. Since the mandating of competitive (negotiated) commissions, the amount of free research that firms can profitably provide has been greatly reduced. For example, discount brokerages announce that their commissions are low in large part because they offer no research opinions to customers. Even at large institutional investment banks, much of the important securities analysis has moved from investment banks to the ultimate buyers of securities. This research done by institutions that purchase securities for their portfolios is called buy-side research.

[5] Trading and Brokerage

In addition to underwriting and selling newly issued securities, investment banks also trade already-issued securities. Aftermarket trading may be simply a brokerage function, in which the investment bank acts as an agent for customers' orders, or it may involve a dealer function, whereby the investment bank carries an inventory of the securities and speculates for its own account as well. Profits from securities trading may account for 25 percent or more of a firm's profit in a typical year.

The Glass-Steagall Act does not preclude commercial banks from acting as agents or brokers but merely prohibits commercial banks from holding inventory as dealers. Thus, in the pure brokerage function, it has always been possible for commercial banks to compete directly with investment banks. Until now, commercial banks did not generally take advantage of their brokerage capabilities for private debt and equity securities, except for servicing a few large clients in their trust departments.

[a] Market Making in Listed Securities. Investment banking firms are divided into two categories: firms that are members of the NYSE and nonmember firms.

NYSE member firms are expressly prohibited from making a market (i.e., holding a trading inventory) in the securities listed on the exchange, because the NYSE is a central auction market, where all trades in the securities listed are brought to a single specialist for pricing and reporting. Nonmember firms, however, are free to make a market in unlisted securities (i.e., securities traded on the National Association of Securities Dealers Automatic Quotation (NASDAQ) system). Most NYSE member firms are active dealers in the NASDAQ markets, as are most nonmember firms. The specific securities in which individual firms make a market vary greatly from firm to firm and within the same firm over time.

[b] Market Making in OTC Securities. Unlisted securities, called over-the-counter (OTC) securities, offer a major market-making opportunity for major investment banks. Frequently, the OTC securities in which an investment bank makes a market are the companies or municipalities that are underwriting clients of the bank. Investment banking firms that make a market in an OTC security are automatically shown on the NASDAQ system when the security's call letters are called. Some small, low-volume stocks are traded without being quoted on the NASDAQ system. Prices for these securities are listed on a daily or weekly sheet (the "pink sheet") circulated to broker-dealers.

To be a market maker, a firm must post a bid and asked price and be willing to make at least a minimum number of purchases (100 shares) at that price. Because market making involves a commitment of the investment bank's own funds, this activity is closely controlled and centralized at the firm's headquarters, where expert personnel can monitor the exposure of trading positions. Much of the market making in securities is centralized in New York City, the headquarters for most major firms. Regional firms, however, are often significant market makers in companies in their own region.

Securities trading is a major profit center for many investment banks as well as an important follow-up activity in supporting the securities of important underwriting clients. Profits from trading may account for 25 percent to 50 percent or more of a firm's revenues and profits in a typical year.

[c] Pure Arbitrage. Arbitrage is closely connected with market making in the trading room of an investment bank. The essential difference between market making and pure arbitrage is that the latter involves the simultaneous buying and selling of a security in two separate markets to take advantage of an illogical price differential. For example, if a share of stock, for some reason, is trading at different prices on the NYSE and the Pacific Coast Stock Exchange, the investment bank arbitrage desk will sell the higher-priced share and simultaneously buy the lower-priced share, counting the difference as profit. In pure arbitrage, there is no risk whatsoever. Since investment banks pay no commissions on their own trades, the arbitrage desks of investment banks can usually spot and exploit pure arbitrage opportunities before they are large enough to be profitable to the general public. Not only are arbitrage activities profitable for investment banks, they also provide a service by keeping the markets efficient.

[d] Risk Arbitrage. The term "risk arbitrage," although frequently heard, is a definitional misnomer because, technically, the term "arbitrage" means a riskless simultaneous transaction. The term "risk arbitrage" has crept into the language of investment banking to describe a transaction that includes the purchase and sale of two separate equity securities upon the announcement of a merger. For example, if security A is selling for $30 and security B is selling for $10, and a merger is announced in which company A is offering one share of its stock for two shares of company B stock, the risk arbitrage trader could purchase 20,000 shares of company B for $2 million and sell short 10,000 shares of Company A for $3 million. At the consummation of the merger, the receipt of 10,000 B shares would allow the covering of the short, and $1 million would be profit. The risk of the transaction is that if the merger does not occur, for legal or other reasons, the prices of the two securities may move in unpredictable ways and cause considerable loss.

Because this type of arbitrage is risky, it can be highly profitable for the astute trader. In an active arena of mergers and acquisitions, risk arbitrage between merger partners provides a large profit center for numerous investment banks. For that reason, it has also been the area where insider trading charges have been most prevalent, and investment banks must be exceedingly cautious that they trade only on information that is truly public and known in the market.

[e] Block Trading of Debt and Equity. Block trading at investment banks refers to the purchase and sale of large blocks of stock, most often owned by institutions, that are too big for the floor of the major exchanges. The major exchanges have special rules for block trading that allow member firms to trade large issues of listed securities off the floor of the exchange; however, the price at which the blocks trade must be reported to the exchange to give information to the investing public.

Because block trading may be effected through the use of the capital of the investment bank, it is another illustration of the riskiness of the trading business. If mutual fund A, for example, wishes to sell 175,000 shares of security X, the block trader may purchase the shares even though there is a visible buyer for only 150,000 of the shares. The unsold shares are carried in inventory with all of the accompanying price risk until they can be sold. Similarly, an investment bank may make a commitment to sell a large block that it does not own. The price risk in this transaction relates to the ability of the firm to acquire the stock at a price lower than the price it agreed to in the sale.

For a firm to be successful in the block trading of either debt or equity, it must have substantial capital to risk in holding securities in inventory. This greatly reduces the number of firms active in the block trading business. In addition, good block traders are expected to have wide contacts with large customers and a good feel for the market.

[f] Government Bond Trading. The trading of government bonds (federal, state, and local) is generally done in a separate trading department of the investment bank. This is one activity in which investment banks compete directly with commercial banks, as the Glass-Steagall Act specifically exempts government bond underwriting and trading from its provisions. The largest government federal government bond departments (in both commercial and investment banks) are classified as official U.S. government bond dealers and are permitted to bid for new federal bond issues and to trade directly with the Federal Reserve Bank of New York.

Bond dealers are high-volume, low-margin operations, with many of the same risk-return characteristics as block trading, and in major investment banks, the government bond desk has significant profit potential.

[6] Options and Derivative Securities

One of the most important investment banking developments in recent years is the invention, sale, and distribution of new types of securities often called derivative securities. These instruments, which include options, futures, forward contracts, and swaps, are often referred to as preferred equities redeemable with common stock (PERCS) or liquidity option notes (LYONs), reflecting attributes well suited to the risk reduction requirements of a buying or selling client. The securities are actively traded in a separate financial engineering, derivative securities, or options department. Their purpose is to allow for the hedging of risk in complex and fast-moving worldwide financial markets, and they are particularly important in hedging interest rate risk, currency risk, and commodities prices.

2.03 FEE-BASED SERVICES

Augmenting the underwriting, sales and brokerage, and trading functions in investment banks is a series of fee-based services conducted by the corporate finance department or various other departments of the firm. (See Figure 2-7 for a breakdown of the revenues and expenses of NYSE firms.) The most important fee-based services include private placements, mergers and acquisitions (M&As), financial consulting, and real estate investment and brokerage.

[1] Private Placements

For many firms, the public issuance of securities is neither feasible nor preferable. Reasons may include the small size of the issue, a need for speed in issuance, complexity or nonstandard nature of the securities, a desire for minimal public disclosure, or a host of other factors that can make a public underwriting difficult. Capital for these clients is often raised through a private placement sold to institutions such as insurance companies, pension funds, or trusts. For a fee, investment banks design and market private placements, and private placements are a significant countercyclical business activity for the bank, as the level of publicly underwritten debt and equity offerings fluctuates.

[2] Mergers and Acquisitions

Since the late 1960s, most major investment banks have been active in representing buyers and/or sellers in all types of business combinations. This activity is usually managed from specialized M&A departments with expert personnel active in both soliciting and negotiating deals. Included in M&A work are both friendly and hostile

FIGURE 2-7

Revenues and Expenses of NYSE Firms Doing Public Business (1988–1990)

Source: Securities Industry DataBank

	1988	1989	1990
Revenues			
Commissions	$ 8,791	$10,151	$ 8,878
Gains (losses) on trading accounts	11,299	12,343	13,175
Gains (losses) on investment accounts	1,394	488	(283)
Profits (losses) from underwriting and selling groups	5,158	4,120	3,243
Margin interest	3,029	3,723	3,075
Mutual fund sales	1,413	1,580	1,669
Account supervision	1,885	2,226	2,241
Research	23	27	18
Commodities	1,382	1,408	1,686
Other: Securities related	14,693	20,338	17,389
Other: Securities unrelated	2,762	3,134	2,942
Total revenues	$51,829	$59,537	$54,034
Expenses			
Registered rep. compensation	$ 7,581	$ 7,539	$ 6,868
Clerical and administrative	9,281	9,103	8,789
Other employee compensation	530	837	877
Salaries for partners and voting stockholder officers	1,349	1,346	1,182
Floor brokerage and clearance	1,756	1,855	1,731
Communications	2,549	2,374	2,222
Data processing	737	711	685
Occupancy and equipment	3,052	3,163	3,092
Promotional costs	1,004	955	878
Interest expense	16,308	24,070	22,717
Error account and bad debt losses	438	422	296
Other expenses	4,754	5,320	4,859
Total expenses	$49,337	$57,695	$54,196
Net income before taxes	$ 2,492	$ 1,842	$ (162)

Note: Dollars in millions, unconsolidated.

takeovers, with firms specializing in specific types of mergers. For example, some firms refuse to represent buyers in unfriendly acquisitions. Other firms have become quite expert in defending companies from hostile takeovers.

The level of merger activity in the 1980s was so extraordinarily high that it became a significant source of profit for many Wall Street firms, although a self-correcting mechanism in the level of M&As has slowed the pace of merger activity, as shown in Figure 2-8. M&A work is an expanding function of many full-service firms, despite the fact that commercial banks compete as aggressively in M&As as they do in private

FIGURE 2-8

Growth in M&As (1981–1990)

Source: Sanford C. Bernstein & Co., Inc.

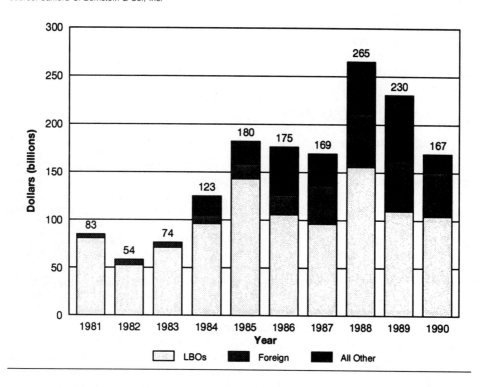

placements. The preponderance of the major mergers, however, are still handled by investment banks. Compensation for M&A work may be on a retainer basis, a percentage of the transaction, or both. The commission for a single successful purchase or sale can run into millions of dollars.

[3] Financial Consulting

The expertise of the corporate finance and trading departments of investment banks is available to assist clients in planning their financial strategy. Among the services provided may be consulting relating to the optimal capital structure, liquidity management, dividend policy, or fairness opinions in connection with the price of mergers. Fee-based financial consulting may be emphasized during slow periods in the market, when regular underwriting and trading activities are not as active. The reputations of many major investment banks in the financial consulting field have grown to the point that it is a significant source of income and competitive advantage for firms that perform it well.

[4] Real Estate Investment and Brokerage

During the 1980s, large institutional investors became increasingly interested in the investment opportunities afforded by real estate. Major investment banks responded by opening real estate departments or real estate subsidiaries to assist these real estate–oriented investors, frequently becoming brokers in the purchase and sale of large commercial properties, including office buildings, shopping centers, and even agricultural land.

2.04 FUNDS MANAGEMENT

[1] Merchant Banking

The term "merchant banking" does not have a universally agreed-on meaning in U.S. investment banks. It has its origins in the United Kingdom, where there is a tradition of certain financial institutions, called merchant banks, directly investing partners' funds in both the loans and equity of their customers. Commercial banks in the United States are precluded from this type of activity, but investment banks are free to pursue merchant banking side by side with their underwriting and trading activities.

For years, investment banks raised funds but did not invest their own funds in their clients' businesses. The reason for such a "no-invest" policy was to minimize conflicts of interest and competition with clients. The advent of heavily leveraged buyouts of companies, however, induced many investment banks to invest their own funds in the debt and equity of clients. Such investments, their monitoring, and their holding for resale at a later date are called merchant banking.

The risks of merchant banking are high, but the rewards have been substantial for many firms. An active merchant banking group can consume considerable amounts of capital within the firm, and it is often an important adjunct to the M&A group, especially when it is only possible to effect an acquisition if the investment bank itself is willing to supply some of the capital for the purchase. In that regard, merchant banking's relation to the M&A department is similar to the bank's willingness to hold and inventory securities to support the trading desk.

[2] Portfolio Management

Investment banks also assist both institutional and individual investors through fee-based fiduciary management of portfolios. This activity closely resembles that of the trust department of a major commercial bank, where discretionary investment authority is delegated to the firm. Investment management has taken on an even larger role in many investment banks with the expansion of mutual funds sold by the large investment banking firms.

[3] Mutual Funds

Many investment banks sponsor mutual funds as a way to generate fiduciary fee income and to provide a diversified product for their sales force. Domestic and international equity funds, long-term bond funds, short-term bond funds, and money market funds are some of the products offered. The funds themselves are owned by the fund share-holders, but the investment management of the assets in the fund can be a significant profit center for the investment bank. Most often, mutual fund management companies and investment management departments are organized as wholly owned subsidiaries of the investment bank.

[4] Venture Capital

A major financial reality of the last two decades is the huge requirement for funds for new ventures. The riskiness of these investments requires special expertise; hence, numerous investment banks have venture capital funds that they both sponsor and manage. These funds are a source of both fee income and incentive return to the bank if the fund performs well. In some instances investment banks invest their own funds as well in venture activities.

[5] Tax Shelters

Tax shelters are a variation on the mutual fund and venture capital business that relates specifically to investment funds that take advantage of the favorable tax treatment accorded to certain specific types of investments. The most common tax shelters relate to oil and gas, real estate, minerals and mining, and agriculture. Few investment banking firms are active in all of these industries; rather, they specialize in originating and distributing tax shelter investments in particular industries or group of industries.

2.05 SYNDICATE SYSTEM

The syndicate system is a creation of the investment banking industry to share risk in the underwriting and distribution of the securities. It is integral to the investment banking function. Understanding the syndicate system requires definitions of the following terms.

[1] Manager

The syndicate manager is the firm that originates the issue and deals directly with the client company (issuer). Prior to the formation of a syndicate, the manager is responsible for working with the client in designing the issue, preparing the legal and accounting documents as required by the SEC, and holding due diligence meetings with prospective investors, at which time the securities and the company are explained to investors. These meetings are oral presentations of the prospectus material, with time for questions.

Most important among the legal requirements for a new issue is the preparation of the prospectus that outlines, in legal form, all of the relevant facts, especially the risks for the issuing company.

When more than one manager is involved in the origination of the issue, the issue is said to have comanagers. There is an increasing trend in the investment banking business toward comanagerships, since the competitiveness of the industry has quickened, and corporations increasingly prefer to have a relationship with more than one investment banker. When there are comanagers, however, one firm generally takes the lead in dealing with the client and in managing the syndicate: for example, selecting participants and keeping track of the selling effort across firms. That manager is designated as the manager running the books and is called the lead manager or book-running manager.

[2] Underwriting Group

The group of firms invited by the manager or comanagers to share the risk of underwriting the issue, the underwriting group, guarantees to accept a fixed number of securities at a price promised to the seller. The traditional purpose of the underwriting group was to ensure that there was enough financial capacity to absorb the issue if the market did not permit a quick resale. It is the underwriting syndicate that appears in the public announcements of the issue printed in the financial press. These announcements are most often called tombstone advertisements, because of the style in which they are printed. A representative tombstone ad is shown in Figure 2-9.

[3] Selling Group

The selling group represents the firms that actually sell the issue to investors. In issues for which the demand is great, the selling group and the underwriting group are nearly identical. Major underwriters prefer to sell their entire underwritten commitment rather than give up the commission to rival firms. In other issues, the selling group may be quite different and may include many more firms than the underwriting group. Most often, the selling group contains smaller retail firms that are not invited to take a major underwriting position. Figure 2-10 shows the major global underwriters, and Figure 2-11 shows the major domestic underwriters.

[4] Compensation in the Underwriting Syndicate

The basis for compensation in an underwriting syndicate is the spread, the difference between the price paid to the issuer and the price at which securities are sold to the public. In equity offerings, the spread may range from as low as 2 percent to a maximum of 10 percent of the offering price. In debt issues, the price spread typically ranges from a low of 0.5 percent to as high as 2 percent, with typical spreads in the 1 percent to 1.5 percent range. If a managing underwriter deems that the normal spread or maximum allowable spread is inadequate to compensate for the risk of the issue, additional compensation to the underwriters may be provided in the form of options (warrants) on the stock or, in some instances, in direct fees for planning the offering. Such extra payments to the underwriters, however, tend to be rare and to be associated only with highly speculative first public offerings.

The spread, in turn is divided among the syndicate as follows: The managers (or comanagers) receive 15 percent to 20 percent, the underwriters receive 10 percent to

FIGURE 2-9

Sample Syndication Tombstone Advertisement

2,489,750 Shares

Common Stock
(par value $.001 per share)

Price $20 Per Share

Upon request, a copy of the Prospectus describing these securities and the business of the Company may be obtained within any State from any Underwriter who may legally distribute it within such State. The securities are offered only by means of the Prospectus, and this announcement is neither an offer to sell nor a solicitation of an offer to buy.

Goldman, Sachs & Co.   **Montgomery Securities**

Bear, Stearns & Co. Inc.   **The First Boston Corporation**   **Alex. Brown & Sons**
Incorporated

A.G. Edwards & Sons, Inc.   **Kemper Securities, Inc.**   **Lehman Brothers**

Merrill Lynch & Co.   **PaineWebber Incorporated**   **Robertson, Stephens & Company**

Smith Barney, Harris Upham & Co.   **Dean Witter Reynolds Inc.**   **Advest, Inc.**
Incorporated

Sanford C. Bernstein & Co., Inc.   **William Blair & Company**   **Dain Bosworth**
Incorporated

Furman Selz   **McDonald & Company**   **Piper Jaffray Inc.**
Incorporated   Securities, Inc.

Rauscher Pierce Refsnes, Inc.   **Raymond James & Associates, Inc.**

Sutro & Co. Incorporated   **Tucker Anthony**   **Wheat First Butcher & Singer**
Incorporated   Capital Markets

Crowell, Weedon & Co.   **First Manhattan Co.**   **Gruntal & Co., Incorporated**

C.J. Lawrence Inc.   **Scott & Stringfellow, Inc.**   **Stifel, Nicolaus & Company**
Incorporated

April 7, 1993

FIGURE 2-10

Top Global Underwriters of Debt and Equity

Source: Securities Data Company, Inc.

Manager	Amount	1992 Market Share	1991 Market Share
Merrill Lynch & Co., Inc.	$ 150.7	13.3%	13.0%
Goldman, Sachs & Co.	119.6	10.6	10.1
Shearson Lehman Brothers Inc.	106.2	9.4	8.3
The First Boston Corporation	98.7	8.7	9.0
Kidder, Peabody & Co. Incorporated	81.0	7.1	6.0
Salomon Brothers Inc.	80.3	7.1	5.8
Morgan Stanley Group Inc.	72.5	6.4	6.9
Bear, Stearns & Co. Inc.	53.4	4.7	3.9
J.P. Morgan Securities Inc.	29.2	2.6	2.0
Prudential Securities Incorporated	28.6	2.5	2.0
Top 10	$ 820.30	72.4%	67.0%
Industry total	$1,133.10	100.0%	100.0%

Note: Dollars in billions.

30 percent, and the selling firms receive 50 percent to 75 percent. Of course, if the managing firm sells all of the securities it has underwritten, that firm will retain the entire spread. In modern investment banking compensation, the major portion of the spread goes to the managers and the sellers, with less to the underwriters. Of course, since the underwriters and sellers of the issue tend much more to be the same firms, the breakdown in the spread is a less important consideration than it once was.

[5] Underwriting Hierarchy and Reading a Tombstone Advertisement

The tombstone ads that appear in the financial press, usually after the issue has been sold, contain a great deal of information about the syndication process.

A tombstone ad contains the issuer's name, followed by the size of the issue (number of shares or dollar amount of bonds), followed by the price to the public. The name of the manager or comanager appears on the top line. Should there be more than one manager, the firm appearing on the left-hand side of the first line is the firm that is running the books.

The underwriting syndicate follows the manager's line, usually in alphabetical order. The syndicate is divided into groups representing major participants, submajor participants, second bracket participants, and regional firms.

Each separate group in the tombstone is recognizable by a new alphabetical order. It is accepted practice in the syndicate system for each member firm in a given group to participate equally in the underwriting, i.e., to accept underwriting responsibility for an equal number of shares to the other firms in that group. Furthermore, the major

FIGURE 2-11

Top Domestic Underwriters

Source: Investment Dealers' Digest *(Jan. 6, 1992), p. 24*

Manager	Jan. 1, 1991–Dec. 31, 1991				Jan. 1, 1990–Dec. 31, 1990			
	Amount	Rank	%	Issues	Amount	Rank	%	Issues
Merrill Lynch & Co., Inc.	$101,757.7	1	17.4	1,209	$ 55,680.0	1	17.8	710
Goldman, Sachs & Co.	72,774.1	2	12.4	1,017	39,003.6	2	12.5	462
Shearson Lehman Brothers Inc.	70,544.8	3	12.0	1,453	19,903.6	7	6.4	459
The First Boston Corporation	57,468.9	4	9.8	956	32,267.1	3	10.3	525
Kidder, Peabody & Co. Incorporated	50,099.0	5	8.5	1,721	21,662.4	6	6.9	644
Morgan Stanley Group Inc.	48,030.5	6	8.2	564	31,207.6	5	10.0	324
Salomon Brothers Inc.	43,652.4	7	7.4	626	32,232.2	4	10.3	378
Bear, Stearns & Co. Inc.	33,407.0	8	5.7	1,089	19,346.7	8	6.2	536
Prudential Securities Incorporated	18,429.0	9	3.1	613	12,711.4	9	4.1	334
Donaldson, Lufkin & Jenrette, Inc.	11,181.7	10	1.9	324	6,585.7	10	2.1	298
PaineWebber Incorporated	10,230.5	11	1.7	356	5,970.6	11	1.9	169
J.P. Morgan Securities Inc.	10,072.2	12	1.7	212	3,532.6	14	1.1	96
Alex. Brown & Sons	7,475.9	13	1.3	65	2,834.4	18	0.9	32
Smith Barney, Harris Upham & Co. Incorporated	6,336.8	14	1.1	255	3,504.8	15	1.1	117
Dean Witter Capital Markets	5,559.7	15	0.9	37	5,263.7	12	1.7	24
Industry totals	$585,970.0			11,968	$312,110.0			6,064

Note: All domestic issues (full credit to lead manager). Dollars in millions.

group typically underwrites somewhat fewer shares than the managers, the submajor group underwrites still fewer shares than the major group, and so forth. Thus, the underwriting income (and risk) for a firm is directly correlated to its position in the tombstone ad. Over long periods, reading tombstone ads can provide an important indicator of the competitive strength of an investment bank in the underwriting business. Observers of tombstone ads follow the rise and fall of firms on Wall Street with great interest.

2.06 COMPETITION AMONG INVESTMENT BANKING FIRMS

In recent years, there has been a large increase in the degree of competition among investment banking firms. This competition has been heightened by increased activity by commercial banks in areas formerly handled exclusively by investment banks. Of course, commercial banks are still precluded from underwriting, selling, and trading private debt and equity securities.

Thus, the day of complete competition between commercial and investment banks has not yet arrived. To understand the basis of the new competition within investment banking, some review of traditional competition in investment banking is in order.

[1] Traditional Competition

Prior to the last decade, the investment banking industry was organized primarily around the negotiated underwriting. In this system, corporations maintained a relationship with their investment bank that was similar to the relationship they had with their accounting firm or law firm. It was a rare event for a corporate client to change investment bankers without good reason, such as a change in the personnel handling the account or a major dispute about pricing. Occasionally, firms changed investment bankers owing to disappointment in the research coverage of the firm, but, by and large, an investment banking relationship was long term in nature.

The competitive position of underwriters was also typified by a large degree of specialization. Several major firms, called origination firms, concentrated on originating deals that were then syndicated and distributed to the selling groups. The originating firms were major institutional firms with strong corporate finance staffs and a long history of stable client relationships. On the other hand, major distribution firms were often retail firms or wire houses with a large network of salespersons and selling offices.

A major shift in this relatively stable competitive environment occurred during the 1970s, when many of the strong selling firms openly began to solicit underwriting business. The result was that a number of the historical investment banking relationships were the object of intense competition. Implicit in this new competition was a desire on the part of many selling firms to obtain more of the management and underwriting fees that accompanied new offerings.

[2] Increased Emphasis on Distribution

Traditionally, major underwriting firms had significant power over the distribution firms because they had the ability to withhold securities (i.e., product) from the distribution firms if they were excessively aggressive in soliciting underwriting clients. Thus, a major distribution firm or wire house needed underwritings to supply its sales force with securities to sell. Newly issued securities were particularly important to firms with large sales forces because the selling commissions on new issues are often two to three times larger than commissions on other sales. For years, the complementary relationship between originating firms and distribution firms had the effect of perpetuating a certain stability in the industry. Major underwriting firms were generally judged to be important competitors according to four basic criteria:[2]

1. *Clients.* The clientele list of a major investment bank was its strongest asset. Given the stability of client relationships, a good clientele list was an assurance of major status in the competitive hierarchy of investment banking firms. The firms that brought many deals to market were the ones invited to participate in other firms' underwritings in a major way.

2. *Capital.* The capital requirements of the NYSE assure that the firms that are to be major underwriters must have enough capital to be in compliance with the regulations during the period of an underwriting. Thus, inadequately capitalized firms were automatically precluded from major underwriting participation. As the size of issues has grown in recent years, the importance of the capital requirement has grown proportionately.

3. *Selling power.* Ultimately, underwritings must be sold. The distribution capability of a major underwriter can be in the form of in-house sales capability or the ability to put together a strong syndicate of distribution firms, usually wire houses. In the final analysis, the distribution capability of the major firms is really tested only in the marketplace.

4. *Strong syndicate department.* The effectiveness of syndicate managers within firms is a key variable in maintaining major investment bank position. Since syndicate managers are dealing with other firms on a regular basis, the reputation of these partners for effective and dependable performance is critical in maintaining the position of their firms as major investment banks.

2.07 CHOOSING AN UNDERWRITER

In a negotiated underwriting, an issuing corporation's choice of underwriter is a major decision. Underwriters may be supermajor and major national firms, strong regional firms, or small specialty houses that have established a reputation for excellence in certain industries, such as high technology, petroleum, transportation, or municipal finance. This reputation is based on an established clientele and a cultivated market for the securities of the industries in which they specialize.

The choice among underwriting firms is often not a scientific one. Nonetheless, some guidelines may be important. The services of the firm include assisting the issuer in choosing debt, equity, or various other more complex securities, such as convertible bonds, debt with warrants, or preferred stock. In some instances, the investment banker may even be consulted on the currency in which a security is to be denominated if access to international capital markets is possible.

Increasingly, issuing companies have become expert in designing their own securities; thus, for some companies, the outside expertise of the investment banker in structuring the deal has become less important. Thus, the advice of the corporate finance professionals in the investment bank may be less important than other factors in choosing an underwriter. Some of these other factors are the following:

---

[2] See "Investment Banking: Power Structure in Flux," *Harvard Business Review* (Mar.–Apr. 1971), pp. 136–152.

- *Relative importance of the client to the firm.* Many corporations must make the imprecise judgment whether it is better to be a major client of a smaller investment bank or a less important client of a well-known major firm. Smaller, regional firms tend to compete in tailor-made service for smaller, regional clients; larger firms tend to concentrate their expertise in Fortune 1000 companies. However, many exceptions to these size groupings are evident.

- *In cases where the issue is to be marketed, regional firms have a particular advantage in marketing stocks that are of interest primarily to regional clientele.* Alternatively, many regional issuers wish to sell their securities nationally, which leads them to a national underwriter. It should be noted, however, that many regional firms can support a national selling effort by inviting a national firm to comanage the issue. Some emerging companies find the combination of a regional and a national firm to be the best combination of strengths for marketing their securities.

- *Aftermarket attention.* The choice of an underwriter also frequently depends on the issuer's assessment of the strength of the underwriter in making an orderly market in the securities after issuance, especially if the firm is not listed on a major exchange. If the firm is listed, the underwriter can be expected to follow the securities (particularly equity) by writing appropriate research reports to keep interest in the stock high. Firms develop reputations based on the extent to which they support their underwriting clients in the aftermarket. Ultimately, the choice of an underwriter depends on the service the client can expect before and after the issuance. In the competitive world of modern underwriting, clients can be and frequently are the object of great attention from more than one investment banker. After the decision is made to proceed with a given firm, however, the competitive activity subsides significantly and the cooperative relationship of a negotiated underwriting commences.

[1] Changes in Underwriting Relationships

A major increase in competition in the issuance of securities took place in the early 1980s with the inauguration of Rule 415 of the SEC. Under Rule 415, publicly traded securities that are already reporting on a quarterly basis to the SEC may register securities in advance of their issuance through shelf registration. Securities so registered may then be sold at any time in the coming year by a process closely resembling competitive bidding.

Under the rule, the firm simply announces its intention to issue all or part of the securities registered under the shelf registration and receives offers from investment banks for the securities. If the offers are acceptable to the firm, the issue is sold; if they are not, the issue can be delayed temporarily or indefinitely. The clear result of Rule 415 is that corporations may have multiple relationships with investment banks and may use different banks in sequence over a short period.

Some observers have noted that Rule 415 has revolutionized the process of issuing securities, with the entire industry becoming much more transaction-driven and much less relationship-driven. Underwriters today simply bid for securities for resale, and many traditional relationships have diminished.

In a Rule 415 transaction, the speed with which announcements and sales are made makes it exceedingly difficult to form a large traditional syndicate. Thus, the purchasing firm may take the entire issue for its own account. Alternatively, a limited number of comanagers are invited to underwrite and sell the entire transaction. Preselling is at a minimum, so investment banks must be willing to take more securities into inventory for longer periods.

Many traditional major investment banking firms have argued strongly that Rule 415 is not good for either issuers or the investment banking community. On the other hand, some of the large nontraditional underwriters have tended to support Rule 415 because it gives access to major clients for a number of nontraditional underwriters.

[2] Pricing an Issue

After the underwriter is chosen, pricing the issue is the major remaining step in a successful deal. To understand the pricing process, it is important to recognize that there are two major constituencies in an offering: sellers and buyers. The interests of these two parties are opposite: Sellers wish a high price for their securities; buyers want a low price.

In a debt or equity issue already traded in the market, the pricing problem is significantly reduced, since investment bankers are expected to price the security near the existing market, most often the previous day's closing price. Some deviation from the previous day's price may occur if that price is not considered representative owing to an unusually small trading volume. Thus, securities are occasionally priced at a small premium or discount from the last close.

For securities that are being publicly offered for the first time, the pricing decision carries considerably more risk. In new issues, there is no objective measure of the correct price. Underwriters in this instance usually attempt to price the issue according to indications of interest that are received by the syndicate manager from the syndicate members. These indications of interest are not firm, however, until the final pricing is done; thus, the element of risk is never completely eliminated. Only after an offering is over and distributed can a judgment be made about the report price.

To supplement indications of interest, the managing underwriter typically gathers data on similar companies in the industry to estimate intrinsic worth on a comparative basis. Factors included in the intrinsic worth calculation are earnings, growth rates in earnings, capital structure, dividend history, general company visibility and reputation in the industry, and industry outlook. All of these enter into a final pricing decision on the offering date.

At the time of the pricing recommendation of the underwriter, the issuer has the option of accepting or declining the final price. If the price is not accepted by the issuer, the offering cannot proceed. The issuer simply loses the out-of-pocket expenses of preparing the issue. These expenses are not small and consist mostly of legal and accounting costs. The underwriter loses the cost of time in preparing the offering, as well as the opportunity cost of the revenue of a successful offering. Since underwriters and clients have a large investment in preparing for the issue, and since they tend to work together closely in the preoffering period, it is rare that they cannot agree on the final offering price at the issuance date. Final negotiations can be stormy, however.

[3] Successful Offering

In first public offerings of equity, the pricing decision is generally considered successful if the price of the stock rises to a small premium of between 5 percent and 10 percent in the 20 days following the issue. If the stock rises quickly by more than 15 percent,

FIGURE 2-12
Capital Positions of Major Investment Banks

	Jan. 1, 1991		Jan. 1, 1990		Offices		Jan. 1, 1991 Employees		Jan. 1, 1991 RRs	
	Capital	Rank	Capital	Rank	Number	Rank	Number	Rank	Number	Rank
Merrill Lynch & Co., Inc.[a]	$9,566,989	1	$10,048,452[b]	1	510	2	39,000	1	11,800	1
Shearson Lehman Brothers Inc.	5,406,125	2	6,152,000	2	427	5	33,326	2	9,550	2
The Goldman Sachs Group, L.P.[a]	4,700,000[c]	3	4,018,000[d]	3	21	49	6,822	9	669	21
Salomon Brothers Inc.	4,419,700	4	3,619,759	4	17	51	4,520	14	961	14
Morgan Stanley Group Inc.[a]	3,380,435	5	2,648,000	5	12	65	7,079	8	543	24
PaineWebber Group Inc.	1,552,909	6	1,523,131	7	267	7	12,746	5	4,873	5
The First Boston Corporation	1,471,419	7	1,568,189	6	10	69	4,218	15	252	45
Dean Witter Reynolds Inc.	1,405,000	8	1,429,000	9	499	3	16,609	4	7,053	3
Bear, Stearns & Co. Inc.[a]	1,387,666	9	1,444,095	8	13	62	5,558	10	1,728	8
Prudential Securities Incorporated	1,224,281	10	1,322,074	10	336	6	17,000	3	6,000	4
Smith Barney, Harris Upham & Co. Incorporated	1,012,000	11	927,000	11	98	11	7,200	7	2,600	7
Donaldson, Lufkin & Jenrette, Inc.[a]	919,000	12	900,000	12	16	54	3,250	16	425	30
Kidder, Peabody & Co. Incorporated	619,642	13	616,045	14	55	22	5,067	12	1,367	13
The Bank of Tokyo Trust Company	601,937	14	682,830	13	NG[e]		1,059	33	NG[e]	
Nomura Securities International, Inc.	520,444	15	375,702	17	3		620	49	103	78

Firm									
J.P. Morgan Securities Inc.	16	506,837	468,761	15	6	90	854	40	188	54
Citicorp Securities Markets, Inc.	17	474,449	463,649	16	3		343	82	274	43
A.G. Edwards, Inc.	18	375,550	341,412	18	432	4	8,416	6	4,153	6
Wood Gundy Inc.	19	283,159	NG[e]		41	28	1,863	23	482	26
Kemper Securities Group, Inc.	20	278,747	NG[e]		178	8	4,800	13	1,670	9
Charles Schwab & Co., Inc.	21	270,201	328,593	19	130	9	2,950	17	1,418	12
Daiwa Securities America Inc.	22	270,115	218,168	28	3		400	72	91	86
UBS Securities Inc.	23	261,694	293,040	20	1		510	55	83	90
Oppenheimer & Co., Inc.	24	248,108	247,871	24	12	65	2,253	19	682	20
Dillon, Read & Co. Inc.	25	241,596	251,461	23	5		584	52	96	83
Van Kampen Merritt Inc.	26	239,035	237,896	26	14	60	407	71	24	
Deutsche Bank Capital Corporation	27	231,883	260,560	21	1		265	95	92	85
The Nikko Securities Co. International, Inc.	28	223,316	231,526	27	4		275	93	60	
Kemper Financial Services, Inc.	29	209,292	NG		1		452	63	30	
Nesbitt Thomson Inc.	30	203,511	148,631	36	33	33	1,500	30	450	29

Note: Dollars in thousands.

[a] Firm's capital is the sum of long-term borrowings and ownership equity.
[b] As of December 29, 1989.
[c] As of November 30, 1990.
[d] As of November 24, 1989.
[e] Information either not given, not available, or not applicable.

there is evidence that the security was underpriced, and the issuer may be less than satisfied with the offering. If it rises less than 5 percent, purchasers of the stock may be dissatisfied with its performance and may become early sellers, putting severe downward pressure on the price. A security that fails rapidly in the aftermarket is generally not considered good, even for the issuer, because the market for subsequent issues may be compromised by the poor price performance of the prior issue.

Investment bankers must satisfy both the sellers and the buyers of their securities, and the syndicate department ultimately is responsible for maintaining this sensitive balance. The syndicate manager stands in the middle between the corporate finance department representing the issuer and the sales department representing the buyer. It is not an easy task to balance the interests of these two constituencies; yet, an investment bank will thrive in the long run only to the extent that its reputation for good pricing decisions is intact. A firm with a reputation for underpricing will lose issuing clients. A firm with a reputation for overpricing will lose purchasers of its issues over time.

2.08 CAPITAL REQUIREMENTS

Few issues in investment banking loom as large as the tremendous need for capital to finance growth in the industry. During the last 30 years, the partnership form of organization was typical of investment banking firms, with a resulting chronic shortage of capital to finance the activities of the firms. To a major extent, the 1980s brought a revolution in the financing of investment banking firms and a trend toward the corporate form of organization as a means of increasing the permanent capital available for growth.

Capital is needed primarily to finance customer receivables (credit extended for customer purchases), trading account inventories, merchant banking, and huge underwriting commitments. While some of the funds for these activities are available through bank borrowings and other liabilities, ultimately the ability of a firm to grow or to do major business in underwriting, block trading, and retail services depends on the amount of equity capital at its disposal. Firms that do not have that capital run out of borrowing capacity and are simply not able to compete as effectively.

[1] Partnership Form

The partnership form of organization in the industry dates back to the 1700s, when there were few formal written contracts between firms and the full personal liability of partners was essential to the confidence of other firms doing business. Until 1970, for example, the NYSE refused membership to firms that were not partnerships, the rationale being that liability without limit for traders on the floor was integral to the functioning of the exchange. In 1970, however, the investment banking firm of Donaldson, Lufkin & Jenrette, Inc. pioneered the concept of the public corporation as a form of organization for an investment bank. It issued $12 million of new equity and started a trend that has influenced the subsequent organization of many prominent firms.

The advantages of the corporate form in both capital accumulation and retention are great. In partnerships, when the partners resign or retire, most wish to take their capital with them. Some partnerships have managed to overcome this problem by agreement that partners can withdraw their capital only over a period of years after leaving the firm. This agreement allows other partners to replenish the capital with their own funds. With the corporate form of organization, however, capital is permanent for the firm (excluding reductions from losses or dividends), and the firm may expand its capital when necessary by issuing new equity to the public. Furthermore, as owners wish to withdraw capital, they may do so by selling their shares in the public market, leaving the capital of the firm intact. The capital positions of the major national investment banks are shown in Figure 2-12.

[2] Mergers for Added Strength

An extension of the corporate form of organization in investment banking firms has been the sale of these firms to financial and nonfinancial holding companies. An example of such a sale has been the purchase of Dean Witter Reynolds Inc. by Sears, Roebuck & Co. or the purchase of Kidder, Peabody & Co. Incorporated by General Electric. The impact of these mergers and others of a similar nature has yet to be completely felt, but it is generally agreed that the capital strength of these new firms gives them some important competitive advantages in coping with the large capital requirements of a modern trading and underwriting function. What remains unclear is whether the innovative spirit and entrepreneurial culture of investment banking can be maintained in the corporate form of organization, especially under the umbrella of a nonfinancial holding company.

Suggested Reading

Benston, G.J. *The Separation of Commercial and Investment Banking: The Glass-Steagall Act Revisited and Reconsidered.* New York: Oxford University Press, 1990.

Birmingham, S. *Our Crowd.* New York: Harper & Row, 1969.

Bloch, E. *Pricing a Corporate Bond Issue: A Look Behind the Scenes.* New York: Federal Reserve Bank of New York, 1964.

——. *Inside Investment Banking.* Homewood, Ill.: Dow Jones-Irwin, 1989.

Brooks, J. *Once in a Golconda.* New York: Harper & Row, 1969.

Caroso, V.P. *Investment Banking in America: A History.* Cambridge, Mass.: Harvard University Press, 1970.

Eccles, R.G., and D.B. Crane. *Doing Deals.* Boston: Harvard Business School Press, 1988.

Friend, I., et al. *Investment Banking and the New Issues Market.* New York: World Publishing Co., 1967.

Hayes, S.L., III. "Investment Banking Power Structure in Flux." *Harvard Business Review* (Mar.–Apr. 1971), pp. 136–152.

——. "The Transformation of Investment Banking." *Harvard Business Review* (Jan.–Feb. 1979), pp. 153–170.

Hayes, S.L., III, and P.M. Hubbard. *Investment Banking: A Tale of Three Cities.* Boston: Harvard Business School Press, 1990.

Hayes, S.L., III, et al. *Competition in Investment Banking*. Cambridge, Mass.: Harvard University Press, 1983.

Logue, D., and J. Lindvall. "The Behavior of Investment Bankers: An Econometric Investigation." *Journal of Finance,* Vol. 29 (Mar. 1974), pp. 203–215.

Parker, G.G.C., and D. Cooperman. "Competitive Bidding in the Underwriting of Public Utility Securities." *Journal of Financial and Quantitative Analysis* (Dec. 1978), pp. 885–902.

Pepe, R., ed. *Securities Industry Yearbook*. New York: Securities Industry Association, 1991.

Perez, R.C. *Inside Investment Banking*. New York: Praeger, 1984.

Toto, G. and G. Monahan, eds. *Securities Industry Association 1991 Fact Book*. New York: Securities Industry Association, 1991.

Van Horne, J.C. *Financial Management and Policy,* 9th ed. Englewood Cliffs, N.J.: Prentice-Hall, Inc., 1992.

Wechsberg, J. *The Merchant Bankers*. Boston: Little, Brown, 1966.

Chapter 3

The Money Markets

ALAN G. JIRKOVSKY

3.01 DEFINITION OF THE MONEY MARKET

The money market represents one type of U.S. and international capital market. Its focus is on short-term financial instruments, typically with original maturities of less than one year. The money market is a collection of markets involving various money market instruments: short-term obligations of the federal government and federal agencies, commercial banks' certificates of deposit (CDs), federal funds (fed funds), banker's acceptances (BAs), repurchase agreements (RPs), and commercial paper (CP). The price (or interest rate) of each instrument is determined by supply in the market, credit conditions, and the overall state of the economy.

In addition, the money market has a primary component and a secondary component. The primary market provides a mechanism for quickly raising short-term financing to meet cash needs. The secondary market exists in order that participants can readily buy and sell short-term financial assets as their cash needs or positions change.

The money market is not centralized; rather, it is a communication system that links all parts of the country and many foreign financial centers. Although there are many participants, activity is centered on commercial banks, primary government security dealers, commercial paper dealers, BA dealers, money market brokers, and the New York Federal Reserve (Fed). (The Fed makes use of the money market to implement monetary policy.)

[1] Participants in the Money Market

Money market securities characteristically have a relatively high degree of safety. There is minimum risk of default or capital loss, although events in various financial markets may have an influence on the risk factor. The short-term aspect of the market allows for minimal time exposure on the part of the lender and less price volatility due to rate fluctuations. The high credit standing of the customer and the securities' short maturity are the chief reasons for the high degree of liquidity in the market.

Borrowers in the money market are the U.S. Treasury, government agencies, commercial banks, securities dealers, large finance companies, and well-known nonfinancial companies. Price differentiation exists in this market. This differentiation is influenced by the market's relative perception of each borrower's credit standing, the supply of a particular customer's debt instruments already in the market, and how a customer approaches the market. The Treasury provides the base rates. In addition to the bond market, the Treasury makes use of the money market because there is a ready demand for its short-term securities. Banks use the money market for funding through issuance of CDs and BAs and for managing cash positions through fed funds borrowings and lendings. Financial and nonfinancial companies fund working capital needs through the issuance of CP.

Suppliers of funds in the market include commercial banks, state and local governments, large nonfinancial companies, nonbank financial institutions, foreign banks, and individuals participating either directly or through money market funds. The Fed acts as both a supplier and borrower of funds in its implementation of monetary policy. Banks use the market to invest short-term excess funds through fed funds and securities, knowing that they can sell the securities again to get back their cash. Local governments often use the money market to invest funds temporarily (from tax revenues or bond issues) that may be committed for future use. Corporations holding excess cash receipts in anticipation of paying expenses often invest in short-term

FIGURE 3-1

Outstanding Volume of Selected Money Market Instruments (May 1992)

Source: Federal Reserve Bulletin

Instrument	Outstanding Volume	Average Daily Volume of Transactions[a]
Treasury bills	$618.2[b]	$36.6
BAs	38.4	NA
CP (all issuers)	533.7	21.3

Note: Dollars in billions.

[a] Transactions (market purchases and sales) of U.S. government primary security dealers reporting to the Fed.

[b] Data for June 1992.

instruments. Proceeds from corporate bond issues also may be channeled into the money market until needed. In addition, many participants are involved from a speculative standpoint, trying to profit from the movements of security prices. Figure 3-1 shows current volume outstanding and approximate daily trading volume for several money market instruments.

3.02 ROLE OF THE FEDERAL RESERVE IN THE MONEY MARKETS

The Fed is the largest single participant in money markets, after the Treasury's primary issuance activity. The Fed influences short-term interest rates more than any other factor. It also implements monetary policy through the Federal Reserve Open-Market Committee (FOMC) and through direct interaction by the Fed's open-market trading desk with the money markets.

The primary responsibility of the Fed is to contribute to the stability and growth of the national economy. This translates into a combination of goals of stable prices, high employment levels, and a stable dollar in foreign exchange markets. The Fed further attempts to accomplish these goals by regulating the overall growth in the money supply through adjusting the level of bank reserves and the fed funds rate.

[1] Money Supply and Bank Credit

The Fed uses three basic tools in implementing policy: reserve requirements, the discount rate, and open-market operations. Reserve requirements are the percentages of deposits that banks must put aside, and the discount rate is the minimum level of interest at which banks are permitted to borrow from the Fed. "Open-market operations" refers to the Fed's activity in buying and selling securities to adjust the level of reserves. In recent times, however, changes in reserve requirements and the dis-

FIGURE 3-2

Components of Monetary Aggregates (July 1992)

Source: Federal Reserve Statistical Release No. H.6 (Oct. 1992)

Component	Amount
M1	
Currency	$ 279.0
Demand deposits	315.6
Other checkable deposits	358.5
Traveler's checks	7.8
Total M1	960.8
M2	
M1	$ 960.8
Savings deposits	1,134.3
Small-denomination time deposits	941.7
Overnight RPs, overnight Eurodollars, general-purpose money market mutual funds, money market deposit accounts	423.9
Total M2	3,460.8
M3	
M2	$3,460.8
Large-denomination time deposits	388.5
Term RPs, term Eurodollars, institutional money market funds	313.7
Total M3	4,163.0
L	
M3	$4,163.0
Savings bonds	145.9
Short-term Treasury securities	337.9
BAs	21.7
CP	347.5
Total L	5,018.6

Note: Seasonally adjusted dollars in billions.

count rate have become less significant in the Fed's actions, while open-market operations have actually become the primary tool of Fed policy.

The Fed has defined four levels of money supply, the most important being M1, M2, and M3. These levels reflect varying degrees of liquidity. Figure 3-2 provides a breakdown of the various components of the different money supplies as of July 1992.

As Figure 3-2 shows, the money supply, however defined, is made up mainly of bank deposits. M1 consists primarily of nonbank balances that support transactions, funds that are readily spendable. M2 adds components of funds that are not considered to be transaction balances, such as savings accounts. M2 also includes bank money market accounts and money market mutual funds. M3 adds short-term institutional investments. All Fed member banks and all other depository institutions are required to hold reserves against these deposits in the form of non-interest-bearing deposits at one of the 12 regional Fed banks. The amount of these reserves is based on percentages of the various deposits that banks hold. The reserves held at the Fed facilitate the entire U.S. payment mechanism. The Fed operates as a clearinghouse for checks drawn on one bank and deposited in another. Reserve deposits also make it easy for the Fed to circulate currency. Yet, the most important function of reserves is the control of bank credit.

[2] Federal Reserve Policy and Strategies

The Fed's long-term goal is to promote sustainable growth in the economy while holding price levels stable and controlling inflation. To the extent that excessive growth in the money supply leads to inflation and disrupts true economic growth, the Fed's role would seem to be one of controlling monetary growth. Monetary policy, however, is only one factor that affects the economy. Fiscal policy and foreign trade deficits also play important roles. While the Fed cannot directly control the money supply, it influences money supply through control of bank reserves.[1] For example, if the economy is expanding too fast and appears to be heading toward unacceptable inflation, the Fed tries to limit the growth in bank credit by tightening reserves. If the economy is slowing toward recession, the Fed is supposed to ease credit by expanding reserves. This tightening and easing of credit must be finely balanced, as the Fed's goals of price stability and full employment are often in conflict.

Furthermore, the Fed sets annual targets for growth in monetary aggregates, targets that are consistent with the desired level of economic activity. These money supply targets are then translated into a target for reserve growth. As with money supply, there are many factors that influence reserves, such as currency in circulation, Fed float, U.S. government deposits with the Fed, and Fed-owned foreign deposits and securities. However, the Fed has tended to focus on M1.

Owing to the proliferation of negotiable order of withdrawal (NOW) accounts, the relationship between growth in the narrow measure (M1) and the economy began to diverge greatly. As a consequence, the Fed has focused on controlling the broader aggregates, M2 and M3.

Fed strategies also changed over time. Throughout the 1970s, the Fed's strategy was aimed at achieving a certain level of money growth by controlling interest rates. The connection between interest rates and reserve growth broke down sometime in the mid-1970s. The Fed could no longer operate this way. Accordingly, on October 6, 1979, then–Fed Chairman Paul Volcker announced that the Fed would approach money control directly by establishing target growth in the nonborrowed reserves component of the money stock. By tightening nonborrowed reserves, banks would

---

[1] The level of deposits in the banking system, and hence bank credit, is related through the reserve deposit multiplier. For example, $1 million in reserves supports $8,333,333 in deposits under a 10 percent reserve requirement. The deposit expansion factor is determined as follows:

$$\frac{1}{\text{Required reserve}} = \frac{1}{10\%} = 10$$

Therefore, each dollar of increased reserves translates into a 10-fold expansion of bank deposits.

be forced either to borrow from the Fed discount window or to compete for scarce reserves, leading to sharp increases in the fed funds rate. The higher rates would translate into higher borrowing costs and decrease demand for business and consumer loans. The Fed believed that this would lead to a break in the inflation spiral. This approach proved successful in controlling inflation but caused greater instability in interest rates.

In 1982, the Fed shifted its policy again. While the nonborrowed reserve target approach worked to reduce inflation, it produced a great deal of volatility in rates. Therefore, the Fed again began to set targets for fed fund rates, the rates banks pay to borrow reserves from other banks. The result in the mid-1980s through the early 1990s has been less volatility in rates.

[a] FOMC and the Directive. The Fed's main policy tool is open-market operations. Open-market operations are directed by the FOMC. Members of the FOMC include the 7-member board of governors, the president of the New York Fed, and 4 of the 11 presidents of the other Fed districts, who serve on a rotating basis.

The FOMC generally meets once every four weeks. The committee reviews macro goals, the economy, money supply, and bank credit. The current monetary policy is set to reflect desired reserve targets and the fed funds ranges. The FOMC then issues a directive that reflects its decision. This directive becomes part of the operating instructions for the manager of the System Open-Market Account, or the Fed's trading desk located in the Federal Reserve Bank of New York. All open-market activity takes place through this desk.

[3] Operations of the Open-Market Desk

The Fed has basically two objectives in mind in its daily open-market activity. First is the need to offset short-term fluctuations in reserves caused by changes in float in the system, activities of the Treasury, and other operating factors that influence reserves but that are beyond the Fed's control. Second is to maintain the targets for reserve growth and the fed funds rate. A decision is reached as to whether security purchases or sales are necessary to prevent credit tightness or excessive reserve expansion. The Fed adds or drains reserves by buying or selling Treasury securities. Every morning at 11:15 Eastern standard time, the Fed conference call is placed. This call links the open-market account manager in New York, a member of the Board of Governors in Washington, D.C., and an FOMC member from another Fed district bank. The decision to buy or sell securities is reaffirmed. The manager then instructs the traders accordingly.

Traders start a process called the go-around. The signal is flashed to the primary dealers that a buy or a sell is about to happen, and traders ask dealers for their bid or offer prices on the securities. After comparing the various bids and offers, the Fed selects the best set of prices and calls back the dealers selected to complete the deal. The Fed tends to enter the market at the same time each day, usually between 11:40 A.M. and 11:50 A.M. Eastern standard time.

In adding reserves, the open-market desk either will buy securities or will enter into RPs. The Fed will do RPs for its own account, known as system RPs, or for customers such as foreign central banks, known as customer RPs. RPs are agreements to buy securities on the condition that they are bought back at a specific price at some time in the future. The Fed decides between buying securities or doing RPs according to whether it is seeking to increase reserves permanently or attempting to offset some temporary uncontrollable fluctuation caused by some operating factor. System RPs have a direct impact on reserves; customer RPs may or may not, depending on the customer's use of the funds. When the Fed's open-market desk enters the market, it does so in a significant way. Typical Treasury bill transactions may range from $1 billion to $1.25 billion. Bonds may go from $800 million to $1 billion, and the RP activity may be in the $1 billion to $4 billion range. These transactions represent a single day's activity.

[4] Fed Watching

In the money market, interest rate forecasting is paramount. Participants in the market do what they do because of some feel for the direction of short-term interest rates. For example, banks structure their liabilities on the basis of their outlook, shortening maturities if a drop in rates is expected or lengthening in anticipation of an upturn in rates. Security dealers and portfolio managers position securities or sell short depending on their expectations. Ultimately, the outlook for interest rates is influenced by the level of economic activity, expectations for inflation, credit demands, the value of the dollar on world currency markets, and the Fed's current policies.

A change in the fed funds rate affects all short-term rates almost directly. Therefore, it is necessary to try to determine the Fed's plan of action in order to guess the direction of rates. Speculation as to what the Fed is doing or is going to do is reached through a sophisticated surveillance activity known as Fed watching. Fed watching is the examination of all information, the scanning of any market activity that might signal the Fed's intentions for money supply, and the Fed's target for the fed funds rate.

Fed watchers typically follow a systematic procedure. Each month, the Fed releases the minutes of the previous month's FOMC meetings. The minutes provide information on reserves, money supply targets, and the fed funds rate. Watchers then track these components against the targets, as well as quarterly gross national product (GNP) growth. If the actual M1 or M2 has been exceeding the targets, a Fed tightening might be expected. Of course, the Fed also could have shifted its targets, but that will not be known until the next month. Watchers then pretend that they are the FOMC and review economic trends and capital markets to try to anticipate whether changes in targets might occur. Thus, Fed watching tends to have a very short-term focus, shorter than the monthly growth patterns.

3.03 INSTRUMENTS IN THE MONEY MARKET

[1] Treasury Bills

Treasury bills are short-term debt obligations of the Treasury and make up the largest dollar volume of any instrument in the money markets. They represent the highest form of liquidity of all instruments in the money market because of their lack of credit risk, the variety of maturities, and the constant supply of new instruments in the market. Treasury bills have played an ever increasing role in the government's debt management program since their inception in 1929. Before the mid-1940s, the amount of bills outstanding at any given time was usually less than $2.5 billion. Current out-

FIGURE 3-3

Outstanding Volume of Treasury Bills

Source: Treasury Bulletin No. FD:2

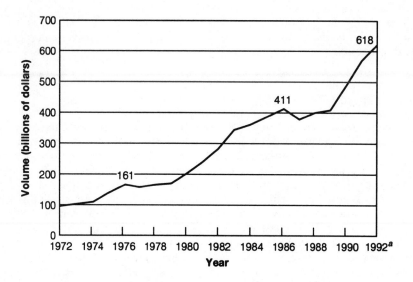

[a] June 1992.

standing volume is about $406 billion. Recent growth in the Treasury bill market is illustrated in Figure 3-3.

Treasury bills are sold on a discount basis, the difference between the price paid and par, reflecting the interest earned over the period to maturity. Various maturities have been issued, but bills are now issued in 91-day (3-month), 182-day (6-month), and 364-day (1-year) maturities. Prior to 1970, bills were issued in minimum denominations of $1,000. The minimum denomination today is $10,000 par value with $5,000 increments thereafter.

[a] Treasury Bill Auction. Every week the Treasury offers new three-month and six-month bills through its regular auction. On Tuesday of each week, the amount of the next Treasury offering is set. At this time "WI," or "when issued," trading is allowed. In other words, bills can be bought and sold between dealers before the actual auction occurs. Settlement in these transactions takes place after the auction. The auction is held on Monday, with delivery and payment taking place on the next Thursday.

Bids appear in two forms, competitive and noncompetitive. Noncompetitive bids specify the dollar amount of bills to be purchased. The price is determined by the average of all competitive bids accepted. Noncompetitive bids, awarded up to $1 million, assure that a buyer will not miss an opportunity by bidding too low or pay too much by bidding on the high side.

Competitive bids are placed by large investors and dealers and specify both an amount and a price that the investor is willing to pay. In addition, each subscriber in the auction may enter multiple competitive bids specifying quantities he or she is willing to buy at different prices.

Bids are submitted to the various Fed banks before the close of bidding at 1:00 P.M. Eastern standard time each Monday. At that time, all bids are tabulated and submitted to the Treasury for allocation. The Treasury first sets aside an amount sufficient to fill all noncompetitive bids. The competitive bids are then allocated, starting with the highest bid and moving down the list until the remaining bills have been sold. The term "stop-out price" refers to the last bid or lowest price at which securities are awarded. Those who have bid below the stop-out price receive no bills. The noncompetitive bids are charged the average price derived from the total of the competitive bids awarded. Noncompetitive bids usually make up less than 15 percent of the total auction, although occasionally they rise above this level.

The volume of bills issued each week is quite large. The typical three-month bill auction is currently near $12 billion, and the weekly six-month bill issue is about the same. In addition, every fourth Thursday, the Treasury sells one-year bills. The average issue size recently has been in excess of $14 billion.

For an example of the size of the Treasury's auction, examine the week of November 9, 1992. On that day, the Treasury auctioned $11.5 billion in three-month bills and $11.8 billion in six-month bills. The average discount rates for the three-month and six-month bills were 3.10 percent and 3.31 percent, respectively. For the three-month bills, tenders totaled $35.0 billion out of the $11.8 billion actually issued. Noncompetitive bids totaled $1.6 billion, or 13.4 percent of the total awarded. The six-month bills received $42.4 billion in bids and $980 million in noncompetitive bids, or 8.3 percent.

As can be seen from the tender numbers, the market demonstrates the ability to absorb large volumes of Treasury securities. Therefore, the Treasury has great flexibility in its debt management program. The auction process also keeps the Treasury from having to second-guess the market on rates. The rates are determined by the auction, and the Treasury merely picks the volume it will issue.

Because of their liquidity and minimum credit risk, Treasury bills appeal to a wide range of money market investors. The minimum denomination of $10,000 and the fairly easy procedures the Fed has set up for noncompetitive bids make bills a safe, attractive investment for individuals. However, two developments have cut into individuals' direct demands for bills. First is the change in the Fed's Regulation Q that allowed financial institutions to issue six-month "money market certificates" with rates tied to six-month Treasury bills. Many individuals found it more convenient to make deposits at their banks than to purchase bills through the auction. Other changes in Regulation Q that eliminated many rate ceilings on deposits made such deposits competitive with many money market instruments. Second is the growth in money market mutual funds. These funds allow individuals to invest in pools of money market securities and receive professional management of their funds for nominal fees. Both bank deposits and mutual funds have given individual investors the ability to invest small amounts at competitive rates in something other than Treasury bills. One benefit of a fund or bank deposit is that an investor can liquidate a portion of funds at any time. An owner of a Treasury bill must sell the entire bill if cash is needed. However, to the majority of Treasury bill purchasers, this is not an issue.

Another group of investors is commercial banks. Banks hold bills in their own portfolios as investments primarily for liquidity management purposes and buy bills for their securities-trading accounts. Many commercial banks have active trading departments that buy and sell Treasury securities in order to provide liquidity to their investor clients. But, more important, these departments actively speculate in short-term price movements of securities and therefore may generate significant trading profits through selling bills.

Still another class of investors is that of foreign investors. Their holdings increased rapidly as many of the oil-importing countries found Treasury bills to be good investments. In fact, many foreign investors that speculate in foreign exchange markets actually invest in bills with the dollars they have purchased. Central banks of other countries that may obtain dollars in currency support operations also invest in bills. The Fed is another major holder through its FOMC operations. Other investors include state and local governments, which use the bill market to invest tax receipts and proceeds from bond issues before these funds are needed. Another major participant has been added to the market through the rapid growth of money market mutual funds.

[b] Treasury Bill Yield Calculations. Treasury bills are a discount instrument, unlike an interest-bearing or coupon security. That means that the security is purchased at a discount from its par value, which is then paid at maturity. The difference between par and the discount value is the interest earned. Another distinguishing feature of Treasury bills is that the discount value and rate are calculated as if there were 360 days in a year. Thus, bills are calculated on an "actual over 360" basis, meaning the actual number of days for the bill against a 360-day year. These conventions and those used for other instruments can make direct comparisons of quoted yields among various instruments misleading.

For example, examine the amount of discount on a 91-day $1 million bill sold at a 7 percent discount rate. The first step is to compute the amount of the discount, which is determined by the following:

$$\text{Amount of discount} = \text{par value} \times \text{discount rate} \times \frac{\text{actual number of days}}{360}$$

For this example,

$$\text{Amount of discount} = \$1,000,000 \times 7\% \times \frac{91}{360} = \$17,694.44$$

Therefore, the price paid for the bill would be

$$\text{Price} = \text{par value} - \text{discount value} = \$1,000,000 - \$17,694.44 = \$982,305.56$$

If the price was given, the discount rate could be calculated using this formula:

$$\text{Discount rate} = \frac{360}{91} \times \frac{\$1,000,000 - \$982,305.56}{\$1,000,000} = 7\%$$

However, the discount rate differs from the true or actual yield. In this example, the investor is putting up $982,305.56 for 91 days and will receive $17,694.44 in interest. Therefore, the true yield is the amount of interest divided by the principal invested and adjusted for the number of days invested to come up with an annual yield. Because this is an actual yield calculation, 365 days in a year are used rather than 360 days. If a leap year is involved, 366 days are used.

$$\text{Yield} = \frac{\text{discount (or interest)}}{\text{price}} \times \frac{365}{\text{number of days}}$$

$$= \frac{\$17,694.44}{\$982,305.56} \times \frac{365}{91} = 7.23\%$$

Note that the actual yield is higher than the discount rate, which was 7 percent in this example. An alternative way of stating the previous formula, using the discount rate rather than the discount price, is

$$\text{Yield} = \frac{365 \times \text{discount rate}}{360 - (\text{discount rate} \times \text{number of days})}$$

Sometimes, reference may be made to "money market yield" in a comparison of rates.

The calculation of money market yield merely replaces "365 days" in the previous formulas with "360 days." The formulas here are useful in computing yield for Treasury bills with maturities of less than 6 months. They are also useful for bills with maturities of over 6 months if the yield comparison is to be made on a simple interest basis. Simple interest merely takes the amount of interest earned divided by the principal on an annualized basis. Compounding of interest is not considered. In other words, if an investor lent $1 million for one year and received $80,000 in interest, the simple interest yield would be 8 percent.

Yields can be computed in various ways, each having a different meaning for those investing funds. The key is to place investment alternatives on a comparable basis. In the money market, discount securities and coupon securities are made comparable by calculating their bond equivalent yield. Bond equivalent yield is based on an assumption of semiannual interest with compounding of interest.

To clarify this point, look at Treasury notes, coupon instruments with maturities of one year or longer. An 8 percent Treasury note of $1 million would pay $80,000 in interest over the year in two equal installments of $40,000 after six months, and $40,000 again after one year. The first payment is assumed to be reinvested at 8 percent[2] for the remaining half of the year, and the total interest received would be

$$\$40,000 + (\$40,000 \times 8\% \times 0.5 \text{ year}) + \$40,000 = \$81,600$$

The second term represents the extra interest from investing the first coupon payment for one-half year at the stated yield of 8 percent. This is the compounding of interest.

On a simple interest basis, the yield would be

$$\frac{\$81,600}{\$1,000,000} = 8.16\%$$

However, the bond equivalent yield, which assumes semiannual compounding with interest reinvested at the same rate as the yield, would be 8 percent.

Take a $1 million 1-year bill at a discount rate of 8 percent and go through the steps from computing the discount to the bond equivalent yield. Bear in mind that a 1-year bill is for 52 weeks or 364 days.

---

[2] In bond equivalent yield calculations, the coupon payments are assumed to be reinvested at a rate equal to the bond equivalent yield. The bond equivalent yield is solved for as an internal rate of return problem.

$$\text{Discount} = \$1,000,000 \times 8\% \times \frac{364}{360}$$

$$= \$80,888.89$$

$$\text{Price} = \$1,000,000 - \$80,888.89 = \$919,111.11$$

$$\text{Simple interest yield} = \frac{\$80,888.89}{\$919,111.11} \times \frac{365}{364} = 8.82\%$$

Now, the formula for the bond equivalent yield for a bill with one year to maturity can be expressed as[3]

$$\text{Yield} = 200 \times \left(\sqrt{\frac{\text{par}}{\text{price}}} - 1 \right)$$

$$= 200 \times \left(\sqrt{\frac{\$1,000,000}{\$919,111.11}} - 1 \right)$$

$$= 8.62\%$$

The coupon instrument sold at a yield of 8 percent had a bond equivalent yield of 8 percent, while the 1-year bill sold at an 8 percent discount rate has a bond equivalent yield of 8.62 percent, a higher yield to the investor.

For Treasury bills with maturities of over six months and less than one year, the calculation of bond equivalent yield is quite complex. It involves computing a partial period compounding of interest. Therefore, bond equivalent yields for various instruments are usually provided on bond dealers' quote sheets. These quote sheets provide amounts outstanding, bid and ask prices, maturity and coupon information, and equivalent yields and other data for the various securities that a dealer is trading. Computer programs and calculators also have been developed to compute these yields.

[c] Trading of Treasury Bills. The Treasury markets typically open around 9:00 A.M. Eastern standard time each day and close around 3:30 P.M. Eastern standard time. At the opening, the market is very active as the direction of the market (up or down) is being determined. When the Fed becomes active (Fed time), the market virtually quits, and the pace often picks up just before the market closes.

Treasury bills usually trade at very narrow spreads between the bid (buy) price and the ask (sell) price. The newer the bill, the narrower the spreads. For example, a new

---

[3] This formula is derived from the basic relationship

$$\text{Par} = \text{price} + \text{interest} = \text{price} + \left(\text{price} \times \frac{\text{yield}}{2} \right) + \left(\text{price} \times \frac{\text{yield}}{2} \times \frac{\text{yield}}{2} \right) + \left(\text{price} \times \frac{\text{yield}}{2} \right)$$

for semiannual interest, where the second term equals the first half-year's interest compounded for the second half-year and the third term is the last half-year's interest.

$$\text{Par} = \text{price} \times \left[1 + \text{yield} + \left(\frac{\text{yield}}{2} \right)^2 \right]$$

$$= \text{price} \times \left(1 + \frac{\text{yield}}{2} \right)^2$$

or

$$\sqrt{\frac{\text{Par}}{\text{price}}} - 1 = \frac{\text{yield}}{2}$$

3-month bill may have a bid-ask spread of 2 to 4 basis points. One basis point on a 90-day bill of $1 million is worth $25.[4] As the bills age, the spread becomes wider. The spread on a bill that is 4 weeks old may be as high as 10 basis points.

[2] Federal Agency Securities

One of the fastest-growing components in the credit markets has been the debt of federal agencies. The federal agencies are financial intermediaries with the purpose of administering selected lending programs of the U.S. government. Over time, Congress has targeted specific economic sectors for credit assistance, most notably agriculture and housing. Federal agencies were formed to provide this assistance by developing consistent flows of funding to those sectors. Agencies perform their function by issuing debt in both money markets and the capital markets, then channeling the proceeds to lending institutions through direct loans or the purchase of loans originated by the institutions.

There are basically two major categories of Federal agencies: federally sponsored agencies and government-owned agencies. Government-owned agencies have the full financial backing of the U.S. government. Many of these agencies provide credit to small businesses, students, and communities financing development projects. These agencies typically raise funds through the Federal Financing Bank, a centralized financing authority supervised by the Treasury. Federally sponsored agencies are not really agencies of the government, but are privately owned by the financial institutions and borrowers they support and have only limited backing by the government. In some cases this support is in the form of an ability to borrow from the Treasury or, by authorization of the Treasury, to buy securities. These agencies originally were started with government capital but have since paid back these funds, becoming private. There are six federally sponsored agencies that are exclusively involved in lending to the housing and agriculture sectors. Three of the agencies are the Federal Land banks, the Federal Intermediate Credit banks (FICBs), and Banks for the Cooperatives, which together make up the Farm Credit System. The other three are the Home Loan Bank Board (HLBB), the Federal National Mortgage Association (FNMA), and the Federal Home Loan Mortgage Corporation (FHLMC), which support the housing market. The Government National Mortgage Association (GNMA) is a government-owned agency that is also involved with supporting the housing market.

The Farm Credit System agencies are the oldest of the federally sponsored agencies. The system is made up of a nationwide family of banks and local associations completely owned by the farmers and their cooperatives that use them. There are 12 Federal Land banks that make long-term loans to farmers and rural residents for purchasing farmland, homes, equipment, and livestock, and for construction repair. The FICBs make short-term and intermediate-term loans to farmers. The 12 FICBs are entirely owned by the local Production Credit Associations, which in turn are owned by their farm members. The 12 district Banks for Cooperatives provide credit to co-

---

[4] The value of a basis point, 0.01 percent, for a Treasury bill is 27.7777 cents per day remaining per $1 million.

$$0.01\% \times \frac{1 \text{ day}}{360 \text{ days}} \times \$1,000,000 = \$0.27777$$

$$\$0.27777 \times 90 \text{ days} = \$25.00$$

FIGURE 3-4

Combined Outstanding Debt of Selected Federally Sponsored Agencies

Source: Federal Reserve Bulletin No. 1.44

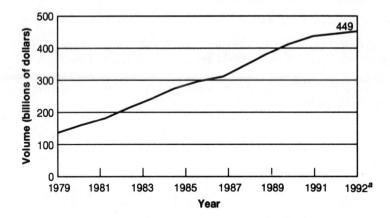

operatives owned by farmers. The credit may be for working capital or to finance buildings and equipment. In addition, the Central Bank for Cooperatives, owned by the district banks, participates with the district banks in financing larger loans.

The HLBB, through its 12 regional districts, provides funds to member institutions, which include all federally chartered savings and loan associations (S&Ls) and other mortgage lending institutions such as state-chartered S&Ls and mutual savings banks. The HLBB provides liquidity to their members when cyclical loan growth and disintermediation cause demand for funds. Longer-term funds are also provided in order to stimulate the housing industry on a continuing basis. The FNMA's responsibility is to provide assistance to the mortgage market when money is tight and funds are difficult to get in the market. This is accomplished by purchasing Federal Housing Administration, Veterans Administration, and conventional loans from banks, S&Ls, and mortgage bankers and in turn often packaging them into mortgage-backed securities that are sold to investors.

[3] Growth of Agency Debt

As noted earlier, the debt from federal agencies has grown extremely fast. In 1965, securities outstanding from federally sponsored agencies totaled $13.8 billion. By 1970, that amount had grown to $39 billion, and then to $79 billion in 1975. At the end of 1991, the combined debt of these agencies stood at $443 billion. Figure 3-4 provides a recent history of the growth in the volume of selected federal agency debt outstanding.

Federally sponsored agencies issue two types of short-term debt. One is coupon securities—similar to Treasury notes—and the other is discount securities—similar to Treasury bills. Bonds are sold on a periodic basis, while discount notes are sold on a continuous basis, with a range of maturities being offered. While bonds are sold through a selling group assembled by the agency's fiscal agent, discount notes typically are sold through a small group of dealers associated with the agency.

The Federal Land banks, FICBs, and Banks for Cooperatives sell their debt jointly through Farm Credit "consolidated systemwide" bonds and notes. Each month, the system offers six-month and nine-month bonds with minimum denominations of $5,000. The issuing takes place in book entry form only, meaning that an actual paper certificate is not provided to the issuer. Instead, a computer record is kept at the Fed in the account of the purchasing institutions. The institution itself keeps the records of individual investors for which it holds the securities. Discount notes are issued by the system on a daily basis with maturities ranging from 5 to 270 days. These securities come in certificate form only, with minimum denominations of $50,000.

The HLBB sells bonds with maturities of over 1 year and short-term discount notes. These discount notes are sold daily at maturities of 30 to 270 days. The minimum denomination has been set at $50,000 to deter small savers from withdrawing deposits from the agencies' members in order to buy the securities.

The FNMA also sells discount securities in the 30-to-270-day range. The minimum denomination is $5,000. However, a minimum purchase of $50,000 is required to help prevent disintermediation. The FHLMC began issuing discount notes in 1981 with maturities of under 1 year and a minimum par amount of $25,000. Federal agencies use the same price and maturity conventions as Treasury securities. Therefore, the discount price, discount rate, and bond equivalent yield calculations are found using the same formulas as for Treasury securities.

[a] Primary and Secondary Markets. The agencies follow a similar method for marketing their coupon certificates. Each agency has a fiscal agent located in New York that assembles a selling group whenever an issue is to come to market. These selling groups are nationwide and include security dealers, dealer banks, and brokerage houses. These participants in turn distribute securities to individual investors. Because securities are issued under an act of Congress, they are exempt from Securities and Exchange Commission registration. Discount notes are offered continuously through a small number of dealers.

Most issues follow a typical procedure. The fiscal agent announces to the selling group the size of the issue. The selling group (as many as 140 dealers in the case of the HLBB) is polled for the level of interest in the issue. Dealers bid for the securities with no rate specified or provide subject bids that specify a minimum rate at which they will take the issue. Dealers are then allocated specific positions of the total to be sold. The next step is pricing, with the objective being to sell close to or at par. The fiscal agent may receive input on pricing from the Treasury and a large group of its dealers. The agent then sets the price or more specifically the yield. Members of the selling group receive a fee for the distribution.

The selling group usually maintains an active secondary market. The growth in the secondary market has paralleled the growth in agency securities outstanding. This market is more developed than that of any private asset. Most dealers are in the market every day trading agency securities, although not to the same extent as Treasury securities. The bid-ask spreads in agency securities are wider than in government securities, while liquidity is less. One factor that has increased the attractiveness of agencies has been the development of RPs in these securities. Agency securities are now part of the Fed repurchase operation. The Fed also purchases agency securities as part of its open-market operations. These factors have increased the willingness of dealers to position larger amounts of agency securities and in turn have improved the market.

[b] Advantages of Agency Securities for Investors. Agency securities provide investors with certain benefits that may not be found in other money market securities. The risk perception compares favorably to that of the Treasury. Some agencies are backed up by a limited authority to borrow from the Treasury. There is a spread over government securities, so the yield is higher for roughly the same perceived level of risk. Agency securities, except for FNMA securities, are exempt from state and local taxes. The liquidity, although less than that of government securities because of the smaller issue size, is greater than for most other money market instruments. Also, there are some specific advantages for banks. Agency securities are collateral for borrowing at the Fed and qualify for collateral for Treasury tax and loan accounts. They are also public securities that can be held without limit by national banks.

[4] Federal Funds

Fed funds are short-term loans made between financial institutions in immediately available funds. That is, there is no delay in transferring the funds from one account to another. Fed funds can be considered the most liquid of money market instruments for two reasons. The great majority of the transactions have a maturity of one day, and because of the mechanism by which these funds flow through the Fed, in most cases they are instantaneously transferred from seller to buyer. Since there is a great incentive to keep these balances at a minimum, the reserves that banks are required to hold against their deposits pay no interest. Alternatively, the fed funds market provides this opportunity. Also, fed funds can provide an economical funding source for large banks, as these funds are often cheaper than other alternatives for bank financing. Not all participants in the money market can buy or sell fed funds. Regulation D restricts access to the market to certain financial institutions, typically depository institutions.

[a] History of Fed Funds. In the early 1920s, some banks that had to borrow periodically from the Fed to meet their reserve requirements began to realize that there were other banks that often had surplus reserves that were not invested. With the dawning of this awareness, banks began to trade fed funds with each other. In the 1930s and 1940s, trading in fed funds became stagnant as most banks experienced excess reserves. During World War II, banks used the large supply of Treasury bills as a trading vehicle to settle reserve positions. As banks discovered that trading bills was not the easiest way to exchange reserves, fed funds transactions picked up again.

Today, the fed funds market provides an attractive investment for retail banks that may have short-term surplus funds. Virtually all banks have access to the market. However, a small bank, because of its size, may not be able to place its surplus funds with a large money center bank but might be able to place as little as $50,000 overnight in a regional bank at a rate just slightly below market rates. The regional bank, in turn, might be able to combine these transactions and place the total with a money center bank. In fact, large banks have realized the value of cultivating a network of correspondents and other banks that are willing to sell them funds on a daily basis.

The money center banks, therefore, provide their network banks with competitive market rates for even small amounts and also back the small banks with offers to sell them funds if necessary. Most trades are done directly between banks, but the market has been enhanced by the development of fed funds brokers. These brokers put together the vast array of participants, respecting the anonymity of whoever stands behind the various bids and offers until a deal is closed. This function is especially helpful when a bank is attempting to do a large funding without disclosing its intention. Brokers typically deal in large amounts, handling virtually no transactions for less than $55 million.

Before the early 1960s, banks used fed funds strictly for reserve settlements. Today, many large banks rely on fed funds as a component of their overall funding mix, and not merely as a means of adjusting reserve balances.

[b] Transactions in the Market. Fed funds are immediately available funds because of the manner in which the transactions take place. For example, correspondent banks maintain demand deposits with a major bank to support various services. When the correspondent wants to sell funds to the bank, it calls with instructions to move funds from its demand deposit account. The next day, the bank moves the funds back into the correspondent's account with interest added. Although the borrowing bank has to pay interest on the fed funds, it receives the full benefit of the funding amount because it does not incur any reserve requirement, as it does for a demand deposit. A second illustration involves banks selling to each other through their reserve accounts at the Fed. When a transaction is completed, the banks instruct the Fed to move funds from the seller's reserve account to the buyer's reserve account. The next day, the Fed is instructed to reverse the transaction, including any payment of interest. When different Fed districts are involved, the transaction takes place through the FedWire, the Fed-owned electronic payment transfer system.

Activity in the fed funds market usually varies according to the week. All banks are required to keep reserves against their deposits and to settle their reserve position at the Fed on alternate Wednesdays. Reserve requirements are determined by the average deposit balances a bank holds over a two-week period. This reserve maintenance period starts on a Thursday and ends the second Wednesday following, which results in a 14-day period. By that Wednesday, banks seek to make up shortfalls that might have existed throughout the maintenance period. However, a bank that finds itself with excess reserves on Wednesday will forgo profit opportunities for carrying uninvested funds, since the Fed pays no interest. Banks do not want to be long in their reserve positions, nor do they desire to be short. Therefore, a wild scramble might take place as all the banks attempt to adjust their reserve accounts at the same time. If reserves are tight in the marketing owing to the FOMC's activity, it is not unheard of for the fed funds rate jump to 10 percent or more above normal trading ranges. If excess reserves are large in the system, the rate may drop as low as 1 percent to 2 percent, which to a selling bank is still better than the Fed's "offer" of 0 percent.

Besides overnight fed funds, a limited amount of term fed funds is sold. These funds may have a term of anywhere from 2 days to over 1 month, priced at a fixed rate. Small banks buying funds may have to provide collateral in the form of government securities. These are known as secured fed funds transactions. The rate quoted on fed funds is an add-on rate, using a 360-day basis. Therefore, the interest on a $50 million overnight transaction quoted a 7.5 percent is

$$\$50,000.000 \times 7.5\% \times \frac{1}{360} = \$10,416.67$$

If the deal is done through a broker, an additional cost of about 50 cents per \$1 million per day is paid by both the buyer and the seller. This transaction thus would cost each participant \$25 in brokerage fees.

If this rate is to be calculated on an annual equivalent basis for comparison with another money market instrument, it is necessary to adjust for actual days. On a simple interest basis, the 7.5 percent quoted rate would be

$$7.5\% \times \frac{365}{360} = 7.6\%$$

It should be noted that the simple interest calculation provides an annualized rate for one day. It does not take into account compounding of interest, which is daily on overnight funds. If daily compounding were taken into account, the 7.5 percent quoted rate would have an effective annualized cost of 7.9 percent.[5] The aggregate volume of fed funds traded daily is impossible to determine, because funds may be bought and sold several times during a day. Institutions with an excess reserve position at the Fed make up the lending side of the market. This includes commercial banks, federal government agencies, S&Ls, mutual savings banks, agencies and branches of foreign banks, and government security dealers.

[5] Repurchase Agreements

RPs at first appear to be a fairly complex type of money market instrument. They represent a means of borrowing money by selling securities to the lender of the funds and simultaneously entering into an agreement to repurchase those securities at a later date. The amount at which the securities are bought back is more than that for which they were sold. The difference represents the interest on the loan. In effect, the transaction is a secured form of lending in which the securities sold are the collateral for the loan. In most cases, the term of the RP is overnight, but it may be several days, several weeks, or longer. A continuous contract RP is a series of overnight loans that are automatically renewed each day unless terminated by either party.

The RP market provides short-term investment opportunities to corporations, state and local governments, and other nonbank investors that cannot sell directly into the fed funds market and find that other investments have maturities too long for their needs. The secured nature adds an extra dimension of attractiveness to investors. Banks find the RP market to be a useful source of short-term funding and an economic one, since the rate tends to trade below that of fed funds. Banks have large volumes of securities in their investment portfolios and trading accounts, both of which provide the collateral. The rate on RPs is one of the lowest in the money markets, mainly because of the secured nature of the transaction. In addition, there are no reserve

---

[5] The effective cost of fed funds with daily compounding of interest for a quoted add-on rate of 7.5 percent is derived as follows:

$$\left(1 + \frac{7.5\%}{360 \text{ days}}\right)^{365} = 1 + \text{annual effective rate}$$

$$= 7.9\%$$

requirements for banks on RP funds as long as the securities used are either U.S. government or federal agency securities. Besides banks, government securities dealers use the RP market to fund their security positions and for arbitrage gains through RPs and reverse RPs. A factor that has helped develop the RP market into one of the largest and most active sectors of the money market has been the increased sophistication of cash management techniques among firms. When rates were not as high or as volatile, firms would pay little attention to excess balances in their demand deposit accounts. Opportunity costs were not a major consideration, but as rates rose, so did the incentive to seek investment opportunities for idle funds. The secured nature of RPs and the settlement in immediately available funds make an available interest-bearing demand deposit readily available to businesses.

A discussion on RPs is not complete without a look at "reverses." A reverse RP is the same transaction as an RP but seen from the viewpoint of the lender of the funds. The lender provides funds while receiving a security, in other words, reversing in. The lender then resells the security at maturity and rereceives the funds. Banks and security dealers will often reverse in a security, thus lending funds. Subsequently, they may repurchase that security to borrow funds. Of course, when the original reverse matures and the security must be returned to the customer, the bank must purchase a like security in the market to be returned. Reversing in and repurchasing out the same security is done because large banks and dealers can usually achieve a positive, although small, spread with this transaction. When the maturities of the RP and the reverse RP are the same, this is called running a matched book. However, dealers may often mismatch the maturities of the RPs and reverse RPs to increase their spread.

Interest on RPs is negotiated at the time of the transaction, and the rate is usually influenced by the current fed funds rate. The rate is not at all determined by the securities bought or sold. They serve solely as collateral for the loan. The rate on overnight RPs usually is slightly less than the overnight fed funds rate, approximately 25 basis points, with the lower rate due to the collateralized nature·of the transaction.

The rate on RPs is an add-on rate using a 360-day basis. Therefore, the amount of interest is

$$\text{Interest} = \text{principal amount} \times \text{RP rate} \times \frac{\text{number of days}}{360}$$

The simple effective interest is computed in the same way as for fed funds, by multiplying the quoted rate by 365/360.

A lender of funds wants the collateral to serve its intended purpose. The value of the securities purchased must be at least equal to the funds provided. Therefore, RPs are priced using the market value of the security, not the par value. The normal practice in the market used to be to price "flat"; that is, on coupon securities, any interest that accrued over the term of the RP was ignored. For overnight RPs, this presents little concern, but considerable risk is involved with the practice of term RPs. A borrower who repurchases out a security expects to obtain the full value of that security at the time of repurchase including any interest accrued over the period. While the borrower has received funds reflecting the value of the security, it has received nothing representing the interest. If the lender should go bankrupt or fail to return the securities, the borrower may lose this accrued interest. The convention now is to price with accrued interest, adjusting the value both at the initiation of the transaction and at maturity.

Another risk in a term RP is that as rates change, the market value of the securities also change. A lender that entered a transaction 100 percent collateralized may have something less than that in the future if the market should drop. Because of this possibility, most term RPs are done with the lender of funds, the party reversing in securities, reserving the right to reprice the value of the collateral to adjust for any drop in security prices. Repricing can be done anytime during the agreement, but there are usually no set periods. Often repricing is a formal part of the RP. This reduces some of the risk to the lender.

As part of its FOMC activities, the Fed plays an active role in the RP market. Permanent changes in the reserve position are accomplished through outright purchases or sales of securities. But any temporary adjustments are carried out by the Fed's doing system RPs, purchasing the securities from dealers if adding reserves or doing reverse RPs if draining reserves.

[6] Negotiable Commercial Certificates of Deposits

Negotiable CDs are one of the principal sources of bank funding. They also represent a major liquid asset with attractive yields for investors. Negotiable CDs were introduced in 1961.

A CD is a negotiable instrument that represents a large time deposit liability of a bank. The certificate specifies the dollar amount of the deposit, the rate of interest to be paid (usually a fixed rate), and the final maturity of the deposit. The minimum size of a negotiable CD is $100,000, although normally CDs are issued in pieces of $1 million or larger to facilitate trading in the secondary market. The minimum legal maturity for CDs is 7 days. More typical maturities are in the one-to-three-month range or six months. Some issuance takes place at one year and beyond, but there is very sporadic activity at these maturities. The majority of CDs are issued by the large money center banks. Interest rates on CDs are higher than on similar-maturity government securities because of the level of credit risk associated with banks.

[a] History and Regulation of Negotiable CDs. Early CDs were in the form of time deposits with an agreement to leave funds in deposit for a specified period. Time deposits, however, provided no liquidity to investors. They were not negotiable, and ownership of the deposit could not be sold or transferred. As corporations and individuals became more sophisticated in their cash management techniques, the instruments in the money market became more attractive than regular bank time deposits or demand deposits. Banks were growing, and many were finding that their need for funds could not be met through their traditional deposit sources. In 1961, First National City Bank (Citibank) began offering negotiable CDs in response to the need for funds. At the same time, Discount Corporation of New York announced that it would make a secondary market for the negotiable CDs of money center banks. Soon, other banks began issuing similar CDs.

Regulation on CDs has changed considerably over the years. When first developed, CDs were subject to the Fed's Regulation Q, which governs the maximum interest rate that can be paid on various deposits. Although the Regulation Q rate ceiling was increased from time to time, the change to a new level usually lagged prevailing rate increases on other money market instruments. Therefore, banks were periodically kept out of the CD market because they could not pay investors competitive rates. In 1969, the rate ceiling so constrained banks that they massively shifted to the Euromarkets to generate deposits. In 1973, the Fed dropped Regulation Q on CDs of $100,000 and larger, making them directly competitive with all other money market instruments. Another regulation affecting CDs is Regulation D, which specifies what amount of reserves have to be held against these deposits. The effect of this regulation has been an effective cost to the banks that is higher than the quoted rate. Over time, Regulation D has changed, with the amount of reserves on CDs decreasing. Currently, there is a zero percent reserve requirement on CDs.

[b] **Primary Market.** Most banks attempt to place their new CD issues directly with investors rather than through CD dealers. One immediate advantage of this approach is that the banks avoid the dealers' commissions. Moreover, this gives banks more control over where the CDs go. Banks would prefer to place CDs only with investors that would hold their securities until final maturity. Large issuers of CDs tend to be in the primary market on a continuous basis and do not wish to see their efforts and costs unduly influenced by secondary trading in their outstanding securities. If a dealer took a large position in a bank's CDs with the idea of selling as soon as a profit could be made, the price of a bank's primary issue could be harmed if the bank was "writing into the market," or issuing its paper, at the same time that a dealer was selling its paper. Too great a supply of a bank's CDs drives the rate up, costing the bank more. That is not to say that dealers cannot provide a benefit to the banks. If a dealer is offering a competitive rate or an issuer has a big job to do, CDs will be placed directly with the dealer. Banks frequently use a funding instrument that was designed to provide liquidity but would prefer that no one trades this instrument.

One of the benefits of banks' funding is that CDs offer some flexibility in the maturities in which they can be issued. Banks may seek different maturities for liquidity reasons, interest rate risk reasons, or simply price. Of course, the market has something to say about how much can be issued and for what time frames. Banks indicate their desires for various maturities by their posted rates. An aggressive, or relative high, three-month rate says that a bank is actively seeking that pricing tenor, while a weak, or low, six-month rate shows little or no interest in that maturity. Rates are set through communications with other banks and dealers over the phone to determine what is trading in the market. Each participant quotes a "CD run," or list of rates across the maturity scale at which he or she is prepared to do business. Loyal customers who may regularly be large buyers of a bank's CDs may be given a preferential rate. Size also matters: A bank may be willing to pay a slightly higher rate for $25 million than for $100,000.

Negotiable CDs are settled in immediately available funds. Interest is paid at maturity for issues up to one year and on a semiannual basis, as in a coupon security, for longer-term CDs. Rates are quoted on an interest-bearing basis, not a discount basis. The calculation of interest is based on actual days to maturity with a 360-day year. To contrast an interest-bearing instrument that has interest due at maturity with a discount instrument, examine a Treasury bill and a CD, both quoted at 8 percent with a 91-day maturity for $1 million.[6]

$$\text{Yield on 8\% Treasury bill} = \frac{365 \times 8\%}{360 - (8\% \times 91)} = 8.28\%$$

---

[6] One would not normally see a Treasury bill and a CD with like maturities quoted at the same rate.

$$\text{Yield on 8\% CD} = 8\% \times \frac{365}{360} = 8.11\%$$

This yield calculation applies to any fixed-rate CD with a maturity of 1 year or less. The effective yield for the Treasury bill is greater, owing to its being quoted on a discount basis. Interest on the 91-day CD is computed by the following:

$$\$1,000,000 \times 8\% \times \frac{91}{360} = \$20,222.22$$

Interest is computed on the entire par value, because the instrument is not discounted.

The all-in cost, or total cost, of a CD to a bank also includes the cost of reserves and Federal Deposit Insurance Corporation (FDIC) insurance.[7] Reserves mean that the entire proceeds of the CD are not available for funding purposes, because a portion must be deposited with the Fed. Effectively, a higher cost to the bank is created for the remaining funds that can be used. If a bank issues a $1 million CD at 8 percent and the reserve rate is 3 percent,[8] the amount of funds available would be

$$\$1,000,000 \times (1 - 0.03) = \$970,000$$

If the term of the CD is 90 days, the amount of interest paid would be $20,000. The 8 percent is applied to the total par amount of the CD because that is what the investor has provided. The rate on the available funds is

$$\frac{\$20,000}{\$970,000} \times \frac{360}{90} = 8.25\%$$

An easier way to state the effective rate is

$$\frac{\text{Nominal rate}}{1 - \text{reserve rate}} = \frac{8\%}{1 - 0.03} = 8.25\%$$

And the equivalent yield on a 365-day basis is

$$8.25\% \times \frac{365}{360} = 8.36\%$$

FDIC insurance presently adds 23 basis points to the cost of the deposit. Therefore, the all-in equivalent cost to the issuer of a CD quoted at 8 percent is about 8.48 percent. Of course, the investor does not receive any extra yield. Reserves and FDIC insurance merely increase the effective all-in cost to the bank of the amount of available funds.

Besides the fixed-rate, fixed-maturity CD described so far, there are several other variations of this instrument. One is the "roly-poly CD" developed by Morgan Bank in 1977. The idea of this instrument was to provide long-term money (two to five years) to the bank and short-term liquidity to the investor. An investor signs a contract that specifies that it would have a deposit with the bank for possibly five years. Instead of a certificate with a five-year maturity, the investor receives a series of six-month CDs with the five-year rate. Each six months, the investor is required to renew his

---

[7] Banks that are insured by the FDIC are required to pay a fee equal to 0.23 percent of their deposits on an annualized basis.

[8] The current reserve requirement on a 90-day CD is zero. To illustrate the calculation, the 3 percent previous requirement is used.

FIGURE 3-5

Time Deposits at Commercial Banks

Source: Federal Reserve Bulletin No. 1.21

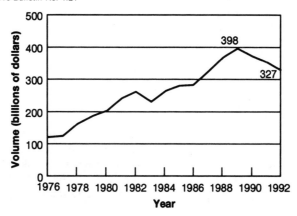

Note: Annual averages of large reporting banks.

deposit for another six months. If it needs funds, it can always sell the current six-month certificate. Variable-rate CDs are another variation. Here, the investor commits to a fixed period from six months to four years with intermediate roll-over periods. At each roll-over, commonly at three-month or six-month periods, a new interest rate is set. Consequently, the CD floats with the current level of rates at each roll-over. The benefit to the investor is that it receives a premium over the normal three-month or six-month rates. Variable-rate CDs typically are large transactions ranging from $50 million to $200 million for large banks.

The volume of CDs has grown dramatically since the removal of Regulation Q rate ceilings. Volumes fluctuate owing to changes in loan demand and are influenced by such factors as the growth of alternative instruments such as money market accounts at banks. The volume of large time deposits, shown in Figure 3-5, at large commercial banks, of which CDs are the major component, is over $300 billion.

[c] **Secondary Market.** There are currently about 16 dealers in CDs; roughly 10 of them are banks. Dealers serve 2 functions. One is to assist in the primary issuance of a bank. Dealers take the issue from the bank at a marked-up yield and sell it through their distribution network to other investors, often making a 5-to-10-basis-point spread on the transaction. The second and more important function is the making of a secondary market. Dealers are willing at all times to quote bids and offers to their customers or other dealers. The wide range of issuers and maturities of CDs leads to an unpredictable supply, and so dealers do not run short positions in CDs. They do, however, carry long positions that at times may be very large. These positions are usually financed through the RP market. The willingness of dealers to hold inventories in CDs is what provides the liquidity in the market.

Dealers, like investors, are aware of the differences in credit risk and liquidity of the different issuers. Before 1974, all top banks traded at about the same level. Regionals and smaller banks traded at somewhat higher rates. In 1974, problems at Franklin National and elsewhere in the U.S. banking industry prompted the market to reevaluate the risk classification. Investors began to pay more attention to the financial strengths and weaknesses of individual institutions, demanding higher premiums from some. Today, investors make even greater distinctions between banks, often relying on credit ratings supplied by independent rating agencies.

[7] Banker's Acceptances

A BA is one of a group of instruments known as bills of exchange or time drafts. It pays a certain amount of money at a specified time in the future. It is created by a bank as a substitution of the bank's creditworthiness for that of the borrower. The bank promises unconditionally to pay the face value of the draft at maturity. A BA is a negotiable instrument that can be sold in the money market to raise funds.

[a] **What Is a BA?** BAs developed out of a need to provide credit for transactions involving the shipment of goods, especially in international trade. If a seller ships goods to a buyer for settlement upon delivery, the seller runs the risk that the buyer might not be able to pay; the buyer, of course, does not want to pay before receiving the goods. Through a BA, the bank guarantees payment to the seller by "accepting" a time draft drawn on it by the buyer. The buyer is obligated to make payment to the bank.

In a typical transaction, after a bank agrees to provide its guarantee, a letter of credit is issued on behalf of the buyer. The letter of credit authorizes the buyer to draw a draft on the bank for an indicated amount. The draft specifies the time from presentation at which the funds are payable. The letter of credit also specifies terms the seller must meet before the bank will accept the draft. These terms may include documentation proving that the goods have been shipped. After the goods are shipped, the seller forwards any required documents, along with the time draft, to the buyer's bank. At this time, the bank indicates its guarantee to pay the draft by stamping it "accepted," which is accompanied by the signature of a bank officer. At this point, the acceptance, guaranteed by the bank, belongs to the seller. A seller that wants cash immediately can sell or discount the acceptance with the accepting bank. The value is determined by the going discount rate in the market for acceptances, which is a function of the rates for alternative money market instruments. The bank now can keep the acceptance or rediscount it into the money market. If it is rediscounted, the final investor will present the acceptance to the bank at maturity and collect the face amount, as shown in Figure 3-6.

[b] **History.** The passage of the Federal Reserve Act of 1913 gave national banks permission to accept time drafts. Before that, major acceptance activity had been taking place in Europe in sterling-denominated acceptances. The Fed, as part of its monetary policy in the early years, offered to buy BAs at quoted rates at any time. This did much to foster the development of the market, which continued to grow until the Great Depression resulted in a decline in international trade, leading to a decline

FIGURE 3-6

A BA Transaction

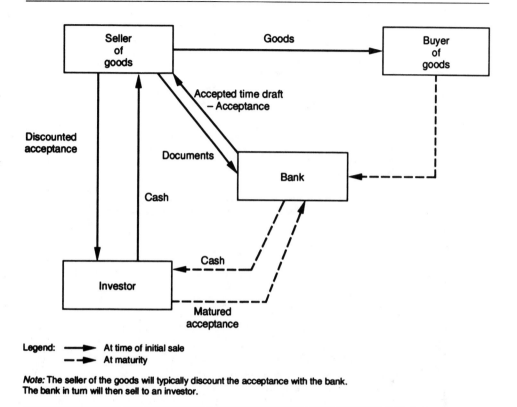

Legend: ——▶ At time of initial sale
         - -▶ At maturity

Note: The seller of the goods will typically discount the acceptance with the bank.
The bank in turn will then sell to an investor.

in acceptances. After World War II, the market began to grow as international trade picked up. Fed banks were authorized to buy and sell acceptances for their own accounts in 1955. This too promoted the market. From 1969 to 1970, when the high level of rates and Regulation Q ceilings prevented them from issuing CDs at competitive levels, banks turned toward acceptances as a form of lending and raising funds. Growth was rapid in the 1970s, and in 1977 the Fed decided not to purchase acceptances outright for its own account through open-market operations. It did, however, decide to continue to do RPs in acceptances and to buy for the accounts the Fed manages on behalf of foreign central banks. Figure 3-7 shows the growth in acceptances outstanding since 1966.

BAs have several advantages for banks. By rediscounting BAs in the market, banks can finance their customers' credit needs without tying up any of their own funds. Thus, BAs are a good financing alternative when credit is tight. BAs that meet certain Fed criteria for eligibility do not incur reserve requirements when rediscounted. Finally, acceptances can be very profitable for banks. A commission is paid to the bank upon creation of the acceptance. A bank also has an opportunity to make a spread

FIGURE 3-7

Outstanding Volume of BAs

Source: Federal Reserve Bulletin No. 1.32

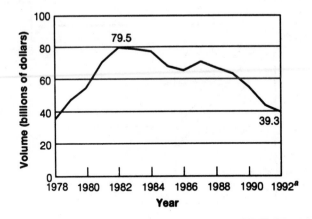

between the initial discount and the rediscount at a later time. The process is no more difficult than issuing CDs.

The borrower also has advantages. Banks are limited by Fed regulation as to how much in loans they can extend to any single customer. BAs fall under a separate limit from this legal lending limit, allowing additional extensions of credit if necessary. Often the cost of the acceptance, including the commission, is less than the all-in cost of a traditional credit transaction. For small and intermediate-size firms, it is often cheaper than issuing CP, which may not even be possible for some. Yet, the fixed commission causes borrowing costs to be much higher should the acceptance be prepaid.

Investors have a high degree of liquidity and safety in BAs. Yields on 90-day acceptances are closely in line with rates on 90-day CDs. The instrument is a liability of the accepting bank and also an obligation of the drawer of the draft. An active dealer market exists, providing good liquidity to the investor. Investors include state and local governments, savings institutions, foreign central banks, insurance companies, investment funds, banks, and individuals.

[c] Market. Yields on BAs, as with Treasury bills, are quoted on a discount basis. Most BAs have three-month maturities, although they also exist in a variety of other maturities of up to six months for eligible acceptances. Banks attempt to create acceptances in sizes that will facilitate secondary trading. Thus, a large deal may be broken up into several smaller BAs, or a series of small deals may be packaged. Typical trading sizes are usually in multiples of $1 million. Anything less than this amount is considered an odd lot. A round lot today in the dealer market is $5 million.

There is a wide diversity of credit quality in the market. Dealers quote a series of

FIGURE 3-8

Outstanding Volume of Commercial Paper

Source: Federal Reserve Bulletin No. 1.32

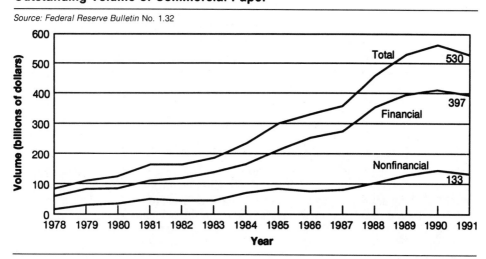

banks on the run; however, investors' perceptions of the various issuers influence what dealers hold. Dealers do not hold short positions because of the range of credit quality and the variety of maturities at which BAs are created. Instead, they hold fairly large inventories. The secondary market in BAs is much like the secondary market in CDs.

[8] Commercial Paper

CP is a short-term, generally unsecured promissory note sold in bearer form. Payment of the paper is backed by the issuing firm's financial health, liquidity, and earnings power. Issuers of CP include both financial and nonfinancial firms, usually large corporations that tend to have the highest credit ratings.

By the end of 1991, total CP outstanding had reached about $530 billion, as shown in Figure 3-8. CP is typically sold on a discount basis, with rates quoted as discount rates. It also may be sold on an interest-bearing basis, as with a CD. The calculation that equates the quoted discount rate to an equivalent yield is the same as that used for a Treasury bill. Thus, a 7.5%, 45-day CP rate has an effective yield of

$$\frac{365 \times 7.5\%}{360 - (7.5\% \times 45)} = 7.68\%$$

CP is a very flexible funding instrument. Typical CP transactions range from $1 million on up, although smaller-denomination paper down to $100,000 is sometimes issued. Most paper issued falls in the 7-to-45-day maturity range.

Issuers of CP include finance companies on a continuous basis, nonfinancial companies issuing for short-term or seasonal needs, and bank holding companies that finance their non-bank-related activities with paper. In addition, many foreign companies, both banks and nonfinancial institutions, have become issuers of CP. To issue paper successfully, an issuer must have a backup line of credit with a bank and a credit rating. Even with very short maturities, because of the large volumes any one firm might have out in the market, there can be substantial risk that a firm cannot pay at maturity or roll over its paper. For that reason, firms maintain lines of credit from banks equal to roughly 100 percent of their outstandings. These lines act as insurance to investors and cost the issuer a fee.

Also, virtually all CP is rated by at least two of four rating agencies. The four agencies are Moody's Investor Services, Standard & Poor's Corporation, Fitch Investor Service, and Duff and Phelps Inc. Firms must pay an annual fee to the agencies to get rated. The ratings are based on firms' financial strength and are an indicator of their ability to meet their obligations. These ratings strongly influence the rate paid in the market. There has been considerably greater concern over credit quality since 1970, when the Penn Central went bankrupt, defaulting on $82 million in paper. Immediately after the default, many companies found it difficult to roll over their own paper and were forced to rely on their backup lines and other means of raising funds. The advent of CP ratings from the agencies was a direct result of the Penn Central case.

Another cost, along with interest, fees for lines, and rating agency fees, is the operational cost of issuing. Of the over 1,800 firms that issue paper, fewer than 80 issue directly into the market. All others issue through CP dealers, which are made up of investment banks and, more recently, commercial banks, which, owing to Securities and Exchange Commission regulation, must act in the capacity of a broker. The standard dealer commission for issuing paper is 0.10 percent to 0.12 percent of the value of paper placed. For this fee, the dealer provides a ready source of investors willing to buy the issuer's paper at an attractive rate for the issuer. Direct issuers, such as the large finance companies, are in the market every day. Some may be issuing several hundred million dollars at a time and have total outstandings in the billions of dollars. These volumes make it easy for a firm to justify the use of its own sales force. Smaller and less frequent issuers cannot afford their own sales staff and go through dealers, paying the commission. For $100 million of paper outstanding, this cost amounts to $100,000 to $120,000 per year. Although attempts have been made to change the process, CP still involves the physical delivery of a note. The issuer must pay a fee to an issuing and paying agent, often a commercial bank, for the printing and delivery of these notes and the payment to the investor at maturity. In setting up a CP program, an issuer also incurs some initial legal expense.

CP transaction takes place entirely in one day: The issuer decides how much paper to issue; it is marketed by the issuer or dealer, and the paper is delivered and payment is made. During the day, while funds are coming into the issuer from the proceeds of selling new paper, investors are presenting maturing paper for payment. The issuer is often drawing down funds during the day to make various payments. The physical delivery of the paper and the flow of funds is a fairly intensive process that is normally flawlessly done. Strict attention is paid to credit quality and the ratings, because investors want to receive their money promptly when a note matures.

Interest rates on CP are higher than on Treasury bills of comparable maturity. The spread widens when money is tight. One reason for the spread is the credit risk associated with paper. The other relates to the fact that there is virtually no secondary market in paper. Nonetheless, CP is a cheap alternative to bank loans.

The lack of a secondary market of any magnitude may be due to a combination of factors. Foremost is that the paper market is more heterogeneous than the CD market.

There is a wide range of issuers with various credit ratings and a variety of maturities, although mostly short. Paper of different issuers, even with the same rating, is not readily interchangeable. Another reason is that many investors tend to hold to maturity, perhaps because the maturities tend to be very short. Dealers that sell paper and direct issuers buy back paper from an investor if cash is needed. As a rule, however, dealers do not speculate in running CP positions as they may with other money market instruments. As a result, secondary activity is substantially less than 5 percent of daily volume.

3.04 EURODOLLAR MARKET

[1] Definition and History

The term "Eurodollars" refers to dollars on deposit in a bank physically located outside of the United States. Although the majority of Eurodollar deposits are held in Europe, the term also refers to dollar deposits in other locations such as Tokyo, Hong Kong, and Singapore. When a deposit is moved from a U.S. bank to a foreign bank, a Eurodollar deposit is created. Eurodollars, regardless of where deposited, never really leave the United States; that is, the recipient institution itself redeposits them in its U.S. bank. The ownership of those dollars is what is transferred. Also, Eurodollars never leave the United States regardless of where they are lent. Again, this is because behind every Eurodollar, there is a corresponding deposit by the offshore bank in the United States. (See Chapters E3 and F4 in the *Handbook of Modern Finance*. See Chapter 3 in the *Handbook of Financial Strategy and Policy*, and Chapter 4 in the *Handbook of International Finance*.)

The Euromarkets developed as substitutes to their domestic counterparts, providing certain advantages. The term "Euromarkets" more precisely means external markets, i.e., markets that operate outside of the traditional financial markets. Thus, the Eurodollar market is not a part of the domestic U.S. dollar market, although it is closely linked through international transactions. The term "Euro" reflects the geography of its origins rather than the scope of its function.

In foreign lending and borrowing involving the traditional domestic markets, all transactions are subject directly to the rules and institutional arrangements of the countries and markets involved. By locating the market for credit in a particular currency outside of the country of that currency, these jurisdictions are circumvented. Differences in rates and terms in the Euromarkets exist because of the inapplicability of various regulatory constraints in the domestic markets.

For example, no reserve requirements are incurred on Eurodollar deposits. Also, there have never been interest rate restrictions on Eurodollar deposits as there were on domestic CDs under Regulation Q. The absence of regulations and other hindrances enables the Eurodollar market to operate more efficiently, economically, and competitively.

The origins of the Eurodollar market date back to the 1950s, when Eastern European governments decided to transfer their dollar deposits from the United States to Europe because they feared their seizure by U.S. claimants and because they wanted to establish credit lines in Europe. Other events continued to contribute to the further growth of the market, such as Regulation Q rate ceilings on domestic CDs in the 1960s and the recycling of OPEC dollars during the oil crisis of the 1970s.

The main issuers of Eurodollar deposits are foreign branches of U.S. banks, although other foreign banks are major issuers, including U.K., Canadian, Swiss, German, French, and Japanese banks. Investors or depositors are large corporations, central banks and other government bodies, supranational institutions such as the Bank for International Settlements, and wealthy individuals. The locations of Eurodollar activity are centered primarily in London and New York. Singapore and Hong Kong also have developed into Eurodollar centers, but to a much lesser degree owing to a lack of natural supply of dollar activity. And to avoid taxes, many exotic booking centers have developed from time to time in such places as Bahrain, Nassau, and the Cayman Islands.

[2] Eurodollar Time Deposits

Investors in the Eurodollar market have the choice between two major instruments. One is the Eurodollar time deposit, which makes up the bulk of the deposits. Time deposits are for fixed periods; once deposited, they remain with the bank until maturity. They are also nonnegotiable. An initial investor can not sell a time deposit to another investor. In rare cases, a bank and its customer may agree to "break" a deposit, and the bank pays the investor early. The maturities of time deposits can range from one day to several years, with the majority of transactions taking place in the seven-day to six-month range. Rates are negotiated between the bank and depositor and are based on market conditions and the bank's need for funds. Rates on deposits in the Eurodollar market are higher than in the domestic market. The higher rates can be justified because of the higher competitive framework and the lack of statutory regulation, such as reserve requirements, in the Euromarket.

[a] **Interbank Market.** The bulk of Eurodollar time deposit activity takes place in the interbank market, made up of Eurobanks from all over the world that are actively lending and borrowing money back and forth with other participants. Banks that do not have deep access to funds from third-party depositors are willing to pay slightly more to obtain funds from other banks in the interbank market. A bank that has just received a Eurodollar deposit will have a use for those funds. If funding a loan is not required, that bank will place the funds with another bank. This asset on the bank's books is referred to as a placement and represents a deposit with the other bank. That deposit may be lent to a third party or placed again in another bank. Several levels of interbank placements may often be made before funds deposited in the market find their way to an ultimate borrower. In determining how much one bank may be willing to deposit in another bank, each bank sets up credit lines or limits with other banks based on the creditworthiness of those institutions. This process is intended to limit risk. Lines are often reciprocal between banks. Therefore, if a bank wishes to receive deposits from another bank, it must be prepared to place funds with that bank from time to time. Banks are sometimes active in placement activity only to foster relationships in order to develop a form of insurance should they need funds in the future. The normal bid-ask spread in the interbank markets is about 0.125 percent. Running a matched book in placements and deposits is usually not done only for the bid-ask spread. Banks often mismatch the maturities of their placements and deposits to achieve a higher net spread between borrowing and binding rates.[9]

---

[9] A higher return from mismatching maturities of placements and deposits is possible with a sloping yield curve. For a positively sloped curve, longer maturities command a higher rate than shorter maturities.

What banks pay for funds in the interbank market is in part affected by tiering. Tiering refers to the classification of banks according to their creditworthiness. The top tier banks pay the best rates, although others are respectively scaled. The credit differentiation varies from time to time and becomes more pronounced in those periods when the financial community perceives potential banking problems.

[b] Eurodollar CDs. Eurodollar CDs (Euro CDs) are much like domestic dollar CDs, except that they are issued offshore in Eurodollars by the foreign branch of a U.S. bank or by a foreign bank. Euro CDs are dollar-denominated negotiable instruments that evidence a deposit in a Eurobank for a specific rate and a specific period. The first Euro CD was issued by Citibank in 1966. Today, virtually all Eurobanks issue Euro CDs. The market is primarily in London, and so the term "London dollar CDs" is sometimes used.

Euro CDs are issued in denominations of $1 million and up, although occasionally $500,000 pieces may be issued. Maturities can range from overnight to five years, with most of the activity concentrated in the short maturities, such as three and six months. Euro CDs are quoted on an interest-bearing basis with a 360-day year, like domestic CDs. Interest is paid at maturity or usually on an annual basis if the term is greater than one year.

Euro CD rates run higher than domestic CD rates and are a little lower than interbank rates, usually about 0.125 percent less for comparable maturities, primarily because CDs have liquidity. An active secondary market exists where spreads on bid and offer rates are about 0.125 percent. The secondary market is not as well defined as the domestic CD market.

The major issuers of Euro CDs are the top U.S. banks, U.K. banks, Canadian bank branches, Japanese branches, and branches of regional U.S. banks. Tiering in price takes place along the same lines as Euro time deposits, with the top banks paying the best rates. Some CDs (tranche CDs) are sold in several portions to appeal to smaller investors and are offered for sale in a fashion analogous to a security issue.

[c] Risk. The higher rates in the Eurodollar market are explained in part by the perceived higher level of risk compared with the domestic markets. Since there should be no credit risk differential between a U.S. bank and its London branch, the difference in perceived risk is one of geographic jurisdictions. Any Eurodollar transaction must clear through a bank in the United States, regardless of where the deposit or loan originates. Therefore, at least two governments are involved, the U.S. government and the government of the nation where the branch is located. A risk is that either government could intervene in the payment of funds. A depositor outside of the United States runs the risk that the United States might restrict the disposition and transfer of foreign-held funds, known as nonresident convertibility. This is a remote possibility. A second risk is that the government of the country in which the Eurobank operates may seize the assets of the bank. This is country or sovereign risk and varies by country. These risks contribute to the rate differential between the domestic market and the Euromarket.

3.05 INTEREST RATE BEHAVIOR AND RELATIONSHIPS

Movements in interest rates for the various money market instruments are highly correlated, as would be expected. This is due in part to the large degree of substitutability among instruments. Banks, for example, are able to use a variety of instruments at different maturities to meet their funding needs. Funding shifts can take place between fed funds, domestic CDs, Eurodollar deposits, and BAs, to name just a few. At the same time, investors are able to choose among instruments according to their perceptions of credit quality, rate forecasts, and other factors. This substitutability of both issuers and investors causes changes in rates in one sector of the money market to be transmitted almost immediately to other sectors. The pattern, relationships, and volatility of some recent money market rates are shown in Figure 3-9.

The most volatile rate, and the key to all other rate movements, is the fed funds rate. It is directly responsive to changes in the level of nonborrowed reserves in the banking system, which is a function of the Fed's strategy in controlling the money supply. Also, a change in the discount rate causes an immediate change in the fed funds rate.

The rates on Treasury bills are a kind of benchmark for the remaining term instruments in the market. Changes in the fed funds rate have an immediate impact on the 90-day bill rate. Treasury bills are the main instrument in the money market and have a very broad and sensitive market of their own. Most open-market purchases and practically all sales by the Fed are done in Treasury bills. This explains part of the tie to the fed funds rate. Another important factor in this linkage is dealers' cost of financing their positions. Most positions are financed with overnight RPs, whose rates move directly with the fed funds rate. If 90-day bill rates are significantly above the fed funds rate, dealers can carry their positions at positive spreads. They are inclined to buy more bills, driving the price up through demand. Thus, the rate declines until it is more in line with the fed funds rate. If the bill rate was significantly under the fed funds rate, the positions would be at a negative carry and would prompt dealers to sell. The selling would force the price down and the yield up until the rates came closer in line. Thus, the cost of financing has a major influence on the bill rates.

Other maturities of government securities are affected almost as rapidly by the 90-day bill rate. For example, the 6-month bill is viewed by dealers as an extension of the 90-day bill, and its rate moves accordingly. In investing, the dealer weighs a decision whether to buy a 6-month bill or a 90-day bill that can be rolled over for a second 90-day bill at its maturity. The decision is a function of the relative yields between 90 days and 6 months, and the forecast of the movement in interest rates 90 days in the future.[10] The dealer's actions and the actions of other dealers in the market influence the yield on the 6-month bill. Movements in the government rates in turn influence all of the other instruments. Spreads between each money market security and Treas-

---

[10] An investor, whether it plans on holding a security for 90 days or 180 days, will relate the 6-month rate to the current 90-day rate plus its forecast of what the new 90-day rate will be 90 days from now. The relationship is explained as

$$\left(1 + \frac{r_{6\text{-month}}}{360} \times 180\right) = \left(1 + \frac{r_{90\text{-day}}}{360} \times 90\right) \times \left(1 + \frac{r'_{90\text{-day}}}{360} \times 90\right)$$

where:

$r_{6\text{-month}}$ = current 6-month rate

$r_{90\text{-day}}$ = current 90-day rate

$r'_{90\text{-day}}$ = the market's expectation of the 90-day rate 90 days in the future

If this relationship is not apparent in the yields reflected in the market, investors will prefer one maturity over the other, influencing the prices until the relationship is back in line. Further explanation appears in any discussion on the term structure of interest rates.

FIGURE 3-9

Short-Term Interest Rates

Source: Federal Reserve Bulletin No. H.15

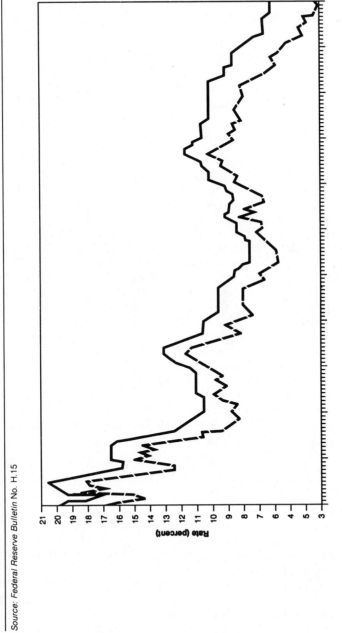

Note: Monthly averages. Horizontal axis labels are for January of each year shown.

FIGURE 3-10

Spreads Between Various Money Market Rates
(January 1988–October 1992)

	Average Spread	High	Low	Variability[a]
90-day BAs to 90-day Treasury bills	0.56%	1.55%	0.10%	0.34%
90-day CDs to 90-day Treasury bills	0.59	1.58	0.11	0.33
90-day Euro CDs to 90-day Treasury bills	0.65	1.54	0.11	0.37
90-day CP to 90-day Treasury bills	0.69	1.76	0.20	0.39
Prime to 90-day CDs	1.98	3.08	0.89	0.52

Note: Weekly rates. Spreads are between rates adjusted to equivalent yields.

[a] Variability expressed as standard deviation.

ury bills of like maturity are influenced by a variety of factors. Perceived credit of the issuer is one. The implicit guarantee of the government explains why agency securities are a bit higher than bills, even though they track very closely. CDs track still a little higher because of the credit risk associated with banks. These spreads, however, are not cast in concrete and do change from time to time. The liquidity of an instrument also influences the relative spread. This explains part of the price differential between domestic CDs and Euro CDs, which tend to have a less liquid secondary market. The supply of a particular instrument in the market influences its relative price or yield. A scarce supply will drive up the price and cause the rate to drop. A final factor is whether the markets are tight or money is easy. For most instruments, the spreads are much narrower over government securities when money is easy. Examples of several spreads are shown in Figure 3-10.

The interrelationship of rate movements among instruments is almost instantaneous, because participants in the money market have reached new levels of sophistication and knowledge. Many dealers and traders use computers and sophisticated statistical techniques to monitor various spread and yield relationships. When a price or yield moves out of line, it is flagged immediately, traders react accordingly, and market forces tend to drive it back in line.

[1] Volatility in Rate Levels

Before fall of 1979, the Fed's policy was to control bank reserves by controlling the fed funds rate; thus, rates were not highly volatile. Target levels for the rate were set, and a narrow range of variability was allowed. On October 6, 1979, the Fed shifted its policy to controlling the level of reserves and letting rates move freely. The result was dramatically increased volatility in the fed funds rate, as shown in Figure 3-11. One also sees that more recently volatility in the fed funds rate has dropped. This is due to the Fed's shift in policy again; now, while not completely focusing on the fed funds rate, the actions of the Fed are aimed toward more stability in rates.

Figure 3-12 illustrates the average levels and variability in three key rates over two

FIGURE 3-11

Weekly Effective Fed Funds Rate (1979–November 1992)

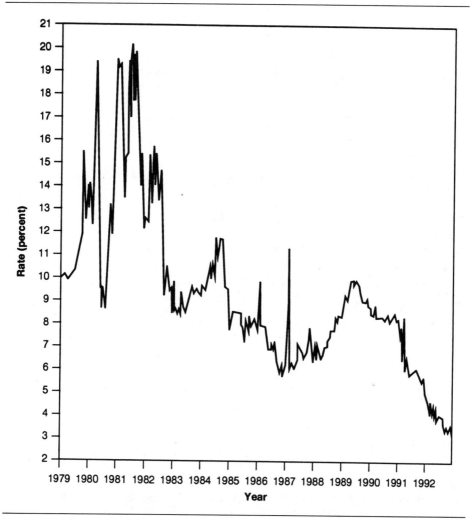

distinct periods. The high variability, as measured by the standard deviation, is noted in the October 1979–1982 period, as is the rather dramatic reduction in the more recent period. There are somewhat regular patterns of rate variability, some being seasonal or cyclical. For example, the business cycle influences the pattern of short-term rates. When the economy slows and the demand for credit falls, rates tend to fall. Then, as the recovery begins and credit demands increase, rates rise. The short-term patterns in rates are affected by the fundamentals of Fed policy, supply and types of securities being issued by the Treasury, loan demand at banks, and other factors.

FIGURE 3-12

Interest Rate Variability

	High	Low	Average	Standard Deviation
1970–October 1979				
Fed funds	13.55%	3.18%	6.94%	2.35%
90-day CDs	12.66	3.54	7.11	2.19
Prime rate	13.50	4.63	7.90	2.09
October 1979–1982				
Fed funds	20.06%	8.42%	13.27%	3.44%
90-day CDs	20.58	8.15	13.07	3.27
Prime rate	21.50	10.50	15.48	3.26
1983–May 1988				
Fed funds	11.77%	5.71%	7.86%	1.57%
90-day CDs	11.75	5.49	7.85	1.63
Prime rate	13.00	7.50	9.53	1.63
June 1988–October 1992				
Fed funds	10.01%	2.95%	6.97%	2.08%
90-day CDs	10.26	3.07	7.01	2.05
Prime rate	11.50	6.00	9.11	1.65

Note: Average weekly rates.

[2] Prime Rate and Bank Lending

While no longer as significant an indicator of the cost of bank loans, the prime rate still acts as a barometer of general lending activity in the market. The prime rate, commonly referred to as the reference rate, is unique in that although it is influenced by changes in short-term money market rates, it is an administered rate. The prime rate changes when banks decide to change it, and not necessarily when the market dictates it should change. Bank loans are not a part of the money market, but there is a direct relationship. First, to many corporate borrowers, short-term bank loans are only one alternative to raise funds; others include CP or the Eurodollar market. Second, the prime rate is a short-term rate and thus an indicator of supply and demand forces in the short-term market. As bank CDs and the fed funds rates increase, banks typically respond with an increase in the prime rate. The size of the increase is usually an indicator of how banks view their funding pressure in the market. A 0.25 percent change is common, while a 0.50 percent change is very significant.

The prime rate over time has been recognized as the rate announced by banks as being what they charged to their most creditworthy customers. But now that the most creditworthy customers often borrow at effective rates less than the prime rate, this interpretation has changed. That is why the prime rate is now referred to as the reference rate. The prime rate was first established in the 1930s. First set at 1.5 percent, it did not change until 1947. From then through the 1960s, the prime changed very infrequently. Before 1970, the greatest number of prime rate changes in a single year

FIGURE 3-13

Bank Prime Lending Rate

Source: Federal Reserve Bulletin No. H.15

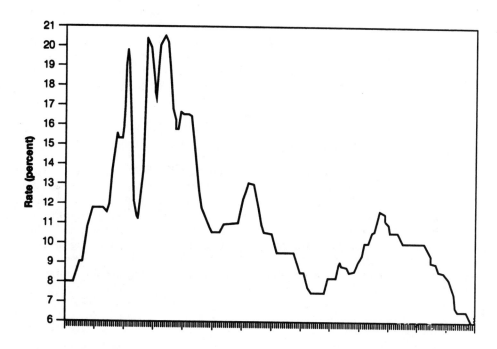

Note: Monthly averages. Horizontal axis labels are for January of each year.

was five, in 1968. Since 1970, changes in the prime rate have been much more frequent and pronounced in response to the generally higher level of rates and increased volatility. Figure 3-13 shows the recent history of the prime rate.

In the late 1960s and early 1970s, extreme public and political pressure was applied to banks to keep them from increasing the prime rate, even though banks' cost of funds had been increasing. As one response to this pressure, some banks went to "formula" prime, based on some function of market-determined rates. Some tied the prime rate to a moving average of CP rates, under the rationale that CP was an alternative borrowing rate. Another formula was based on a spread over commercial CDs. Thus, changes in the prime rate appeared to be less an arbitrary move by banks to raise rates and more a market-determined development.

Today, the prime rate is more reflective of a bank's cost of purchased funds and therefore tied more closely to money market conditions, which explains its higher volatility and levels over the current decade. Competition among banks to retain top customers along with customers' access to other sources of funds, like the Euromarket and CP, has forced banks to make loans available to their customers using pricing formulas other than the prime rate, with the prime rate being used more for consumer lending rates such as home equity lines. Many loans today are priced off a bank's various costs of funds such as Eurodollars or CDs. Thus, fewer and fewer corporations are borrowing from banks at the prime rate. The prime rate is still influenced, however, by what banks pay for their CDs, Eurodeposits, and fed funds. Meanwhile, financial markets, the stock market, and foreign exchange markets still react when the prime rate changes.

3.06 FINANCIAL FUTURES AND OTHER HEDGING INSTRUMENTS

A relatively recent development in the money markets has been the rapid growth in financial futures contracts, financial options contracts, forward rate agreements (FRAs), and interest rate swaps. (See Chapters 9 and 10 in this book; Chapter B1 in the *Handbook of Modern Finance*; and Chapter 1 in the *Handbook of Securities and Investment Management*.) As interest rates have continued to experience great volatility, these instruments have grown in popularity as a means of protecting investors from price fluctuations and borrowers from adverse lending costs and have also given traders and speculators in financial markets new ways of taking risk for a profit.

[1] Financial Futures

A financial futures contract is a contract to buy or sell a particular financial instrument at a specific date in the future for a specific price. It can be used to lock in a price today for a financial instrument that will not be bought or sold until some future time. The buyer or seller thus transfers the risk of a change in price to another party. This hedging of risk has been the single most important factor contributing to the growth of the financial futures market.

The first financial futures contract was traded in October 1975, when a market was opened for GNMA certificates. This was followed in January 1976 by a futures contract in 90-day Treasury bills, the most popular trading contract. Besides Treasury bills, financial futures contracts exist in Treasury bonds and Treasury notes, 90-day bank CDs, and 90-day Eurodollars. Financial futures markets also exist in various foreign currencies. Futures have shown such growth and popularity that it is not unusual for daily volume and total positions in the Treasury bond and Treasury bill futures markets to exceed the volume and positions in the underlying Treasury cash securities markets. Recent average trading volume in Treasury bill futures has been in the 5,000-to-10,000-contract range. In terms of dollars, this represents $5 billion to $10 billion in underlying bills.

Financial futures are used by investors and institutions to lock in or guarantee a specific interest rate for investing or borrowing sometime in the future, i.e., to hedge interest rate exposure. A hedge of a future investment rate is known as a long hedge. In such a case, the investor buys a futures contract that guarantees delivery of a security sometime in the future at a price and yield determined now. For example, if the investor knew that it wanted to buy Treasury bills three months from now because of a scheduled cash inflow, it would buy the appropriate bill contract that would guarantee a price on bills to be delivered in three months. The standard bill contract is for $1 million. The value of the contract moves with interest rates. If, three months from now, Treasury bill rates drop, the value of the contract will have increased. This increase in the value of the contract offsets the lost interest from investing at the lower rate.

Institutions can hedge their borrowing costs in a similar manner. Hedging the costs of borrowing involves selling a futures contract, which is called a short hedge. If rates should go up, the cost of borrowing would increase. However, the value of the futures contract would decrease and the sale could be covered at a lower cost, resulting in a gain to the seller. This gain should offset the increase in borrowing cost caused by the higher rate.

Financial futures prices parallel movements in prices in the underlying cash instruments, but these fluctuations in prices are not always precisely equal to changes in the cash markets. Thus, the hedger really is exchanging the risk of absolute price movement in a security for the risk of volatility in the relationship between cash and futures. This risk in the price relationship is known as basis risk. The amount of basis risk incurred is a function of the cash instrument. An investor hedging the purchase of a Treasury bill incurs one level of basis risk by using the Treasury bill futures contract. An institution trying to hedge the cost of its prime rate loan through shorting a Treasury bill contract will incur a much greater basis risk, since there is volatility not only between the cash market and the futures market but also between the prime rate and the Treasury bill rate. However, this volatility is much less than with no hedge at all.

Arbitrage transactions between cash and futures minimize the basis risk; in other words, they ensure a somewhat stable relationship between the two. For example, the current yield in the cash market of three-month and six-month Treasury bills implies a projection of what three-month bills will be three months into the future. This is known as the cash forward rate or forward-forward rate. The current futures contract, given the proper period, also implies the three-month bill rate three months into the future. Normally, these implied rates in the two markets should be close. If it is assumed that they were not, imagine that an investor held a six-month bill with an implied three-month forward rate of 7.25 percent and that the futures contract three months from now is priced at 7.5 percent. The investor would be likely to sell the cash security and buy the futures contract (provided that the difference between the extra yield of 0.25 percent three months from now makes up any lost yield in the current period). Selling the cash drives the yield up, and buying the futures pushes the yield down, closing the gap between the two rates. Likewise, if the cash yield were higher than the futures, the investor would buy the cash and sell the futures. Such activity tends to keep the cash and futures prices in a steady relationship.

[2] Other Hedging Instruments

As participants looked for additional ways to hedge interest rate risk, options contracts on financial instruments and options on futures contracts tied to financial instruments came into popularity. More recently, FRAs and interest rate swaps were developed to hedge risk.

[a] Options. An options contract gives the buyer the privilege of buying or selling the underlying instrument at a fixed price sometime in the future. (See Chapter A9.) The important difference between an option and a futures contract is that the holder of the option is not obligated to buy or sell but rather can exercise the option at his discretion. There are two basic types of options contracts: a call, which gives the buyer the right to buy the underlying instrument at a specific price, and a put, which gives the buyer the right to sell at a specified price. The buyer exercises the put or call if it is in its best financial interest. Otherwise, the buyer may let the option expire, and nothing happens.

There are five basic elements in any options contract:

1. The underlying security refers to the instrument that may be bought with a call or sold with a put (in the financial markets, there are options on both cash instruments and futures contracts).
2. The strike price is the price at which the security is bought or sold if the option is exercised.
3. The expiration date is when the option contract becomes void.
4. The premium is the price paid for the option.
5. The size of the contract specifies the value, usually par, of the underlying instruments.

A U.S.-style option can be exercised up to and including the expiration date, while a European-style option can be exercised only on the expiration date.

The premium paid for an option is based on how long a period exists until expiration, the time value, and the difference between the current price of the underlying instrument and the strike price, the intrinsic value. A call option is "in the money" if the underlying instrument has a value higher than the strike price. In such a case, the holder could exercise the option, buying a security at the strike price and then selling it in the market, making a profit. A put option is in the money if the strike price is higher than the price of the underlying instrument. The opposite of these two situations means the respective contracts are "out of the money." "At the money" refers to a situation where the strike price is equal to the current value.

In hedging strategies, an option has the benefit of offering downside protection and upside gain. An investor in money market instruments that is concerned about a drop in interest rates may buy at the money call option, for example, on the Eurodollar futures contract. It should be kept in mind that a futures contract increases in value as rates drop and decreases in value if rates rise, as with a cash instrument. If rates drop when the investor is due to roll over the money market instrument, the investor would exercise the call and sell the futures contract for a profit. This profit offsets the lost interest on the lower-yielding investment that was rolled over. If rates increase, the investor would roll over the investment at the higher rate and just let the option expire. Thus, the investor has downside protection yet can still gain if rates go in its favor. This differs from the futures hedge, which locks in a specific rate. For this privilege, the buyer of the option of course pays a premium, while the buyer of the futures does not.

Options currently exist for Treasury notes, bonds, and bills and on Eurodollar futures for exchange-traded options. A variety of options on various instruments can be bought through the over-the-counter market, which basically represents nonstandard contracts negotiated with the seller. Buyers and sellers of financial options currently include dealers, investment banks, commercial banks, and nonfinancial corporations. These participants use options to hedge as well as for trading speculation.

[b] FRAs. An FRA is a contract between two parties, each wishing to protect itself against an adverse future movement in interest rates. FRAs grew out of the forward-forward rate agreements that developed in the interbank market, primarily in London. Banks for some time were entering into agreements where they would guarantee a deposit or placement rate for another bank at some point in the future. A typical deal was to guarantee a three-month interest rate three months in the future. FRAs are a formalized version of the forward-forward market and began in 1983. Banks and corporations are major participants. The contracts offer tailor-made hedges for almost any size or maturity and thus offer an alternative to interest rate futures for hedging purposes.

The FRA is a contract between two parties to exchange short-term interest rate payments over a predetermined period in the future. The buyer of an FRA locks in a fixed rate of interest, while the seller locks in a floating rate. No principal loan or deposit is exchanged between the parties. Instead, the FRA is settled at the beginning of the predetermined period, with one party compensating the other for any differences between the original short-term rate and the actual market rate on the settlement date. For example, someone who wants to lock in the three-month interest rate at three months from now would buy a "threes against sixes" FRA with the forward rate agreed on by the buyer and seller for a notional amount of principal that the buyer wants to hedge. Three months from now, if the three-month rate is less than the agreed-on rate, the seller would pay the buyer a sum of money representing the difference between the interest earned at the market rate versus what would have been earned at the agreed-on rate. If the market rate three months from now is higher than the agreed-on rate, the buyer would pay the seller a sum representing the difference in interest. The majority of FRAs today are based on Eurodollar rates, although others are available.

[c] Interest Rate Swaps. Interest rate swaps cover a longer time horizon for hedging purposes than do the other instruments discussed so far. An interest rate swap is based on a notional principal amount that never gets exchanged like an FRA. Based on this notional amount, two parties enter into a contract where one participant agrees to make a fixed-rate payment of interest and the other participant agrees to make a floating-rate payment of interest. These payments are exchanged between the two parties. The parties swap fixed-rate and floating-rate payments. In the agreement, dates are set for when payments are to be made, at which time the floating rate and the final maturity date are set. The fixed rate is also agreed on. If, for example, the swap is six months floating against five years fixed, each six months the current six-month rate will be compared against the agreed-on five-year rate and the payments will be swapped. Typically, only a net payment is made.

For example, suppose one party has a floating-rate loan priced off of the six-month Eurodollar rate with a five-year maturity; this party would prefer to have a fixed-rate loan to avoid future fluctuations in interest expense. It could enter into an interest rate swap with another party where it would agree to make fixed-rate payments for the next five years in exchange for receiving floating-rate payments based on the six-month Eurodollar rate. Each six months, it would receive a sum of money that represents the amount of interest on the notional amount of the swap based on the then-current six-month rate. The first party would take those funds and pay the actual interest owed on the floating-rate loan. It must also pay the other party a sum based on the notional amount and the fixed rate of interest agreed to at the start of the deal.

The party with the loan in effect has converted the floating-rate loan to a fixed-rate loan through the swap. Thus, the first party has hedged against changes in the six-month rate. The major participants in the swap market are banks, which will manage a portfolio of swaps arranged between various corporations. Many nonfinancial corporations are now also running their own swap books.

Suggested Reading

Cargill, Thomas F. *Money, The Financial System and Monetary Policy*. Englewood Cliffs, N.J.: Prentice-Hall, Inc., 1986.

Coats, W.L., Jr. "How to Improve Control of the Supply." *The AEI Economist* (Mar. 1981).

Dufey, Gunter, and Ian H. Giddy. *The International Money Market*. Englewood Cliffs, N.J.: Prentice-Hall, Inc., 1978.

Fabozzi, Frank J., and Irving M. Pollack, eds. *The Handbook of Fixed Income Securities*, 3rd ed. Homewood, Ill.: Dow Jones-Irwin, 1991.

Felix, Richard, ed. *Commercial Paper*. London: Euromoney Publications Plc, 1987.

Henning, Charles N., William Pigott, and Robert Haney Scott. *Financial Markets and the Economy*, 5th ed. Englewood Cliffs, N.J.: Prentice-Hall, Inc., 1988.

Hetzel, Robert L. *Monetary Policy in the Early 1980s*. Federal Reserve Bank of Richmond, Working Paper 84-1. Richmond, Va.: 1984.

Homer, Sidney, and Martin L. Leibowitz. *Inside the Yield Book*. Englewood Cliffs, N.J.: Prentice-Hall, Inc., 1972.

Instruments of the Money Market. Federal Reserve Bank of Richmond. Richmond, Va.: 1981.

Jones, David M. *Fed Watching and Interest Rate Projections: A Practical Guide*, 2nd ed. New York: New York Institute of Finance, 1989.

Malkiel, Burton. *The Term Structure of Interest Rates: Expectations and Behavior Patterns*. Princeton: Princeton University Press, 1966.

The Market for Federal Funds and Repurchase Agreements. Board of Governors of the Federal Reserve System, Staff Study, 1979.

Melton, William C., and Jean M. Mahr. "Bankers Acceptances." *Federal Reserve Bank of New York Quarterly Review* (Summer 1981), pp. 39–55.

Ritter, Lawrence S., and William L. Sibler. *Money*. New York: Basic Books, Inc., 1984.

Rothstein, Nancy H., and James McLittle. *The Handbook of Financial Futures*. New York: McGraw-Hill, 1984.

Stigum, Marcia. *The Money Market*, 3rd ed. Homewood, Ill.: Dow Jones-Irwin, 1990.

Van Horne, James C. *Financial Market Rates and Flows*. Englewood Cliffs, N.J.: Prentice-Hall, Inc., 1978.

Walmsley, Julian. *The New Financial Instruments*. New York: John Wiley & Sons, Inc., 1988.

Chapter 4

Mathematics of Finance: Money and Time

T. Craig Tapley

The areas covered in this chapter include (1) time value of money; (2) bank loans; (3) bond analysis; and (4) futures contracts. It is assumed that the reader has some understanding of the problem that needs to be solved. If not, other chapters in this book discuss the relevant underlying economic and financial theory.

4.01 TIME VALUE OF MONEY

"Time value of money" is a generic term that encompasses all aspects of converting cash flows at one point in time to their equivalent values at another point in time. The starting point is that a dollar today is worth more than a dollar one year from today. Depending on the problem to be analyzed, the interest rate may be referred to as a discount rate, a compounding rate, an opportunity cost, a cost of capital, a yield to maturity, or a growth rate. Whichever name is used, if the problem if one of converting a value at one point in time to its equivalent value at another point in time, the basic calculations remain the same.

[1] Definitions of Variables

i = interest or discount rate on an annual basis

A = periodic annuity payment

M = number of compounding or discounting periods within a year

N = number of years

t = intermediate time periods, usually between 0 and N

FV = future or compounded value

PV = present or discounted value

$FVIF(i\%, N)$ = compound value interest factor at i percent for N periods

$PVIF(i\%, N)$ = present value interest factor at i percent for N periods

In addition, the subscript a refers to a regular annuity, the subscript ad refers to an annuity due, and the subscript p refers to a perpetuity. All other variables are defined within the text.

[2] Compounding of a Single Sum

The compounding of a single sum is the conversion of an earlier (present) value into an equivalent later (future) value. The use of the terms "earlier" and "later" makes clear that the reference point need not be real time. The future value depends on the present value, the applicable interest rate, and the number of compounding periods.

[a] Calculation of a Future Value. The future value of a single sum, compounded at an interest rate of i percent for N periods, is calculated as

$$FV = PV\,[(1 + i)^N]$$
$$= PV\,[FVIF(i\%, N)]$$

FIGURE 4-1

Future Value of a Single Sum

Period	1%	2%	3%	4%	5%	6%	7%	8%	9%	10%	12%	14%	15%	16%	18%	20%	24%	28%	32%	36%
1	1.0100	1.0200	1.0300	1.0400	1.0500	1.0600	1.0700	1.0800	1.0900	1.1000	1.1200	1.1400	1.1500	1.1600	1.1800	1.2000	1.2400	1.2800	1.3200	1.3600
2	1.0201	1.0404	1.0609	1.0816	1.1025	1.1236	1.1449	1.1664	1.1881	1.2100	1.2544	1.2996	1.3225	1.3456	1.3924	1.4400	1.5376	1.6384	1.7424	1.8496
3	1.0303	1.0612	1.0927	1.1249	1.1576	1.1910	1.2250	1.2597	1.2950	1.3310	1.4049	1.4815	1.5209	1.5609	1.6430	1.7280	1.9066	2.0972	2.3000	2.5155
4	1.0406	1.0824	1.1255	1.1699	1.2155	1.2625	1.3108	1.3605	1.4116	1.4641	1.5735	1.6890	1.7490	1.8106	1.9388	2.0736	2.3642	2.6844	3.0360	3.4210
5	1.0510	1.1041	1.1593	1.2167	1.2763	1.3382	1.4026	1.4693	1.5386	1.6105	1.7623	1.9254	2.0114	2.1003	2.2878	2.4883	2.9316	3.4360	4.0075	4.6526
6	1.0615	1.1262	1.1941	1.2653	1.3401	1.4185	1.5007	1.5869	1.6771	1.7716	1.9738	2.1950	2.3131	2.4364	2.6996	2.9860	3.6352	4.3980	5.2899	6.3275
7	1.0721	1.1487	1.2299	1.3159	1.4071	1.5036	1.6058	1.7138	1.8280	1.9487	2.2107	2.5023	2.6600	2.8262	3.1855	3.5832	4.5077	5.6295	6.9826	8.6054
8	1.0829	1.1717	1.2668	1.3686	1.4775	1.5938	1.7182	1.8509	1.9926	2.1436	2.4760	2.8526	3.0590	3.2784	3.7589	4.2998	5.5895	7.2058	9.2170	11.703
9	1.0937	1.1951	1.3048	1.4233	1.5513	1.6895	1.8385	1.9990	2.1719	2.3579	2.7731	3.2519	3.5179	3.8030	4.4355	5.1598	6.9310	9.2234	12.166	15.916
10	1.1046	1.2190	1.3439	1.4802	1.6289	1.7908	1.9672	2.1589	2.3674	2.5937	3.1058	3.7072	4.0456	4.4114	5.2338	6.1917	8.5944	11.805	16.059	21.646
11	1.1157	1.2434	1.3842	1.5395	1.7103	1.8983	2.1049	2.3316	2.5804	2.8531	3.4785	4.2262	4.6524	5.1173	6.1759	7.4301	10.657	15.111	21.198	29.439
12	1.1268	1.2682	1.4258	1.6010	1.7959	2.0122	2.2522	2.5182	2.8127	3.1384	3.8960	4.8179	5.3502	5.9360	7.2876	8.9161	13.214	19.342	27.982	40.037
13	1.1381	1.2936	1.4685	1.6651	1.8856	2.1329	2.4098	2.7196	3.0658	3.4523	4.3635	5.4924	6.1528	6.8858	8.5994	10.699	16.386	24.758	36.937	54.451
14	1.1495	1.3195	1.5126	1.7317	1.9799	2.2609	2.5785	2.9372	3.3417	3.7975	4.8871	6.2613	7.0757	7.9875	10.147	12.839	20.319	31.691	48.756	74.053
15	1.1610	1.3459	1.5580	1.8009	2.0789	2.3966	2.7590	3.1722	3.6425	4.1772	5.4736	7.1379	8.1371	9.2655	11.973	15.407	25.195	40.564	64.358	100.71
16	1.1726	1.3728	1.6047	1.8730	2.1829	2.5404	2.9522	3.4259	3.9703	4.5950	6.1304	8.1372	9.3576	10.748	14.129	18.488	31.242	51.923	84.953	136.96

N																				
17	1.1843	1.4002	1.6528	1.9479	2.2920	2.6928	3.1588	3.7000	4.3276	5.0545	6.8660	9.2765	10.761	12.467	16.672	22.186	38.740	66.461	112.13	186.27
18	1.1961	1.4282	1.7024	2.0258	2.4066	2.8543	3.3799	3.9960	4.7171	5.5599	7.6900	10.575	12.375	14.462	19.673	26.623	48.038	85.070	148.02	253.33
19	1.2081	1.4568	1.7535	2.1068	2.5270	3.0256	3.6165	4.3157	5.1417	6.1159	8.6128	12.055	14.231	16.776	23.214	31.948	59.567	108.89	195.39	344.53
20	1.2202	1.4859	1.8061	2.1911	2.6533	3.2071	3.8697	4.6610	5.6044	6.7275	9.6463	13.743	16.366	19.460	27.393	38.337	73.864	139.37	257.91	468.57
21	1.2324	1.5157	1.8603	2.2788	2.7860	3.3996	4.1406	5.0338	6.1088	7.4002	10.803	15.667	18.821	22.574	32.323	46.005	91.591	178.40	340.44	637.26
22	1.2447	1.5460	1.9161	2.3699	2.9253	3.6035	4.4304	5.4365	6.6586	8.1403	12.100	17.861	21.644	26.186	38.142	55.206	113.57	228.35	449.39	866.67
23	1.2572	1.5769	1.9736	2.4647	3.0715	3.8197	4.7405	5.8715	7.2579	8.9543	13.552	20.361	24.891	30.376	45.007	66.247	140.83	292.30	593.19	1178.6
24	1.2697	1.6084	2.0328	2.5633	3.2251	4.0489	5.0724	6.3412	7.9111	9.8497	15.178	23.212	28.625	35.236	53.108	79.496	174.63	374.14	783.02	1602.9
25	1.2824	1.6406	2.0938	2.6658	3.3864	4.2919	5.4274	6.8485	8.6231	10.834	17.000	26.461	32.918	40.874	62.668	95.396	216.54	478.90	1033.6	2180.0
26	1.2953	1.6734	2.1566	2.7725	3.5557	4.5494	5.8074	7.3964	9.3992	11.918	19.040	30.166	37.856	47.414	73.948	114.47	268.51	612.99	1364.3	2964.9
27	1.3082	1.7069	2.2213	2.8834	3.7335	4.8223	6.2139	7.9881	10.245	13.110	21.324	34.389	43.535	55.000	87.259	137.37	332.95	784.63	1800.9	4032.2
28	1.3213	1.7410	2.2879	2.9987	3.9201	5.1117	6.6488	8.6271	11.167	14.421	23.883	39.204	50.065	63.800	102.96	164.84	412.86	1004.3	2377.2	5483.8
29	1.3345	1.7758	2.3566	3.1187	4.1161	5.4184	7.1143	9.3173	12.172	15.863	26.749	44.693	57.575	74.008	121.50	197.81	511.95	1285.5	3137.9	7458.0
30	1.3478	1.8114	2.4273	3.2434	4.3219	5.7435	7.6123	10.062	13.267	17.449	29.959	50.950	66.211	85.849	143.37	237.37	634.81	1645.5	4142.0	10143.
40	1.4889	2.2080	3.2620	4.8010	7.0400	10.285	14.974	21.724	31.409	45.259	93.050	188.88	267.86	378.72	750.37	1469.7	5455.9	19426.	66520.	a
50	1.6446	2.6916	4.3839	7.1067	11.467	18.420	29.457	46.901	74.357	117.39	289.00	700.23	1083.6	1670.7	3927.3	9100.4	46890.	a	a	a
60	1.8167	3.2810	5.8916	10.519	18.679	32.987	57.946	101.25	176.03	304.48	897.59	2595.9	4383.9	7370.1	20555.	56347.	a	a	a	a

Note: FVIF(*i*%,N) = (1 + *i*)^N.

a FVIF > 99,999.

The value $(1 + i)^N$ is called the future value interest factor of a single sum. Future value interest factors for various values of i and N have been calculated and are presented in Figure 4-1.

> **EXAMPLE:** Assume that $100 is deposited in a savings account paying interest at an annual rate of 5 percent. This $100 and any interest earned is left on deposit for five years. What is the value of this account at the end of five years?
>
> $FV = \$100(1.05)^5$
>
> $\quad = \$100[FVIF(5\%, 5)]$
>
> $\quad = \$100(1.2763) = \$127.63$

In this example, the savings account has a value of $127.63 at the end of five years. The value consists of the initial deposit of $100 (principal) plus accumulated interest. The year-by-year accumulation of interest is as follows:

Year	Beginning Balance	Interest	Interest on Interest	Total Interest for Year	Ending Balance
1	$100.00	$5.00	$0.00	$5.00	$105.00
2	105.00	5.00	0.25	5.25	110.25
3	110.25	5.00	0.51	5.51	115.76
4	115.76	5.00	0.79	5.79	121.55
5	121.55	5.00	1.08	6.08	127.63

If the earned interest had been withdrawn at the end of each year, the interest calculated for the subsequent period would always be based on a beginning balance of $100. This would give total interest earned for the five-year period of $25. The difference between this value and the actual interest earned of $27.63 arises because the interest is left on deposit to earn interest itself. This interest-on-interest is the basis for all compounding.

> **EXAMPLE:** In 1983, the earnings per share of *XYZ* Corporation were $2.34. These earnings grew at an annual rate of 7 percent over the next 10 years. What were the earnings per share in 1993?
>
> $FV = \$2.34(1.07)^{10}$
>
> $\quad = \$2.34[FVIF(7\%, 10)]$
>
> $\quad = \$2.34(1.9672) = \$4.60$

[3] Discounting of a Single Sum

The conversion of a later value into an earlier value is called discounting and is the inverse process of compounding. The question is, What present value, when compounded, will be equal to the future value.

[a] Calculation of a Present Value.
As already shown, the general equation for a future value may be written as

$FV = PV[(1 + i)^N]$

If this equation is solved for present value, the resulting equation is

$$PV = FV\left[\left(\frac{1}{1+i}\right)^N\right]$$

$$= FV[PVIF(i\%, N)]$$

The value $1/(1 + i)^N$ is called the present value interest factor of a single sum. Present value interest factors for various values of i and N have been precalculated and are presented in Figure 4-2.

It should be clear that compounding and discounting are inversely related, since

$$PVIF(i\%, N) = \frac{1}{FVIF(i\%, N)}$$

EXAMPLE: X is currently renting a house but has an option to purchase it in two years at a price of \$80,000. If X can earn an annual interest rate of 6 percent on his savings, how much does he have to deposit today in order to have the total purchase price in two years?

$$PV = \$80,000\left[\left(\frac{1}{1.06}\right)^2\right]$$

$$= \$80,000[PVIF(6\%, 2)]$$

$$= \$80,000(0.8900) = \$71,200$$

EXAMPLE: In 1993, Y's stock portfolio had a value of \$25,469.68. Y has held this portfolio for 10 years and has earned an annual rate of return of 9.8 percent. How much did Y invest originally?

Figure 4-2 does not contain interest factors for 9.8 percent, but the present value may be easily calculated with any calculator.

$$PV = \$25,469.68\left[\left(\frac{1}{1.098}\right)^{10}\right]$$

$$= \$25,469.68(0.3926238) = \$10,000$$

[4] Regular Annuity

An annuity is a series of periodic payments with the size of each payment being the same for each period. In a regular annuity, the payments occur at the end of each period. An example is an installment loan where the first repayment takes place at the end of the first installment period, not when the loan is originally made. It is possible to convert this series of payments into either a future value or a present value.

[a] Future Value: Time-Line Analysis. The future value of an annuity can be evaluated as the sum of the future value of the individual cash flows comprising the annuity. This is easily seen diagrammatically through a time-line analysis.

FIGURE 4-2

Present Value of a Single Sum

Period	1%	2%	3%	4%	5%	6%	7%	8%	9%	10%	12%	14%	15%	16%	18%	20%	24%	28%	32%	36%
1	0.9901	0.9804	0.9709	0.9615	0.9524	0.9434	0.9346	0.9259	0.9174	0.9091	0.8929	0.8772	0.8696	0.8621	0.8475	0.8333	0.8065	0.7813	0.7576	0.7353
2	0.9803	0.9612	0.9426	0.9246	0.9070	0.8900	0.8734	0.8573	0.8417	0.8264	0.7972	0.7695	0.7561	0.7432	0.7182	0.6944	0.6504	0.6104	0.5739	0.5407
3	0.9706	0.9423	0.9151	0.8890	0.8638	0.8396	0.8163	0.7938	0.7722	0.7513	0.7118	0.6750	0.6575	0.6407	0.6086	0.5787	0.5245	0.4768	0.4348	0.3975
4	0.9610	0.9238	0.8885	0.8548	0.8227	0.7921	0.7629	0.7350	0.7084	0.6830	0.6355	0.5921	0.5718	0.5523	0.5158	0.4823	0.4230	0.3725	0.3294	0.2923
5	0.9515	0.9057	0.8626	0.8219	0.7835	0.7473	0.7130	0.6806	0.6499	0.6209	0.5674	0.5194	0.4972	0.4761	0.4371	0.4019	0.3411	0.2910	0.2495	0.2149
6	0.9420	0.8880	0.8375	0.7903	0.7462	0.7050	0.6663	0.6302	0.5963	0.5645	0.5066	0.4556	0.4323	0.4104	0.3704	0.3349	0.2751	0.2274	0.1890	0.1580
7	0.9327	0.8706	0.8131	0.7599	0.7107	0.6651	0.6227	0.5835	0.5470	0.5132	0.4523	0.3996	0.3759	0.3538	0.3139	0.2791	0.2218	0.1776	0.1432	0.1162
8	0.9235	0.8535	0.7894	0.7307	0.6768	0.6274	0.5820	0.5403	0.5019	0.4665	0.4039	0.3506	0.3269	0.3050	0.2660	0.2326	0.1789	0.1388	0.1085	0.0854
9	0.9143	0.8368	0.7664	0.7026	0.6446	0.5919	0.5439	0.5002	0.4604	0.4241	0.3606	0.3075	0.2843	0.2630	0.2255	0.1938	0.1443	0.1084	0.0822	0.0628
10	0.9053	0.8203	0.7441	0.6756	0.6139	0.5584	0.5083	0.4632	0.4224	0.3855	0.3220	0.2697	0.2472	0.2267	0.1911	0.1615	0.1164	0.0847	0.0623	0.0462
11	0.8963	0.8043	0.7224	0.6496	0.5847	0.5268	0.4751	0.4289	0.3875	0.3505	0.2875	0.2366	0.2149	0.1954	0.1619	0.1346	0.0938	0.0662	0.0472	0.0340
12	0.8874	0.7885	0.7014	0.6246	0.5568	0.4970	0.4440	0.3971	0.3555	0.3186	0.2567	0.2076	0.1869	0.1685	0.1372	0.1122	0.0757	0.0517	0.0357	0.0250
13	0.8787	0.7730	0.6810	0.6006	0.5303	0.4688	0.4150	0.3677	0.3262	0.2897	0.2292	0.1821	0.1625	0.1452	0.1163	0.0935	0.0610	0.0404	0.0271	0.0184
14	0.8700	0.7579	0.6611	0.5775	0.5051	0.4423	0.3878	0.3405	0.2992	0.2633	0.2046	0.1597	0.1413	0.1252	0.0985	0.0779	0.0492	0.0316	0.0205	0.0135
15	0.8613	0.7430	0.6419	0.5553	0.4810	0.4173	0.3624	0.3152	0.2745	0.2394	0.1827	0.1401	0.1229	0.1079	0.0835	0.0649	0.0397	0.0247	0.0155	0.0099
16	0.8528	0.7284	0.6232	0.5339	0.4581	0.3936	0.3387	0.2919	0.2519	0.2176	0.1631	0.1229	0.1069	0.0930	0.0708	0.0541	0.0320	0.0193	0.0118	0.0073
17	0.8444	0.7142	0.6050	0.5134	0.4363	0.3714	0.3166	0.2703	0.2311	0.1978	0.1456	0.1078	0.0929	0.0802	0.0600	0.0451	0.0258	0.0150	0.0089	0.0054
18	0.8360	0.7002	0.5874	0.4936	0.4155	0.3503	0.2959	0.2502	0.2120	0.1799	0.1300	0.0946	0.0808	0.0691	0.0508	0.0376	0.0208	0.0118	0.0068	0.0039
19	0.8277	0.6864	0.5703	0.4746	0.3957	0.3305	0.2765	0.2317	0.1945	0.1635	0.1161	0.0829	0.0703	0.0596	0.0431	0.0313	0.0168	0.0092	0.0051	0.0029
20	0.8195	0.6730	0.5537	0.4564	0.3769	0.3118	0.2584	0.2145	0.1784	0.1486	0.1037	0.0728	0.0611	0.0514	0.0365	0.0261	0.0135	0.0072	0.0039	0.0021
25	0.7798	0.6095	0.4776	0.3751	0.2953	0.2330	0.1842	0.1460	0.1160	0.0923	0.0588	0.0378	0.0304	0.0245	0.0160	0.0105	0.0046	0.0021	0.0010	0.0005
30	0.7419	0.5521	0.4120	0.3083	0.2314	0.1741	0.1314	0.0994	0.0754	0.0573	0.0334	0.0196	0.0151	0.0116	0.0070	0.0042	0.0016	0.0006	0.0002	0.0001
40	0.6717	0.4529	0.3066	0.2083	0.1420	0.0972	0.0668	0.0460	0.0318	0.0221	0.0107	0.0053	0.0037	0.0026	0.0013	0.0007	0.0002	0.0001	a	a
50	0.6080	0.3715	0.2281	0.1407	0.0872	0.0543	0.0339	0.0213	0.0134	0.0085	0.0035	0.0014	0.0009	0.0006	0.0003	0.0001	a	a	a	a
60	0.5504	0.3048	0.1697	0.0951	0.0535	0.0303	0.0173	0.0099	0.0057	0.0033	0.0011	0.0004	0.0002	0.0001	a	a	a	a	a	a

Note: $PVIF(i\%, N) = \dfrac{1}{(1 + i)^N}$.

a The factor is zero to four decimal places.

EXAMPLE: Assume that $100 is deposited at the end of each year for five years and that each deposit earns an annual interest rate of 5 percent. What is the total value of the deposits at the end of five years?

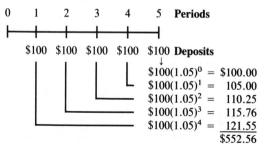

$100(1.05)^0 = $100.00
$100(1.05)^1 = 105.00
$100(1.05)^2 = 110.25
$100(1.05)^3 = 115.76
$100(1.05)^4 = \underline{121.55}$
$552.56

The future value of this five-year annuity is $552.56. Since this is a regular annuity, *all deposits occur at the end of the period*. This means that the last deposit is compounded forward zero years. Note that the value of any number raised to the zero power is one.

[b] Future Value: Calculations. The future value of a regular annuity may be calculated as follows:

$$FV_a = A[(1 + i)^0] + A[(1 + i)^1] + \cdots + A[(1 + i)^{N-1}]$$

$$= A\ [(1 + i)^0 + (1 + i)^1 + \cdots + (1 + i)^{N-1}]$$

$$= A\left[\sum_{t=0}^{N-1} (1 + i)^t\right]$$

$$= A\left[\frac{(1 + i)^N}{i} - \frac{1}{i}\right]$$

$$= A[FVIF_a(i\%, N)] = A\left[\sum_{t=0}^{N-1} FVIF(i\%, t)\right]$$

Future value interest factors for a regular annuity for various values of i and N have been precalculated, and are presented in Figure 4-3.

EXAMPLE: X has just had a child and has decided that starting on the child's first birthday, X will deposit $1,000 each year for the child's college education. If X makes 18 deposits and each earns a 6 percent annual rate of return, how much will the child have for college when he turns 18?

$$FV_a = \$1,000\left(\frac{1.06^{18}}{0.06} - \frac{1}{0.06}\right)$$

$$= \$1,000[FVIF_a(6\%, 18)]$$

$$= \$1,000(30.905) = \$30,905$$

[c] Present Value: Time-Line Analysis. The present value of an annuity can be calculated using a time-line analysis and the same example that was used for future value: $100 is deposited each year for five years and the annual interest rate is 5 percent. The present value of this regular annuity is then equal to

FIGURE 4-3

Future Value of an Annuity

Period	1%	2%	3%	4%	5%	6%	7%	8%	9%	10%	12%	14%	15%	16%	18%	20%	24%	28%	32%	36%
1	1.0000	1.0000	1.0000	1.0000	1.0000	1.0000	1.0000	1.0000	1.0000	1.0000	1.0000	1.0000	1.0000	1.0000	1.0000	1.0000	1.0000	1.0000	1.0000	1.0000
2	2.0100	2.0200	2.0300	2.0400	2.0500	2.0600	2.0700	2.0800	2.0900	2.1000	2.1200	2.1400	2.1500	2.1600	2.1800	2.2000	2.2400	2.2800	2.3200	2.3600
3	3.0301	3.0604	3.0909	3.1216	3.1525	3.1836	3.2149	3.2464	3.2781	3.3100	3.3744	3.4396	3.4725	3.5056	3.5724	3.6400	3.7776	3.9184	4.0624	4.2096
4	4.0604	4.1216	4.1836	4.2465	4.3101	4.3746	4.4399	4.5061	4.5731	4.6410	4.7793	4.9211	4.9934	5.0665	5.2154	5.3680	5.6842	6.0156	6.3624	6.7251
5	5.1010	5.2040	5.3091	5.4163	5.5256	5.6371	5.7507	5.8666	5.9847	6.1051	6.3528	6.6101	6.7424	6.8771	7.1542	7.4416	8.0484	8.6999	9.3983	10.146
6	6.1520	6.3081	6.4684	6.6330	6.8019	6.9753	7.1533	7.3359	7.5233	7.7156	8.1152	8.5355	8.7537	8.9775	9.4420	9.9299	10.980	12.135	13.405	14.798
7	7.2135	7.4343	7.6625	7.8983	8.1420	8.3938	8.6540	8.9228	9.2004	9.4872	10.089	10.730	11.066	11.413	12.141	12.915	14.615	16.533	18.695	21.126
8	8.2857	8.5830	8.8923	9.2142	9.5491	9.8975	10.259	10.636	11.028	11.435	12.299	13.232	13.726	14.240	15.327	16.499	19.122	22.163	25.678	29.731
9	9.3685	9.7546	10.159	10.582	11.026	11.491	11.978	12.487	13.021	13.579	14.775	16.085	16.785	17.518	19.085	20.798	24.712	29.369	34.895	41.435
10	10.462	10.949	11.463	12.006	12.577	13.180	13.816	14.486	15.192	15.937	17.548	19.337	20.303	21.321	23.521	25.958	31.643	38.592	47.061	57.351
11	11.566	12.168	12.807	13.486	14.206	14.971	15.783	16.645	17.560	18.531	20.654	23.044	24.349	25.732	28.755	32.150	40.237	50.398	63.121	78.998
12	12.682	13.412	14.192	15.025	15.917	16.869	17.888	18.977	20.140	21.384	24.133	27.270	29.001	30.850	34.931	39.580	50.894	65.510	84.320	108.43
13	13.809	14.680	15.617	16.626	17.713	18.882	20.140	21.495	22.953	24.522	28.029	32.088	34.351	36.786	42.218	48.496	64.109	84.852	112.30	148.47
14	14.947	15.973	17.086	18.291	19.598	21.015	22.550	24.214	26.019	27.975	32.392	37.581	40.504	43.672	50.818	59.195	80.496	109.61	149.23	202.92
15	16.096	17.293	18.598	20.023	21.578	23.276	25.129	27.152	29.360	31.772	37.279	43.842	47.950	51.659	60.965	72.035	100.81	141.30	197.99	276.97
16	17.257	18.639	20.156	21.824	23.657	25.672	27.888	30.324	33.003	35.949	42.753	50.980	55.717	60.925	72.939	87.442	126.01	181.86	262.35	377.69

N																				
17	18.430	20.012	21.761	23.697	25.840	28.212	30.840	33.750	36.973	40.544	48.883	59.117	65.075	71.673	87.068	105.93	157.25	233.79	347.30	514.66
18	19.614	21.412	23.414	25.645	28.132	30.905	33.999	37.450	41.301	45.599	55.749	68.394	75.836	84.140	103.74	128.11	195.99	300.25	459.44	700.93
19	20.810	22.840	25.116	27.671	30.539	33.760	37.379	41.446	46.018	51.159	63.439	78.969	88.211	98.603	123.41	154.74	244.03	385.32	607.47	954.27
20	22.019	24.297	26.870	29.778	33.066	36.785	40.995	45.762	51.160	57.275	72.052	91.024	102.44	115.37	146.62	186.68	303.60	494.21	802.86	1298.8
21	23.239	25.783	28.676	31.969	35.719	39.992	44.865	50.422	56.764	64.002	81.698	104.76	118.81	134.84	174.02	225.02	377.46	633.59	1060.7	1767.3
22	24.471	27.299	30.536	34.248	38.505	43.392	49.005	55.456	62.873	71.402	92.502	120.43	137.63	157.41	206.34	271.03	469.05	811.99	1401.2	2404.6
23	25.716	28.845	32.452	36.617	41.430	46.995	53.436	60.893	69.531	79.543	104.60	138.29	159.27	183.60	244.48	326.23	582.62	1040.3	1850.6	3271.3
24	26.973	30.421	34.426	39.082	44.502	50.815	58.176	66.764	76.789	88.497	118.15	158.65	184.16	213.97	289.49	392.48	723.46	1332.6	2443.8	4449.9
25	28.243	32.030	36.459	41.645	47.727	54.864	63.249	73.105	84.700	98.347	133.33	181.87	212.79	249.21	342.60	471.98	898.09	1706.8	3226.8	6052.9
26	29.525	33.670	38.553	44.311	51.113	59.156	68.676	79.954	93.323	109.18	150.33	208.33	245.71	290.08	405.27	567.37	1114.6	2185.7	4260.4	8233.0
27	30.820	35.344	40.709	47.084	54.669	63.705	74.483	87.350	102.72	121.09	169.37	238.49	283.56	337.50	479.22	681.85	1383.1	2798.7	5624.7	11197.9
28	32.129	37.051	42.930	49.967	58.402	68.528	80.697	95.338	112.96	134.20	190.69	272.88	327.10	392.50	566.48	819.22	1716.0	3583.3	7425.6	15230.2
29	33.450	38.792	45.218	52.966	62.322	73.639	87.346	103.96	124.13	148.63	214.58	312.09	377.46	456.30	669.44	984.06	2128.9	4587.6	9802.9	20714.1
30	34.784	40.568	47.575	56.084	66.438	79.058	94.460	113.28	136.30	164.49	241.33	356.78	434.74	530.31	790.94	1181.8	2640.9	5873.2	12940.6	28172.2
40	48.886	60.402	75.401	95.025	120.79	154.76	199.63	259.05	337.88	442.59	767.09	1342.0	1779.0	2360.7	4163.2	7343.8	22728	69377	a	a
50	64.463	84.579	112.79	152.66	209.84	290.33	406.52	573.76	815.08	1163.9	2400.0	4994.5	7217.7	10435	21813	45497	a	a	a	a
60	81.669	114.05	163.05	237.99	353.58	533.12	813.52	1253.2	1944.7	3034.8	7471.6	18535	29219	46057	a	a	a	a	a	a

Note: $\text{FVIF}_a(i\%,N) = \dfrac{(1+i)^N}{i} - \dfrac{1}{i}$.

[a] $\text{FVIF}_a > 99{,}999$.

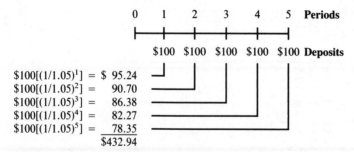

$$\$100[(1/1.05)^1] = \$\ 95.24$$
$$\$100[(1/1.05)^2] = \ \ 90.70$$
$$\$100[(1/1.05)^3] = \ \ 86.38$$
$$\$100[(1/1.05)^4] = \ \ 82.27$$
$$\$100[(1/1.05)^5] = \ \ \underline{78.35}$$
$$\$432.94$$

The present value of this regular annuity is $432.94. It may be found by discounting the individual cash flows that compose the annuity.

[d] Present Value: Calculations. The present value of a regular annuity may be calculated as follows:

$$PV_a = A\left[\left(\frac{1}{1+i}\right)^1\right] + A\left[\left(\frac{1}{1+i}\right)^2\right] + \cdots + A\left[\left(\frac{1}{1+i}\right)^N\right]$$

$$= A\left[\left(\frac{1}{1+i}\right)^1 + \left(\frac{1}{1+i}\right)^2 + \cdots + \left(\frac{1}{1+i}\right)^N\right]$$

$$= A\left[\sum_{t=1}^{N}\left(\frac{1}{1+i}\right)^t\right]$$

$$= A\left[\frac{1}{i} - \frac{1}{i(1+i)^N}\right]$$

$$= A[PVIF_a(i\%, N)] = A\left[\sum_{t=1}^{N} PVIF(i\%, t)\right]$$

Present value interest factors for a regular annuity for various values of i and N have been calculated and are presented in Figure 4-4.

EXAMPLE: X has agreed to make a three-year loan at an annual interest rate of 8 percent. If the annual repayments will be $1,746.15, what is the original amount of this loan?

$$PV_a = \$1,746.15\left[\frac{1}{0.08} - \frac{1}{(0.08)(1.08)^3}\right]$$

$$= \$1,746.15[PVIF_a(8\%, 3)]$$

$$= \$1,746.15(2.5771) = \$4,500$$

[e] Relationship Between Future Value and Present Value. There is a relationship between the future value and the present value of an annuity, although it is not an inverse relationship. In the prior time-line examples, where $100 was deposited each year for five years at an annual interest rate of 5 percent, the values found were

$$FV_a = \$552.56$$

$$PV_a = \$432.94$$

FIGURE 4-4

Present Value of an Annuity

Number of Payments	1%	2%	3%	4%	5%	6%	7%	8%	9%	10%	12%	14%	15%	16%	18%	20%	24%	28%	32%
1	0.9901	0.9804	0.9709	0.9615	0.9524	0.9434	0.9346	0.9259	0.9174	0.9091	0.8929	0.8772	0.8696	0.8621	0.8475	0.8333	0.8065	0.7813	0.7576
2	1.9704	1.9416	1.9135	1.8861	1.8594	1.8334	1.8080	1.7833	1.7591	1.7355	1.6901	1.6467	1.6257	1.6052	1.5656	1.5278	1.4568	1.3916	1.3315
3	2.9410	2.8839	2.8286	2.7751	2.7232	2.6730	2.6243	2.5771	2.5313	2.4869	2.4018	2.3216	2.2832	2.2459	2.1743	2.1065	1.9813	1.8684	1.7663
4	3.9020	3.8077	3.7171	3.6299	3.5460	3.4651	3.3872	3.3121	3.2397	3.1599	3.0373	2.9137	2.8550	2.7982	2.6901	2.5887	2.4043	2.2410	2.0957
5	4.8534	4.7135	4.5797	4.4518	4.3295	4.2124	4.1002	3.9927	3.8897	3.7908	3.6048	3.4331	3.3522	3.2743	3.1272	2.9906	2.7454	2.5320	2.3452
6	5.7955	5.6014	5.4172	5.2421	5.0757	4.9173	4.7665	4.6229	4.4859	4.3553	4.1114	3.8887	3.7845	3.6847	3.4976	3.3255	3.0205	2.7594	2.5342
7	6.7282	6.4720	6.2303	6.0021	5.7864	5.5824	5.3893	5.2064	5.0330	4.8684	4.5638	4.2883	4.1604	4.0386	3.8115	3.6046	3.2423	2.9370	2.6775
8	7.6517	7.3255	7.0197	6.7327	6.4632	6.2098	5.9713	5.7466	5.5348	5.3349	4.9676	4.6389	4.4873	4.3436	4.0776	3.8372	3.4212	3.0758	2.7860
9	8.5660	8.1622	7.7861	7.4353	7.1078	6.8017	6.5152	6.2469	5.9952	5.7590	5.3282	4.9464	4.7716	4.6065	4.3030	4.0310	3.5655	3.1842	2.8681
10	9.4713	8.9825	8.5302	8.1109	7.7217	7.3601	7.0236	6.7101	6.4177	6.1446	5.6502	5.2161	5.0188	4.8332	4.4941	4.1925	3.6819	3.2689	2.9304
11	10.3676	9.7868	9.2526	8.7605	8.3064	7.8869	7.4987	7.1390	6.8052	6.4951	5.9377	5.4527	5.2337	5.0286	4.6560	4.3271	3.7757	3.3351	2.9776
12	11.2551	10.5753	9.9540	9.3851	8.8633	8.3838	7.9427	7.5361	7.1607	6.8137	6.1944	5.6603	5.4206	5.1971	4.7932	4.4392	3.8514	3.3868	3.0133
13	12.1337	11.3484	10.6350	9.9856	9.3936	8.8527	8.3577	7.9038	7.4869	7.1034	6.4235	5.8424	5.5831	5.3423	4.9095	4.5327	3.9124	3.4272	3.0404
14	13.0037	12.1062	11.2961	10.5631	9.8986	9.2950	8.7455	8.2442	7.7862	7.3667	6.6282	6.0021	5.7245	5.4675	5.0081	4.6106	3.9616	3.4587	3.0609
15	13.8651	12.8493	11.9379	11.1184	10.3797	9.7122	9.1079	8.5595	8.0607	7.6061	6.8109	6.1422	5.8474	5.5755	5.0916	4.6755	4.0013	3.4834	3.0764
16	14.7179	13.5777	12.5611	11.6523	10.8378	10.1059	9.4466	8.8514	8.3126	7.8237	6.9740	6.2651	5.9542	5.6685	5.1624	4.7296	4.0333	3.5026	3.0882
17	15.5623	14.2919	13.1661	12.1657	11.2741	10.4773	9.7632	9.1216	8.5436	8.0216	7.1196	6.3729	6.0472	5.7487	5.2223	4.7746	4.0591	3.5177	3.0971
18	16.3983	14.9920	13.7535	12.6593	11.6896	10.8276	10.0591	9.3719	8.7556	8.2014	7.2497	6.4674	6.1280	5.8178	5.2732	4.8122	4.0799	3.5294	3.1039
19	17.2260	15.6785	14.3238	13.1339	12.0853	11.1581	10.3356	9.6036	8.9501	8.3649	7.3658	6.5504	6.1982	5.8775	5.3162	4.8435	4.0967	3.5386	3.1090
20	18.0456	16.3514	14.8775	13.5903	12.4622	11.4699	10.5940	9.8181	9.1285	8.5136	7.4694	6.6231	6.2593	5.9288	5.3527	4.8696	4.1103	3.5458	3.1129
25	22.0232	19.5235	17.4131	15.6221	14.0939	12.7834	11.6536	10.6748	9.8226	9.0770	7.8431	6.8729	6.4641	6.0971	5.4669	4.9476	4.1474	3.5640	3.1220
30	25.8077	22.3965	19.6004	17.2920	15.3725	13.7648	12.4090	11.2578	10.2737	9.4269	8.0552	7.0027	6.5660	6.1772	5.5168	4.9789	4.1601	3.5693	3.1242
40	32.8347	27.3555	23.1148	19.7928	17.1591	15.0463	13.3317	11.9246	10.7574	9.7791	8.2438	7.1050	6.6418	6.2335	5.5482	4.9966	4.1659	3.5712	3.1250
50	39.1961	31.4236	25.7298	21.4822	18.2559	15.7619	13.8007	12.2335	10.9617	9.9148	8.3045	7.1327	6.6605	6.2463	5.5541	4.9995	4.1666	3.5714	3.1250
60	44.9550	34.7609	27.6756	22.6235	18.9293	16.1614	14.0392	12.3766	11.0480	9.9672	8.3240	7.1401	6.6651	6.2402	5.5653	4.9999	4.1667	3.5714	3.1250

Note: $PVIF_a(\%, N) = \dfrac{1}{i} - \dfrac{1}{i(1+i)^N}$.

Time value of money calculations convert a value at one point in time to its equivalent value at another point in time. Thus, these values are equivalent:

$$PV_a = FV_a[PVIF(i\%, N)]$$
$$= \$552.56[PVIF(5\%, 5)]$$
$$= \$552.56(0.7835) = \$432.94$$
$$FV_a = PV_a[FVIF(i\%, N)]$$
$$= \$432.94[FVIF(5\%, 5)]$$
$$= \$432.94(1.2763) = \$552.56$$

Another way of looking at PV_a is that it is the amount one would have to deposit today to create an annuity. In this example, if $432.94 is deposited at an annual interest rate of 5 percent, $100 can be withdrawn each year for five years. After the fifth withdrawal, the balance should be zero.

Year	Beginning Balance	Interest	Withdrawal	Ending Balance
1	$432.94	$21.65	$100.00	$354.59
2	354.59	17.73	100.00	272.32
3	272.32	13.62	100.00	185.94
4	185.94	9.30	100.00	95.24
5	95.24	4.76	100.00	0.00

This ability to convert a value at one point in time to its equivalent value at another point in time is the basis and primary function of time value of money calculations.

[5] Annuity Due

The only difference between a regular annuity and an annuity due is that *the cash flows associated with an annuity due occur at the beginning of the period.* An example is life insurance, where the first payment is made when the contract is signed.

[a] **Future Value: Time-Line Analysis.** The calculation of future value for an annuity due can be demonstrated using the same values already applied to a regular annuity: $100 is deposited each year for five years at an annual interest rate of 5 percent. Now, however, the payments occur at the beginning of each period. The future value is then equal to

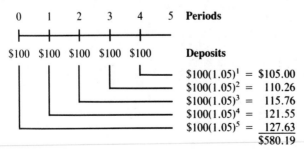

$100(1.05)^1 =$	$105.00
$100(1.05)^2 =$	110.26
$100(1.05)^3 =$	115.76
$100(1.05)^4 =$	121.55
$100(1.05)^5 =$	127.63
	$580.19

The future value of this five-period annuity due is $580.19. Since deposits are now

made at the beginning of the period, the last deposit is compounded forward one period.

[b] Future Value: Calculations. The future value of an annuity due may be calculated as follows:

$$\begin{aligned}
FV_{ad} &= A[(1 + i)^1] + A[(1 + i)^2] + \cdots + A[(1 + i)^N] \\
&= A[(1 + i)^1 + (1 + i)^2 + \cdots + (1 + i)^N] \\
&= A\left[\sum_{t=1}^{N} (1 + i)^t\right] \\
&= A\left[\sum_{t=1}^{N} FVIF(i\%, t)\right] \\
&= A[FVIF_{ad}(i\%, N)]
\end{aligned}$$

The tables do not contain future value interest factors for annuities due. However, there is a direct relationship between the interest factor for a regular annuity and the interest factor for an annuity due.

If a final payment had been made in period N, an N-period annuity due could be evaluated as an $(N + 1)$-period regular annuity. The compounding factor associated with this payment is $(1 + i)^0 = 1$. Therefore, the future value interest factor associated with an N-period annuity due is equal to the interest factor for an $(N + 1)$-period regular annuity minus 1.

$$\begin{aligned}
FV_{ad} &= A\left[\sum_{t=0}^{N} (1 + i)^t - 1\right] \\
&= A\left[\frac{(1 + i)^{N+1}}{i} - \frac{1}{i} - 1\right] \\
&= A[FVIF_a(i\%, N + 1) - 1]
\end{aligned}$$

Alternatively, if an N-period annuity due was treated as a regular annuity, its future value would be found as of the last payment date or at period N. Since we are dealing with an annuity due, it is necessary to find its value one period later, or as of time-period $N + 1$. Therefore, the future value associated with an N-period annuity due is equal to the future value of an N-period regular annuity compounded forward one period, or

$$FV_{ad} = A[FVIF_a(i\%, N)](1 + i)$$

EXAMPLE: The annual premium on X's insurance policy is $445. If the insurance company invests the premiums to earn 7 percent after all fees to the company, what is the cash value of this policy after 29 years?

$$\begin{aligned}
FV_{ad} &= \$445\left(\frac{1.07^{30}}{0.07} - \frac{1}{0.07} - 1\right) \\
&= \$445[FVIF_a(7\%, 30) - 1] \\
&= \$445(93.460) = \$41,590.05
\end{aligned}$$

The future value of this 29-year annuity due (payments in years 0 through 28, evaluated at year 29) is $41,590.05. Its value is calculated by first finding the interest factor for a 30-year regular annuity and then subtracting 1 from this value. This new interest factor is then multiplied by the annuity payment.

Alternatively, the future value of this 29-year annuity due may also be calculated as

$$FV_{ad} = \$445[FVIF_a(7\%, 29)](1.07)$$
$$= \$445(93.460) = \$41,590.05$$

[c] Present Value: Time-Line Analysis. The same example may be used to demonstrate the calculation of present value for an annuity due. Deposits of $100 are made each year for five years at an annual interest rate of 5 percent. Each deposit is made at the beginning of the period. The present value of this annuity due is then equal to

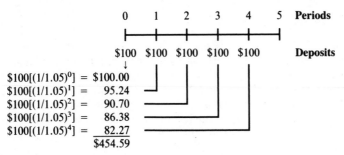

The present value of this five-period annuity due is $454.59. If a payment had not been made at time-period 0, this would have been equal to a four-period regular annuity.

[d] Present Value: Calculations. The present value of an annuity due may be calculated as follows:

$$PV_{ad} = A\left[\left(\frac{1}{1+i}\right)^0\right] + A\left[\left(\frac{1}{1+i}\right)^1\right] + \cdots + A\left[\left(\frac{1}{1+i}\right)^{N-1}\right]$$

$$= A\left[\left(\frac{1}{1+i}\right)^0 + \left(\frac{1}{1+i}\right)^1 + \cdots + \left(\frac{1}{1+i}\right)^{N-1}\right]$$

$$= A\left[\sum_{t=0}^{N-1}\left(\frac{1}{1+i}\right)^t\right]$$

$$= A\left[\sum_{t=0}^{N-1} PVIF(i\%, t)\right]$$

$$= A[PVIF_{ad}(i\%, N)]$$

The tables do not contain present value interest factors for annuities due. However, once again there is a direct relationship between the interest factor for a regular annuity and the interest factor for an annuity due.

If an initial payment had not been made at time-period 0, an N-period annuity due could be evaluated as an $(N - 1)$-period regular annuity. The discounting factor associated with this initial payment is $[1/(1 + i)^0] = 1$. Therefore, the interest factor associated with an N-period annuity due is equal to the interest factor for an $(N - 1)$-period regular annuity plus 1.

$$PV_{ad} = A\left[\sum_{t=1}^{N-1}\left(\frac{1}{1+i}\right)^t + 1\right]$$

$$= A\left[\frac{1}{i} - \frac{1}{i(1+i)^{N-1}} + 1\right]$$

$$= A[PVIF_a(i\%, N - 1) + 1]$$

Alternatively, if an N-period annuity due is treated as a regular annuity, its present value would be found as of one period before the first payment date or at time-period -1. Since we are dealing with an annuity due, we actually want to find its value one period later, or as of period 0. Therefore, the present value associated with an N-period annuity due is equal to the present value of an N-period regular annuity compounded forward one period, or

$$PV_{ad} = A[PVIF_a(i\%, N)](1 + i)$$

EXAMPLE: X has an opportunity to purchase a whole life insurance policy. X may either make annual payments of \$375, starting today, for the next 19 years (20 payments) or make a single payment today. If the applicable annual interest rate is 6 percent, what is the value of the single payment that X would be required to make today?

$$PV_{ad} = \$375\left[\frac{1}{0.06} - \frac{1}{0.06(1.06)^{19}} + 1\right]$$

$$= \$375[PVIF_a(6\%, 19) + 1]$$

$$= \$375(12.1581) = \$4,559.29$$

The present value of this 20-payment (years 0 to 19) annuity due is \$4,559.29. Its value is calculated by first finding the interest factor for a 19-year regular annuity and then adding 1 to this value. This new interest factor is then multiplied by the annuity payment.

Alternatively, the present value of this 20-year annuity due may also be calculated as

$$PV_{ad} = \$375[PVIF_a(6\%, 20)](1.06)$$

$$= \$375(12.1581) = \$4,559.29$$

[6] Perpetuities

A perpetuity is an annuity that has an infinite life or time to maturity. One example of a perpetuity is the British Consol Bond, so called because it consolidated the debt incurred during the Napoleonic Wars. These bonds will never mature but promise to pay a constant amount in interest each year. Another example of a perpetuity is preferred stock that has an infinite maturity but (for most types of issues) has a fixed payment each year (i.e., the dividend).

[a] **Calculations.** The future value of a perpetuity is a trivial solution. Since it will provide an infinite number of cash payments with an infinite total dollar value, its

compounded value must also be infinite. The same is not true for the present value of a perpetuity. The present value of a perpetuity may be written as

$$PV_p = A\left[\sum_{t=1}^{\infty}\left(\frac{1}{1+i}\right)^t\right]$$

Because of the infinite life of the annuity and because the cash flow is the same in each period, this equation reduces to a simpler form:

$$PV_p = A\left(\frac{1}{i}\right)$$

EXAMPLE: The preferred stock of *XYZ* Corporation pays an annual preferred dividend of $10 per share. If *X* requires a 16 percent annual rate of return, how much should *X* pay for this preferred stock?

$$PV_p = \$10\left(\frac{1}{0.16}\right)$$

If *X* pays $62.50 for this preferred stock, he would receive a 16 percent rate of return by receiving a $10 dividend each year.

$$\$10 = \$62.50(0.16)$$

[b] Annuities as Differences of Perpetuities. The present value and future value interest factors for regular annuities may be calculated as

$$FVIF_a(i\%, N) = \left[\frac{(1+i)^N}{i} - \frac{1}{i}\right]$$

$$PVIF_a(i\%, N) = \left[\frac{1}{i} - \frac{1}{i(1+i)^N}\right]$$

These equations may be obtained by considering an annuity as the difference between two perpetuities.

The cash flows associated with an *N*-period annuity are equal to the cash flows associated with a perpetuity starting at time-period 0, minus the cash flows associated with a perpetuity starting at period *N*. This may be represented by the following time-line analysis.

The future value of an *N*-period annuity—its value at time-period *N*—requires that both of the perpetuities also be evaluated at time-period *N*. The value of the perpetuity starting at period 0 evaluated at period 0 is

$$PV_p = A\left(\frac{1}{i}\right)$$

To transform this value into its equivalent value at time N, it must be compounded forward N periods.

$$FV_p = A \left(\frac{1}{i}\right) [(1 + i)^N]$$

The value of the perpetuity starting at time-period N evaluated at time-period N is

$$PV_p = A \left(\frac{1}{i}\right)$$

The future value of the N-period annuity is the difference between these two perpetuities:

$$FV_a = A \left(\frac{1}{i}\right) [(1 + i)^N] - A \left(\frac{1}{i}\right)$$

$$= A \left[\frac{(1 + i)^N}{i} - \frac{1}{i}\right]$$

The present value of an N-period annuity—its value at time-period 0—also requires that both of the perpetuities be evaluated as of time-period 0. The value of the perpetuity starting at time-period 0 evaluated at period 0 is

$$PV_p = A \left(\frac{1}{i}\right)$$

The value of the perpetuity starting at time-period N evaluated at time N is

$$PV_p = A \left(\frac{1}{i}\right)$$

To transform this value into its equivalent value at time 0, it must be discounted back N periods.

$$PV_p = A \left(\frac{1}{i}\right) \left[\left(\frac{1}{1 + i}\right)^N\right]$$

The present value of this N-period annuity is the difference between the two perpetuities:

$$PV_a = A \left(\frac{1}{i}\right) - A \left(\frac{1}{i}\right) \left[\left(\frac{1}{1 + i}\right)^N\right]$$

$$= A \left[\frac{1}{i} - \frac{1}{i (1 + i)^N}\right]$$

[7] Nonannual Periods

The previous examples all used annual compounding and discounting periods. However, the general equations that have been presented are also applicable to nonannual periods. If there are M periods per year, the procedure is to divide the annual interest rate by M and to multiply the number of years by M.

[a] Future Value: Calculations. The future value of a single sum with M compounding periods per year is equal to

$$FV = PV\left[\left(1 + \frac{i}{M}\right)^{N*M}\right]$$

$$= PV\left[FVIF\left(\frac{i}{M}\%, N*M\right)\right]$$

EXAMPLE: X deposits $100 for a period of five years at an annual interest rate of 12 percent. What is the future value if compounding occurs semiannually?

$$FV = \$100\left[\left(1 + \frac{0.12}{2}\right)^{5*2}\right]$$

$$= \$100[FVIF(6\%, 10)]$$

$$= \$100(1.7908) = \$179.08$$

EXAMPLE: Y deposits $500 for a period of one year at an annual interest rate of 6 percent. If compounding occurs daily, what is the value of this amount at the end of one year?

$$FV = \$500\left[\left(1 + \frac{0.06}{365}\right)^{1*365}\right]$$

$$= \$500(1.0618313) = \$530.92$$

Interest in the preceding example was calculated using a 365-day year (366 days during a leap year). This is referred to as exact interest and is the basis that most banks use to calculate daily interest. However, there are other securities, such as commercial paper, Treasury bills, and repurchase agreements (RPs), where quotations are based on a 360-day commercial year. Regardless of whether a 360-day or a 365-day year is used, the general procedure is the same.

A special case of nonannual periods is continuous compounding. The future value of a single sum under continuous compounding is equal to

$$FV = PV[e^{i(N)}]$$

where e has an approximate value of 2.7182818.

EXAMPLE: Z deposits $1,000 for a period of 10 years at an annual interest rate of 5 percent, but interest is compounded continuously. What is the future value of this amount at the end of 10 years?

$$FV = \$1,000[e^{0.05(10)}]$$

$$= \$1,000(1.64872) = \$1,648.72$$

[b] Present Value: Calculations. The present value of a single sum with M compounding (discounting) periods per year is equal to

$$PV = FV\left[1 \Big/ \left(1 + \frac{i}{M}\right)^{N*M}\right]$$

$$= FV \left[PVIF \left(\frac{i}{M} \%, N^*M \right) \right]$$

EXAMPLE: If the annual interest rate is 12 percent but interest is compounded on a semiannual basis, what is the value of $100 to be received at the end of five years?

$$PV = \$100 \left[1 \Big/ \left(1 + \frac{0.12}{2} \right)^{5*2} \right]$$

$$= \$100[PVIF(6\%, 10)]$$

$$= \$100(0.5584) = \$55.84$$

EXAMPLE: If the annual interest rate is 8 percent but interest is compounded quarterly, what is the present value of $5,000 to be received in 10 years?

$$PV = \$5,000 \left[1 \Big/ \left(1 + \frac{0.08}{4} \right)^{10*4} \right]$$

$$= \$5,000[PVIF(2\%, 40)]$$

$$= \$5,000(0.4529) = \$2,264.50$$

Continuous discounting is once again a special case. The present value of a single sum under continuous discounting is equal to

$$PV = FV \left[\frac{1}{e^{i(N)}} \right]$$

$$= FV \left[e^{-i(N)} \right]$$

EXAMPLE: If the annual interest rate is 5 percent but discounting is on a continuous basis, what is the present value of $1,000 to be received at the end of 10 years?

$$PV = \$1,000 \left[\frac{1}{e^{0.05(10)}} \right]$$

$$= \$1,000[e^{-0.05(10)}]$$

$$= \$1,000(0.6065307) = \$606.53$$

[c] Annuities: Calculations. The interest factors associated with annuities are equal to the sum of the interest factors associated with the individual cash flows comprising the annuities. Therefore, the rules that were applied to compounding and discounting individual cash flows, with nonannual periods, also apply to annuities.

$$FV_a = A \left[FVIF_a \left(\frac{i}{M} \%, N*M \right) \right]$$

$$PV_a = A \left[PVIF_a \left(\frac{i}{M} \%, N*M \right) \right]$$

The timing of the annuity payment each period must be considered. It is possible to calculate the present value and the future value of an annuity where the payment periods do not equal the compounding periods. For simplicity, assume that the payment periods match the compounding periods.

EXAMPLE: The annual interest rate is 16 percent (compounded quarterly), and an annuity consists of a $25 cash flow to be received every three months (quarterly) for five years. This means that X receives or pays out 20 quarterly cash flows of $25 each. The future value and present value are calculated as

$$FV_a = \$25 \left[\sum_{t=0}^{19} \left(1 + \frac{0.16}{4}\right)^t \right]$$

$$= \$25 \left[\frac{(1 + 0.16/4)^{5*4}}{0.16/4} - \frac{1}{0.16/4} \right]$$

$$= \$25[FVIF_a(4\%, 20)]$$

$$= \$25(29.778) = \$744.45$$

$$PV_a = \$25 \left\{ \sum_{t=1}^{20} \left[1 \Big/ \left(1 + \frac{0.16}{4}\right)^t \right] \right\}$$

$$= \$25 \left[\frac{1}{0.16/4} - \frac{1}{(0.16/4)(1 + 0.16/4)^{5*4}} \right]$$

$$= \$25[PVIF_a(4\%, 20)]$$

$$= \$25(13.5903) = \$339.76$$

Continuous compounding and discounting are once again a special case. For annuities, however, the special case either assumes a stream of receipts received continuously over time or requires the use of integral calculus. Therefore, this special case is not discussed here.

[d] Annual and Effective Rates. For nonannual periods, it is also possible to use what is referred to as the effective annual rate. For instance, if the stated annual interest rate is 5 percent but compounding is on a semiannual basis, interest is earned at the rate of 2.5 percent per six-month period. Over one year, the effective annual interest rate is

$$1.025(1.025) - 1 = 0.050625 = 5.0625\%$$

This effective annual interest rate is greater than the stated annual interest rate. This is because interest on interest is being earned at a faster rate. Once this effective annual interest rate has been found, it may be used to compound or discount a cash flow on an annual basis.

EXAMPLE: Find the present value of $100 to be received in five years if the stated annual interest rate is 8 percent, but discounting is performed on a quarterly basis.

Step 1. The effective annual interest rate is equal to

$$\left(1 + \frac{0.08}{4}\right)^4 - 1 = 0.0824322 = 8.24322\%$$

Step 2. The present value, using the effective annual interest rate, is

$$PV = \$100 \left(\frac{1}{1.0824322^5} \right)$$

$$= \$100(0.6729713) = \$67.30$$

This is the same value that would be found using a quarterly rate of 2 percent.

$$PV = \$100 \left[1 \Big/ \left(1 + \frac{0.08}{4} \right)^{5*4} \right]$$

$$= \$100[PVIF(2\%, 20)]$$

$$= \$100(0.6730) = \$67.30$$

It is necessary to know whether a quoted annual rate is a stated annual rate that implicitly assumes nonannual periods or an effective annual rate that already incorporates the nonannual periods. Usually the answer is found by the context in which it is used. For instance, yields on corporate bonds are a stated annual rate, and one half of the stated rate applies to each six-month period. On the other hand, bankers are required to specify the effective annual rate, in addition to the stated rate, on loans.

[8] Solving for *N*, *A*, or *i* and Linear Interpolation

The equations that have been developed for the time value of money calculations imply that given all other variables, it should be possible to solve for the number of periods, *N*; the value of the annuity payment, *A*; or the interest rate, *i*.

[a] **Solving for *N*.** For simple cash flows, *N* is an easy variable to solve for, especially if one has access to a financial calculator. The solution procedure is demonstrated by the following example.

EXAMPLE: At an annual interest rate of 6 percent, how long will it take for $100 to double in value?

METHOD 1
This problem may be set up as either a future value or a present value problem. The general form is

$$\$200 = \$100[FVIF(6\%, N)]$$

or

$$\$100 = \$200[PVIF(6\%, N)]$$

If a financial calculator is used, the following values are supplied:

Future value = $200

Present value = $100

Interest rate = 6%

Solving for N gives a value of 11.895661 years. This solution may be verified by the following calculations.

$$FV = \$100[(1.06)^{11.895661}] = \$200$$

$$PV = \$200\left[\left(\frac{1}{1.06}\right)^{11.895661}\right] = \$100$$

METHOD 2

This problem may also be solved using interest factor tables and linear interpolation to arrive at an approximation for N. Here, present value interest factors are used.

$$\$100 = \$200[PVIF(6\%, N)]$$

$$\Rightarrow [PVIF(6\%, N)] = \frac{\$100}{\$200} = 0.5$$

According to Figure 4-2, when the interest rate is 6 percent, the present value interest factor takes on a value of 0.5 somewhere between $N = 11$ (PVIF $= 0.5268$) and $N = 12$ (PVIF $= 0.4970$). Now, imagine the following set of lines:

$N = 11$	$N = ?$	$N = 12$
PVIF $= 0.5268$	PVIF $= 0.50$	PVIF $= 0.4970$

These two lines are exactly the same length. The top line is labeled in units of discounting periods, and the bottom line is labeled in units of present value interest factors. The length of the top line is one period, and the length of the bottom line is 0.0298 present value interest factor units.

Since the two lines are exactly the same length, the length of the top line from $N = 11$ to $N = ?$ is equivalent to the length of the bottom line from PVIF $= 0.5268$ to PVIF $= 0.50$, or 0.0268 present value interest factor units. The portion of the bottom line represented by 0.0268 present value interest factor units is

$$(0.0268/0.0298) = 0.8993 = 89.93\%$$

or 89.93 percent of its length. Therefore, the distance from $N = 11$ to $N = ?$ must be 89.93 percent of the length of the top line. Since the total length of the top line is one period, the distance from $N = 11$ to $N = ?$ must be equal to

$$(1 \text{ period})(0.8993) = 0.8993 \text{ periods}$$

This implies that $N = ?$ is equal to

$$11 + 0.8993 = 11.8993 \text{ periods}$$

This compares to the exact answer of 11.895661 periods. Some difference between the two is expected, since interpolation attempts to represent a complex polynomial relationship as a linear function.

The general procedure for interpolation may be expressed as follows:

$$N = N_1 + \left[\frac{FVIF(i\%, N_1) - FVIF(i\%, N)}{FVIF(i\%, N_1) - FVIF(i\%, N_2)}\right](N_2 - N_1)$$

Using the values from the prior example results in

$$N = 11 + \left(\frac{0.5268 - 0.5000}{0.5268 - 0.4970}\right)(12 - 11) = 11.8993 \text{ periods}$$

[b] Solving for A. The following example outlines the procedures to calculate the amount of a periodic annuity payment.

EXAMPLE: X's child will enter college in five years, and X would like to have $10,000 saved by that time. The annual interest rate on X's savings is 12 percent, but interest is compounded monthly. How much should X deposit each month, starting one month from today, so that he will have $10,000 at the end of of five years?

The $10,000 is now a future value, and the annuity payment may be calculated as

$$\$10,000 = A[\text{FVIF}_a(1\%, 60)]$$

$$= A(81.669)$$

$$A = \frac{\$10,000}{81.669} = \$122.45$$

[c] Solving for i. For simple cash flows (single sums or annuities), i may be calculated in a manner similar to the way the value of N was calculated; either a financial calculator or interpolation of interest factor tables may be used. In addition, the interest rate associated with the future value and present value of single sums may be calculated using any calculator that has a power function key (y^x).

EXAMPLE: What is the annual interest rate that will allow $35 to grow to $100 over a period of 10 years?

METHOD 1

This problem may be solved as either a present value or a future value problem. Using future value interest factors, this problem is represented by the following equation.

$$\$100 = \$35 [(1 + i)^{10}]$$

$$\Rightarrow (1 + i)^{10} = \frac{\$100}{\$35} = 2.8571429$$

Taking the tenth root of both sides of this equation yields the following:

$$(1 + i) = (2.857149)^{1/10} = 1.1106909$$

$$\Rightarrow i = 1.1106909 - 1 = 0.1106909 = 11.06909\%$$

METHOD 2

Linear interpolation may be used to determine an approximation for i. Figure 4-1 shows that a future value interest factor of 2.8571 lies between an interest rate of 10 percent (FVIF = 2.5937) and an interest rate of 12 percent (FVIF = 3.1058). The interpolated value then is equal to

$$i = 0.1 + \left(\frac{2.5937 - 2.8571}{2.5937 - 3.1058}\right)(0.12 - 0.1) = 0.110287053 = 11.0287053\%$$

EXAMPLE: A regular annuity pays $25 every three months for five years. If the present value of this annuity is $347.41, what is the stated annual interest rate and what is the effective annual interest rate?

Step 1. If i' is the interest rate per quarter, the problem may be represented by the following equation:

$$\$347.41 = \$25[PVIF_a(i', 20)]$$

$$\Rightarrow PVIF_a(i', 20) = \frac{\$347.41}{\$25} = 13.8964$$

In Figure 4-4, an interest factor of 13.8964 is found to lie between an interest rate of 3 percent (IF = 14.8775) and an interest rate of 4 percent (IF = 13.5903). The interpolated value then is equal to

$$i' = 0.03 + \left(\frac{14.8775 - 13.8964}{14.8775 - 13.5903}\right)(0.04 - 0.03) = 0.0376 = 3.76\%$$

Step 2. The interest rate 0.0376 is a quarterly interest rate. The stated annual interest rate equals

$$i = 0.0376(4) = 0.1504 = 15.04\%$$

The effective annual interest rate is

$$i = (1.0376)^4 - 1 = 0.1591 = 15.91\%$$

[9] Newton's Approximation Technique

It is impossible to use interest factor tables and linear interpolation to determine the interest rate when dealing with complex cash flows. As an example of a complex cash flow, consider a loan of $4,800 with repayments of $1,000 each year for five years and a $2,200 balloon payment in the sixth year. The cash flows associated with this loan may be presented as follows:

Year	Cash Flow
0	$4,800
1	− 1,000
2	− 1,000
3	− 1,000
4	− 1,000
5	− 1,000
6	− $2,200

The interest rate on this loan must be such that the present value of the cash repayments in years 1–6 is exactly equal to the amount borrowed in year 0. This also means that the present value of all cash flows in years 0–6 added together must equal zero.

[a] Calculation of the Interest Rate. If x equals $[1/(1 + i)]$, the functional form for the present value of these cash flows may be written as

$$f(x) = 0 = \$4,800\ (x^0) - \$1,000\ (x^1) - \$1,000\ (x^2) - \$1,000\ (x^3) - \$1,000\ (x^4)$$
$$- \$1,000\ (x^5) - \$2,200\ (x^6)$$

The value for i that solves this equation is the interest rate on this loan. However, since the equation is a sixth-degree polynomial, it must be solved by an iterative process, which is too complex to be dealt with here.

4.02 BANK LOANS AND EFFECTIVE INTEREST RATES

When money is borrowed from a bank, the stated interest rate, also referred to at times as the simple or regular interest rate, may be much lower than the effective interest rate on the loan. Because of this, the Truth-in-Lending Act now requires all financial institutions to state the effective interest rate or annual percentage rate (APR) on the loan. The APR depends on the type of loan that is taken out.

[1] Definitions of Variables

i = stated or simple interest rate

P = principal amount borrowed

CB = percentage of the loan that must be kept on deposit as a compensating balance

APR = annual percentage rate or effective interest rate

[2] Straight Loan

A straight loan, also called a term loan, is one where both the principal and interest are repaid at the end of the borrowing period. Interest expense is equal to the stated interest rate times the principal amount borrowed.

[a] Calculations. The APR on a straight loan is equal to the stated rate on an annual basis. To illustrate this, assume that $1,200 is borrowed for a term of one year at a stated rate of 10 percent. The interest expense is equal to

$1,200(0.1) = $120

At the end of one year, the principal amount of $1,200 and interest of $120 must be repaid. The APR is then equal to

$$APR = \frac{P(i)}{P}$$
$$= \frac{\$1,200(0.1)}{\$1,200}$$
$$= 0.1 = 10\%$$

The reason that the APR and the stated rate are the same is that the borrower has the use of the entire $1,200 for the whole year. It is the early repayment or nonuse of the principal borrowed that increases the APR.

[3] Discounted Loan

In a discounted loan, the interest is prepaid at the time of borrowing. The usual procedure is for the financial institution to deduct the interest expense from the proceeds that the borrower receives.

[a] Calculations. If $1,200 is borrowed on a discounted basis for one year at a stated interest rate of 10 percent, the amount that the borrower actually receives is equal to

$1,200 - $1,200(0.1) = $1,080

This is equal to the principal amount borrowed minus the interest expense. At the end of the year, the borrower makes a total repayment (of principal) of $1,200. This is equivalent to borrowing $1,080 for one year and paying total interest of $120. The APR can be calculated as the interest expense divided by the amount of funds that the borrower actually has the use of.

$$\text{APR} = \frac{\$120}{\$1,080}$$

$$= 0.1111 = 11.11\%$$

The general formula for the effective rate on a discounted basis is

$$\text{APR} = \frac{i}{1 - i}$$

$$= \frac{0.1}{0.9}$$

$$= 0.1111 = 11.11\%$$

[4] Compensating Balance

There are times when a financial institution will agree to a loan only if a percentage of the loan, called the compensating balance, is kept on deposit with the institution. If the borrower's balances are already sufficient to cover the required compensating balance, this requirement will not affect that borrower's effective rate. However, if the borrower must keep a portion of the loan proceeds on deposit with the institution, this will reduce the total funds available for the borrower's use, thus increasing the effective rate.

[a] Calculations. The specific calculation of APR depends on the type of loan and the actual amount of the loan required as a compensating balance.

EXAMPLE: A loan of $1,200 is made for a term of one year at a stated interest rate of 10 percent. The compensating balance requirement is 15 percent of the amount of the loan. What is the APR on this loan?

The amount that must be kept on deposit as a compensating balance is equal to

$1,200(0.15) = $180

This means that the borrower has the use of

$1,200 − $180 = $1,020

for the year. At the end of the year, the borrower will repay the $1,200 of principal plus $120 in interest. The effective rate is equal to

$$\text{APR} = \frac{\$120}{\$1,200 - \$180} = 0.1176 = 11.76\%$$

The general equation for the effective rate may be written as

$$\text{APR} = \frac{i}{1 - \text{CB}}$$

$$= \frac{0.1}{0.85} = 0.1176 = 11.76\%$$

EXAMPLE: The sum of $1,200 is borrowed on a discounted basis for one year at a stated interest rate of 10 percent. In addition, a compensating balance equal to 20 percent of the amount of the loan is required. What is the APR?

The amount of prepaid interest on this loan is equal to

$1,200(0.1) = $120

The amount of the compensating balance is equal to

$1,200(0.2) = $240

Therefore, the borrower has the use of

$1,200 − $120 − $240 = $840

for the year. At the end of the year, the borrower will repay $1,200 of principal. The effective interest rate is equal to

$$\text{APR} = \frac{\$120}{\$1,200 - \$120 - \$240} = 0.1429 = 14.29\%$$

The general equation for the effective rate may be written as

$$\text{APR} = \frac{i}{1 - i - \text{CB}}$$

$$= \frac{0.1}{0.7} = 0.1429 = 14.29\%$$

[5] Installment Loan

An installment loan is one that requires periodic payments of principal and interest during each installment period. For bank loans, the installment period is usually each month or each quarter. The installment payment is the same for each period and is therefore equivalent to an annuity.

[a] Calculations. An approximation of the effective rate may be found as follows: If $1,200 is borrowed on a 12-month installment basis at a stated interest rate of 10 percent, the principal owed is reduced to zero by the end of the year. Therefore, on average, the borrower has the use of

$$\frac{\$1,200 + 0}{2} = \$600$$

for the entire year. At a stated interest rate of 10 percent, the total interest expense is still $120. An approximation of the effective rate would then be

$$\frac{\$120}{\$600} = 0.2$$

The true effective rate may be found in the following manner. The total amount to be repaid over the year is $1,200 in principal and $120 in interest, or a total of $1,320. If this amount is repaid on a monthly basis, the monthly payments are equal to

$$\frac{\$1,320}{12} = \$110$$

These monthly payments consist of a principal repayment plus interest on the unpaid balance of the loan.

The effective rate can be analyzed in terms of present value concepts. The financial institution has agreed to loan the borrower $1,200 today (the present value) in return for an annuity stream of $110 each month for 12 months. The true effective interest rate is simply the discount rate that equates the present value of the $110 annuity stream with the beginning value of $1,200.

$$\$1,200 = \$110 \left[\sum_{t=1}^{12} \left(\frac{1}{1+i} \right)^t \right]$$

$$\Rightarrow i = 0.014976663 = 1.4976663\%$$

This is the interest rate per month. On an annual basis, the true effective interest rate is

$$APR = (1.014976663)^{12} - 1 = 0.1952883 = 19.52883\%$$

However, financial institutions are not actually required to report the true effective interest rate as the APR. Rather, they may report a noncompounded form of this rate by taking (in this example) the monthly rate and multiplying it by 12. This would give

$$APR = 0.014976663(12) = 0.179719956 = 17.9719956\%$$

The main advantage of this form of APR is that it simplifies the calculation of the effective rate per period (simply divide by 12 to obtain the monthly rate). This, in turn, is useful when dealing with installment loans with a maturity greater than one year. However, it should be noted that even though it is legal for financial institutions to report this rate, it will always be less than the true effective rate being charged to the borrower.

[6] Discounted Installment Loan

Like a regular discounted loan, interest on a discounted installment loan is prepaid. The principal is then repaid in equal periodic payments.

[a] Calculations. The effective interest rate for a discounted installment loan is found in much the same manner as for a regular installment loan. If $1,200 is borrowed on a 12-month installment basis with prepaid interest at a stated rate of 10 percent, the borrower prepays $120 in interest. This gives the borrower usable funds, initially, of $1,080. The monthly payments consist only of a repayment of principal, since interest has been prepaid. The monthly payments are equal to

$$\frac{\$1,200}{12} = \$100$$

The effective interest rate is then calculated as follows:

$$\$1,080 = \$100 \left[\sum_{t=1}^{12} \left(\frac{1}{1 + i} \right)^t \right]$$

$$i = 0.016593678 = 1.6593678\%$$

$$APR = (1.016593678)^{12} - 1 = 0.218341 = 21.8341\%$$

Again, this is the true effective rate. The rate actually reported to the borrower will usually be

$$APR = 0.016593678(12) = 0.199124136 = 19.9124136\%$$

[7] Amortization Schedule

An amortization schedule specifies the principal and interest repayments for each period of an installment loan. As such, it also specifies the ending principal balance after each periodic repayment.

[a] Calculations. It has previously been determined that a one-year, $1,200 installment loan at a stated interest rate of 10 percent has an effective monthly interest rate of 1.4976663 percent. It has also been shown that the monthly payment for this loan is $110, composed of a principal repayment and interest on the remaining balance. To derive an amortization schedule, the following calculations must be made for each period.

Interest payment = (beginning balance)(0.014976663)

Principal repayment = $110 − interest payment

Ending balance = beginning balance − principal repayment

An amortization schedule for the $1,200 installment loan would look as follows:

Month	Beginning Balance	Interest Payment	Principal Repayment	Ending Balance
1	$1,200.00	$ 17.97	$ 92.03	$1,107.97
2	1,107.97	16.59	93.41	1,014.56
3	1,014.56	15.19	94.81	919.75
4	919.75	13.77	96.23	823.52
5	823.52	12.33	97.67	725.85
6	725.85	10.87	99.13	626.72
7	626.72	9.39	100.61	526.11
8	526.11	7.88	102.12	423.99
9	423.99	6.35	103.65	320.24
10	320.34	4.80	105.20	215.14
11	215.14	3.22	106.78	108.36
12	108.36	1.64	108.36	0.00
		$120.00	$1,200.00	

4.03 BOND ANALYSIS: NON-INTEREST-BEARING SECURITIES

Non-interest-bearing securities are also referred to as discounted securities. Unlike regular corporate bonds, which pay periodic interest (i.e., pay a coupon), interest is earned on these bonds by their appreciation in price over time. That is, these securities originally sell for less than their maturity or face value. All other factors being constant, the price approaches the face value as the time to maturity approaches zero. Note that this is not the same thing as a coupon bond that is selling at a discount.

[1] Definitions of Variables

d = discount rate as a percentage of the face value

D = dollar value of the discount

F = face or maturity value of the security

P = current price of the security

Y = equivalent bond yield of the security

i_J = simple interest rate using a J-day year

P' = price per dollar of face value

t_M = time remaining until maturity

t_H = time held by the original investor

[2] Discount Rates and Pricing

The discount rate determines the dollar value of the discount or the difference between the price and the maturity value. At times, this is also referred to as the quoted yield of the security. For most securities, such as Treasury bills and commercial paper, the discount rate is stated as a 360-day-year annual rate. All subsequent calculations must take into account the actual number of days until maturity.

[a] Calculation of the Dollar Discount. As stated previously, the discount rate is based on a 360-day year. The dollar discount is determined by the discount rate, the face value of the security, and the number of days until maturity. The general equation for the dollar discount is

$$D = F(d)\left(\frac{t_M}{360}\right)$$

EXAMPLE: An investor has just purchased a 6-month (180-day) Treasury bill. The face value of this security is $10,000, and the discount rate is 9.75 percent. What is the dollar value of the discount for this security?

$$D = \$10,000(0.0975)\left(\frac{180}{360}\right) = \$487.50$$

Intuitively, this security promises to pay a discount of 9.75 percent or $975 if held for one year. Since the investor will hold this security for half a year, it is entitled to half of the discount, or $487.50.

[b] Calculation of Price. The price of a discounted security is equal to the face value minus the dollar discount. It may be calculated by either of the following two formulas:

$$P = F - D$$

$$P = F\left[1 - \frac{d(t_M)}{360}\right]$$

EXAMPLE: What is the price of a 180-day, $10,000 face value Treasury bill if the discount rate is 9.75 percent?

METHOD 1

The dollar discount associated with this security, calculated in the previous section, is $487.50. Therefore, the price is equal to

$$P = \$10,000 - \$487.50 = \$9,512.50$$

METHOD 2

The price may also be calculated as follows:

$$P = \$10,000\left[1 - \frac{0.0975(180)}{360}\right] = \$9,512.50$$

[c] Calculation of the Discount Rate. Given the face value of the security, the time to maturity, and either the dollar discount or the price, the annual discount rate may be calculated using the following equations:

$$d = \frac{D}{F}\left(\frac{360}{t_M}\right)$$

$$d = \left(\frac{F - P}{F}\right)\left(\frac{360}{t_M}\right)$$

EXAMPLE: What is the annual discount rate for a 180-day Treasury bill with a face value of $10,000 and a current price of $9,512.50?

METHOD 1

The dollar discount is equal to

$$D = \$10,000 - \$9,512.50 = \$487.50$$

This implies that the discount rate is equal to

$$d = \left(\frac{\$487.50}{\$10,000}\right)\left(\frac{360}{180}\right) = 0.0975 = 9.75\%$$

METHOD 2

The discount rate may also be calculated as

$$d = \left(\frac{\$10,000 - \$9,512.50}{\$10,000}\right)\left(\frac{360}{180}\right) = 0.0975 = 9.75\%$$

[3] Equivalent Simple Interest Rate

Since an investor pays less than the face value of the discounted security, the interest rate earned, which is based on price, must be greater than the discount rate, which is based on the face value. The usual procedure is to state this simple interest rate on the basis of a 365-day year.

[a] Calculations. The simple interest rate is a function of the original price paid and the amount of price appreciation earned over the investment horizon. Allowing the subscripts b and s to represent the *buying price* and the *selling price*, the simple interest rate may be calculated as

$$i_{365} = \left(\frac{P_s - P_b}{P_b}\right)\left(\frac{365}{t_H}\right)$$

If an investor holds the security until it matures, the price appreciation will be equal to the dollar discount at time of purchase; no return is earned from changes in the general level of market interest rates. The simple interest rate may then be calculated as

$$i_{365} = \frac{365(d)}{[360 - d(t_M)]}$$

EXAMPLE: If an investor purchases a 90-day Treasury bill for $9,500 and sells it in 45 days for $9,750, what is the simple interest rate, or the rate of return, that the investor earns on this investment?

$$i_{365} = \left(\frac{\$9,750 - \$9,500}{\$9,500}\right)\left(\frac{365}{45}\right) = 0.21345 = 21.345\%$$

EXAMPLE: An investor purchases a 180-day Treasury bill at a price of $9,512.50. This Treasury bill has a face value of $10,000 and a discount rate of 9.75 percent. If the investor holds this security until it matures, what is the simple interest rate on this investment?

METHOD 1

The simple interest rate may be calculated as

$$i_{365} = \left(\frac{\$10,000 - \$9,512.50}{\$9,512.50}\right)\left(\frac{365}{180}\right) = 0.1039 = 10.39\%$$

METHOD 2

The simple interest rate may also be calculated as follows:

$$i_{365} = \frac{365(0.0975)}{360 - 0.0975(180)} = 0.1039 = 10.39\%$$

[4] Effective Return

The simple interest rate that was calculated in the previous section assumed an add-on type of interest. The distinction between add-on interest and compound interest is not really important except in the direct comparison of securities with different maturities. In other words, an investor must be concerned with the actual investment horizon.

[a] Calculations. Assume that an investor has an investment horizon of 120 days, and that 120-day Treasury bills have a discount rate of 10 percent and 30-day Treasury bills have a discount rate of 10.25 percent. The equivalent simple interest rate for these two securities would be

$$\text{120-day: } i_{365} = \frac{365(0.1)}{360 - 0.1(120)} = 0.1049 = 10.49\%$$

$$\text{30-day: } i_{365} = \frac{365(0.1025)}{360 - 0.1025(30)} = 0.1048 = 10.48\%$$

For the 120-day Treasury bill, the simple interest rate of 10.49 percent assumes that the investor could earn

$$0.1049\left(\frac{120}{365}\right) = 0.0345 = 3.45\%$$

every 120 days. For the 30-day security, the simple interest rate of 10.48 percent assumes that the investor could earn

$$0.1048\left(\frac{30}{365}\right) = 0.0086 = 0.86\%$$

every 30 days.

From the simple interest rates of 10.49 percent and 10.48 percent, it might appear that the investor would be better off purchasing the 120-day security. However, assume that over the 120-day investment horizon the investor believes that it could purchase either the 120-day security at a discount rate of 10 percent or 4 consecutive 30-day securities each at a discount rate of 10.25 percent. In the second case, 1 security matures every 30 days, and the proceeds are reinvested in a new 30-day security, so the investor actually earns compound interest. The effective rate of return for the 30-day Treasury bills is equal to

$$\text{30-day: } i_{365} = \left\{ \left[1 + \left(\frac{0.1048}{365} \right) (30) \right]^{120/30} - 1 \right\} \left(\frac{365}{120} \right) = 0.1062 = 10.62\%$$

Because of compounding, the investor is better off, in terms of effective return, if it is able to invest in 4 consecutive 30-day Treasury bills, each with a discount rate of 10.25 percent.

If the investment horizon is 360 days and if each of these securities could be rolled over at their stated discount rate, the effective rates of return would be

$$\text{120-day: } i_{365} = \left\{ \left[1 + \left(\frac{0.1049}{365} \right) (120) \right]^{360/120} - 1 \right\} \left(\frac{365}{360} \right) = 0.1086 = 10.86\%$$

$$\text{30-day: } i_{365} = \left\{ \left[1 + \left(\frac{0.1048}{365} \right) (30) \right]^{360/30} - 1 \right\} \left(\frac{365}{360} \right) = 0.1099 = 10.99\%$$

[5] Equivalent Bond Yield

The equivalent bond yield, also referred to as the coupon yield equivalent, is reported on most bond dealers' quote sheets. Its purpose is to make possible direct comparisons between the interest earned on discount securities and the yield to maturity on coupon-paying bonds. Since most coupon securities pay interest on a semiannual basis, the time to maturity for the discount security is important in determining its equivalent bond yield.

[a] Calculations: Fewer Than 182 Days. A coupon bond with fewer than 182 days to maturity will make no coupon payments until it matures. Thus, its yield to maturity is already on an equivalent basis to the simple interest rate of a discounted security, and the discounted security's equivalent bond yield is equal to its simple interest rate.

EXAMPLE: What is the equivalent bond yield for a 95-day Treasury bill with a quoted discount rate of 11.5 percent?
Since the time to maturity for this security is less than 182 days, the equivalent bond yield is equal to the simple interest rate, which is equal to

$$Y = \frac{365(0.115)}{360 - (0.115)(95)} = 0.1202 = 12.02\%$$

[b] Calculations: More Than 182 Days. A coupon bond with more than 182 days to maturity will make a coupon payment before it matures. To calculate the equivalent bond yield for a discounted security with more than 182 days to mature, it must be treated as if it too paid interest on a semiannual basis. The formula for the equivalent bond yield is

$$Y = \frac{-[2(t_M)/365] + 2((t_M/365)^2 - \{[2(t_M)/365] - 1\}[1 - (1/P')])^{1/2}}{\{[2(t_M)/365] - 1\}}$$

EXAMPLE: A 225-day Treasury bill has a quoted discount rate of 12 percent. What is the equivalent bond yield on this security?

Step 1. $P' = \left[1 - \dfrac{0.12(225)}{360}\right] = 0.925$

Step 2. The equivalent bond yield is then equal to

$$Y = \frac{-[2(225)/365] + 2((225/365)^2 - \{[2(225)/365] - 1\}[1 - (1/0.925)])^{1/2}}{\{[2(225)/365] - 1\}}$$

$$= 0.1299 = 12.99\%$$

This says that there would be no difference, all other factors being held constant, between holding a 225-day Treasury bill with a discount rate of 12 percent and holding a 225-day coupon bond with a yield to maturity of 12.99 percent.

4.04 BOND ANALYSIS: INTEREST-BEARING SECURITIES

Most corporate bonds, as well as municipals and Treasury notes and bonds, pay interest on a semiannual basis. To find the interest paid during the year, multiply the par value (face or maturity value) of the bond by the annual coupon rate. This amount is then divided by 2 to determine the amount of interest paid every 6 months. It is important to know that corporate securities use a 180-day coupon period—a commercial year of 360 days or 30 days per month, whereas government securities use an exact year of 365 days (366 days for a leap year). In addition, corporate securities are delivered 5 business days after the sale, whereas government securities are delivered the same day or the day after the sale. Prices for these securities are calculated as of the delivery date. Finally, if a bond is sold between coupon dates, it will have accrued interest since the last coupon date. This accrued interest must be added to the quoted price to determine the actual amount that the investor is required to pay.

[1] Definitions of Variables

C = annual coupon rate

F = face, par, or maturity value of the bond

P = quoted price for the bond

P' = price per dollar of face value

N = number of coupon periods remaining

Y = yield to maturity or the discount rate used in present value calculations

AI = amount of accured interest

AI' = accrued interest per dollar of face value

AY = approximation of the actual yield

CY = approximation of the yield to call

$$RY = \text{approximation of the actual realized yield}$$
$$RCY = \text{realized compounded yield}$$
$$SF = \text{sinking fund payment}$$
$$TVR = \text{terminal value ratio of cash flows at maturity to original price}$$
$$t_{PM} = \text{time from purchase until maturity in days}$$
$$t_{PS} = \text{time from purchase until settlement of maturity in days}$$
$$t_H = \text{time held by the original investor since the last coupon date}$$
$$t_C = \text{time remaining until call in years}$$
$$t_M = \text{time remaining until maturity in years}$$
$$t_{IH} = \text{investor's time horizon}$$
$$t_{CD} = \text{actual number of days between coupon periods}$$
$$PV = \text{present value of future cash flows}$$
$$PVIF(Y/2\%, N) = \text{present value interest factor for a single sum at an annual yield of } Y \text{ percent for } N \text{ six-month periods}$$
$$PVIF_a(Y/2\%, N) = \text{present value interest factor for an annuity at an annual yield of } Y \text{ percent for } N \text{ six-month periods}$$

[2] Accrued Interest

When a bond is sold between coupon dates, the price actually paid by an investor is equal to the present value of all future cash flows to be received. This value is greater than the quoted price by the amount of accrued interest, where the accrued interest is equal to the portion of the next coupon to be received that is owed to the original owner of the bond. The actual calculation of accrued interest depends on whether the security is a corporate security or a government security.

[a] Calculations: Corporate Securities. Accrued interest on corporate securities is calculated using a 180-day coupon period. All months within the coupon period are assumed to have 30 days. The accrued interest may be calculated as follows:

$$AI = F\left(\frac{C}{2}\right)\left(\frac{t_H}{180}\right)$$

EXAMPLE: Assume that a 9 percent coupon bond with a face value of $1,000 has just been purchased. Interest on this bond is paid semiannually, and it has been 45 days since the last coupon payment. What is the accrued interest on this bond?

$$AI = \$1,000\left(\frac{0.09}{2}\right)\left(\frac{45}{180}\right) = \$11.25$$

This amount is added to the bond's quoted price to determine the amount actually paid by the purchaser.

[b] Calculations: Government Securities. Unlike corporate securities, government securities use the actual number of days within the coupon period to determine the amount of accrued interest. This period may range from 181 days to 184 days. The accrued interest may be calculated as follows:

$$AI = F\left(\frac{C}{2}\right)\left(\frac{t_H}{t_{CD}}\right)$$

Example: A Treasury bond with a face value of $100,000 is issued with a coupon rate of 8.75 percent. Coupon payment dates for this bond are November 15 and May 15. If this bond is purchased on January 5, what is the value of accrued interest?

There are 181 days between November 15 and May 15, and 184 days between May 15 and November 15. If the date of sale is included, there are 51 days between November 15 and January 5. The amount of accrued interest may be calculated as follows:

$$AI = \$100,000\left(\frac{0.0875}{2}\right)\left(\frac{51}{181}\right) = \$1,232.73$$

[3] Yield to Maturity

The yield to maturity is the discount rate that is used to determine the present value of all future cash flows to be received. The yield is reported on an annual basis but is an add-on interest rate. That is, one half of the reported yield is the correct rate to use per six-month period for coupon bonds with semiannual payments of interest.

[a] **Calculation of Yield.** For interest-bearing securities, the calculation of yield to maturity is the same as finding the internal rate of return (discount rate) for a complex cash flow. For instance, assume that a five-year, 9 percent coupon, corporate bond is purchased for $961.39. If this bond pays interest on a semiannual basis, what is its annual yield?

METHOD 1
A 9 percent coupon rate implies that this bond will pay

$$\$1,000\left(\frac{0.09}{2}\right) = \$45$$

every 6 months for 5 years (10 6-month periods). In addition, since it is a corporate bond, it will pay a maturity value of $1,000. The pricing equation for this bond is then equal to

$$\$961.39 = \$45\left[\sum_{t=1}^{10}\left(\frac{1}{1 + (Y/2)}\right)^t\right] + \$1,000\left[\left(\frac{1}{1 + (Y/2)}\right)^{10}\right]$$

$$= \$45\left[PVIF_a\left(\frac{Y}{2}\%,10\right)\right] + \$1,000\left[PVIF\left(\frac{Y}{2}\%,10\right)\right]$$

This equation may be solved for Y with either a financial calculator or an iterative solution process such as Newton's Approximation Technique.

METHOD 2
The yield to maturity for this bond may also be solved using bond tables. (A portion of a bond table is presented in Figure 4-5). The first step in using bond tables is to

FIGURE 4-5

Bond Pricing Table (Coupon Rate = 9.0%)

Yield	1 Year	2 Year	3 Year	4 Year	5 Year	6 Year	7 Year	8 Year	9 Year	10 Year
7.00	101.90	103.67	105.33	106.87	108.32	109.66	110.92	112.09	113.19	114.21
7.25	101.66	103.20	104.64	105.98	107.23	108.39	109.48	110.48	111.42	112.30
7.50	101.42	102.74	103.96	105.10	106.16	107.14	108.05	108.90	109.69	110.42
7.75	101.18	102.28	103.29	104.23	105.10	105.91	106.66	107.35	107.99	108.59
8.00	100.94	101.81	102.62	103.37	104.06	104.69	105.28	105.83	106.33	106.80
8.25	100.71	101.36	101.96	102.51	103.02	103.49	103.93	104.33	104.70	105.04
8.50	100.47	100.90	101.30	101.67	102.00	102.31	102.60	102.86	103.10	103.32
8.75	100.23	100.45	100.65	100.83	101.00	101.15	101.29	101.42	101.54	101.64
9.00	100.00	100.00	100.00	100.00	100.00	100.00	100.00	100.00	100.00	100.00
9.25	99.77	99.55	99.36	99.18	99.02	98.87	98.73	98.61	98.50	98.39
9.50	99.53	99.11	98.72	98.37	98.05	97.75	97.49	97.24	97.02	96.82
9.75	99.30	98.67	98.09	97.56	97.09	96.65	96.26	95.90	95.57	95.28
10.00	99.07	98.23	97.46	96.77	96.14	95.57	95.05	94.58	94.16	93.77
10.25	98.84	97.79	96.84	95.98	95.20	94.50	93.86	93.29	92.76	92.29
10.50	98.61	97.36	96.22	95.20	94.28	93.45	92.69	92.01	91.40	90.85
10.75	98.38	96.92	95.61	94.43	93.36	92.41	91.54	90.77	90.06	89.43
11.00	98.15	96.49	95.00	93.67	92.46	91.38	90.41	89.54	88.75	88.05
11.25	97.93	96.07	94.40	92.91	91.57	90.37	89.30	88.33	87.47	86.69
11.50	97.70	95.64	93.80	92.16	90.69	89.38	88.20	87.15	86.21	85.37
11.75	97.47	95.22	93.21	91.42	89.82	88.39	87.12	85.98	84.97	84.07
12.00	97.25	94.80	92.62	90.69	88.96	87.42	86.06	84.84	83.76	82.80
12.25	97.03	94.39	92.04	89.96	88.11	86.47	85.01	83.72	82.57	81.55
12.50	96.80	93.97	91.46	89.24	87.27	85.53	83.98	82.61	81.40	80.33
12.75	96.58	93.56	90.89	88.53	86.44	84.60	82.97	81.53	80.26	79.13

refer to the portion of the table that lists yields for the particular coupon rate of interest; in this problem, that would be the 9 percent coupon table. The next step is to convert the current price of the bond to its percentage of par value; this is how bond prices are reported in the financial press. In this example, the price would be reported as 96.14. Scan across the columns until a time to maturity of five years is reached; then scan down the rows until the price closest to 96.14 is found. This corresponds to a yield of 10 percent.

[b] Approximation of Yield. The yield to maturity is the solution to a complex polynomial function. However, there are several formulas used by the industry that are quite simple and provide a close approximation of the true yield. For instance, if an investor plans to hold a bond until it matures, an approximation for the true yield may be calculated as follows:

$$AY = \frac{[F(C) + (P_M - P_P)/(t_M)]}{(P_M + P_P)/(2)}$$

where the subscripts M and P refer to the *maturity price* and *purchase price* of the security, respectively.

EXAMPLE: A 9 percent coupon bond has five years to maturity. If an investor paid $961.39 for this bond and it will mature for $1,000, what is the approximate yield to maturity for this bond?

$$AY = \frac{[\$1,000(0.09) + (\$1,000 - \$961.39)/5]}{(\$1,000 + \$961.39)/2}$$

$$= 0.0996457 = 9.96457\%$$

This result is very close to the true yield of 10 percent.

Today, many bonds issued by corporations are callable. This means that the corporation may force the early retirement of the bonds. The usual procedure is to defer the first call date for a period after the initial issue of the bond (e.g., five years). After this period, the bonds may be called by the corporation. If the bond is called, the investor will receive the bond's maturity value plus a call premium, usually a maximum of one year's interest. However, the bondholder then forgoes the right to any other coupons on the bond.

If the bond is selling for more than its maturity value plus one year's interest, there is a very good chance that the bond will be called at the first call date. The yield to call will usually be less than the corresponding yield to maturity. If it is, the financial press will usually report the yield to call as the bond's yield. An approximation for the yield to call may be calculated as follows:

$$CY = \frac{[F(C) + (P_C - P_P)/t_C]}{(P_C + P_P)/2}$$

where the subscripts C and P refer to the *call price* and the *purchase price*, respectively.

EXAMPLE: A 9 percent coupon bond is purchased for $1,213.55. The time to maturity for this bond is 20 years, but it is callable in three years at a call price of $1,090. What are the approximate yield to maturity and yield to call?

$$AY = \frac{[\$1,000(0.09) + (\$1,000 - \$1,213.55)/20]}{(\$1,000 + \$1,213.55)/2}$$

$$= 0.0717 = 7.17\%$$

$$CY = \frac{[\$1,000(0.09) + (\$1,090 - \$1,213.55)/3]}{(\$1,090 + \$1,213.55)/2}$$

$$= 0.0424 = 4.24\%$$

Finally, an investor that sells a bond before maturity may be interested in the actual realized yield on this bond. An approximation for this realized yield may be calculated as

$$RY = \frac{[F(C) + (P_S - P_P)/t_{IH}]}{(P_S + P_P)/2}$$

EXAMPLE: A 9 percent coupon bond is purchased for $865. It is sold for $950 after being held for four years. What is the approximate realized yield for this bond?

$$RY = \frac{[\$1{,}000(0.09) + (950 - \$865)/4]}{(\$950 + \$865)/2}$$

$$= 0.1226 = 12.26\%$$

[c] Government Securities During the Final Coupon Period. The yield on government securities during the final coupon period may be calculated as

$$Y^* = \left[\frac{1 + (C/2)}{(P' + AI') - 1}\right]\left[\frac{2(t_{CD})}{t_{PM}}\right]$$

This is the value that will be quoted as the bond's yield, but it is only an approximation of the true yield. To obtain the true yield, two corrections may have to be made:

1. Since $2(t_{CD})$ will never be exactly equal to 365 days, the approximate yield must be adjusted by the factor $365/2(t_{CD})$.

2. It is possible that the bond will not mature on a business day (this is true for most securities). Therefore, the time from purchase to settlement will not be equal to the time from purchase to maturity. If this is the case, the approximate yield must be adjusted by the factor t_{PM}/t_{PS}.

This implies that the true yield is equal to

$$Y = Y^*\left[\frac{365}{2(t_{CD})}\right]\left[\frac{t_{PM}}{t_{PS}}\right]$$

EXAMPLE: An investor settles on an 8 percent Treasury bond on September 17, 1992. This bond pays coupons on November 15 and May 15 and matures on November 15, 1992. The maturity value of this bond is $100,000, the current quoted price is $99,960.48, and the amount of accrued interest is $2,717.39. What is the approximate yield and the true yield on this security?

Step 1. There are 184 days between May 15 and November 15. There are 125 days between May 15 and September 17, and 59 days between September 17 and November 15. However, November 15, 1992 is a Sunday. Therefore, the settlement of maturity will not occur until the following day, which is 60 days from the date of purchase.

Step 2. The amount of accrued interest (given in this example) can be calculated as

$$AI = \$100{,}000\left(\frac{0.08}{2}\right)\left(\frac{125}{184}\right) = \$2{,}717.39$$

The accrued interest per dollar of face value is then equal to

$$AI' = \frac{\$2{,}717.39}{\$100{,}000} = 0.0271739$$

Step 3. The quoted price, which does not include accrued interest, is $99,960.48. The price per dollar of face value is then equal to

$$P' = \frac{\$99{,}960.48}{\$100{,}000} = 0.9996048$$

Step 4. The approximate yield on this security may now be calculated as follows:

$$Y^* = \left[\frac{1 + (0.08/2)}{(0.9996048 + 0.0271739) - 1} \right] \left[\frac{2(184)}{59} \right]$$

$$= 0.080314343$$

Step 5. The true yield, which is nothing more than a simple interest rate, may then be calculated as

$$Y = 0.080314343 \left[\frac{365}{2(184)} \right] \left[\frac{59}{60} \right] = 0.078331947 = 7.8331947\%$$

It can be shown that this value is the true yield, expressed as a simple interest rate, for this security.

Step 1. The interest rate earned over the 60 days from purchase to the settlement of maturity is equal to

$$0.078331947 \left(\frac{60}{365} \right) = 0.012876484 = 1.2876484\%$$

Step 2. If a simple interest rate of 1.2876484 percent is earned on an initial investment of

$$\$99,960.48 + \$2,717.39 = \$102,677.87$$

after 60 days the investment should have an ending value equal to

$$\$102,677.87(1.012876484) = \$104,000$$

which is exactly equal to the maturity value and the final coupon that will be received on November 16.

[d] Realized Compounded Yield. Some people believe that a *coupon bond's* yield to maturity is the rate of return that they will actually earn (realize) if they hold the bond to maturity. This is usually incorrect. The yield to maturity is nothing more than the bond's internal rate of return and, as such, is a statistical artifact; it is simply the discount rate that when applied to the bond's cash flows will give a present value equal to the price. The only time that it will also be equal to the realized compounded yield (return actually earned) is when the reinvestment rate for the bond's intermediate cash flows is exactly the same as the bond's yield to maturity.

A bond's yield to maturity will understate (or overstate) the realized compounded yield when the true reinvestment rate is greater than (or less than) the calculated yield to maturity. Figure 4-6 illustrates this relationship for a 10 percent coupon bond that pays $50 in interest every 6 months, has 10 years until it matures, and is originally priced to sell at par (that is, its yield to maturity is equal to the coupon rate). If the annual reinvestment rate is also 10 percent (5 percent per 6-month period), the terminal value of the cash flows received plus the interest earned from the reinvestment of those cash flows will be equal to $2,653.30: $1,000 from the maturity value of the bond, $1,000 to be received in the form of coupon payments, and $653.30 from reinvesting the coupons every 6 months to earn a 5 percent, 6-month rate. Given the starting value of $1,000 and the terminal value of $2,653.30, the terminal value ratio is equal to

FIGURE 4-6

Realized Compounded Yields at Different Reinvestment Rates

	Reinvestment Rates		
	8%	10%	12%
Total coupons	$1,000.00	$1,000.00	$1,000.00
Reinvestment income	488.90	653.30	839.28
Terminal value of coupons	$1,488.90	$1,653.30	$1,839.28
Payoff at maturity	1,000.00	1,000.00	1,000.00
Total terminal value	$2,488.90	$2,653.30	$2,839.28
Initial price	$1,000.00	$1,000.00	$1,000.00
Terminal value ratio	2.4889	2.6533	2.8393
Realized compounded yield	9.329%	10.000%	10.713%

Note: Ten percent coupon, 10-year bond, priced at par.

$$TVR = \frac{\$2,653.30}{\$1,000} = 2.6533$$

The realized compounded yield can then be calculated as

$$RCY \Rightarrow 2.65330 = \left[1 + \left(\frac{RCY}{2}\right)\right]^{20}$$

$$\Rightarrow \quad RCY = 2(2.65330^{1/20} - 1) = 0.1 = 10\%$$

If the stated annual reinvestment rate is only 8 percent (4 percent per six-month period), the realized compounded yield on an annual basis will be equal to 9.329 percent, and if the stated annual reinvestment rate is 12 percent, the realized compounded yield will be equal to 10.713 percent.

This example shows that it may be unwise for an investor to rely too heavily on the yield to maturity that is reported for a bond. Since reinvestment rates do change over time and may certainly be expected to differ from the yield to maturity, the realized compounded yield may be the only correct measure of the return actually earned by the investor.

[4] Bond Pricing

The quoted price of a bond is equal to the present value of the future cash flows to be received minus the accrued interest. Bonds are priced as of the delivery date. Corporate bonds assume a 180-day coupon period, whereas government securities use the exact number of days within the coupon period. Thus, for bonds not selling at a coupon date, a distinction must be made between corporate and government securities.

[a] Calculation of a Price at a Coupon Date. If a bond is purchased for delivery at a coupon date, accrued interest will be zero. If the bond pays interest on a semiannual basis, all future cash flows to be received will be discounted over full periods at one half of the quoted yield to maturity.

EXAMPLE: A 10 percent coupon bond has a quoted yield of 9.8 percent. If interest on this bond is paid semiannually and the bond has 10 years to maturity, what is its current price?

Step 1. Since this bond is being priced at a coupon date, its accrued interest is zero.

Step 2. This bond will make 20 semiannual payments of $50, starting 6 months from today, and a final maturity payment of $1,000.

Step 3. The appropriate discount rate is equal to one half of the quoted yield, or 4.9 percent per six-month period.

Step 4. The current price is equal to the present value of all future cash flows to be received discounted at the six-month rate:

$$P = \$50 \left[\sum_{t=1}^{20} \left(\frac{1}{1.049} \right)^t \right] + \$1,000 \left(\frac{1}{1.049} \right)^{20}$$

$$= \$1,012.57$$

[b] Calculation of a Price Between Coupon Dates: Corporate Securities. When a corporate bond is sold between coupon dates, accrued interest is calculated using a 180-day coupon period. The price that an investor must pay is equal to the quoted price plus the accrued interest, which is simply the present value of all future cash flows to be received. This section demonstrates straightforward present value calculations and two additional pricing methods used by the industry.

EXAMPLE: On June 8, 1992, a 10 percent coupon bond with a quoted yield of 6 percent is purchased. This bond makes interest payments on March 15 and September 15 and matures on September 15, 1993. What is the quoted price (add-interest price) and the actual price (flat price) for this bond?

This bond will be delivered for settlement after five business days (one week) or on June 15, 1992. All calculations are made as of the delivery date. The cash flows and timing for this bond may be represented as follows.

Date	Cash Flow
June 8, 1992—sale	
June 15, 1992—delivery	
September 15, 1992	$ 50
March 15, 1993	50
September 15, 1993	1,050

The delivery date of June 15, 1992 falls halfway between the last coupon payment and the next coupon payment (90 days). Accrued interest on this bond may be calculated as

$$AI = \$1,000 \left(\frac{0.1}{2} \right) \left(\frac{9}{180} \right) = \$25$$

METHOD 1

To find the present value of the cash flows, the following steps may be used.

Step 1. Calculate the price of the bond as of the next coupon payment date. This price will not include the next coupon to be received:

$$PV = \$50 \left[\left(\frac{1}{1.03}\right)^1\right] + \$1,050 \left[\left(\frac{1}{1.03}\right)^2\right]$$

$$= \$1,038.27$$

Step 2. Add to the calculated price the next coupon to be received:

$$PV = \$1,038.27 + \$50$$

$$= \$1,088.27$$

This is the present value of all future cash flows to be received, evaluated as of the next coupon date.

Step 3. Discount this new value back to the actual delivery date:

$$PV = \$1,088.27 \left[\left(\frac{1}{1.03}\right)^{90/180}\right]$$

$$= \$1,072.30$$

This is the flat price or the price that the investor actually has to pay.

Step 4. To calculate the quoted price or add-interest price, subtract the accumulated interest:

$$P = \$1,072.30 - \$25$$

$$= \$1,047.30$$

METHOD 2

The flat price may also be calculated as a one-step process:

$$PV = \$50 \left[\left(\frac{1}{1.03}\right)^{90/180}\right] + \$50 \left[\left(\frac{1}{1.03}\right)^{270/180}\right]$$

$$+ \$1,050 \left[\left(\frac{1}{1.03}\right)^{450/180}\right]$$

$$= \$1,072.30$$

This is the same price as calculated under Method 1. For this particular problem, there is a slight rounding error when the two industry methods are used.

METHOD 3

The first industry method demonstrated here calculates the quoted or add-interest price. The calculation follows.

Step 1. Using the current yield, calculate the price as of the last coupon payment date. This would be as of March 15, 1992 and would be equal to

$P_{M83} = \$50[\text{PVIF}_a(3\%, 3)] + \$1,000[\text{PVIF}(3\%, 3)]$

$\qquad = \$1,056.57$

Step 2. Using the current yield, calculate the price as of the next coupon payment date. This would be as of September 15, 1992 and would be equal to

$P_{S83} = \$50[\text{PVIF}_a(3\%, 2)] + \$1,000[\text{PVIF}(3\%, 2)]$

$\qquad = \$1,038.27$

Step 3. Determine the price appreciation or depreciation over the coupon period:

$\$1,056.57 - \$1,038.27 = \$18.30$ of depreciation

Step 4. Determine the proportion of the total price appreciation or depreciation that is applicable to the period from the last coupon date to the delivery date:

$\$18.30 \left(\dfrac{90}{180}\right) = \$9.15$

Step 5. The quoted or add-interest price is equal to the price at the last coupon date plus (minus) the applicable price appreciation (depreciation) since the last coupon date.

$P = \$1,056.57 - \$9.15$

$\quad = \$1,047.42$

Step 6. The flat price, or actual payment required at delivery, is equal to the quoted price plus accrued interest.

$PV = \$1,047.42 + \$25.00$

$\qquad = \$1,072.42$

METHOD 4

This industry method calculates the flat price of the bond. The steps are as follows:

Step 1. Using the current yield, calculate the price as of the last coupon date. This would be as of March 15, 1992 and would be equal to

$P_{M83} = \$50[\text{PVIF}_a(3\%, 3)] + \$1,000[\text{PVIF}(3\%, 3)]$

$\qquad = \$1,056.57$

Step 2. Using a 180-day coupon period, find the amount of interest that would result in a 6 percent annual yield if this bond had been bought at the last coupon date and held until the delivery or settlement date.

$\text{Interest} = \$1,056.57 \left(\dfrac{10.06}{2}\right)\left(\dfrac{90}{180}\right)$

$\qquad = \$15.85$

Step 3. The flat price is equal to the price at the last coupon date plus the applicable interest that results in the current yield of 12 percent.

$PV = \$1,056.57 + \$15.85$

$\quad = \$1,072.42$

Step 4. The quoted price is equal to the flat price minus the amount of accrued interest.

$$P = \$1,072.42 - \$25.00$$
$$= \$1,047.42$$

[c] Calculation of a Price Between Coupon Dates: Government Securities. The price of a government note or bond may also be calculated as the present value of all future cash flows to be received. However, as was true for accrued interest, the exact number of days between coupon payment dates, as well as the exact number of days between the last coupon payment date and the date of delivery, must be determined.

EXAMPLE: A $9\frac{3}{8}$ government bond is purchased for delivery on June 22, 1992. The face value of this bond is $100,000 and the current yield is 6 percent, and it pays interest semiannually on May 15 and November 15. If this bond matures on November 15, 1994, what is the quoted price of this bond and what price is actually paid?

Step 1. There are 184 days between May 15 and November 15. There are 38 days between the last coupon date and the date of delivery and 146 days between the date of delivery and the next coupon date.

Step 2. Accrued interest on this bond is equal to

$$AI = \$100,000 \left(\frac{0.09375}{2}\right)\left(\frac{38}{184}\right)$$

$$= \$968.07$$

Step 3. The applicable discount rate is one half of the quoted yield, or 3 percent per six-month period. However, the purchaser has to wait 146/184 of a period before receiving its first coupon. The timing and the amount of all cash flows to be received is presented in the following table.

Date of Payment	Amount	Period Until Receipt
November 15, 1992	$ 4,687.50	146/184
May 15, 1993	4,687.50	1 + 146/184
November 15, 1993	4,687.50	2 + 146/184
May 15, 1994	4,687.50	3 + 146/184
November 15, 1994	104,687.50	4 + 146/184

Step 4. The present value of the cash flows to be received is equal to

$$PV = \$4,687.50 \left[\left(\frac{1}{1.03}\right)^{(146/184)}\right] + \$4,687.50 \left[\left(\frac{1}{1.03}\right)^{(1 + 146/184)}\right]$$

$$+ \$4,687.50 \left[\left(\frac{1}{1.03}\right)^{(2 + 146/184)}\right] + \$4,687.50 \left[\left(\frac{1}{1.03}\right)^{(3 + 146/184)}\right]$$

$$+ \$104,687.50 \left[\left(\frac{1}{1.03}\right)^{(4 + 146/184)}\right]$$

$$= \$108,387.90$$

This is the amount that is actually paid on delivery for this bond.

Step 5. The quoted price is equal to the flat price minus the amount of accrued interest.

$$P = \$108,387.90 - \$968.07 = \$108,419.83$$

[d] Government Securities During the Final Coupon Period. Remember from earlier discussion that the yields on government securities during their final coupon period are expressed as a simple interest rate. Given the quoted yield, which may not be equal to the true yield, the actual price of a government security may be calculated as follows:

$$P' = \left[\frac{1 + C/2}{1 + [Y^*(t_{PM})]/[2(t_{CD})]}\right] - AI'$$

EXAMPLE: On June 30, 1992, an investor settles on a 9.75 percent government coupon bond with a quoted yield of 5.25 percent. This bond has a face value of $100,000 and matures on September 15, 1992. What is the quoted price for this bond and what price is actually paid?

Step 1. There are 184 days from the last coupon payment (March 15) to the date the bond matures. There are 107 days from the last coupon payment to the delivery or settlement date and 77 days from the settlement date to the maturity date.

Step 2. The accrued interest on this bond is equal to

$$AI = \$100,000 \left(\frac{0.0975}{2}\right)\left(\frac{107}{184}\right)$$

$$= \$2,834.92$$

Since the face value of this bond is $100,000, the accrued interest per dollar of face value is equal to

$$AI' = \frac{\$2,834.92}{\$100,000} = 0.0283492$$

Step 3. The quoted price on this bond, per dollar of face value, is equal to

$$P' = \left[\frac{1 + (0.0975/2)}{1 + [(0.0525)(77)]/[2(184)]}\right] - 0.0283492$$

$$= 1.0090054$$

which, since the face value of this bond is equal to $100,000, implies that

$$P = \$100,000(1.0090054) = \$100,900.54$$

Step 4. The actual price that the investor is required to pay is equal to

$$PV = \$100,900.54 + \$2,834.92 = \$103,735$$

It can be shown that this price results in the quoted yield of 5.25 percent. If the yield is 5.25 percent, this implies that the yield per six-month period is equal to

$$\frac{0.0525}{2} = 0.02625$$

However, for the last coupon period this is the simple interest rate for a 184-day period.

Since the investor holds the bond for only 77 days, the applicable simple interest rate for its holding period is

$$0.02625 \left(\frac{77}{184} \right) = 0.010985$$

If the investor purchases the security for a total price of \$103,735.46 and earns a simple interest rate of 1.0985 percent, the ending value of its investment should be equal to

$$\$103,735.46(1.101985) = \$104,875$$

which is exactly equal to the maturity value of this security plus the final coupon to be received.

[5] Premiums and Discounts on Coupon Bonds

If a bond's price is greater than par (yield less than the coupon rate), the bond is selling at a premium. If a bond's price is less than par (yield greater than the coupon rate), the bond is selling at a discount. The calculation of a bond's current price was discussed previously. Once the current price is known, the premium or discount on the bond is simply the difference between this price and the par or maturity value of the bond. However, there is another method that uses the difference between the coupon rate and the quoted yield to determine the amount of premium or discount for the bond.

[a] **Calculation of a Discount.** The amount of discount for a bond is equal to the present value of an annuity stream that represents the difference between the coupon rate and the quoted yield.

EXAMPLE: On April 1, 1992, an investor takes delivery of a 5 percent coupon bond. This bond has a face or par value of \$1,000 and pays interest on April 1 and October 1. This bond matures on October 1, 1996, and the current yield to maturity is 6 percent. What is the amount of discount for this bond?

METHOD 1

Calculate the current price for this bond. It is equal to

$$P = \$25[\text{PVIF}_a(3\%, 9)] + \$1,000[\text{PVIF}(3\%, 9)]$$
$$= \$961.07$$

The discount for this bond is then equal to

$$\text{Discount} = \$1,000.00 - \$961.07$$
$$= \$38.93$$

METHOD 2

Any discount on this bond will be due to the difference between the coupon rate of 5 percent and the current yield of 6 percent. For this security to sell at par with a yield of 6 percent, it would have to pay interest of \$30 every six months. Since it actually pays only \$25 every six months, this is a difference of \$5. This difference of \$5, which will occur at each coupon date, is what lowers the price of the bond below its par value. However, this difference can be evaluated as an annuity and its present value determined by discounting it at the current yield to maturity.

Discount = $5[PVIF$_a$(3%, 9)]

= $38.93

The current price of this bond is therefore equal to

P = $1,000.00 − $38.93

= $961.07

[b] Calculation of a Premium. The same logic that was used to calculate the amount of the discount may also be used to calculate the amount of the premium.

EXAMPLE: On April 1, 1992, an investor takes delivery of a 5 percent coupon bond. This bond has a face or par value of $1,000 and pays interest on April 1 and October 1. This bond matures on October 1, 1996, and the current yield to maturity is 4 percent. What is the amount of the premium for this bond?

METHOD 1

The current price for this bond may be calculated in a straightforward manner. The price is equal to

P = $25[PVIF$_a$(2%, 9)] + $1,000[PVIF(2%, 9)]

= $1,040.81

The amount of the premium is therefore equal to

Premium = $1,040.81 − $1,000.00

= $40.81

METHOD 2

Since the current yield on this bond is 4 percent, it would have to pay $20 in interest every six months for it to sell at par. It actually pays $25 in interest every six months. This difference of $5, which will occur at each coupon date, is what increases the price of this bond above its par value. This difference may be evaluated as an annuity and its present value determined by discounting it at the current yield to maturity.

Premium = $5[PVIF$_a$(2%, 9)]

= $40.81

The current price of this bond is equal to

P = $1,000.00 + $40.81

= $1,040.81

[6] Amortization and Accumulation Schedules

Although a coupon bond may sell at either a premium or a discount, at maturity its add-interest price must be equal to its par or face value. This decrease in the amount of the premium or discount occurs because of a rolldown in the bond's maturity. Discounts are said to be accumulated over time, while premiums are said to be amortized over time.

Another way of phrasing this is that when a bond is selling at a premium (yield less than the coupon rate), the realized yield will be equal to the coupon income *less* the decrease in the market price of the bond. If a bond is selling at a discount (yield greater than the coupon rate), the realized yield will be equal to the coupon income *plus* the increase in the market price of the bond.

EXAMPLE: On April 1, 1992, an investor takes delivery of a 5 percent coupon bond. This bond has a face value of $1,000 and pays interest on April 1 and October 1. The bond matures on October 1, 1996, and the current yield is 6 percent. Construct an accumulation schedule for this bond.

The price of this bond at each coupon date may be calculated using the following formula:

$$P = \$25[PVIF_a(3\%, N)] + \$1,000[PVIF(3\%, N)]$$

where N is the number of six-month periods until maturity. The amount of accumulation is the change in the market price over each coupon period. The required dollar return, so as to earn the quoted yield, is equal to the yield on a six-month basis times the market price of the bond at the beginning of the coupon period. This is also equal to the coupon income received plus the accumulation of discount. This may be presented as shown below:

Evaluation Date	Coupon Income	Accumulation	Required Return	Market Value
April 1, 1992	—	—	—	$ 961.07
October 1, 1992	$25	$3.83	$28.83	964.90
April 1, 1993	25	3.95	28.95	968.85
October 1, 1993	25	4.07	29.07	972.91
April 1, 1994	25	4.19	29.19	977.10
October 1, 1994	25	4.31	29.31	981.41
April 1, 1995	25	4.44	29.44	985.86
October 1, 1995	25	4.53	29.58	990.43
April 1, 1996	25	4.71	29.71	995.15
October 1, 1996	25	4.85	29.85	1,000.00

To illustrate, on April 1, 1992, the market price of this bond was $961.07. To earn a 3 percent yield over the next six months, an investor must earn a total dollar return of

$$\$961.07(0.03) = \$28.83$$

This required return of $28.83 will be composed of $25.00 in coupon income plus an increase in the market price of $3.83.

EXAMPLE: On April 1, 1992, an investor takes delivery of a 5 percent coupon bond. This bond has a face value of $1,000 and pays interest on April 1 and October 1. This bond matures on October 1, 1996, and the current yield is 4 percent. Construct an amortization schedule for this bond.

The price of this bond at each coupon date may be calculated using the following formula

$$P = \$25[\text{PVIF}_a(2\%, N)] + \$1,000[\text{PVIF}(2\%, N)]$$

where N is equal to the number of six-month periods until maturity. The amount of amortization is the change in the market price over each coupon period. The required dollar return, so as to earn the quoted yield, is equal to the yield on a six-month basis times the market price of the bond at the beginning of the coupon period. This is also equal to the coupon income minus the amortization of the premium. This may be presented as follows:

Evaluation Date	Coupon Income	Amortization	Required Return	Market Value
April 1, 1992	—	—	—	$1,040.81
October 1, 1992	$25	$4.18	$20.82	1,036.63
April 1, 1993	25	4.27	20.73	1,032.36
October 1, 1993	25	4.35	20.65	1,028.01
April 1, 1994	25	4.44	20.56	1,023.57
October 1, 1994	25	4.53	20.47	1,019.04
April 1, 1995	25	4.62	20.38	1,014.42
October 1, 1995	25	4.71	20.29	1,009.71
April 1, 1996	25	4.81	20.19	1,004.90
October 1, 1996	25	4.90	20.10	1,000.00

To illustrate, on April 1, 1992 the price of this bond was $1,040.81. To earn a 2 percent yield over the next six months, the investor must earn a total dollar return of

$$\$1,040.81(0.02) = \$20.82$$

This required return of $20.82 will be composed of $25.00 in coupon income less the decrease in the market price of $4.18.

[7] Sinking Funds

A bond with a sinking fund provision requires the corporation to make periodic deposits, usually with the bond's trustee, which sum will be sufficient to redeem the bond in full at maturity. This is done either by investment of the periodic payments until maturity or by the periodic repurchase of outstanding bonds. This section concentrates on the former method.

[a] Calculations: Size of the Sinking Fund Payment.

Once the size and maturity of a bond issue are known, a corporation needs to determine the size of the sinking fund payment that is required. The solution to this is nothing more than the solution to a future value of an annuity problem.

EXAMPLE: A corporation issues $1 million worth of bonds on September 1, 1992 with a maturity date of September 1, 1997. The indenture agreement specifies that the corporation must make semiannual payments to a sinking fund administered by the bond's trustee. Assume that the corporation will make its first payment to the sinking fund on March 1, 1993 and its last payment on September 1, 1997. If the deposits will earn an effective rate of 8.16 percent (4 percent per semiannual period), what is the size of the sinking fund payment?

This is nothing more than a 10-period annuity problem, whose future value must be equal to the maturity value of the bond.

$$\$1,000,000 = SF[FVIF_a(4\%, 10)]$$
$$= SF(12.006)$$
$$\Rightarrow SF = \frac{\$1,000,000}{12.006}$$
$$= \$83,291.69$$

EXAMPLE: Consider the prior example, but now assume that the first payment takes place on September 1, 1992 and the last payment takes place on March 1, 1997. What is the size of the sinking fund payments?

This is now an annuity due problem, whose solution is represented by the following equation:

$$\$1,000,000 = SF[FVIF_{ad}(4\%, 10)]$$
$$= SF[FVIF_a(4\%, 11) - 1] = SF[FVIF_a(4\%, 10)][1.04]$$
$$= SF(12.486)$$
$$\Rightarrow SF = \frac{\$1,000,000}{12.486}$$
$$= \$80,089.70$$

[b] Calculations: Number of Sinking Fund Payments. When a corporation issues a bond with a sinking fund provision, it must be sure that it will be able to meet both the sinking fund and interest payments on the bond each period. This fact may act to restrict the number of sinking fund payments (maturity of the bond) that are possible.

EXAMPLE: Assume that a firm wishes to issue $1 million of 10 percent coupon bonds. These bonds will pay interest on a semiannual basis, but the firm can guarantee only $125,000 for each six-month period toward the interest and sinking fund payments. What is the minimum number of sinking fund payments possible?

Since interest is paid each six months, the possible contribution to the sinking fund is as follows:

Total semiannual payment	$125,000
Less: Interest	(50,000)
Sinking fund contribution	$ 75,000

The number of sinking fund payments required now depends on the rate of return that the firm is able to earn on its deposits. If it can earn 3 percent each six months and the first payment is made six months from the date of issue, the number of payments needed to accumulate the maturity value of $1 million may be found as a regular annuity problem:

$$\$1,000,000 = \$75,000[FVIF_a(3\%, N)]$$

$$\Rightarrow FVIF_a(3\%, N) = \frac{\$1,000,000}{\$75,000}$$

$$= 13.333$$

The value for N may then be found either by linear interpolation or by the use of a financial calculator:

$N = 11.38$ 6-month periods

$= 5.69$ years

Since firms do not issue bonds with maturities of 5.69 years, the firm should extend the period and issue a bond with a maturity of 6 years. The actual sinking fund payment required may then be calculated as

$$\$1,000,000 = SF[FVIF_a(3\%, 12)]$$

$$= SF(14.192)$$

$$\Rightarrow SF = \frac{\$1,000,000}{14.192}$$

$$= \$70,462.23$$

4.05 BOND ANALYSIS: ADDITIONAL ISSUES

This section discusses some additional issues for fixed-income securities. These issues include measures of risk, rolling yield, duration and immunization, and duration versus convexity.

[1] Definitions of Variables

N = number of discounting periods

P = current price

Y = yield to maturity or discount rate

D_1 = duration of a fixed-income security

n = years of maturity; $2n$ = remaining coupon payments

M = maturity value

P' = predicted price given a change in yield

D^* = modified duration

CV = convexity

CV^* = modified convexity

HV = horizon volatility

CF_t = cash flow received at the end of period t

$PVIF(i\%, N)$ = present value interest factor of a single sum at a discount rate of i percent for N periods

$PVIF_a(i\%, N)$ = present value interest factor of an annuity at a discount rate of i percent for N periods

[2] Measures of Risk

Traditional measures of risk for fixed-income securities are the yield value of a thirty-second, the price value of one basis point, and the percent price volatility. Another measure that has been advocated is the horizon volatility. It specifies the basis point change in return that will result from a one basis point change in yield. However, let us first discuss the traditional measures of risk or volatility.

[a] **Yield Value of a Thirty-Second.** Price quotes for bonds are reported in values of percentage points and thirty-seconds of par. The yield value of a thirty-second gives the change in yield that will result from a change in price of one thirty-second ($0.03125).

For instance, assume that a five-year, 8 percent coupon bond is currently selling for $102\frac{5}{32}$ to yield 7.4752 percent. If its price goes up to $102\frac{6}{32}$, its new yield will be 7.4677 percent. Therefore, a price increase of $\frac{1}{32}$ results in a 0.0075 percent (0.75 basis points) decrease in yield. The value 0.75 is the yield value of a thirty-second for this bond. Given this value, it is possible to obtain a close approximation to the exact yield change for any given change in price.

[b] **Price Value of One Basis Point.** If the yield value of a thirty-second for a security is known, it is easy to obtain the price value of one basis point for that security. The price value of one basis point indicates how much the price will increase (or decrease), in terms of percent of par, for every basis point decrease (or increase) in yield.

In the previous example, the yield value of a thirty-second was 0.75 basis points. This implies that the price value of one basis point is equal to

$$\frac{-0.03125}{\pm 0.75} = \pm 0.04167$$

This says that if the yield on the bond in the example goes from 7.4752 percent up to 7.4852 percent (one basis point), the price will drop by approximately $0.04167, expressed as a percent of par.

[c] **Percent Price Volatility.** The percent price volatility is the price value of one basis point as a percentage of the bond's current price. In the prior example, the percent price volatility is equal to

$$\frac{\$0.04167}{\$102.15625} = 0.0004079 = 0.04079\%$$

[d] **Horizon Volatility.** The total return for a bond incorporates the percentage change in price over the investment horizon. Although price may vary during this investment period, it is only the change at the horizon that is important in determining the bond's actual return. This concept of price change at the horizon is incorporated into a measure called the horizon volatility. It measures the basis point change in return, given the basis point change in yield over the investment horizon.

EXAMPLE: A six-year, 8 percent coupon bond is selling at par (8 percent yield). Over a one-year investment horizon, this bond rolls down to a five-year, 8 percent coupon bond with a yield of 7.4752 percent. What is the horizon volatility of this bond?

The horizon volatility may be calculated as follows:

Step 1. Look at the bond at the end of the investment horizon. It has previously been shown that the yield value of a thirty-second for a five-year, 8 percent coupon bond with a yield of 7.4572 percent is 0.75 basis points. Therefore, the percent price volatility at the horizon may be calculated as follows:

Decimal value of a thirty-second	0.03125
Yield value of a thirty-second	÷ 0.75000
Price value of one basis point	0.04167
Horizon price	÷ 102.15625
Percent price volatility	0.04079%

Step 2. Now consider the bond at the beginning of the investment period. The horizon volatility may be calculated as follows:

Percent price volatility at the horizon	0.04079%
Current price/horizon price ($100.00/$102.15625)	÷ 0.97889
Percent price change at the horizon, expressed as a ratio of current and horizon price	0.04167
Translation factor to convert to basis points	× 100.00000
Horizon volatility	4.16700

This says that the investment period return should increase by 4.167 basis points for every basis point decrease in yield. Note that the horizon volatility is very similar to the price value of one basis point. This occurs because it has been assumed that the bond is originally selling at par.

The use of the horizon volatility may be illustrated by the prior example. Over the one-year investment horizon, the yield went from 8 percent down to 7.4572 percent. This is a decrease of 52.48 basis points (0.5248 of one percent). Using the concept of horizon volatility, this implies a return from price appreciation of

$$0.005248(4.167) = 0.0218684 = 2.18684\%$$

The actual return from price appreciation would be

$$\frac{\$102.15625 - \$100}{\$100} = 0.0215625 = 2.15625\%$$

The advantage of horizon volatility is that it allows for the rapid calculation of returns under differing scenarios of yield changes. It may also be used to determine an approximation for a bond's rolling yield.

[3] Measures of Return: Rolling Yield

The yield curve specifies how much additional yield may be obtained from an increase or decrease in the maturity of a fixed-income security. A basic problem with this yield is that it assumes that the security is held until it matures. Therefore, it is difficult to directly compare securities with different maturities. One way around this problem is to calculate a rolling yield, which specifies the holding period return for all maturities over some predefined investment horizon.

The rolling yield acts as a benchmark return. It assumes that the yield curve will remain constant over the investment period. Each security will then have positive (or negative) price appreciation as the security rolls down (or up) the yield curve over time. This is somewhat unrealistic in that some changes in the "shape" and the level of the yield curve over time would be expected. However, the rolling yield at least gives us a starting point for further scenario analyses of return.

[a] Calculations. The rolling yield consists of three items:

1. Coupon income

2. Reinvestment income

3. Price appreciation

EXAMPLE: A five-year, 10 percent coupon bond is currently selling at par. The investment horizon is one year, and the current yield on a four-year security with equivalent risk is 9 percent. What is the rolling yield for this security?

Coupon income. Over the investment period, $100 ($50 every six months) in coupon income is paid out. Since this bond is selling at par, the return from this coupon income will be equal to

$$\frac{\$100}{\$1,000} = 0.1 = 10\%$$

Reinvestment income. There is also a return associated with the first $50 of coupon income that is paid, since it may be reinvested for a six-month period. Although the exact reinvestment rate may vary, assume that an appropriate reinvestment rate would be 5 percent for the six-month period. This implies that the reinvestment income is equal to

$$\$50(0.05) = \$2.50$$

which implies a return from reinvestment income of

$$\frac{\$2.50}{\$1,000} = 0.0025 = 0.25\%$$

Price appreciation. If the yield curve remains constant, at the end of the investment horizon the purchaser will hold a four-year, 10 percent coupon bond with a yield to maturity of 9 percent. The price of this bond would be

$$P = \$50[\text{PVIF}_a(4.5\%, 8)] + \$1,000[\text{PVIF}(4.5\%, 8)]$$

$$= \$1,032.98$$

Thus, total price appreciation is

$$\$1,032.98 - \$1,000 = \$32.98$$

which implies a return from price appreciation of

$$\frac{\$32.98}{\$1,000} = 0.03298 = 3.298\%$$

The rolling yield is then equal to

$$0.1 + 0.0025 + 0.03298 = 0.13548 = 13.548\%$$

In the prior example, the rolling yield of 13.548 percent is greater than the current yield for the five-year security of 10 percent. This is always true with an upward sloping yield curve, and the reverse is true with a downward sloping yield curve.

The advantage of the rolling yield is that it acts as a benchmark return for making further comparisons. It may also be combined with the concept of horizon volatility to perform scenario analysis. For example, if the yield curve remains constant for this investment period, the five-year security will have a realized return of 13.548 percent. The yield curve is not actually expected to remain constant across time. However, assume the horizon volatility for the five-year bond has been calculated. If the yield of this bond at the end of the investment horizon is expected to differ from 9 percent, this difference would be multiplied by the horizon volatility. This amount would then be added to or substracted from the rolling yield to obtain an approximation of the realized return under the new scenario of a change in the yield curve. Since this process may be computerized, scenario analysis becomes quite easy to do.

[4] Duration and Immunization

Reinvestment rate risk (i.e., changes in market yields) is a major concern to those investors that have purchased fixed-income securities. Increases (or decreases) in the reinvestment rate will increase (or decrease) reinvestment income from the coupons received. At the same time, they will decrease (or increase) the applicable market price of the security if it must be sold. A concept that has been used to "immunize" against reinvestment rate risk is duration.

Duration may be considered to be the weighted average maturity for a fixed-income security. As such, it takes into consideration that some of the cash flows associated with a bond (the coupons) will be received before maturity. There are many different ways to calculate this average maturity, including some that consider the stochastic process driving changes in the yield curve. However, this discussion concentrates on the traditional measure of duration, also referred to as D_1.

[a] **Calculation of Duration.** Duration is a weighted average measure of maturity with the case flows weighted by the time remaining until they are received. The formula for the duration of an N-period bond is as follows.

$$D_1 = \sum_{t=1}^{N} \frac{(t)(CF_t)/(1 + (Y/2))^t}{P}$$

where the weighted cash flows are discounted at the bond's current yield and the sum is divided by the current price of the bond.

EXAMPLE: What is the duration of a two-year, 8 percent coupon bond that pays interest semiannually and is selling at par?

Periods Until Receipt of Cash Flow		Cash Flow		Weighted Cash Flow	Present Value at 4%
1	×	$ 40	=	$ 40	$ 38.46
2	×	40	=	80	73.96
3	×	40	=	120	106.68
4	×	1,040	=	4,160	3,555.99
					$3,775.09

The duration of this bond is then equal to

$$D_1 = \frac{\$3,775.09}{\$1,000} = 3.77509 \text{ 6-month periods}$$

EXAMPLE: What is the duration of a three-year, 8 percent coupon bond that pays interest semiannually and is also selling at par?

Periods Until Receipt of Cash Flow		Cash Flow		Weighted Cash Flow	Present Value at 4%
1	×	$ 40	=	$ 40	$ 38.46
2	×	40	=	80	73.96
3	×	40	=	120	106.68
4	×	40	=	160	136.77
5	×	40	=	200	164.39
6	×	1,040	=	6,240	4,931.56
					$5,451.82

The duration of this bond is equal to

$$D_1 = \frac{\$5,451.82}{\$1,000} = 5.45182 \text{ 6-month periods}$$

[b] Duration of Portfolios. The duration of a portfolio is considered to be equal to the weighted average duration of the securities comprising the portfolio.

EXAMPLE: Consider the two securities in the examples in the previous section. If an investor invests 86.6 percent of its funds in the two-year security and 13.4 percent of its funds in the three-year security, what will be the duration of the resulting portfolio?

$$D_1 = 3.77509(0.866) + 5.45182(0.134) = 4 \text{ 6-month periods}$$

[c] Immunization of a Portfolio. Duration is said to immunize against reinvestment rate risk if the duration of the portfolio (security) is equal to the time remaining in the investment horizon.

EXAMPLE: Consider the portfolio in the prior example. It has a duration of two years, and its weighted yield is

$$0.08(0.866) + 0.08(0.134) = 0.08 = 8\%$$

If the investment horizon is two years and the investor holds this portfolio, a one-time change in the reinvestment rate should still allow it to earn an 8 percent realized yield. To illustrate this, assume that right after this portfolio is purchased the reinvestment rate will either remain at 8 percent or there will be a one-time change to either 7 percent or 9 percent.

Reinvestment Rate	Weight	Security	Coupon Income	Capital Gains	Interest on Interest	Total Dollar Return	Realized Compounded Yield
7%	0.866	2 year	$138.56	$0.00	$ 7.45	$146.01	7.94%
7	0.134	3 year	21.44	1.27	1.15	23.86	8.36
7	1.000	Portfolio	$160.00	$1.27	$ 8.60	$169.87	8.00
8	0.866	2 year	$138.56	$0.00	$ 8.54	$147.10	8.00%
8	0.134	3 year	21.44	0.00	1.32	22.76	8.00
8	1.000	Portfolio	$160.00	$0.00	$ 9.36	$169.86	8.00%
9	0.866	2 year	$138.56	$0.00	$ 9.64	$148.20	8.06%
9	0.134	3 year	21.44	− 1.25	1.49	21.68	7.64
9	1.000	Portfolio	$160.00	−$1.25	$11.13	$169.88	8.00%

No matter what happens to the reinvestment rate, the realized compounded yield will remain 8 percent. Increases (or decreases) in reinvestment income are exactly offset by decreases (or increases) in capital gains at the time of sale.

However, there are some serious problems with duration. It was no accident that both of the securities in the prior example had current yields of 8 percent and that they both had shifts of the reinvestment rate to either 7 percent or 9 percent. For duration to immunize a portfolio effectively, parallel shifts of a flat yield curve are required. Another problem is the assumption that the reinvestment rate would change immediately after the purchase of the securities and would remain at that rate until the end of the investment period. This assumption is unrealistic, and the portfolio must be reimmunized every time a coupon is received or there is a change in the market rate of interest (almost continuously). As a practical matter, most investors will reimmunize only periodically, e.g., every six months to a year. Even with all its faults, using duration to immunize a portfolio, if it is done with some thought, will greatly reduce the amount of reinvestment rate risk.

[5] Duration Versus Convexity[1]

In the previous section it was shown that duration can be used to immunize a portfolio of fixed-income securities. However, actual price volatility, given a change in yield, is also related to the maturity of a bond and the size of the change in yield. Duration, in terms of its ability to accurately predict the percentage price change for a given change in yield, may therefore not be optimal when considering long-term bonds with large changes in yield. The relationship between duration, changes in yield, and percentage change in a bond's price may be defined as

---

[1] The author would like to thank Richard W. McEnally, the Meade Willis Professor of Investment Banking at the University of North Carolina at Chapel Hill, for bringing the subject of convexity to his attention and for demonstrating how it can be used to better approximate percentage price changes.

$$\frac{\Delta P}{P} = (-D^*)(\Delta Y) \tag{4.1}$$

which implies

$$P' = P + P(-D^*)(\Delta Y) \tag{4.2}$$

where:

$$-D^* = \text{modified duration} = \frac{-D_1}{1 + (Y/2)}$$

For example, assume a 10 percent coupon bond that pays $50 in interest every six months, has 20 years until it matures, and is originally priced at par (that is, its yield to maturity is equal to the coupon rate). The duration of this bond is equal to 9.008475 6-month periods, while the modified duration is equal to 8.5795 6-month periods. If the interest rate on this bond increases from 10 percent to 10.5 percent, the approximate percentage price change will be equal to

$$\frac{\Delta P}{P} = -8.5795(0.005) = -0.0428975 = -4.28975\%$$

and

$$P' = \$1,000 + \$1,000(-8.5795)(0.005) = \$957.1025$$

versus an actual price of $958.53 and an actual percentage price change of

$$\frac{\$958.53 - \$1,000}{\$1,000} = -0.04147 = -4.147\%$$

This is a fairly close approximation, but it is not exact, and the larger the change in the interest rate (yield), the more inexact it becomes. This occurs because the predicted price as calculated using Equation 4.2 is linear in modified duration, whereas the actual change in price is convex. Using the previous example (bond originally priced at par to yield 10 percent), Figure 4-7 shows the actual price versus the price predicted using Equation 4.2, where the new interest rate varies between 0 and 20 percent. It is clear from this figure that Equation 2 is not a good predictor of prices for large changes in yields.

Figure 4-7 also demonstrates that a bond's actual price is indeed convex with respect to changes in yield. This is true for all "straight" bond issues but is not the case for bonds that include an "option" feature, such as callable bonds. The price of a callable bond is equal to the price to the investor of an equivalent straight bond less the price to the issuer of the option to call. As interest rates decrease, the value of the option to call increases. Because of these offsetting effects, the actual increase in the price of a callable bond may be less than the increase in price for an equivalent straight bond. This, in turn, leads to negative convexity.

The degree of convexity for a bond is dependent on the coupon rate, the current interest rate, the bond's maturity value, and the time remaining until the bond matures. Convexity can be calculated as

$$CV = \sum_{t=1}^{2n} \left[\frac{t}{2} + \left(\frac{t}{2}\right)^2 \right] \left\{ \frac{(C/2)/[1 + (Y/2)]^t}{P} \right\} + (n + n^2) \left\{ \frac{M/[1 + (Y/2)]^{2n}}{P} \right\}$$

Using the concept of modified convexity, in conjunction with modified duration, we can now get a better approximation for the percentage change in a bond's price for a given change in the yield. The relationship is

FIGURE 4-7

Actual Prices Versus Equation 4.2 Prices

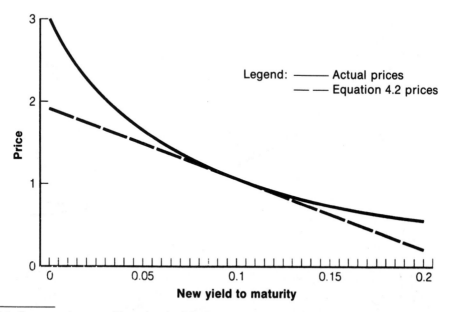

Note: Ten percent coupon, 20-year bond, originally priced at par.

$$\frac{\Delta P}{P} = (-D^*)(\Delta Y) + 0.5(CV^*)(\Delta Y)^2 \tag{4.3}$$

where:

$$CV^* = \text{modified convexity} = \frac{CV}{[1 + (Y/2)]^2}$$

and

$$P' = P + P[(-D^*)(\Delta Y) + 0.5(CV^*)(\Delta Y)^2] \tag{4.4}$$

Note that the percentage change in price is now defined by a quadratic equation and is no longer linear; modified convexity now helps to offset the degree of linearity specified by modified duration. Still using the prior example (bond originally priced at par to yield 10 percent), Figure 4-8 shows the actual price versus the price predicted using Equation 4.4, where the new yield again varies between 0 and 20 percent. Also note that unlike the use of modified duration, which always understates the true price of the bond, the inclusion of modified convexity leads to an overstatement of the price when the yield increases.

Figure 4-9 compares the extent to which Equations 4.2 and 4.4 understated and overstated the actual price of the bond used in the prior examples. This figure also shows that both formulas give fairly good approximations for small changes in yield but for large changes Equation 4.4 is superior.

It should also be noted that the difference in percentage price changes predicted

FIGURE 4-8
Actual Prices Versus Equation 4.4 Prices

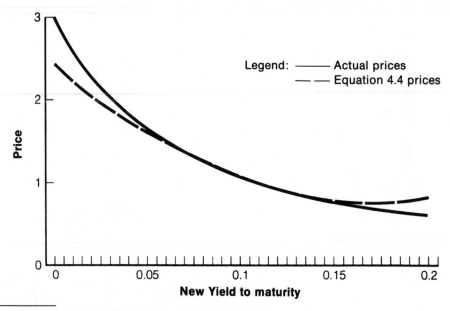

Note: Ten percent coupon, 20-year bond, originally priced at par.

by Equations 4.1 and 4.3 gets smaller as the starting yield gets larger. This is because both modified duration and modified convexity decrease as the starting yield increases but modified convexity decreases at a faster rate and therefore becomes less important. Figure 4-10 shows the values for original price, modified duration, modified convexity, actual percentage change in price, and predicted percentage price changes using Equations 4.1 and 4.3 for a 0.5 percent increase in yield, where the *starting* yield now varies from 0 percent to 20 percent. For this bond, the difference in predicted percentage price changes using Equations 4.1 and 4.3 decreases as the starting yield moves towards 20 percent.

4.06 FUTURES AND FORWARDS

A forward contract is an agreement between a buyer and a seller of a commodity that cifies the price that will be paid for the commodity when it is delivered at a future date. It has been said that futures contracts are simply marketable forward contracts that are traded on regulated exchanges. However, profit and loss on futures contracts is calculated each day (i.e., value is marked to market) and is debited or credited against the margin account. Forward contracts are not marked to market.

Futures contracts are traded on many different commodities, including grains, livestock, food, fibers, metals, petroleum, currencies, Treasuries (bills, notes, and bonds),

FIGURE 4-9

Equation 4.2 Versus Equation 4.4

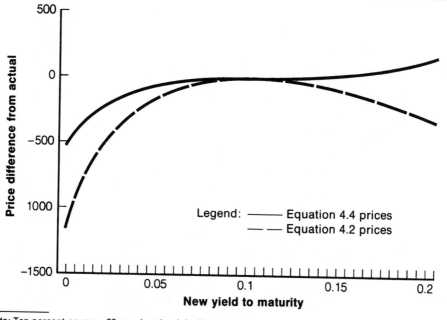

Note: Ten percent coupon, 20-year bond, originally priced at par.

and indexes (stock, munis, Eurodollar, major market, and so forth). This section concentrates on one particular contract, a 90-day Treasury bill futures contract.

[1] Definitions of Variables

D = dollar value of discount

P = current price

d_J = discount rate or yield for security J

t_J = time from delivery or settlement until maturity for security J

RP = implified term RP rate

SY = strip yield rate

IFR = implied forward rate

$_Ji_M$ = simple interest rate or equivalent bond yield for security J based on an M-day year

The subscripts c and f refer to a *cash security* and a *futures security*, respectively.

[2] Pricing Relationships

Treasury bill futures contracts on the International Monetary Market (IMM) are quoted in terms of an index value where the index is equal to 100 minus the discount rate. The

FIGURE 4-10

Predicted Percentage Price Changes for a 0.5 Percent Increase in Yield

Original Starting Yield	Original Price	Modified Duration	Modified Convexity	Actual Percentage Change	Percentage Change Predicted by Equation 4.1	Percentage Change Predicted by Equation 4.3
0.000	$3,000.00	13.5000	239.0833	−0.0647	−0.0675	−0.0645
0.005	$2,805.94	13.2487	232.5672	−0.0635	−0.0662	−0.0633
0.010	$2,627.75	12.9958	226.0697	−0.0623	−0.0650	−0.0622
0.015	$2,463.99	12.7417	219.5995	−0.0611	−0.0637	−0.0610
0.020	$2,313.39	12.4867	213.1652	−0.0599	−0.0624	−0.0598
0.025	$2,174.76	12.2311	206.7755	−0.0587	−0.0612	−0.0586
0.030	$2,047.05	11.9754	200.4391	−0.0575	−0.0599	−0.0574
0.035	$1,929.31	11.7200	194.1645	−0.0563	−0.0586	−0.0562
0.040	$1,820.66	11.4651	187.9601	−0.0551	−0.0573	−0.0550
0.045	$1,720.32	11.2112	181.8341	−0.0539	−0.0561	−0.0538
0.050	$1,627.57	10.9586	175.7944	−0.0527	−0.0548	−0.0526
0.055	$1,541.76	10.7077	169.8484	−0.0515	−0.0535	−0.0514
0.060	$1,462.30	10.4589	164.0033	−0.0504	−0.0523	−0.0502
0.065	$1,388.65	10.2124	158.2658	−0.0492	−0.0511	−0.0491
0.070	$1,320.33	9.9687	152.6420	−0.0480	−0.0498	−0.0479
0.075	$1,256.89	9.7280	147.1376	−0.0469	−0.0486	−0.0468
0.080	$1,197.93	9.4906	141.7576	−0.0458	−0.0475	−0.0457
0.085	$1,143.08	9.2569	136.5066	−0.0447	−0.0463	−0.0446
0.090	$1,092.01	9.0269	131.3885	−0.0436	−0.0451	−0.0435
0.095	$1,044.41	8.8011	126.4067	−0.0425	−0.0440	−0.0424
0.100	$1,000.00	8.5795	121.5637	−0.0415	−0.0429	−0.0414
0.105	$958.53	8.3625	116.8618	−0.0404	−0.0418	−0.0404
0.110	$919.77	8.1500	112.3025	−0.0394	−0.0408	−0.0393
0.115	$883.50	7.9423	107.8868	−0.0384	−0.0397	−0.0384
0.120	$849.54	7.7395	103.6150	−0.0375	−0.0387	−0.0374
0.125	$817.70	7.5417	99.4872	−0.0365	−0.0377	−0.0365
0.130	$787.82	7.3489	95.5027	−0.0356	−0.0367	−0.0356
0.135	$759.75	7.1613	91.6605	−0.0347	−0.0358	−0.0347
0.140	$733.37	6.9787	87.9591	−0.0339	−0.0349	−0.0338
0.145	$708.53	6.8013	84.3968	−0.0330	−0.0340	−0.0330
0.150	$685.14	6.6290	80.9713	−0.0322	−0.0331	−0.0321
0.155	$663.08	6.4619	77.6802	−0.0314	−0.0323	−0.0313
0.160	$642.26	6.2998	74.5207	−0.0306	−0.0315	−0.0306
0.165	$622.59	6.1427	71.4897	−0.0299	−0.0307	−0.0298
0.170	$603.99	5.9905	68.5841	−0.0291	−0.0300	−0.0291
0.175	$586.39	5.8433	65.8005	−0.0284	−0.0292	−0.0284
0.180	$569.71	5.7008	63.1353	−0.0278	−0.0285	−0.0277
0.185	$553.89	5.5630	60.5850	−0.0271	−0.0278	−0.0271
0.190	$538.87	5.4299	58.1458	−0.0265	−0.0271	−0.0264
0.195	$524.61	5.3012	55.8140	−0.0259	−0.0265	−0.0258
0.200	$511.05	5.1769	53.5858	−0.0253	−0.0259	−0.0252

Note: Twenty-year bond paying $50 every six months, original yield varying from zero to 20 percent.

basic contract is for $1 million of 90-day Treasury bills. The contracts are deliverable in the third week of March, June, September, and December. Treasury bill futures contracts use the same equations for price, dollar discount, discount rate, simple interest rate, and equivalent bond yield that were developed previously for non-interest-bearing securities.

[a] Calculations. The only difference between the pricing of a cash Treasury bill and a Treasury bill futures contract is that the number of days used in the calculations for the futures contracts is measured from the day of settlement (delivery) until maturity. In pricing cash Treasury bills, this number is measured from the date of the purchase of the security until maturity.

EXAMPLE: Assume that the IMM quote for a 90-day Treasury bill futures contract, for delivery in 11 days, is 87.76. This gives a discount rate of

$$d = 100\% - 87.76\%$$
$$= 12.24\% = 0.1224$$

This discount rate is stated on the basis of a 360-day year and as a percentage of par value. If this futures contract is purchased and held for delivery, in 11 days the purchaser will receive a 90-day cash Treasury bill and will be guaranteed a price of

$$P = \$1,000,000 \left[1 - \frac{0.1224(90)}{360} \right]$$
$$= \$969,400$$

This implies that the amount of the dollar discount is equal to

$$D = \$1,000,000 - \$969,400$$
$$= \$30,600$$

The simple interest rate, or the equivalent bond yield since this contract is less than 182 days, is equal to

$$i_{365} = \frac{365(0.1224)}{360 - 0.1224(90)}$$
$$= 0.128 = 12.8\%$$

Another value that is often useful in calculating profit and loss is the value of an "01." For a 90-day Treasury bill futures contract, this is equal to $25. It says that the price of the contract will increase (or decrease) by $25 for each basis point decrease (or increase) in the discount rate.

[b] Hedging. Treasury bill futures contracts may be used to hedge against price level risk, but they cannot be used to hedge against spread variation risk.

EXAMPLE: X plans to invest in $1 million worth of 90-day cash Treasury bills in June. It is now March, and June Treasury bill futures contracts have a yield (discount rate) of 8 percent. X is concerned about the rate that he will actually be able to earn in June. If X would be satisfied with an 8 percent rate, he can lock this rate in by purchasing a 90-day Treasury bill futures contract in March; he will have created a long hedge. In June, when X takes delivery of the futures contract, he will receive 90-day cash Treasury bills at a guaranteed price of

$$P = \$1,000,000 \left[1 - \frac{0.08(90)}{360} \right]$$

$$= \$980,000$$

No matter what the actual rate is on cash Treasury bills in June, X will have guaranteed himself an 8 percent rate. By the use of this long hedge, X has gotten rid of downside price level risk (changes in the level of interest rate) as well as upside potential. Although this is often cited as an example of a perfect hedge, the requirements of margin money and marking to market actually make this hedge less than perfect.

EXAMPLE: To illustrate spread variation risk, assume now that Y plans to purchase 90-day cash Treasury bills in May instead of June. Y would also use the June futures contracts to hedge, since there are no May contracts, but Y is now exposed to spread variation risk. Assume that in May, when Y takes off the hedge and purchases the cash Treasury bills, Y faces an upward-sloping yield curve. Also assume that the yield on 90-day cash Treasury bills is 9 percent, while the yield on June Treasury bills futures contracts is 9.5 percent (approximately equal to the yield on 120-day cash Treasury bills). Y would then have obtained the following effective yield from its hedged position:

Futures	
Value at sale (9.5%)	$976,250
Value at purchase (8%)	980,000
Loss on futures position	$ 3,750

Cash Treasury bills	
Value at purchase (9%)	$977,500
Loss on futures position	3,750
Effective price of cash Treasury bills	$981,250

Y's effective discount rate is then equal to

$$d = \left(\frac{\$1,000,000 - \$981,250}{\$1,000,000} \right) \left(\frac{360}{90} \right) = 0.075 = 7.5\%$$

The effective discount rate is 50 basis points less than the original yield of 8 percent on the futures contract when Y initiated the hedge. This is exactly equal to the spread between the cash security (9 percent) and the futures contract (9.5 percent) when the hedge was lifted. If the yields had been reversed—i.e., cash 9.5 percent and futures 9 percent—the effective discount rate would have been 8.5 percent, or 50 basis points higher than the original yield on the futures contract. This is the basis of spread variation risk: It is not known what the spread will actually be when the hedge is taken off.

Also note that the effective price has increased from $980,000 to $981,250. This difference of $1,250 is exactly equal to the value of an "01" times the ending spread of 50 basis points.

$$\$25(50 \text{ basis points}) = \$1,250$$

[3] Interest Rate Parity

If the pure expectations theory of the term structure is correct (see Chapter B1 in the *Handbook of Modern Finance* and Chapter 1 in the *Handbook of Securities and*

Investment Management for a complete discussion of interest rates) and if markets are efficient, rates on futures contracts should be equal to the implied forward rates on equivalent cash securities. In practice, these rates are usually not the same. Therefore, investors must know how to calculate implied forward rates from cash securities and strip yields from futures securities if they are to make correct investment decisions.

[a] Implied Forward Rates. Assume that an investor has a 180-day investment horizon and only 2 possible investment strategies: (1) It can invest in a 180-day cash Treasury bill (security 1) with a discount rate of 9 percent or (2) it can invest in 2 consecutive 90-day cash Treasury bills (securities 2 and 3), where the first cash Treasury bill (security 2) has a discount rate of 8 percent.

If the pure expectations theory of the term structure is correct, there should be no difference between the two strategies. This means that the two discount rates that are known (securities 1 and 2) must imply the value of the third (security 3). There are two methods to determine this implied forward rate.

METHOD 1

The first step is to convert the known discount rates to simple interest rates over their maturity life:

$$_1i_{365} = \frac{365(0.09)}{360 - 0.09(180)}$$

$$= 0.0955497 = 9.55497\%$$

$$_1i_{180} = 0.0955497\left(\frac{180}{365}\right)$$

$$= 0.0471204 = 4.71204\%$$

$$_2i_{365} = \frac{365(0.08)}{360 - 0.08(90)}$$

$$= 0.0827664 = 8.27664\%$$

$$_2i_{90} = 0.0827664\left(\frac{90}{365}\right)$$

$$= 0.0204082 = 2.04082\%$$

Given the simple interest rates for the 90-day and the 180-day securities, the implied simple interest rate for a 90-day cash security, starting in 90 days, must be equal to

$$_3i_{90} = \frac{1.0471204}{1.0204082} - 1$$

$$= 0.0261779 = 2.61779\%$$

$$_3i_{365} = 0.0261779\left(\frac{365}{90}\right)$$

$$= 0.1061663 = 10.61663\%$$

Given the simple interest rate on the basis of a 365-day year, the corresponding discount rate is equal to

$$d = \frac{360(i_{365})}{365 + t(i_{365})}$$

Therefore, using the data gives the following implied forward discount rate for security 3:

$$\text{IFR} = \frac{360(0.1061663)}{365 + 90(0.1061663)}$$

$$= 0.102 = 10.2\%$$

Method 2

The implied forward discount rate may also be calculated directly from the following equation:

$$\text{IFR} = \left\{1 - \frac{1 - (d_1 t_1/360)}{1 - (d_2 t_2/360)}\right\} \left(\frac{360}{t_3}\right)$$

Using the data in this example yields the following.

$$\text{IFR} = \left\{1 - \frac{1 - [0.09(180)/360]}{1 - [0.08(90)/360]}\right\} \left(\frac{360}{90}\right)$$

$$= 0.102 = 10.2\%$$

[b] Futures Rates and Implied Forward Rates. The rate just calculated of 10.2 percent is the implicit discount rate for the 180-day cash Treasury bill over the last 90 days of its life. Another way of saying this is that the discount rate of 9 percent for 180 days is equal to an 8 percent discount rate for the first 90 days and a 10.2 percent discount rate for the last 90 days. This discount rate of 10.2 percent should be compared to the discount rate for a 90-day Treasury bill futures contract for delivery in 90 days. If the futures rate is greater than 10.2 percent, it is better to purchase a 90-day cash Treasury bill and, at the same time, a 90-day Treasury bill futures contract for delivery in 90 days. If the futures rate is less than 10.2 percent, it is better to purchase the 180-day cash Treasury bill.

EXAMPLE: Using the data from the previous example, assume that the implied forward rate is 10.2 percent but the futures rate is 11 percent. If $1 million is invested in the 180-day cash Treasury bill with a simple interest rate of 9.55497 percent, as already calculated, the ending value of the investment after 180 days would be equal to

$$\$1,000,000\left[1 + 0.0955497\left(\frac{180}{365}\right)\right] = \$1,047,120.40$$

The alternative strategy is to invest in a 90-day cash Treasury bill and a 90-day Treasury bill futures contract for delivery in 90 days. The simple interest rate for the 90-day cash Treasury bill (already calculated) is equal to 0.0827664. The simple interest rate for the futures contract, with a discount rate of 11 percent, is equal to

$$i_{365} = \frac{365(0.11)}{360 - 0.11(90)}$$

$$= 0.1146815 = 11.46815\%$$

This means that the ending value of the $1 million investment under this strategy is equal to

$$\$1,000,000 \left[1 + 0.0827664 \left(\frac{90}{365}\right)\right] \left[1 + 0.1146815 \left(\frac{90}{365}\right)\right] = \$1,049,262.90$$

[c] Strip Yields. Just as the discount rates on cash securities may be used to derive an implied forward rate, the discount rates on futures contracts may be used to derive something called the strip yield. For instance, the strip yield for a 180-day cash Treasury bill is the rate implied by the discount rates on a 90-day cash Treasury bill and a 90-day Treasury bill futures contract for delivery in 90 days. The strip yield may be calculated with the following formula:

$$SY = \left\{\left[1 - \frac{d_c t_c}{360}\right]\left[(d_f)\left(\frac{t_f}{360}\right) - 1\right] + 1\right\}\left(\frac{360}{t_c + t_f}\right)$$

EXAMPLE: Assume that the yield on a 155-day cash Treasury bill is 10 percent and the yield on a 90-day Treasury bill futures contract, to be delivered in 155 days, is 9 percent. The strip yield, or the implied discount rate for a 245-day cash Treasury bill, is then equal to

$$SY = \left\{\left(1 - \frac{0.1(155)}{360}\right)\left[0.09\left(\frac{90}{360}\right) - 1\right] + 1\right\}\left(\frac{360}{155 + 90}\right)$$

$$= 0.0949 = 9.49\%$$

If the actual yield for the 245-day cash Treasury bill is greater than 9.49 percent, it is better to purchase the 245-day security. If the actual yield is less than 9.49 percent, it is better to purchase the 155-day cash Treasury bill and, at the same time, the 90-day Treasury bill futures contract for delivery in 155 days.

[4] Repurchase Agreements

Many Treasury bill dealers finance their inventories or purchases with RPs, also known as repos. With a repo, the dealer "borrows" the money to finance the purchase by simultaneously selling the security to a repo investor. (This description is somewhat simplified.) At the same time, the dealer agrees to repurchase the security at a designated time in the future. The total amount that the dealer must pay at this future time will be equal to the original price of the security (the amount borrowed) plus interest on the amount borrowed. The stated interest rate on a repo, the term RP rate, is stated on the basis of a 360-day year.

[a] Implied RP Rates. If a dealer finances a Treasury bill with a repo for only part of the Treasury bill's life, the dealer is said to have created a tail. For instance, if the dealer finances a 180-day Treasury bill for the first 90 days using a term RP, he or she has created a 90-day tail at the end of the repo period. The dealer's ultimate objective is, of course, to purchase the 180-day Treasury bill at one price and to sell the 90-day tail at a higher price. However, the actual price that he or she will be able to obtain for the 90-day tail depends on the current discount rates at the time of sale. One way for the dealer to insure against unfavorable rate level changes would be to sell a 90-day Treasury bill futures contract, for delivery in 90 days, when he or she originally purchases the 180-day cash Treasury bill.

The actual profit on this deal depends not only on the cash and futures prices but also on the term RP rate. It should be clear that there will be a term RP rate whereby the dealer would just break even. This rate is called the implied repo rate. It may be calculated as follows:

$$RP = \left(\frac{d_c t_c - d_f t_c}{360 - d_c t_c}\right)\left(\frac{360}{t_{RP}}\right)$$

EXAMPLE: Assume that the discount rate on a 180-day cash Treasury bill is 10 percent and that the discount rate on a 90-day Treasury bill futures contract, to be delivered in 90 days, is 9 percent. The implied repo rate is then equal to

$$RP = \left[\frac{0.1(180) - 0.09(90)}{360 - 0.1(180)}\right]\left(\frac{360}{90}\right)$$

$$= 0.1157895 = 11.57895\%$$

If the actual term RP rate is equal to the implied repo rate, the dealer will just break even. This can be demonstrated with a cash-in, cash-out analysis.

Assume that an investor has purchased $1 million (face value) of 180-day cash Treasury bills at a discount rate of 10 percent. It intends to finance this Treasury bill for the first 90 days using a repo, where the term RP rate is 0.1157895. In addition, the investor has sold a 90-day Treasury bill futures contract for delivery in 90 days at a yield of 9 percent. Over the 90-day period, the investor's cash-in, cash-out positions are as follows:

Transaction	Cash-In	Cash-Out
Purchase 180-day cash Treasury bills at 10%		$ 950,000
Borrow purchase price using 90-day term RP	$ 950,000	
Deliver 90-day tail against the futures contract at 9%	977,500	
Repay term RP borrowings		950,000
Pay term RP interest at 0.1157895 (90/360) or 2.89474%	_____	27,500
Total cash positions	$1,927,500	$1,927,500

If the actual term repo rate is less than the implied repo rate, the investor will make a profit. If the rate is greater, the investor will have a loss.

Suggested Reading

Cheney, John M., and Edward A. Moses. *Fundamentals of Investments*. New York: West Publishing Company, 1992.

Duffie, Darrell. *Futures Markets*. Englewood Cliffs, N.J.: Prentice-Hall, Inc., 1989.

Fabozzi, Frank J., and T. Dessa Fabozzi. *Bond Markets, Analysis and Strategies*. Englewood Cliffs, N.J.: Prentice-Hall, Inc., 1989.

Gould, Bruce G. *The Dow Jones-Irwin Guide to Commodities Trading*. Homewood, Ill.: Dow Jones-Irwin, 1973.

Kaufman, George G. *The U.S. Financial System: Money, Markets and Institutions,* 2nd ed. Englewood Cliffs, N.J.: Prentice-Hall, Inc., 1983.

Kolb, Robert W. *Understanding Futures Markets*. Glenview, Ill.: Scott, Foresman and Company, 1985.

Leibowitz, Martin L. *Total Return Management: A Goal Oriented Framework for Bond Portfolio Analysis*. New York: Salomon Brothers, 1979.

Levine, Sumner N. *Investment Manager's Handbook*. Homewood, Ill.: Dow Jones-Irwin, 1980.

Loosigian, Allan M. *Interest Rate Futures*. Homewood, Ill.: Dow Jones-Irwin, 1980.

Maginn, John L. and Donald L. Tuttle. *Managing Investment Portfolios: A Dynamic Process*. Sponsored by The Institute of Chartered Financial Analysts. New York: Warren Gorham Lamont, 1983.

Powers, Mark J., and David J. Vogel. *Inside the Financial Futures Markets*. New York: John Wiley & Sons, 1981.

Radcliffe, Robert C. *Investment: Concepts, Analysis, and Strategy*, 2nd ed. Glenview, Ill.: Scott, Foresman, 1987.

Schwarz, Edward W. *How to Use Interest Rate Futures Contracts*. Homewood, Ill.: Dow Jones-Irwin, 1979.

Schwarz, Edward W., Joanne M. Hill, and Thomas Schneeweis. *Financial Futures: Fundamentals, Strategies, and Applications*. Homewood, Ill.: Richard D. Irwin, Inc., 1986.

Stigum, Marcia. *Money Market Calculations: Yields, Break-Evens, and Arbitrage*. Homewood, Ill.: Dow Jones-Irwin, 1981.

———. *The Money Market: Myth, Reality, and Practice*. Homewood, Ill.: Dow Jones-Irwin, 1978.

Van Horne, James C. *Financial Market Rates and Flows*, 2nd ed. Englewood Cliffs, N.J.: Prentice-Hall, Inc., 1984.

Chapter 5

The Long-Term Bond Market

RICHARD W. MCENALLY

5.01 INTRODUCTION

The long-term bond market provides a major channel for the flow of capital to corporations and governmental bodies. It is also a significant outlet for the investment funds of individuals and institutions. This chapter reviews the market from both perspectives. The emphasis is on the decisions these participants must make in issuing or investing in bonds, and in particular, on the risk-return consequences of these decisions.

5.02 BASIC SECURITY ATTRIBUTES

The classic long-term bond essentially consists of a package of two promises: a promise to make a series of equal payments at semiannual intervals over the life of the bond (called the coupon or coupon payment), and a promise to make a significantly larger lump-sum payment at the end of the life of the bond (called the payoff at maturity, maturity value, or par value). By convention, the dimensions of long-term bonds are usually discussed on a basis of $100 of par value. Thus, the size of the coupon stream is specified by reference to the coupon rate, or dollar coupons per $100 of par value per year, it being understood that each semiannual coupon payment consists of half of this number of dollars. The coupon rate, name of issuer, and year in which the bond pays off are usually sufficient to identify a bond. For example, a bond market price quotation for the "Eastman Kodak 8⅝ of '16" refers to an issue of Eastman Kodak that makes semiannual payments of $4.3125 per $100 of par value until some time in the year 2016, at which time it makes a final semiannual coupon payment of $4.3125 plus a payment of $100 per $100 of par value. (From standard sources, such as *Moody's Bond Record* or *Standard & Poor's Bond Guide,* it can further be determined that the end of the life of the bond, or its maturity date, is June 15, 2016; the implication is that the semiannual payments will be made every June 15 and December 15 through this date.)

The price quotation on this particular bond might be given as 85⅜. Following the "per 100" convention, this means a price of $85.375 per $100 of par value. It is also understood that the bond is priced "with interest" unless otherwise stated, meaning that the purchaser must pay the seller the proportion of a coupon that has been earned since the last coupon payment, the accrued coupon. (If a bond does not trade with interest, it is said to trade flat.) For example, if this bond was purchased on January 15 at 85⅜, the invoice price would be

$$\$85.375 + \$4.3125(1/6) = \$85.375 + \$0.719 = \$86.094$$

per $100 of par value purchased.[1] Most bonds are denominated in units of $1,000 of par value. Therefore, the Eastman Kodak 8⅝ of '16 would actually be priced at $853.75 per bond, and each bond would provide semiannual coupons of $43.125 and would pay off at $1,000 at maturity.

---

[1] This example assumes that exactly 1 month, representing one sixth of a coupon period, has elapsed since the last coupon payment and that five sixths of a coupon period remains. Therefore, it is consistent with the "day count" convention for corporate bonds, where it is assumed that a year consists of 12 months of equal length with 30 days in each. For some fixed-income securities, such as U.S. government bonds, actual days are counted. Full details on day count conventions are given by Bruce M. Spense, Jacob Y. Graudenz, and John L. Lynch, Jr., *Standard Securities Calculation Methods* (New York: Security Industry Association, 1973).

With respect to maturity, a distinction is sometimes made between notes, which are loosely defined as securities with 7 to 10 or fewer years to maturity at the time of issue, and bonds, which have initial maturities in excess of 7 to 10 years. However, both types of issues are customarily referred to generically as bonds. In the subsequent discussion, observations that are made about bonds are also intended to apply to notes unless stated otherwise.

Individual bond issues have a number of important attributes aside from issuer, coupon rate, maturity date, and price. Some of these arise from specific provisions in the contract between the issuer and purchasers, called the indenture, while others are due to external influences, such as the Tax Code and the markets in which the bonds trade.

[1] Features of the Indenture

[a] **Security Status.** Some bonds are secured by claims on specific assets of the issuer, so that in the event of default (a failure to make a cash payment as contractually scheduled) the bondholders have a claim on the assets or the proceeds from their liquidation. Such bonds are frequently referred to as mortgage bonds, collateralized bonds, or collateralized trust bonds. Others simply represent a general obligation of the issuer; they are often called debentures. The claims represented by more junior bonds (subordinated debentures) rank behind the claims of mortgage bondholders, general obligation bondholders, or other unsecured creditors.

[b] **Call Provisions.** Borrowers frequently reserve the right to pay off a bond issue prior to maturity. Call provisions permit them to do this. A typical call provision specifies that under certain conditions, the issuer can retire bonds by paying the holder a call price, the par value plus a call premium. Thus, calling a bond is akin to prepaying a home mortgage, and the call premium is analogous to a prepayment penalty.

There are actually three types of call provisions, with rather different motivations underlying each. The most critical from the viewpoint of both the borrower and lender, frequently referred to as a refunding provision or refunding restriction, is intended to permit the issuer to take advantage of a reduction in borrowing costs subsequent to issuance of the bonds. Such a provision typically includes a deferred call period during which that bond issue cannot be called for the purpose of refinancing at lower interest rates. For example, the issue might be noncallable for refunding purposes during the first 5 or 10 years of its life. At the end of the deferred call period, the bond becomes callable for refunding purposes at a schedule of prices set out in the indenture. A common initial price, or call premium, is one year's coupons. These call prices generally decline over the life of the issue and are frequently equal to par in the last few years of the issue's life. As subsequent discussion will demonstrate, investors prefer that bonds be fully noncallable for refunding purposes, while the borrower obviously prefers to be able to refund as quickly and cheaply as possible. Notes are usually noncallable over their entire life.

Bond issuers also normally reserve the right to call a bond issue for purposes unrelated to refunding. Bonds frequently issued by for-profit corporations typically can be refunded for business purposes, such as financial reorganization. Moreover, if the issue has a sinking fund provision, as subsequently discussed, it will usually be callable for purposes of permitting the issuer to meet the sinking fund requirements. A separate schedule of call prices will be provided in the indenture for each of these types of call.

Business-purpose and sinking fund call provisions are considered uncontroversial by most bond issuers and buyers.

[c] Sinking Fund. Provision may be made for the gradual repayment of a bond issue over its life rather than in one lump sum at maturity. Sinking fund clauses accomplish this objective. The term "sinking fund" tends to conjure up a process in which the borrower sets aside a sum of money each year so that at the maturity date of the bond issue there is a large pool of cash to pay off the bonds. In fact, sinking funds now rarely operate in this way; rather, they provide for the actual retirement of a portion of the bond issue at periodic intervals. For example, the indenture might specify that for a bond issue with an initial term to maturity of 25 years, the issuer must retire 5 percent of the bond issue annually, beginning at the end of the sixth year of the bond's life. Such a sinking fund, which will retire 95 percent of the issue prior to the final maturity date, would be regarded as a "strong" sinking fund. A "weak" sinking fund might retire only 15 percent or 20 percent of the issue prior to maturity. Notes normally have no sinking fund provisions.

The indenture usually specifies that sinking fund requirements can be met by calling the necessary bonds, and then retiring or canceling them. Sometimes the indenture contains a "doubler," a provision that gives the issuer the option of retiring additional bonds through a sinking fund call if it so chooses. If the bond issue is sold to the general public, the issuer typically has the option of meeting sinking fund requirements by tendering bonds acquired in the open market, an option which can be very valuable if the bonds trade in the marketplace below the call price.

[d] Equity Features. Some bonds issued by for-profit corporations are convertible, meaning that they can be exchanged for the common stock of the issuer at a ratio specified in the indenture. This feature has considerable appeal for the buyer owing to the capital gains potential, especially when the market value of the stock into which the bond can be converted is of the same order of magnitude as the bond's price.

Other bonds are designed to accomplish substantially the same purpose by being sold initially with warrants attached. Such warrants are rights to purchase the issuer's common stock at a specified price that often represents or comes to represent a discount to the market. Warrants are frequently detachable; that is, they can be traded separately from the bond.

In some cases, the associated bond can be used at its par value to pay for the common stock even when its market price is other than par. Such a bond, called a usable bond, is especially attractive to the buyer when it sells for less than par because it effectively provides a means of exercising the warrants at a discounted price. Bonds with warrants are viewed by some issuers as an especially effective means of tapping a number of investor interests, such as the desire for pure income, aggressive capital gains, or an intermediate position, with a single security issue.

[e] Other Indenture Items. Bonds have traditionally been quite stylized in form. However, in the early 1970s, a much wider variety of features began to be designed into bond issues. These innovations were largely a response to the high and varying interest rates of the period. Some help investors avoid or at least better manage risks to which they are particularly sensitive, while others are intended primarily to provide similar benefits to the issuer. Regardless of the nature of the innovation, this process represents an effort to "complete" markets and thereby make both parties better off in net by providing some combination of features that did not previously exist or could not be created by market participants. The following details a number of such innovations.

OID bonds. The objective of completing markets is typified by original issue discount (OID) bonds, which are bonds whose coupon rate at the time of issuance is below yields on roughly equivalent securities. Thus, these securities are issued at prices below par, or at discounts. The extreme form of the OID is a bond with a zero coupon. Zero-coupon bonds are therefore single-payment obligations, bonds with only a payoff at maturity and no stream of annuity payments. The first OID bond to attract wide attention, the Martin Marietta 7s of 2011, were marketed in March of 1981, and for several years thereafter, a large number of low- or zero-coupon bonds were issued by other corporate borrowers. Maturities on the low-coupon issues have ranged from 3 to 20 years, while maturities on the zero-coupon bonds have been confined to 10 or fewer years. Such issues have a number of attractions in different types of portfolio management situations.

In the United States, investors must recognize ordinary taxable income on the straight-line amortization of discount on bonds issued initially at a discount. The associated tax on OIDs would be burdensome to tax-paying investors, especially in the case of the zero-coupon issues, where there is no cash flow from the bond to pay the tax. For this reason, purchases of OIDs in this country have largely been for tax-exempt investment, including pension funds and individual retirement accounts. However, OIDs have been quite popular in some foreign countries in which capital gains are not taxed and the discount amortization is regarded as a capital gain item. OIDs were also initially quite attractive to corporate issuers. Yields were possibly somewhat below those on current coupon bonds of comparable maturity. Moreover, for tax purposes, the issuer was allowed to deduct interest expense equal to the straight-line amortization of the discount, in addition to any coupon interest. This had the effect of making the after-tax cost of the OIDs to the issuer quite modest, especially in a double-digit interest rate environment. However, the Internal Revenue Service (IRS) soon began to require "scientific" amortization of the discount, in which the allowable interest expense was equal only to the yield to maturity on the bond times the accumulated value of the initial sales proceeds invested at this yield. Since this ruling, the issuance of OIDs by corporations has been more limited.

Options on amount or time of payoff. Options features on bonds, even bonds without equity features, are not new. The call option, for example, has been a common feature of corporate bonds for many years. However, many of the newer options features give the buyer rather than the issuer the right to make a change. One common variation relates to the time of payoff of the principal. Puttable or retractable bonds can be submitted to the issuer on certain dates for early payment, while the time of repayment of extensible bonds can be delayed at the option of the holder. In effect, such options have the effect of shifting some of the effects of changing interest rates from the lender to the borrower. Some issues have also been marketed with contingent takedown options that give the investor the option of increasing the size of the investment at some point after the initial issue date. The consequence of this option is similar to those that shift maturities; specifically, it acts as a partial shield to the investor against declining interest rates.

Exchangeable issues. Preferred stocks are corporate equities that usually carry a fixed dividend that must be paid before any dividends can be paid on common shares.

(Such preferred stocks are discussed in more detail in Chapter 7.) Corporations can deduct interest expense in computing federal income taxes, but dividends on preferred stocks are not deductible. On the other hand, corporations that receive dividends pay taxes on only 70 percent of the dividends, under current statutes, while they are taxed in the entirety on interest received. Thus, it is advantageous for corporate investors to receive dividends, and for corporations that are not paying taxes owing to loss carryforwards or the like, there is no incremental tax burden to the corporations paying dividends versus interest. In recent years, a number of corporations that are not paying taxes have issued exchangeable convertible preferred stocks, or preferred stocks that can be exchanged for bonds at the option of this issuer. The idea is that these issues will be held by corporations initially, and they will accept a lower yield than they would require on a debt instrument because of the favorable tax treatment of the dividend. Then, if and when the issuing corporation begins to pay taxes, it will execute the exchange and reap the benefits of paying tax-deductible interest. Most issues of this type are convertible exchangeable preferreds; that is, they are both convertible into common stock at the option of the holder and exchangeable for bonds at the option of the issuer.

Bonds with floating rates. Short-term interest rates tend to move closely with the rate of inflation, and thus a series of short-term investments can at least partially insulate the investor against inflation. Moreover, short-term investments are relatively immune to price erosion from increasing interest rates, since they quickly mature at par. A series of short-term borrowings can also be attractive to fund users whose asset returns tend to be tied to interest rates, such as commercial banks. However, many borrowers prefer to lock up sources of funds, and many investors wish to commit funds for lengthy periods. In addition, it is expensive when the fixed costs of a security issue or portfolio investment must be spread over only a short interval. In response to these considerations, a number of borrowers have issued long-term bonds whose coupons are periodically adjusted according to the level of some short-term interest rate series. The result is a security whose price does not deviate much from par as interest rates fluctuate. Such floating rate issues vary in many details, including the frequency of the adjustment and the rate series to which they are tied. A number of them have limitations on the size of the adjustment that can take place at any reset date or on the bands within which the rates can fluctuate. Some also have options permitting either the borrower or the lender to convert them to fixed-income issues.

[2] Nonindenture Bond Features

[a] **Marketability.** Marketability or liquidity refers loosely to the degree to which bonds can be bought or sold quickly and with minimum price concessions. One extreme in marketability is represented by directly or privately placed bonds, which are sold initially to one or very few institutional investors rather than to the general investment public. Such direct placements or private placements have no marketability, except perhaps occasionally, in a specially negotiated transaction.

[b] **Quality of Promise.** A bond places an obligation on the issuer to do things in the future, frequently in the far distant future, sometimes 40 years or more. Unfortunately, bond issuers do not always keep their promises. Bond quality refers to the

FIGURE 5-1

Descriptions of Bond Ratings

Moody's	S&P	
Investment Grade		
Aaa	AAA	Highest quality available; "gilt edge"; ability to repay is extremely strong
Aa	AA	High quality, with only slightly less ability to pay than highest grade
A	A	Upper medium grade, with strong ability to repay, possibly with some susceptibility to adverse economic conditions or changing circumstances
Baa	BBB	Medium grade, with adequate ability to pay at the present time
Speculative		
Ba	BB	Has speculative elements, with only moderate ability to pay
B	B	Speculative issues, currently making contractual payments
Caa	CCC	Issues of poor quality that may be in default on contractual payments
Ca	CC	Highly speculative issues, characterized by major uncertainties, often in default
C	C	In default, with poor prospects
	C1	Interest not being paid
	D	In default, with interest and/or principal payments in arrears

Note: Moody's applies the modifiers 1, 2, and 3 to each of the classifications from Aa through B where 1 denotes the high end of the rating, 2 a midrange rating, and 3 the lower end of the rating. S&P applies the modifiers plus (+) and minus (−) to show relative standing within the rating, where + denotes the upper end and − the lower end; unsigned ratings denote bonds in the intermediate range of the rating.

likelihood that the borrower will be willing and able to discharge its obligations fully and in a timely manner.

A common guide to bond quality is the rating assigned to a specific bond issue by one of the rating agencies, such as Moody's, Standard & Poor's (S&P), and Duff and Phelps. (See Chapter C1 in the *Handbook of Modern Finance* and Chapter 1 of the *Handbook of Short-Term and Long-Term Financial Management* for details on credit analysis.) Figure 5-1 summarizes the rating scheme of the first two of these agencies. Although the ratings are influenced by many specific, measurable attributes of the issuer or the specific bond issue, in the final analysis they are judgment calls by the agencies. It is noteworthy that the ratings appear to incorporate assessments of bond marketability in addition to pure default risk considerations, although there is dispute as to the extent to which this is so. Investors are quite interested in the possibility of these agency ratings being changed. The agencies all have "watch lists" on which bonds are placed when the rating is being reevaluated, usually in response to some episodic event such as an acquisition or a new securities offering.

Sometimes the quality of the promise of specific debt issues is enhanced by guarantees given by third parties. For example, the U.S. government guarantees the payment of coupons and principal on some bonds issued by U.S. shipping companies for the construction of vessels that meet specified criteria. Coverage by private insurance against default, a common feature of municipal bonds, has also appeared in the corporate bond market. Obviously, such guarantees can increase the creditworthiness of the bonds, but it should be equally obvious that the guarantee is at best only as good as the guarantor and that its value may be reduced by potential problems in forcing the guarantee to be made good.

[c] Tax Status. Bonds vary considerably in the tax treatment of the coupon income they provide and any capital gain or losses that result from owning them. Moreover, the tax treatment of these components of return is frequently different at the federal and state levels. Such tax considerations are obviously of the utmost importance to the investor and hence to the issuer.

[d] Eligibility. Frequently, a body that is in a position to do so will specify that only certain types of debt issues can be used to fulfill some objective. Such debt is then said to be eligible for that purpose. For example, many municipalities specify that any of their funds placed with a depository institution must be backed by an especially segregated pool of federal government securities, and the insurance commissioners in some states restrict investment by insurers doing business in that state to an approved list of securities. Such eligibility may well have a bearing upon the approved securities' values, other characteristics being equal.

5.03 MAJOR BOND ISSUER CHARACTERISTICS

Bonds are essentially nothing more than contracts, and as such they can and do have almost an infinite number of variations. This section describes typical attributes of bonds issued by some of the major borrowers in the long-term bond market. However, in the bond area, as in other fields of business and finance, there is no substitute for reading the contract—the indenture—and acquiring other relevant information.[2]

[1] U.S. Treasury Issues

The federal government is a major borrower in the long-term bond market, one whose relative importance has increased dramatically over the years and whose securities have come to represent a point of departure in bond design, pricing, and the like.

Long-term debt issued by the U.S. Treasury is conventional with respect to coupon and maturity payment patterns, with initial term to maturity varying widely up to about 30 years. Such debt represents an unsecured general obligation of the U.S. government. It has no sinking fund features. A limited number of U.S. Treasury issues are callable in the last 5 years of their life only. Specific issues are formally denoted as bonds or notes. Notes initially are limited to maturities of 10 or fewer years and tend to be issued in larger amounts and thus have more marketability than bonds.

Owing to the taxing and money creation powers of the U.S. government, Treasury

---

[2] A standard source of information on debt issues of the United States and its agencies is *Handbook of Securities of the United States Government and Federal Agencies*, published biannually by The First Boston Corporation. Information on other types of debt issues may be found in the various Moody's manuals, including the *Industrial Manual, OTC Industrial Manual, Public Utilities Manual, Transportation Manual, Bank and Finance Manual,* and *Municipal and Government Manual.* The last of these also covers U.S. government and agency debt.

debt is regarded as free of default risk. For this reason, and because of its large quantity outstanding, both in total and with respect to specific issues, it is much more marketable than other forms of long-term debt. Marketability does vary considerably among issues, however, with the longer term to maturity, less recent, and smaller issues exhibiting considerably less marketability than large short-term issues. Recently issued Treasury securities, sometimes referred to as on-the-run issues, are regarded as actively traded and highly marketable and for this reason tend to serve as reference securities when the level of yields or prices in the bond markets is under scrutiny.

Treasury debt is subject to federal income taxes, and under current regulations both coupon receipts and realized capital gain or loss are taxed as ordinary income. However, Treasury securities are exempt from taxation at the state or local levels.

[2] Agency Issues

An increasing fraction of U.S. government borrowing operations over the years has been conducted by the federal agencies. These agencies fall into two categories. One are bodies created by the government to discharge specific tasks such as housing financing, rural electrification, or farmland acquisition. The other category of agency is the Federal Financing Bank (FFB), a superagency through which borrowing for other agencies is conducted. The agencies discharge their financing function by borrowing in the public markets and then relending to the constituents they serve. (To date, the FFB has borrowed directly from the Treasury almost entirely and therefore has not tapped the public markets to any material degree.) Agency debt is conventional with respect to coupon and maturity and normally does not have special features such as call or sinking fund provisions. Its credit quality varies. Issues of some agencies, such as the Government National Mortgage Association (GNMA), are guaranteed by the full faith and credit of the U.S. government, while other issues, such as Federal National Mortgage Association (FNMA) debt, are only backed by the strength of the agency itself plus a strong implication that in the event of financial difficulty, the agency would be assisted by the federal government. Agency debt tends to be quite marketable although less marketable than direct debt of the Treasury, in part because individual issues are of considerably smaller size.

At the federal level, the taxation of agency debt parallels that of U.S. Treasury debt; it is fully taxable. However, the tax status of agency debt at the state and local level varies according to the issuing agency; some is taxed and some is tax exempt. For this reason and because of the differing nature of the federal guarantee, there is no substitute for knowing the characteristics of the individual issue under consideration.

[3] Corporate Debt

"Corporate debt" is a term usually reserved for the debt issued by for-profit business enterprises. Because of the power of the contract, and because patterns of funds needed by corporations vary widely, there is considerably more variety in characteristics of corporate bonds outstanding than in issues of the federal government and its agencies. Nevertheless, some generalizations are possible. The typical corporate bond is conventional in its pattern of coupon flows and payoff at maturity and is callable following a deferred call period, usually 5 or 10 years. Coupon income and capital gain or loss are subject to taxation as ordinary income at the federal level and are taxed as well at the state and local level in whatever way other forms of ordinary income and capital gain or loss are taxed. Except for occasional issues guaranteed by the federal government, all corporate debt is formally subject to default risk. Obviously, credit quality varies widely. However, bonds issued by some large, stable corporations are regarded as virtually as safe as Treasury debt, while debt of companies in poor financial straits (junk bonds) may be viewed as having so much default risk that it trades virtually as common stocks. Corporate bonds also vary widely in marketability, although even under the best of conditions, marketability is nowhere close to that of Treasury or agency debt.

It is typical and useful to subdivide corporate bonds according to the issuer, with common subdivisions being industrial bonds (i.e., those issued by an unregulated enterprise), utility bonds, transportation bonds, and financial bonds, depending on the nature of the business and its regulation. Finer subdivisions are also possible; for example, the market appears to make a clear distinction among the bonds issued by a telephone company, an electric utility, and a gas pipeline, and indeed, it even appears to distinguish among bonds of electric utilities according to the primary fuel source.

With respect to the 4 major categories of issuer, industrial bonds typically provide more generous call protection to the investor than utility bonds; an initial deferred call period of 10 years is common. The majority of industrial bonds are unsecured, and most have some sort of sinking fund provision. Utility bonds typically offer no more than 5 years of call protection (this is frequently mandated by the regulatory authority), and are secured by mortgages on specific property. While many utility bonds appear to have sinking fund provisions, the indentures in such cases usually enable the utility to satisfy the sinking fund by pledging additional property. Traditionally, such pledges of additional property were routine, so that in practice there was no effective sinking fund. However, in recent years, with smaller capital construction programs and reduced needs for funds, utilities have increasingly met sinking fund requirements by retiring debt rather than pledging additional property. With the exception of the fact that transportation company bonds are frequently secured, it is not possible to generalize about features for transportation and financial bonds.

Corporate notes are typically noncallable over their life, have no sinking fund provisions, and are unsecured. Long-term corporate debt, as observed previously, is sometimes placed directly with investors rather than sold to the general investment public. By restricting the number of investors to which an issue is marketed and sold, the issuer can avoid registration of the issue with the Securities and Exchange Commission (SEC) and the associated disclosures and expenses. The traditional investors in direct placements (i.e., the larger life insurance companies and some pension funds) maintain professional staffs to analyze credit risk and negotiate direct placement loans. Since the issuer negotiates directly with the lender, it is possible to tailor a directly placed bond issue to accommodate the special needs of the issuer, whereas a publicly placed bond issue must be rather standard in its terms and conditions. For these reasons, two broad types of corporate bond issues tend to be dominant in the direct placement market. The prototypical direct placement is issued by smaller companies that wish to raise amounts of money that would be below the threshold for public issues (i.e., $10 million), that do not have established financial records, or that have specialized financing needs. The direct placement market is also used by large, financially strong corporate borrowers that wish to raise money for specialized projects or that otherwise have constraints or other unique considerations that are not easily explained within the strictures of a prospectus. For example, much of the debt issued to finance the North Slope petroleum pipeline was privately placed, presumably because of the temporary strain this financing put on the borrowers' balance sheets and because of the necessity to present plans and forecasts in marketing the debt. In the 1980s, the direct placement market was also a popular source of funding for leveraged buyouts (LBOs), recapitalizations, and other actions that greatly increased the debt burden of well-established firms.

Aside from specialized indenture covenants designed to accommodate specific borrower or lender requirements, privately placed corporate debt is usually similar to publicly placed debt, with one exception: the issuer does not have the option of acquiring bonds in the marketplace in order to meet sinking fund requirements. An aspect of directly placed debt that is attractive to the borrower is the ability to negotiate changes in indenture covenants during the life of the issue, something that is much more difficult with publicly placed issues that have widely distributed ownership.

In the 1980s, a large market evolved for high-yield or junk bonds. As these terms imply, such debt is below investment grade and consequently carries yields that are higher than the yields on conventional, investment-grade debt. There are three primary sources of high-yield bonds: smaller, emerging companies that in former times might have been able to borrow only in the private placement market; large, well-established companies that have extremely high levels of debt as a result of LBOs or recapitalizations; and "fallen angels," companies whose debt was initially higher grade but that have fallen on hard times. The proponents of high-yield bonds as an investment vehicle acknowledged that losses due to default are larger on such debt than on investment-grade debt, but they argued that on average these losses would be more than compensated for by the high yields. Thus, they claimed a well-diversified portfolio of high-yield bonds should have higher realized returns even after default losses, especially if the securities in it were carefully selected. They also contended that the prices of high-yield bond issues should be more stable than those of high-grade debt. Another factor contributing to the development of the high-yield market was that underwriters of such bonds generally made a market in them after issuance. As high-yield investing became more accepted and popular, there was some tendency for yields on junk bonds to decline relative to other segments of the fixed-income securities markets.

The historical record between the postwar era and the 1987 stock market crash supported the claims that the realized returns on junk bonds routinely exceeded the investment returns on high-grade corporate debt and default-free Treasury debt. However, in the postcrash era, a number of junk bond issues went into default, and others were eliminated through exchanges that left investors with even less-desirable paper. The dramatic increase in defaults probably reflected poor business conditions and increasingly lower-quality debt, and possibly an aging process at work; since bonds typically do not begin to default until several years after they are issued, defaults might be expected to increase as the stock of low-grade debt becomes older. Normally, defaulting bonds do not result in a total loss of value for investors. However, even when the amount of recovery is considered, current evidence suggests that investors in junk bonds in the 1970s and 1980s on average did not do well as investors in higher-grade debt. Still, recent strengthening of corporate balance sheets and the elimination of the lowest-quality junk debt could reverse this result in the future.

[4] International Bonds

An even more significant development than the junk bond market has been the internationalization of bond markets and fixed-income investment, a development that has been underway for years but has accelerated only recently.

Loosely speaking, international bonds are those that are issued in a market or denominated in a currency other than those of the borrower. International investing, however, involves taking a position in a market or currency other than those of the lender.

Major categories of international bonds include Eurodollar bonds and foreign bonds. Eurodollar bonds, which normally represent borrowings of U.S. corporations, are denominated in dollars but sold initially in Europe and traded primarily in Europe. Thus, the market but not the currency is different from that of the issuer. Since Eurodollar bonds are not registered with the SEC, they cannot be purchased at issue by U.S. investors. They pay interest annually. Foreign bonds are issued in both a different market and currency from those of the borrower. Yankee bonds are representative. These are borrowings by foreign entities denominated in dollars that are issued and traded in the United States. They pay semiannual interest. Other examples of foreign bonds include Samurai bonds, denominated in yen and issued in Japan, and Bulldog bonds, denominated in pounds and issued in the United Kingdom. International bonds can be issued by governments as well as business corporations.

In addition to the more typical risks of bonds, international fixed-income investing involves exposing the portfolio to currency risk when the securities are denominated in a currency other than that of the investor, to the risk of markets that behave differently from the investor's domestic market when the securities trade in another market, or both. Investors engage in such investment when they buy in a market or currency other than their own. For example, a U.S. investor that purchases Eurodollar bonds in the aftermarket engages in international investment, as does the U.S. investor that purchases Bulldog bonds. But a Japanese investor that purchases U.S. Treasury bonds is also engaging in international investing; even though the bonds themselves are not foreign when viewed by the issuer, they are foreign pay to the Japanese investor.

The internationalization of the long-term bond markets is significant for at least three reasons. First, it greatly increases the set of opportunities to both the borrower and the lender, thereby enhancing the chances for reducing borrowing costs or raising investment returns. For example, roughly half of the world's bonds are denominated in currencies other than dollars, so a U.S. investor that considers foreign pay issues approximately doubles the universe of fixed-income investment alternatives. Second, it may have the effect of integrating the world's long-term bond markets, causing the level and behavior of yields to be increasingly alike around the world. Third, it may provide a potential avenue for increased diversification in bond portfolio management.

[5] Mortgage-Related Debt

Residential and commercial mortgages have long been a popular investment medium with some types of institutional investors, such as savings and loan associations (S&Ls) and life insurance companies. However, their popularity has been limited by a number of factors, including the need for specialized skills in the lending process and their comparative lack of marketability. While circumstances remain much the same for commercial mortgages, they are now quite different in the residential mortgage area. Over the past two decades or so, a variety of arrangements have evolved that permit investors to place funds into home mortgages without any direct connection with the lending process.

Under the most common arrangement, involving mortgage pools, participations, or pass-throughs, shares in packages of mortgages assembled by lenders are sold to investors, which then receive a pro rata share of monthly mortgage payments less a fee for the administration of the pool. The prototype of this type of arrangement, and by far the largest, is the GNMA program. GNMA pass-throughs, as they are called, are packages of Veterans Administration and Federal Housing Authority mortgages that have full faith and credit guarantees of the U.S. government, and they have an active aftermarket. A number of participations packaged by other federal agencies and by private lenders are similar in form but usually incorporate some sort of private mortgage insurance. Such instruments have become a popular alternative to corporate bonds in individual and institutional investment portfolios because of their safety, marketability, and yield characteristics. Their popularity has been hampered, however, by uncertainty regarding the pattern of cash flows that arises from the wide flexibility accorded the homeowner for mortgage prepayment and possibly by their lack of familiarity.

Collateralized mortgage obligations (CMOs) represent a response by the market to institutional investor dissatisfaction with the prepayment uncertainty and widely dispersed cash flows of conventional pass-throughs. CMOs are bonds collateralized by whole loan mortgages or mortgage pass-through securities and in this respect are much like mortgage-backed bonds. What distinguishes them is the pattern of investor payoff. A CMO is divided into multiple payoff pools or subissues, called tranches, five being a common number. The cash flow generated by the underlying collateral, to the extent that it exceeds the amount required to pay interest, is used to pay off the tranches in order, beginning with the first, shortest, or fastest-pay tranche. After the fastest-pay tranche is paid off, residual cash flow goes to pay off the second-fastest tranche, and so on. This arrangement does not eliminate prepayment uncertainty, but it does compartmentalize such uncertainty. It also converts fairly long-lived mortgages into securities of varying average lives. Thus, the purchaser of the fastest-pay tranche, for example, knows that it will pay out quite quickly despite the actual pattern of prepayments, while the buyer of the slowest-pay tranche is confident of having funds invested for a comparatively long period. A number of CMOs have specialized features, such as guarantees that the rate of repayment will adhere to some schedule.

Real estate mortgage investment conduits (REMICs) were created by the Tax Reform Act of 1986 (TRA 1986) to resolve a tax issue that had arisen with CMOs: the possibility that the Internal Revenue Service (IRS) might levy taxes on both the mortgage trust and the holders of the individual claims. The legislation creating REMICs specifically provides that there should be no taxation at the entity level. REMICs consist of regular and residual interests. The regular interest holders have debtlike claims, with unconditional entitlement to receive a specified principal amount and interest at a specified rate. There may be a number of regular interests. The residual interest holders receive everything else, specifically the excess cash remaining after bondholders and expenses have been paid. The residual interest is treated as equity in the underlying assets. There can be only one class of residual interest.

Several federal agencies and large private lenders have also issued mortgage-backed bonds, which in essence are nothing more than bonds secured by mortgages.

[6] Other Available Instruments

In addition to the securities previously described, some other long-term bondlike security forms are available to borrowers, lenders or both. While mortgage-backed securities are by far the most popular form of issue backed by financial assets, the process of collateralizing marketable securities by financial assets, or securitization, has become much more pervasive. Such issues have included securities backed by automobile loans, by consumer charge accounts, and by computer leases. These asset-backed securities can be quite attractive to investors if their yields are perceived as adequate in comparison with the security features, including risks. Securitization can also be attractive to the originators of the underlying financial assets, many of which sell the assets to investment banking firms that actually create and market the asset-backed securities. Such firms get both the asset and any related borrowing off the balance sheet in return for a quick infusion of cash, and they can often retain the lucrative business of servicing the underlying financial assets.

Securitization is only one of many examples of financial innovation that increases the range of financing and investment alternatives available to borrowers and lenders. Another important form of innovation is securities repackaging, creating new securities forms from existing traded securities.

One of the most important forms of securities repackaging has been bond stripping. The rise in popularity of original discount bonds, described previously, was accompanied by recognition of a fact that should have been evident in any event: The conventional coupon bond, combining an annuity stream and a single-payment loan due at the bond's maturity, represents something of a compromise for investors. Therefore, a number of brokerage firms and investment bankers began to unpackage conventional bonds by selling claims on the coupon stream and the maturity payment separately. The usual practice was to acquire a block of Treasury securities, place them in trust, and market claims on the two streams at prices that in the aggregate exceed the cost of the underlying bonds. The coupon stream could also be marketed as a series of separate single-payment claims.

In 1985, the Treasury got into the act by allowing the component parts of all Treasury notes and bonds with at least 10 years' initial maturity to be traded separately. In so doing they effectively created Treasury zeros. These securities, called STRIPS (Separate Trading of Registered Interest and Principal of Securities) have come to dominate the zero-coupon bond market.

Municipal bonds are debt securities issued by states, localities, and special state-chartered governmental bodies. The coupon income (but not capital gain or loss) on municipal debt has traditionally been exempt from federal income taxes, and specific issues may enjoy favorable tax status at the state and local level as well. Municipal bonds, because of the large number of small issues, as a group tend to be much less marketable than conventional Treasury and corporate bonds. However, for investors, they represent a viable alternative to long-term, conventionally taxed debt. Also, some corporate borrowing takes place through the medium of industrial revenue bonds, bonds issued by a municipal body to construct a facility leased to an industrial user with the lease payments pledged by the municipal body to pay off the debt.

TRA 1986 contains provisions that restrict the volume of tax-exempt municipal debt as well as the uses of the proceeds. Fundamentally, tax-exempt debt can no longer be used by local governments to finance corporate activity; the financing of actual government operations has been unaffected by the changes. In response to such strictures, some governmental bodies have begun to issue taxable municipal debt, bonds that are fully subject to federal taxation for industrial development purposes. So far, the volume of such debt issuance has been small.

5.04 INVESTMENT CONSIDERATIONS: YIELD, PRICE, AND RISK

[1] Price and Yield Calculations

The yield to maturity on a bond is the discount rate that equates the discounted present value of all future cash flows, coupons as well as principal repayments, to the current price. At this point, it is simply necessary to understand that the yield of a security is essentially nothing more than the dollars of return per $100 of initial investment it provides the investor per year. The yield on a bond is the basic measure of its cost to the issuer and the investment return it provides to the investor. It is also a proxy for bond price, since once the coupon and term to maturity of a bond is known, its price can be determined by its promised yield; the converse is also true.

Yield to maturity has at least four interpretations, each with somewhat different implications for long-term bond investment. First, it is the rate of return an alternative investment must earn just to duplicate the pattern of funds flows from the bond. For example, if the bond's purchase price was deposited in a savings account that earned a rate of interest equal to the yield to maturity, it would be possible periodically to withdraw from the savings account sums of money just equal to the bond's coupons over its life and have an amount of money just equal to the principal or par value of the bond remaining in the savings account. Second, it is equal to the geometric average of the periodic rates of return that the investor will realize if the investor holds the bond over its entire life. While realized returns on long-term bonds vary from period to period, on average they must be equal to the yield to maturity. Third, it is the rate of return that is earned from holding the bond over a single period, provided that its yield to maturity does not change. That is, if the bond's yield to maturity is the same at the beginning and the end of a period, the total return over the period, considering coupons and capital gain or loss, will be just equal to this yield to maturity. Fourth, it is at that rate that funds invested in the bond will grow over its life, provided that the coupons are reinvested to earn this rate of return.

In dealing with yields, one must understand the assumption that is used with respect to the compounding interval. As observed in the preceding discussion, bonds originating in the United States normally pay coupon interest semiannually, while some foreign bonds, especially European issues, pay interest only at annual intervals. The yields that are customarily quoted on these securities assume compounding at either semiannual or annual intervals as well.[3] Yields that are quoted on other types of fixed-income investments, such as S&L time deposits, often make still other assumptions about the compounding interval. Thus, care should be exercised in comparing yields on different types of investments. It is also worth keeping in mind that by convention, the yields that are stated on bonds that pay interest semiannually are twice the semiannual rate of compounding. For this reason, conventional yield numbers understate the rate of growth of fixed-income portfolios when coupon income is reinvested. For example, if a coupon bond yielding 12 percent is held and the coupons are reinvested at this rate, the funds actually grow at the following rate:

$$(1.06^2 - 1)(100\%) = 12.36\%$$

---

[3] It has become a common practice in the Eurobond market to quote two yields. One is the Association of International Bond Dealers (AIBD) yield, an annual-compounding yield consistent with the annual coupon payment of these securities. The other is the semiannual yield equivalent, the yield a security making coupon payments semiannually would have to offer in order to afford the same annual return as the bond in question.

[2] Effect of Taxes

Investors are frequently interested in the yield an investment will provide after allowance for the burden of taxes. Such a yield can be obtained by modifying the equation for the standard bond price-yield relationships to place all cash flows on an after-tax basis. As previously noted, the Internal Revenue Code requires that investors treat as ordinary income any gain that results from buying at a discount a bond initially issued at par. However, the tax on this gain need only be paid at maturity. Since this treatment gives the investor the use of the tax until the bond matures, it has the effect of raising the after-tax yield on a discount bond slightly compared to that of a par bond with an equivalent pretax yield. The IRS also allows any premium that is paid over par to be amortized, or written off, on a straight-line basis over the life of the bond. This treatment gives such bonds slightly higher yields after tax than do par bonds with equivalent pretax yields.

[3] Promised Versus Expected Yields

The cash payments from investing in some bonds, such as those issued by the Treasury, are certain. In most situations, however, the possibility of default exists. In such circumstances the conventional yield to maturity probably overstates the rewards that the marketplace is expecting to obtain from the investment. Thus, in the mind of the investment community, the promised or nominal yield is adjusted downward by the probability of default to something more like an expected yield. It is customary in discussions of the bond markets to treat nominal yields as though they are certain. However, it is well to keep in mind that these are high-side proxy measures for the anticipated investment rewards on which the market is actually operating.

[4] Yield Changes, Price Changes, and Reinvestment Considerations

Fluctuating interest rates lead to two kinds of risks for fixed-income investors: price risk and reinvestment rate risk. Rising interest rates raise yields on individual bonds and lower their prices. That is the bad news. However, the good news is that any funds that are reinvested subsequently, including the proceeds from coupons and maturing bonds, earn higher rates of return. The relationships are reversed if interest rates decline: Bond prices tend to rise, but reinvestment must proceed at lower rates of return. Much attention is given in fixed-income investment to managing these two types of risks. Moreover, attention is now directed to portfolio management techniques that effectively attempt to offset these two types of risks.

In dealing with long-term bonds from either the issuer's or the investor's viewpoint, it is essential to have an understanding of the relationships between coupon, maturity, and price on the one hand, and price changes on the other as yields change. A knowledge of the meaning, role, and determinants of reinvestment rates and realized compound yields is also critical. These relationships are reviewed in Chapters A4 and B1 of the *Handbook of Modern Finance*; Chapter 4 in this book; and Chapter 1 in the *Handbook of Securities and Investment Management*. It is also desirable to understand the concepts of duration and convexity, presented in Chapter 4 of this book as well. Managers must understand why bonds with different characteristics have different yields. Investors also must understand if they are to take advantage of anticipated changes in yields, or if they wish to assess the interest rate-induced price risk of an investment situation.

FIGURE 5-2

Yields of Selected Long-Term Bonds

	June 1989	Dec. 1989	June 1990	Dec. 1990	June 1991	Dec. 1991	June 1992	Dec. 1992
U.S. government bonds[a]								
1 year	8.44%	9.72%	8.10%	7.05%	6.36%	4.38%	4.17%	3.71%
2 year	8.41	7.78	8.35	7.31	6.96	5.03	5.05	4.67
3 year	8.37	7.77	8.40	7.47	7.39	5.39	5.60	5.21
5 year	8.29	7.75	8.43	7.73	7.94	6.19	6.48	6.08
10 year	8.28	7.84	8.48	8.08	8.28	7.09	7.26	6.77
30 year	8.27	7.90	8.46	8.24	8.47	7.70	7.84	7.44
Federal agencies: 10 years[b]	9.01	8.31	9.09	8.63	8.35	7.59	7.52	7.17
Municipals: 20 years[a,c]	7.02	6.98	7.24	7.09	7.13	6.69	6.49	6.22
Aaa corporates[a,d]	9.10	8.86	9.26	9.05	9.01	8.31	8.22	7.98
Baa corporates[a,d]	10.03	9.82	10.22	10.43	9.96	9.26	9.05	8.81
Aa industrials[b,e]	9.75	9.30	9.85	9.83	9.13	8.75	8.40	8.25
Aa utilities[b,e]	10.00	9.45	10.05	10.00	9.13	8.75	8.55	8.20
Preferred stocks[a]	8.96	8.75	9.01	8.72	8.26	7.62	3.06	7.45

[a] From *Federal Reserve Bulletin* (various issues); monthly averages.

[b] From Salomon Brothers, Inc., published in *Federal Reserve Bulletin* (first of month).

[c] *Bond Buyer* series *Inside the Yield Book*.

[d] Seasoned, long term.

[e] New issue, 20-year.

5.05 PRICING OF LONG-TERM BONDS

Thus far, this chapter has reviewed the features of long-term bonds, identified features associated with the bonds of different types of issuers, and briefly reviewed some aspects of bond yields. This section puts all this material together by looking at the price determinants of specific bond issues. In other words, the question of how the marketplace values the various features of bonds is addressed. As a framework for discussion, the numbers contained in Figure 5-2 are used, which show yields at selected points in time for a representative sample of securities. (See Chapter B1 in the *Handbook of Modern Finance* and Chapter 1 in the *Handbook of Securities and Investment Management* for a discussion of interest rate determinants.)

[1] Term to Maturity

In Figure 5-2, the first six rows contain yields on Treasury bonds of varying maturity. Such bonds are ideal for appraising the effects of term on yield, because in other respects they are about as "pure" or homogeneous as one can hope for; they are free of default risk, and their prices or yields are largely unaffected by many special features, such as call provisions or sinking funds. The plot of such Treasury security yields against term to maturity is called the yield curve. An example of a yield curve

FIGURE 5-3

Yields of Treasury Securities (June 30, 1992)

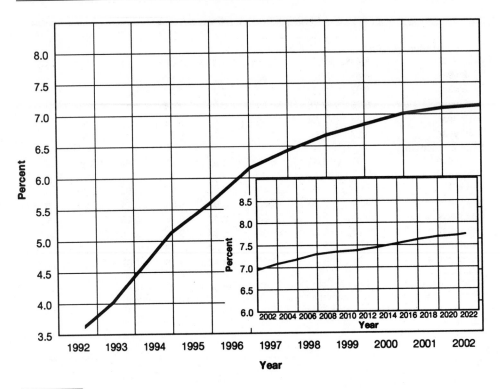

Note: Based on closing bid quotations. The curve is fitted by eye and based only on the most actively traded issues. Market yield on coupon issues due in less than three months are excluded.

is given in Figure 5-3. To a considerable extent, most other types of securities are "priced off the Treasury yield curve"; that is, their yields and prices tend to be based on the yields of Treasury securities of comparable maturity, with adjustment for risks and other considerations.

The Figure 5-2 yields do not display a consistent pattern across the different maturities at each time point. The incremental yield between bonds of different maturities is not constant. However, there is an overall tendency for the yields to increase with term to maturity, especially in the shorter maturities. This pattern is consistent with the generally accepted conception of the yield-maturity relationship, as shown in Figure 5-3. The ideal yield curve rises with term to maturity, rapidly at first, then at a decreasing rate, until it is almost horizontal at the longest maturities.

The usual explanation for this shape of the ideal yield curve is based on the effect of term to maturity on the price change–yield change relationship. As discussed in Chapter B1 in the *Handbook of Modern Finance* and Chapter 1 in the *Handbook of Securities and Investment Management*, the longer the maturity of a bond, the greater is the percentage change in its price for a given change in yields. Therefore, if investors are adverse to fluctuations in the value of their bond investments, as seems likely,

FIGURE 5-4

**Return Volatility and Term to Market for U.S. Government Bonds
(Quarterly, 1965–1977)**

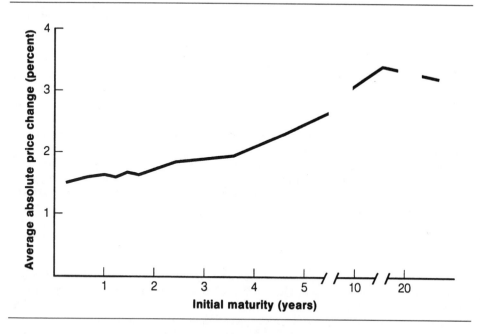

and if interest rates vary by approximately the same amount across bonds of different terms, the additional price fluctuation of longer-term bonds should cause them to be viewed as more risky and investors should demand higher yields to compensate them for bearing this risk. Longer-term bonds do tend to have greater price fluctuation, as illustrated in Figure 5-4, despite their tendency to have lower yield fluctuations, also illustrated in Figure 5-2. (However, this tendency is only a tendency, and it is not always so; but a careful analysis of the data in Figure 5-2 reveals that average yield change increases with term to maturity up to maturities of 10 years.) Apparently, the increasing responsiveness of longer-term bond price to changes in yield overpowers, at least in part, the dampening in yield variation of longer-term bonds. It is also evident from Figure 5-4 that the actual price fluctuation of longer-term bonds increases at a decreasing rate. Thus, the pattern of price change versus maturity provides a plausible explanation for the shape of the normal yield curve. As is discussed in Chapter B1 of the *Handbook of Modern Finance* and Chapter 1 of the *Handbook of Securities and Investment Management*, this explanation is frequently referred to as the liquidity premium hypothesis for the term structure of interest rates.

What about the situations in which the yield curve departs from this normal shape? Chapter B1 of the *Handbook of Modern Finance* and Chapter 1 of the *Handbook of Securities and Investment Management* also deals with this problem. The most widely accepted theory of the term structure, the expectations hypothesis, attributes departures from the normal shape to widely held beliefs that yields will rise in the future, in the case of upward-sloping yield curves, or fall in the future when the yield curve is downward-sloping. While the yield curve may embody generally held expectations of future interest rates, it is widely recognized that these implicit forecasts are often far off the mark. Consistent with this observation, some fixed-income portfolio managers consciously "bet" against the yield curve. For example, they might go long when the yield curve is steeply upward-sloping and the visible rewards for buying long are great, or go short when the yield curve is downward-sloping and it is possible to obtain a certain high return in place of an uncertain capital gain.

In periods when the yield curve has a substantial upward slope, some investment managers use an investment operation called riding the yield curve to exploit this slope. In essence, what they do is buy securities of longer maturity than the average maturity they wish in their portfolios and then hold these securities to a point at which their maturities are shorter than they wish to hold (including the point at which they actually mature). In this way, they attain their average maturity target. At the same time, by buying longer, initially higher-yielding bonds, they raise the average yield on their portfolio above the yield that would result from maturities more closely matching their target. As the securities shorten in maturity and trade at lower yields, they can produce capital gains, provided they are not held to maturity. While riding the yield curve is most popular with short-term securities, it is also encountered in long-term bond portfolio management.

[2] Marketability

The seventh row of Figure 5-2 shows yields on long-term bonds issued by the federal agencies. These yields are always above those on Treasury securities of comparable maturity—10 years, for example, in the table. Several factors may account for this yield difference, including possible differences in perceived credit quality and institutional considerations such as eligibility. However, it is likely that a major factor is the lower marketability of the agency issues in comparison with the Treasury issues. In any event, it is generally accepted that more marketable bond issues command higher prices and thus carry lower yields. Possibly the clearest example of this proposition, though it is difficult to document, is in the pricing of privately placed versus publicly placed corporate debt, where, it is frequently asserted, a yield increment of 25 to 50 basis points (one quarter to one half of a percentage point) on the direct placements is demanded by the marketplace.

[3] Quality of the Promise

Rows 9 and 10 of Figure 5-2 show the yields on long-term publicly placed corporate debt rated Aaa and Baa by Moody's. In both cases, these yields are above those on comparable-maturity federal agency and Treasury bonds. It is not possible to ascribe the yield differential between the Aaa bonds and the two types of government issues exclusively to differences in the quality of the promise (marketability considerations, tax considerations, and more subtle features such as differences in call risk and sinking fund features probably play a role as well), but differences in default risk almost surely account for much of the yield differential between the two grades of corporate bonds.

In a preceding section, a distinction was drawn between promised or nominal yields, of which the yields in Figure 5-2 are representative, and yields expected by the marketplace after adjustment downward for anticipated acts of default. An obvious question and one that is extremely important for fixed-income investment is whether expected yields are also greater for bonds of lower quality, i.e., whether a pure risk premium is built into the yield structure in addition to the more obvious actuarial adjustment for defaults. If there is such a risk premium, a strategy of investing in lower-quality bonds should generate superior investment returns over time. This is the thinking underlying investment in junk bonds discussed previously.

Many believe that there is such a risk premium, basing their argument either on the theoretical ground that the marketplace should extract a reward for bearing default risk or on the empirical observation that in postwar years lower-grade bonds have generated higher returns than lower-grade bonds. Others are not sure. They observe that there are a large group of investors, life insurance companies being frequently mentioned, that have widely diversified portfolios, considerable expertise in evaluating risk, and long investment horizons. Such investors may well be able to tolerate default risk and happily do so if the expected returns for such a strategy exceed those for a lower risk strategy. As discussed previously, the evidence is inconclusive; it depends on what period is being examined.

[4] Tax Considerations

Rows 8 and 13 of Figure 5-2 show respectively the yields on municipal bonds and preferred stocks, which illustrate a more general point about taxation and bond prices. It is hardly surprising that the municipal bond yields are uniformly below those on corporate bonds of equivalent quality, as the coupon income from the municipals is exempt from federal taxation. Tax-paying investors therefore find it advantageous to purchase these bonds despite their comparatively low yields because, after taxes, the yields are at least as high as those that they can obtain on fully taxed securities. In effect, what is happening is that investors are focusing on after-tax yields and pricing bonds accordingly, while yields that are customarily quoted are pretax yields. Therefore, the lower pretax yields reflect the value of the special tax feature.

The yields on preferred stocks also reflect such tax considerations, but less obviously. From the figure it is evident that this particular series of preferred stock yields is uniformly lower than the yields on Aaa corporate bonds, a phenomenon that may, seem very peculiar at first blush, as the corporate bonds represent a senior claim and the preferred stocks a very junior claim on essentially the same assets and income stream. However, tax considerations make this phenomenon very rational. As noted previously, dividend income is 70 percent tax exempt when received by a corporate taxpayer. Therefore, to tax-paying corporate investors in fixed-income securities, the preferred stock dividends are largely tax-free. Considering yield only, they can purchase preferred stocks, bidding their prices up and forcing their yields down, until the point at which the yields after taxes to them are just equal to those of equivalent-quality fully taxed securities. The result is pretax lower yields on these partially tax-sheltered securities than on fully taxed fixed-income securities. This consideration tends to reduce the attractiveness of preferred stocks to investors that are not tax-paying corporations.

[5] Refunding Call Features

Most longer-term corporate issues become refundable at the option of the issuer sometime during their life. Such call features unequivocally reduce the attractiveness of the bonds to investors and therefore increase the yields on the bonds in the marketplace. The prospect of call is unappealing to investors for two reasons.

First, it tends to result in a price ceiling on the bond. If interest rates decline and prices approach the call price, the knowledge that the bond is subject to being called at that price causes prospective investors to be unwilling to pay much more for it. Even if the bond is not currently callable, if it will soon become callable the knowledge of that possibility will have a similar impact. This effective price ceiling puts a lid on the capital gains that can be realized from the bond should interest rates drop, and the opportunity to make large capital gains on bonds is not something fixed-income portfolio managers pass up lightly.[4]

The second reason investors do not like refunding call is the reinvestment problem it poses. If interest rates have declined to the point that the issuer finds it attractive to replace the bonds with funds borrowed at a lower rate, it follows that the long-term investor is going to be forced to roll over funds at a lower interest rate and therefore will suffer a loss. This is so even when the bond carries a substantial call premium, since the call price inclusive of the premium is below the price at which the bond would sell if not constrained by the prospect of call.

The same considerations that make a refunding call unattractive to the investor make it very rewarding to the issuer. Even though the issuer must often pay more than par for the bond in order to effect its call, the reduced interest expense over the life of the original issue can more than compensate. A message here for both issuers and purchasers of bonds with call provisions is that the apparent level of yields on such issues may be overstated. The increased probability of subsequent call for bonds issued under such conditions means that over the original maturity horizon, the issuer will likely not pay as much nor will the investor earn as much as the initial yield on the bonds implies. The effect, then, is to shave off the apparent peaks in interest rates.[5]

In addition to lowering averaged realized lifetime returns, call provisions have the effect of increasing the uncertainty regarding lifetime returns. This uncertainty tends to raise the promised yields investors demand on callable bonds at the time of issue. Prepayments on mortgage pass-through securities have a similar effect. It is likely that the high level of prepayment uncertainty on conventional mortgage pass-through securities has caused the level of yields on such instruments to be higher than it otherwise would be. As noted previously, CMOs and REMICs were devised largely to reduce this uncertainty. If they are successful, the result should be lower average yields on these improved securities, ultimately resulting in lower interest rates to mortgage borrowers.

[6] Sinking Fund Provisions

As noted previously, most corporate bonds carry sinking funds of varying intensities. Provided that the issue is selling at a discount, the presence of such sinking funds tends to reduce the yield demanded by the marketplace. This yield effect is sometimes

---

[4] Because of this effective price ceiling, bonds whose prices are artificially held down by it, or "cushion bonds," can sometimes be bought at yields that are abnormally high in the prevailing interest rate environment. These bonds are "cushioned" against price declines if interest rates rise, at least to a point, because their prices are artificially low. However, the change in effective maturity that can occur when the marketplace's horizon shifts from the point at which call is expected to the maturity date of the issue can produce substantial price declines if rates rise enough to make call unlikely.

[5] For evidence on the effect of call in reducing yields at local peaks over the years 1956–1964, see F.C. Jen and J.E. Wert, "The Effect of Call Risk on Corporate Bond Yields," *Journal of Finance,* Vol. 22 (Dec. 1967), pp. 637–651.

attributed to risk considerations, the idea being that the sinking fund results in gradual paydown of the issue and avoids any "crisis at maturity" that might occur if a large balloon of debt becomes due at one time. Such an explanation probably has some validity, especially for bonds of less creditworthy issuers. The fact that a sinking fund reduces the effective term to maturity of a bond is probably also important in reducing yields.

However, another, more subtle influence is possibly more significant in explaining the reduced yield. Sinking fund provisions of publicly placed bonds normally give the issuer the option of calling the bonds or of acquiring them in the marketplace in order to satisfy the debt reduction requirement. If the bonds are selling at a discount, the issuer can save money by acquiring them below par rather than calling them at or above par. Indeed, under these circumstances the issuer can bid very aggressively for the bonds and still come out ahead. This possibility is not lost on the more sophisticated fixed-income investors, and in recent years they have routinely attempted to "collect" bonds with strong sinking funds and a limited floating supply in hopes of subsequently reselling them to the issuer. The result, of course, is lower yields than the bonds would otherwise carry.

It should be evident, however, that the sinking fund provision can be a two-edged sword. For bonds selling at a premium, the sinking fund call can serve very much as a refunding call even when the bonds are not currently refundable or are callable for refunding only at a higher price. This adverse effect of the sinking fund provision can be especially pronounced when the issue has a doubler provision allowing the issuer to increase the size of the sinking fund call at its option.

From the issuer's viewpoint, the option to acquire the bonds in the aftermarket rather than pay them off at par or above is a valuable one; it means that if interest rates rise over the life of the issue, the effective interest expense may be considerably less than is suggested by the initial price and coupon. The fact that directly placed bonds do not carry this option reduces their attractiveness as a means of raising capital.[6]

[7] Security Status

Despite what intuition might suggest, debt indenture covenants that give bondholders a claim on some assets of the issuer do not usually appear to have a major effect on bond yields. Indeed, casual observation almost suggests that the opposite may be so. It is almost as though issuers secure bonds only if their intrinsic creditworthiness is such that they must do so in order to obtain financing, and the market, recognizing this, demands a higher yield from such issuers. The worth of claims on specific assets probably lies more in the power they give bondholders over the operations of the issuer than in the realizable value of the assets in question, many of which have low marketability. A possible exception may be found in the transportation industries, where some types of equipment, by virtue of being highly mobile and reasonably marketable, constitute good enough security to actually reduce the risk exposure of the investors. Recent evidence does tend to the conclusion that when other considera-

---

[6] See A.J. Kalotay, "Sinking Funds and the Realized Cost of Debt," *Financial Management*, Vol. 12 (Spring 1982), pp. 43–54.

tions are equal, secured bonds will carry somewhat lower yields than unsecured issues.[7]

[8] Industry of Issuer

Rows 11 and 12 of Figure 5-2 show two types of corporate bond yields, the yields on newly issued industrial bonds and utility bonds rated Aa. It is readily apparent that the industrials have lower yields than the equivalent utilities. It is not totally evident why this is so. Professional bond portfolio managers frequently attribute it to supply-demand considerations, pointing out that there is a rather steady flow of new utility bonds, owing to their financing programs, while the new supply of industrial bonds, especially high-quality ones, is rather limited. The result may be something of a scarcity factor at work. One would think that the market would not pay more than a rational price for any security, including an industrial bond, simply because it is rare, but it may be that utility bonds are not perfect substitutes for industrial bonds because of some consideration such as portfolio diversification.

A more likely possibility is that utility and industrial bonds are not actually equivalent securities. As noted previously, the industrials usually carry sinking fund provisions while the utilities do not, and they usually are issued with more initial call protection than the utilities, and both of these differences may increase the value of the industrials relative to the utilities. The perceived credit quality of industrial bonds may also be higher than equivalently rated utility bonds. For example, the market may be responding to the greater flexibility of the industrials than the regulated utilities to enter or leave markets, raise or lower prices, and the like. In any event, the higher yield on utility than industrial bonds is a quite noticeable characteristic of bond pricing that is probably representative of other yield differences among various sectors of the long-term bond market.

[9] Coupon Level or Price Discount

All of the features reviewed previously in this section are built into the specification of the bond: its term to maturity, sinking fund status, and the like. However, another important attribute in determining yields of bonds is the coupon rate or something that is closely akin to it, the discount of the price from par. Since most bonds are initially issued with coupons approximately equal to prevailing yields to maturity and hence with prices approximately equal to par, this coupon level or price discount phenomenon is confined to bonds that have been outstanding for some time in a rising interest rate environment. The nature of the relationship, which is a quite pronounced one, is that the yield to maturity tends to be lower as the coupon is lower and as the price discount from par is higher.

In former years, when capital gains were taxed at a rate that was much more favorable than the rate on ordinary income, the built-in capital gain of discount bonds was

---

[7] G.S. Roberts and J.A. Viscone, "The Impact of Seniority and Security Covenants on Bond Yields: A Note," *Journal of Finance,* Vol. 39 (Dec. 1984), pp. 1,597–1,602.

an obvious attraction of such issues.[8] Such tax considerations are no longer a major factor. However, the implicit call protection provided by the low coupon or price discount on otherwise callable bonds remains attractive to investors. It should be readily evident that the risk of call on a callable bond with, e.g., a 10 percent coupon exceeds the risk of call on an 8 percent coupon bond, and its risk of call in turn exceeds that on a 6 percent bond, as interest rates would have to fall progressively further before it would pay the issuer to call the lower-coupon bonds to replace them with even lower-cost debt capital. Indeed, a low coupon is the best protection against call that is available; bonds with deferred call periods will one day become callable, and call premiums will decline over time, but a bond with a low coupon will always retain that characteristic. In order to obtain this call protection, investors will sacrifice some yield to maturity on bonds where call is a possibility, such as corporate bonds.

[10] Seasoning

It is frequently alleged by professional bond managers that a process of "seasoning" operates in the bond market, whereby newly issued bonds yield more than similar bonds that have been outstanding for some time. This seems rather unlikely, and in fact one might expect that the yield differences would be in the opposite direction, as it is generally agreed that the marketability of newly issued bonds exceeds that of seasoned issued. Indeed, such evidence as exists suggests that the seasoning effect is actually due to a tendency for the seasoned bonds to carry coupons below those on the new issues, with the effects noted in the prior section.[9]

[11] Recapitulation and Interpretation

The bottom line, then, is that the yield of a bond or its mechanically derived price depends on many things. Term to maturity is important, as are coupon level and marketability considerations, for both government-issued and corporate bonds. Moreover, for corporate bonds, features of the indenture, including sinking fund and call provisions, are important, as is the identity of the issuer itself and the credit quality of the instrument. These considerations are significant in designing a bond issue or in structuring a bond portfolio because of their influence on the yield or cost of the issue.

It is noteworthy that while the prices and yields of bonds with different features tend to rise and fall together, the relative prices of these features change over time. For example, in Figure 5-2, it can be seen that the yield spreads between the different lines, representing different sectors of the bond market, do not remain constant. Therefore, in designing an issue or structuring a portfolio, one is concerned not only with the typical price of some characteristic or sector but also with the current price relative to other alternatives. In one environment, a company may issue intermediate-term

---

[8] Even when capital gains and ordinary income are taxed at the same rate, discount bonds are a more attractive investment than bonds selling at par. The tax on the capital gain can be deferred until the bond matures, producing an economic gain. There is also a modest advantage in bonds selling above par compared with par bonds, because the premium can be amortized on a straight-line basis as a reduction in the income from the bond.

[9] J.D. Martin and R.M. Richards, "The Seasoning Process for Corporate Bonds," *Financial Management*, Vol. 11 (Summer 1981), pp. 41–48.

rather than long-term bonds, or currently callable rather than deferred call bonds, because the structure of bond market prices or yields suggests that it is relatively cheap to do so. In a similar manner, portfolio managers, who obviously have more flexibility than bond issuers, may frequently shift among different bond market sectors, depending on their assessment of the risks and rewards in doing so.

5.06 INVESTMENT MANAGEMENT OF FIXED-INCOME PORTFOLIOS

Professional investment managers customarily separate the management of fixed-income securities from the management of other assets, such as equities, and refer to this package of securities as the fixed-income portfolio. Presumably, this practice is a reflection of characteristics, objectives, and concerns of fixed-income portfolios and portfolio management that differentiate them from other types of investment problems. Moreover, fixed-income portfolios differ among themselves in terms of their objectives and concerns, and for this reason quite different management techniques are appropriate in dealings with the various kinds of portfolios.

[1] Portfolio Objectives and Concerns

Fixed-income portfolios appear to fall into three categories. A common type of portfolio, one that is probably representative of traditional fixed-income investment management, is intended to provide a steady and reliable flow of spendable income over time, where income is equated with coupon payments by the security issuer. Portfolios created for the benefit of foundations, educational institutions, charities, and other eleemosynary institutions are prototypes; many portfolios managed for the benefit of individuals (such as the income beneficiary in an income beneficiary–remainderman trust) are also representative of this type. Mature pension funds in the liquidation phase are also essentially income portfolios, even though they draw on both principal and the income stream to provide benefits. The portfolio and beneficiary are frequently tax exempt or in modest tax brackets. Primary concerns in the management of such portfolios are things that could impair the income stream, such as acts of default, widespread exercise of call options by issuers, and the possibility of having to reinvest maturing bonds at low interest rates. These income portfolios tend to be managed conservatively, and they have traditionally stressed a passive, buy-and-hold investment posture, although there has been a trend toward more active management in the last two decades.

A second sort of fixed-income portfolio, at the opposite end of the spectrum from the income-oriented portfolio, is those in which total returns, considering both coupon income and capital gain or loss, are the investment objective. The fixed-income component of balanced mutual funds, portfolios of aggressive individual investors, and occasionally fixed-income holdings of pension funds in the growth phase typify such total return-oriented investment. In portfolios of this type, fixed-income securities are effectively no more than another type of investment medium, albeit one with somewhat distinctive features that have an effect on management practices. Tax considerations can be critical, as in the case of portfolios managed aggressively for individual accounts. In the management of such portfolios, changes in value and the things that affect value, such as changes in the level of interest rates and in the relative prices or yields in the various fixed-income sectors, are the name of the game. The objective is to structure the portfolio to best exploit these kinds of market changes. Total return investment tends to be active rather than passive and may involve frequent trading. In recent years, this type of fixed-income security investment has become quite popular.

A third type of fixed-income portfolio is managed with an eye to accumulation of value. Such portfolios typically have a long time–horizon and a continuing commitment to fixed-income securities; cash income flows, as well as other cash flows such as those resulting from maturing bonds, are reinvested in the portfolio. The portfolio is frequently tax exempt. Bond funds representing pooled individual retirement accounts typify this type of investment, and many pension funds in the growth or accumulation stage are managed in this manner. The overall objective is to generate the maximum amount of value at some point or series of points in the future, subject to keeping risk levels within tolerable limits. Therefore, the major task is profitable initial investment and reinvestment of portfolio flows, and reinvestment risk is the primary concern. The style of management of such portfolios is in a stage of flux. Traditionally, they were managed in a very passive manner. Over time, this passive investment has tended to give way to a more active style, but recently there has been a considerable move back to what are essentially passive techniques rooted in the application of technology to fixed-income investment.

[2] Portfolio Management Practices and Techniques

Fixed-income portfolio management has not traditionally been among the more dynamic areas of investment management. The image of the investor that buys newly issued bonds and locks them away until they mature has a substantial basis in reality. However, since the mid-1960s, fixed-income investment managers describe themselves as becoming much more aggressive, or "active." This increased activity is probably attributable to two specific developments in addition to a general rethinking of investment practices that has affected all areas of investments. First, the heightened volatility of interest rates and bond prices has made it prospectively more rewarding to seek out opportunities for gain and to avoid losses if possible. Second, increased marketability in the bond market and the greater relative importance of the more liquid government bond market together have made active management more feasible than before. It is interesting, though, that there has been something of a swing back to passive investment management. The difference is that the new passive investment management has its basis in caution rather than in indolence, and much of it incorporates new, theoretically suggested responses to reinvestment rate risk and other problems.

[a] Credit Analysis and Management. Regardless of the portfolio objective, the matter of bond quality must always be addressed. Fixed-income investment management has traditionally been described as a negative art, one in which the manager identifies a universe of bonds that meet specified portfolio criteria and then proceeds to eliminate those that pose unacceptable risk, such as poor credit quality. However, actual portfolio management practices with respect to credit analysis and the assessment of default risk vary widely. Many managers implicitly accept the proposition that the agency ratings of credit quality (e.g., Moody's and S&P) provide reasonably satisfactory representations of default risk, especially when the costs of additional analysis are considered, and do little or no further credit analysis. Others also seem to accept this proposition but routinely go through standardized credit analysis for the purpose of providing checks on the rating agencies and possibly satisfying regulatory bodies to whom they are accountable, some of whom require independent credit analysis.

At the other extreme, some fixed-income investment managers feel that there are enough situations in which specific bonds are both misrated by the agencies and traded according to these improper ratings to make it worthwhile to seek them out through detailed, extensive credit analysis. For obvious reasons, these managers tend to be associated with large fixed-income portfolios. Their objective is to identify for purchase bonds with higher credit quality than is consistent with the bonds' market yields and to avoid bonds whose yields are excessively low compared with their real default risk. Sometimes they also seek to identify bonds that will be rerated by the agencies before this rating is reflected in the bonds' prices so that they can trade them profitably.

Practices with respect to default risk levels that are tolerated in the portfolio also vary widely. The case for investing in high-yield or junk bonds has been presented previously. On the other hand, many portfolios, especially those that are more traditionally managed, adhere to a policy of high-quality holdings only. This stance is consistent with the notion that high yield alone cannot compensate for low quality, since it may take many years of earning a percentage point or two higher yield to compensate for the loss of principal value that may occur in the event of default.[10] However, it may also be motivated by more subtle considerations. Low-quality bonds are much more susceptible to breaks in price simply because of heightened concern in the marketplace about the prospect of default. A high-quality strategy avoids exposure to such market risk. It also simplifies the problem when a portfolio manager is trying to accomplish a pure play on some other bond-pricing element, such as attempting to exploit an anticipated change in interest rates. In addition, because the returns of lower-grade bonds are more highly correlated with returns on common stocks, presumably because the level of concern about the prospect of default varies with the same forces that drive the stock market, high-quality bonds can provide more diversification to a portfolio that contains common stocks.[11]

Both high-quality and low-quality investment strategies are consistent with most bond portfolio objectives. An intermediate posture toward bond quality, one popular with active, total return–oriented investment managers, is driven by a feeling that sometimes the price of quality in terms of forgone yield is very cheap and sometimes very dear. Therefore, these managers monitor the yield spreads among bonds of different quality and structure their portfolios according to the size of this spread and anticipations of the way in which it will change. This approach toward bond portfolio management is representative of a more general approach to portfolio management, which will be addressed later.

---

[10] Such a stance is typified by the observation of Graham, Dodd, and Cottle in their classic work *Security Analysis,* where they observe: "Deficient safety cannot be compensated by an abnormally high coupon rate alone." Since they are talking about new-issue bonds, "coupon rate" is analogous to yield to maturity. Benjamin Graham, David Dodd, and Sidney Cottle, *Security Analysis: Principles and Techniques* (New York: McGraw-Hill, 1962), p. 310.

[11] See R.W. McEnally, "Some Portfolio-Relevant Risk Characteristics of Long Term Marketable Securities." *Journal of Quantitative and Financial Analysis,* Vol. 8 (Sept. 1973), pp. 565–585.

[b] Maturity Management. The maturities within a bond portfolio clearly represent one of its significant dimensions. Although this is another area of fixed-income investment management in which there have been changes in recent years, three types of portfolios representing different approaches or strategies towards maturity management have traditionally been identified.

The most obvious and conventional of these strategies results in "laddered" or spaced-maturity portfolios. With laddering, the maturities in the portfolio are scheduled in such a way that a reasonably stable proportion of the portfolio matures at regular intervals. The funds received from maturing bonds might be paid out to beneficiaries of the portfolio or they might be reinvested, depending on the investment objective and time horizon of the portfolio. If the portfolio is in a distribution phase, the laddered maturities effectively avoid the risk of having to sell bonds in an unfavorable interest rate environment. If the portfolio is oriented toward the production of income or the accumulation of value, the laddering strategy avoids the risk of having a large proportion of the portfolio exposed to reinvestment at the yields available at any given point in time. In effect, reinvestment risk is effectively managed through diversification of reinvestment across time. Therefore, this strategy is essentially passive rather than active, and it is more appropriate for income-oriented or accumulating portfolios than for total-return-oriented portfolios.

At the opposite extreme is the strategy that results in "bullet" portfolios, portfolios concentrated around a single maturity date. Bullet portfolios can be consistent with both passive and active management. For example, if either an income-oriented portfolio or an accumulating portfolio has a specific liquidation date, the strategy of investing in bonds maturing at or shortly before that date is an obvious and frequently advocated one. (As shall be seen, however, there may be better strategies in the case of accumulating portfolios.) However, bullet portfolios are more frequently associated with actively managed total-return-oriented portfolios, where the target of the bullet may be a distant maturity date, a near one, or some position in between, depending on the portfolio manager's expectations of the pattern of change in interest rates and the conviction with which these expectations are held.

Another maturity strategy that is occasionally encountered results in "barbell" portfolios, portfolios that are concentrated approximately equally in short-maturity and long-maturity securities. The result, therefore, is to structure the portfolio into a very defensive segment and a very aggressive segment, with the hope that the aggressive segment will provide returns and the defensive segment will reduce risk in a way that will perform better than alternative maturity patterns. This strategy appears to owe some of its popularity to "what if" experiments conducted with historical bond price and yield data. In such experiments, the barbell strategy frequently appears to produce more returns than laddered or bullet strategies with the same average portfolio maturity. However, it has been suggested that such experiments are flawed because they concentrate on maturity rather than duration. Since duration increases at a decreasing rate with term to maturity, a barbell portfolio should have a shorter duration and lower price volatility than any other equivalent-maturity portfolio; thus, it is asserted, these experiments do not actually hold risk constant among the portfolios.[12]

---

[12] G.O. Bierwag and G.C. Kaufman, "Bond Portfolio Strategy Simulations: A Critique," *Journal of Financial and Quantitative Analysis*, Vol. 13 (Sept. 1978), pp. 519–528.

[c] Sector Management. A sector is any identifiable segment of the bond market within which securities share a similar characteristic. Obviously, bonds of different quality or different maturity ranges represent segments of the bond market. Other segments might be defined by reference to the coupon level of bonds, the identity of their issuer, the extent of their call protection, or their sinking fund features. Even in passive investment it is desirable to formulate guidelines regarding the sectoral composition of the portfolio. These guidelines presumably reflect the situation of the portfolio with respect to its objectives, risk tolerance, tax status, and the like and also reflect the portfolio manager's perceptions of the reward-risk trade-offs in the various sectors.

Sectoral considerations play an especially substantial role in active portfolio management. As previously emphasized, yield spreads among the various segments of the bond market are not constant over time. Many bond portfolio managers routinely monitor the yield spread relationships among sectors of the bond market very closely and move funds from sectors that appear to be relatively overvalued (excessively low relative yields) to those that seem relatively undervalued (excessively high relative yields) based on historical relationships, supply-demand analysis, or their intuition. In this way, they hope to pick up value by participating in favorable relative price movements, even when the general direction of bond prices is neutral or unfavorable. Movement among bonds of varying quality or maturity simply represents two types of sector management.

[d] Bond Swapping. Most professional bond managers are of the opinion that temporary price disparities occasionally develop among bonds that are substantially identical, differing only in the identity of the issuer within a rating grade or having only slight differences in coupon or term to maturity. They frequently attempt to profit from these disparities by swapping relatively overpriced bonds in their portfolios for relatively underpriced bonds offered to them by dealers. This activity within sectors resembles movement among bond sectors, but it is both less risky and less prospectively rewarding, owing to the similarity of the bonds involved. However, the difference is one of degree, and many bond swaps do have an element of sector management about them. The transactions often are actual swaps; that is, one package of bonds is traded for another, usually with some boot (called the takeout or giveup) going along with one package. In order to encourage dealers to bring them prospective trades, portfolio managers who actively trade bonds routinely provide dealers with inventories of their portfolio holdings and keep the dealers informed of their preferences for trades. Active traders may well turn over their portfolios a number of times a year in this manner. Such bond swapping is compatible with passive styles of portfolio management, but many managers also view it as a profitable supplement to more aggressive bond portfolio management.

[e] Active Management by Means of Scenario Analysis. Scenario analysis is in essence nothing more than a systematic, integrated approach to sector management. It was suggested previously that a common technique in active total return portfolio management involves varying the portfolio maturity to exploit anticipated changes in interest rates. As has been seen, the responsiveness of a fixed-income security's price (or the value of a portfolio of fixed-income securities) to changes in the interest rate tends to increase with term to maturity; that is, longer-duration securities or portfolios display more price responsiveness to changes in their yield. Knowing these relationships, the portfolio manager might extend maturities when interest rates are expected to decline, hoping to maximize the increase in value, or maturities might be decreased when interest rates are expected to rise, in order to minimize price erosion. A similar strategy might be adopted with respect to coupon level; since smaller coupons tend to accentuate responsiveness of price to interest rate changes and increase duration, the portfolio manager might reduce portfolio coupon levels in the first instance and increase them in the second. Equivalent strategies might also be formulated with respect to other bond characteristics, such as quality, call provisions, or identity of issuer.

Provided that the expected changes in interest rates or yields do occur and the changes are large, these strategies should work fairly well. However, they might not be so effective for smaller changes, especially those that are generally expected. For example, when interest rates are generally anticipated to decline, this expectation will become built into the structure of prices and yields on securities of different maturities in a way that negates easy gains from a maturity-based portfolio strategy. Similarly, there is a tendency for the prices of low-coupon bonds to be bid up prior to large decreases in yields, to the extent that holding a portfolio of low-coupon bonds during such a period is not as rewarding as holding a portfolio of intermediate or current coupon bonds.[13] No doubt the market also prices the potential gains from other bond features, such as call protection, in a similar manner. The point is that effective bond strategies cannot operate simply on the basis of mechanical effects of bond characteristics on the bond yield change–price change relationship. Attention must also be given to the way these characteristics are priced in the marketplace. (Strategies based on the mechanical relationships should work when yield changes are substantial, however, because large changes are almost always partly unanticipated; presumably, the market only prices out the effects of anticipated changes.)

Over the years, bond portfolio managers have learned to deal with the effects of market anticipations on active portfolio strategies by working with "what if" or scenario analysis. For example, in attempting to structure the maturity dimensions of a portfolio, a manager with a one-year horizon might forecast what the yield curve would look like in one year. The manager would then take the observable beginning-of-year yield curve and work out the total returns, considering both coupon yield and changes in value, that would occur with bonds of different initial maturity if the yield curve changed over the year in the manner forecasted.[14] In this way, an optimum maturity strategy could be determined by taking into account both the initial market pricing of maturity and the anticipated changes in yields. Similar analyses could be conducted for bonds of different coupon levels, call protection, and the like.

This general approach has served portfolio managers well, but it has also been limited by difficulties arising from dealing with only one bond characteristic at a time and concentrating on a single "best" future forecast. A number of computer-based proprietary systems have been developed for conducting such scenario analysis in a

---

[13] M.D. Joenk, H.R. Fogler, and C.E. Bradley, "The Price Elasticity of Discounted Bonds: Some Empirical Evidence," *Journal of Financial and Quantitative Analysis*, Vol. 13 (Sept. 1978), pp. 559–566.

[14] Mechanically, the manager would assume a bond with a coupon equal to the yield read off the initial yield curve at the initial maturity of interest, and compute its price at the yield on the forecast yield curve at the new term to maturity, equal to the initial maturity reduced by one year in this case; the total return for this initial maturity would then be equal to the initial yield, adjusted for the length of the holding period, plus the computed price change.

more extensive and systematic fashion. These systems usually require forecasts of the yield curve and prices of other major bond attributes. Frequently, they permit multiple forecasts with probabilities attached to each. The systems then take the existing structure of yields and work out the total return outcomes from portfolios of different configurations. Many of them can be applied to specific existing portfolios of securities in order to identify issues that are particularly desirable or undesirable. Those that permit multiple forecasts with associated probabilities can also be used to quantify the risk as well as the statistically expected return of alternative portfolio configurations. Unfortunately, the major impediment to the use of such techniques remains the difficulty of forecasting future prices with enough accuracy to make the exercise worthwhile.

[f] Managing Reinvestment Rate Risk in Accumulating Portfolios. For a number of reasons, most notably high levels of interest rates and the increasing importance of pension fund investment in fixed-income portfolio management, the problem of controlling reinvestment rate risk received considerable attention in the 1980s. At least three approaches to this problem have evolved.

Dedicated portfolios. The reinvestment rate problem exists only when there are portfolio proceeds to be reinvested; when there is no reinvestment, there is no problem. Occasionally investment situations arise or can be created when it is possible to structure a portfolio of bonds whose pattern of cash flows, including both coupon payments and principal repayments, exactly duplicates the pattern of cash demands placed on the portfolio. A standard example is provided in the pension context by a mature, fully funded pension fund that must simply pay off a stream of defined benefits, which at least actuarially can be predicted with a high degree of accuracy. Such a set of circumstances can also be created by segregating the retired portion of the beneficiaries of a more general pension plan. It is then a fairly straightforward mathematical programming problem to construct a portfolio whose cash flows not only exactly duplicate this pattern of benefits but also do it with the lowest possible initial investment. While the use of dedicated portfolios is basically a passive form of investment management, it is possible to inject an element of active management into the process by engaging in simple like-for-like swaps that do not alter the portfolio's cash flow pattern. In the pension area, a number of consultants and investment managers are prepared to help specify the pattern of cash flow needs, to identify and construct the minimum cost portfolio, and to administer the actual liquidation of the portfolio.

Immunization. Many portfolios face patterns of funds flow needs that simply cannot be addressed by dedicated portfolios. For example, using only conventional bonds it is not possible to construct a portfolio that will have all of its cash flows occurring in 6.5 years, but such targeted funds needs do arise in practice. One approach to this problem is investment in zero-coupon bonds of the appropriate maturity, and indeed much of the popularity of zeros is that they provide an easy means of response. However, a drawback of zeros is that they often do not provide yields as high as those available on coupon bonds.

Using a technique called immunization, it is possible, at least conceptually, to provide any specified pattern of funds flows with investment in coupon bonds while fully protecting the portfolio against uncertainties due to changing reinvestment rates. This technique became quite popular in the United States in the first half of the 1980s, especially in pension fund applications. Immunization involves the second use of duration referred to earlier. Although the technique is attributable to the English actuary E.M. Redington,[15] an article published in 1971 by Fisher and Weil generated the awareness of and interest in the technique on which its current popularity is based.[16]

The basic point of immunization is quite simple. If the weighted average duration of a portfolio is always kept equal to the time remaining until the end of the investment horizon, that portfolio is immune to the effects of changing interest rates. The realized rate of return on the portfolio will at worst be equal to its yield to maturity, and it may exceed this yield. The appropriate weighted average duration is one in which durations of the individual securities are weighted by their proportionate contributions to the total market value of the portfolio.

Understanding why duration works is not so simple. The proof that it works is algebraic and complex, but basically what happens is that price risk and reinvestment risk are just offset. An immunized portfolio will have a life in years that exceeds the time remaining until the end of the investment horizon. (Recall that the duration of a conventional coupon-paying bond is always less than its term to maturity.) Therefore, at the end of the horizon the portfolio must be liquidated through sale rather than through the maturing of the securities in the portfolio. This implication, of course, is quite contrary to the conventional wisdom to the effect that the prudent, minimum-risk strategy is to invest the portfolio in securities that mature at the end of the investment horizon. With immunization, an increase in market yields, which reduces the value of the portfolio when it is liquidated at the end of the investment horizon, is just offset by the added income that results from investment intermediate coupons at the higher yields. Conversely, with a decrease in market yields, the value of the portfolio at the end of the investment horizon increases, but this capital gain is just offset by the loss of terminal portfolio value that occurs owing to the necessity to reinvest intermediate portfolio flows at the lower yields.

Reality is never quite as kind as the assumptions of theory. The immunization concept is based on some somewhat unrealistic assumptions, but many of the complications of reality turn out to be surmountable in practice. A number of immunization programs that were implemented in the late 1970s and early 1980s have subsequently reached their liquidation horizon. The vast majority of these were successful in achieving their return goals. When there have been problems, they were mostly due to defaults and premature calls rather than to any fundamental failure of immunization.

The most substantial problem in implementing immunization strategies is the lack of sufficiently long durations. For conventional coupon bonds, duration increases with term to maturity only to a point. Under present interest rate conditions, this point is approximately 12 years for Treasury bonds selling at par. Unfortunately, 12 years is not very long in comparison with many fixed-income investment horizons (e.g., the 40 years or more that might be associated with a pension fund portfolio or a life insurance company portfolio). Zero-coupon Treasury securities have made it possible to extend durations. Some effort has also been made to respond to this problem by expanding the universe of securities considered for inclusion in the immunizing portfolio to include common stocks and interest rate futures.

Immunization is a passive investment strategy in the sense that the portfolio is not

---

[15] F.M. Redington, "Review of the Principles of Life-Office Valuation," *Journal of the Institute of Actuaries*, Vol. 78 (1952), pp. 286–315.

[16] L. Fisher and R.L. Weil, "Coping With the Risk of Interest Rate Fluctuation: Returns to Bondholders from Naive and Optimal Strategies," *Journal of Business*, Vol. 44 (Oct. 1971), pp. 408–431.

managed aggressively to take advantage of anticipated changes in interest rates, but portfolio trading and swapping that does not alter the duration of the portfolio is not inconsistent with immunization and may add value. As with dedicated portfolios, a number of consultants and investment managers are prepared to design and implement immunization programs to meet specific investment needs.

Contingent immunization. A variation on immunization that permits active portfolio management, labeled "contingent immunization" by its developer, Martin Leibowitz of Salomon Brothers, Inc., has attracted considerable attention in the fixed-income investment community.[17] Under contingent immunization, the portfolio is actively managed as long as doing so is rewarding; immunization is only implemented if it appears necessary in order to achieve a predetermined target return or target value for the portfolio over some investment horizon. At each periodic review point, a portfolio "trigger value" is determined; this value is the minimum value the portfolio must have at that point in order to reach the target value if it is then immunized at prevailing interest rates. If the actual portfolio value is above this trigger, active management continues; if not, the portfolio is immediately immunized. Therefore, in a very real sense contingent immunization is not and may not become immunization at all. Immunization is simply a fallback position to which the portfolio sponsors or managers have made a commitment if they are unsuccessful with active management. However, contingent immunization does respond to a frequent criticism of conventional immunization; that is, while it limits the losses that can occur from adverse reinvestment, it also eliminates the possibility of reaping the gains that active portfolio management may bring.

[g] Indexing. The practice of indexing a portfolio, or constructing it so that its composition and performance are similar to those of some broad market index has been popular in equity investment for a number of years. Until recently, indexing has been infrequent in fixed-income investment. In contrast to the situation in the equities market, there was no substantial evidence that the long-term bond market was so efficient as to justify such a passive investment approach, nor were there generally accepted indexes of the market such as the S&P 500 for stocks. A number of major brokerage firms, including Merrill Lynch, Salomon Brothers, and Shearson Lehman, now provide an elaborate set of fixed-income indexes, and several of these are emerging as standard representations of the long-term bond market. It is also possible to construct customized indexes from indexes maintained by these firms for different market sectors, maturities, and the like. Moreover, there is increasing evidence casting doubt on the ability of active fixed-income managers to produce superior returns relative to the risks that are assumed.[18] As a result of these two developments, indexing is starting to show up in fixed-income investment.

It is not practical to hold all of the bonds in a standard index. Several approaches are used to duplicate the index. One is essentially a sampling approach, in which the bonds in the index are cross-classified into "cells" (e.g., 10-to-15-year AA industrials) and an effort is then made to keep a fraction of the portfolio equal to the representation

---

[17] M.L. Leibowitz and A. Weinberger, "The Uses of Contingent Immunization," *Journal of Portfolio Management,* Vol. 8 (Fall 1981), pp. 51–55.

[18] Fredric A. Nelson, "Indexing Fixed-Income Investments," *Innovations in Fixed-Income Investments and Markets,* Richard W. McEnally, ed. (Charlottesville, Va.: The Institute of Chartered Financial Analysts, 1987), pp. 57–63.

of each cell in the index in selected bonds that fall within the cell. Another approach simply attempts to duplicate the characteristics on the index on average, so that on average the bonds that are held have the same duration, coupon level, quality, and the like. More complex approaches attempt to "optimize" the portfolio by seeking the highest expected return while meeting index characteristic constraints. As in the equity investment area, value-added indexing is sometimes practiced by managers who attempt to replicate an index while seeking out especially attractive securities and avoiding those that are expected to perform poorly.

[h] International Bond Investing. In the last decade, many fixed-income investors have altered their portfolio policy guidelines to allow investment in non-U.S. bonds. This move parallels an earlier move to international equity investment. It seems to have two themes.

Some international fixed-income investors are attracted by the opportunity to add a currency play dimension to their potential investment strategies. They recognize that changes in the relative value of currencies in which bonds are denominated can add a large element of gain or loss to more familiar sources of return. For example, when the dollar declined against most other major currencies in the mid-1980s, annual returns from nondollar bonds to a dollar-based investor in excess of 40 percent were not uncommon. Strategic international investors may also be attracted to high-yield foreign bonds when they feel that the yields of issues denominated in a particular currency are more than adequate to offset likely losses due to any decline in the value of the currency against the dollar.

Another set of international bond investors are motivated by the sheer magnitude of the foreign bond markets and a perceived potential for risk reduction from diversifying into such bonds. As pointed out earlier, the non-U.S. bond market is very large, and simply for this reason some portfolio managers wish to have some exposure to it. Others have observed that because currencies change in relative value and interest rates do not move uniformly worldwide, the intercorrelation among returns of U.S. and foreign bonds is low enough to make diversifying into foreign issues a means of reducing portfolio risk. Such diversification is perceived to be especially attractive because foreign bonds do not have obviously lower returns than domestic issues. Much the same arguments were responsible for the move toward international equity investment that began a decade ago.

At this time, many U.S.-based investors in foreign bonds are using managers domiciled in the country of interest. Most are also confining their investment to government issues, foreign borrowings of U.S. corporations, or bonds of other familiar issuers such as major banks and multinational corporations. With the passage of time and increased experience with foreign bond markets, it is likely that more U.S. investors will do their own foreign investment and will become more venturesome in defining the admissible set of investments.[19]

[i] Portfolio Insurance. Portfolio insurance is a portfolio management strategy that attempts to achieve at least a minimum return when asset values are declining while maintaining some participation in upside moves. The strategy can be implemented

---

[19] A useful survey of international fixed-income investment is provided in Richard W. McEnally, ed., *International Bonds and Currencies* (Charlottesville, Va. and Homewood, Ill.: The Institute of Chartered Financial Analysts and Dow Jones-Irwin, 1985).

using options, futures, or rebalancing strategies, but its essence is to increase exposure to the asset in question as values rise and decrease exposure as values decline.

In equity investment, portfolio insurance enjoyed a surge of increasing popularity until the stock market crash in October 1987. The strategy has been much less popular in fixed-income investment, at least as an explicit portfolio management technique. However, it has been observed that many fixed-income portfolios implicitly employ a form of portfolio insurance.[20] The reasoning is that rising interest rates, which reduce bond values, also tend to shorten durations and thereby reduce the portfolio's exposure to subsequent rate changes. Conversely, falling rates simultaneously increase bond values and lengthen durations, thereby raising exposure to interest rate change. Such tendencies can be overcome by conscious shifts in portfolio duration as interest rates change.

[j] Interest Rate Futures. Futures contracts are now traded on a number of fixed-income securities, including Treasury bills, Treasury notes, Treasury bonds, and GNMA pass-throughs. The uses of such futures contracts in investment management, including the management of long-term bond portfolios, are legion. However, the common element in most fixed-income investment applications is that they use the high liquidity and leverage potential of futures to make portfolio adjustments more quickly and more dramatically than would be possible by changing the fundamental composition of the portfolio itself. For example, a portfolio manager who becomes concerned about upward movements in interest rates can quickly shift much of this risk to others by shorting interest rate futures, whereas actually liquidating the portfolio might be expensive and time-consuming. Therefore, interest rate futures have reduced or largely eliminated many of the traditional encumbrances to aggressive, creative bond portfolio management techniques.

5.07 PORTFOLIO PERFORMANCE EVALUATION

Evaluation of investment performance is important as an aid to identifying superior or inferior managers and as a means of improving subsequent investment performance. The state of the performance evaluation art is not as advanced in the fixed-income area as in equity investment, but a number of consultants have begun to market performance evaluation products for fixed-income portfolios. Most of these products are oriented toward portfolios managed for total returns, and most have two goals: to compare the performance of the actual portfolio with some external benchmark and to decompose the performance into its major elements.

Two types of performance benchmarks are typically employed. As in the equity investment area, portfolio performance is often compared to indexes designed to reflect general market returns. However, this approach may be inappropriate if a bond portfolio is restricted from investment in some sectors of the bond market because of policy or other considerations. In these circumstances, performance evaluation is usually driven by comparison with the results of a guideline or baseline portfolio representing an agreed-on "ideal" or "neutral" composition for the portfolio in question. By reference to subindexes of bond market returns, discussed previously, it is a fairly easy

---

[20] See Nelson, *op. cit.*, pp. 57–63.

matter to determine what the performance of the unmanaged baseline portfolio would have been.

Regardless of the standard of comparison, performance evaluation then normally proceeds by analyzing the differences in the returns of the managed portfolio and the benchmark according to the elements that generate these differences. Typical decomposition schemes usually isolate the effects on differential returns of (1) a maturity or duration strategy that represents a departure from the benchmark; (2) a sectoral balance that is different from the benchmark; and (3) superior selection of securities from within a sector. Some performance evaluation approaches also isolate the contribution of bond-swapping activity separately.

Suggested Reading

McEnally, Richard W., ed. *Innovations in Fixed-Income Investments and Markets.* Charlottesville, Va.: The Institute of Chartered Financial Analysts, 1987.
———, ed. *International Bonds and Currencies.* Charlottesville, Va. and Homewood, Ill.: The Institute of Chartered Financial Analysts and Dow Jones-Irwin, 1985.
Fabozzi, Frank J., ed. *The Handbook of Fixed Income Securities,* 3rd ed. Homewood, Ill.: Dow Jones-Irwin, 1991.

Chapter 6
Municipal Securities

Timothy W. Koch

6.01 INTRODUCTION

State and local governments have long relied on municipal securities as a means of financing their varied activities. Short-term securities mature within one year and are typically issued to fund either temporary imbalances between operating expenditures and receipts or capital outlays in anticipation of permanent financing from a long-term bond placement. They are repaid when anticipated tax or bond revenues are received. Long-term securities, in contrast, mature beyond one year and are typically issued to fund capital assets, such as schools, water and sewer treatment facilities, hospitals, and housing projects. Repayment is from tax receipts or project revenues generated over the life of the underlying facilities.

As indicated in Figure 6-1, the volume of municipal securities outstanding has grown dramatically in recent years and changed structurally in terms of composition.[1] At the end of 1945, $14.8 billion in municipals was outstanding, with long-term public-purpose bonds composing 98 percent of the total and short-term securities 2 percent. During the mid-1970s, municipalities began to issue long-term industrial development bonds (IDBs), whose proceeds were effectively used by businesses for private purposes. At year-end 1991, the volume of outstanding municipals had grown to over $1.1 trillion. Of this total, however, long-term public-purpose bonds comprised only 76 percent, while long-term industrial use bonds accounted for 19 percent. Short-term securities peaked at over 9 percent of outstandings in 1970 but have since fallen to about 5 percent.

Since 1986, the changing federal tax environment has altered municipal market activity. Certain classes of securities, such as large IDBs, have lost their tax exemption, and various investors have seen the yield advantage of municipals lessen or disappear entirely. Thus, both the supply of municipals and the composition of holdings by investor groups will differ sharply in future years. The data for industrial use bonds from 1985 to 1992 reflect the supply constraints, as outstandings were virtually the same in 1992 as in 1985, indicating no net new issues. Industrial development bonds thus declined as a fraction of total outstandings.

6.02 TAX EXEMPTION AND MUNICIPALS

Ever since the U.S. Congress implemented a federal income tax in 1913, interest income from municipal securities has been excluded from taxation. This exemption was based largely on a U.S. Supreme Court ruling in 1895 that municipal property and revenues were not subject to federal taxes because such taxes violated the prohibition against one government unit's interfering in the constitutional affairs of another. A 1954 revision specifically excluded municipal interest from taxable income. In April 1988, however, the Supreme Court overruled the 1895 decision and stated that Congress can constitutionally tax municipal interest and property, if it desires. Thus, while the exemption remains in effect, investors are at risk that the tax treatment of both existing and new securities could change.

Municipals continue to be subject to other taxes. If, for example, an investor realizes

---

[1] With the Tax Reform Act of 1986, some securities issued by state and local governments pay interest that is fully taxable to all investors. These securities are labeled taxable municipals. Throughout this chapter, the term "municipal securities" refers to issues that pay tax-exempt interest.

FIGURE 6-1

State and Local Government Debt Outstanding (1945–1992)

Source: Flow of Funds Accounts, Year-End Outstandings, Board of Governors of the Federal Reserve System (Washington, D.C.: 1992)

Year	Public Purpose		Private Purpose	Total
	Short Term	Long Term	Industrial Use Bonds	
1945	$ 0.3	$ 14.5	—	$ 14.8
1950	1.3	23.1	—	24.4
1955	2.1	43.8	—	45.9
1960	3.5	67.3	—	70.8
1965	5.5	94.8	—	100.3
1970	13.3	131.1	—	144.4
1975	18.6	195.8	$ 9.4	223.8
1980	14.9	288.0	62.6	365.4
1985	18.9	515.7	208.3	743.0
1990	45.6	808.8	201.2	1055.6
1991	52.4	840.1	208.8	1101.4
1992[a]	46.0	867.4	212.7	1126.1

Note: Dollars in billions.
[a] Through June 1992.

a capital gain from holding a municipal, the price appreciation is subject to tax.[2] Many states and local governments similarly tax municipal interest and/or levy personal property taxes against municipal holdings. Figure 6-2 classifies states into four categories depending on whether they have an income tax or exempt any municipal interest from taxation. Most states with income taxes exempt interest on bonds issued within the state but tax interest from municipals issued outside the state. The figures in parentheses indicate the effective tax rate on bonds issued by out-of-state borrowers.

6.03 RELATIVE YIELDS ON MUNICIPAL AND TAXABLE SECURITIES

Pretax yields on municipal securities are lower than yields on otherwise comparable taxable securities because municipal interest is exempt from federal income taxes. Investors willingly accept these lower yields as long as the after-tax return is greater. The appropriate yield comparison is thus between relative after-tax yields. In the determination of the relative after-tax yields, the following variables are defined:

R_t = pretax taxable yield
R_m = pretax municipal yield
T_t = investor's marginal tax rate on taxable income
T_m = investor's marginal tax rate on municipal interest

---

[2] Price appreciation to par on original issue municipal discount bonds is viewed as interest and is thus tax exempt. Any price increase over par is taxed as a capital gain.

FIGURE 6-2

Types of Bonds Exempted From State Income Taxes

Source: Gabriele, Hueglin, and Cashman, Inc., *Guide to State and Local Taxation of Municipal Bonds* (New York, 1981)

	Exempted Bonds	States		
Group 1	No income tax	Alaska (0) Florida (0.6) Nevada (0)	South Dakota (0) Texas (0) Washington (0)	Wyoming (0)
Group 2	Exempt all bonds from state income tax (with state income tax in force)	Indiana (1.4) Nebraska (0)	New Mexico (0) Utah (0)	Vermont (0)
Group 3	Exempt all in-state and tax all out-of-state	Alabama (4) Arizona (4.2) Arkansas (3.5) California (5.5) Connecticut (6.2) Delaware (6.8) Georgia (3.5) Hawaii (4.9) Idaho (3.8) Kentucky (4.5) Louisiana[a] (3.1)	Maine (5) Maryland (3.8) Massachusetts (5.4) Michigan (4.1) Minnesota (9.9) Mississippi (2) Missouri (3.3) Montana (6.4) New Hampshire (2.5) New Jersey (1.3) New York (7)	North Carolina (4.8) North Dakota (4.2) Ohio[b] (2.6) Oregon (5) Pennsylvania (3.3) Rhode Island (4.3) South Carolina (3.5) Tennessee (3) Virginia (2.9) West Virginia (7.9)
Group 4	Exempt some in-state and tax all out-of-state	Colorado[c] (4.7) Illinois (1.3)	Iowa (6.9) Kansas (6.8)	Oklahoma (3) Wisconsin (5)

Note: Effective state tax rate appears in parentheses. Tax rates are based on 9 percent coupon par bonds and include applicable personal property taxes.

[a] Out-of-state bonds bought before January 1, 1980 are exempt. Those purchased thereafter are taxable.

[b] Ohio has a personal property tax on some in-state bonds.

[c] Most in-state bonds issued before May 1, 1980 are taxable. Those issued thereafter are exempt.

Note that T_t represents the combined federal tax rate and state and local income tax rate on normal taxable income, while T_m represents the applicable state and local tax rate on municipal interest and property. The after-tax return on each type of security equals the pretax yield times one minus the relevant marginal tax rate, so that the yield comparison is

$$R_t(1 - T_t) \gtreqless R_m(1 - T_m) \tag{6.1}$$

Suppose, for example, that an investor resides in a state with a 6 percent tax on normal taxable income as well as municipal interest and pays federal income taxes at a 28 percent rate. If the yields on taxable and municipal securities of comparable risk and maturity are 10 percent and 8 percent, respectively, the after-tax municipal yield of 7.52 percent exceeds the after-tax taxable yield of 6.6 percent, making the municipal more attractive. Other yield comparisons, assuming varying interest rates and tax rates, are summarized below:

	R_t	T_t	R_m	T_m	$R_t(1 - T_t)$		$R_m(1 - T_m)$
1.	10%	34%	8.0%	6%	6.60%	<	7.52%
2.	11	31	8.0	3	7.59	<	7.76
3.	10	28	7.2	0	7.20	=	7.20
4.	9	21	7.0	6	7.11	>	6.58
5.	10	18	8.0	3	8.20	>	7.76

In the first two instances, the after-tax return on the municipal security exceeds the after-tax return on the taxable security. In the third instance, an investor paying federal taxes at 28 percent and no state taxes would be indifferent between the two securities because both provide an identical 7.2 percent after-tax return. Taxable securities produce the higher returns in the last two cases.

[1] Indifference Tax Rates

In general, if T_t substantially exceeds T_m, an investor will find that municipals offer higher after-tax returns at prevailing interest rates. If T_t is relatively low, an investor will find that taxables typically yield more. This is demonstrated by comparing the first two yield relationships with the last two in the previous example. Relative municipal and taxable yields change, so that the last investor that views these securities as substitutes earns equal after-tax returns and is thus indifferent. Viewed alternatively, the marginal tax rates of the indifferent investor determine the ratio of pretax municipal to taxable yields. Let T_t^* and T_m^* equal the indifferent investor's marginal tax rates. Then

$$\frac{R_m}{R_t} = \frac{(1 - T_t^*)}{(1 - T_m^*)} \tag{6.2}$$

Most discussions of relative tax-exempt and taxable yields ignore taxes on municipals, so that T_m^* is assumed to equal zero. In terms of Equation 6.2, analysts thus focus on the ratio of municipal to taxable yields, which equals one minus an implied T_t^* at the margin. Investors that pay taxes at rates above T_t^* prefer municipals, while those that pay taxes at rates below T_t^* prefer taxables. Figure 6-3 presents the values of the ratio of the prime grade municipal to the Treasury rate $(1 - T_t^*)$ from 1970 to 1992 using quarterly averages of municipal and Treasury yields for securities of various maturities, assuming that T_m^* equals zero.

The rate ratio indicates a persistent pattern in indifference rates across maturities prior to 1990. An indifference to the rate represents the marginal federal income tax rate at which an investor would earn the same after-tax yield on a taxable and a municipal security, if taxes are paid at that rate. Specifically, the rate ratio systematically increases with maturity, since the 1-year rate ratio is always lower than the 10-year rate ratio, which in turn is lower than the 20-year rate ratio. Thus, the indifference tax rate is highest for 1-year securities and decreases with maturity. From 1970 through 1988, T_t^* averaged 43 percent for 1-year securities, 31 percent for 10-year securities, and only 27 percent for 20-year securities. This relative ranking of indifference rates remained the same regardless of the shape of the Treasury yield curve or the level of interest rates.

Since 1990, however, the relative relationship has changed as the 1-year rate ratio has occasionally exceeded the 10-year ratio. This represents a dramatic shift in indifference tax rates and thus the yield comparison. The cause of the shift appears to be

FIGURE 6-3

Ratio of Municipal Yields (R_m) to Treasury Yields (R_t) on Securities of Comparable Maturity

Source: An Analytical Record of Yields and Yield Spreads, Salomon Brothers (1992)

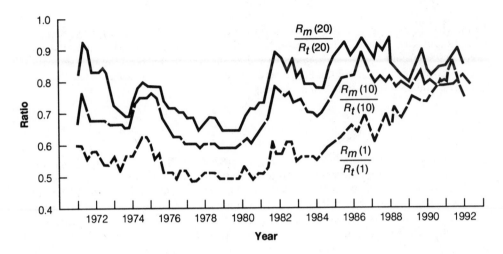

Note: Maturity in years appears in parentheses.

market participants' response to the Tax Reform Act of 1986 (TRA 1986). Under provisions of TRA 1986, commercial banks have largely withdrawn from the municipal market as investors. Individuals now buy the majority of municipal issues. Generally, short-term municipal yields have increased relative to short-term taxable yields to attract additional funds from individuals. Thus, the indifference tax rate for one-year securities has declined.

The implication of the traditional rate relationship and recent change is that investors need to examine the yield comparison across maturities carefully before buying. The same investor may prefer municipals at one maturity but Treasuries at another. In the future, this relationship should be more volatile, reflecting increasingly varied borrowing and investing activity.

Clearly, T_m does not equal zero for many investors, so the previous discussion is simplistic. In many states, T_m is zero for in-state securities and positive for out-of-state securities (see Figure 6-2). In this instance, otherwise comparable municipals from two states will provide different after-tax returns if they carry the same pretax yields. Investors would subsequently prefer in-state securities and thus bid pretax yields on in-state bonds below those on similar out-of-state bonds, bringing the after-tax yields closer together. In terms of Equation 6.2, the ratio of municipal to taxable yields will be bid higher for out-of-state bonds when T_m is greater than zero. Thus, the higher the state tax rate on out-of-state municipals, the lower the yield on in-state municipals compared with the yield on out-of-state municipals.[3]

[2] Tax-Equivalent Yields

Brokers and bond analysts often compare yields on municipals and taxable securities by converting tax-exempt yields to tax-equivalent yields. This conversion does nothing more than transform an after-tax municipal yield to its pretax equivalent for an investor paying taxes at a marginal rate T_t. Again, T_m is typically assumed to be zero. Thus, the quoted tax-equivalent yield on a municipal paying R_m from Equation 6.2 is

$$\text{Tax-equivalent yield} = \frac{R_m}{(1 - T_t)} \tag{6.3}$$

An individual subject to a 28 percent federal tax rate would subsequently be indifferent between a municipal that pays 7.5 percent interest and a taxable paying 10.42 percent. It is clear that investors can compare yields on a pretax basis by means of tax-equivalent yields or on an after-tax basis using Equation 6.1.[4]

6.04 SHORT-TERM MUNICIPAL SECURITIES

Most state and local governments are subject to constitutional restrictions that require balanced operating budgets. Thus, they are effectively prohibited from financing a deficit operating budget with long-term bonds. Many units subsequently use short-term securities to help fund temporary discrepancies in the timing of receipts and expenditures, with the expectation that the debt will be repaid once the receipts appear. Short-term municipals carry maturities ranging from one month to one year and are normally sold in $25,000 denominations. The volume of outstanding short-term securities has shown little growth, averaging from 4 percent to 9 percent of total municipals outstanding. Different types of instruments are described in the following paragraphs.

[1] Tax, Revenue, and Bond Anticipation Notes

Three types of tax-exempt notes dominate short-term municipals. Tax anticipation notes (TANs) are issued to fund normal operating expenditures before a state or local government receives tax collections. The issuing government pledges the expected taxes as the source of repayment. Revenue anticipation notes (RANs) similarly fund expenses with repayment pledged from expected nontax revenue sources, such as federal grant receipts or state financial aid to localities. Finally, bond anticipation notes (BANs) are issued to finance capital expenditures prior to the placement of long-

---

[3] Kidwell, Koch, and Stock (1984) document this effect and estimate the relative magnitudes of average interest savings by state for a sample of municipal bonds.

[4] Practically, tax-equivalent yields should also recognize that T_m does not equal zero. The relevant calculation of an effective tax-equivalent yield is thus $R_m(1 - T_m)/(1 - T_t)$. This yield equals 10.54 percent in the previous example if a 3 percent state tax rate applies to all income, including municipal interest.

term bonds with investors. Principal and interest on the short-term securities are paid from the proceeds once the bonds are issued. Consider the case where a municipality plans to build a water treatment plant but prevailing long-term bond rates are viewed as being too high. The municipality may issue BANs and use the proceeds to start construction. Once market conditions warrant issuing long-term bonds, the BANs will be redeemed. If this timetable exceeds one year, the BANs are normally rolled over or reissued at the maturity of the initial offering. Each of these notes is typically a general obligation of the issuer. They pay the full amount of interest at maturity and normally are noncallable by the issuer.

[2] Tax-Exempt Commercial Paper

States and localities with large borrowing requirements and frequent access to the money markets can issue municipal commercial paper. Like its private-sector counter-part, this short-term debt carries maturities between 30 and 270 days and represents unsecured, promissory notes of the borrower. The minimum denomination is now as low as $25,000, with most issues equal in volume to at least $1 million. Because the borrowers are well known and relatively active in the market, investors view the securities as exhibiting low default risk and a high degree of marketability. Interest rates on municipal commercial paper are thus often lower than rates on similar-maturity tax-exempt notes by as much as one percent.

[3] Variable-Rate and Floating-Rate Notes

States and localities occasionally issue variable-rate and floating-rate notes to finance a broad range of expenditures. The peculiar feature of these notes is that the interest rate varies periodically to reflect changes in current market conditions. Variable-rate demand notes that are repriced weekly are common, but repricing can occur once a month, once a quarter, or semiannually. Typically, the interest rate is tied to some base rate, such as the rate on three-month Treasury bills. Consider, for example, a variable-rate municipal note priced at 75 percent of the weekly three-month Treasury bill auction rate. If the bill rate is set at 8 percent, the variable-rate note will yield 6 percent. Each week the Treasury auctions new three-month bills, and interest on a weekly variable-rate note will change coincidentally with the auction rate. An increase in the bill rate to 8.63 percent would thus raise the note rate to 6.45 percent.

Floating-rate municipal notes are similarly priced off some taxable base rate. Here, however, the frequency of the base rate change may vary, so that repricing is not at systematic or predictable intervals. The process is the same in that interest on floating-rate notes changes whenever the relevant base rate changes. Floating-rate municipals are particularly attractive to investors because they pay up to one percent more than short-term municipal funds and may be puttable to the original issuer.

[4] Municipal Securities With Put Options

Many municipals carry a put feature, which allows the investor the option prior to final maturity to return the security to the issuer and demand payment of principal at par. Most variable-rate and floating-rate notes described earlier and some long-term bonds have this feature. When an investor puts a bond back to the issuer, the borrower normally has five days to make payment. In most cases, the borrower tries to sell the security to another investor through the original dealer and thus avoid refunding the debt.

Variable-rate and floating-rate notes carry put options that normally can be exercised at the same interval when the market interest rate is reset. Thus, these notes are puttable weekly, quarterly, or semiannually. Many longer-term bonds are puttable at intervals shorter than one year or annually. As such, they are short-term securities. Interest rates on long-term put bonds are reset at the exercise date for each put option and thus trade at prices comparable to those of municipal notes, even though final maturity may exceed one year.

6.05 LONG-TERM MUNICIPAL BONDS

State and local governments issue long-term municipal bonds to finance capital expenditures on projects where the benefits accrue for more than one year. Issues for public purposes range from the construction of schools, hospitals, highways, and utility plants to expenditures for equipment, police cars, and pollution control facilities. Issues for private-sector benefit similarly cover a broad range of purposes under the general label of IDBs.

[1] General Characteristics

Municipal bonds exhibit the same basic features as other long-term fixed-income securities, except that the issuer can be any state or local government or one of their political subdivisions. Each issue specifies a final maturity when the entire principal borrowed is repaid. Even though the final principal payment may be scheduled for 30 years after the original issue date, most municipals are offered as serial bonds, where a portion of the total principal matures each year. The size of each periodic interest payment is determined by a set coupon rate indicating the percentage of the bond's par value that is paid annually to bondholders. While this rate is stated as an annual percentage, most municipal bonds pay coupon interest semiannually equal to one half of the annual coupon rate. Finally, each underlying bond carries a market yield or price that is determined by prevailing market conditions. Bonds sold at par carry a price stated at 100 percent with the market rate of interest equal to the bond's coupon rate. A bond is sold at a discount when the quoted price is less than 100 percent of par, such that the effective market yield exceeds the bond's coupon rate. A premium bond, in contrast, is priced above 100 percent of par and carries a market yield below the associated coupon rate.

[2] Tombstone Advertisement

Figure 6-4 presents a typical tombstone advertisement for a new issue bond offering by the city of New York. Tombstone ads provide summary information regarding a bond's basic features. The top of the ad indicates that the municipal unit is issuing

FIGURE 6-4

Tombstone Notice of City of New York General Obligation Bonds

---

All of these Bonds having been sold, this announcement appears as a matter of record only:

In the opinion of Bond Counsel, interest on the Bonds will be exempt from personal income taxes imposed by the State of New York or any political subdivision thereof, including the City. Assuming continuing compliance with the provisions of the Internal Revenue Code of 1986, as amended, as described in the Official Statement, interest on the Bonds will not be includable in the gross income of the owners thereof for Federal income tax purposes. See "Section IX: Other Information—Tax Exemption" as described in the Official Statement for certain provisions of the Code that may affect the tax treatment of interest on the Bonds for certain Bondholders.

New Issue/December 3, 1991

$1,269,100,000

The City of New York

General Obligation Bonds, Fiscal 1992 Series B

The Bonds will be issued as registered bonds and registered in the name of Cede & Co., as nominee of The Depository Trust Company, New York, New York, which will act as securities depository for the Bonds. Purchasers will not receive certificates representing their ownership interest in the Bonds purchased. Interest will be payable semi-annually, beginning February 1, 1992 and on each August 1 and February 1 thereafter. The Bonds are subject to redemption prior to maturity as described in "Section II: The Bonds—Optional Redemption", in the Official Statement.

Amount	Due Feb. 1	Rate	Price or Yield	Amount	Due Feb. 1	Rate	Yield
$50,035,000	1992	4½ %	100%	$46,910,000	2007	7½%	7.80 %
52,440,000	1993	5.60	100	22,225,000	2008	7½	7.80
50,845,000	1994	6.20	100	22,225,000	2009	7½	7.80
48,510,000	1995	6.70	100	22,215,000	2010	7¾	7.875
48,500,000	1996	?	100	22,215,000	2011	7¾	7.875
51,090,000	1997	7.10	7.15	22,215,000	2012	7¾	7.875
53,070,000	1998	7.20	7.30	22,215,000	2013	7¾	7.875
60,080,000	1999	7.30	7.45	22,700,000	2014	7¾	7.875
72,745,000	2000	7.40	7.55	24,610,000	2015	7¾	7.875
68,100,000	2001	7½	7.60	22,250,000	2016	?	7.85
69,145,000	2002	7½	7.65	28,225,000	2017	?	7.85
72,025,000	2003	7½	7.70	29,985,000	2018	7	7.85
72,195,000	2004	7½	7.75	32,845,000	2019	7	7.85
57,235,000	2005	7½	7.80	33,310,000	2020	?	7.85
68,940,000	2006	7½	7.80				

(Plus accrued interest from December 3, 1991)

The Bonds are offered subject to prior sale, when, as and if issued by the City and accepted by the Underwriters, subject to the approval of the legality of the Bonds by Brown & Wood, New York, New York, and Barnes & Darby, New York, New York, Bond Counsel to the City, and subject to certain other conditions. Certain legal matters in connection with the preparation of the Official Statement will be passed upon for the City by Lord Day & Lord, Barrett Smith, New York, New York. Certain legal matters will be passed upon for the Underwriters by Rogers & Wells, New York, New York, and Wood, Williams, Rafalsky & Harris, New York, New York. It is expected that the Bonds will be available for delivery through the facilities of The Depository Trust Company in New York, New York, on or about December 3, 1991.

J.P. Morgan Securities Inc.

Bear, Stearns & Co. Inc.	**Dillon, Read & Co. Inc.**	**The First Boston Corporation**
Goldman, Sachs & Co.	**Lehman Brothers**	**Merrill Lynch & Co.**

BT Securities Corporation	Donaldson, Lufkin & Jenrette Securities Corporation	First Albany Corporation
Grigsby Brandford Powell Inc.	Manufacturers Hanover Securities Corporation	Morgan Stanley & Co. Incorporated
PaineWebber Incorporated	Prudential Securities Incorporated	Pryor, McClendon, Counts & Co., Inc.
Samuel A. Ramirez & Co., Inc.	Muriel Siebert & Co., Inc.	Smith Barney, Harris Upham & Co. Incorporated
Dean Witter Reynolds Inc.	Artemis Capital Group, Inc.	Chemical Securities, Inc.
First Chicago Capital Markets, Inc.	Kidder, Peabody & Co. Incorporated	WR Lazard, Laidlaw & Mead Incorporated
Lebenthal & Co., Inc.	Roosevelt & Cross Incorporated	Tucker Anthony Incorporated

$1.269 billion in new general obligation bonds. A statement appears above the principal amount that summarizes the expected income tax treatment of the issue.[5]

The middle section states that the bonds will be registered with interest payable semiannually each August 1 and February 1, starting in 1992. As the bonds are general obligation bonds, interest and principal payments are secured by the full faith, credit, and taxing authority of the city of New York. The data section summarizes the issue's financial characteristics. The bond has only serial principal components that mature on February 1 of successive years from 1992 to 2020. For example, $50.035 million in bonds matures on February 1, 1992, $52.44 million matures on February 1, 1993, and so forth. The final maturity date is just over 28 years from the date of issue.

The rate column indicates the fixed coupon rate on the underlying securities for each serial issue. In this instance, the coupon rate on the shortest-term issue is 4.5 percent. Coupon rates on subsequent issues increase systematically to 7.75 percent for bonds maturing in the years 2010–2015. The last five serial components carry a coupon rate of 7 percent. The price or yield column indicates whether the bond was offered at par (100 percent) or at a discount where the yield noted exceeds the coupon rate. Note that the first five serial components were sold at par, while the remainder were sold at a discount with the market yield increasing with maturity.

The bottom of the ad lists the primary underwriters that purchased the bonds from the city of New York and sold them to investors. These firms represent the members of an underwriting syndicate that won the right to place the bonds through a competitive bidding process. This bid process is described later and compared with direct placements.

[3] General Obligation Bonds

Municipal bonds are generally classified as either general obligation or revenue bonds, depending on how the issuer commits to raising funds to repay principal and interest. In fact, many municipals are of neither type in a pure sense but rather hybrids that incorporate features of each.

General obligation bonds typically finance essential public-purpose expenditures for education, roads, water treatment facilities, and other general community services. Principal and interest payments are secured by the issuer's full faith, credit, and taxing authority. Thus, a governmental unit pledges to raise taxes, if necessary, to meet debt service requirements. This is the strongest commitment a municipal borrower can make. The likelihood of default is thus typically low depending on the viability of the issuer's tax base and ability to increase tax collections.

General obligation bonds exhibit two characteristics that differentiate them from other municipals. First, voters within the issuer's jurisdiction generally must approve any new bond offering. This derives from the government's authority to raise taxes in support of the debt service as voters essentially ratify a possible tax increase. Second, there is no direct association between who uses the facility financed and who pays for it. School bonds represent a common example. Principal and interest payments are covered by property taxes, so that all property owners in the community finance the schools rather than just those families with children in school. Not surprisingly, voter

---

[5] The legal opinion also stated that interest would not be included as a tax preference item for federal income taxes and is thus not subject to the federal alternative minimum tax.

approval limits the volume of new issues because many individuals prefer not to pay more in taxes for many projects or purposes. The data in Figure 6-1 support this, showing that the growth in long-term public-purpose bonds fell well below that for private-purpose bonds after 1970. Many states have also placed ceilings on the total amount of outstanding general obligation debt at any point in time.

[a] Unlimited Tax Bonds. These bonds are the municipal equivalent of Treasury securities. Issuers commit to raise taxes, either by increasing marginal tax rates or expanding the tax base, to cover all debt service of the underlying bonds. Thus, unlimited tax bonds exhibit few defaults and pay relatively low rates compared with other municipals.

[b] Limited Tax Bonds. Whenever a government unit is restricted in terms of how much it can raise taxes to service debt, its securities are referred to as limited tax bonds. This often occurs when municipalities specify a maximum property tax rate in support of school expenses. If property values and local demographics deteriorate, the issue may go into default. These bonds subsequently involve more risk than unlimited tax general obligations.

[c] Double-Barreled Bonds. These bonds are secured by a government's taxing and credit authority in addition to specific revenues from a project. They are commonly associated with water treatment facilities. Here, the issuer collects user fees to cover operating expenses and make the mandatory debt service payments. Only if the fees are insufficient does the issuer raise taxes to cover the deficiency. This twofold security often makes these bonds lower-risk than other general obligations from an investor's perspective.

[4] Revenue Bonds

State and local governments issue revenue bonds to finance projects that produce specific revenues that are, in turn, used to make principal and interest payments. Hospital revenue bonds represent one example, where the bond proceeds finance the expansion of hospital facilities and equipment. Debt service is secured by anticipated user fees and related hospital revenues. Unlike general obligations, revenue bonds do not require voter approval and there are few restrictions regarding the amount of revenue debt that can be issued. Because each bond is backed by a specific revenue source, default risk varies with the strength and predictability of the underlying revenue stream. Some revenue bonds thus exhibit low risk, while others are extremely risky. Investors should carefully review a revenue bond prospectus, however, because it is often difficult to determine which entity and what revenues actually support debt service.

Revenue bonds are generally referred to by the source of revenues pledged against debt service. Public-purpose revenues can be classified as user fees (water, sewer, hospital, and electric fees), tolls (transportation charges), or special assessments (university and housing revenues). Private-purpose revenues typically consist of lease payments from private firms that use facilities leased from municipalities.

[a] User Fee Bonds. These revenue bonds are backed by specific revenues obtained from user charges levied against services obtained from the project financed with the bond proceeds. Gas and electric bonds compose the largest segment of this market, followed by hospital bonds and water and sewer bonds. Some hospital bonds have demonstrated considerable risk, because the underlying revenue streams became unpredictable owing to uncertainty over patient usage rates and changes in federal Medicaid and Medicare payments.

[b] Transportation Bonds. Many revenue bonds are associated with transportation facilities and are thus secured by tolls or related user charges. Bonds for the construction and maintenance of highways, bridges, and tunnels have long dominated this category of securities. However, municipalities have used these bonds to finance airports and loading docks secured by landing fees and dock charges.

[c] Special Obligation Bonds. These bonds are backed by specific revenues obtained by an issuer that are not directly linked to user charges. University revenue bonds, for example, are often issued to finance construction of dormitory facilities. Because student dormitory fees do not cover the full debt service, a university pledges tuition and other revenues as security. Housing revenue bonds are similarly issued to construct housing for the disadvantaged with the periodic mortgage payments pledged against obligated principal and interest payments. Frequently, the issuing government subsidizes the users, so that the mortgage payments must be supplemented with grant revenues to meet debt service requirements.

[d] Industrial Use Bonds. As the name suggests, these bonds are tax exempt but the proceeds are used by the private sector. One type of security, IDBs, is typically issued by a local government's economic development authority for the purchase or construction of a facility. This facility is then leased to a private firm so that the lease payments cover the debt service on the bonds. Thus, state and local governments essentially transfer their ability to borrow at subsidized rates to private firms. Another type consists of pollution control bonds, which are issued to finance the purchase of equipment to reduce or eliminate pollution produced by private firms.

Figure 6-1 shows the enormous growth in industrial use bonds from 1975 to 1985. During this time, the volume of these outstanding bonds increased from just $9.4 billion, or 4.2 percent of the total, to $208.3 billion, equal to 28 percent of the total. Viewed differently, from 1975 to 1985, industrial use bonds accounted for over 40 percent of all net long-term issues. While the bulk of these bonds went to finance small commercial enterprises, other uses included mass transit facilities, convention and sports centers, and rental housing. Because public funds should be used for public purposes, state and local governments justified the use of these bonds as a stimulant to local economic development by attracting and retaining businesses that employ local citizens and ultimately add to the tax base.

Tax experts, however, argued that IDBs abused the tax system because private firms obtained the benefits of the state and local government tax exemption. The federal government was thus subsidizing selected firms in the private sector. Bond experts further argued that the increased volume of IDBs drove tax-exempt rates higher, which penalized state and local government borrowers pursuing legitimate public purposes. Because of these perceived abuses, Congress eliminated the use of IDBs for many purposes in TRA 1986 and placed state-by-state caps on other private-sector uses.[6] These changes reduced the volume of industrial use bonds such that the outstanding volume declined after 1986. (See Figure 6-1.)

[e] Moral Obligation Bonds. Moral obligation bonds are revenue bonds that carry an additional guarantee by a state or municipality to meet debt service requirements if the original anticipated revenues are not forthcoming. Typically, the issuing government authority establishes a debt reserve fund as secondary collateral supporting the bond offering. Proceeds from the debt reserve fund are used only when the issuer's normal revenues are insufficient to make obligated principal and interest payments. In this instance, the appropriate governmental unit is morally obligated to replenish the reserve fund or make the actual debt service payments. The obligation, however, is not legally binding, so bond investors must rely on the good faith of the issuer. Moral obligation bonds were first issued in 1960 by the New York State Housing Finance Agency. Not surprisingly, they pay rates above those on otherwise comparable general obligation bonds.

[f] Zero-Coupon and Stripped Municipals. Since the early 1980s, brokers have offered zero-coupon municipal bonds, associated primarily with housing authorities, to investors. Maturities normally range from 10 to 30 years. Zero-coupon bonds pay no coupon interest but instead are sold at steep discounts from par. An investor earns income because the bonds appreciate in value over time and pay the full par value at maturity. This price appreciation represents tax-exempt interest. For example, a $5,000 par value zero-coupon bond maturing in 20 years is priced at $710 to yield 10 percent compounded semiannually. A buyer invests little up-front cash, knows the exact appreciation rate at all intervals, and knows the value of the bond at maturity. The fact that there is no reinvestment risk makes zero-coupon bonds extremely attractive to individuals who are saving for long-term purposes, such as a child's education or retirement.

However, municipal zero-coupon bonds possess several disadvantages. First, they are more volatile in price than coupon-bearing securities with the same maturity. Thus, if rates rise, prices on zero-coupon bonds fall more than prices on coupon-bearing municipals. Similarly, if rates fall, zero-coupon bonds appreciate more. Second, most zero-coupon bonds are callable, and the relative penalty to the investor from having a zero-coupon bond called is greater than that for having a coupon security called. This results because price appreciation on a zero-coupon bond is greatest in the last years of the instrument. If interest rates decline and a zero-coupon bond is called early, an investor receives little appreciation. Finally, even though municipal interest is exempt from federal income taxes, an investor has to pay applicable state and local taxes annually on the price appreciation, even though no cash is actually received, until final maturity. To compensate for these costs and risks, municipal zero-coupon bonds typically carry yields approximately 50 basis points above yields on otherwise comparable coupon-bearing municipals.

TRA 1986 further authorized the technique of stripping municipal securities into components and selling each part as a zero-coupon security. Like stripped Treasuries, stripped municipals separate coupon payments on a bond from the principal payments. Each single payment or stream of payments is then sold as a separate security. Stripped

---

[6] The section on TRA 1986 describes specific features of the act and subsequent market impacts.

municipals are equivalent to zero-coupon bonds, except that they carry maturities that are much shorter. By stripping coupons, a dealer can sell municipal zero-coupon bonds with maturities ranging from 1 year to 10 years, maturities that were previously nonexistent.

[5] Mini-Munis

Historically, municipal securities have been sold in denominations of $25,000 or more. Individual investors with limited resources thus found it difficult to buy individual securities and still adequately diversify their portfolios. In 1979, the state of Massachusetts sold $1 million in municipals in denominations as low as $100. Such instruments naturally appealed to individuals rather than corporate investors. With the growth in individual investor interest in municipals, many states and localities are offering "mini-munis" to attract additional funds. These securities are zero-coupon bonds that typically pay $5,000 at maturity. With maturities ranging from 5 to 25 years, they are sold at a deep discount and can be purchased for relatively small amounts. The attraction for issuers is that small-denomination offerings may bring new funds to the market that otherwise would go elsewhere.

As small-denomination discount instruments, mini-munis carry considerable risk. While they pay attractive interest rates, investors have a difficult time selling them prior to maturity because the market is so thin. In addition, because the coupon rate is fixed through maturity, the bonds swing widely in price when market interest rates change. Thus, mini-munis are extremely price-volatile. They appeal mostly to investors who can hold these instruments to maturity.

6.06 TAX REFORM ACT OF 1986 AND MUNICIPAL SECURITIES

TRA 1986 dramatically altered the structure of the municipal securities market. On the supply side, Congress determined that the growth in private-purpose bonds was out of control and cost too much in lost tax revenues. Borrowers were also perceived to be taking unwarranted advantage of arbitrage opportunities by advance-refunding outstanding debt and investing the proceeds in higher-yielding assets. TRA 1986 subsequently restricted tax-exempt issues of certain types of municipal securities. On the demand side, TRA 1986 lowered marginal tax rates for both corporate and individual investors and modified the alternative minimum tax (AMT). Most important, TRA 1986 eliminated commercial banks' ability to deduct interest expense on liabilities used to finance the purchase of most new municipals. Only small-issue, public-purpose municipals were exempted. This change makes most municipals unattractive to banks as investors. Banks that once dominated the group of investors in municipals will generally withdraw from the market.

[1] Supply Effects

[a] Classes of Municipal Securities. One clear intent of TRA 1986 was to limit private-purpose tax-exempt securities and thus the federal subsidy of private-sector borrowing costs. This was accomplished by creating four categories of municipal secu-

rities, each subject to different restrictions. The term "private activity bonds" was used to designate issues for nonessential public purposes.[7]

Governmental-purpose bonds. Traditionally, public-purpose municipals were classified as "governmental-purpose" bonds. This category includes both general obligation and revenue bonds where the proceeds are used to finance essential public needs. As a test, issuers must use at least 90 percent of the proceeds for governmental or public-purpose expenditures. In the case of output contracts, such as with investor-owned utilities, the nongovernmental portion of outlays cannot exceed $15 million. Interest on these bonds continues to be tax exempt, and issuers have no restrictions on how much they can borrow in this form.

Capped private activity bonds. In lieu of IDBs, TRA 1986 created a category of tax-exempt private activity bonds. Interest on these bonds continues to be tax exempt as long as gross issues within each state do not exceed a volume cap. For 1988 and thereafter, each state's volume cap is set at the higher of $50 per capita or $150 million. Securities subject to the cap include mortgage revenue bonds, multifamily housing bonds, student loan bonds, and small-issue IDBs.[8] Issues lose their exemption if the volume cap is violated.

Uncapped private activity bonds. A select group of private activity bonds remains tax exempt without any volume caps on issues. The list includes bonds issued for veterans' mortgages, not-for-profit groups such as universities and hospitals, and expenditures for airports, docks, and solid waste facilities.

Taxable private activity bonds. All other private-purpose bonds that formerly qualified for tax exemption are now labeled as taxable bonds. Issuers have lost the interest subsidy from the exemption and must pay higher taxable rates. General-purpose bonds that are most affected include nonmanufacturing bonds, small issue IDBs, industrial pollution control bonds, and bonds for local community sports and convention centers. Figure 6-5 summarizes the range of prospects potentially financed by taxable municipal bonds.

[b] Arbitrage and Advance Refunding. Many municipal borrowers took advantage of yield differences by advance-refunding outstanding debt but using the new issue proceeds to purchase higher-yielding assets rather than pay off the old debt. The net arbitrage profit added to operating revenues and made it worthwhile to allow the debt to remain outstanding for several years. TRA 1986 limited the number of times each issuer could refinance outstanding debt and restricted the size of arbitrage earnings.

[2] Demand Effects

[a] General Provisions. TRA 1986 contained several general provisions that reduced the overall demand for municipals at prevailing rates. First, it lowered individual marginal income tax rates to a maximum 33 percent and corporate rates to a maximum

---

[7] This discussion draws heavily from Peterson (1987).

[8] To meet the small-issue requirement, a borrower has the choice of a limit where the total amount of new and outstanding IDBs associated with the project and user cannot exceed $1 million or a limit of $10 million on capital outlays by the primary user over a six-year period around the issue date.

FIGURE 6-5

Candidate Securities and Transactions for Taxable Bonds

Source: J. E. Peterson, "Examining the Impacts of the 1986 Tax Reform Act on the Municipal Securities Market," *National Tax Journal*, Vol. XL (Sept. 1987), pp. 403–418

- Projects that fail to meet tighter new standards defining governmental-purpose bonds: Private organizations now may use no more than 10 percent of tax-exempt bond proceeds either directly or indirectly or where private-purpose loans exceed 5 percent of proceeds.
- Projects for which issuers lack sufficient debt capacity under the state per capita debt allocation for private activity financing: The new tax law increases the types of projects that must share in the allocation of lower ceilings.
- Private universities and other Internal Revenue Code Section 501(c)(3) organizations that face limits of $150 million on nonhospital tax-exempt bonds that may be outstanding at any time.
- Public power and resource recovery issuers that face tighter limits on the output contracts they may have with nonexempt entities such as investor-owned utilities.
- Facilities specifically ineligible for tax-exempt financing including facilities for sports, conventions, trade shows, parking, industrial parks, and enterprise development.
- Economic development projects, particularly for urban redevelopment, industrial parks, and enterprise development.
- Multifamily housing programs that fail to meet stricter tests for low-income eligibility.
- Cash flow borrowings (tax anticipation) that do not meet tighter arbitrage standards on the amount and period for seasonal financing.
- Advance refundings for single-family housing bonds and IDBs that are blocked from using tax-exempt securities: The recent drop in long-term rates in the taxable market makes more taxable refundings of tax-exempt debt become economically viable.
- Certain projects financed with private activity bonds that cannot finance all issuance costs under the 2-percent-of-proceeds limitation.
- Obligations backed, directly or indirectly, by federal government guarantee.
- Manufacturing (and farming) small-issue IDBs, which lost tax exemption in 1990.
- Single-family mortgage revenue bonds, which lost tax exemption in 1989.

34 percent. In general, municipal rates will have to increase relative to taxable rates for the same investors to find municipals attractive. Second, TRA 1986 reduced the attractiveness of municipals to banks by eliminating the deductibility of bank carrying costs for the purchase of "nonqualified" municipals. The lost deduction lowers after-tax municipal yields below yields on taxables so that banks will no longer invest in these securities. Third, TRA 1986 provided that property-casualty insurance companies would pay a tax on a fraction of their municipal interest earned. While after-tax municipal yields are still attractive to these firms, the size of the yield advantage is reduced.

It appears that Congress will raise the marginal tax rates during the Clinton administration. The current proposal recommends raising the top rates to 36 percent and 39.6 percent from the current 31 percent maximum. The recognition that tax rates will soon rise served to drive municipal yields lower relative to taxable yields as investors bought municipals in an attempt to shelter income even before Congress formally raises the rates.

[b] AMT. TRA 1986 further extended the reach of the AMT, which has altered relative yields on tax-exempt securities. Both the individual and the corporate AMT

FIGURE 6-6

Summary of Tax Rates on Income From Municipal Securities Under Various Provisions of TRA 1986

Source: J.E. Peterson, "Examining the Impacts of the 1986 Tax Reform Act on the Municipal Securities Market, *National Tax Journal,* Vol. XL (Sept. 1987), pp. 403–418

Investor Group and Type of Tax	Class of Municipal Security	
	Governmental[a]	Private Sector[b]
Individuals		
Regular income[c]	0	0
AMT	0	21.0%
Corporations		
Regular income	0	0
AMT		
Preference income	0	20.0
Excess book income[d]	10.0%	10.0
Property and Casualty Companies		
Regular income	5.1	5.1
AMT		
Preference income	11.5	20.0
Excess book income[e]	11.5	20.0

[a] Governmental and IRC Section 501(c)(3).

[b] Not included are private activity bonds that are fully taxable.

[c] Not including tax on Social Security income prorated to tax-exempt income.

[d] Not including the 0.12 percent Superfund tax on excess book income exceeding $2 million.

[e] Bonds acquired before August 8, 1986 are taxed at 10 percent under the excess book income.

apply only when they create a larger tax liability for the taxpayer than does the regular income tax. For individuals, interest earned on all nonessential bonds (private activity bonds) issued after August 7, 1986, is designated a preference item and is subject to the 21 percent AMT rate. For corporations other than property-casualty insurers, an AMT rate of 20 percent applies to preference items, which are the same as those for individuals. In addition, 50 percent of "book income" is included as a preference item, where book income includes interest earned on essential government all-purpose bonds. The applicable tax rates, summarized in Figure 6-6, are higher but are applied similarly for property-casualty insurers. Again, current proposals under the Clinton plan, if passed, would raise the AMT higher than the figures noted here.

6.07 DEMAND FOR MUNICIPALS BY INVESTORS

The exemption of interest income from the federal income tax effectively restricts the demand for municipal securities to investors that pay the highest marginal tax rates.

FIGURE 6-7

Major Investors in State and Local Government Debt: Holdings as a Percentage of Total Municipals Outstanding

Source: *Flow of Funds Accounts, Year-End Outstandings,* Board of Governors of the Federal Reserve System (Washington, D.C.: 1992)

Year	Total Debt	Commercial Banks	Property-Casualty Insurance Companies	Individuals Directly	Money Market and Mutual Funds	Other
1960	$ 70.8	25.0%	11.4%	43.5%	—	20.1%
1965	100.3	38.7	11.3	36.3	—	13.7
1970	144.4	48.6	11.8	31.9	—	7.7
1975	223.8	46.0	14.9	30.4	—	8.7
1980	365.4	40.7	22.0	28.0	1.7%	7.6
1985	743.0	31.1	11.9	40.8	9.4	6.7
1990	1055.6	11.1	13.0	52.8	18.3	4.8
1991	1101.4	9.4	12.6	52.6	20.6	4.8
1992[a]	1126.1	8.8	12.5	51.3	22.6	4.8

Note: Dollars in billions.

[a] Through June 1992.

Such investors are willing to accept lower pretax yields on municipals because they earn higher after-tax returns. Historically, three investor groups, namely, banks, property-casualty insurance companies, and individuals, purchased virtually all of the municipal securities offered. Commercial banks and property insurers were the only financial firms that paid taxes at high enough marginal rates to make municipals attractive. Others, such as life insurance companies and savings and loans, were subject to low effective tax rates because they had better tax-sheltered investment alternatives. They subsequently found tax-exempts unattractive or, like pension funds, were exempt from taxation. Individuals pay taxes across a broad range of tax rates, with those in the highest marginal brackets acquiring most of the tax-exempts within this group.

Figure 6-7 presents a percentage breakdown of investors' municipal holdings for selected years listed in Figure 6-1. Individuals' holdings are divided into direct purchases of bonds and securities held indirectly as money market and mutual fund shares. As indicated, the relative importance of each investor group changed dramatically in the 1980s from prior years. Through 1980, commercial banks were the dominant investor group, owning almost 49 percent of tax-exempts in 1970 (over 50 percent in 1972) and well over 40 percent throughout the 1970s. By 1985, however, bank holdings had dropped to 31 percent, with the percentage falling rapidly in later periods. Property insurers' holdings have, in contrast, been relatively stable, from 11 percent to 15 percent of outstandings. Around 1980, when underwriting profits were large, they did invest considerably more in tax-exempts. Finally, individuals, who were second to banks before 1980, now dominate the market. At the end of 1985, they directly owned 41 percent of all municipals and another 9 percent indirectly. Their holdings increased to a combined 74 percent at mid-year 1992.

[1] Commercial Banks

Banks that paid federal income taxes historically found that tax-exempts provided greater after-tax yields than all alternative fixed-income securities. At prevailing interest rates, banks paying taxes at the full corporate tax rate always found that municipals yielded more than Treasuries, agency securities, and mortgage-backed securities. Aggressive banks would subsequently structure their portfolios where income from loans and taxable securities covered deductible expenses net of noninterest income. Tax-exempt interest and other tax-sheltered income then comprised the bulk of reported net income.

During the late 1970s, banks started to withdraw from the municipal market. TRA 1986 accelerated the process by making most municipals unattractive investments to banks. The initial decline in bank investments in the late 1970s was caused by large banks' use of alternative tax-sheltered investments and a general decline in bank profitability. With fewer profits to shield and an increase in tax sheltering by means of foreign tax credits, investment tax credits, and accelerated depreciation from leasing operations, banks purchased fewer municipals. TRA 1986, in contrast, directly targeted bank municipal investments as an abused tax shelter and subsequently changed the tax laws so that after-tax yields on most municipals dropped below after-tax taxable yields.

[2] Qualified Versus Nonqualified Securities

For many years, banks were the only taxpayers that could borrow, invest the proceeds in municipals, and still deduct their entire interest expense. Individuals and others whom the Internal Revenue Service (IRS) determined had tried this were not allowed to deduct any of their borrowing costs from income. Not surprisingly, some banks used this opportunity to arbitrage by issuing certificates of deposit (CDs) and using the proceeds to buy tax-exempts. In 1983, Congress revised the tax laws to deny banks a deduction for 20 percent of their total interest expense associated with financing new municipal purchases. This reduced the yield advantage for municipals over taxables, but municipals still yielded more after taxes.

TRA 1986 went the next step by creating two types of municipals as viewed from a bank's investment perspective. One type, qualified municipals, retains the 80 percent deductibility of carrying costs for new purchases. TRA 1986 increased the lost deduction for the other type, nonqualified municipals, to 100 percent of associated carrying costs for new municipal purchases. All bonds acquired on or before August 7, 1986 were grandfathered in, as the tax changes applied only to new municipal purchases. Banks that buy nonqualified securities after this date can thus deduct none of their associated interest expense. The lost deduction effectively represents a tax on municipal interest, so that the after-tax yield on nonqualified municipals is well below that on similar taxable securities.[9] Thus, banks should not invest in nonqualified municipals.

In order for a municipal security to be classified as a qualified bond, a local government unit cannot issue more than $10 million in bonds per year and the proceeds must be used for essential public purposes. The issuer obtains a legal opinion that the offering meets the small-issue, public-purpose criteria. The bond contract also contains a provi-

---

[9] Chapter 17 of *Bank Management* by Timothy Koch describes the mechanics of the tax computation and provides examples for a hypothetical bank.

sion that stipulates that the effective coupon rate will be increased retroactively if a qualified bond is ultimately deemed to be nonqualified. State debt offerings are automatically classified as nonqualified bonds.

While the 80 percent deductibility of carrying costs lowers after-tax yields on qualified municipals, it still ensures a relative yield advantage over similar maturity taxables. Banks purchase only qualified issues, and this concentrated demand activity, in turn, lowers pretax yields on qualified securities below those on similar nonqualified securities. Estimates of this yield difference range from 25 basis points to 55 basis points depending on bond maturity and credit rating. Thus, banks should be the only investors in qualified municipals. Other investors can earn high risk-adjusted yields on nonqualified securities.

[3] Property-Casualty Insurance Companies

At the end of 1991, property insurers held almost $140 billion in municipals, or 12.6 percent of total outstandings. This ranked them behind individuals, banks, and mutual funds. Like banks, property insurers pay taxes at the full corporate rate on most of their earnings. Tax-exempt rates have therefore always exceeded after-tax rates on taxable bonds for fully taxed firms. Property insurers thus determine how many municipals they want to purchase by estimating expected profits and sheltering as much income as possible from taxes. The magnitude of their municipal purchases, in turn, closely tracks the cyclical nature of insurance underwriting, rising when profits are expected to be high and falling when profits are expected to be low.

Property insurers use tax-exempt securities and equities to shelter income. Even though they can deduct 80 percent of stock dividends from taxable income, property insurers have a bias for municipals. This derives from state insurance regulations that link the amount of insurance a firm can write to its statutory surplus. When calculating statutory surplus, most states value bonds at cost and stocks at market values. Changes in stock prices thus change surplus, while changes in bond prices do not. In particular, a decline in bond values due to a rate increase does not lower the amount of business a firm can write.

TRA 1986 altered property insurance companies' tax positions, but not as dramatically as that of banks. Two provisions directly reduced the value of tax-exempt interest. First, property insurers must include 15 percent of tax-exempt interest (and excluded dividends) in taxable income when computing their regular income tax. This feature, labeled proration, effectively provides for the taxation of a small fraction of previously tax-exempt interest. Second, the expanded AMT adds tax preference items to taxable income and applies a flat 20 percent tax rate. Tax-exempt interest (and excluded stock dividends) are included as preference income and also taxed through "excess book income" provisions. Figure 6-6 demonstrates that private- and public-purpose tax-exempts are treated differently.[10]

The tax provisions lowered but did not eliminate the yield advantage of municipals relative to taxable bonds. Thus, property insurers still prefer municipal securities and should remain substantial investors. They generally prefer long-term securities because of the higher yields on long-term municipals relative to short-term municipals and, historically, they have purchased large amounts of revenue bonds. Recent estimates

---

[10] See Peterson (1987).

from *Best's Aggregates and Averages* suggest that over 65 percent of property insurers' tax-exempt bond holdings mature beyond 10 years. Similar estimates indicate that they own over 50 percent of all outstanding revenue bonds.

[4] Individuals: Direct Investment

Since 1980, individual investors have dominated the municipal market. By the end of 1991, individuals directly owned almost 53 percent of all outstanding municipals and indirectly owned another 21 percent via money market and longer-term mutual funds. From 1985 through 1991, when banks liquidated $128 billion in municipals (net of new purchases), individuals directly purchased $276 billion, while fund holdings increased by over $157 billion. Given that total municipals outstanding rose by only $358 billion over this period, individuals purchased 121 percent of net new issues.

Historically, individuals' demand for municipals has been quite volatile. When banks and property insurers purchased large amounts, individuals' purchases were small, and vice versa. The underlying reason related to how various investors reacted to municipal rate changes. Because banks and property insurers paid taxes at the full corporate rate, municipals always yielded more after taxes than comparable taxable securities. Small changes in rates did not induce additional purchases. Individuals, in contrast, paid taxes at rates ranging from 14 percent to 50 percent and as a group have always been quite sensitive to interest rate changes. Whenever state and local governments needed to borrow, they could induce additional purchases from individuals by raising municipal rates relative to taxable rates. Higher relative rates appealed to investors in lower marginal tax brackets, who previously found municipals unattractive. Thus, movements in the rate ratios in Figure 6-3 varied directly with individuals' municipal purchases as a fraction of total net issues.

The general withdrawal of banks as major investors in municipals thus changes the structure of the municipal market and municipal yields. Because states and municipalities must now rely more on individual investors, who represent the marginal investor in municipals, they pay yields that are closer to comparable taxable yields (the municipal to taxable rate ratio equals one minus the indifference tax rate) and have less certainty regarding what the prevailing municipal yield will be at the time of issue. This is revealed in Figure 6-3 as the rate ratios converged after 1986 because of an increase in the short-term rate ratio. Now, individuals represent the marginal investor at all maturities.

[5] Money Market and Mutual Funds

As indicated in Figure 6-1, individuals' holdings of municipals through money market and mutual funds rose sharply after 1980. By 1991, they accounted for 20.6 percent of all municipal investments, only slightly below the holdings of banks. While both types of funds represent a means for individuals with limited resources to invest in municipals and obtain the benefits of diversification, the underlying return and risk characteristics differ significantly.

[6] Tax-Exempt Money Market Funds

Individuals who purchase any money market or mutual fund shares essentially own a claim on the interest and principal payments of securities purchased by fund managers.

Money market fund managers invest the proceeds from individuals in a variety of the short-term tax-exempt securities discussed earlier, including TANs, BANs, variable-rate notes, and bonds with short-term put options. They collect the contracted interest and principal, which they then pass through to shareholders less a servicing fee. Typically, the shares are categorized as units that maintain a fixed value of $1. Each security is valued at its amortized cost under the assumption that interest accrues continuously until maturity. Thus, changes in a security's market value between the time an investor purchases and sells units are ignored, and there is no subsequent price risk where an investor will receive less than the initial investment. Interest is allocated to shareholders as additional units.

Investors can often acquire units with an initial investment as low as $1,000. Most money market funds offer shareholders check-writing privileges against their outstanding balance. Clearly, this type of fund represents a vehicle for high-tax-bracket individuals to temporarily park funds in a highly liquid form until the proceeds are needed elsewhere. Because of the low default risk associated with short-term municipals and the persistent upward slope in the municipal yield curve, quoted yields on tax-exempt money market funds are below those on long-term bonds and bond funds.

[7] Tax-Exempt Bond Funds

Bond funds are structured similarly to money market funds except that fund managers use the proceeds to buy long-term municipal bonds. Investors have a choice between two types of long-term mutual bond funds: open-end funds and unit investments trusts (UITs). As the name suggests, an open-end fund allows new investors to purchase shares at any time and allows existing shareholders to add to their investment or liquidate shares at any time. Thus, open-end fund managers are constantly buying and selling securities to invest new receipts, meet redemption requests, and generally maximize returns on the entire portfolio. These funds typically charge low fees. Interest payments on bonds held by the fund are passed through to shareholders, but there is no distribution of principal. These funds thus have an unlimited life.

A UIT, in contrast, is a type of closed-end bond fund that sells shares to investors at origination and invests the proceeds in municipal bonds. Initial sales charges are quite large, ranging from 5 percent to 9 percent. After origination, the fund manager does not purchase any additional bonds and may sell bonds only under duress, such as when some of the bonds are expected to default or shareholders in the fund try to redeem their shares and no new investors can be found. Owning shares in a UIT is similar to owning a bond directly. Interest on the underlying bond portfolio is paid periodically and principal is returned when bonds either are called, are sold, or simply mature. Once the final principal payment is made, the trust no longer exists.

Investors in both types of bond funds are subject to price risk. With a UIT, an investor purchases a fixed number of units, initially valued at $100 or $1,000 per value of the underlying securities. With an open-end fund, an investor receives units at the prevailing share price equal to the principal value of the portfolio adjusted for the number of shares outstanding. Whenever the level of interest rates rises, the value of the units or shares declines just as it does with a bond. Whenever the level of rates falls, the units and shares increase in value. An investor's net return thus varies with interest earned and the associated price appreciation or depreciation between the time of purchase and sale of the underlying units.

Bond funds are attractive because they provide diversification benefits for relatively

FIGURE 6-8

Municipal Bond Credit Ratings

Explanation	Moody's	S&P	Default Risk Premium
Best quality; smallest degree of risk	Aaa	AAA	Lowest
High quality; slightly more long-term risk than top rating	Aa1	AA+	
	Aa2	AA	
	Aa3	AA−	
Upper medium grade; possible impairment in the future	A1	A+	
	A2	A	
	A3	A−	
Medium grade; lack outstanding investment characteristics	Baa1	BBB+	
	Baa2	BBB	
	Baa3	BBB−	
Speculative issues; protection may be very moderate	Ba1	BB+	
	Ba2	BB	
	Ba3	BB−	
Very speculative; may have small assurance of interest and principal payments	B1	B+	
	B2	B	
	B3	B−	
Issues in poor standing; may be in default	Caa	CCC	
Speculative in a high degree; with marked shortcomings	Ca	CC	
Lowest quality; poor prospects of attaining real investment standing	C	C	
		D	Highest

small dollar investments. Investors can similarly select a fund that appeals to their specific situation. For example, distinct bond funds exist that specialize in (1) insured bonds; (2) bonds issued only within a certain state and thus exempt from state income taxes; (3) bonds with well-defined maturities, such as intermediate-term funds (average maturities of from 3 to 9 years) and long-term funds (average maturities of 20 to 30 years); and (4) junk bond funds. Thus, investors can buy shares that reflect ownership in securities that are quite comparable to individual bonds and compatible with individual investment objectives. Of course, relative yields and price risk differ across all types of funds.

6.08 MUNICIPAL MARKET CHARACTERISTICS

[1] Bond Ratings and Default Risk[11]

Investors typically do not formulate the probability of default themselves but use credit ratings and written reports provided by ratings services or investment bankers. A borrower defaults anytime it fails on the promise to pay coupon interest and/or principal

---

[11] Portions of this section were coauthored with David Kidwell and originally appeared in the first edition of the *Handbook of Modern Finance* (1985).

FIGURE 6-9

Municipal Note and Commercial Paper Credit Ratings

Explanation	Moody's		S&P	
	Note	Commercial Paper	Note	Commercial Paper
Highest degree of safety	MIG 1	P-1[a]	SP-1	A-1 +
Very strong degree of safety	MIG 2	P-1[a]	SP-2	A-1
Strong degree of safety	MIG 3	P-2	SP-3	A-2
Satisfactory degree of safety	MIG 4	P-3		A-3

[a] Moody's assigns a single credit rating to securities in the top two categories.

at the agreed-on time. The degree of default risk inherent in a security can be measured as the difference between the rate paid on a risky security less the rate on a default-free security, with all other factors being held constant. That difference is called the default risk premium, and it varies systematically over the business cycle. Default risk premiums widen during periods of economic decline and narrow during periods of economic expansion.

[a] Credit Rating Agencies. The two major credit rating agencies are Moody's Investor Service and Standard & Poor's (S&P). Both rank securities in order of the perceived probability of default and publish ratings as letter grades. The rating scheme they use for municipal bonds is shown in Figure 6-8. The highest-credit-quality bonds, those with the lowest default risk, are rated triple-A. As the perceived default risk of a bond increases, the bond rating declines, and the lower a bond's credit rating, the higher the yield it carries.

Bonds rated in the top four rating categories, Aaa to Baa for Moody's and AAA to BBB for S&P, are called investment-grade bonds. State and federal laws frequently require commercial banks, insurance companies, pension funds, and other financial institutions to purchase securities rated as investment-grade quality. Moody's may also assign a bond the abbreviation "Con." (for "conditional") which means that the credit rating is conditional on (1) completion of a project; (2) demonstrated earnings for projects with little operating experience; (3) rental income beginning once the project is completed; or (4) some other limiting factor. Likewise, S&P uses the letter "P" to indicate a provisional rating that is intended to be removed after completion of a project or at the start of earning income.

Moody's and S&P also rate short-term municipal paper; Moody's rates municipal notes and commercial paper and S&P rates only commercial paper. Figure 6-9 shows the rating schemes used by the two agencies. As with bond ratings, the higher the quality rating, the lower the security's default risk and the lower the yield on the security. All of the rating categories shown in Figure 6-9 are considered to be of investment-grade quality by both Moody's and S&P, and the agencies also produce written reports for investors on the issues that they rate.

The rating agencies consider a number of factors when assigning a bond a credit rating. For general obligation bonds, among the most important areas are (1) the issuer's debt structure, so that the overall debt burden can be determined; (2) the issuer's ability and discipline in maintaining a balanced budget; (3) the quality and viability of the issuer's tax base; and (4) the issuer's overall socioeconomic environment—population growth, employment distribution, diversification of industry, real estate property valuation, and trends for future growth. For revenue bonds, many of the same factors are considered, but more emphasis is placed on the quality and stability of the project's expected cash flow and the quality of the project's management. Once a bond rating is assigned to a particular issue, the rating is periodically reviewed by the rating agency and is subject to change. A lower rating increases the future borrowing cost of the issuer and may limit the issuer's access to money and capital markets. Finally, there is evidence that bond rating agencies do a reasonable job of classifying bonds according to their probability of default. Empirical studies report a high correlation between credit ratings assigned by agencies and actual default experience.

[b] Credit Quality Problems. Until the 1970s, state and local government securities experienced few defaults. No major defaults had occurred since the Great Depression of the 1930s. However, the 1970s and early 1980s were periods marked by high inflation and economic instability. As a result of these turbulent economic times, many municipalities, especially large cities, suffered serious financial difficulties, which caused investors to reassess the credit standings of municipal securities in general.

The most dramatic of these financial difficulties was the default of New York City on its debt obligations in the summer of 1975. The default, the largest in the nation's history, brought to light the legal and political difficulties involved in a large-scale municipal default. In the wake of New York City's default, other large northeastern cities (e.g., Boston, Buffalo, Cleveland, Detroit, Philadelphia, and Newark) suffered degrees of financial difficulty and found their credit costs soaring. Most noteworthy of the previously mentioned cities is Cleveland, which defaulted in December 1978. The most widely publicized default is that of the Washington Public Power Supply System, which in 1983 defaulted on $2.25 billion worth of bonds used to finance two nuclear power plants. Interestingly, in 1981 these bonds carried credit ratings of A1 (Moody's) and A+ (S&P).

The decade of the 1980s was not good for many municipalities that pursued aggressive spending programs by borrowing heavily to finance the outlays. With the recession of the early 1990s, receipts were not forthcoming and the municipal securities went into default. One of the most notorious responses was that of Bridgeport, the most populous city in Connecticut, which declared chapter 9 bankruptcy. Not surprisingly, yields on the city's $207 million in outstanding bonds jumped as bondholders tried to liquidate. In Bridgeport's case, the city was trying to get court help in revising labor contracts that were deemed burdensome and was able to meet interest and principal payments on its debt.

Municipalities and municipal bonds were also involved in the failure of Executive Life, a large California insurance company. Many different municipalities created public finance authorities, which borrowed large sums, presumably to finance useful capital projects such as low-income housing or to subsidize loans to farmers. Instead of spending the bond proceeds on the projects, the borrowers purchased guaranteed investment contracts (GICs) offered by Executive Life. Often, the objective of the municipality was to earn the positive carry on the funds, the difference between the yield on the GIC and the lower tax-exempt interest rate on the municipal bond, rather than to invest in the announced project. California regulators closed Executive Life in April 1991, sharply lowering the value of the GICs. Investors in municipal bonds whose proceeds were used to buy Executive Life GICs in turn suffered as the municipalities defaulted.

[2] Disclosure

It is often difficult to assess the probability of default with municipals because borrowers provide limited financial information in support of a debt offering. Unlike corporate bonds, which are subject to federal registration requirements, municipal disclosure requirements are set by each state, where applicable. A 1988 survey conducted by the National Association of State Auditors, Controllers, and Treasurers reported that 14 states required the filing of some form of official statement summarizing relevant financial and demographic information before an issuer could take an offering to market. An additional 22 states required such information for a select group of borrowers only, and the remaining 14 states did not require any disclosure.

Without disclosure, borrowers must either generate the information themselves, obtain it from an alternative source, or go without it. Recent concerns over the lack of disclosure have produced two important responses. First, the Securities and Exchange Commission approved a plan that has municipal borrowers place key financial, demographic, and economic data in an electronic data base. This information is then sold to any interested party. Second, a variety of municipal bond brokers now provide such information to the public. For example, Kenny S&P Information services and Bloomberg Financial Markets provide background data on most municipal primary security offerings. In addition, the Public Securities Association, a municipal trade group, provides research reports with relevant data and issue features. This is a first step toward reducing the search costs in assessing municipal default risk. If successful, it should improve liquidity in the municipal market and thereby lower risk premiums inherent in municipal interest rates.

[3] Underwriting Process

States and municipalities have a choice in the new-issue (primary) market as to whether they offer their securities for competitive sale or enter into a negotiated sale, with the lowest-cost method normally being selected. In a competitive sale, issuers offer their securities to the public through groups of underwriters that submit sealed bids for the right to handle the bonds. The issuer stipulates the appropriate principal amount and maturity structure and often provides guidelines concerning the size of coupons on different serial bonds. Each bid stipulates which coupons are associated with each maturity, the price (yield) the underwriter will pay for each serial bond, and any premium or discount offered. The lowest-cost bid is determined by calculating either a net interest cost or true interest cost measure of average borrowing costs for the entire offering.

In a negotiated sale, the issuer works directly with a single group of underwriters under a contract that stipulates the risks that each party bears and the requisite fees. There are no competing bids, and the underwriter has the exclusive right and obligation to distribute the securities. The underwriter again structures the bond offering's coupons and prices to minimize overall interest expense to the issuer by having securities that can be presold to selected investors.

Underwriting municipal bonds is normally handled by commercial banks and investment banks, with the latter dominating the market. This occurs largely because commercial banks have been prohibited by law from underwriting most revenue bonds. With most issues, the underwriter is actually a group or syndicate of banks and security dealers, rather than one firm, which allows each participant to reduce its risk. The tombstone ad in Figure 6-4, for example, lists 28 members of the underwriting syndicate with the lead firm, J.P. Morgan Securities Inc., listed first. Because underwriters effectively buy the bonds from the issuer before they actually place them with investors, they bear the risk that they might not sell all of the securities and/or that interest rates may rise such that prices fall and they suffer a loss. Not surprisingly, most competitive bids are submitted close to when the bonds go to market so that an underwriter has a good understanding of prevailing conditions. Many smaller underwriters, in fact, restrict their activity to a certain type of municipals for which they have a local monopoly or special expertise.

While municipal underwriting was a lucrative business through the early 1980s, firms overexpanded and drove profit margins lower. By early 1989, many investment banks had withdrawn from the business. Still, *The Bond Buyer* estimated that underwriter compensation had fallen by almost 50 percent from $23 per $1,000 of bonds in 1984 to just $12 per $1,000 by the early 1990s.

[4] Bond Insurance

Many investors have difficulty analyzing the credit quality of municipal bonds issued by small, lesser-known municipalities and their political subdivisions. Without appropriate incentives, they avoid these issues or require huge yield premiums to justify their investment. Many states and municipalities have circumvented this problem by obtaining bond insurance. Such insurance presumably lowers borrowing costs by more than the insurance premium. Insured bonds were so well received that from 1985 to 1987, almost 25 percent of all long-term issues were insured.

Municipal bond insurance consists of an unconditional guarantee by a property-casualty insurance company that it will make the contracted interest and principal payments on outstanding debt in the event of a default by the issuer. Note that the insurer is simply obligated to make the promised payments in a timely fashion and that the full principal outstanding is not repaid at default. The initial insurance premium is paid at the time of issue, either by the municipality or the underwriters, and the policy is noncancelable after insurance is guaranteed.

Bond insurance has an obvious appeal to many investors, but there are costs. Foremost is the fact that investors may pay the insurance premium by accepting a lower yield on the insured securities. The yield differential between insured and uninsured bonds typically ranges from 20 to 100 basis points, depending on the size of the issue and prevailing economic conditions. If municipal defaults are few and/or small, the added security comes at a high cost. Investors are also simply substituting the insurers' ability to repay the debt in lieu of the original issuer. If the insurers' capital to insured risk is low, the value of the insurance may also be low.

Still, insured bonds possess two attractive features in addition to the security. First, insured bonds are more liquid than uninsured bonds. This trait is extremely valuable, since many municipal securities are issued by relatively unknown units. During an economic downturn or other times of market distress, uninsured bonds attract fewer bids and at considerably lower prices than insured bonds. Second, insurance provides some protection against rating changes. While municipal defaults are infrequent, the rating agencies routinely downgrade municipal issues from one rating category to another. This action typically lowers the prices of the underlying bonds, as investors scramble to liquidate the unwanted securities. Downgrading does not affect insured municipals to the same degree because the property insurers' risk profile does not necessarily change with the issuer's risk profile. Thus, the downward price pressure is less.

There are four main groups that provide municipal bond insurance: the American Municipal Bond Assurance Corporation, which is owned primarily by Citicorp; the Municipal Bond Insurance Association, owned by five of the largest property insurance companies; the Financial Guarantee Insurance Company, owned by General Electric and several investment banks; and the Bond Investor's Guaranty, owned by a group of smaller property insurers. Each carried a triple-A rating by Moody's and S&P in 1991, and their combined capital totaled almost $2 billion. Bonds backed by these groups subsequently receive the same rating.

6.09 SLOPE OF THE MUNICIPAL YIELD CURVE

It is well known that short-term yields on municipal securities are almost always below yields on similar-quality longer-term securities. The city of New York general obligation bonds described in Figure 6-4 demonstrate this for reoffering yields on the serial bond issues. In particular, the one-year yield equals 4.5 percent and the yield at each successive maturity increases to where the 24-year yield reaches 7.5 percent. The same positive slope in the municipal yield curve also appears when averages of market yields on similarly rated securities are used, as demonstrated in Figure 6-10. Interestingly, the positive slope persists over all stages of the business cycle and regardless of whether the Treasury yield curve is sloping up or down. The steepness of the slope appears to follow a pattern, however. When interest rates increase sharply and are relatively high, as they were in 1973–1975 and 1978–1980, the slope is relatively low. The slope is highest when interest rates are relatively low.

Analysis attribute the positive slope to a variety of factors. The dominant influence is market segmentation and the investment behavior of banks. Commercial banks historically dominated investors by purchasing the majority of municipals issued. Because of the short-term liabilities, commercial banks had a strong preference for short-term municipals and largely avoided buying 20-year or longer securities. They therefore bid short-term municipal yields low relative to comparable maturity taxable yields. Thus, the implied indifference tax rate (T^*) for one-year securities from Figure 6-3 is close to the full corporate tax rate. Because banks purchased a smaller portion of longer-term municipals offered, issuers had to place these securities with individual investors, who paid taxes at lower marginal tax rates. Thus, T^* decreased with maturity (see Figure 6-3), or the ratio of the municipal to the taxable interest rate increased with maturity. In general, the fewer securities that banks purchased relative to net municipal issues, the more individuals purchased and the steeper was the slope of the municipal yield curve. Figure 6-10 demonstrates, for example, that the slope has remained high after 1980 when banks accelerated their withdrawal from the municipal market.

A second factor that imparts an upward bias to the yield curve is the relative riskiness of long-term versus short-term municipals. Most short-term municipals exhibit very low default risk, while default risk and risk premiums on yields increase with

FIGURE 6-10

Differences in Municipal Yields by Maturity

Source: Data from *An Analytical Record of Yields and Yield Spreads,* Salomon Brothers (1992)

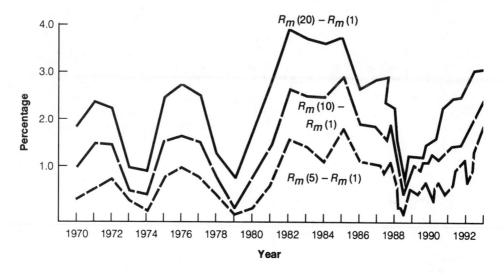

Note: Maturity in years appears in parentheses.

maturity. Thus, even with a flat yield curve determined by constant interest rate expectations, long-term yields would exceed short-term yields. Long-term municipals generally exhibit more price risk and are less marketable, which adds to the risk premium required on a long-term bond. Still, it seems unlikely that risk premium alone can induce a permanent upward bias in the municipal yield curve.

TRA 1986 accentuated the movement of commercial banks out of municipals, which, in turn, altered the municipal yield curve. Banks no longer find qualified municipals at just any maturity attractive. By withdrawing from the market, the effect should be greatest at short maturities where the banks' investment was proportionately the greatest. After TRA 1986, short-term yields increased relative to long-term yields so that the municipal yield curve flattened. The data after 1985 in Figure 6-10 support this.

State and local governments have found it difficult to take advantage of the persistent upward slope in the yield curve. Most government units have constitutional requirements that they run balanced operating budgets and use long-term debt to permanently finance capital expenditures. Thus, they cannot substitute between short-term and long-term securities simply to take advantage of relative yields. Still, the positive slope at least partly explains the growth in variable-rate demand notes and put bonds. Because these instruments carry maturities beyond one year yet are priced comparably with short-term municipals consistent with the repricing frequency of the floating rate or put option, they allow issuers to move down the yield curve at lower market yields.

6.10 MUNICIPAL BOND FUTURES

In June 1985, the Chicago Board of Trade opened trading in a municipal bond futures contract based on the value of *The Bond Buyer*'s Municipal Bond Index (MBI). The MBI is based on a portfolio of 40 bonds representing a cross-section of the municipal market. Each included bond has at least 19 years remaining until maturity, has a fixed coupon payable semiannually, has a reoffering price between 95 and 105, is rated A or higher by Moody's, has at least a $50 million term principal component, and is callable at par with at least 7 years remaining until first call. The bonds can be either general obligations or revenue bonds. The MBI futures contract is valued at $1,000 times the MBI.[12] Because there is no single deliverable security to satisfy expiration day closing of all futures positions, the MBI futures contract provides for cash settlement. Thus, rather than deliver municipal bonds for cash at delivery, traders value the 40 bonds in the index, calculate the MBI, and simply mark their positions to market and exchange cash.

Municipal market participants can benefit from the MBI futures contract to the extent that they use the contract to hedge their cash positions. A state or municipal borrower, for example, would hedge its borrowing costs on a new debt issue by selling MBI futures contracts. If a government unit expects to issue debt in the near future, it faces the risk that municipal bond rates might rise in the interim and its borrowing costs would increase. Of course, its borrowing costs would decrease if rates fell. Selling MBI futures reduces this risk because the value of the short futures position varies in the opposite direction to the anticipated cash market borrowing. If municipal rates increase, the MBI futures contract typically decreases in value. Thus, losses in the cash market in the form of higher borrowing costs are at least partially offset by profits in futures, as the borrower could buy back its futures position at a lower price.

An investor that anticipates having funds to buy municipal bonds in the near future could buy futures contracts to hedge against an opportunity loss if municipal rates fell. Again, the purchase of MBI futures (long position) increases in value when futures rates decline and decreases in value when futures rates increase. If the investor hedges and cash market municipal rates decrease, the lost interest income would be at least partially offset if MBI futures rates fell coincidentally and the hedger sold the position at a profit. Hedging generally works because cash market and futures rates normally move in the same direction. If they do not change by equal amounts, and normally they do not, the hedger is exposed to this basis risk.[13] Finally, note that had interest rates moved in the opposite direction in the two previous examples, a hedge would have gained in the cash market but lost with the futures position. Hedging thus reduces the potential for windfall gains.

One of the MBI futures contract's major weaknesses is that it is based on a portfolio of bonds. Because the municipal market is so diverse, few bonds exhibit the same interest sensitivity. Thus, rate changes on a single issuer's securities may not track

---

[12] The interested reader can obtain literature from the Chicago Board of Trade that explains the actual calculation of the index and MBI futures contract price.

[13] The basis equals the cash price minus the futures price, or the futures rate minus the cash rate.

rate changes one to one for the MBI portfolio. This increases basis risk and makes a hedge result less predictable. Still, investors with a portfolio of municipals have been able to track movements in the MBI fairly closely.

Suggested Reading

Brucato, P., R. Forbes, and P. Leonard. "The Effects of State Tax Differentials on Municipal Bond Yields." *Municipal Finance Journal* (Fall 1991).

Cooner, James. *Investing in Municipal Bonds*. New York: John Wiley & Sons, Inc., 1987.

Fabozzi, Frank, et al., eds. *The Municipal Bond Handbook*. Vols. 1 and 2. Homewood, Ill.: Dow Jones-Irwin, 1983.

Fortune, P. "Municipal Bond Yields: Whose Tax Rates Matter?" *National Tax Journal,* Vol. XLI (June 1988), pp. 219–233.

Government Finance Officers Association. *Disclosure Guidelines for State and Local Government Securities,* 1988.

Hein, Scott, Timothy Koch, and Scott MacDonald. "The Changing Role of Commercial Banks in the Municipal Securities Market." Working Paper, 1992.

Kidwell, D., and T. Koch. "Market Segmentation and the Term-Structure of Municipal Yields." *Journal of Money, Credit and Banking,* Vol. 15 (Feb. 1983), pp. 40–55.

Kidwell, D., T. Koch, and D. Stock. "The Impact of State Income Taxes on Municipal Borrowing Costs." *National Tax Journal,* Vol. XXXVII (Dec. 1984), pp. 551–561.

Kidwell, D., E. Sorenson, and J. Wachowitz. "Estimating the Signaling Benefits of Debt Insurance: The Case of Municipal Bonds." *Journal of Financial and Quantitative Analysis,* Vol. 22 (Sept. 1987), pp. 299–313.

Koch, Timothy. *Bank Management*. Hinsdale, Ill.: The Dryden Press, 1992.

Mitchell, K., and M. McDade. "Preferred Habitat, Taxable/Tax-Exempt Yield Spreads, and Cycles in Property/Liability Insurance." *Journal of Money, Credit and Banking,* Vol. 24 (Nov. 1992), pp. 528–552.

Neubig, T., and M. Sullivan. "The Implications of Tax Reform for Bank Holdings of Tax-Exempt Securities." *National Tax Journal,* Vol. XL (Sept. 1987), pp. 403–418.

Peek, J., and J. Wilcox. "Tax Rates and Interest Rates on Tax-Exempt Securities." *New England Economic Review* (Jan./Feb. 1986), pp. 29–41.

Peterson, J.E. "Examining the Impacts of the 1986 Tax Reform Act on the Municipal Securities Market." *National Tax Journal,* Vol. XL (Sept. 1987), pp. 393–402.

Peterson, J.E., R. Doty, R. Forbes, and D. Barque. "Initiatives and Issues in Municipal Bond Disclosure." *Government Finance Review* (Dec. 1988).

Phelps, Bruce. *Understanding the MOB Spread*. Chicago Board of Trade Research Report. Chicago: 1986.

Chapter 7

Corporate Equities

J. Peter Williamson

7.01 CAPITAL STRUCTURE OF MODERN CORPORATIONS

Traditionally, corporations have been financed through three types of capital: common stock, preferred stock, and debt. The once-clear distinctions among these three kinds of financial instrument have become somewhat blurred over the years, as hybrid instruments have been concocted to combine characteristics of two or all three of the traditional forms of capital.

7.02 COMMON STOCK

While many corporations are free of debt, and most corporations do not have preferred stock outstanding, it is hard to imagine a corporation without common shareholders. Common stock is the fundamental ownership interest in the corporation.[1]

[1] Characteristics of Common Stock

[a] **Limited Liability.** Historically, the most important attribute of common stock, as opposed to a proprietorship or a partnership interest, is limited liability. The predecessor to the modern business corporation, the joint stock company, generally did not confer limited liability on holders of its shares of stock. If the joint stock company got into financial difficulties, the stockholders could be held liable for its debts, just as general partners are liable for the debts of their partnership. (The American Express company was a joint stock company until 1965, when it became a corporation.) As corporations replaced joint stock companies, state legislatures wrestled with the question of whether shareholders should be relieved of liability for corporate obligations. Today, limited liability is accepted as a normal characteristic of shares in a business corporation: No matter what financial difficulties the corporation may find itself in, neither it nor its creditors can demand any contribution from its common shareholders.

There may still be a few cases where common shares are "assessable." In these cases, the original subscribers to the shares of a corporation agree to pay up to a certain amount for their shares, but not all at once. For example, if the agreement was to pay $100 per share, the corporation might have asked for a $10 down payment and then followed up with further assessments as money was needed, until the full $100 had been collected. It might take several years before this series of assessments was completed, and in the meantime the shareholders were obligated to pay up on assessment or forfeit their shares. One still encounters the terminology "fully paid

---

[1] There has been some interesting speculation as to whether one could construct business corporations without common stock. For example, suppose corporation A owns all of the shares of corporation B, which owns all of the shares of corporation C, which owns all the shares of corporation A. There now appears to be a closed circle that as a whole is owned by no one. Imagine that A is incorporated in New York state, B is incorporated in the Netherlands Antilles, and C is incorporated in France. Why might an arrangement like this be attractive? Suppose that family members occupy all of the directorships and the management positions in the three companies. They pay themselves well, enjoy comfortable perquisites, and pass these benefits down from generation to generation, not through estates subject to taxes but simply by replacing executives and directors. Whether or not such an arrangement is feasible, it would certainly be quite extraordinary and far from the experience of most investors and business corporations.

and nonassessable," referring to shares for which the holders cannot be held liable for any further payments.

There are a few exceptions to limited liability, but these generally apply not to individual shareholders or pure investors but to parent companies with respect to the shares of stock they hold in their subsidiary corporations. If the subsidiary is inadequately financed, or particularly where the parent misleads creditors of a subsidiary to think that they can rely on the credit of the parent, the courts may "pierce the corporate veil" and hold the parent company liable for the obligations of the subsidiary.

[b] Voting Rights. Fundamental to common shares are voting rights, including the right to elect directors. The simplest arrangement is 1 vote per common share, but not all corporations are organized in this way. There is a long tradition of corporations owned and controlled by a single family turning to the public market to raise capital through the sale of new shares but preserving the family control. The usual device was to designate the family shares as class A, and to create another class of shares, class B, to sell to the public. In all respects except voting rights, the shares of the two classes would be identical, but the shares in class A might carry 5, 10, 20, or more votes per share, while the shares in class B carry only 1 vote per share. This means that the number of shares in class B could be much larger than the number in class A, but the family would still possess over half of the votes. In extreme cases, the class B shares carried no votes at all for directors. For some years, there has been a campaign in the United States against this separation of ownership from voting power, in favor of a one share–one vote rule. The New York Stock Exchange (NYSE) has refused since 1926 to list nonvoting common shares.

The Securities and Exchange Commission (SEC) attempted in 1988 to impose the one share–one vote rule on all corporations listed on the major stock exchanges (principally the NYSE and the American Stock Exchange). Securities Exchange Act Rule 19c-4 was accepted by the exchanges, which in turn imposed a one share–one vote rule on all of their listed companies. In 1990, however, the Court of Appeals for the District of Columbia invalidated the rule as inconsistent with purposes of the Securities Exchange Act.[2] The real impetus for the rule had come from the plans of a number of corporations to create class A and class B differential voting rights, not to protect the control position of a particular family but to ward off corporate raiders by concentrating voting power in a friendly minority group and making it impossible for the outsider to gain a majority of the votes, even after buying a majority of the outstanding shares. With the invalidation of Rule 19c-4, the exchanges no longer impose a one share–one vote rule, although both exchanges have proposed a requirement of shareholder approval before the voting power of existing public shareholders may be reduced. The National Association of Securities Dealers, on the other hand, decided to continue the one share–one vote rule for the companies traded on the National Association of Securities Dealers Automated Quotation (NASDAQ).[3]

Cumulative voting for directors is required by the statutes of some states and autho-

---

[2] Business Roundtable v. Securities & Exch. Comm'n, 905 F2d 406 (DC Cir. 1990).

[3] For a discussion of the significance and demise of Rule 19c-4, see R.J. Gilson, "Regulating the Equity Component of Capital Structure: The SEC's Response to the One-Share, One-Vote Controversy," *Journal of Applied Corporate Finance*, Vol. 5 (Winter 1993), pp. 37–43. On the effect of dual-class recapitalizations that reduce voting rights on the monitoring of management, see R.C. Moyer, R. Rao, and P.M. Sisneros, "Substitutes for Voting Rights: Evidence From Dual Class Recapitalizations," *Financial Management*, Vol. 21 (Autumn 1992), pp. 35–47.

rized by others. Under cumulative voting, each shareholder possesses a number of votes equal to the number of shares held multiplied by the number of directors to be elected. The shareholder may then place all of those votes on one candidate for director or spread them over more than 1 candidate. Cumulative voting permits the holder of less than half of the shares voted to elect some directors, while straight (noncumulative) voting enables the owner of over half of the shares to elect all of the directors. For example, if there are 1,000 shares outstanding and 5 directors to be elected, under cumulative voting a total of 5,000 votes will be cast. If there are 6 candidates for the 5 directorships, a holder of more than one sixth of the shares outstanding can be sure of electing a director. This is because one sixth of 1,000 shares is 166.67 shares and 167 shares carry 835 votes, which can all be cast for 1 candidate. The remaining shareholders together have 4,165 (5,000 minus 835) votes. No matter how these votes are spread over 5 candidates, it is impossible for each of the 5 to receive over 833 votes. So the candidate receiving the 835 votes from the owner of 167 shares must receive more votes than at least 1 of the 5 opponents and therefore must be elected.

The benefit to minority shareholders of cumulative voting can be reduced by the practice of "classifying" boards of directors (unless the courts find classified boards inconsistent with state constitution–mandated cumulative voting, as has happened in some states). For example, a board of directors might consist of 15 members, with 5 to be elected each year for a 3-year term. This means that only 5 directors are elected at a time, and a larger minority block of shares is required to elect a director than would be the case if the entire 15-member board were elected at once. In addition, even in the case of cumulative voting, a holder of a majority of the corporation's shares may have to wait a year before electing a majority of the board.

[c] Proxies. Strictly speaking, the right to vote recognized by a corporation is a function not of who actually owns the shares but of who is the shareholder "of record," the shareholder listed on the corporation register of shareholders. The corporate by-laws generally confer the right to vote on those that are listed on the corporate register as of the "record date," which is likely to be sometime prior to the meeting at which the voting takes place. A shareholder that purchases shares between the record date and the meeting, generally does not have the right to vote, unless it can persuade the seller (whose name was on the register at the record date) to give the new owner a proxy to vote the shares.

Generally, any registered shareholder is entitled to give a proxy to someone else, who then has the right to vote the shares. Most large corporations do not anticipate that many shareholders will actually attend an annual meeting and vote in person, so they routinely mail out proxies for those shareholders to send back, authorizing representatives of the management to vote for them. Some corporate bylaws require that proxies be registered with the corporation before the annual meeting in order to be usable. Generally speaking, a proxy is revocable. That is, the shareholder can change its mind after giving it to someone and decide to vote the shares itself or to give the proxy to someone else. Any proxy automatically revokes a prior-dated proxy.

Most managements of large companies solicit proxies from shareholders. There are various reasons for this. Usually a quorum, in the form of shares represented at the meeting either by owners in person or by proxies, is required before any business can be transacted. Without proxies many corporations would never achieve a quorum. At the same time, the management would like its own slate of directors to be elected and any other business of the meeting to be settled to its satisfaction.

The rules of the SEC governing the use of proxies apply to corporations listed on stock exchanges plus a great many other publicly held corporations. These rules prescribe various disclosures that must accompany a proxy and give the shareholders some flexibility in how the proxy may be used. Currently, corporations must comply with greatly expanded disclosure rules calling for explanations of executive compensation, among other things.

[d] Dividends. Common shareholders generally cannot force a corporation to pay them any dividends. The payment of dividends lies within the discretion of the board of directors. (See Chapter E3 in the *Handbook of Modern Finance* and Chapter 3 in the *Handbook of Financial Strategy and Policy* for a discussion of the dividend decision.) In a famous case early in this century, the Dodge Brothers were successful in forcing the Ford Motor Company to pay them dividends over the objections of Henry Ford.[4] However, this was an unusual case, in which the court concluded that Henry Ford was withholding dividends in a purely arbitrary way without concern for the best interests of the stockholders.

The discretion of directors to declare dividends to common shareholders is further circumscribed by law. Generally, dividends may not be paid in cash or other property if the result would be impairment of the capital of the corporation, which is supposed to serve as a cushion to protect creditors. In general, the capital consists of money supplied to the corporation by the stockholders and designated as capital. The earned surplus, the cumulative retained earnings of the corporation, is not a part of this capital and is available for dividends.

There are four dates connected to the payment of dividends that are important. First is the date of declaration. On that date, the directors of the corporation announce their decision to have the corporation pay a dividend and the amount of that dividend. The announcement also states the second date, the record date. Dividends are distributed to those that are listed on the official register of shareholders. Shareholders that purchased their shares after the record date will not receive the dividend; the corporation will mail the dividend check not to them but to the parties that sold them the shares. The third date, the "ex-dividend" date, is specified by the stock exchanges. Anyone that purchases shares on or after this date, under the stock exchange rules, is not entitled to the dividend. Anyone that purchases before the ex-dividend date is entitled to the dividend. The ex-dividend date is set by the stock exchanges so that transactions before that date will reach the transfer books before the record date and transactions after the ex-dividend date will reach the transfer books after the record date.

Many corporations in a phase of rapid growth do not pay dividends, preferring to use what cash they have to finance the growth. Other corporations are opposed to the payment of cash dividends as a matter of principle, even though they have the cash available, reasoning that dividends are taxed to shareholders at ordinary income tax rates and that many shareholders do not need the dividends and would rather not pay the taxes. These corporations are likely to use their cash to repurchase shares from shareholders. The corporation may make an offer to the shareholders to purchase a certain number of shares, and the shareholders that wish to receive some cash and are prepared to pay a tax on the gain realized on the shares they sell accept the offer, while other shareholders do not.

---

[4] Dodge v. Ford Motor Co., 204 Mich. 459, 170 NW 668 (1919).

Stock dividends. Stock dividends are dividends distributed in common shares rather than in cash or other property. Some would argue that they are worthless and that the corporation is wasting the expense of the paper work that accompanies a stock dividend. For example, assume that a shareholder owns 100 shares of stock in a corporation that has 1 million shares outstanding. The directors of the corporation declare a 5 percent stock dividend, which means that 50,000 new shares of stock will be distributed and the shareholder will receive 5 of them. The shareholder now owns 105 shares but still owns 1 ten-thousandth of the corporation, just as it did before the distribution. The corporation has exactly the same assets it had before the distribution and exactly the same earning capacity (except that it has spent some money on mailing and bookkeeping). The market price of the shares falls after the stock goes ex-dividend, so that the 105 shares are worth about what 100 shares used to be worth.

Some shareholders, however, apparently do not see the difference between a cash and a stock dividend. Five percent in stock is as good as 5 percent in cash to them, and if there are many such shareholders, the price after the dividend may hold up. Sometimes, too, the cash dividend per share is maintained, so that as the number of shares rises by 5 percent, the total cash dividends paid by the corporation also rises by 5 percent; thus, an increase in the value of the shareholdings may appear to be due to the five extra shares the shareholder received, when in fact it is due to the increase in cash dividends it will receive on 105 shares rather than on 100 shares.

Stock dividends in the form of common shares distributed to holders of common shares are free of federal income tax when they are distributed only if the stockholder is not given a choice between the receipt of stock dividends and the receipt of cash dividends. When those dividend shares are sold, the gain or loss resulting is capital gain or loss, just as if some of the original shares were sold, with the cost of the original shares spread over both the original and the dividend shares.

The accounting rule for modest stock dividends (not over 25 percent) involves a transfer of earned surplus to capital and capital surplus in the amount of the fair market value of the shares distributed as a dividend. The bookkeeping treatment for larger stock dividends is generally the same as for stock splits.

Stock splits. A corporation generally splits its stock when the price seems to have gotten too high. It is hard to tell how high is too high, but most managements have some feeling for what a popular range for the price of their company's stock is. Hence, keeping the stock price within a popular range encourages investment and therefore tends to maximize the value of the shares.

A two-for-one stock split is equivalent to a 100 percent stock dividend. Where a shareholder had one share before, that shareholder has two shares after the split or dividend. A three-for-two split leaves the shareholder with three shares for every two old shares and is equivalent to a 50 percent stock dividend. The accounting treatment differs somewhat from that described for smaller stock dividends. There is no transfer from earned surplus to capital or capital surplus. If the shares have a par value, the par value is generally split. Since the number of shares has increased, the product of the number of shares outstanding and the par value will remain the same.

[2] Sale and Purchase of Common Stock

Common shares in a business corporation are normally freely transferable. Whether they are marketable is another matter. The term "marketability" refers to the ease with which one can buy and sell shares. The most marketable shares are those in large corporations with substantial volumes of shares traded every day on major markets like the NYSE. There are always willing buyers and sellers and brokers that can match them up. However, for a very small corporation with few if any shares changing hands from one year to the next, marketability may be almost nonexistent. In addition, shares may not even be freely transferable. Sometimes transferability is restricted by the terms under which the shares were originally issued. For example, investors taking a major position in the stock ownership of a corporation may be required to agree to hold the stock for a certain period or to sell it only through a public offering registered with the SEC. So-called letter stock is stock that is subject to a letter of agreement setting out the conditions upon which it may be transferable. A corporation with a tax loss carryover risks losing the benefit of the carryover if there is a change in control of the corporation, so it may be appropriate to restrict share transfers that could bring about such a change.

Small and closely held corporations frequently have agreements among the shareholders limiting transferability of shares and often providing that a shareholder that wishes to sell must offer the stock first to the remaining shareholders or to the corporation itself. Finally, there are statutes limiting the percentage a single shareholder or shareholder group may own in corporations engaged in various industries and limiting foreign ownership of certain corporations. Transferability, of course, assumes some sort of market. The shares in several thousand U.S. business corporations are traded on the various stock exchanges and over-the-counter (OTC) market. The shares in many thousands more corporations are not traded in any public market, and finding a buyer or seller may be quite difficult.

In general, a common shareholder cannot be forced to sell its shares in a corporation, nor can the shareholder force the corporation to purchase those shares. There are some important exceptions to these propositions. The state corporation law or the charter of the individual corporation may provide that shareholders that object to certain major transactions (such as sale of substantially all of the corporate assets) may insist on being bought out by the corporation at a fair price. And where a purchaser makes an offer for all of the outstanding stock of a corporation and the offer is accepted by a large enough majority, the minority may be compelled to sell as well, although with the right to demand an appraisal and a fair price. The Delaware "short merger" statute brings about this result if the purchaser can persuade the holders of at least 90 percent of the shares to sell.

A corporation is generally free to purchase shares of its stock in the market, and these shares become treasury stock, available for resale or sometimes for issue to employees upon the exercise of stock options.

[3] Authorized and Outstanding Shares and Preemptive Rights

Before shares can be outstanding, i.e., issued by the corporation and held by shareholders, they must be authorized. Generally, the directors vote to authorize a certain number of new shares and a majority vote of the shareholders is required to complete the formality. The authorized shares are then available for issue to new or existing shareholders.

The corporation laws of some states and some corporate charters give shareholders preemptive rights to the new shares when they are issued. This means that if new shares are to be sold, the shares must be offered first to existing shareholders such that they can maintain their proportionate ownership of the corporation. Even in the absence of statutory preemptive rights or rights prescribed by the corporate charter, some corporations choose to issue new shares by way of a rights offering, in which each shareholder may be issued, e.g., one right to buy a share for every five shares already owned. The right generally entitles the holder to purchase a share at a price somewhat below the current market price, which gives value to the right and provides an incentive for the shareholders to exercise the rights and purchase the shares or to sell the rights to someone who will exercise them. The result can be a low-cost distribution of the new shares, avoiding the expense of the more common underwritten offering, where the shares are sold to an investment banking firm or group of firms that in turn offers the shares to the public.

The theoretical value of a right is easily calculated. Suppose that there are 1,000 shares outstanding and for each 5 shares held the shareholders are given the right to purchase 1 new share, so that 200 rights are distributed. Suppose the market value of the 1,000 shares outstanding before the rights offering is $40 each, for a total value for the corporation of $40,000. Now suppose that the new shares are offered at a 20 percent discount from the $40 market value, or $32 each. The value of the corporation after the new shares have been sold should be $40,000 (the original value) plus 200 times $32 (the new money coming in), or $46,400, and the value of each share (there will be 1,200 outstanding after the new offering) should then be $46,400 divided by 1,200, or $38.67. Since one right entitles a shareholder to buy for $32 a share that is worth $38.67, the value of a right should be $6.67.

A question is sometimes raised about the loss to shareholders, which see the market price of their shares fall from $40 to $38.67. Those shareholders had the opportunity to purchase new shares at only $32, and this opportunity makes up for the decline in share price. Alternatively, if the shareholders sold their rights for $6.67 each, they lost nothing.

[4] Par and No-Par Stock

Par value is simply a price per share stipulated in the articles of incorporation. During the early history of stock corporations, this was the price at which the stock was first issued to shareholders. As time went on, there seemed to be no reason why a corporation should not charge its first shareholders more than the par value for its shares, although it should not be allowed to charge less. The rule today is simply that par value shares may not be issued by a corporation at less than par. The par value device was supposed to protect creditors of a corporation by indicating exactly what the capital of a corporation is. Most state corporation statutes prohibit the payment of dividends if the payment would impair this capital. The protection is not worth much if the corporation simply establishes a very low par value for its shares. For example, there is generally nothing to stop the corporation from establishing the par value at $1 per share but issuing those shares for $1,000 each. The sale of 100 shares will raise $100,000 for the corporation, but its technical capital will be only $1,000, and only this $1,000 is then to be protected for the creditors against the distribution of dividends.

No-par shares have been allowed in the United States since 1912. The directors must decide what portion of the proceeds of sale of no-par shares is to be allocated to stated capital, and this stated capital is not available for common dividends.

[5] Warrants for the Purchase of Common Shares

The owner of a warrant has the right to purchase a fixed number of shares of common stock at a predetermined price during a specified period. (Some warrants are perpetual.) Warrants are generally created by a corporation to facilitate the sale of debt or preferred stock. The purchasers of the debt or the preferred stock will receive a certain number of warrants for each bond or each share of preferred stock that they buy. At the time the warrants are issued, the price at which they can be exercised is generally somewhat above the current market price of the corporation's common shares. At that point, no one is going to exercise the warrants, but the expectation on the part of the buyers is that the share price will rise over time until the exercise price for the warrant becomes a bargain. For example, if the shares are selling at $30 and the warrants entitle the holders to buy shares at $40 over the next five years, the hope of the warrant holder is that the share price will rise well above $40 within five years. The use of warrants to sell debt or preferred stock makes sense only if the management has good reason to think that the warrants are not as valuable as the investors think they are. To the extent that new investors are permitted to buy common stock at less than the fair value of that stock at some date in the future, the existing shareholders are disadvantaged.

[6] Share Repurchases

The practice of some corporations of using surplus cash to repurchase their own common shares rather than paying dividends is intended essentially to accommodate the varying preferences of shareholders, some of which want cash from the corporation and others of which do not. There are other reasons for share repurchases, including the creation of a supply of shares to take care of the exercise of employee stock options, and sometimes the corporate management simply concludes that the most profitable investment available is in the corporation's own shares.

There are a number of techniques that a corporation may employ in repurchasing its shares. At one time, the most common was the fixed-price offer. The management would announce to its shareholders the number of shares it wished to repurchase, the time during which the offer would be open, and the price the corporation would pay for all shares tendered by shareholders and accepted by the corporation. Should the number of shares offered by the shareholders exceed the number the corporation was willing to purchase, less than 100 percent of the offered shares would be accepted. In the 1980s, a second technique became popular: the Dutch auction. In a Dutch auction repurchase, the corporation announces the total number of shares it will repurchase and for how long the offer will remain open, but instead of setting a single price, it sets a range of prices. The shareholder responding to the tender must specify how many shares are offered to the corporation at what price (within the range). The corporation then determines the lowest price that allows it to repurchase the number of shares it was seeking. All of the shares are actually purchased at this single price. This means that in the end, all of the tendering shareholders receive the same price, but only shares offered at this or a lower price are accepted by the corporation. If a shareholder names too high a price, that shareholder may have no shares accepted. Naming too low a price simply increases the likelihood that the price paid will be low.

The Dutch auction is arguably the most satisfactory way in which to treat the tendering shareholders and the remaining shareholders fairly.[5]

[7] Valuation of Common Stock

[a] **Discounted Cash Flow and Intrinsic Value.** Security analysts whose livelihood depends on the ability to value common stocks may rely on a number of valuation methods. (See Chapter D6 in the *Handbook of Modern Finance* and Chapter 10 in the *Handbook of Short-Term and Long-Term Financial Management*.) The formal method that is most widely recognized is based on the work of John Burr Williams, who, in his book *The Theory of Investment Value* (1938), set forth the rule of present worth. The rule says that the value of a share of stock is the discounted present value of all of the dividends that the holder of the share can expect to receive, shown mathematically as

$$V = \frac{d_1}{(1 + r_1)} + \frac{d_2}{(1 + r_1)(1 + r_2)} + \frac{d_3}{(1 + r_1)(1 + r_2)(1 + r_3)} + \cdots$$

$$+ \frac{d_n}{(1 + r_1)(1 + r_2)(1 + r_3)(1 + r_n)}$$

where V is the intrinsic value of the share, d_1 is the dividend to be received in a year, d_2 is the dividend to be received in two years, d_3 is the dividend in the third year, and so on up to d_n, the dividend in the nth year, and r_1 is the rate of return on the investment required by the shareholder in the first year, r_2 is the required rate the second year, and so on up to r_n, the required rate in the nth year.

A possible objection to the equation is that it assumes that the corporation pays dividends, and not all corporations do. The answer is that shares in a corporation have no value unless there is the prospect that at some time there will be a distribution of corporate assets to the shareholders. There need not be regular annual dividends—many of the ds in the equation may be zeros—but there must be some expectation of a positive d at some time. Even the use of corporate funds to redeem shares can be a sufficient d (although it is not, strictly speaking, a dividend).

A second possible objection is that the shareholder does not anticipate holding the share to infinity, but rather expects to sell it. Suppose that the shareholder expects to sell it at the end of the third year. Then, for this shareholder,

$$V = \frac{d_1}{(1 + r_1)} + \frac{d_2}{(1 + r_1)(1 + r_2)} + \frac{d_3}{(1 + r_1)(1 + r_2)(1 + r_3)} + \frac{P_3}{(1 + r_1)(1 + r_2)(1 + r_3)}$$

where P_3 is the stock price at the end of the third year. But Williams's rule would say that the best estimate of P_3 is given by

$$P_3 = \frac{d_4}{(1 + r_4)} + \frac{d_5}{(1 + r_4)(1 + r_5)} + \cdots + \frac{d_n}{(1 + r_{n-1})(1 + r_n)}$$

resulting in the original equation for V.

While Williams's rule seems to stand as sound theory, it is virtually unusable without some simplifying assumptions, and these assumptions create serious weaknesses.

---

[5] See D.B. Hausch, D.E. Logue, and J.K. Seward, "Dutch Auction Share Repurchases: Theory and Evidence," *Journal of Applied Corporate Finance*, Vol. 5 (Spring 1992), pp. 44–49.

First, generally assuming that $r_1 = r_2 = r_3$ and so on flies in the face of the well-known fact that the yield curve is not flat across all maturities. That is, the yield on a one-year debt instrument is not the same as the yield on a five-year instrument. But since it is almost impossible to deal with different values for r in determining V, analysts are forced to the assumption of equal values and have to explain that the resulting r is some sort of average required rate over the indefinite future.

Second, generally the values of d_1, d_2, d_3 and so on are assumed to follow a steady growth rate. Careful users of the discounted cash flow (DCF) model may try to allow for varying growth. For example, in the 1960s Molodovsky proposed that most successful companies go through a period of rapidly rising earnings (and dividends), but that as the companies mature, their growth rate drops to that of their industry, which he approximated as the rate of growth in the economy as a whole.[6] The user of his model now has to estimate two growth rates and the period for the first. It is hard to be sure that the result will be much better than would be the case with a single growth rate, and, if it is, why not go to three growth rates or four? As a practical matter, the multiple growth rate model does not seem to have achieved any wide acceptance.

The single growth rate assumption converts d_1 into $d_0(1+g)$, where g is the annual growth rate and d_0 is the dividend for the year just past. Similarly, d_2 becomes $d_0(1 + g)^2$ and so on, and the model now becomes

$$V = \frac{d_0(1 + g)}{(1 + r)} + \frac{d_0(1 + g)^2}{(1 + r)^2} + \frac{d_0(1 + g)^3}{(1 + r)^3} + \cdots + \frac{d_0(1 + g)^n}{(1 + r)^n}$$

This expression has the enormous virtue that it can be converted by a little algebra into

$$V = \frac{d_0(1 + g)}{(r - g)}$$

This equation assumes that dividends are paid annually. Because most companies pay dividends quarterly, it is best to substitute $1 + g/2$ for $1 + g$.

The assumption of a single growth rate deserves more attention. First, there is no evidence that investors think in terms of a single growth rate to infinity. One would expect that if this growth rate were of interest to investors, someone would attempt to supply estimates, but no analyst appears to offer estimates of growth rates to infinity. Yet the DCF method is treated as though it represents the investors' thought process. There is probably no way around the assumption; the model is too difficult to use without it. A serious weakness has been introduced, however, because the analyst is forced to come up with the growth rate expected by investors to infinity when there is no reason to believe that investors have any such growth rate in mind.

Estimating the growth rate is no simple matter, and the value of V is very sensitive to that rate (the growth rate, g, must be smaller than the discount rate, r; otherwise, the value of V is indeterminate). There seem to be no published sources of professional growth rate forecasts to infinity, although forecasts for shorter periods can be found. Analysts' forecasts of five-year growth rates in earnings are available from at least two services: the Institutional Brokers Estimate System (IBES) and Zacks Investment Research. Both organizations collect forecasts from analysts at brokerage firms and distribute them to subscribers.

---

[6] The last of a series of articles by Molodovsky was "Common Stock Valuation," *Financial Analysts Journal*, Vol. 21 (Mar.–Apr. 1965), pp. 104–123.

Gordon[7] proposed a method for estimating g that takes the form

$$g = br + sv$$

where g is the expected growth rate to perpetuity, b is the fraction of earnings retained and reinvested in the business, r is the rate of return on book common equity, s is the funds raised from the sale of new stock as a fraction of the existing common equity, and v is the fraction of the funds raised from the sale of stock that accrues to those that were shareholders before the new financing took place (owing to differences between the market and book values of the shares). It turns out that sv is generally very small compared to br, so g is essentially br. The tests that Gordon employed to validate his growth measure were based on electric utility data for the period 1958–1968, but more recent testing indicates the method does not work well. In 1990, Gordon conceded that the method is not reliable and that investors rely primarily on security analysts' forecasts.

Finally, r must be estimated. Some would use the capital asset pricing model (CAPM), some would use the arbitrage pricing theory, and some would use a risk premium methodology for this determination. (These topics are discussed in Chapter B2 of the *Handbook of Modern Finance* and Chapter 2 in the *Handbook of Securities and Investment Management*.)

[b] P/E Ratios and Relative Value. From an investor's point of view, the value of a stock relative to the value of other stocks may be more interesting than the intrinsic value, and, perhaps more important, one may have more confidence in a relative valuation than in an intrinsic valuation.

It is also true that price/earnings (P/E) ratios can be used to establish intrinsic value, and the ratio of the price to the earnings per share of a stock is probably the most popular quality measure of the stock. If quality is made up of a number of characteristics of a company, the normal P/E ratio at any time is a function of various measurable characteristics of the company. To determine this function, an analyst examines a large number of companies at a particular point in time and relate their P/E ratios to the relevant characteristics. Having found the function, the analyst can determine the normal P/E ratio for each of the companies and compare the normal ratio with the actual ratio to see which corporations are relatively underpriced or overpriced. Whitbeck and Kisor[8] proposed three characteristics of a company from which the normal P/E ratio could be deduced. These were the expected growth rate in earnings per share (provided by security analysts); the expected dividend payout ratio; and the standard devia tion measuring the variability in expected earnings around the expected growth trend line.

A close approximation to the Whitbeck and Kisor model has been used by IBES, which reported each month (up to May 1992, when it stopped updating its model) on the parameters of its P/E growth model.

The three variables in the IBES model are the median five-year earnings growth estimate (obtained from brokerage firm security analysts), the coefficient of variation calculated from the various five-year earnings growth forecasts, and the dividend payout ratio. IBES ran a regression each month, using these three characteristics for most of the stocks in the Standard & Poor's 500 index, as well as the actual P/E ratios for

[7] Myron J. Gordon, *The Cost of Capital to a Public Utility* (1974).

[8] V.S. Whitbeck and M. Kisor, Jr., "A New Tool in Investment Decision-Making," *Financial Analysts Journal* (May–June 1963), pp. 55–62.

those stocks, to establish a relationship. For May 1992, for example, the relationship was:

P/E = 0.97(median annual growth rate forecast for next 5-year period)

+ 0.12(coefficient of variation among the growth rate forecasts)

+ 0.09(dividend payout ratio) − 0.1

For May 1992, the average P/E ratio for the set analyzed was 15.7. The annual growth rate forecast was 11.7 percent, the coefficient of variation was 6.3, and the dividend payout ratio was 40.7. To use the model, one supplies from the data collected by IBES the median annual growth rate forecast for a particular stock, the coefficient of variation for that stock, and the dividend payout ratio for that stock. The ''normal'' P/E ratio is then calculated with the coefficients shown previously and compared to the actual P/E ratio. If the actual ratio is below the normal ratio, the stock is under-priced and is a buy. If the actual ratio is above the normal ratio, the stock is overpriced and is a sell. The model may actually be more useful for determining undervalued and overvalued industries or segments of the market than for identifying individual stocks that are overpriced or underpriced.

Analysts who use a P/E ratio to establish the true or intrinsic value of a stock generally rely on intuition to come up with the appropriate ratio and multiply it by the earnings (or perhaps normal earnings) to come up with a valuation. The IBES model and similar models offer a perhaps more scientific way of getting at the most appropriate P/E ratio.

7.03 PREFERRED STOCK

The majority of business corporations do not use preferred stock at all. The reason is very simple: Interest paid on debt is deductible for income tax purposes, while dividends paid on preferred stock are not. However, there is a further tax distinction between interest on debt and preferred dividends that to some extent offsets the disadvantage: Interest received is taxed at ordinary income tax rates to all taxable recipients, but dividends paid to taxable corporations are treated in a special way. If the receiving corporation owns 20 percent or more of the paying corporation, the former is allowed to deduct 80 percent of the dividend. If the receiving corporation owns less than 20 percent, it is allowed to deduct 70 percent of the dividend. (Until the 1986 tax changes, the deduction was 85 percent, regardless of the percentage ownership.) For example, for a casualty insurance company, that is likely to be paying federal corporate income taxes at a 34 percent rate and that maintains a substantial investment portfolio, the interest on a bond is fully taxable at 34 percent, while the dividends on a preferred stock are only 30 percent taxable (after the 70 percent deduction). Therefore, the effective tax rate on the dividend is 30 percent of 34 percent, or 10.2 percent.

For most corporations, the inability to deduct preferred dividends paid is not sufficiently offset by the dividends-received deduction to a corporate investor, and therefore preferred stock is not a useful source of capital. Corporations with very low effective tax rates (because of very little taxable income) might find the issue of preferred stock attractive. The ideal combination would seem to be an issuer with a very low effective tax rate and an investor with a very high effective tax rate.[9] The reduction in the dividends-received deduction to 70 percent or 80 percent, as described previously, from the 85 percent that was permitted before 1986 has reduced the number of cases where effective tax rates favor the use of preferred stock.

Until the 1980s, preferred stock was used fairly heavily by public utilities. Regulators appear to favor the use of preferred stock, and, during the 1970s, utilities were making heavy investment in plant, which required substantial financing. To avoid excessive use of debt, utilities found preferred stock to be a cheaper source of capital than common stock. In the 1980s, utilities were spending less on plant, and industrial and financial issuers replaced utilities as the major sellers of preferred stock.

For financial issuers, there was a special reason for favoring preferred stock. In 1981, the Federal Reserve Board classified perpetual preferred stock as "primary capital" at a time when banks generally found the sale of common stock to be unattractive yet were in great need of expanded primary capital. At about the same time, adjustable-rate preferred stock was introduced and proved to be an attractive substitute for banks for floating-rate notes or a succession of short-term notes.

Industrial corporations found preferred stock especially useful in mergers and as a defensive weapon against threatened takeovers. A voting preferred issue could be placed in friendly hands to help ward off outsiders seeking control of a corporation. In the case of a merger, it was often convenient for the purchaser to issue preferred stock as part of the price paid if the purchaser was likely to have a low effective tax rate as the result of high leverage.

A certain amount of preferred stock is often issued in cases of bankruptcy. The holders of debt may be persuaded to accept preferred stock in place of some of the debt. The corporation's ability to defer the payment of preferred dividends offers a considerable benefit in times of financial stress and may offer the prospect of recovery for a bankrupt corporation that is acceptable to the debt holder that sees little chance that the debt will be repaid in full.

Preferred stock (or "preference" stock, as it is sometimes called; the distinction is discussed later) is senior to common stock but junior to debt in the hierarchy of classes of capital. First, preferred shares are generally entitled to a dividend that must be paid before dividends may be paid to the common shareholders. Second, on dissolution of the corporation, preferred shareholders are entitled to receive the par value of their shares (or some stated value) before the common shareholders receive anything. Third, although preferred shareholders generally are not entitled to vote for directors (they are generally entitled to vote on any changes in bylaws or articles of incorporation that would affect their rights), if the preferred dividends have not been paid for a certain period the holders of the preferred shares are often entitled to elect a certain number of directors (and in some cases to elect a majority of the board).

Convertible preferred stock has some especially useful properties, making it popular in many cases despite the tax disadvantages.

[1] Preferred Dividends

The dividend on a preferred stock is generally fixed and is expressed either as a percent or as a dollar amount. A 6 percent preferred pays a dividend (generally quarterly) of

---

[9] The hypothesis was set forth in I. Fooladi and G. Roberts, "On Preferred Stock," *Journal of Financial Research* (Winter 1986), pp. 319–324. See A.L. Houston, Jr. and C.O. Houston, "Financing With Preferred Stock," *Financial Management,* Vol. 19 (Autumn 1990), pp. 42–54 for empirical test results confirming the hypothesis.

6 percent per year of the par or stated value of the preferred. If the par value is $100, the dividend is $6, probably paid at the rate of $1.50 per quarter. The same dividend might simply be stated as $6 per share.

Preferred shareholders, like common shareholders, do not have a legal right to dividends. The payment of preferred dividends is a matter of the directors' discretion. From the corporation's point of view, the fact that debt holders have a legal claim against the corporation that could lead to bankruptcy for its failure to pay interest, while the preferred shareholders have no such claim for failure to pay dividends, can be an important advantage of preferred stock (but not generally important enough to offset the tax disadvantage). However, as long as preferred dividends are not paid, there can be no dividends on the common shares. If the failure to pay preferred dividends goes on long enough, the preferred shareholders may be able to elect their own representatives to the board, and possibly control the board.

An important distinction is one between "cumulative" and "noncumulative" preferred dividend rights. If the preferred dividend is cumulative, any missed dividends must be made up before there can be any common dividends. Occasionally, one finds that preferred shares are quoted at a price well above the par or stated value because the corporation has failed to pay preferred dividends for some time. In such cases, there are significant "cumulated unpaid preferred dividends," and there is an expectation that the corporation's fortunes may be improving and that the arrearage will be paid off soon in order to pave the way for resumption of common dividends. If the dividend is noncumulative, however, missed dividends are gone forever. There is no bar to common dividends if the current preferred dividend payment is made. A noncumulative preferred stock is generally a very unattractive instrument in the hands of an investor unless it carries some other special rights.

A participating preferred stock is one that is entitled to dividends beyond the promised rate. If the corporation prospers and common stock dividends increase, this preferred stock participates in the prosperity by way of extra dividends.

Since the early 1980s, a number of new types of preferred stock have been introduced. For the most part, these innovations have sought to create a preferred stock that benefits from the dividends-received deduction to corporate investors but in other respects closely resembles corporate debt. The objective was to shift financing from debt instruments to some kind of preferred instrument to benefit from the tax advantage. Congress responded by reducing the dividend-received deduction in 1986 from 85 percent to 80 percent or 70 percent. Corporations best able to make use of the new types of preferred stock are those with relatively low effective tax rates, but even those with normal or high effective tax rates were attracted to these new types of preferred stock for other reasons (including the building of primary capital by banks).[10]

---

[10] One must be careful that the exotic types of preferred stock will be treated for tax purposes as preferred stock and that the dividends will be treated as preferred dividends. The risk is that the Internal Revenue Service and the courts might conclude that the instrument is really a debt instrument and that the payment is really interest and not a dividend. The usual rule will apply that a dividend must be distributed out of "earnings and profits" of the paying corporation. If the corporation has no earnings and profits, either cumulated or current, for tax purposes no distribution will be a dividend. In addition, the Internal Revenue Code requires a 46-day holding period for variable-rate preferred stock, so it is customary to change the rate every 49 days. See S.G. Frost and S.D. Conlon, "Adjustable Rate Preferred Stock Still Provides Many Tax Benefits," *The Journal of Taxation,* Vol. 73 (Oct. 1990), pp. 244–252.

[a] **Adjustable-Rate Preferred.** Corporate treasurers are accustomed to investing surplus cash in short-term fixed-income securities such as bank certificates of deposit, Treasury bills, or commercial paper. Their primary concern is preservation of principal value; income that can be earned on these funds is a secondary concern. It occurred to some corporate treasurers and investment bankers in 1982 that if one could combine the characteristics of these short-term fixed-income instruments with the tax benefits (the dividends-received deduction, for a corporate investor) of preferred dividends, the resulting hybrid instrument could be very attractive to corporate treasurers. Chemical New York Corporation (the parent of Chemical Bank) issued the first adjustable-rate cumulative preferred stock. The dividend rate was set initially at 14.2 percent, to be adjusted quarterly to equal one half of 1 percent over the highest of (1) the Treasury bill rate; (2) the 10-year constant-maturity U.S. government rate; and (3) the 20-year constant-maturity U.S. government rate. The expectation was that this quarterly adjustment would keep the price of the preferred stock at or very close to its par value of $50 per share and initial price. As interest rates rose, so would the yield on the preferred stock, and as interest rates fell, so would the yield. A number of other financial institutions proceeded to offer adjustable-rate preferred stock. In fact, there were 91 such offerings from May 1982 through June 1984. All of them used the same 3 interest rates as a reference point, offering various premiums above the highest of the rates. Some of the issues had "collars," meaning that there were maximum and minimum dividend yields specified.

The adjustable-rate preferred issues did not experience the stability in price that had been hoped for. One reason was that while the adjustable yield may have taken care of price volatility arising from changes in interest rates, it did not protect against volatility arising from changes in the credit standing of the issuer. Fresh versions of variable-rate preferred stocks were devised to deal with both the change in interest rates and possible changes in credit standing. First, various kinds of conversion privileges were tried. The adjustable-rate preferred stock might be convertible into common shares, with the conversion ratio changing to maintain the value of the preferred stock. Different ways of setting the variable rate from time to time were also tried; then a much more effective alternative was discovered in the Dutch auction.

[b] **Auction-Rate Preferred.** The auction-rate preferred stock is an adjustable-rate preferred stock that has the dividend rate reset through a Dutch auction. Potential buyers participate by indicating the amount of the preferred stock that they are prepared to buy at a particular yield. Holders of the shares indicate whether they are offering any for sale, and, if so, how many and below which dividend yield. An agent appointed by the company determines the yield at which the market clears, i.e., the yield at which the offers to purchase equal the offers to sell. Auction-rate preferred stock achieved substantial popularity, with the market reaching over $5 billion by 1986.[11]

[c] **Remarketed Preferred.** Following close on the heels of the auction-rate preferred stock was remarketed preferred stock. Remarketed preferred stock is another perpetual preferred stock whose variable dividend rate is reset periodically by a remar-

---

[11] The use of auction-rate preferred stock is compared to the issue of commercial paper in D.T. Winkler and G.B. Flanigan, "Default Risk Premia in the Near-Cash Investment Market: The Case of Auction-Rate Preferred Stock Versus Commercial Paper," *Journal of Financial Research*, Vol. 14 (Winter 1991), pp. 337–343.

keting agent. The holder of the preferred stock can elect to continue to hold the shares for a 49-day period at the new rates or tender the shares for sale. It is the responsibility of the agent to reset the 49-day rate to cause the remarketed preferred stock to trade at par value.

There has been fierce competition between auction-rate preferred and remarketed preferred stock. Auction-rate preferred stock was an innovation of J.P. Morgan, and many other firms have followed its lead. Remarketed preferred stock was invented by Merrill Lynch, which continues to be its major proponent. There are those who agree with Merrill Lynch that a dealer can do a more effective job than investors operating through a Dutch auction and those who maintain that no dealer is a satisfactory substitute for an auction open to investors.

[2] Callable Preferred Stock

Some preferred stocks are perpetual, as is common stock. There is no provision for the corporation's ever paying off the preferred holders and redeeming their shares, short of dissolution of the corporation. Some, like debt instruments, have a specified redemption date, when the corporation will redeem the shares at their par or stated value. A call feature is common; this gives the corporation the right (but not the obligation) to call the shares for redemption at a specified price or a series of specified prices at a specified time or at a number of specified times at the corporation's choice.

The most obvious reason for the corporation's wanting the preferred to be callable is that during a period when interest rates are lower than when the preferred was issued, it may be possible to replace the outstanding issue with a new preferred at a lower dividend cost. In late 1992 and early 1993, for example, with interest rates at their lowest level in many years, a number of corporations were calling their callable preferred stocks issued at times of high interest rates and therefore carrying high dividend rates, and replacing them with either debt or other preferred stocks at much lower cost. Such a call is highly beneficial to the corporation but not at all beneficial to the holder, who loses the high dividend and must reinvest the proceeds upon redemption at a relatively low rate. The expectation that the call privilege will be used to benefit the corporation at the expense of the holder is, of course, one aspect of the initial transaction in which the investor agrees to purchase the preferred stock. The more unattractive the call feature appears to the investor, presumably the greater must be the specified dividend to induce an investment.

[3] Preference Stock

One sometimes finds that the balance sheet of a corporation includes both preferred and preference stock. In this case, the preference stock is generally junior to the preferred stock and senior to common stock. Its right to dividends and to a redemption payment if the corporation is dissolved will be subordinated to the rights of the preferred stock, but with respect to common stock it will look like a preferred stock.

Preference stock is likely to be issued when the corporation would like to issue more preferred stock but for some reason cannot. For example, it is quite common for the corporation's articles of incorporation to require a vote of the preferred stockholders or to prescribe a dividend coverage test before more preferred stock is issued. The requirement might be that new preferred stock may be issued only if the previous 12 months' net income after taxes would be enough to cover the preferred dividends (including dividends on the new shares to be issued) one and one-half times. If the coverage test cannot be met or if the vote of the preferred shareholders cannot be obtained and the corporation prefers not to issue common stock, the only way to raise equity capital may be by way of preference stock.

[4] Valuation of Preferred Stock

The value of a perpetual preferred stock, nonparticipating and nonconvertible, is usually computed as the discounted present value of an infinite stream of constant dividends. This is just d/r, where d is the annual dividend in dollars and r is the rate of return demanded by the investor. To investors that demand a return of 8 percent a year on preferred shares carrying a $6 annual dividend, the value of a share is $6 divided by 0.08, or $75. Establishing the appropriate discount rate is not a trivial matter and raises the same questions as does the determination of the discount rate in establishing the intrinsic value of a share of common stock.

If the preferred stock is participating, the value of the participation must be added to the value of the assured dividend. The participation will take the form of a function of the common dividend, as a rule, so the DCF flow method for valuing a stream of common dividends can be applied to value the stream of participating dividends.

Where the preferred stock is not perpetual but has a redemption date or is at least callable, the valuation process must take into account the date of redemption or call. In this case, valuing the preferred stock is similar to putting a price on a bond with a fixed maturity and possible call features. More sophisticated models for the valuation of preferred stock involving option-pricing theory are not discussed here.[12]

7.04 CONVERTIBLE SECURITIES

Debt instruments convertible into common stock have some of the characteristics of debt and some of the characteristics of common stock. Convertible preferred stock has some of the characteristics of preferred stock and some of the characteristics of common stock. This section examines only the conversion privilege itself.

[1] Convertible Preferred and Convertible Debt Instruments

A convertible preferred stock can be exchanged, at the shareholder's option, for common stock; the same is true for a convertible bond. The conversion of the preferred stock may be 1 for 1, i.e., 1 share of common stock for each share of convertible preferred stock, or it may be 4 for 1 or any ratio at all. Sometimes the conversion terms are expressed as a conversion price rather than a ratio; this will almost always be the case for a convertible bond or debenture. The ratio is the par or stated value of the preferred stock (or the face value of the bond or debenture) dividend by the

---

[12] For a discussion of valuation models for nonconvertible preferred stock, see E.J. Ferreira, M.F. Spivey, and C.E. Edwards, "Pricing New Issue and Seasoned Preferred Stocks: A Comparison of Valuation Models," *Financial Management*, Vol. 21 (Summer 1992), pp. 52–62. The perpetuity-pricing model is compared to Merton's option-pricing-theory-derived model and a second option-pricing-theory-derived model that incorporates further conditions.

conversion price. A conversion price of $25 where the par value of the preferred stock is $100 corresponds to 4 shares of common stock per share of preferred stock. A conversion price of $25 where the face value of the debenture is $1,000 corresponds to 40 shares of common stock per debenture.

As in the case of warrants, the usual purpose of a conversion feature is to make preferred stock or bonds or debentures more salable. The purchaser anticipates that the value of common shares will rise and that the conversion will be profitable at some point in the future. From the issuing corporation's point of view, there are significant differences between the use of warrants and the use of convertible preferred stock or debt instruments. In the case of the warrants, their exercise brings fresh cash into the corporation. In the case of the convertibles, no new cash comes in, but preferred stock or debt disappears from the corporation's balance sheet and is replaced by common stock. Some corporations see the latter transformation as an attractive way to replace debt with common stock, more or less automatically, as long as the stock price rises sufficiently to induce the conversion.

The point in time when conversion is likely to take place is generally a function of the dividends on the common and preferred stock and the coupon interest on the debt. Since there are protective features pertaining to preferred and debt instruments that do not pertain to common stock, those that convert their preferred stock or their debt instruments are sacrificing some of these protective features. The inducement to convert will be the achievement of higher income. If the dividends on the shares into which the preferred stock can be converted are somewhat higher than the dividends being paid on the preferred stock, there is an incentive to convert. Similarly, if the dividends on the common shares are greater than the interest being paid on the debt convertible into those shares, there is an incentive to convert the debt instruments.

Generally, convertible preferred and convertible debt instruments are also callable, which enables the corporation to force conversion. When there is a call, the holders of the convertible preferred or debt instruments are confronted with a choice either to convert or to have their preferred or debt instruments redeemed at the par or face value, which is generally less than the value of the common stock into which they could be converted. The result is that all or virtually all of the convertible instruments are converted into common stock. A common stock price that never quite reaches the point where conversion is attractive can present serious difficulties to a corporation.

Convertible preferred stock is especially useful in a new venture when the founders are seeking capital from investors. The investors would probably purchase common stock so as to share in the benefits of the expected success were it not for the risk that the life of the corporation might be short, and in a liquidation all of the shareholders, including the founders and the investors, would share the assets. The result might be that the money supplied by the investors would simply pass in large part to the founders. If the investors are issued convertible preferred stock, however, they can enjoy all of the benefits of common stock if the company succeeds but also be entitled to their money back, up to the value of the assets of the corporation, if it fails. It is not necessary that the preferred stock carry any dividend in this case. The investors are not interested in preferred dividends; they are interested in participating in a rising share value with protection in case the venture fails.

Brennan and Schwartz have suggested the reason why a convertible preferred or debt instrument may be especially useful in a case where there is disagreement between the management of the company and the investors as to the riskiness of the venture.[13]

---

[13] Michael Brennan and Eduardo Schwartz, "The Case for Convertibles," *The Revolution in Corporate Finance*, 2nd ed. (1992).

A convertible preferred stock can be thought of as consisting of a straight preferred stock and an option on common stock, and a convertible debt instrument can be thought of as a straight debt instrument combined with an option on common stock. The more risky the venture, the less valuable the straight preferred or debt instrument for any given dividend yield or coupon. At the same time, the more risky the venture, the more valuable the option on the common stock. If the management attributes a relatively low risk to the venture and the investors attribute a relatively high risk, the management will value the straight preferred or debt instrument higher than the investors do, but the investors will value the option higher than the management does, and the two differences will offset each other. It is perhaps easier to reach agreement on financing terms when a convertible instrument is used than it could be in the case of straight preferred or straight debt.

[2] Preferred Equity Redemption Cumulative Stock

Preferred equity redemption cumulative stock (PERCS) is a kind of convertible preferred stock invented by Morgan Stanley and first effectively brought to the market in 1991. PERCS automatically convert to common stock at the end of the three years (unless they are called by the issuer during that period). A cap is set on the conversion value, generally at about 30 percent above the common stock price when the preferred stock is issued. At the end of the three years, if the common stock is trading at or below the cap, holders of the PERCS receive one share of common for each PERCS share. If the common stock is trading above the cap, the holders of the PERCS receive less than one share, with the conversion ratio adjusted so that the market value of the common issued equals the cap. Those familiar with call options will realize that the investor is in effect purchasing a share of common stock and giving the corporation a call option at the cap price. The investor is compensated for giving up the call option by an unusually high yield. For example, General Motors offered an 8 percent dividend on its PERCS issued in 1991, when the common stock was yielding 3.9 percent. The initial popularity of PERCS seems to have been based on the attractiveness of an immediate high yield in a generally low-yield market. And from the issuer's point of view, PERCS are helpful if the credit rating is strained, since the rating agencies generally consider PERCS equivalent to common stock. Since the explosion of offerings in 1991 and 1992, more thought appears to have been given to the precise trade-off involved in these shares. The valuation question concerns whether the extra dividend yield received by the holders of PERCS is a fair price for the call option given to the issuer. There may be a tendency for investors to place a lower value on that option than does the issuer, in which case it is easy to satisfy both parties.

7.05 VALUATION OF WARRANTS, OPTIONS ON COMMON STOCK, AND CONVERTIBLE DEBT OR PREFERRED STOCK

A call option entitles the holder to purchase common shares at a specified price, the exercise price, up to a specified date, the expiration date. There are a number of valuation models for call options, including the Black-Scholes model.

A warrant to purchase common stock is a kind of call option and is valued in the same way. A convertible preferred stock can be thought of as a combination of a straight preferred stock (i.e., a nonconvertible preferred stock) and an option on common stock. For example, a preferred share that carries a $6 dividend and that is also convertible into a share of common stock can be thought of as a combination of a

FIGURE 7-1

Holdings of Common and Preferred Stock (Not Including Mutual Fund Shares) (1982–Third Quarter 1992)

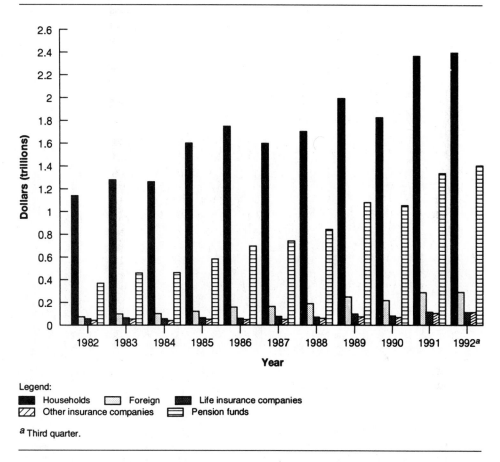

Legend:

■ Households   ▢ Foreign   ▨ Life insurance companies
▨ Other insurance companies   ▤ Pension funds

a Third quarter.

straight $6 preferred share and an option to purchase a common share. If the return required by investors on a straight preferred stock is 8 percent, the value of the straight preferred component is $6 divided by 0.08, or $75. The $75 value can be turned into a common share at any time up to a specified date. An option valuation model helps analysts find the value of an option to buy a common share at an exercise price of $75, with an expiration date that is the same as that of the conversion privilege. The value of the convertible preferred stock is then $75 per share plus the value of the option.

7.06 OWNERSHIP OF EQUITY SECURITIES

Figure 7-1 shows the holdings of common and preferred stock (not including mutual fund shares) of 5 major ownership groups from 1982 through the third quarter of 1992.

FIGURE 7-2

New Security Issues and Borrowing by U.S. Corporations (1982–1991)

Source: Federal Reserve Bulletin (various issues)

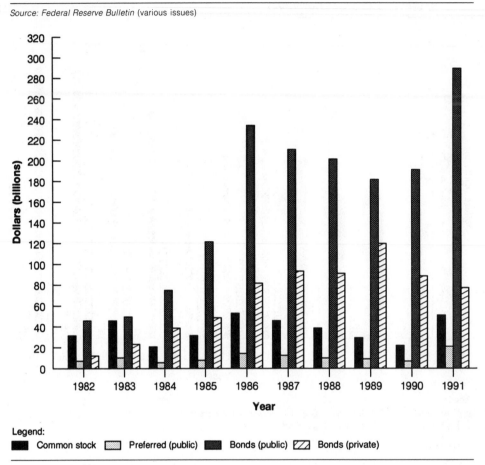

It is clear that over the nearly 11 years, the holdings of households generally increased, but the rate of increase was much greater for pension funds. Much of this rapid growth was due to a shift by state and local government retirement funds into common stocks. One might guess that over the next decade, institutional holdings will rise to equal the holdings of households.

7.07 MARKETS FOR EQUITY SECURITIES

[1] Primary Market

The sale of a new issue of common stock by a large corporation is generally underwritten, which means that the corporation actually sells the stock to an investment banker

FIGURE 7-3

Percentage of Total U.S. Share Volume

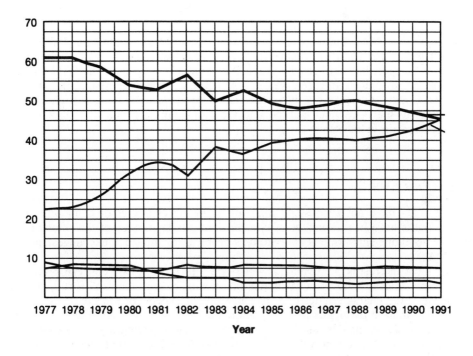

Note: The NASDAQ stock market's percentage of total U.S. share volume has grown substantially since its inception, doubling over the last 15 years.

or group of investment bankers, which in turn resells the stock, frequently through other investment banking firms, to institutions and individuals. Preemptive rights and rights offerings are sometimes made directly by a corporation to its own shareholders, but even in these cases, an investment banking firm is generally enlisted with an agreement to purchase any shares that are not taken up by the existing shareholders. Another way of selling new shares to existing shareholders is through dividend reinvestment plans, under which the shareholders agree that their dividends will be used to purchase more shares for them.

Figure 7-2 shows statistics on new offerings of common and preferred stock and of bonds over the 10-year period 1982–1991. Bond offerings tend to follow interest rates, with corporations relying more on short-term debt than bonds when interest rates are high (as in 1982) and then financing heavily through bonds when rates are low (as in 1991). Common stock offerings have been consistently low compared to bond offerings, and preferred stock offerings have been even lower. In fact, during the late 1980s and early 1990s, net offerings of common stock actually became negative. The popularity of leveraged buyouts and management buyouts absorbed more common stock than was being put on the market.

[2] Secondary Market

For many years, the dominant market in which stockholders bought from and sold to each other was the NYSE. Far more stock issues are traded in the OTC market than on the exchanges, but until recent years, the volume of trading in the OTC market had been much smaller. In recent years, NASDAQ has greatly increased the volume in the OTC market. Figure 7-3 shows the shift over the past 10 years of trading from the NYSE to the NASDAQ market, and the indications are that this market may become larger in volume than the NYSE.

7.08 CONCLUSION

Recent years have not seen many innovations in the character of common stock. Voting rights have been a matter of concern, and the legitimacy of deviations from the one vote–one share rule is likely to be a problem for the stock exchanges and for NASDAQ.

The most interesting innovations, which are still in progress, concern preferred stock. One series of innovations is in the direction of constructing an instrument that has most of the characteristics of a debt instrument except for the tax deductibility of interest and the dividends-received deduction. This kind of instrument is clearly aimed at satisfying the demand from corporate investors paying regular tax rates. A second line of innovation has to do with creating preferred stock that seems very much like common stock but has a lower cost to the issuing corporation. PERCS are an example. Both lines of innovation involve convertibility of the preferred stock into common stock.

As long as there is money to be made through satisfying investor demand for instruments that have unique and valuable characteristics and satisfying the demand on the part of issuers for instruments that can lower their cost of capital, the stream of innovations will continue to flow.

Chapter 8

Trading Markets

Thomas E. Copeland

Hans R. Stoll

8.01   ECONOMICS OF TRADING MARKETS

A market in which a financial instrument, such as a share of stock or an option, can be sold and resold is called a secondary market. One type of secondary market is a trading market. Trading markets are distinguished from negotiated markets or private placement markets (such as the venture capital market) in which resale of a financial instrument usually is difficult. Trading markets are also distinguished from new issues markets, the purpose of which is to raise new capital rather than to trade existing securities.

[1]   Function of Trading Markets

From the investor's perspective, the function of a trading market is to provide liquidity at fair prices. Investors seek liquidity for three reasons: first, because they have new information about a particular security; second, because they wish to save out of current consumption (buy securities) or dissave (sell securities); and third, because a change in their attitude toward risk warrants a change in the composition of their portfolios. Liquidity is achieved if investors can trade large amounts of securities without affecting price. Prices are fair if they reflect the underlying value of the security correctly.

From society's perspective, the function of trading markets is to summarize correctly the information that investors have about securities and to set prices so as to allocate resources to their proper uses. While trading in outstanding securities involves no allocation of new resources, prices in trading markets are essential for determining how savings will be allocated among competing uses. For example, in the stock market, the ability of a company to sell additional shares as well as its decision about paying out earnings depends on the stock price. In the commodities markets, farmers' planting decisions and storage decisions depend on the futures price.

[2]   Allocational Efficiency

A market is said to be allocationally efficient if the prices of securities in that market are "right" in the sense that they give the correct signals for the allocation of resources. Allocational efficiency has two aspects. First, it requires informational efficiency: The market for gathering information is efficient if the marginal benefit to society of gathering more information is equal to the marginal cost to society of gathering that information. When this occurs, securities analysts are doing their job. Second, allocational efficiency requires pricing efficiency: The available information is quickly and correctly reflected in securities prices. Pricing efficiency means that traders react quickly to new information and cause it to be reflected correctly in security prices. It also means that no market participant is so large as to be able to affect prices in the absence of new information.

If a trading market is allocationally efficient, certain propositions about that market follow. First, investing in that market is said to be a fair game. This means that investors can expect to earn a normal return that is commensurate with the risk assumed, but they cannot expect to earn more. This normal return is available whether or not the investor carries out research. Indeed, research based on publicly available information, whether technical or fundamental, has no benefit, because, by the definition of allocational efficiency, public information is already reflected in securities prices. Profits can be made only by predicting information that will cause prices to change.

The second proposition that follows is that new information, with which one might make a superior forecast of security price changes, is hard to get. If a market is informationally efficient, many security analysts compete for new information, with the result that none has consistent access to superior information. While a security analyst may occasionally discover new information and make superior predictions, those superior investment results tend to be offset by the costs of acquiring information. Informational efficiency does not rule out the possibility of acquiring nonpublic information; it implies only that such information is costly to acquire.

[3] Operational Efficiency

A market is said to be operationally efficient if the commissions of brokers and the bid-ask spreads of dealers are as low as possible for the level of services rendered by these intermediaries. Trading markets provide three categories of service: (1) communication and execution; (2) clearing, settlement, and record keeping; and (3) market making. The mechanisms by which investors that desire to trade find each other, establish mutually satisfactory prices, and execute transactions are through the services of brokers or agents and through various communication devices ranging from face-to-face communication on the floor of an exchange to telephones to sophisticated computer communication systems. After a transaction has been agreed on, title and money must change hands and records of the transaction must be established on the account of the customer, on the account of the issuer, and by various intermediaries. This service is generally performed by the broker and ranges from physical transfer of certificates of ownership to transfers by means of book entries in a computer system. Finally, since investors' brokers are not always able to find the other side of a transaction immediately, the services of dealers, which stand ready to buy or sell for their own accounts as principals, may be required. Dealers must be compensated for their costs, which include the risk associated with keeping an inventory of securities. Dealers' compensation comes from the fact that they purchase securities at a bid price and resell them at a higher ask price.

Figure 8-1 illustrates the concept of operational efficiency. The demand curve represents the shares that securities buyers would like to buy at alternative prices, and the supply curve represents the shares that securities sellers would like to sell at alternative prices. The intersection of demand and supply gives the equilibrium price, p^*, and the volume of trading, v^*, in the absence of transaction costs. In an allocationally efficient market, the equilibrium price reflects "all that is knowable" in the sense described previously. Trading volume arises because investors disagree about what they know and because portfolio adjustments and liquidity needs necessitate trading even in the absence of information.

Investors are not generally able to trade at p^* because of the cost of maintaining trading markets. Buyers buy at the ask price of the dealer, p_a, and pay a commission, c, to the broker. Sellers sell at the bid price of the dealer, p_b, and pay a commission, c. The difference between the buyer's price and the seller's price is

$$(p_a + c) - (p_b - c) = p_a - p_b + 2c$$

which is the bid-ask spread of the dealer plus two commissions. Transaction costs cause investors to reduce their volume of trading from v^* to v. The amount of the

FIGURE 8-1

Operational Efficiency

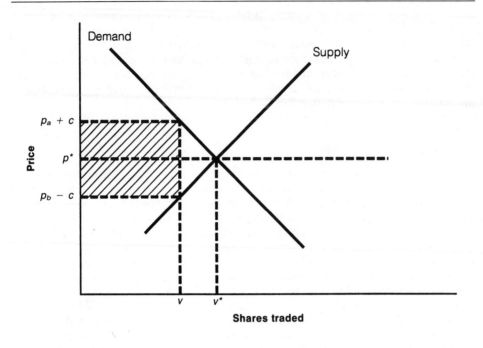

reduction depends on the slope of the demand and supply schedules. A trading market is operationally efficient if the bid-ask spread and commission charges are as low as possible for a given level of services.

The revenues of the securities industry are then given by $(p_a - p_b + 2c)v$, the shaded rectangle, i.e., the amount earned per share traded multiplied by the number of shares traded. The welfare of the securities industry depends critically on the size of this rectangle and on the cost to the industry of rendering its transaction services. The size of the rectangle depends on the charge per transaction (the vertical distance) and the volume of trading (the horizontal distance).

[4] Types of Markets

Trading markets may be classified by security type or by their organizational form. The major security types are equity (common and preferred stock) and debt. Debt instruments range from short-term money market instruments such as Treasury bills and banker's acceptances to long-term bonds issued by the U.S. government, by corporations, or by state and local governments. Futures contracts and option contracts have also increased in importance. The markets for these four financial instruments are examined in greater detail later in this chapter.

Trading markets may differ in their organizational structures. Financial instruments may be traded in a dealer or an auction market, in a continuous market or a call market, in an over-the-counter (OTC) market, or on an exchange. In a pure dealer market, investors, represented by their brokers, always trade with a dealer at the dealer's bid or ask price. In a pure auction market, investors, represented by their brokers, trade directly with each other. If a satisfactory price cannot be arrived at, the investor must wait to trade. In a continuous market, trading in the security takes place at all times. In a call market, trading takes place at specific times of the day, when the security is "called" for trading. A continuous market requires the participation of a dealer that is willing to trade immediately, while a call market can operate without dealers.

An exchange is a physical location where trading takes place. An OTC market is not a physical location; rather, it is a communications network using telephones and computers. Most exchange markets in the United States are continuous auction markets, which combine features of a dealer market and an auction market. Investors, represented by their brokers, have the opportunity to trade directly with each other to the extent that they are present at the same time at the same physical location on the floor of the exchange, but they can also trade with a dealer (e.g., the specialist on the New York Stock Exchange (NYSE) and the scalper on the commodities exchange) who is willing to provide liquidity at a price that is reflected in his bid-ask spread. OTC markets are dealer markets in which investors, or brokers representing investors, trade with dealers, not directly with each other. In the United States, most debt instruments are traded in an OTC dealer market, as are certain equity securities. No major U.S. securities market is a pure call auction market, since all U.S. markets are aimed at maintaining continuous trading. This has not always been so. The NYSE, for example, began as a call auction market in which particular securities were traded at particular times during the day. The Paris Bourse and the Tel Aviv Stock Exchange operate today according to the principles of a call auction market.

[5] Types of Orders

In all trading markets, investors may give their brokers a range of instructions. A market order instructs the broker to trade at the best price available under current market conditions. A limit order instructs the broker to trade at a specified price or better. A limit buy order specifies a price below the current market price. A limit sell order specifies a price above the current market price. Limit orders also specify how long the order is to remain outstanding. Frequently, the decision to use a market order or limit order depends on the trading activity in the security. In an inactive market, it may be advisable to use a limit order because market prices deviate from their "correct" value and because the bid-ask spread may be large. In an active market, market prices deviate less from their "correct" value and spreads are smaller. Thus, a market order is satisfactory. A stop order instructs the broker to trade when the market reaches a specified price. Once the price is reached, a stop order becomes a market order. A stop buy order specifies a price above the current market and would be used to limit losses on a short position. A stop sell order specifies a price below the current market and would be used to limit losses on a long position.

Since a limit order specifies prices away from the current market price, it must be held until the market price hits the limit price. Trading markets differ in their procedure for holding limit orders. In some markets, all limit orders in a particular security are centrally held. For example, on the Chicago Board Options Exchange (CBOE), all limit orders are held by an order book official who has no duties other than to handle limit orders and who is compensated by a portion of the broker's commission when limit orders are executed. On the NYSE, limit orders are held by the specialist, who receives floor brokerage when he or she executes limit orders on behalf of other brokers. In other markets, such as the OTC and futures markets, limit orders are held by individual market makers. There appear to be significant benefits to centralizing limit orders: When limit orders are dispersed, each broker must check the market price continuously to see if it is approaching the limit prices of the broker's customers; when they are centralized, considerable duplication of effort is avoided.

[6] Regulation of Trading Markets

Several government agencies regulate trading markets. The Securities and Exchange Commission (SEC), established in 1934, oversees trading in equities, corporate bonds, options, and municipal bonds. The Commodities Futures Trading Commission (CFTC) regulates trading in futures contracts. The U.S. Department of the Treasury oversees trading in government securities.

Federal regulation of the securities markets rose out of the stock market crash of 1929 and the investigation of pools and other manipulative devices that was carried out by the Senate Committee on Banking and Currency. The Securities Act of 1933 (1933 Act) applies to new issues of securities. It requires registration by the issuer, the underwriter, and control persons, as well as requiring the provision of a prospectus to all potential purchasers. Antifraud provisions are contained in Section 17(A) of the act.

The Securities Exchange Act of 1934 (1934 Act) applies primarily to trading in already issued securities, that is, to trading markets. Major sections of the 1934 Act are concerned with full disclosure, antifraud, and antimanipulation provisions. Periodic reporting requirements of the 1934 Act provide for disclosure by listed corporations. The 1934 Act also regulates the business conduct of brokers and dealers that are members of exchanges. Under the principle of self-regulation, the SEC has, with certain exceptions, only indirect oversight responsibility over exchanges and their members and leaves to the exchanges the responsibility for enforcing the explicit provisions of the 1934 Act. The Maloney Act of 1938 extends the authority of the SEC to include the supervision of the OTC market. The Maloney Act provides for the registration of any qualified association of brokers and dealers, and the National Association of Securities Dealers (NASD) is registered pursuant to this act. SEC regulations prohibit trading on the basis of material inside information. Under Section 16 of the 1934 Act, specific prohibitions and disclosure requirements are imposed on corporate officers, directors, and holders of 10 percent or more of the stock. Under the more general Section 10(b) of the 1934 Act, which is a general prohibition of manipulation or deceptive trading, less specific prohibitions apply to other investors that are recipients of inside information.

The CFTC, established in its present form by an act of Congress in 1974, is responsible for overseeing trading in all futures contracts. Prior to 1974, only trading in the agricultural commodities was formally regulated, and that authority rested with the Commodity Exchange Authority housed within the Department of Agriculture.

Although the Treasury has no formal authority to regulate government securities markets, it maintains oversight of these markets and, with the help of the Federal

FIGURE 8-2

Equity Trading Markets in the United States (1991)

Source: NYSE, *Fact Book, 1992;* NASDAQ, *Fact Book, 1992;* AMEX, *Fact Book, 1992*

Market	Number of Companies	Dollar Volume of Trading[a]	Market Value of Listings[a]
NYSE	1,885	$1,520	$3,713
AMEX	860	41	124
Regionals	—	204[b]	—
NASDAQ	4,094	693	510

[a] Dollars in billions.
[b] Includes dually listed stocks.

Reserve Board, conducts periodic studies of the structure and functioning of the government securities market.

8.02 EQUITY TRADING MARKETS

[1] Major Trading Markets

[a] **Exchange Markets.** The NYSE is the principal market for trading equities in the United States. At the end of 1991, the NYSE listed the common stocks of 1,885 companies with a total market value of $3,713 billion. The annual dollar volume of trading was $1,520 billion in 1991 (see Figure 8-2).

The right to trade on the floor of the NYSE is conferred by ownership of one of 1,336 seats. Seats may be purchased and sold, and the price of a seat reflects the value to a broker of having access to the floor. As of December 1991, seat prices were approximately $430,000. The majority of seats on the NYSE are owned by commission house brokers, who are partners in brokerage firms that execute orders for the public. At the end of 1991, 329 member firms, each with one or more seats, dealt directly with the public. Approximately 400 seats are owned by specialists, who do not deal directly with the public. The remaining seats are held by floor brokers, who execute orders on the floor on behalf of other brokers, or by floor traders, who trade for their own account. In 1991, approximately 190 member firms, each with one or more seats, did not deal directly with the public.

The American Stock Exchange (AMEX) lists the shares of smaller companies not listed on the NYSE. At the end of 1991, 860 companies were listed on the AMEX. The market value of these firms was $124 billion at the end of 1991, and 1991 dollar volume was $41 billion. Equities are also traded on regional exchanges: the Philadelphia, Midwest, Pacific Coast, Boston, Cincinnati, Inter-Mountain, and Spokane Exchanges. Most of the volume on these exchanges is in stocks that are also listed on the NYSE or AMEX. The number of companies listed solely on regional exchanges is small.

Trading activity in NYSE- or AMEX-listed stocks is reported on a consolidated tape no matter where the transaction is executed. In addition to the regional exchanges, a certain amount of trading in listed securities is carried out on the National Association of Securities Dealers Automated Quotation (NASDAQ) system of the OTC market. The tape reports information on the number of shares and the price of each transaction.

[b] OTC Market. Whereas an exchange market is a physical location, an OTC market is a communications network connecting customers to the physically dispersed dealers that make up the market. One of the most dramatic developments in the securities industry in the last 20 years has been the development and growth of NASDAQ, an automated quotation system for facilitating trading in stocks that was developed by the NASD in 1971. Prior to the introduction of NASDAQ, dealer quotations in OTC securities were supplied daily on printed "pink sheets" and reflected closing quotations for the previous day. At the end of 1991, 4,094 companies with equity securities valued at $510 billion were listed solely on NASDAQ.

NASDAQ is a dealer market made up of approximately 425 dealers that stand ready to buy and sell the securities in the system. Each stock has at least two dealers. In 1991, the average number of dealers per stock was 10.1, with 290 stocks having more than 20 dealers. Individual dealers may make markets in as many as 300 to 400 stocks. Access to NASDAQ occurs at various levels. Possession of a level 1 terminal allows a broker to determine the inside quote, the highest bid price of any dealer and the lowest ask price of any dealer. At the end of 1991, 205,000 terminals with level 1 capability existed. A terminal with level 2 capability allows a broker to determine the bid and ask prices of each dealer in a stock. Dealers in NASDAQ possess terminals with level 3 capability, which, in addition to allowing level 1 and level 2 capability, also permit the dealers to enter price quotations for the stocks in which they make a market.

The trading information provided on NASDAQ depends on the security. For over 2,500 securities, termed national market securities, NASDAQ provides volume of trading and transaction price data comparable to listed securities, as well as bid and ask prices. For less active securities, only bid and ask data are provided.

[2] The Trading Public

Until 1960, trading in common stocks was primarily the province of individual investors. Since then, however, there has been substantial growth in the role of institutional investors. This growth arises in part from the desire of individual investors to achieve diversification, professional management, and freedom from the mechanics of managing a stock portfolio. In part, it reflects the growth of pension funds and other forms of institutionalized saving. The major institutional investors are mutual funds and pension funds. According to NYSE statistics, institutional investors held 39 percent of U.S. equity in 1991. The importance of institutional trading activity is reflected in the statistics on block trading—trading in amounts of 10,000 shares or more—shown in Figure 8-3. In 1965, 2,171 block trades, amounting to 3.1 percent of reported share volume, were recorded. In 1991, 981,077 block transactions, accounting for 49.6 percent of reported share volume, were recorded. There is no gainsaying the tremendous growth in this form of trading.

FIGURE 8-3

NYSE Large Block Transactions of 10,000 Shares or More

Source: NYSE, *Fact Book, 1992*

Year	Number of Transactions	Reported Share Volume (Thousands)	Percentage of Reported Share Volume
1965	2,171	48,262	3.1
1970	17,217	450,908	15.4
1975	34,420	778,540	16.6
1980	133,597	3,311,132	29.2
1985	539,039	14,222,272	51.7
1991	981,077	22,474,383	49.6

[3] Specialists and Other Dealers

Central to the operation of the NYSE and other U.S. exchanges is the specialist system. Each stock on the NYSE is traded at a "post." The post is manned by several specialists and their clerks. Today, it is complemented by an array of electronic equipment for communicating information and assisting in the trading and trade reporting process. Each specialist is assigned one or more stocks, the number depending on the activity in the stock and the market-making capability of the specialist. No stock is currently assigned to more than one specialist. As a dealer, the specialist is responsible for maintaining a fair and orderly market by buying shares for his or her own account when other buyers are not available or selling shares for his or her own account when other sellers are not available. In this way, continuous trading is maintained.

The specialist also maintains the book of limit orders and acts as a broker's broker in executing these limit orders against incoming market orders. The specialist bid-ask quote frequently represents the book on one side. SEC data suggest that the specialist's income from activities as broker and as dealer are approximately equal.

The specialist system has been criticized because each specialist has a monopoly franchise. This lack of competition among specialists may allow each specialist to quote a wider bid-ask spread than would be the case under competition.

The specialist system has also been criticized because it combines the functions of broker and dealer. First, there is concern that conflict may arise between the interests of specialists acting for their own accounts and the interests of their customers. Second, because specialists have privileged knowledge of the book of limit orders, they have information not available to the public. For example, knowing how many buy orders on the book are just below the current market price reduces the specialist's risk in taking a long position in a stock and provides information about future supply and demand that is not generally available.

Over the years, a variety of changes in the specialist system have been urged. It has been argued that the specialist's functions as broker and dealer should be separated. Another suggestion is that the book of limit orders be made public, thereby eliminating the specialist's privileged knowledge of the book. With television monitors, this proposal is quite feasible. Finally, it has been urged that there be more competition among specialists. Partly in response to this suggestion, the NYSE introduced a new category of floor member in 1978—a registered competitive market maker (RCMM). However, the RCMM's participation must be requested by a floor official; he or she does not compete directly on an equal basis with the specialist. Other attempts at instituting direct competition among specialists on the floor of the NYSE have tended to fail, in large part because of the natural tendency of businesspersons in continuous and generally friendly contact to share markets, and in part because of the physical structure of the NYSE floor, which makes competition difficult.

While direct competition among specialists on the floor of the NYSE is unlikely today, specialists' pricing decisions are constrained by a variety of competitive forces. First, specialists on other exchanges and dealers in the OTC market with which the NYSE is linked electronically may compete with the specialist on the floor of the NYSE if the specialist spread is too wide. Second, the specialist faces competition from traders in the crowd at the post, who trade for their own accounts, and from brokers in the crowd, who hold customer market orders. Third, the specialist faces competition from limit orders of investors. For example, any seller who judges the specialist bid price to be too low may enter a limit order to sell at a somewhat higher price. In doing so, the customer must weigh the cost of delay in executing the order against the benefit from trading at a better price. Last, the specialist faces competition from "upstairs" market makers who arrange large block transactions. The relatively low capitalization of most specialists and the absence of sophisticated communications equipment has relegated specialists largely to making smaller-size markets on the floor of the exchange on the basis of face-to-face communication. Upstairs market makers trade large blocks for institutional customers, usually as brokers but not infrequently as dealers with respect to at least part of the block. While such transactions must be brought to the floor for execution under NYSE rules, the trade is for all intents and purposes completed upstairs. Upstairs market makers or block positioning firms compete with each other in making markets in large blocks in a wide range of stocks.

The absence of direct competition on the floor of exchanges is not typical of the OTC market. As already noted, on the NASDAQ system, the average stock attracts in excess of 10 competing dealers, with many stocks attracting more than 20 competing dealers.

[4] Execution Process

[a] Standard Transactions. The principal steps in executing standard-size stock market transactions (neither very large, such as a block transaction, nor very small, such as an odd-lot transaction) are depicted by the flow chart in Figure 8-4. The customer deals with a registered representative, who has passed a certifying examination conducted by the NASD. The registered representative is able to supply a certain amount of advice and can provide market information regarding the last transaction price and price quotations of dealers in the securities of interest to the customer. The customer places an order with the registered representative, which is transmitted to the back office of the brokerage firm and is time-stamped. If the stock is listed on the NYSE, the order is automatically sent to the floor broker on the NYSE. Sometimes the back office may investigate other markets, such as regional exchanges or NASDAQ, on which the stock is also traded.

If the order is a market order, the floor broker takes the order to the specialist's post and asks the specialist for a quote and perhaps his or her size at that quote.

FIGURE 8-4

The Execution Process

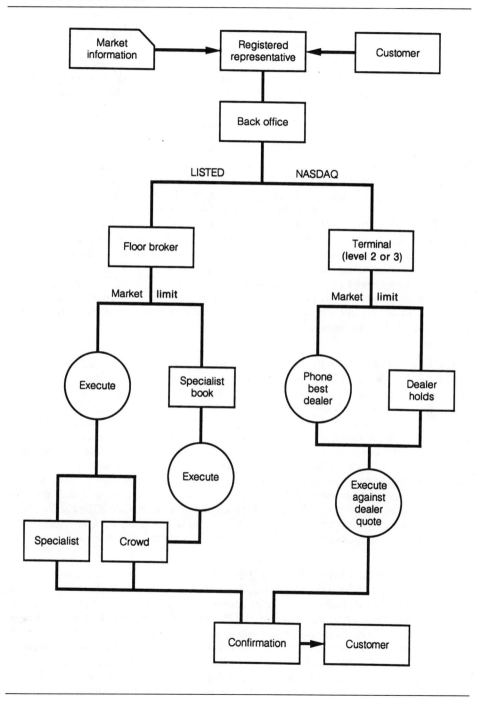

Usually, the transaction is executed immediately with the specialist, unless other brokers standing in the crowd at the same time offer a better price. Usually, an order is completed in a single transaction. However, large orders, particularly in inactive stocks, may require several transactions at different prices to complete. Upon completion of the transaction, price and volume information is immediately entered into the exchange's computer and printed on the consolidated tape. The floor broker also reports the terms of the transaction to his or her back office. A confirmation of the transaction, which indicates the price, the commission, the market, and whether the broker acted as principal or agent, is also prepared and sent to the customer and the registered representative.

If the order is a limit order, the floor broker gives it to the specialist for entry in the specialist's book. Suppose the stock last traded at 30½. A limit order to sell at 32 would be entered by the specialist in his or her book. If the market price rises so that the specialist's quote is 31¾ to 32, the ask price at 32 would represent the book (even if the specialist wished to sell at 32, the customer has priority). At that point, the limit order will be executed against the next incoming market buy order.

In the case of NASDAQ securities, the back office must check its level 2 or level 3 terminal to determine which dealers in NASDAQ quote the best price. That dealer is then telephoned, and, in the case of a market order, immediate execution takes place. Again, the order may be broken up if the market maker is unwilling to trade the entire amount at his quote. Individual market makers hold limit orders of their own customers as well as the customers of other brokers not making a market in the stock. As in the case of listed securities, the confirmation is prepared immediately after the transaction and sent to the customer and the registered representative by the back office of the customer's firm.

[b] Block Trades. Usually, large blocks cannot be executed according to the standard procedure just described, because no one in the market has the capital necessary to take the other side of such a transaction. As a result, certain block trading firms with substantial capital have come forward to make a market in large blocks. These firms may act as dealers with respect to all or part of a block. They are also knowledgeable about other institutional investors in the market and, with the assistance of various computer communications systems, are frequently able to find institutional customers to take all or part of the other side of the transaction. After a transaction has been negotiated in the upstairs trading room of the block trading firm, brokers representing the institutions on both sides of the transaction meet on the floor of the NYSE for formal execution of the trade. Frequently, a block trades at a price different from that of the last sale. For example, a block may trade at 37, down from a last sale of 38. In that case, buy limit orders between 37 and 38 are executed at the block price, 37.

[c] Small Orders. Orders for fewer than 100 shares are termed odd-lot orders. At one time, odd-lot transactions were made by two odd-lot trading firms that purchased and sold odd lots for their own account and offset any imbalances between odd-lot purchases and sales by transactions on the floor of the exchange. Today, these odd-lot trading firms have disappeared and odd lots are handled directly by the specialist. Certain large brokerage firms also execute odd-lot transactions for their customers.

A major trend in the securities markets is the development of automated systems for routing and executing small orders, including small round lots as well as odd lots. An order-routing system automatically directs an order to the execution location and thereby bypasses the need for a floor broker and other intermediary handling that is required in standard transactions. Trade reports are sent back through the same order-routing system. For example, the NYSE's designated order turnaround (DOT) system automatically routes orders to the appropriate specialist post for execution by the specialist using normal procedures. Execution is not automatic.

Automatic (or nearly automatic) execution systems exist on the regional exchanges (PACE on the Philadelphia Stock Exchange, SCOREX on the Pacific Coast Exchange, and MAX on the Midwest Exchange). These systems are called derivative pricing systems because automatic execution is usually at the bid or ask quote in other markets. In certain cases the specialist on a regional exchange has an opportunity to better the quote in other markets. Certain NASD dealers that are not members of the NYSE also make markets in NYSE-listed stocks at low transaction costs.

The NASDAQ market has implemented the small order execution system (known as SOES), which allows small orders of 1,000 or fewer shares to be executed automatically against the best bid or ask price without the need for telephone contact. In addition, brokerage firms often automatically execute customer orders on their in-house systems.

Academicians have long argued that the process of matching buyers and sellers is largely a clerical task that could be automated. Under the pressures of increased volume and the need to economize, brokerage firms are coming to the same conclusion.

[5] Clearing Process

After a trade has been executed, securities and money must change hands within five business days of the trade date, on the settlement date. The clearing process can be cumbersome, costly, and time consuming if each broker must contact every other broker with whom it has traded on a given day or if settlement must be made with individual brokers by physical delivery of certificates. The paperwork crisis of 1969–1970, in which failures to deliver reached new highs and back offices were overwhelmed by the unprecedented volume of trading, gave rise to major improvements and automation of the clearing and settlement system. While the tremendous volume of trading during the October 1987 crash was handled surprisingly well, the crash provided additional impetus to expand and improve clearing procedures.

Basically, two tasks are carried out in the clearing process: trade comparison and settlement. Trade comparisons are made through the facilities of a clearing corporation that receives reports of each transaction from the brokers participating in the transaction. The largest clearing corporation is the National Securities Clearing Corporation (NSCC), established in 1977 as a successor to clearing corporations affiliated with the NYSE, AMEX, and the NASD. The NSCC is the first clearing corporation registered as a national clearing corporation pursuant to the Securities Acts Amendments of 1975. Many brokers do not clear for themselves but instead establish correspondent relationships with brokers that participate in the NSCC. The facilities manager of NSCC is the Securities Industry Automation Corporation (SIAC), established in 1972 and jointly owned by the NYSE and AMEX. SIAC owns and maintains computers and operates a variety of trading and clearing systems.

The first four days of the clearing period are devoted to the trade comparison process and to resolving any discrepancies in the transaction information provided by parties to a transaction. Unmatched trades are flagged, and advisory notices are sent to participants that fail to report a transaction reported by the contra side. While much of this process is already automated, further enhancements to allow on-line processing of uncompared transactions are currently being developed. For example, the NASD has developed the trade acceptance and reconciliation system, which allows participants in the NSCC to receive on-line trade comparison information.

The second step in the clearing process, the final settlement, is also automated and usually carried out through computer book entries. The key change permitting the use of book entry settlement has been the immobilization of securities certificates, which has been made possible by the increased willingness of brokers and financial institutions, such as banks, to forgo physical delivery of certificates. Instead, certificates are immobilized at a securities depository. The principal depository is the Depository Trust Company (DTC), founded in 1973 as a successor to the NYSE Central Certificate Service. The DTC is owned by the NYSE, AMEX, the NASD, and major participants (brokers and banks); it is regulated by the SEC and, as a limited trust company, by the Federal Reserve System and New York state. Because participants in the DTC keep securities in the name of a nominee, Cede & Company, shares may be transferred among participants in the DTC without the need for transfer on the issuer's books.

Final settlement is usually accomplished through a continuous net settlement (CNS) procedure. On the fourth day after a transaction, each NSCC participant is informed of the *net* obligation to deliver (or receive delivery of) securities in each issue traded four days before. The NSCC guarantees the contra side of each transaction. Simultaneously, each participant is informed of its total money obligations for all transactions executed four days before, with payment due to or due from the NSCC. The NSCC then directs the DTC to transfer securities from net sellers and to net buyers.

A schematic of this procedure, in which the NSCC is the focal point, is shown in Figure 8-5. The line connecting each clearing broker to the NSCC, as spokes in a wheel, indicates that the broker settles its position directly vis-à-vis the NSCC. Prior to the NSCC, the daily balance order system was usually employed. Under this procedure, each broker would settle with respect to every other broker with whom it had traded, and certificates would be delivered physically between all trading partners. Clearly, such a system is inefficient, especially since certificates would have to be redelivered frequently. A modified balance order system is currently in use by the NSCC for securities not eligible for CNS. However, in that system the NSCC determines obligations between pairs of brokers so that no redelivery of certificates is required.

In Figure 8-5, the spokes of the wheel extend beyond the clearing brokers to introducing brokers that clear on a correspondent basis and to customers. Introducing brokers do not clear for themselves and frequently do not hold customer securities. An introducing broker may act on a "fully disclosed basis," in which case customers know the name of the clearing broker and the clearing broker settles the individual customer accounts of the introducing broker. Alternatively, the introducing broker may act on an "omnibus basis," in which case the clearing broker only settles accounts vis-à-vis the introducing broker, leaving to the introducing broker the task of maintaining the accounts of individual customers. Today, most clearing brokers have direct customer links, but there is a tendency for some clearing brokers to specialize in providing wholesale clearing services for other brokers.

The final ring in the clearing process depicted in Figure 8-5 is the customer. Customer-side settlement (as opposed to street-side settlement, as just discussed) varies according to whether the customer wants delivery of securities or is willing to hold securities in street name. If securities are kept in street name, the only record of the transaction is the confirmation and the customer's monthly statement. If the customer seeks delivery, the broker must send certificates to the transfer agent, who records a

FIGURE 8-5

The Clearing Process

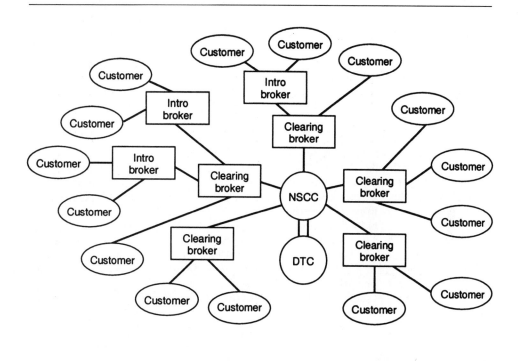

change of ownership on the books of the issuer and mails certificates to the customer. In the past, the desire of large institutional investors, such as bank trust departments, to receive delivery of certificates slowed the clearing process substantially. Today, major custodian banks are members of the DTC and are willing to accept book entry transfer.

[6] Cost of Trading

The services of a trading market are not provided without cost. The information, execution, and clearing systems are costly to establish and to maintain. Brokers and dealers recover these costs and make a profit by charging a commission (when acting as agents) or buying at the bid price and selling at the ask price (when acting as dealers).

[a] **Commissions.** Commission charges must cover the costs of the registered representative (about 40 percent of the commission) and all of the other costs in the execution process, including any floor brokerage paid to other brokers.

Prior to May 1, 1975 (May Day), commissions on the NYSE were fixed at a minimum. As a result of the Securities Acts Amendments of 1975, commissions are determined competitively, as are most other prices in the U.S. economy. Since May Day, average commission rates have declined, and the decline has been particularly dramatic in the case of large institutional orders. According to the SEC, commissions on institutional orders dropped from 0.84 percent of the price in 1975 to 0.36 percent of the price in 1980. Commissions on smaller orders did not decline as much—from 1.73 percent of the price in 1975 to 1.39 percent of the price in 1980. Commissions vary by type of stock and type of service provided. Commission rates tend to be higher for small, less actively traded stocks than for large, actively traded stocks. Discount brokerage firms charge lower commissions than full-service firms that offer more counseling and advice.

[b] Bid-Ask Spread. While not appearing on a customer's confirmation, the bid-ask spread is a real cost of trading in securities markets. The cost is reflected in a higher price paid by the buyer and a lower price received by the seller. In the typical NYSE stock, the spread is 25 cents or less. There is considerable variation in the spread of different stocks according to the volume of trading in the stock, the price of the stock, the volatility of the stock, and other factors.

Commissions and bid-ask spreads also declined in the 1980s. Institutional investors often pay as little as 3 cents per share, and individuals can find it possible to trade at as little as 15 cents per share. In the NASDAQ market, institutions often pay no commission; the broker earns only the bid-ask spread. In fact, some dealers are willing to pay 1 or 2 cents per share to retail brokers that send them a steady stream of orders to execute. These reduced trading costs reflect the effects of competition among markets and brokers for the order flow.

[7] Margin Trading

Investors may borrow funds to help finance the purchase of securities. The initial margin requirement, set by the Federal Reserve Board, determines the fraction of the purchase price that customers must finance out of their own funds. Since January 3, 1974, the margin requirement has been 50 percent, which means that investors that wish to purchase $1,000 worth of common stock must supply $500 of their own money and may borrow the rest. All listed stocks and a large number of NASDAQ stocks are eligible for margining.

Investors that borrow from their broker must keep shares in street name as collateral for the broker's loan. An interest rate ranging from 0.5 percent to 3 percent above the broker's call money rate is charged. An account that falls below the initial margin requirement is restricted, and the equity of the account must be increased before additional securities can be purchased. The minimum maintenance margin requirement at which the customer must supply additional funds or face liquidation of position is established by self-regulatory organizations such as the NYSE, where the rate is currently 25 percent. The exchanges sometimes establish special margin requirements for individual issues that exhibit unusual volume or price volatility. Individual brokers also have the option of setting higher minimum maintenance margins for their customers.

[8] Short Selling

Short selling is the sale of a security that the investor does not own. In order to make delivery within the five-day settlement period, the security must be borrowed from another investor. There are three parties involved in a short sale: the short seller, the buyer of the shares sold short, and the lender of the shares.

Lenders will not lend shares unless they are at least as well off as they would be by keeping the shares. This means that lenders must receive any dividends paid on the stock (which must be paid by the short seller) and must be guaranteed that the shares can be returned upon demand. This requirement is met by the establishment of an escrow account, which is marked to market daily so that it always contains sufficient funds to buy back the shares in the market should the lender wish them to be returned. Frequently, the lender demands an additional premium for the time and trouble involved in lending shares.

The buyer receives shares as if it were involved in an ordinary transaction. It owns the shares and receives dividends from the company. The lender does not own the shares, although it is in the same economic position as if it did. The dividend is paid not by the company but by the short seller.

The short seller must supply margin equal to 50 percent of the current market price of the shares. However, no loan is required. Indeed, the seller (or broker) receives the proceeds of the short sale, which can be invested to earn interest. According to SEC regulations, short selling is permissible only on an uptick (i.e., only after the price has increased by at least an eighth of a point).

Short selling is used in a variety of ways. Investors that believe the stock price will fall sell short in the hope of buying back the shares at a later date at a lower price. Short selling also is used frequently in arbitrage situations, such as a merger. If company A, currently selling at $40 per share, is taking over company B, currently selling at $30 per share, and if the takeover offer is a one-for-one exchange of shares, arbitragers might sell A short and buy B. If the merger goes through, the arbitragers can cover their short position with the shares of A received in the merger. A variety of other arbitrage or semiarbitrage opportunities can arise with respect to the same security traded in different markets or with respect to related securities such as options.

[9] Financial Integrity of Securities Firms

Customers are concerned about the financial integrity of their brokerage firms because they leave securities in street name or because they temporarily leave idle funds with their broker (free credit balances). Even customers who pay fully for securities and demand delivery bear some risk in the period between the trade date and the final delivery date of the certificates. Risks exist because securities left in street name and margined by the customer may be pledged as collateral for bank loans to the broker or may be lent out, and free credit balances may be used by the brokerage firm for the firm's activities. Should a brokerage firm fail, the customer is in the position of any other creditor seeking redress in bankruptcy court.

Society is concerned with the financial integrity of brokerage firms because failure of a brokerage firm may precipitate a lack of confidence in other brokerage firms and may produce a cumulative run on brokerage firms not unlike the bank runs of the 1930s.

Two types of safeguards protect customers: insurance and regulatory constraints on the brokerage firm. As a result of the paperwork crisis of 1969–1970, a decline in the market shortly thereafter, and the resulting failure of a number of brokerage firms, Congress created the Securities Investor Protection Corporation (SIPC), which insures customer accounts. The SIPC is financed by assessments on brokerage firms.

Regulatory constraints take two forms: a net capital requirement and segregation requirements. These requirements are administered directly by the SEC or by self-regulatory organizations such as the NYSE or the NASD. The net capital requirement limits the amount by which a brokerage firm's indebtedness may exceed its net capital. (Net capital is assets minus liabilities.) For the purpose of the net capital rule, assets are subject to a reduction in value, or "haircut," the amount of which depends on the liquidity of the asset, and liabilities exclude certain subordinated loans that are included in equity. The SEC has established a net capital ratio (i.e., liabilities divided by net capital), at which the brokerage firm is subject to examination and a restriction on its activities.

Under segregation requirements, customers' securities that have been paid for in full must be segregated. Segregation is in bulk, not by individual customer name. Cash received as the proceeds of short sales on behalf of customers is also segregated.

[10] Changing Structure of the Stock Market

In the past 20 years, the stock market has experienced rapid change that has led to increased competition among securities firms and between securities firms and other financial intermediaries. The factors responsible for these changes are threefold. First, the computer and improved communications technology have reduced the cost of serving many customers in different locations desiring different services. In effect, reduced costs of communication and record keeping have increased the extent of the market and thereby promoted competition among more financial institutions across a broader geographical area.

Second, technological developments and the growth of pension funds and other forms of institutionalized saving have produced a new class of large investors. With respect to securities markets, these institutional investors have substantial bargaining power, and they have been an important force in stimulating competition and improved service in the provision of brokerage services.

Third, regulatory changes in the securities industry have removed impediments to competition. Pressure from the Antitrust Division of the Department of Justice as well as other pressures produced a change in regulatory philosophy at the SEC and in Congress that culminated in the passage of the Securities Acts Amendments of 1975. These amendments abolished fixed commission rates on the NYSE and called for increased competition in all aspects of the securities industry.

[a] **NMS.** Among other things, the Securities Acts Amendments of 1975 called for a reduction in direct government regulation of securities exchanges and a greater reliance on competition within the framework of a single national market system (NMS). This system would not be restricted to a specific physical location, and communication and trading through a computer could replace face-to-face communication and trading on an exchange floor. Access to an NMS would be available to any qualified broker or dealer.

To satisfy congressional criteria, an NMS would need three key elements: (1) a computerized national transaction reporting system that records and reports all transactions wherever they take place; (2) a computerized national central limit order book (CLOB) that lists limit order prices of investors as well as bids and offers of dealers; and (3) a mechanism to "lock in" a transaction on the computer when an acceptable price is observed in the CLOB.

A national transaction-reporting system, the consolidated tape, is in place for listed securities. However, the remaining two elements of an NMS are not operational on a national basis. While there are no technological obstacles, the establishment of an NMS has been hindered by the cost of implementing these features. In addition, many brokers that benefit from the current trading procedures oppose the speedy establishment of an NMS and the greater competition that an NMS would imply. The SEC has also decided to let an NMS evolve rather than to impose a specific blueprint.

Some evolution is occurring toward linking various physical markets to produce an NMS. The various regional exchanges and NASDAQ are linked to each other and to the NYSE through the intermarket trading system (ITS), which allows an order received in one market to be executed at a better price in another market. The ITS does not allow automatic execution; however, it is an efficient communications link between markets.

[b] NYSE Rule 390. NYSE Rule 390 requires that all NYSE member firms' transactions as principal be brought to the floor of the NYSE. A major debate revolves around the status of NYSE Rule 390. Those in favor of its complete abolition argue that abolition would remove restrictions on the market to which orders are sent and would therefore remove the remaining obstacles to the implementation of the NMS. Those opposed to the abolition of NYSE Rule 390 are concerned about market fragmentation and the loss of order flow. In particular, floor members of the NYSE are concerned that markets for all transactions will be made upstairs, directly between investors and brokers, without the need to bring such orders to the floor of the exchange. Opponents also argue that NYSE Rule 390 should not be relaxed before procedures for protecting limit orders in different markets are established. On June 11, 1980, the SEC, in its Rule 19C-3, prohibited the application of NYSE Rule 390 to securities listed after April 26, 1979. This experiment in the relaxation of NYSE Rule 390 did not change trading procedures materially because the use of the ITS is cumbersome and order-routing procedures automatically channel orders to the NYSE floor.

[c] Alternative Routes to an NMS. While the debate is continuing with respect to exchanges and securities listed on exchanges, substantial progress toward a national market system for OTC securities has been made and NASDAQ has been upgraded to provide data on transactions as well as dealer quotations. Furthermore, since all dealer quotations are displayed simultaneously, it is a small step to the automatic execution of orders against the best bid or ask, and such an automatic execution system is currently possible for small orders.

Thus, forces leading to an NMS appear to have been set in motion. An NMS is likely to arise as a result of the further development of the ITS link, or, if this link proves unworkable, other markets such as NASDAQ may grow in importance. In future years, stock trading, like bond trading, may be conducted over communication links connecting physically dispersed locations, at least for institutional-size transactions. The role of exchanges may be greatly diminished.

8.03 DEBT MARKETS

Although less familiar to the public, debt markets are larger and more liquid than stock markets. Debt markets may be categorized by maturity: Money markets trade short-term, highly liquid debt instruments such as Treasury bills, banker's acceptances, and federal funds. Capital markets for debt trade longer-term securities such as U.S. government bonds, municipal government bonds, and corporate bonds. In this discussion, debt markets are categorized by issuer.

[1] U.S. Government Debt Markets

The large deficits of the U.S. government through the 1970s and 1980s have resulted in huge primary and secondary markets for Treasury bills, notes, and bonds as well as for the debt of U.S. government agencies such as the Government National Mortgage Association, Federal Intermediate Credit Banks, Federal Home Loan Banks (FHLBs), Federal Land Banks, and Federal Farm Credit Banks (FFCBs). By far the largest primary market is for Treasury securities.

[a] **U.S. Government Securities.** The form of Treasury debt with the shortest term is called a Treasury bill. It is a promise to pay a stipulated amount (called the face of the bill) on a stated maturity date. There are no intermediate payments such as coupons. Most bills are issued with original maturities of either 91, 182, or 364 days. The secondary market for Treasury bills is extremely competitive and highly efficient. More than 40 dealers continuously provide bid and ask quotations and will purchase and sell bills for their own inventory and at their own risk. The bid-ask spreads are quite small, frequently no more than one or two basis points (a basis point is one hundredth of one percent), and standard-size transactions range from $5 million to $25 million. There is a large interdealer market that is fully computerized. The best quotes of the dealer community appear continuously on computer screens, thereby eliminating the need to make a large number of phone calls to uncover the best price. This automation and the size of transactions makes the Treasury bill market perhaps the most efficient and liquid in the world.

Treasury notes and Treasury bonds are coupon bonds with original issue maturities of 1 year or more. Notes usually have maturities ranging from 1 to 10 years; bonds may have any maturity but typically mature in 25 to 30 years from their issue date. All Treasury coupon bonds are exchanged in secondary markets on an accrued-interest basis. In addition to the transaction price of the bond, buyers must compensate sellers for all interest accrued since the last coupon.

Federal agency debt is issued in large blocks. The proceeds are re-lent through local financial intermediaries to ultimately benefit smaller borrowers such as home owners and farmers. There is a fairly active secondary market for federal agency debt. The short-maturity coupon issues of FFCBs and FHLBs trade in very liquid markets.

[b] **Treasury Auctions.** Treasury securities are issued in an auction and may be purchased by submitting a competitive tender stating the yield to maturity (discount rate in the case of bills) the bidder is willing to accept and the quantity to be purchased. The Treasury first totals all noncompetitive bids and then accepts competitive bids starting with the lowest yield until the amount to be sold is reached. In issues with coupons (notes and bonds), the coupon rate is based on the average yield of accepted competitive tenders.

In the Treasury's traditional multiple price auction, competitive bidders pay the price (receive the yield) they bid but are uncertain if they will be allocated the quantity of securities they request. If many bidders bid the same price, partial allocations may be made. Noncompetitive tenders are always accepted but are limited to $1 million per bidder in bills and $5 million per bidder in notes and bonds.

In 1992, the Treasury began to experiment with a single price auction in issues of notes. This new auction procedure was implemented in partial response to the revelation that Salomon Brothers had violated the rule that no bidder may bid for more than 35 percent of an issue and because of concerns that the multiple price auction encouraged collusion among bidders. In a single price auction, bidders continue to bid a price or yield, but the Treasury awards all securities at the highest accepted price (lowest accepted yield). Aggressive bidders may therefore pay a lower price (receive a higher yield) than the price (yield) they bid. The purpose of this procedure is to create incentives for more aggressive bidding and to reduce the incentives for collusive behavior. The Treasury has made a number of other changes in its auction procedures, including opening the auction to dealers and depository institutions that are not classified as primary dealers.

[2] Commercial Bank Liabilities

One of the most liquid of all debt markets is the federal funds market. Fed funds are not securities at all, but rather the purchase or sale of unsecured reserve balances of commercial banks. Banks that have funds in excess of Federal Reserve Bank reserve requirements will lend, usually overnight, to another bank that is short of its reserve requirement. Fed funds conventionally trade in $5 million blocks in a brokered market. About 100 large commercial banks participate in the national market on a daily basis. In addition to overnight loans, fed funds are occasionally lent on a term basis for several weeks or months.

Repurchase agreements (RPs) are collateralized loan contracts. A borrower will sell securities (usually U.S. government or agency securities or certificates of deposit (CDs)) to a lender and simultaneously agree to buy back the same securities at a later date for the same price plus interest. Rates on RPs are usually very close to the rates on fed funds of the same maturity. Although commercial banks are frequent participants in RPs, the major borrowers are government securities dealers. Corporations and municipal governments with money to invest for short periods are major suppliers (lenders) in the RP market. Many of the transactions are made via direct contract between the borrower (a dealer in Treasury securities) and the lender (a corporation or municipal government).

A CD is a negotiable deposit liability of the issuing commercial bank. Because CDs are negotiable, they can be bought or sold in a secondary market. CDs are interest-bearing securities and may sell for a price above or below their face value depending on the market rates of interest at the time. Original-issue CDs are usually sold on a tap basis, which means that commercial banks offer them continuously rather than having a periodic offering of large quantities. Maturities of new CDs are at the option of the buyer but must be for at least 14 days from the original issue. Nonbank broker-dealers also help to sell CDs. In return for a commission fee, the broker locates investors interested in the issue. When an investor is found, the broker then buys the CD from the issuing bank and sells it to the investor on a "bought-as-sold" basis. This procedure exposes the broker to no risk because no inventory is held. The secondary market for CDs is operated by nonbank firms such as Salomon Brothers, First Boston Corporation, and Merrill Lynch. The standard block size is $5 million. Yields on outstanding CDs are usually slightly above those of new issues from the same bank because an investor can tailor a new issue maturity to his or her needs; this is not possible for issues traded in the secondary market.

[3] Corporate Debt Markets

Commercial paper is unsecured short-term corporate debt that pays no coupons. It promises to pay a stated face value upon maturity. Investors receive a return because commercial paper is sold at a discount from its face value. Almost all commercial paper has a maturity of nine months or less when it is originally issued. New issues of commercial paper may be placed directly on a tap basis in denominations of $100,000 with the maturity at the discretion of the buyer, or they may be placed by dealers such as The First Boston Corporation or Goldman, Sachs. Dealer-placed paper is typically sold in $250,000 lots and may be underwritten or brokered. If it is underwritten, the dealer buys the entire issue for its own inventory and takes the risk of reselling it. The issuing corporation pays an underwriting fee in order to avoid the risk. Alternatively, the issue may be placed on a bought-as-sold brokered basis. In this case, the corporation receives a higher price but bears more risk. Although there is no secondary market for directly placed commercial paper, some liquidity is provided because corporations usually stand ready to buy back their own paper if the need arises. In addition, dealers will occasionally bid to buy back paper at a premium of roughly 25 basis points. Thus, the effective bid-ask spread on commercial paper is substantially wider than the spread of 1 or 2 basis points in the more liquid Treasury bill market.

Corporate bonds are interest-bearing corporate debt that usually have original issue maturities of 5 to 30 years. Bonds are issued infrequently in large blocks either through a private placement on a brokered basis with a life insurance company or by means of an underwritten public offering. If the new issue is a public offering, an underwriting syndicate of dealers will form to buy the new bonds from the firm and then resell them to the public. About 6 weeks before the offering date, the issuer files a registration statement with the SEC, although a recent innovation called shelf registration allows the issuer to file as much as a year before the offering and to choose the best time for the offering. The day before a public offering, the members of the underwriting syndicate meet with the issuing firm to decide on the coupon rate and offering price for the bonds. If the yield is too high, the issuer might withdraw; if it is too low, the syndicate may break up because the bonds will be too hard to sell. After the price, coupon rate, and terms of the bond are established, a final prospectus is filed with the SEC. The offering is then sold at a common price to the public on a subscription basis. If the issue is sold out, the members of the underwriting syndicate divide their profits, but if the issue is not sold, the syndicate may break up and the members try to sell the bonds for whatever price they can.

Secondary trading of registered corporate bonds occurs in a nonbank dealer market because the Glass-Steagall Act expressly prohibits commercial banks from acting as dealers in corporate securities. Investors that wish to transact in corporate bonds contact their broker, which then contacts a dealer that will offer bid and ask quotes. Trading in corporate debt is relatively infrequent, and, as a result, the market is very thin. Weeks may pass between transactions in a particular security.

[4] Municipal Government Debt

Municipal bonds are the interest-bearing debt of municipal governments or their agencies. Their most important feature is that their coupon interest income is not subjected to federal income taxes. Note, however, that capital gains on municipal debt are taxable. Municipal debt is usually classified by the type of security underlying it. General obligation bonds are secured only by the general revenues of the municipality. Revenue and authority bonds for the construction of all highways, ports, parking facilities, utilities, or public housing are secured by the revenue streams that they bring in.

Municipal securities are issued by means of a process that is a hybrid of the unrestricted competition of Treasury auctions and the negotiated underwriting of corporate debt. Although the bonds are advertised for sale to the public, they are offered on an all-or-nothing basis. In practice, this restricts bidding to syndicates of broker-dealers that buy a new issue and then reissue it to the public. The Glass-Steagall Act does not prohibit commercial banks from participating in municipal bond syndicates. Competition among syndicates may affect the interest paid by municipalities. Richard West (1966) found that municipalities that received only a single bid had to pay an average premium of 23 basis points above prevailing market rates.

The secondary market in municipal securities has several tiers. Recent offerings with large outstanding volumes are traded actively through the dealer activities of large banks and nonbank broker-dealers. Next, there is a dealer market, which trades a large variety of smaller issues. Finally, there is an extremely thin market for the small issues of local school districts and local governments. The bid-ask spread on a municipal bond may be as low as 0.25 percent on an actively traded issue or as high as 5 percent on inactive issues.

8.04 FUTURES MARKETS

Futures markets are the most rapidly growing of all trading markets. While futures contracts in agricultural commodities have been traded since before the turn of the century, rapid expansion in the number of contracts has occurred only recently with the advent of futures on financial instruments. Futures exchanges in the United States and their more actively traded contracts are shown in Figure 8-6.

[1] Nature of a Futures Contract

A futures contract is just that, a contract. In a futures contract, the buyer (the long) agrees to buy an asset (such as wheat, a foreign currency, gold, or a Treasury bill) at a later date at a price established when the contract is initiated. The seller (the short) agrees to sell the underlying asset at maturity at the price specified. Neither the underlying asset nor the purchase price specified in the contract changes hands when the contract is initiated. Both parties to the contract must, however, deposit margin, usually about 10 percent of the contract value. This margin is different from margin in the stock market or bond market, in which payment and delivery are made at the trade date. Margin in futures markets is a performance guarantee and is required from both the buyer and seller. Interest-earning assets may be pledged to meet the margin requirement.

FIGURE 8-6

U.S. Futures Markets and Active Futures Contracts

Exchange	Grains and Oilseeds	Livestock and Meat	Food, Fiber, and Wood	Metals and Oil	Debt Instruments	Currencies	Equity Instruments
Chicago Board of Trade	Corn Soybeans Wheat Soybean meal Soybean oil Oats	Iced broilers		Silver Gold	Treasury bonds Treasury notes Municipal bonds		Major market index
Chicago Mercantile Exchange and international money market		Live cattle Pork bellies Live hogs Feeder cattle	Lumber		Treasury bills Bank CDs Eurodollars	U.K. pound Deutsche mark Swiss franc Canadian dollar Japanese yen	S&P 500 stock index
New York Commodity Exchange Inc.				Gold Copper Silver			
New York Futures Exchange							NYSE composite index
New York Cotton Exchange			Orange juice Cotton		Treasury notes	Dollar index	
Kansas City Board of Trade	Wheat						Value Line stock index
Minneapolis Grain Exchange	Wheat						
Mid-America Commodity Exchange and monetary market	Wheat Corn Oats Soybeans Rough rice	Live cattle Live hogs		Silver Gold	Treasury bonds Treasury bills	Deutsche mark U.K. pound Japanese yen Canadian dollar Swiss franc	
New York Mercantile Exchange				Platinum Palladium Heating oil Unleaded gasoline Crude oil Natural gas Gasoline			
Coffee, Sugar, and Cocoa Exchange			Coffee Sugar #11 Cocoa				

While most futures contracts call for delivery of the underlying asset at maturity, delivery can be avoided by taking an offsetting position before maturity. Thus, a long in March wheat futures can avoid receiving delivery of wheat in March by selling March wheat futures prior to the maturity month. Delivery is rare in futures markets because participants that wish to possess the underlying asset usually prefer to purchase the asset in the cash market, where the grade and delivery point of the asset can be more precisely specified; they prefer to use the futures markets as a temporary hedge while the cash market transaction is being arranged. Certain new contracts, such as stock index futures, do not call for delivery but call for cash settlement. In cash settlement, traders make a gain or loss measured as the difference between the contract price and the cash price of the underlying asset at maturity.

An active and liquid futures market is possible only for standardized assets. Standardization is necessary so that each participant knows precisely what is being bought and sold. However, even an asset like wheat is not inherently perfectly standard: Different grades of wheat are grown. As a result, futures contracts are written in terms of a standard grade but permit delivery of other grades at a premium or discount from the standard contract price. Broadening the delivery terms limits the ability of anyone to control the available supply so as to engineer a corner or short squeeze in the delivery month. While broadening the definition of the assets acceptable for delivery limits the danger of price manipulation in the delivery month, too broad a definition limits the hedging usefulness of a futures contract because the relationship between the future price and the cash price is no longer very precise. This conflict between precise standardization and a broad definition to avoid manipulation in the delivery month is inherent in the design of most commodity contracts.

Another important feature of futures contracts is the number of delivery months. Agricultural commodities have approximately 6 delivery months at any moment, extending approximately 15 months into the future (for example, in October, the delivery months for wheat are December of the current year and March, May, July, September, and December of the next year). Other futures contracts, such as silver and some of the financial futures, have delivery months extending more than 2 years into the future. Again, the contract design involves a balancing of objectives. Having too many contract months reduces the liquidity in any one of the contract months, while having too few contract months limits the usefulness of the contract.

[2] Trading Mechanics

As in the stock market, anyone interested in trading futures contracts establishes an account at a brokerage firm and deals with an account executive who has passed an examination on commodity futures markets and is registered with the CFTC. Customers are also required to sign a "risk disclosure statement" that describes the risks involved in trading futures contracts.

As in the stock market, market orders, limit orders, or stop orders may be used (with variations). There is no limit order book in futures markets. Instead, each broker holds its own "deck" of orders, including limit orders. In futures markets, spread orders are also possible. A spread order calls for the simultaneous purchase and sale of futures contracts of different delivery months in the same underlying asset.

As in the stock market, orders are first routed to a firm's back office and then to the trading floor of the appropriate exchange. The trading floor is quite different from the trading floor of a stock exchange because there is no single specialist making a

FIGURE 8-7

Illustration of Trading and Settling in Futures Markets

Time	Buyer	Seller	Cumulative Contract Volume	Open Interest	Price	Cumulative Profit			
						A	B	C	D
1	A	B	1	1	4.00	0	0	0	0
2	C	A	2	1	4.01	0.01	-0.01	0	0
3	C	D	3	2	3.98	0.01	0.02	-0.03	0

Note: Long positions = short positions = open interest. Total profits of all traders at any point in time are zero.

market at a particular location. Instead, there is a large trading pit filled with brokers and traders dealing directly with each other by means of hand signals and voice contact. Many traders act as brokers on behalf of their customers. Others, scalpers, are very short-term traders who perform the same function as dealers in the stock market. Scalpers trade for their own account; they buy at a bid price when there is excessive public selling and sell at an ask price when there is excessive public buying. Others, day traders and position traders, take speculative positions for their own account.

A price reporter enters price information into a computer next to the trading pit. The information is displayed on the floor and disseminated worldwide. Information on transaction size is not reported. Volume and open interest are reported only on the following day by the clearinghouse of the commodities exchange. Volume is the number of contracts traded in a day; open interest is the number of contracts outstanding at the end of the day.

The clearinghouse is central to the proper functioning of a futures exchange. It compares and settles transactions carried out on the floor of the exchange. Not all brokerage firms are members of the clearinghouse, and those that are not clear through a clearinghouse member. The clearinghouse facilitates trading by interposing itself between the buyer and seller after a transaction has been agreed on. This makes possible an active secondary market for buyers and sellers, since positions can now be reversed by dealing with the clearinghouse without having to deal with the original parties to the contract.

The illustration in Figure 8-7 may clarify the process. Assume that the commodity is December wheat and that all transactions are for one contract (5,000 bushels). At time 1 the contract is opened for trading, and A and B agree to trade at a price of $4 per bushel. Volume is one contract and open interest is one contract. The clearinghouse becomes the buyer to B and the seller to A. When A becomes a seller at time 2, the clearinghouse is the buyer to A. Since A is now a buyer and seller of the same contract on the books of the clearinghouse, its position is closed out by the clearinghouse (and it makes a profit of 1 cent). In effect, C replaces A as the offsetting long to B's short position, without B's knowledge. At time 2, cumulative volume has increased by one to two contracts, while open interest remains at one. When C buys a second contract from D at time 3, cumulative volume and open interest each increase by one contract.

A feature of futures markets is that accounts are settled daily with respect to the clearinghouse. Thus, at time 3, C has lost 3 cents a bushel, even though C has not closed out its long position. C must therefore post additional margin, whereas B has excess margin (of 2 cents), which may be withdrawn. Note that long positions always equal short positions and that total profits of all traders are zero.

[3] Purposes of Futures Markets

Futures markets serve two economic functions: (1) They allow price risk to be shifted from the less able or less willing to the more able or more willing and (2) they provide information that is useful to processors and other users of the underlying asset.

In futures markets, risk is shifted from hedgers to speculators. A hedger is a party that holds, processes, or has an obligation to deliver the underlying asset. To limit risk, a hedger establishes a futures market position that is opposite to its cash market position. For example, a storer of a commodity such as wheat (an asset) would sell futures (a liability) to protect against adverse price fluctuations in wheat. Speculators take a position in futures markets opposite to that of hedgers in hopes of making a profit. Evidence suggests that, on average, speculators do not make profits; this, in turn, implies that hedgers receive insurance against price risk at zero cost.

Even in the absence of hedging uses, futures markets can be beneficial because speculators, acting on the best information available to them, cause futures prices to reflect all that is knowable. Thus, the futures market is allocationally efficient in the sense described previously, and futures prices act as useful signals to processors, storers, and farmers. In the absence of futures markets, such information would not be generally available, and producers, storers, and farmers might make decisions based on less complete information.

Neither the risk shifting nor the information function needs to be performed in markets in which prices are certain. Futures markets arise when there is price instability. For example, currency futures only became popular after the advent of flexible exchange rates. The fact that futures markets arise in volatile markets sometimes leads to the incorrect inference that futures markets cause volatile markets.

[4] Stock Index Futures

Futures contracts on stock indexes are among the most actively traded futures contracts. While futures contracts on several indexes are currently traded, the contract on the Standard and Poor's (S&P) 500 index is the most active. Trading and clearing procedures for index futures contracts are the same as for other futures contracts, but index futures differ in that they do not call for delivery of an underlying item. Instead, index futures call for cash settlement. In the case of cash settlement, the holder of a futures contract simply accumulates gains and losses on his position, as shown in Figure 8-7. At the end of the futures contract's life, any remaining holders are simply closed out at the final settlement price. In the case of the S&P 500 futures contract, which expires quarterly, the final settlement occurs on the third Friday of March, June, September, and December at the opening value of the S&P 500 index, as calculated from the opening prices of each of the component stocks in the index. (Prior to June 1987, the closing value of the index was used.) Cash settlement is called for in index futures because of the difficulty of delivering the 500 component stocks of the index in the exact proportions called for by the index.

As in the case of other futures contracts, stock index futures provide a useful risk management tool. For example, by selling stock index futures a portfolio manager can hedge a portfolio of common stocks against a decline in the general market. If the portfolio manager has selected stocks skillfully so that they decline in price less than the market declines (or rise in price more than the market does), the portfolio manager makes gains. Stock index futures can also be used for market timing. A portfolio manager who holds a diversified portfolio but switches between bonds and stocks on the basis of forecasts of market movements can accomplish such switches more rapidly and at lower cost by trading stock index futures than he or she can by trading stocks and bonds. For example, a portfolio manager with $80 million in stocks and $20 million in bonds who wishes to switch to $60 million in stocks and $40 million in bonds could sell $20 million of stocks and buy $20 million of bonds. The commission costs plus the market impact of such a transaction could easily amount to $80,000. On the other hand, the manager could sell stock index futures on $20 million worth of stock (which represents approximately 100 S&P 500 futures contracts). The commission plus the market impact cost of using futures is about $7,500. Stock index futures therefore provide a very low-cost way of moving in and out of the stock market.

[a] **Program Trading.** While stock index futures are the fastest and lowest-cost procedure for trading claims on diversified portfolios of stocks, sometimes money managers wish to trade actual portfolios of stocks. Program trading is the trading of a portfolio of stocks pursuant to a single order. Program trading allows a money manager to buy or sell the S&P 500 index, the S&P 100 index, the Major Market Index (an index of 20 stocks), or other diversified portfolios. While a single order may be given to trade a program, component stocks of the program must still be traded individually. The innovation in program trading is the speed with which program transactions are executed and the fact that broker-dealers will make bids on program trades before the orders are executed and sometimes before the actual composition of the portfolio is known.

[b] **Stock Index Arbitrage.** Stock index arbitrage maintains the appropriate relation between the stock index futures price and the price of the underlying cash index. If stock index futures prices are too high, arbitragers sell stock index futures and purchase the component stocks of the index (a program trade). Sometimes, only a representative subset of the index stocks is purchased. If stock index futures prices are too low, arbitragers purchase stock index futures and sell the component stocks of the index (either as a short sale, which is often difficult, or from a long position). Probably the majority of program trading is associated with the need to buy or sell portfolios of stocks as part of index arbitrage.

The theoretical relation between the stock index futures price and the cash index price can be shown as the following:

$$\frac{F - S}{S} = r - d$$

where:

F = stock index futures price

S = cash price of the stock index

r = riskless rate of interest for the period until maturity of the futures contract

d = dividend yield for the period until maturity of the futures contract

This calculation follows from the fact that the purchase of the index stocks at S and the sale of the futures at F locks in a known return that must, in equilibrium, be equal to the cost of carrying the position. That cost is the interest cost (r) of funds tied up in the stocks less the dividend yield in those stocks (d).

At maturity, the futures positions of arbitragers are automatically closed out according to the cash settlement procedure. If arbitragers wish to remain hedged, they must either roll into new futures contracts or they must dispose of their positions in the underlying stocks. If the underlying stocks are disposed of, arbitragers usually trade them at the opening price on the NYSE on the expiration day of the futures contract because the opening price is the settlement price for the futures contract. By trading the index stocks at the opening price, arbitragers maintain the riskless hedge vis-à-vis the futures market: Any adverse price changes in the individual stocks are offset by beneficial price changes in the futures contract.

[c] Triple Witching Hour. Before June 1987, the triple witching hour (i.e., the last hour of trading on the quarterly expirations of index futures when index options and stock options also expire) witnessed extremely heavy stock market volume and additional stock price volatility as a result of the unwinding of stock index arbitrage positions and the desire of arbitragers to receive the closing price on the expiration day. Substantial program trading during the triple witching hour caused order imbalances in index stocks, and the technical problems of accommodating these imbalances have from time to time resulted in temporary price effects that have averaged about 0.3 percent.

In an attempt to mitigate expiration-day volatility, settlement of the S&P 500 index futures contract was changed from Friday close to Friday opening. If a severe opening order imbalance was observed that would tend temporarily to distort prices, the specialist could postpone the opening until orders on the other side could be accumulated. It was hoped that the use of the opening price would mitigate price pressures that have been observed at the closing price. However, the evidence indicates that volatility was simply shifted from the close to the opening.

[d] Dynamic Portfolio Insurance. Dynamic portfolio insurance is a fairly recent innovation in financial markets first introduced by Leland, O'Brian, and Rubinstein Inc. in the early 1980s. Dynamic portfolio insurance is not really insurance in the traditional sense of the word; rather, it is a form of short-term trading that is designed to provide investors (usually pension funds) with gains when the stock market is rising, while limiting losses when the stock market fails. The pattern of returns is similar to a call option; that is, there is upside gain potential, but downside losses are limited. Dynamic portfolio insurance is usually implemented by the use of stock index futures contracts.

The idea behind dynamic portfolio insurance is quite simple. As the market rises, greater and greater portions of the investor's portfolio are moved into common stocks and out of bonds, and, when the market falls, the portfolio is weighted more toward government bonds and less toward equities. The stock index futures allow this switch between stocks and bonds to be made more quickly and at lower cost than if stocks and bonds were actually traded. For example, the return on a $20 million portfolio of diversified common stocks can be guaranteed over a three-month period by selling three-month stock index futures on $20 million of stock. The difference between the stock index futures price and the current price of that portfolio (plus any dividends paid on the portfolio) is the guaranteed yield on that portfolio. In other words, by selling stock index futures against the portfolio, a stock portfolio has in effect been converted into a short-term debt portfolio.

313

Suppose a pension fund wishes to guarantee a minimum annual return of 5 percent over a five-year horizon at a time when five-year government bonds yield 7 percent yearly. On the basis of the expected return and the likely volatility of stock prices over the five-year horizon, an initial allocation of 30 percent to stocks and 70 percent to bonds might be made. If the stock market goes up more than expected, the pension fund can afford to take additional risk and place a greater proportion of its portfolio in stocks; the cost of such portfolio insurance is that the pension fund does not fully participate in stock market gains (because only 28 percent of the portfolio is initially in stocks). If the stock market goes down, on the other hand, the pension fund must reduce its exposure to risk by taking funds out of stocks and placing the funds in bonds, thereby guaranteeing that the minimum return of 5 percent will be earned.

The fact that dynamic portfolio insurance causes portfolio managers to buy stocks when the market is rising and to sell stocks when the market is falling has caused concern that portfolio insurance is destabilizing, thus adding to market volatility. This criticism seems valid: If all investors blindly follow portfolio insurance strategies, markets would be destabilized. Market stability depends on the existence of a sufficient number of investors concerned with fundamental values and willing to take the other side if portfolio insurance trading results in artificial prices.

8.05   OPTION MARKETS

In the last decade, options contracts became more and more important, because of both the rapid growth of trading on organized options exchanges and the rapid development of option pricing theory. This part of the chapter first describes the nature of various types of options contracts (e.g., puts and calls on various underlying assets such as stocks, bonds, and indexes) and then discusses the development of major options exchanges and the mechanics of trading in them.

[1]   Types of Option Contracts

A call option gives its owner the right to purchase an underlying security, usually a share of stock, at a predetermined price for a fixed interval. For example, at the close of the CBOE on Thursday, January 7, 1993, there were 12 call options on shares of AT&T common stock. Their prices as well as the closing price of AT&T stock are given in the following chart.

Striking or Exercise Price	Maturity Month			AT&T Closing Price
	January	*April*	*July*	
40	$11\frac{3}{4}$	$13\frac{1}{8}$	9	$51\frac{3}{4}$
45	—	—	$8\frac{1}{2}$	$51\frac{3}{4}$
50	2	$3\frac{3}{8}$	$4\frac{1}{2}$	$51\frac{3}{4}$
55	$\frac{1}{16}$	1	$1\frac{3}{4}$	$51\frac{3}{4}$

An investor that purchases an April option with a $50 exercise (or striking) price is betting $3\frac{3}{8}$ that AT&T's stock price, which closed at $51.75, will rise $3.375 above $50 before the third Friday in April 1993. All option contracts mature on the third Friday of the stated month unless it is a holiday. Most options may be exercised any time up to and including their maturity date. When options have this early exercise feature, they are called American options. If they cannot be exercised until maturity, they are called European options.

The other major type of option contract is a put. It gives its owner the right to sell a share of stock at the stated exercise price either any time up to its maturity date (if it is an American put) or at the maturity date (if it is a European put). Shown below are the put options written on AT&T.

Striking or Exercise Price	Maturity Month			AT&T Closing Price
	January	April	July	
50	$3/16$	$1\frac{1}{4}$	$1\frac{3}{4}$	$51\frac{3}{4}$
55	—	—	$4\frac{3}{8}$	$51\frac{3}{4}$

For example, an investor that buys an April put with a $50 exercise price, bets $1.25 that AT&T's stock price will fall from its current level of $51.75 to below $50 sometime before the third Friday in April 1993.

[2] Major Exchanges and Option Instruments

Options are traded on the CBOE, AMEX, the NYSE, and several regional exchanges including the Pacific, the Philadelphia, and the Midwest Exchanges. In addition to puts and calls on common stock, options are also written on stock indexes on foreign currencies and on U.S. government notes and bonds. Options on certain agricultural commodities have also been introduced. The growth in popularity of options contracts is amazing when one recalls that the first standardized option contracts were listed on the CBOE on April 26, 1973.

[3] Contract Standardization and Liquidity

A major reason for the rapid growth of options markets is that they have provided standardization and liquidity in order to facilitate trading. Prior to 1973, all options were traded on the OTC market, where put and call dealers and brokers brought would-be buyers and sellers together, arranged terms, helped with paper work, and charged substantial fees required for the work involved. There was little standardization of contracts, low volume, and virtually no secondary market. A buyer wishing to close out a position prior to expiration could exercise an option, but it was usually too costly to try to find another buyer so that the option could be sold prior to expiration. The obvious advantage of CBOE options is that they have a common exercise price and a common maturity, and all are written on 100 shares of stock. Standardization makes it easy to buy and sell option contracts in the secondary market and avoids the necessity of waiting until maturity to exercise the option.

[4] Mechanics of Trading

The Options Clearing Corporation greatly facilitates trading in listed options because it severs direct links between buyers and sellers in the manner described for futures markets. If a buyer chooses to exercise an option, the Options Clearing Corporation computer will randomly choose a seller that has not closed its position and assign the exercise notice accordingly. The corporation also guarantees delivery of the underlying security if a seller defaults. In addition, the Options Clearing Corporation makes it possible for a buyer to "sell out" of a position and a seller to "buy in" a position at any time. If a trader has offsetting positions, the computer simply eliminates both positions. The Options Clearing Corporation is capitalized with funds provided by clearing members of the options exchanges.

Listed option contracts are protected against stock splits and stock dividends by adjustment of the exercise price and the number of shares underlying the contract. For example, if a firm declares a 50 percent stock dividend, a call option would be adjusted to cover one and one-half times as many shares at two thirds of the original exercise price per share. Listed options are not, however, protected against cash distributions to shareholders, such as dividends or spinoffs. In this case, the option holder must resort to early exercise in order to be protected. For example, in December 1976, General Motors stock was selling for around $75 per share. Call options were outstanding with an exercise price of $60 per share. On the next day, the company was scheduled to go ex dividend with a dividend of $3 per share. This implied that the stock would fall to approximately $72 per share. Before the ex dividend date, the value of the option could not fall below the stock price minus the exercise price, i.e., $15 per share. But the very next day, the stock price would fall to around $72 per share, and the option price would also fall (it fell to 12⅝). On one day, the option was worth $15, and on the next day everyone knew it would fall in value because the call option was not dividend-protected. The only rational thing to do was to exercise the option just before the stock went ex dividend.

Margin requirements are much more complicated for options transactions than for common stock. Investors that purchase or sell options contracts without hedging their position by purchasing the underlying security are said to have naked options positions. No margin is allowed for buyers of naked options. On the other hand, writers (sellers) of naked options must deposit a margin of at least 30 percent of the price of the underlying security plus or minus the amount the call is in the money or out of the money. For example, if AT&T is selling for $67.50, the writer of an April contract for 100 call options at an exercise price of $60 must deposit 30 percent of $67.50 times 100 (i.e., $2,025) plus the in-the-money amount of $750 (i.e., $7.50 per share times 100), for a total of $2,775. The proceeds from the option sale (i.e., $900) may be applied to the margin requirement.

There are further complications to the margin requirements when an investor takes a complex position (e.g., a straddle) using options on the same stock. Since the actual margin requirement will vary among brokers, it is necessary to consult the brokerage house for exact requirements.

[5] Benefits of Options

The standardization of options contracts has facilitated the rapid growth in their popularity. However, the growth could not have occurred unless options provided some fundamental benefits. Those benefits can be found by studying the wide variety of investment strategies that options make possible.

Most obviously, options can be used for sheer speculation. In many cases, a naked option position is much more sensitive to changes in stock prices than is a highly margined position in the same stock.

Another use of options is hedging. For example, the owner of a share of stock that wishes to limit downside risk can hedge by either writing call options or buying put options in the correct hedge ratio. Thus, options may be used as a type of portfolio insurance.

There are an almost unlimited number of combinations of options and the underlying securities that allow investors to tailor the risk and return characteristics to their desired specifications. This variety is, perhaps, the major benefit of options contracts.

8.06 FACTORS AFFECTING TRANSACTION COSTS

Each of the trading markets that have been examined here imposes transaction costs on investors in the form of commissions and the bid-ask spread. These costs are necessary to compensate brokers and dealers for the services they render in providing information, speedy execution, and clearing services.

[1] Bid-Ask Spread

Dealers provide immediacy to investors that do not want to enter limit orders and wait to trade. Dealers are prepared to purchase at the bid price securities they may not want or to sell at the ask price securities they may not have (and need to borrow).

[a] **Breakdown of Dealer Costs.** Dealers' costs of providing immediacy can be broken down into three elements: holding costs, order costs, and information costs. Holding costs represent the costs of holding an inventory of securities that the dealer would prefer not to hold because of the price risk and potential for losses. The possibility of loss is a function of the price variability of the security and the size of the dealers' position. The compensation dealers demand also depend on their willingness to take risk and on the amount of capital they have at their disposal.

Order costs represent the clerical costs of carrying out a transaction, the cost of the dealer's time, and the cost of the physical communications and office equipment necessary to carry out the transaction. To a considerable degree, order costs are fixed with respect to any particular transaction.

Information costs arise if some investors trade with dealers because they have superior information. Since dealers quote a two-sided market based on information available to them, any investor with information not available to the dealers can trade with the dealers at a favorable price. Suppose a dealer quotes 30 to 30½ and an investor has information that the stock will decline below 30. That investor will sell at 30 to the dealer and reap a benefit when (and if) the stock price falls. As Bagehot (1971) first showed, since dealers cannot identify information traders in advance, they must charge a spread large enough to be compensated for the average losses they incur with respect to information traders. Since the spread is charged to all traders, traders without information, in effect, pay the dealers' cost of trading with those that have information.

A related information cost arises if a dealer does not adjust the bid-ask price continuously. In that case, even new public information that justifies a price different from the dealer's current bid and ask allows speedy traders to benefit at the dealer's expense. Copeland and Galai (1983) show that speedy traders benefit because they are able to trade at a bid or ask price based on old information before dealers have time to change their spreads to reflect the new information.

[b] Empirical Evidence. Although all of the factors that affect the bid-ask spread cannot be measured, empirical evidence of Demsetz (1968), Stoll (1978(b)), Tinic (1972), and others (see Cohen et al. (1979)) indicates that the following factors are important empirical determinants of the spread:

- *The volume of trading in a security.* The greater the volume of trading, the easier it is for the dealer to dispose of an unwanted inventory position and the easier it is to cover the fixed costs of handling orders. Securities with high volume therefore tend to have lower spreads than those with low volume.

- *Price volatility.* The greater the variability of return of a security, the greater the risk to the dealer and therefore the larger the spread the dealer tends to charge.

- *Price.* Empirical evidence for the stock market indicates that the higher the price of a stock, the lower the proportional spread. The explanation for this relationship is not totally clear. It appears that price is a proxy for risk and that low price stocks tend to have greater risk and therefore larger proportional spreads. Low-price stocks also have larger proportional spreads because the minimum quoted spread (one-eighth dollar) is a relatively large fraction for stocks selling at low prices.

- *Extent of information trading.* The amount of informational trading measured by turnover (where "turnover" is defined as the ratio of volume of trading to shares outstanding) is positively related to the spread.

- *Degree of competition.* Empirical evidence also indicates that the spread is lower when several dealers are making markets in the same stock. Competition limits the ability of a dealer to charge more than his costs of providing immediacy.

[c] Behavior of the Spread Over Time. After a purchase by a dealer, the dealer tends to lower the bid price because it is less anxious to buy more shares of the same security. Simultaneously, the dealer tends to lower the ask price because it wishes to sell the securities it has acquired. Thus, the spread is frequently unchanged over time even though both the bid and ask price are changed so as to create an incentive for public investors to trade in a way that moves the dealer's inventory back to the desired level.

[2] Commissions

A commission is charged by a broker that acts as an agent and does not assume any price risk, as does a dealer. The commission reflects the costs of executing and clearing an order as well as the costs of advising customers. Large orders tend to be more difficult to execute and clear; they thus require a higher dollar commission. However, the increase in costs is not proportional to the order size, and therefore the proportional commission tends to decline as the size of the order increases.

Empirical studies of commission charges on stock transactions support the view that there are economies of scale in handling larger transactions (Edmister (1978); Stoll (1979), p. 61). The commission as a fraction of the value of the transaction declines with the number of shares traded. If the number of shares traded is held constant, the percentage commission also declines with the price per share.

8.07 FACTORS AFFECTING THE PRICE OF SECURITIES: ALLOCATIONAL EFFICIENCY

[1] Framework for Examining Allocational Efficiency

One of the major structural differences between the U.S. economy and the economies of other developed nations in Europe and Asia is that the dollar volume of trading in trading markets here is a much larger percentage of gross national product than anywhere else. Given this fact, one would hope that the U.S. securities markets operate efficiently.

Allocational efficiency was previously defined to include two aspects: informational efficiency and pricing efficiency. In an informationally efficient market, society gathers relevant information about securities as long as the marginal benefit exceeds the marginal cost. What type of information is relevant? The speculative equilibrium hypothesis, best described by Keynes (1936), is that investors base their investment decisions entirely on the anticipation of other individuals' behavior without any necessary relationship to the actual payoffs that the assets are expected to provide. An alternative viewpoint, called the rational expectations hypothesis, predicts that prices are formed on the basis of the expected future payouts of assets, including their resale value to third parties. Although it is impossible to test these alternative hypotheses empirically, an interesting experimental study using human subjects was conducted by Forsythe, Paltrey, and Plott (1982). They concluded that investors' behavior is better described by rational expectations.

Pricing efficiency is concerned with speed of price adjustment to the arrival of new information in the marketplace. Empirical evidence indicates that market prices react very rapidly, although not instantaneously.

Fama (1970) has provided a framework for analyzing allocational efficiency by partitioning the relevant information set. A market is said to be weak-form efficient if current securities prices fully reflect all historical price information. The implication is that no pattern in past prices can be used to forecast changes in future prices. In other words, technical analysis of price patterns is useless for making systematic capital gains. The next section discusses the empirical evidence that has validated this proposition of weak-form efficiency. The semistrong form of market efficiency arises when prices fully reflect all publicly available information. The implication for investors is that it is impossible to use annual reports of corporations, newspaper articles, or brokerage house newsletters to form trading rules to outperform the market. The next section discusses evidence that supports this hypothesis. Finally, strong-form market efficiency implies that no investor can earn excess returns using any information whether it is publicly available or not. If the strong-form efficiency hypothesis were true, even insiders that have information not available to the marketplace could not earn excess returns. Empirical evidence rejects the strong-form hypothesis.

[2] Empirical Evidence: Are Markets Allocationally Efficient?

Hundreds of academic studies have tested market efficiency; there is not enough space here to report them all. Consequently, a few of the early studies are highlighted here.

The weak form of market efficiency has been tested by using various trading rules based on filters. Alexander (1961) and Fama and Blume (1966) used a filter rule according to which stock is purchased when it rises x percent from its previous low, then held until the price falls x percent from its high. At that time, the stock is sold and a short position maintained until the price goes up x percent. The objective of such a filter rule is to make profits from runs in stock prices. The filter rule tests have two important results. First, filters greater than 1.5 percent could not beat a simple buy and hold strategy. Therefore, the weak form of the efficient market hypothesis is confirmed. Second, although filters smaller than 1.5 percent did beat the market before transaction costs, the profits were completely eliminated by transaction costs as low as 0.1 percent, a rate paid by even a floor trader on the NYSE. This illustrates the relationship between allocational and operational efficiency. If transaction costs are high, there will be a greater illusion of market inefficiency because trading rule profits, before transaction costs, will be high.

The performance of managed portfolios provided a test of the semistrong form of market efficiency. A partial list of studies of the risk-adjusted performance of mutual funds includes work by Friend and Vickers (1965), Sharpe (1966), Treynor (1965), Friend, Blume, and Crockett (1970), Jensen (1968), and Mains (1977). Most studies found that mutual fund performance was neutral on average. Mains (1977) reported that the gross (risk-adjusted) rates of return for 80 percent of the mutual funds were higher than the market but that their net performance, after subtracting management fees and brokerage commissions, was neutral. The implication is that mutual funds can beat the market by just enough to cover their costs of gathering and processing information and the cost of transactions. Hence, the evidence from mutual funds is consistent with market efficiency.

Semistrong-form market efficiency can be tested directly by using the recommendations of the Value Line Investor Survey, which are based on publicly available information. Value Line uses a complex computerized filter rule to predict future performance. Stocks are rated 1 through 5, with 1 being the best performance predicted during the next 12 months. Copeland and Mayers (1982) found statistically significant performance only for Value Line Portfolio 5. However, the measured abnormal performance was small (only 3.05 percent per 6 months) and would have been eliminated by the transaction costs of an active trading strategy based on Value Line recommendations. Hence, the empirical results, once again, are consistent with the semistrong form of market efficiency.

A particularly interesting series of studies by Scholes (1972), Kraus and Stoll (1972), and Dann, Mayers, and Raab (1977) focused on the phenomenon of block trading. As mentioned previously, large blocks of securities are typically not handled by the NYSE specialist; rather, they are placed by the floor trader with customers of the brokerage firm. Once the block has been sold, usually at a discount from its equilibrium price level, it is announced on the NYSE ticker. Semistrong-form market efficiency can be tested by observing the length of time it takes for the stock price to adjust upward to a new equilibrium level. Dann, Mayers, and Raab report that for a sample of large blocks, traders must react within five minutes of the block announcement on the ticker tape in order to earn a positive rate of return after transaction costs. Not only is this evidence consistent with semistrong market efficiency, but it also tells us that market prices react very quickly to news events. Kraus and Stoll and Dann, Mayers, and Raab also reported that if a trader can purchase at the block price, it is possible to earn positive risk-adjusted returns, even after certain transaction costs. This may be interpreted as evidence contrary to the strong form of market efficiency because certain traders can use information that is not publicly available to earn abnormal returns.

A better case for rejecting strong-form efficiency is made by the empirical evidence on insider trading provided by Jaffe (1974) and Finnerty (1976). They formed portfolios that mimicked the trading behavior of corporate insiders. In both studies, the results indicate that insiders can beat the market on a risk-adjusted return basis both when buying and selling securities of their own firms.

The weight of empirical evidence indicates that securities markets (at least in the United States) are allocationally efficient in the weak and semistrong forms but not in the strong form. Individuals possessing information that is not publicly available can and do earn abnormal returns.

8.08 MARKET STABILITY AND THE CRASH OF 1987

On Monday, October 19, 1987, the Dow Jones Industrial Average fell by 508 points, or 22.6 percent, from its close on the preceding Friday. Similarly dramatic price declines were experienced by financial markets in other parts of the world.

The crash focused attention on the adequacy of trading markets in the United States and other countries and on whether markets are structured appropriately to accommodate large price changes with minimum turmoil. The report of the Presidential Task Force on market mechanisms (the Brady Commission Report) recommended "circuit breakers"—trading halts—that would provide time for markets to adjust to major selling imbalances or news events. In the spirit of that recommendation, the Chicago Mercantile Exchange and NYSE jointly announced an agreement to halt trading in stocks and stock index futures under specific conditions.

Much attention has been paid to program trading as a possible contribution to the crash. Program trading means many things, among them portfolio trading, computer trading, index arbitrage, and portfolio insurance. Portfolio trading, the trading of a basket of stocks pursuant to a single order, is a trading innovation that is a natural outcome of the desire of investors to remain diversified against the risk of any individual security. If diversification is a reasonable objective, it is hard to see why portfolio trading would be a bad thing.

Program trading is sometimes interpreted to mean computer trading and order processing because program trades are usually implemented through the NYSE DOT system for small transactions. Given the large volume of trading in today's financial markets and the computerization of upstairs brokerage offices, computer trading and order processing are an essential element in the proper management of order flow. One of the problems on October 19 was the inability of computers to handle the order flow. What is needed is more computer trading, not less.

Sometimes program trading is associated with stock index arbitrage. If the stock index futures price diverges from its theoretical relation to the underlying cash price, baskets of stocks must either be bought or sold to bring the two prices back into line. Stock index arbitrage is a stabilizing force that maintains the appropriate pricing links between stock market indexes and derivative futures and options instruments. Index arbitrage cannot cause a crash. It can, of course, cause all markets to reflect the same underlying forces. On October 19, index arbitrage was impeded by the inability of the NYSE DOT system to handle all of the order flow and by restrictions on program trading. As a result, index futures and cash prices diverged and gave conflicting signals.

Program trading is sometimes associated with computer decision making. A troublesome type of computer decision making is the computerized technical trading rule such as the one used in portfolio insurance–trading strategies. Portfolio insurance–trading strategies can be destabilizing, like other technical trading rules; and there is some evidence that portfolio insurance–trading strategies did destabilize markets on October 19. Strictly speaking, however, portfolio insurance–trading strategies cannot cause a crash; they only respond to other prices. Furthermore, the decision by portfolio insurers to sell stocks must be validated by the absence of buying by other investors at current prices. In other words, prices fall only if other investors also agree that they will not hold stocks at current prices.

The crash also raised concerns about margin trading and differential margins in the stock market, the option market, and the futures market. In view of the tremendous drop in equity options and futures, it is noteworthy that all futures and options market clearing firms were able to meet their obligations. While certain individual investors were overleveraged and failed to meet their obligations to particular brokerage firms, such cases were not frequent enough to precipitate massive failures or massive dislocations in the securities industry. The margining system worked surprisingly well during the crash of 1987.

The difference in margin requirements in futures markets and stock markets caused some to call for greater "consistency" in those requirements. As noted earlier, margins in futures and in stocks mean different things. In addition, the one-day settlement period in futures as against the five-day settlement period in stocks lowers the transaction risk in futures relative to stocks, and this justifies a lower margin level in futures. In other words, margins on stocks and futures need not be the same to insure a comparable level of financial integrity in the two markets.

Separate from the margin issue are the differences in the timing of cash flows after settlement of trades in different markets. Such differences in the timing of payments in different markets can impose strains on a brokerage firm that operates in the different markets. For example, if a brokerage firm makes a profit in the stock market that will not be received for five days while it incurs a loss in the futures market that must be paid immediately, tremendous pressures on its capital will be imposed. On October 19, such pressures brought certain firms close to failure even though they were perfectly hedged over a longer time frame. The differences in the timing of payments thus imposes significant transaction risks. The Brady Commission calls for the unification of clearing systems across marketplaces to reduce this financial risk. The first step in such unification is progress toward one-day settlement in all markets, something that has not yet been achieved in the equity markets.

The trading markets withstood the crash of 1987 admirably. Markets recovered rapidly, and the economy weathered the crash with almost no side effects. The crash did, however, point to areas in the structure of markets that need modification. The exchanges have responded by improving capacity, increasing automation, establishing circuit breakers and other contingency plans, and modifying margins. The increased interdependence of stock markets, futures markets, option markets, and debt markets has also been recognized in the greater coordination among the markets by self-regulatory organizations.

Suggested Reading

Alexander, S.S. "Price Movements in Speculative Markets: Trends or Random Walks." *Industrial Management Review* (May 1961).

Bagehot, W. (pseud.). "The Only Game in Town." *Financial Analysts Journal,* Vol. 27 (Mar.–Apr. 1971), pp. 12–14, 22.

Board of Trade of the City of Chicago. *Commodity Trading Manual.* Chicago, Ill., 1989.

Cohen, K. et al. "Market Makers and the Market Spread: A Review of Recent Literature." *Journal of Financial and Quantitative Analysis,* Vol. 14 (Nov. 1979), pp. 813–835.

Cohen, K., S. Maier, R. Schwartz, and D. Whitcomb. *The Microstructure of Securities Markets.* Englewood Cliffs, N.J.: Prentice-Hall, Inc., 1986.

Copeland, T., and D. Galai. "Information Effects on the Bid-Ask Spread." *Journal of Finance,* Vol. 38 (1983), pp. 1457–1469.

Copeland, T., and D. Mayers. "The Value Line Enigma (1965–1978): A Case Study of Performance Evaluation Issues." *Journal of Financial Economics,* Vol. 10 (Nov. 1982), pp. 289–321.

Copeland, T.E., and J.F. Weston. *Financial Theory and Corporate Policy,* 3rd ed. Chapters 9 and 10. Reading, Mass.: Addison-Wesley, 1988.

Cox, I., and M. Rubenstein. *Options Markets.* Englewood Cliffs, N.J.: Prentice-Hall, Inc., 1985.

Dann, L., et al. "Trading Rules, Large Blocks and the Speed of Price Adjustment." *The Journal of Financial Economics,* Vol. 4 (Jan. 1977), pp. 3–22.

Demsetz, H. "The Cost of Transacting." *Quarterly Journal of Economics,* Vol. 82 (Feb. 1968).

Edmister, R. "Commission Cost Structure: Shifts and Scale Economies." *Journal of Finance,* Vol. 33 (May 1978), pp. 477–485.

Fama, E. "Efficient Capital Markets: A Review of Theory and Empirical Work." *Journal of Finance,* Vol. 25 (May 1970), pp. 383–417.

Fama, E., and M. Blume. "Filter Rules and Stock Market Trading." *Journal of Business,* Vol. 39 (Jan. 1966, special supp.), pp. 226–241.

Finnerty, J.E. "Insiders and Market Efficiency." *Journal of Finance,* Vol. 31 (Sept. 1976), pp. 1141–1148.

Forsythe, R., et al. "Asset Valuation in an Experimental Market." *Econometrica* (May 1982), pp. 537–567.

Friend, I. "The Economic Consequences of the Stock Market." *American Economic Review,* Vol. 52 (May 1972), pp. 212–219.

Friend, I., and D. Vickers. "Portfolio Selection and Investment Performance." *Journal of Finance,* Vol. 20 (Sept. 1965), pp. 391–415.

Garbade, K. "Electronic Quotation Systems and the Market for Government Securities." *Quarterly Review,* Vol. 3 (Summer 1978), pp. 13–20. New York: Federal Reserve Bank of New York.

Jaffe, J. "The Effect of Regulation Changes on Insider Trading." *Bell Journal of Economics and Management Science* (Spring 1974), pp. 93–121.

Jensen, M. "The Performance of Mutual Funds in the Period 1945–64." *Journal of Finance,* Vol. 23 (May 1968), pp. 389–416.

Keynes, J.M. *The General Theory of Employment, Interest and Money.* New York: Harcourt Brace, 1936.

Kraus, A., and H. Stoll. "Price Impacts of Block Trading on the New York Stock Exchange." *Journal of Finance,* Vol. 27 (June 1972), pp. 569–588.

Logue, D. "Market Making and the Assessment of Market Efficiency." *Journal of Finance,* Vol. 30 (Mar. 1975), pp. 115–123.

Mains, N.E. "Risk, the Pricing of Capital Assets, and the Evaluation of Investment Portfolios: Comment." *Journal of Business,* Vol. 50 (July 1977), pp. 371–384.

Peake, J. "The National Market System." *Financial Analysts Journal,* Vol. 34 (July–Aug. 1978), pp. 25–33.

Ritchken, P. *Options: Theory, Strategy and Applications.* Glenview, Ill.: Scott, Foresman, 1987.

Roll, R. "A Simple Implicit Measure of the Effective Bid-Ask Spread in an Efficient Market," *Journal of Finance,* Vol. 39 (Sept. 1984), pp. 1127–1139.

Rubinstein, M. "Portfolio Insurance and the Market Crash." *Financial Analysts Journal,* Vol. 44 (Jan.–Feb. 1988), pp. 38–47.

Scholes, M. "The Market for Securities: Substitution Versus Price Pressure and the Effects of Information on Share Prices." *Journal of Business,* Vol. 45 (Apr. 1972), pp. 179–211.

Schwartz, R. *Equity Markets: Structure and Performance.* New York: Harper & Row, 1988.

Sharpe, W.F. "Mutual Fund Performance." *Journal of Business,* Vol. 39 (Jan. 1966), pp. 119–138.

Shiller, R. "The Volatility of Stock Market Prices." *Science* (Jan. 2, 1987).

Smidt, S. "The Road to An Efficient Stock Market." *Financial Analysts Journal,* Vol. 27 (Sept.–Oct. 1971), pp. 18–20, 64–69.

Stoll, Hans R. *Equity Trading Costs.* Charlottesville, VA: Research Foundation of the Institute of Chartered Financial Analysts, 1993.

———. "Principles of Trading Market Structure," *Journal of Financial Services Research,* Vol. 6 (1992), pp. 75–107.

———. "The Stock Exchange Specialist System: An Economic Analysis." *Monograph Series in Finance and Economics,* No. 2. New York: New York University, Salomon Brothers Center, 1985.

———. "Regulation of Securities Markets: An Examination of the Effects of Increased Competition." *Monograph Series in Finance and Economics.* New York: New York University, Salomon Brothers Center, 1979.

———. "The Pricing of Security Dealer Services: An Empirical Study of NASDAQ Stocks." *Journal of Finance,* Vol. 33 (Sept. 1978(b)), pp. 1153–1172.

———. "The Supply of Dealer Services in Securities Markets." *Journal of Finance,* Vol. 33 (Sept. 1978(a)), pp. 1133–1151.

Stoll, Hans R., and Robert E. Whaley. *Futures and Options.* Cincinnati, Ohio: South-Western Publishing Company, 1993.

———. "Expiration-Day Effects: What Has Changed?" *Financial Analysts Journal* (January–February 1991), pp. 58–72.

Tinic, S. "The Economics of Liquidity Services." *Quarterly Journal of Economics,* Vol. 86 (Feb. 1972).

Treynor, J.L. "How to Rate Mutual Fund Performance." *Harvard Business Review* (Jan.–Feb. 1965), pp. 63–75.

United States Department of the Treasury. *Joint Report on the Government Securities Market.* U.S. Government Printing Office, 1992.

United States Office of the President. *Report of the Presidential Task Force on Market Mechanisms* (Brady Commission Report). U.S. Government Printing Office, 1988.

West, R. "More on the Effects of Municipal Bond Monopsony." *Journal of Business,* Vol. 39 (Apr. 1966), pp. 305–308.

West, R., and S. Tinic. *The Economics of the Stock Market.* New York: Praeger, 1971.

Zwick, B. "The Market for Corporate Bonds." *Quarterly Review* (Autumn 1977), pp. 27–36. New York: Federal Reserve Bank of New York, 1977.

Chapter 9

Option Markets

ANDREW RUDD

9.01 INTRODUCTION

A common lament currently voiced at the major U.S. option exchanges is of the significant decrease in trading volume since the highs of the 1980s. At some exchanges, trading is about one third lower than trading prior to October 1987. The market crash in that month appears to have significantly altered investors' perceptions of the option markets. Investors were gradually regaining confidence in the market when the events of October 1989 again made them wary of stock options.

This decrease in volume has not affected all exchanges or contracts equally, nor has it extinguished the innovative spirit that helped fashion the option markets. In spite of decreased stock option and stock index option volume, U.S. exchanges are constantly in the product development process, searching for new option contracts and affiliations with other exchanges that will offer greater opportunities to investors. For example, most exchanges have experimented with various specifications of index options, such as the Russell Indices in New York and the Financial News Composite Index on the Pacific Exchange. As can be expected, not all of these experiments have been successful, but they are testimony to continuing efforts toward innovation in the options area.

Option market innovations have evolved in three distinct phases. First, U.S. exchanges offered domestic contracts: options on U.S. assets, principally stocks and stock indexes, but also debt instruments, currencies, and commodities. The initial step in this phase was the opening in 1973 of the Chicago Board Options Exchange (CBOE). This was the first exchange devoted entirely to stock options, which until that time were neither well understood nor frequently used. The acceptance of stock option strategies over the intervening years has been discussed often. Suffice it to say that an option industry now exists. This industry has been responsible for supporting the financial viability of many players—investment banks, money managers, and consultants—in the investment marketplace as other areas of business have faltered. This financial contribution is particularly important as the industry has become more global.

Second, exchanges in other countries have offered contracts on their domestic assets. Among the first overseas exchanges were the European Options Exchange (EOE) and the London markets. More recently Paris, Sweden, Switzerland, Germany, Japan, and other countries have followed suit.

The third phase, which is currently under way, is the full globalization of the option industry. This phase includes the offering of contracts on international indexes, the involvement of overseas assets, and the development of cooperative linkages between exchanges in different countries. For example, the American Stock Exchange (AMEX) has developed an affiliation with the EOE and has also listed options on an international index, the International Market Index (IMI), which is an index composed of non-U.S. stocks on which American depository receipts (ADRs) are traded in the United States.

There have been two major developments in the usage and understanding of option contracts and strategies. One development, which coincides with phases 2 and 3 just outlined, is, in short, the increasing internationalization of option exchanges, contracts, and strategies. This development has actually led to the evolution of option trading; new exchanges such as those of Switzerland and Germany are organized in stark contrast to the CBOE and other traditional exchanges.

A second important change involves the development and application of a more robust option theory for interest rate options and options embedded in fixed-interest instruments. Articles by Ho and Lee and Heath, Jarrow, and Morton have been the

326

catalysts of work in this area.[1] Without doubt, major investment banks and other financial institutions are only just beginning to gain experience applying the Heath, Jarrow, and Morton technology, which appears to be the preferred approach of the two.

9.02 EVOLUTION OF OPTIONS

[1] Definition of Option Contracts

Ownership of an option contract simply conveys the right (not the obligation) to undertake either the purchase or sale of an underlying asset at or before a specified date. The distinction between right and obligation is important, since it differentiates the option contract from other similar instruments, such as forward or future contracts, which legally require the owner to fulfill certain obligations. Of course, the owner of the option contract may wish to complete the transaction if it is economically beneficial, but there is no legal duty to do so.

For example, an option to buy an apartment building in San Francisco conveys the right to purchase a specific piece of real estate (the underlying asset) at a certain price at or before a fixed time. If real estate prices fall, the holder of the option may not wish to complete the transaction, in which case the option expires and becomes worthless. Alternatively, the option holder may think it is beneficial to proceed with the transaction, in which case the holder exercises the option and the seller of the option is obligated to fulfill the requirement of the contract to sell the apartment building. Finally, it is conceivable that the option holder, prior to the fixed ending date of the contract, may find another investor or broker willing to purchase the option contract (i.e., purchase the right to purchase the apartment building at a fixed price at or before a fixed time). One of the innovations of the CBOE was the standardization of listed stock option contracts to promote the secondary trading of options.

The purchase price of the option is frequently called the option premium. The fixed price at which the transaction is completed is called the exercise price or the strike price, and the fixed time is called the expiration date or option maturity. There are two types of option contracts: If the option conveys the right to purchase the underlying asset, it is called a call; if the option conveys the right to sell the underlying asset, it is called a put.

The investor that purchases an option is the buyer or holder and is said to hold the option long. Conversely, the investor that sells an option is the writer and is said to have sold the option short. One of the innovations of the option market is that it is particularly easy for an investor to go long or short as desired; an investor may wish to purchase options at one time, write options at another time, or buy and write options simultaneously at a third time.

Another important characteristic of the option contract is the exercise policy: whether the option can be exercised at any time prior to the expiration date or only at the expiration date. If the option can be exercised at any point during its lifetime,

---

[1] T.S.Y. Ho and S. Lee, "Term Structure Movements and Pricing Interest Rate Contingent Claims," *The Journal of Finance*, Vol. XLI (Dec. 1986); David Heath, Robert Jarrow, and Andrew Morton, "Bond Pricing and the Term Structure of Interest Rates: A New Methodology for Contingent Claims Valuation," Working Paper, Cornell University, revised Oct. 1989.

it is called an American option. If the option can be exercised only at maturity, it is called a European option. In fact, all options that trade on organized exchanges, both in the United States and abroad, are American options. Hence, for practical purposes the distinction can be ignored. However, as discussed later in this chapter, theoretical considerations require that the distinction be maintained.

The two types of American options are defined as follows:

1. An American call is an option to buy a fixed quantity of a given underlying asset at a fixed price until a fixed date.

2. An American put is an option to sell a fixed quantity of a given underlying asset at a fixed price until a fixed date.

The underlying asset for the listed stock options traded on the organized exchanges is the common stock of a major corporation. (While options on other underlying assets are becoming increasingly common, in this chapter the underlying asset is a common stock, unless specifically noted otherwise.)

The fixed quantity of the underlying asset referred to in the contract definition is usually 100 shares, although sometimes after the underlying asset undergoes a share split or stock dividend, the number of shares optioned may change. The contract specifications do not change after a cash dividend; options traded on the organized exchanges are said to be payout-unprotected in that there is no adjustment for cash payouts on the underlying asset.

The complete specification of a general option contract includes seven items:

1. Option type: put or call

2. Name of the underlying asset (common stock)

3. Expiration date

4. Exercise price

5. Number of shares of the underlying asset (common stock) optioned

6. Exercise policy: European or American

7. Degree of payout protection

Unless otherwise noted, the organized exchanges set the number of shares at 100, permit exercise prior to maturity (American options), and do not adjust for dividends (payout unprotected).[2] Hence, for listed stock options, investors really need consider only four important items: the option type, the name of the stock, the expiration date, and the exercise price.

[2] Elementary Pricing Relationships

Option exchanges normally establish for each stock six or more standard call and put options that differ only by maturity and exercise price. For example, assume that on a recent date 20 different *XYZ* Corporation calls were traded on the CBOE. The exercise prices, expiration dates, and reported closing prices are given in Figure 9-1.

---

[2] Some options do not trade on one of the organized exchanges but in the so-called over-the-counter market. These options are usually payout-protected and European.

FIGURE 9-1

XYZ Corporation Calls

Exercise Price	Expiration Date		
	April	July	October
$ 65	35.000	*a*	*a*
70	29.625	*a*	*a*
75	24.750	26.000	*a*
80	20.500	20.500	*a*
85	15.125	16.750	*a*
90	10.750	12.875	15.250
95	6.500	10.000	12.000
100	3.250	7.125	9.625
110	0.500	3.125	5.375

a No option is offered.

The first *XYZ* call has an exercise price of $65, was last traded at $35, and expires in April.[3] It is referred to as the *XYZ*/April/65 call. To purchase this call on 100 shares would cost a total of $3,500 plus commissions; a writer of this call of 100 shares would receive $3,500 less commissions and less any collateral the broker may require to ensure performance of the contract.[4] To purchase the *XYZ*/April/110 call on 100 shares would cost only $50 plus commissions. Assume that on this day the closing price of *XYZ* was $99.875, so the purchase cost of 100 shares was $9,987.50 plus commission. How can one explain these price differences?

The holder of the *XYZ*/April/65 call could exercise it immediately, by paying $65 per share to the writer. For the 100-share contract this would cost $6,500, for which the holder would receive stock worth $9,987.50, yielding a profit (before commissions) of $3,487.50. This amount is less than would be obtained by selling the contract in the market, the difference of $12.50 being the value the market places on the right to hold on to the option until expiration. Between the current time and expiration, the stock may rise in price, causing an increase in the value of the option contact. The amount of $3,487.50 is called the intrinsic value of the option and the amount of $12.50 the time value of the option.

The *XYZ*/April/110 call will now be examined. The holder would clearly not exercise the option, since this action would result in the loss of $110 minus $99.875 per share, or $1,012.50 for the 100-share contract. Hence, the intrinsic value of the option is 0, and its time value is the total price of $0.50. In other words, by market consensus the value of holding the option to expiration in the hope that *XYZ* may trade at 1 stage above $110 is $50 per contract. Writers are willing to accept $50 now, and purchasers are willing to spend $50 now in a "bet" on the price of *XYZ* on (or before) the expiration of the option. If the *XYZ* price rises above $110, the purchaser wins and the writer

---

[3] Trading in options continues up to 3 P.M. Eastern time on the third Friday in its expiration month.

[4] The collateral is called margin. See A. Rudd and M. Schroeder, "The Calculation of Minimum Margin," *Management Science* (Dec. 1982), pp. 1368–1379, for further details.

FIGURE 9-2

XYZ Corporation Puts

Exercise Price	Expiration Date		
	April	July	October
$ 65	a	b	b
70	1/16	b	b
75	a	0.125	b
80	a	7/16	b
85	1/16	0.750	b
90	0.25	1 13/16	2 15/16
95	15/16	3.250	4.75
100	2 13/16	5.500	7.00
110	10.25	a	12.75

a No option is offered.
b The option did not trade.

loses to the tune of the difference between the stock price and the exercise price. By comparison, if the *XYZ* price remains below $110, the call expires worthless and the purchaser loses the original call contract premium of $50, which the writer gains.

The smallest intrinsic value is zero and occurs when the exercise price is greater than the stock price; in this situation, the option is said to be out of the money. When the intrinsic value is positive (i.e., the exercise price is less than the stock price), the option is said to be in the money. When the stock price is in the region of the exercise price, the option is said to be at the money. Also, the smallest time value is zero and occurs when there is "no life left in the option," i.e., at the expiration date when the option premium is equal to its intrinsic value.

The situation for puts is similar. Figure 9-2 shows the puts on *XYZ* that traded on the CBOE on a recent date. Only one put with an exercise price of $65 is offered; it is the *XYZ*/April/65 put, but it did not trade during the day. The *XYZ*/April/70 traded, and its last price was $0.0625. Hence, for a 100-share contract, the put would cost only $6.25. Why such a small price for this put? The answer, of course, is that the exercise of the put would require the holder to deliver the underlying *XYZ* stock to the writer in exchange for the $70 (per share) exercise price. Since the stock closed at almost $100, no investor would immediately exercise the put. In fact, the contract value of $6.25 represents the value of a form of insurance against the possibility that *XYZ* will close beneath $70 prior to the maturity of the option.

The *XYZ*/April/110 put last traded at $10.25, or $1,025 for the 100-share contract. Immediate exercise of this put would entail the delivery of *XYZ* stock worth $9,987.50 in return for an aggregate exercise price of $11,000, for a net profit of $1,012.50 per 100-share contract. The holder of the put would therefore be wealthier by $12.50 (before commissions) if the contract were to be sold on the exchange rather than exercised.

As before, the value of the contract if exercised (zero for the *XYZ*/April/75 and $1,012.50 for the *XYZ*/April/110) is called the intrinsic value of the option, and the difference between the option price and the intrinsic value is called the time value.

Puts are in the money when they have positive intrinsic value and out of the money when their intrinsic value is zero. They are said to be at the money whenever the exercise price is very close to the underlying asset price.

These relationships are shown graphically in Figure 9-3. The top panel plots the *XYZ* calls with $65 and $110 exercise prices. The lower panel plots the puts with $70 and $110 exercise prices. Several important points are evident from the figure. First, the time value for different April calls (or puts) need not be the same. For example, investors are willing to pay (for the 100-share contract) only $6.25 time value for the April/70 put but $12.50 for the April/110 put.[5]

Next, the longer the time to maturity, the greater the time value of both the puts and calls. This follows directly from the fact that the longer the time to maturity, the more likely the underlying asset will move to a price where exercise is (more) beneficial. For example, the *XYZ* calls with exercise prices of $100 are all just out of the money. The July options have three months more than the April options, during which the *XYZ* price can increase, driving the call in the money. The additional $3.875 ($7.125 − $3.25) per share represents the consensus value that market participants place on this three-month period. Also, the value of the additional three-month period from July to October is only valued at $2.50 per share; hence, for the $100 exercise price options, the market places greater value on the first three months than on the second. For the calls with $90 exercise prices, however, the reverse is true; purchasing the July rather than April maturity option costs only an incremental $2.125 per obtained share, but purchasing the October rather than July maturity option costs $2.375 incremental per optioned share.

Finally, a curious anomaly shows up with the $80 exercise price calls, where both the April and July options cost $20.50. If this is really true,[6] why would anybody purchase the April option or anybody write the July option? Purchasers would prefer the July call and writers the April call, leading to an imbalance of supply and demand.

A large part of understanding options has to do with isolating the important factors that influence option prices and evaluating an option's time value. One particular method for pricing options is described in detail later in this chapter; however, even at this stage a series of important relationships governing option prices can be enumerated:

- Both put and call prices are the sum of two components: intrinsic value and time value.

- A call's (or put's) intrinsic value is the amount by which the stock price exceeds the exercise price (or exercise price exceeds the stock price).

- Time value for options with some life prior to maturity is always positive; at the expiration date, it is zero. Time value increases with time to maturity, and for any given maturity it tends to be largest for the at-the-money options.

[3] Simple Strategies and Their Profitability

The easiest way to understand the impact of options is to examine various strategies when the options are held to expiration. This analysis is more straightforward than

---

[5] The largest time value for the April puts is associated with the April/100 put. For a 100-share contract on this option, investors are willing to pay 100 times ($2^{13}/_{16} − (100 − 99.875) = $2.6875), or $268.75.

[6] The likely explanations for these prices are that one is more timely than the other or there was an error in reporting the correct closing prices.

FIGURE 9-3

XYZ Corporation Option Prices

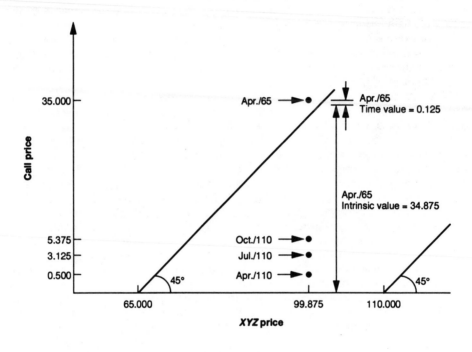

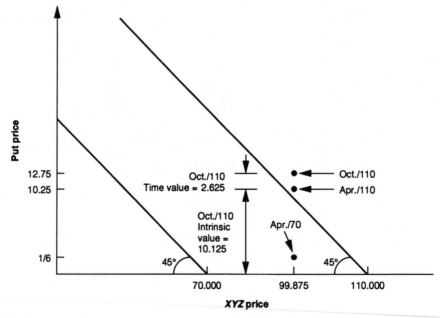

FIGURE 9-4

Profits From Purchasing the April/100 Call

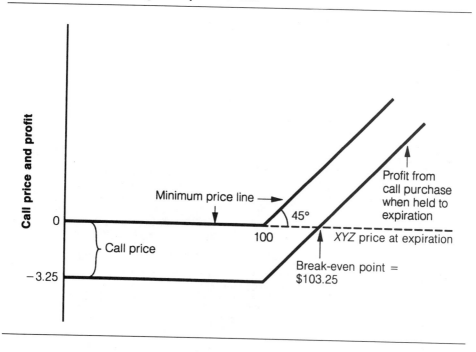

permitting the closing of the option position prior to expiration because, as noted in the previous section, at expiration call prices are simply the amount by which the stock price exceeds the exercise price.

Figure 9-4 shows the profits that accrue to purchasers of the XYZ/April/100 call option. The minimum price line shows the minimum price of the call as a function of the XYZ price at expiration; it is zero up to the point where XYZ trades at $100 and increases $1 for each $1 increase in the stock price beyond $100. As indicated, it is the potential for profitable investment (occurring for the call when the stock price exceeds the exercise price) that forms the basis for option valuation. In order to gain this potential, the buyer pays the call price to the writer, which thereby places itself in the position for a potential loss or contingent obligation. The obligation is the delivery of the stock to the option purchaser at the fixed exercise price, contingent on the stock trading at a greater price.

This analysis indicates that the profits to the call writer are just the mirror image about the horizontal of the call purchaser's profit. The writer's profit as a function of the stock price is given in Figure 9-5. Notice that the positions net each other out; a long and short position in the same call has neither risk nor profit potential. For this reason, investment in options is a zero-sum game; option purchasers profit at the expense of option writers, and vice versa.

Figure 9-6 shows two variants on the simple strategy of purchasing calls. First, notice the effect of changing the exercise price. The lower the exercise price, the greater the minimum price line for every stock price at expiration. In other words,

FIGURE 9-5

Profits From Writing the April/100 Call

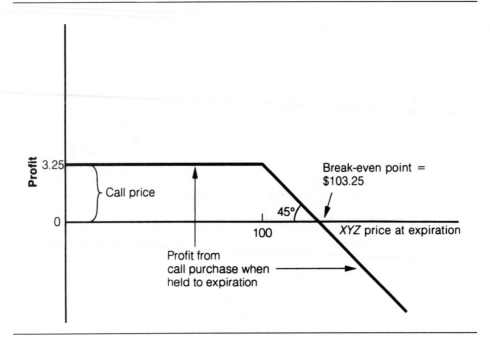

the lower the exercise price, the larger the potential payoff for every stock price. However, the increased payoff potential comes with a higher initial call price; hence, the profits for low stock prices are reduced, while the profits for large stock prices are increased. This is made clear in the figure where the profit line for the April/85 call is superimposed over the profit line for the April/100 call, shown previously in Figure 9-4.

The second variant of the simple strategy is the impact of purchasing more than one call contract. Of course, if the call expires out of the money, the losses are multiplied by the number of contracts held; but when the call expires in the money, each $1 increase in the stock prices causes multiple dollar increases in the option position, depending on the number of contracts held. For example, if two call contracts are held, the sloping part of the profit line will be at 60 degrees to the horizontal.

Figure 9-6 shows a further example of a multiple call position. If 4.7 April/100 calls are held, the total cost will be approximately the same as one April/85 call (4.7 times $3.25 equals $15.275), so the profit corresponding to 4.7 April/100 calls is shown compared with that of the April/85. For stock prices at expiration below $85, the 2 strategies are identical; for stock prices between $85 and a little over $104, the April/85 call provides greater profits (or smaller losses); and for prices in excess of $104, the 4.7 April/100 calls are more beneficial. The choice of strategy depends on the preference of the investor. In this case there is little difference between the 2 profit diagrams at expiration, although prior to expiration the difference is greater, as shown subsequently.

FIGURE 9-6

Profits From Call Purchase Strategies

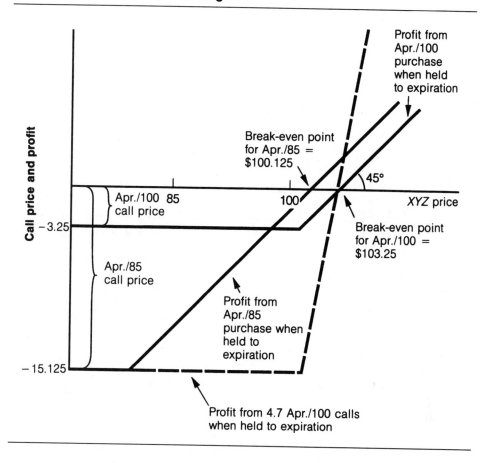

Figures 9-7 and 9-8 show the profit diagrams for a long put and a written put, respectively. Again notice that the sum of the cash flows to the put buyer and writer are zero. In contrast to the diagram for the calls, both the put buyer and put writer can compute their maximum possible loss. The holder of the put (and the holder of the call) has limited liability, so its maximum loss is the option price. The put writer suffers most when the stock price falls to zero, in which case the maximum loss is the exercise price less the initial put price.

More interesting strategies occur when an option is held in conjunction with either another option or the underlying asset. In the latter case, when the underlying asset and the option are held so that profits on one instrument tend to offset losses on the other, the resulting portfolio is called a hedge. The most common hedges are when (1) the underlying asset is held long and the call written (shown in Figure 9-9), and (2) the underlying asset and put are both held long (shown in Figure 9-10).

The hedge in Figure 9-9 shows the case when one share of stock is hedged with one call written at the money. When the hedge is one to one, it is termed a covered

FIGURE 9-7

Profits From Purchasing the April/100 Put

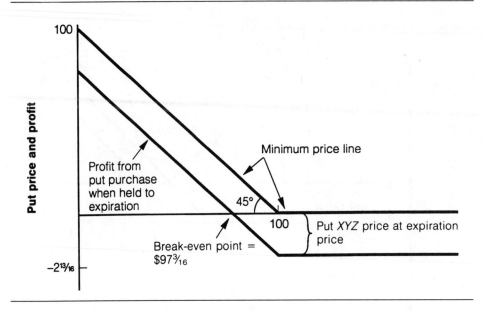

FIGURE 9-8

Profits From Writing the April/100 Put

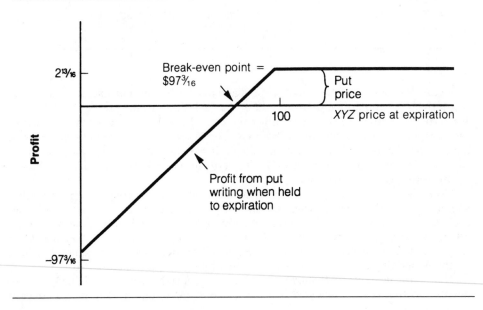

FIGURE 9-9

Profits From a Covered Call Hedge

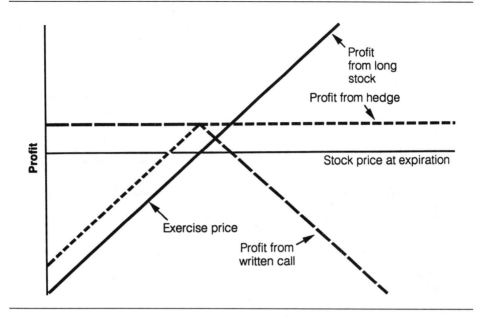

call hedge. The written call provides some income to partially offset the losses on the stock for low stock prices, but it is exercised at high stock prices, substantially reducing the upside profitability of the stock-only position. What is left is a lower-risk portfolio than the original stock holding, similar in shape to the written put diagram shown in Figure 9-8. Figure 9-10 shows the covered put hedge (one at-the-money put held long for every share of stock), which is the same shape as the purchased call diagram shown in Figure 9-4.

The intuition to be gained from Figures 9-9 and 9-10 is important. The indication is that (at least at expiration and subject to a cash adjustment to equate the values of the position) a long stock position can be duplicated with a portfolio containing a long call and a written put, or, equivalently, a long call can be thought of as a long stock position plus a long put. The long stock component gives the call some of the profit characteristics of the underlying asset, while the long put provides insurance against low stock prices at expiration. The relationship between the put and call can be developed further into a series of theorems known as the put-call parity theorems, one of which will be described in the next section.

Figures 9-11 and 9-12 show two representative versions of another option strategy known as a spread. An option spread is a portfolio of calls (or puts) on the same underlying asset where profits on one or more calls (or puts) offset losses on the other calls (or puts). There are an almost endless variety of spreads, each seemingly with a graphic name, designed to capture some part of the stock return distribution.[7] Figure

---

[7] See, e.g., Robert A. Jarrow and Andrew Rudd, *Option Pricing* (Homewood, Ill.: Dow Jones-Irwin, 1983), for further details.

FIGURE 9-10
Profits From a Covered Put Hedge

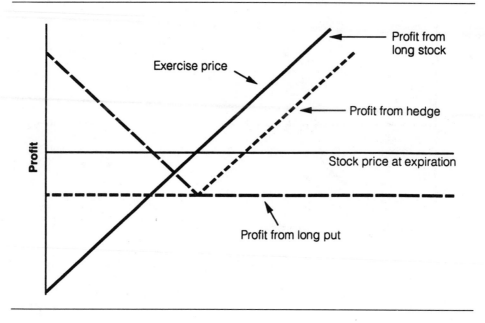

9-11 shows a spread where calls of identical maturity are held; the call with the larger exercise price is written, and the call with the smaller exercise price is purchased. Figure 9-12 shows a similar spread but using put options.

The final strategies introduced here are called combinations. A combination is a portfolio containing puts and calls on the same underlying asset, where the options are either all purchased or all written. The most common combination is called a straddle, and contains a purchased put and a purchased call where both options have the same exercise price and same maturity. The profit diagram for a straddle is shown in Figure 9-13 and appears like a letter V. If the stock price remains close to the common exercise price, the investor shows losses, with the maximum loss equal to the sum of the option prices. If the stock price jumps considerably from the exercise price in either direction, however, the investor can make a profit when one option ends up in the money and the other ends up out of the money (and worthless).

These simple strategies show some of the virtuosity of the option contract. The dominant characteristic by far of an option is that the payoff can be molded to suit the preferences of the investor. The strategies in this section show that highly nonlinear payoff diagrams, which are quite unlike the payoff diagrams for other assets, can be constructed.

[4] Put-Call Parity

For the sake of simplicity, assume that the options are European (i.e., they cannot be exercised prior to maturity) and the underlying asset pays no cash dividends prior

FIGURE 9-11

Profits From a Call Spread

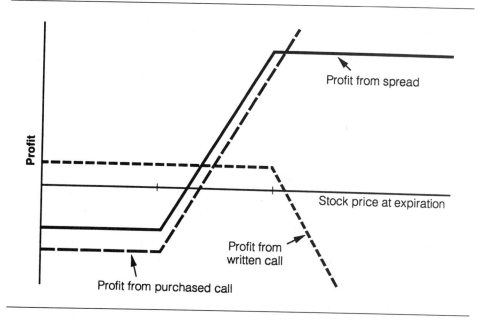

Profit

Profit from spread

Stock price at expiration

Profit from
written call

Profit from purchased call

to the expiration date of the options.[8] The technique used to prove the result is called arbitrage. If two portfolios have exactly the same payoffs for all future states of the world, they must have the same price now. If not, the act of arbitrage would force the two prices to be identical, as investors purchase one portfolio (the "cheap" portfolio) while selling the other (the "expensive" portfolio).

First, C_0, P_0, and S_0 are defined to be the initial (time zero) prices of a call, put, and underlying stock, respectively. Similarly, C_t, P_t, and S_t, are the three prices at the maturity of the options (time t). Let K be the common exercise price of the options and let B_0 be the initial price of a zero-coupon, riskless bond that delivers $1 at time t.

For example, assume that S_0 is $100, K is $100, P_0 is $2.50, and C_0 is $3.50. If the maturity of the option is exactly one month away and the interest rate is one percent per month, then the initial price of the zero-coupon, riskless bond is $B_0 = \$0.99$.

Consider two portfolios. The first is a long call, and the second is composed of a long stock, a long put, and a loan of KB_0 (i.e., the present value of the exercise price payable at option maturity). Figure 9-14 shows the cash flow to these two portfolios. The two cases at possible maturity are (1) the stock price ends up below the exercise price (i.e., the call is out of the money and the put is in the money) and (2) the stock price ends up above the exercise price (i.e., the call is in the money and the put is out of the money).

---

[8] These assumptions can easily be eliminated at the cost of more complex algebra. See *ibid*. for further details.

FIGURE 9-12

Profits From a Put Spread

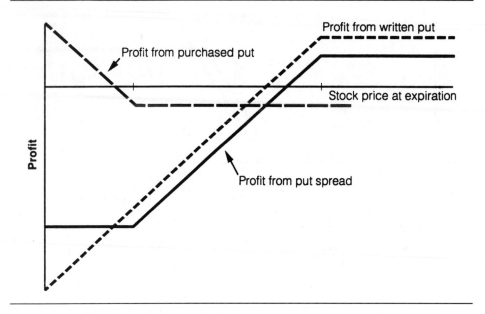

Figure 9-14 shows the values of the two portfolios in these two situations. For the numerical example, the two values are S_t is \$50 and S_t is \$150. As is obvious from the figure, the dollar payoffs from the portfolios are the same, as are the payoffs when written in symbols. Arbitrage, therefore, ensures that the portfolios have the same initial price, which is \$3.50 = \$100 + \$2.50 − \$99. In symbols, this put-call parity equation is given by

$$C_0 = S_0 + P_0 − KB_0$$

That is, the call price is equal to the stock price plus the put price less the present value of the exercise price. If this relationship did not hold, e.g.,

$$C_0 > S_0 + P_0 − KB_0$$

at least under these assumptions, the call could be written and portfolio 2 purchased (obtain loan, then purchase stock and put) to gain risk-free profits.

This put-call parity theorem justifies the intuitive feeling that the call is a levered stock position, with insurance. The stock holding and loan combine to give the levered stock position, and the put provides the insurance, since it eliminates losses should the stock price fall. Moreover the theorem shows that the put and call prices cannot get too far out of line. If they do, arbitrage may be possible to force them back into their natural relationship.[9] This observation underlies the strategies of conversion, which are described in detail later in this chapter.

---

[9] Be aware that certain assumptions that are not true in the real world have been made. Without these assumptions, the put-call parity theorem becomes more complex, and there is not necessarily any unique relationship between puts and calls.

FIGURE 9-13

Profits From a Straddle

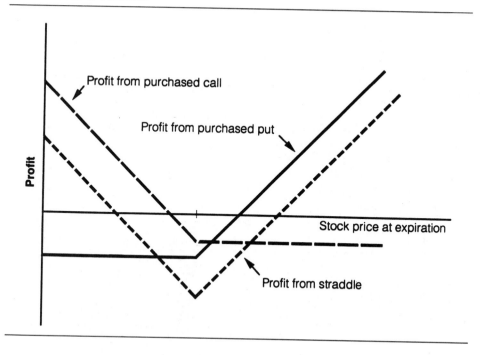

FIGURE 9-14

Cash Flows to the Arbitrage Portfolio

Portfolio	Inital Cash Flow		Cash Flow at Maturity			
			$S_t \leq K$ ($S_t = \$50$)		$S_t > K$ ($S_t = \$150$)	
1. Long call	C_0	$ (3.5)	0	0	$S_t - K$	$ 50
2. Long stock	(S_0)	(100.0)	S_t	0	S_t	150
Long put	(P_0)	(2.5)	$K - S_t$	$50	0	0
Loan of KB_0	$99	K	$(100)	$-K$	$(100)	0
Total	$KB_0 - P_0 - S_0$	$ (3.5)	0	0	$S_t - K$	$ 50

[5] U.S. Exchange–Traded Options

When historians analyze the securities markets over the last quarter of this century, one recurring theme is bound to be the rapid proliferation of new financial instruments. Exchange-traded options are certainly a major part of this proliferation.

The following categories of underlying assets on which the important options are traded can be isolated:

- Common stocks
- Stock indexes
- Fixed-income securities
- Foreign currencies
- Futures contracts (both commodity and financial)

The characteristics of the options within these five asset categories are discussed in turn. The trading strategies are discussed later in this chapter.

[a] Common Stocks. Options on common stocks were originally listed on the CBOE, which was formed for the purpose of trading stock options. In addition to the CBOE, stock options are now traded on the AMEX, the Philadelphia Stock Exchange, the Pacific Stock Exchange, and the New York Stock Exchange (NYSE). The relative importance of the five exchanges is as follows:

	Optionable Stocks (Approximate)	Approximate Percentage			
		Call Volume	Put Volume	Call Open Interest[10]	Put Open Interest
CBOE	180	55.0	70	45	45
AMEX	135	22.5	15	25	25
Philadelphia Stock Exchange	70	12.5	10	18	20
Pacific Stock Exchange	70	9.0	4	9	7
NYSE	25	1.0	1	3	1
		100.0	100	100	100

In total, average daily option volume is approximately 600,000 contracts, which represents approximately 40 percent to 70 percent of the daily volume of trading on the NYSE.

[b] Stock Indexes. Options on approximately 20 stock indexes are currently traded. However, only 3 indexes have any significant volume. These indexes are the Standard & Poor's (S&P) 100 and the S&P 500, which are traded on the CBOE, and the Major Market Index (MMI), which is traded on the AMEX.

The S&P 100 index is a market capitalization weighted index formed from 100 stocks on which options are traded on the CBOE. Because of its construction, it resembles quite closely the S&P 500 and the NYSE composite indexes, and it is not dissimilar to many institutional portfolios. For this reason, options on the S&P 100 may potentially be very useful for hedging market risk in institutional portfolios. Since it is not exactly the same as the S&P 500, synthetic strategies involving the popular S&P 500 futures contract and the S&P 100 option would exhibit basis risk. For this reason, the S&P 500 index option also trades.

[c] Fixed-Income Securities. The CBOE trades options on U.S. government fixed-income securities. These options are usually referred to as interest rate options, since trading in them represents a strategy with respect to interest rates.

---

[10] The open interest represents the number of option contracts outstanding at any particular time.

The CBOE also has two different forms of interest rate options; one has specific U.S. Treasury bonds as specific underlying assets, while the other has U.S. Treasury notes as specific underlying assets. Both have a principal value of $100,000.

There is a general feeling that all the interest rate options contracts have been something of a disappointment. Daily volume is low, as is the contract open interest. There appears to be little doubt that the prime place to hedge interest rate risk through option use is the Chicago Board of Trade (CBT) where the Treasury bond futures options are traded.

[d] Foreign Currencies. In December 1982, the Philadelphia Stock Exchange started trading options on the U.K. pound. In only five months, demand was such that the exchange could list five contracts: pounds, Swiss francs, deutsche marks, Canadian dollars, and yen.

Demand for currency options has remained strong. During the summer of 1988, the Philadelphia exchange—still the only U.S. exchange to list currency options—had successful contracts for the Australian dollar, U.K. pound, Canadian dollar, deutsche mark, French franc, yen, Swiss franc, European currency unit (ECU), and U.K. pound–deutsche mark cross rates. In addition, the exchange had attempted, though less successfully, to promote European-style contracts on several of these currencies.

The contracts appear to be valuable for some financial institutions and corporations. In addition, the increasing global exposure of U.S. pension funds has stimulated demands for products and strategies hedging currency risk.

[e] Futures Contracts. The CBT, Chicago Mercantile Exchange (CME), New York Futures Exchange, Commodity Exchange, Inc. (COMEX), International Monetary Market (IMM), Kansas City Board of Trade, New York Cotton Exchange, New York Mercantile Exchange, and New York Coffee, Sugar and Cocoa Exchange all trade options. The most important option contract is the Treasury bond futures option contract traded on the CBT. The S&P 500 stock index futures option contract, traded on the CME, is also important.

Of lesser importance are the Treasury note contract (traded on the CBT), the Eurodollar contract (traded on the CME), and the currency contracts (traded on the IMM). In general, the options on the agricultural, oil, livestock, and metal futures have been less successful. Occasionally, specific events cause one or more of these contracts to come to life, causing daily volume to exceed several thousand contracts and open interest to climb. The COMEX trades a gold option, while the New York Coffee, Sugar and Cocoa Exchange has sugar, coffee, and cocoa options. Of these options, only the gold, silver, and sugar options have reasonable volumes.

An option on a future is conceptually the same as an option on any other asset. The only thing to remember is that the exercise of an option on a future causes a futures contract to be delivered, rather than, for example, a share of common stock. Having the future as the underlying asset rather than the actual asset is a significant advantage when there is no public market in the actual asset. This is the case with stock indexes and assets. For example, stock indexes are a composite of their constituent securities; hence, to buy or sell the index, one has to buy or sell the constituents, since there is no market for the indexes themselves. There is a market for Treasury bonds, but it is a telephone or over-the-counter (OTC) market between large dealers, and the value of a single Treasury bond is not easy to find. For these assets, for which no public market exists, a futures market occasionally thrives. This is certainly true for the stock indexes and Treasury bonds.

Hence, pricing and trading the underlying asset future is easier than pricing and trading the actual underlying asset. This makes certain strategies (such as hedging where the underlying asset is traded in conjunction with the option) far more effective with the futures option than the actual option.

[6] Non–U.S. Exchange–Listed Options

The growth of option trading in the non-U.S. markets has been even more significant than in the United States. Flourishing markets now exist worldwide. The most notable successes have taken place in Europe. A list of European exchanges that are either currently trading options or planning to do so in the near future is provided here. Other European countries, such as Belgium and Italy, are also actively discussing the possibilities of option trading.

[a] Australia. The option market is based in Sydney and is highly developed. There are listed options (both puts and calls) on approximately 25 major Australian companies, as well as the Australian Stock Exchange (ASX) 20 leaders stock index. The organization of the market is quite similar to that in the United States. In addition, there are options (both puts and calls) on three futures contracts: 90-day bank bills, the All-Ordinaries Share Price Index (a 290-stock capitalization weighted index) and the 3-year and 10-year Commonwealth treasury bonds.

[b] Belgium. The BELFOX exchange in Brussels has several stock (index) options and futures listed. Options exist for four companies and for the market as a whole, represented by the BEL-20 Index. Futures also exist for the BEL-20 Index and for a notional Belgium government bond on the interest rate (BIBOR 3-month).

[c] Canada. Options are traded in three locations in Canada: on the Montreal Stock Exchange, the Toronto Options Exchange, and a network called Trans Canada Options (TCO). On the Montreal Stock Exchange, there are options on 10-year Canadian government bonds, while on the Toronto Options Exchange there is an index option contract on the Toronto 35. This is a 35-stock index composed of major Canadian stocks that is capitalization-weighted with adjustments for float and cross-holdings. In addition, there are options on approximately 50 common stocks and LEAPS on approximately six stocks.

[d] Denmark. Two options on futures trade in Copenhagen; one is a specific Danish bond and the other is the KFX index.

[e] France. As in the Netherlands, options and futures are traded on different exchanges, e.g., the Monep (options) and Matif (futures). Stock options exist on approximately 26 French companies, but the majority of trading arises from the stock index option on the CAC-40. Options on the CAC-120 and CAC-250 are expected in the near future. The Matif is a 2-year-old exchange based in Paris. Several interest-related futures are listed, mainly on government bonds.

[f] Germany. The Deutsche Terminborse (DTB) lists stock options on approximately 15 individual companies and on the DAX. Futures exist on the DAX, Bund, and Bobl (long- and medium-term bonds, respectively) indexes. On the DAX and Bund futures there are also option contracts.

[g] Hong Kong. There is the Hong Seng stock index option contract, in addition to a vibrant market in stock warrants.

[h] Japan. Three exchanges trade options in Japan. On the Tokyo Exchange, the TOPIX stock index option is listed, along with a 10-year bond future option. In Nagoya, there is a 25-stock index option, and in Osaka, there is the Nikkei 225 stock index option.

[i] New Zealand. There are four options on futures contracts in New Zealand. These are the 3-month bill, 5- and 10-year bonds and the TOP 40 stock index.

[j] Netherlands. There are two organized exchanges in the Netherlands: the European Options Exchange (EOE) and the Financiele Termijnmarkt Amsterdam (FTA), both located in Amsterdam. The EOE is the oldest organized option exchange in Europe and trades options on several classes of assets.

[k] Singapore. Three options on futures trade on the SIMEX. These are the 90-day Eurodollar, 90-day Euroyen, and Japanese Nikkei 225 index futures contracts.

[l] Spain. Options trade on bond futures in Barcelona, and options on a 35-stock index (the IBEX) trade in Madrid.

[m] Sweden. Options and futures are traded on the Optionsmaklarna (OM) in Stockholm and exist notional for 17 of the major Swedish stocks, the OMX index, and Swedish government bonds with maturities of 5 years. Futures also exist for underlying instruments like interest rates, bonds with different maturities, and mortgage-backed securities.

[n] Switzerland. The Swiss Options and Financial Futures Exchange (SOFFEX) was launched in the summer of 1988. As of the beginning of 1993, options on 12 Swiss companies and the Swiss market index (SMI) are listed. Futures exist on the SMI, 5-year Swiss franc interest rate, and Swiss government bonds.

[o] United Kingdom. Since the merger of the London International Financial Futures Exchange (LIFFE) and the London Traded Options Market (LTOM), options and futures are traded on a central marketplace. As the leading market in Europe for financial futures and options, the LIFFE offers a wide range of derivatives. Options exist on over 60 companies and the FTSE 100 Index. Furthermore, the LIFFE has 4 options contracts on short-term interest rate futures traded at the exchange (3-month Sterling, 3-month Eurodollar, and 3-month Euromark and Euroswiss) and 3 options contracts on long-term bonds (long gilts, German government bonds, U.S. treasury bonds and Italian government bonds.)

9.03 OPTIONS ON INTERNATIONAL INDEXES

Currently the only international index on which options are traded is the IMI. Options on this index are traded on the AMEX, with the associated futures contracts traded on the Coffee, Sugar, and Cocoa Exchange in New York. Although it is the only international index option, the IMI has not been particularly successful.

The only other nondomestic stock index option is the MMI, which is traded on the EOE in Amsterdam, although volume on this contract is fairly light. The MMI's principal exchange is the AMEX in New York. There are plans to list a Japanese index option, as well as either the actual index or proxies for the Morgan Stanley Capital International, Europe Asia Far East Index (EAFE), and the Financial Times-Actuaries Euro-Pacific Index in the United States. In Europe, the EOE has fairly advanced plans to list a European 100 index. The International Stock Exchange in London has developed a Continental European 100 index, and the Matif in France is developing a broader index for Europe. Both of these indexes will most likely support options and futures.

There is no doubt that the growth of international option strategies will be significant and will parallel the growth of international investment in general. In addition to being able to invest in options underlying the larger international stocks, major institutional investors will soon have access to stock index options for both the major markets and regions. Options for the larger international stocks and stock index options for the more important countries already exist. The use of regional indexes, such as EAFE, as underlying assets for index options is more problematic, as evidenced by the limited success of the IMI. For this reason, the IMI makes an interesting case study.

The IMI is an international index that measures the performance of 50 leading foreign stocks traded in the United States, most in the form of ADRs. It is capitalization-weighted and based in U.S. dollars. Figure 9-15 shows this constituent list, country of domicile for each underlying issue, and percentage weight in the index. The IMI developers wanted to create an index that could be considered a benchmark for performance measurement of international portfolios because of its high correlation to already-established international indexes, and they chose their 50 stocks accordingly.

Only stocks that had a minimum capitalization of $100 million and met certain liquidity constraints were considered for inclusion in the index. The first notable characteristic of the index is the country weights. There are some substantial differences between the IMI and other major indexes. Figure 9-16 shows the country exposures relative to EAFE. The United Kingdom and the Netherlands are significantly overweight, while France, Germany, and Japan are underweight. These country weightings, together with some important industry mismatches (most notably in household durables and appliances) and the substantial concentration among large companies relative to EAFE cause the IMI to track EAFE relatively poorly. Figure 9-17 shows the risk analysis of the IMI relative to EAFE. The annual tracking error is just less than 7 percent, which is high for a diversified, 50-stock portfolio relative to EAFE. The IMI has a beta of significantly less than 1.0, suggesting that it is quite unlike the benchmark EAFE. The IMI will underperform in up markets and outperform in down markets, on average. Most of the tracking error is a result of country, industry, and specific risk.

In general, the design of an international index to support derivatives is more complex than that of a domestic index. The following issues are among the important considerations that should be addressed:

FIGURE 9-15

Constituents of the International Market Index[a]

Name	Weight	Country
News Corporation Ltd.	0.35%	Australia
Pacific Dunlop	0.45	Australia
Broken Hill Proprietary	1.81	Australia
National Australia Bank	0.80	Australia
Novo-Nordisk B	0.22	Denmark
Dresdner Bank A.G.	1.40	Germany
Hong Kong Telecom	1.39	Hong Kong
Montedison	0.59	Italy
Nissan Motor Co., Ltd.	3.39	Japan
NEC Corporation	3.48	Japan
Mitsubishi Bank	8.03	Japan
Sony Corporation	3.20	Japan
Toyota Motor Corp.	8.59	Japan
Tokio Marine & Fire	2.71	Japan
TDK Corporation	0.92	Japan
Hitachi Ltd.	5.62	Japan
Fuji Photo Film Co.	1.96	Japan
Canon Inc.	1.44	Japan
Honda Motor Co., Ltd.	1.93	Japan
Matsushita Electric	5.04	Japan
Kyocera Corporation	1.62	Japan
Ito-Yokado Co., Ltd.	1.93	Japan
Royal Dutch Petroleum	6.98	Netherlands
Unilever NV	2.21	Netherlands
K.L.M.	0.17	Netherlands
Phillips Gloeilampenfab	0.85	Netherlands
Norsk Hydro	1.11	Norway
Norsk Data Class "A"	0.02	Norway
Telefonica de Espana	1.23	Spain
Endesa	1.00	Spain
Banco Central	0.79	Spain
Pharmacia AB	0.21	Sweden
Volvo (AB)	0.26	Sweden
Ericsson B. Free	1.28	Sweden
Asea AB	1.02	Sweden
Electrolux "B" Free	0.48	Sweden
Natl Westminster Bank	1.61	United Kingdom
Imperial Chemical Ind.	2.42	United Kingdom
Hanson	3.28	United Kingdom
Rank Organisation Plc.	0.64	United Kingdom

[a] Constituent list as of May 31, 1990.

(continued)

FIGURE 9-15   (*continued*)

Name	Weight	Country
Smithkline Beecham A	1.04	United Kingdom
Saatchi & Saatchi Co.	0.04	United Kingdom
Reuters Holdings	1.48	United Kingdom
British Petroleum Co.	5.04	United Kingdom
B.A.T. Industries Plc.	3.06	United Kingdom
Barclays Bank Group Plc.	1.82	United Kingdom
Burman Oil Plc.	0.33	United Kingdom
Glaxo Holdings	3.35	United Kingdom
Fisons Plc.	0.72	United Kingdom
Cadbury Schweppes Plc.	0.67	United Kingdom

FIGURE 9-16

Country Exposures

Source: Barr, Rosenburg & Associates

	Percentage IMI	Percentage EAFE	Percentage Difference
Australia	3.41	2.13	1.28
Austria	0	0.44	(0.44)
Belgium	0	1.03	(1.03)
Canada	0	0	0
Denmark	0.22	0.58	(0.37)
Finland	0	0.26	(0.26)
France	0	5.62	(5.62)
Germany	1.40	6.66	(5.26)
Hong Kong	1.39	1.28	0.11
Ireland	0	0	0
Italy	0.59	2.85	(2.26)
Japan	49.87	53.87	(4.00)
Malaysia	0	0.44	(0.44)
Mexico	0	0	0
Netherlands	10.21	2.49	7.72
New Zealand	0	0.24	(0.24)
Norway	1.13	0.51	0.62
Singapore	0	0.68	(0.68)
South Africa	0	0	0
Spain	3.02	1.70	1.32
Sweden	3.26	1.64	1.62
Switzerland	0	3.26	(3.26)
United Kingdom	25.50	14.31	11.19

FIGURE 9-17

Risk Analysis of the IMI Relative to EAFE

Source: Barr, Rosenburg & Associates

Annual standard deviation of EAFE		18.04%
Annual standard deviation of IMI		17.05%
Predicted beta of IMI		0.87
Annual standard deviation of residual return		6.50%
Annual tracking error		6.89%
Decomposition of residual variance		
Country risk	28%	
Industry risk	37	
Risk Index risk	4	
Currency risk	5	
Specific risk	26	
Total	100%	

- *Number of names.* Should the index be broad or narrow? EAFE and similar indexes have some 700 names, which, when associated with their multicurrency origin, make hedging and arbitrage difficult. The range of 100 to 300 names is probably manageable for an international index.

- *Constituent characteristics.* Should the constituents be liquid, be tradable outside of their domestic markets, be optionable, or have other characteristics?

- *Country coverage.* Some countries are more important than others; for example, how necessary is it to have Finland, Malaysia, and Hong Kong represented?

- *Country weighting.* Capital markets in different countries have evolved at different rates as a result of different regulatory environments, financial incentives, and so on, and they may certainly have evolved at different rates according to each country's trade, political importance, and so forth. For this reason, capitalization weighting may not be as acceptable practically as theoretically.

- *Base currency.* In theory, a global or regional index should most appropriately be based in a composite or basket currency such as the special drawing right or ECU. However, this will make marketing the index difficult; hence, a U.S. dollar base is still most appropriate for the United States, the yen is most appropriate for Japan, and so on.

- *Asset weighting.* There is a natural appeal in capitalization weighting, since this scheme incorporates automatic rebalancing. However, other schemes such as equal weighting, gross domestic product weighting, and price weighting, can be used.

9.04 EXCHANGE DEVELOPMENT

Among the more important developments has been the evolution of the actual exchange structure. Starting with the Swedish OM exchange, there are now several entirely electronic option exchanges. The OM structure will soon form the basis for an option exchange in Austria. An alternative structure, which was first developed for the Swiss

SOFFEX market, appears to be somewhat more popular. It has already been enhanced for the German DTB exchange and will also form the basis for the Spanish market in 1991. In general, users of such an electronic exchange are able to place orders from their desktops. The systems allow order entry, automated order matching, trade settlement, margining, price dissemination, and automated trade confirmation.

The system configuration varies, but there are essentially three major components. The first is the exchange's data center, where such things as pricing are focused. Second, regional nodes are set up to be in continual communication with the data center. Third, each user site is tied in to the closest regional node. In this way, each member firm is linked electronically to the exchange, which provides all of the software for quote entry and position maintenance.

Real-time prices are provided by the exchange for use in third-party applications (such as proprietary option-pricing models) through a well-defined interface. This allows member firms to remain independent of the exchange in terms of such things as analytics and accounting while remaining in continual communication with the exchange center as far as price feeds and so on. The biggest advantage of electronic exchanges is that all back office transactions are handled electronically, which dramatically reduces labor costs and errors. A trade confirmation is received within seconds of order entry. The exchange also feeds this confirmation through a back office interface for use in third-party applications, allowing firms to monitor position risk in real time. In addition, an electronic audit trail prevents or at least deters fraud.

One of the disadvantages of electronic exchanges is that the traders do not have a feel for the market, as do those working in traditional trading pits. As can be expected, this complaint is usually heard from traders who started their careers in the pits; newer traders seem to enjoy the advantages of electronic trading.

9.05 OPTION VALUATION

When options are held to expiration, it is fairly easy to perform simple analyses of option strategies. Options, however, have different expiration dates; hence, it is not always realistic to invoke the assumption of holding to expiration. This leads to the need to develop a pricing model for options at every point in time prior to maturity. Several models have been developed for option pricing, but all are fairly complex mathematically.

This section describes the first important approach to option pricing. It was developed in 1973 by Black and Scholes.[11] Although other models have been developed since that attempt either to correct perceived deficiencies or to increase applicability, the Black-Scholes formula retains a substantial following among fund managers, brokers, and option market makers. Before the model is examined in detail, it is helpful first to review briefly how option prices should behave prior to maturity and then to enumerate the factors that influence option prices.

---

[11] The formula was originally published in F. Black and M. Scholes, "The Pricing of Options and Corporate Liabilities," *Journal of Political Economics* (May 1973), pp. 637–659.

[1] Actual Price Line

The price of a call or put at expiration should equal its intrinsic value, namely the excess of the stock price over the exercise price for a call and the exercise price over the stock price for a put. In fact, an American option must be priced at all times no less than its intrinsic value, which forms a lower limit on the option's price, since it can be exercised for this amount at any time. In addition, prior to maturity the option will be priced above this lower bound by an amount equal to the time value. How large can the time value get?

Certainly, one upper bound on the option value is the stock price for the call and the exercise price for the put, since in both cases these prices represent the maximum possible payoffs. Hence, option prices must lie within this region at all times. Figure 9-18 shows the regions for both puts and calls together with typical actual price lines for an option at two dates prior to maturity. The actual price line indicates how the price of the option behaves as a function of the stock price at one point prior to maturity. As time to maturity decreases, the actual price line moves down, until at maturity it "collapses" into the lower bound on the option price, its intrinsic value.

An interesting implication of the actual price line is the computation of the change in option prices for a small change in the underlying asset price. If the stock moves a small amount over a very short interval (so the actual price line does not move toward the option lower price bound), the option price moves along the actual price line. The crucial measurement showing the effect of the stock on the option is the slope of the actual price line; for deep out-of-the-money calls the slope is almost zero (indicating little option price change for a given stock movement), while for deep in-the-money calls, the slope is almost one (indicating that the option price changes almost a dollar for a dollar with the stock).

The slope of the actual price line is frequently called the riskless hedge ratio or the option delta. Its application to hedging is clear: If a number of shares of the underlying asset equal to the slope of the actual price line are purchased for every call written (or every put purchased), the hedge will be riskless over small intervals and for small stock price changes. To see this, consider a call hedge set up in the specified manner. There are two interesting cases to consider. First, suppose the stock price increases. Then the stock component of the hedge will increase by the slope of the actual price line times the stock price increase, which is exactly the loss on the written call. Similarly, if the stock price declines, the loss on the stock component of the hedge is offset by the gain on the call component. In short, the hedge is riskless. Notice that a riskless hedge requires a holding of a greater number of options than shares of stock, since the slope of the actual price line is less than one in absolute magnitude.

A concept related to the option delta is the option elasticity, which measures the rate of return on the option for a given rate of return on the stock. The formula for the elasticity is $(\Delta O/O)/(\Delta S/S)$, where ΔO is the small change in the option price resulting from a small change, ΔS, in the stock price, and O and S are the option and stock prices, respectively. Hence, $\Delta O/O$ is the rate of return on the option and $\Delta S/S$ is the rate of return on the stock. The elasticity can be rewritten $(\Delta O/\Delta S)(S/O)$, where $\Delta O/\Delta S$ is the slope of the actual price line, or option delta, and S/O is the ratio of the stock price to the option price. It can be shown that the option elasticity is greater than one in absolute magnitude (positive for calls, negative for puts). Hence, although

FIGURE 9-18

Actual Price Lines for Calls and Puts

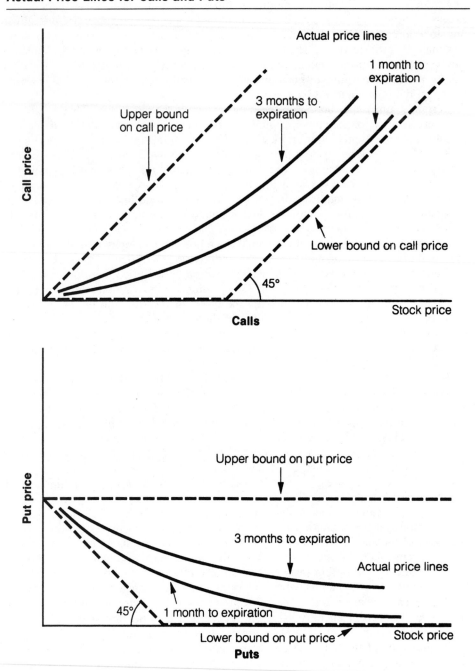

the absolute price change for options will be less than the price change for the stock, the absolute rate of return for options will be greater than for stocks.

[2] Factors Influencing Option Prices

The important characteristics of an option contract that influence the option's value can be separated into three groups by the element they depend on:

1. Underlying asset
2. Option contract
3. Economy in general

[a] Factors That Depend on the Underlying Asset. Included within this group are the price, the volatility, and the dividend policy of the underlying asset. Clearly, the larger the price, the larger the call value and the smaller the put value, since there is a larger potential payoff from the call and a smaller payoff from the put.

The impact of the volatility of the underlying asset is a little more complex. In general, the payoff from the option depends on the distribution of the underlying asset at the expiration of the option. The greater the range of underlying asset prices at expiration, the greater the probability and extent to which the option will be in the money and the greater the potential payoff from the option. Although a greater range of prices also increases the likelihood that the option ends up out of the money, this is not of great importance; if the option ends up a little or a great deal out of the money, its value is still zero. The concept of the range of prices can be made more precise with statistical theory, but it is sufficient here to think of the important measure as being the variability or volatility in the evolution of the stock price between the current date and expiration.

The final factor in this group is the dividend policy of the underlying asset. If the option is European and payout protected, the dividend policy has no effect. For other options, however, there are two distinct effects from the dividend policy. First, cash dividends cause the stock price to fall, which increases put prices and decreases call prices. Second, cash payouts can affect the exercise policy of American options. The latter effect is more complicated to analyze and requires some advanced techniques. Current research seems to indicate, however, that the effect is not of major importance.

[b] Factors That Depend on the Option Contract. The principal factors in this category are the expiration date and the exercise price of the contract; however, all of the characteristics mentioned earlier are relevant. For American options, a longer time to maturity implies greater flexibility of the contract and thus increases its value. Increasing the exercise price decreases the potential payoff from the call and increases the potential payoff from the put. Hence, an increase in the exercise price increases put prices and decreases call prices.

[c] Factors That Depend on the Economy in General. The most important of these factors is the risk-free interest rate. The interest rate enters from the need for discounting future cash flows, in particular the exercise price of the option. Since an increase in the interest rate decreases the present value of the exercise price, there is a tendency for call prices to increase and for put prices to decrease. However, the effect can be more complicated in certain situations; without further assumptions, a definitive conclusion as to the effects of interest rates cannot be reached.

[3] Black-Scholes Formula

The idea of the riskless hedge was used by Black and Scholes to develop a formula for valuing European options on non-dividend-paying underlying assets. Their insight was to use the hedge, instantaneously rebalanced, so that it is riskless over the entire period until maturity of the option. Since the hedge is riskless, it should earn the riskless rate on the funds invested. This fact, together with some high-powered mathematics describing the movement of stocks in continuous time, was sufficient to derive their formula.

The Black-Scholes call valuation formula is

$$C_0 = S_0 N(d_1) - K B_0 N(d_2)$$

where:

C_0 = current call value

S_0 = current call price

K = exercise price

B_0 = price of a riskless zero-coupon bond that matures at the expiration of the option with value $1

$N(d)$ = value of the cumulative standard normal distribution function; this value represents the probability that the value of d or less will be drawn from the distribution

$d_1 = [\log(S_0/KB_0) + 0.5\sigma^2 t]/\sigma\sqrt{t}$

$d_2 = d_1 - \sigma\sqrt{t}$

$\log$ = natural logarithm

t = maturity of the option

σ = volatility of the underlying asset

The formula looks undeniably complex. Fortunately, its interpretation is rather straightforward. The first term, $S_0 N(d_1)$, is the expected value of the stock price given that it exceeds the exercise price (i.e., given that the option ends up in the money) times the probability of the stock price's exceeding the exercise price. Figure 9-19 shows the probability distribution of the stock price at the expiration date. The shaded area represents the part of the probability distribution that exceeds the exercise price. Hence, the first term is the expected value of the shaded area times the probability of being in the shaded area. The second term subtracts the cost of exercising the option, namely, the present value of the exercise price times the probability that the option ends up in the money.

With the exception of the two terms involving the normal distribution, $N(d_1)$ and $N(d_2)$, the remainder of the formula is quite simple. In fact, even the two terms from the normal distribution can be approximated very easily so that the formula can be computed on a hand-held calculator. All of the expected variables appear in the formula: the current stock price, S_0; the volatility of the underlying asset, σ; the exercise price, K (in fact, the relevant term is the present value of the exercise price, KB_0);

FIGURE 9-19

Distribution of Stock Prices at Expiration and the Value of a Call

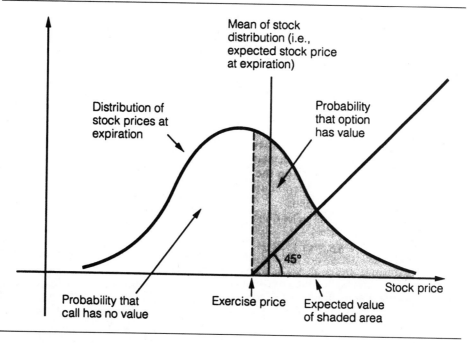

the time to maturity, t; and the riskless interest rate, which is expressed here as the price of a riskless zero-coupon bond, B_0.

It is possible to take derivatives of the formula with respect to these variables to discover their impact on option prices. The exact formulas are not repeated here, but the signs of the derivatives are as follows:

Effect of stock price:	$\partial C_0 / \partial S_0 > 0$
Effect of exercise price:	$\partial C_0 / \partial K < 0$
Effect of time to maturity:	$\partial C_0 / \partial t > 0$
Effect of volatility:	$\partial C_0 / \partial \sigma > 0$
Effect of interest rates:	$\partial C_0 / \partial r > 0$

These results are exactly as anticipated, including the effect of interest rates, about which there is some ambiguity without resorting to a model such as the Black-Scholes formula.

[4] Illustration of Black-Scholes Usage

As an illustration of the formula's usage, reexamine the *XYZ*/April/100 call listed in Figure 9-1. A word of warning is in order: The formula applies exactly only to European payout-protected calls, but listed options are American payout unprotected. In fact, XYZ did not pay a cash dividend between the dates of the prices listed in Figure 9-1 and the expiration of the April options; hence, the issue of dividend payments and payout protection does not arise. Therefore, the formula can be applied without fear of bias from this source. However, the pricing of an American option as if it were a European option is far more controversial. This point is discussed in more detail in the next section, but for now it is worth pointing out that in this case distinction is not important.

As indicated above, five inputs are needed. These are

$S_0 = \$99.875$

$K = 100$

$T = 0.08$ years

$r = 0.085$

$\sigma = 0.255$

The first two of these inputs require no further explanation. The call had exactly four weeks of its life remaining, which has been converted to years. The interest rate on large certificates of deposit was approximately 8.5 percent, which has been taken as a proxy for the interest rate. The last input, the volatility for XYZ, is the most problematic, since it is not directly observable in the market.

There are a number of ways in which the volatility can be obtained. The most common method is to compute the standard deviation of a history of (frequently 180 daily) logarithmic stock returns. Another method is to use the implicit volatility from a prior day; this is the volatility that solves the formula, given that it is the only unknown. Finally, several option services supply estimates of volatility for the various underlying stocks; the estimate from one of these is used here.

It follows from these inputs that under continuous compounding, the price of the zero-coupon bond is

$$B_0 = e^{-rt} = e^{-0.0068} = \$0.99$$

Further:

$$KB_0 = 99$$
$$t = 0.28$$
$$\sigma\sqrt{t} = 0.07$$
$$\sigma^2 t = 0.005$$
$$S_0/KB_0 = 1.009$$
$$\log(S_0/KB_0) = 0.009$$

Now d_1 and d_2 can be computed as

$d_1 = 0.16$

$d_2 = 0.088$

From a table of the cumulative standard normal distribution, it is easy to find that

$N(d_1) = 0.5636$

$N(d_2) = 0.5351$

Hence, the Black-Scholes call price is

$$C_0 = (99.875)(0.5636) - (99)(0.5351)$$
$$= 56.29 - 52.97$$
$$= \$3.32$$

This compares with the reported price of \$3.25. If the inputs are to be believed, the option is slightly undervalued. It probably does not represent a purchase opportunity, however, since commissions and other transaction costs (in particular, the bid-ask spread) are frequently much greater than the mispricing.

[5] Limitations of the Black-Scholes Model

Such an elegant formula as that derived by Black-Scholes is not obtained without making some fairly stringent assumptions. The most important of these are as follows:

- The markets for options and common stock are frictionless.
- The risk-free rate is constant over the life of the option.
- The underlying stock pays no dividends.
- The distribution of stock prices at the end of any finite interval is log-normal with constant variance.

Assumption 1 is a standard assumption in finance theory. Essentially, it guarantees that every investor can construct its desired portfolio without cost. In reality, of course, it is not true for all investors, but it may not be so far in error for brokers and large dealers that prices may be set as if the assumption held.

Assumption 2 is a convenience that can be removed at the expense of greater mathematical sophistication. In fact, the call price is not too sensitive to interest rates, and since rates over the maximum nine-month holding period of listed stock options are not too variable (at least not as variable as the stock price), it is questionable whether the generalized formulas are worth the incremental effort.

Assumption 3 is invoked for two reasons: (1) The payment of cash dividends causes the stock price to change and (at least for the theoretical analysis) some model is required to explain the change; and (2) there is a strong interaction between the early exercise of American options and dividend payments.[12] For example, for sufficiently large dividends (causing a large price drop in the stock on the ex dividend date), it may pay call holders to exercise their options early to capture the dividend. For practical purposes, what is required is a formula for American options on dividend-paying stocks. Unfortunately, general models to value such options are quite complex; hence, for simplicity a number of approximations are frequently made that are based on the Black-Scholes formula. The most common approximation is to apply the formula as it stands but using as input the stock price less the present value of any dividends anticipated prior to the maturity of the option. It can be shown that this approximation is reasonable under many circumstances but that it does not capture the entire divi- dend–early exercise effect.

---

[12] Professor Robert Merton has derived a formula with stochastic interest rates. See his article, "Theory of Rational Option Pricing," *Bell Journal of Economics and Management Science* (Spring 1973), pp. 141–183.

Assumption 4 comes in two parts. First, the distribution of stock prices has to be log-normal and, second, it has a constant variance. A number of option-pricing formulas have been developed that have been based on alternative (and usually more complex) specifications of the underlying stock distribution. None of these formulas has achieved widespread acceptance in the investment community, and it is doubtful if they provide much benefit when applied to listed stock options. In contrast, however, there is good reason to believe that interest rate options and foreign currency options could be more accurately analyzed with the generalized models than with the Black-Scholes formula.

[6] Put Option Valuation

The pricing of European puts on non-dividend-paying stocks is no more difficult than pricing calls. Both the put-call parity theorem and the Black-Scholes formula apply in this situation, so it is trivial to solve for the put value. For example,

$$P_0 = C_0 - S_0 + KB_0$$

and

$$C_0 = S_0 N(d_1) - KB_0 N(d_2)$$

so

$$P_0 = S_0[N(d_1) - 1] - KB_0[N(d_2) - 1]$$
$$= S_0 N(-d_1) - KB_0 N(-d_2)$$

where the last step follows from the well-known relationship that $N(d_1) + N(-d_1) = 1$ and $N(d_2) + N(-d_2) = 1$.

As with the call formula, the derivatives of the put formula can be evaluated with respect to the inputs. These are

Effect of stock price:	$\partial P_0/\partial S_0 < 0$
Effect of exercise price:	$\partial P_0/\partial K > 0$
Effect of time to maturity:	$\partial P_0/\partial t \geq 0$
Effect of volatility:	$\partial P_0/\partial \sigma > 0$
Effect of interest rates:	$\partial P_0/\partial r < 0$

The only surprise among these derivatives is the effect of increasing the time to maturity. For the Black-Scholes European put formula, increasing the time to maturity has no single effect on the put price. This is slightly disconcerting, since it was argued previously that for an American put increasing the time to maturity unambiguously increases the price.

This difference illustrates one of the shortcomings of the European put formula: In many circumstances, it does not provide a very good approximation of the American put price. Certainly, it provides a worse approximation than the European call formula does of American call prices. One reason for this is that there are more occasions when the American put should be exercised early. One extreme example is when the stock price drops to zero before the expiration of the put. There is no point in waiting until expiration to exercise, since the maximum possible payoff from the put (namely, the exercise price) can be gained immediately.

As with the call formula, there are several approximations that can be used to adjust the formula for cash dividends. However, a more satisfactory approach, which accounts for both cash dividend payments and the biases caused by early exercise, is to use a numerical method for evaluating the American put price. The standard numerical procedure is based on an article by Cox, Ross, and Rubinstein and is called the binomial method.[13] It is easily programmed on a computer and is widely used.

The problem with numerical approaches is that they can become computer bound. This occurs particularly with certain interest rate option calculations where the complexity of the computational tree leads to the approach's becoming infeasible for all but the larger computer centers. While there is always a trade-off between accuracy and the computational intensity, in many cases this is not easy to determine beforehand.

An alternative approach is to try to determine an analytical approximation of the American option price. One early attempt in this direction was by Professor Robert Geske, who viewed the American option as a "compound option" (i.e., an option on an option).[14] Unfortunately, this approach is also somewhat computationally intensive. In the mid-1980s, there were several other attempts along this line, but none was particularly successful. However, this strand of research has now become more fashionable, and some results by a research group in London show promise.[15]

[7] How Well Does the Option-Pricing Model Work?

Much effort has been expended testing the Black-Scholes call-pricing formula and its generalizations. However, there has been far less work than one would suspect given the wide usage of the models. (There has been much less effort directed toward testing the option formulas than, for example, the capital asset pricing model.) Further, there has been virtually no empirical research on the pricing of puts.

In general, the empirical work has suggested two major findings.

1. Overall, the option-pricing models work exceedingly well. The average difference between the market and the model prices over all options has tended to be a few cents. Moreover, when the model has indicated that the option was overvalued or undervalued, writing or buying the option has tended to be profitable.

2. There appear to be a number of systematic biases between the market and model prices. For example, out-of-the-money calls tend to have market prices somewhat higher than those predicted by the model. However, the exact nature of the biases and their magnitude is still the matter of some debate.

9.06 OPTION-TRADING STRATEGIES

In this last part, the uses of options in trading strategies are discussed. As with any asset class, a great deal of information about the return characteristics of options can

---

[13] J. Cox et al., "Option Pricing: A Simplified Approach," *Journal of Financial Economics* (Sept. 1979), pp. 229–263.

[14] See R. Geske and H. Johnson, "The American Put Valued Analytically," *Journal of Finance*, Vol. 39 (1984).

[15] S. Gandhi and A. Kooros, "American Option Pricing: An Analytic Approach I" (Unpublished Paper, Imperial College of Science, 1993).

be found by examining the historical performance of a representative index. However, since options have only short lives and may change considerably over very short intervals (e.g., from in the money to out of the money), the construction of a representative option index is not easy. Not only is such an index desirable for learning about the nature of option returns, but it is required for the systematic analysis of an option portfolio manager.

The next topic in this part is a more detailed description of how options affect an equity portfolio. This is an area of increasing academic interest and the subject of a number of recent articles. Finally, some of the most common listed stock option strategies used by institutional investors and the strategies now being employed for index options and debt options are reviewed.

[1] Option Indexes

There are a number of possible uses of asset indexes. For example, the level of a call option index could usefully indicate whether call prices are currently overvalued or undervalued relative to some historical norm. In investment management, two of the most useful applications of a representative index are (1) to develop some intuition about the asset's return characteristics for use in asset allocation decisions and (2) to provide a benchmark for analyzing the performance of option managers. The first use requires a long series of periodic returns from which descriptive characteristics such as the average return, standard deviation, skewness, and, perhaps, beta (systematic risk exposure) are computed. The requirements for the second usage are more subtle. Certainly, the construction of the index should be such that an option manager could replicate the performance of the index (not taking into account transaction costs). In other words, the index should represent a doable strategy. A second requirement is that the index, if used as a benchmark, must be representative of the option manager's style. For example, there is no point in measuring the performance of a manager who buys calls against an index that attempts to capture the returns of a covered call strategy.

There have been a number of attempts over the past few years to compute option indexes.[16] With very few exceptions, they have been designed to capture the relative valuation of calls (or puts). For example, the CBOE publishes a call index and a put index, the CBOE Time Premium Indexes, which measure, respectively, the time values of a hypothetical six-month at-the-money call and put. These indexes suggest whether calls or puts as a whole are currently cheap or expensive relative to the historical record. They provide no indication as to the valuation of individual options or the returns likely to be obtained in the option markets.

Some return indexes are published. These are usually computed by investment consultants or brokers and thus are not as widely disseminated as the value indexes. One of the most comprehensive sets of indexes is that made available by Barr, Rosenburg & Associates (BARRA).[17] BARRA computes 60 indexes, each of which reports the buy-and-hold return of one aspect of the call or put market. For example, two indexes track the overall performance of the call option market and the put option

---

[16] See, e.g., D. Galai, "Option Indices," *Journal of Finance* (May 1979), on which the CBOE Time Premium index is based; G. Gastineau, *The Stock Options Manual* (New York: McGraw-Hill, 1979). *Barrons* publishes the CBOE Time Premium index in its weekly issues.

[17] BARRA is an investment consulting firm based in Berkeley, California.

market, respectively, and two others track the returns on covered call option and covered put option strategies.

[2] Analyzing Option Portfolio Performance

The study of investment outcomes of managed portfolios has three aspects: (1) performance measurement, which is concerned with defining the outcome itself; (2) performance analysis, which attempts to determine, first, whether the outcome arose from skill or from chance and, second, the benefit to the client of the portfolio performance in view of the risks that were taken to produce the reward; and (3) performance attribution, which decomposes the portfolio return into various categories of investment return (e.g., what portion of the portfolio return can be attributed to the return of the airline industry or the relative performance of small versus large capitalization companies) and the return arising from specific management decisions, such as market timing or asset selectivity.

The managed option portfolio is a portfolio of asset positions like any other portfolio, and hence the analysis of option portfolio performance must be a special case of traditional portfolio performance analysis. It is of particular interest because of the option portfolio's relationship to the larger aggregate portfolio of the investor, within which it is usually viewed as an incremental component. In the traditional performance analysis of a portfolio, which is usually only one among the many portfolios belonging to a single investor and managed by multiple managers, the fact that the portfolio is only a part of the client's total assets has usually been ignored. In contrast, reference to a broader context is inescapable with option portfolio analysis, since either a cash pool or a stock portfolio (perhaps even managed by another manager) often serves as collateral.

Performance measurement is most commonly specified in terms of the compound investment return (defined as the ratio of terminal value, including any cash flows, to initial value) on the managed portfolio. Unfortunately, the investment return for an option portfolio is not always defined because the option portfolio may have zero or negative initial value. This is clearly the case with covered call writing, where equity holdings managed elsewhere in the investor's total portfolio serve as collateral for the option-writing strategy. Since the initial value for the option strategy is ambiguous, it is natural to define the investment return in terms of the value of a larger asset portfolio. In theory, the asset portfolio should include all of the assets of the client, whether explicitly linked to the option manager or not, since the use of this base gives results that are accurate in representing the contribution of the option portfolio to the utility of the client.[18]

The logic behind the use of incremental return to the client's total asset base is straightforward. In the absence of the option manager, the client's return can be easily identified. When the option strategy is added, the client experiences an incremental return. Is the increment beneficial or not? Clearly, this is a natural measure of the productivity of the option manager. Indeed, it is natural to study the usefulness of any kind of manager by comparing the performance of the total portfolio that would be held in the absence of his or her activities to the total portfolio including the manager's contribution.

---

[18] It can be shown that under some circumstances, the use of a smaller base is biased against the skillful option manager. For details, see B. Rosenberg and A. Rudd, "Option Performance Analysis,"

Frequently, however, the use of the client's total asset portfolio as the base is rejected because of data collection difficulties, and a smaller base is substituted. There are two obvious candidates for this smaller base: (1) the total value of the assets nominally under the option manager's control, provided that this is a positive and relatively constant number, and (2) the total value of the cash and equity portfolios that are directly related to the option manager, by virtue of the contributions to the cash portfolio and writing options against the equity portfolio. It is important to note that in both cases, the risk-reward trade-off applied to performance analysis must be adjusted.

Performance analysis can be used retrospectively to determine the apparent skill shown by the manager during a historical period, as well as prospectively to predict the likely superior performance of the manager. In either case, the measure of performance should be fair and not gameable. Fairness requires that when money managers are doing their best to improve the circumstances of the client, the money managers who have greater skill should be expected to rank higher on the performance measure than less skillful managers. Further, the manager should not be able to benefit by gaming against the performance method so as to improve the performance ranking without making any contribution to the client.

Both criteria strongly argue for the use of a normal portfolio or normal bogey for each option manager.[19] The normal portfolio represents the typical or neutral position of the manager and serves as a benchmark for active management. The option manager performs active management by making active bets relative to the neutral position. The difference between the managed portfolio return and the normal portfolio return is the active return, which represents the value added by the manager's skill. The active return is independent of the return that arises from the manager's permanent style or strategy.

The use of normal portfolios permits accurate comparisons of the performance of different managers. If comparisons among managers are made without neutralizing the influence of the performance of each manager's long-term orientation or preferred habitat, most likely managers who have concentrated on the sector that has performed best most recently will be erroneously deemed the most skillful. This indicates that performance analysis is solely concerned with the manager's active return.

The manager and client should jointly define the normal option portfolio to reflect the manager's typical investment strategy. The normal portfolio may contain call and put options, the underlying equities and short-term Treasury bills, each with dollar investment values that correspond to the typical dollar values invested in each category. Within the option component of the normal portfolio, weights should be assigned to long-, medium-, and short-maturity and in-the-money, at-the-money, and out-of-the money options so as to best represent the managers' typical strategy and style.

Once the active portfolio returns have been computed, the next step is the analysis of performance. Although some limited implications can be drawn directly from the return series, the more useful results require the adjustment of the active returns for the risk. This analysis requires the use of a risk model for options, which must be integrated with a similar risk model for the underlying securities, to describe the impor-

Proceedings of the Seminar on the Analysis of Security Prices (Chicago: University of Chicago Press, 1981), pp. 37–74.

[19] For further discussion on the use of normal portfolios in option performance measurement, see A. Rudd, "Performance Measurement of Option Portfolios" (Talk at the American Stock Exchange Options Colloquium, March 31, 1981), published in *Transcripts of the 1981 Amex Options Colloquium,* Day Two (Mar. 31, 1981), pp. 24–30.

tant factors influencing option returns and relate them to the factors in the equity market.

Option risk models are discussed in detail in the next section. It is sufficient here to note that the option risk model provides the mechanism for the adjustment for risk and the decomposition of option return to the important factors influencing the option market. Since one of these factors is the underlying stock itself, the option return is related to factors affecting only the option market together with factors that affect the equity market as well. Moreover, because interest rates affect option returns, one can also argue that bond market factors (e.g., the term structure of interest rates) should also be part of this attribution of option performance. This specification is crucial when managers justify an option strategy in terms of factors external to the option market, e.g., when deep in-the-money covered call writing is pursued as a surrogate for a fixed-income strategy.

There are several levels of performance analysis. At the least detailed level of analysis, investment returns are attributed to category timing (as among cash or bonds, equities, and call and put options) and to within-category selectivity. The former reflects the manager's wisdom in devoting funds among the available investment vehicles, while the latter reflects the manager's superior performance, if any, in asset selection within each category.

The next level of analysis, which is exceedingly important for understanding the role of option management in the overall portfolio, reflects a distinction between timing the important factors that influence the equity and option markets (market factor timing) and performance that arises independently of the factors (residual performance). The former reflects the manager's skill in timing the equity market and the options market, relative to the cash market.

Under this approach, the manager's actions in the option market and (if there are any) in the equity market affect the equity portfolio beta and thereby contribute to equity market timing. Option transactions contribute to equity market timing because of the option's linkage to its underlying security. Moreover, option actions also contribute to option market timing. Elements of performance that are not related to active timing of these two markets are attributed to residual performance within each of the investment categories. This analysis underscores the strong effect of option investment on the equity market exposure of the total portfolio. For example, much of the performance contribution of option management relates to deliberate or inadvertent changes in the equity beta.

At the most detailed level of analysis, the performance contributions of individual factors within the markets and of specific returns of individual assets are studied. This framework provides a complete attribution of return and presents the most intricate performance monitor. For example, an option investment is viewed as partial equity and bond positions. Abnormal option return arises from mispricing of the underlying security (i.e., the stock specific return) in addition to the specific return of the option itself, net of any linked effect from the other markets.

[3] Option Risk Models

Option risk models[20] decompose the option return into the important factors influencing the option market, and the underlying stock is one of the important factors. In

---

[20] For further information, see J. Evnine and A. Rudd, "A Multiple Factor Risk Model for Options" (Paper presented at the Joint National ORSA/TIMS Meeting, Apr. 25–27, 1983).

particular, over short intervals, it may be expected that the return on the option in excess of the risk-free rate should approximate the underlying stock excess return times the option elasticity. In symbols,

$$r_0 - r = \eta(r_s - r) + \cdots$$

    where:

        r_0 = return on the option

        r_s = return on the stock

        r = risk-free rate

        η = option elasticity

The term $\eta(r_s - r)$ is therefore the fraction of the option return that can be associated with the underlying security.

The ellipsis dots at the end of the equation indicate that there may be other factors influencing the option return. What are these other factors? Certainly, the same factors that influenced option prices will be important. Note that here the option return rather than price is being modeled; hence, the relevant term in the decomposition is the return on the factor rather than the factor value itself. Since some of the factors (such as exercise price) do not change, they are not relevant in the model of option returns.

A simple model for call return may include the following terms:

Excess call return = return due to underlying stock + return due to change in interest rates + return due to change in variance + return due to autonomous changes in the call market as a whole + specific return

The next step is to estimate the correlations between the various factors. The result is a risk model for options. In concept, this is very similar to the market model for common stocks that is used quite extensively by investment managers. The option risk model has a number of interesting uses. First, it is possible to determine the risk exposure of an option portfolio and hence to determine the risk levels of a combined option-stock portfolio. For example, it is possible to determine the degree of systematic risk and total risk that is reduced by writing options against the underlying equities. Second, performance analysis of option portfolio returns is made more meaningful with a risk model once it is possible to estimate the degree of risk associated with each component of return. Third, it is possible to identify the style of the manager with fair precision and to provide feedback on the manager's judgments. For example, are the active bets that are being made consistent with the level of risk that is being borne? Fourth, there are a number of sophisticated applications where the risk model can be used in conjunction with an optimization program to produce maximally efficient portfolios subject to certain prespecified criteria.

[4] Institutional Listed Stock Option Strategies

The most important listed stock option strategies include those described in the following sections.

[a] Long Calls and Treasury Bills. This strategy is a surrogate for holding long common stocks. The long call holding, which usually comprises approximately 10 percent of the portfolio, provides exposure to the equity market, while the Treasury bill holding provides stability. From the previous discussion, the long call holding has a beta of approximately 9; hence, the beta of the combined call and Treasury bill portfolio is close to 1. The strategy has the advantage that the maximum loss is predefined (the 10 percent call holding), while the potential for the strategy is comparable to the stock-only portfolio.

[b] Cash-Secured Put Writing. Here, the strategy is to deposit the put exercise price in escrow (to provide collateral) while writing the put. When held to expiration, the payoff from the written put is similar to that from the covered call (see Figures 9-7 and 9-8); hence, many investors view cash-secured put writing as covered call writing. One important difference between the strategies is the greater likelihood of the put rather than the call being exercised prior to expiration.

[c] Covered Call Writing. This is by far the most common institutional strategy. The common justifications are that writing calls against an existing equity position provides increased return from receiving the call premiums and reduces the risk of the portfolio. To some extent, there are fallacies in these arguments. First, the additional income from the call premiums is in return for taking the obligation to receive the stock at the exercise price at the option of the call holder. This obligation effectively eliminates the upside potential of the stock. (See Figure 9-9.) Second, there are many ways of reducing the risk of the portfolio (e.g., placing funds in riskless assets). Writing calls is only beneficial if the calls are overvalued (and hence providing incremental return) or the use of the calls is less costly than other assets in reducing risk.

[d] Conversion. This is an arbitrage strategy, based on perceived mispricing between the put and call markets. If the investor believes that put prices are too expensive relative to calls, the put can be written and the call purchased. If the put-call parity theorem discussed previously holds, this strategy would produce riskless profits before transaction costs. Unfortunately, the existence of early exercise causes the conversion strategy to be risky, although if the option prices get too far out of line it can still be a profitable strategy.

[e] Portfolio Insurance. The strategy of portfolio insurance[21] as currently practiced is not a listed stock option strategy. However, since it could be implemented using listed options and is important in fund management, it should be described here.

The assets that every portfolio manager would like to have available are call or put options on his or her portfolios. In other words, if there were listed options (or the options could be fabricated) on every managed portfolio, managers and/or clients could decide whether to hedge the portfolio (by writing calls or purchasing puts). Obviously, listed options on all managed portfolios do not exist, but they can be fabricated.

One method follows directly from the discussion of option valuation presented previously. It was shown that over short intervals, a portfolio containing the correct number (defined as the option delta) of shares of the underlying stock held long and one written call was equivalent to a holding in a riskless bond. This being the case, it is simple to see that the call can be duplicated (over a short period) by a portfolio

---

[21] The original article in this area is by Hayne Leland, "Who Buys Portfolio Insurance?" *Journal of Finance* (May 1980), pp. 581–594. See also R. Ferguson. "Two Approaches to Asset Allocation." *Pensions and Investment Age* (Sept. 19, 1983), p. 38.

containing the correct proportions of the underlying stock and the riskless bond. Of course, these correct proportions must be adjusted through time so that the portfolio can replicate the instantaneous return on the call option.

This simple idea is the basis for developing portfolio insurance strategies. For example, a put on any managed portfolio can be fabricated by "continuously" trading in a particular manner between a riskless bond portfolio and the managed portfolio. Although the idea is very straightforward, its implementation is complex, since methods for dealing with changes in the volatility of the portfolio and minimizing transaction costs, for example, have to be worked out. Several organizations have produced software packages that generate the rebalancing transactions to insure portfolios using this form of dynamic trading strategy. In addition, many investment managers based in several countries offer services to insure or "protect" portfolios under a wide variety of conditions.

The other method for constructing an option on a portfolio is to select a portfolio of options that behaves like the desired option by means of the use of an option risk model. Basically, the approach is to compute the exposures of the managed equity portfolio to the factors of return. From these exposures, it is possible to compute the exposures of the hypothetical option on the managed portfolio to the factors of return influencing the option market. The final step requires the use of an optimization program, in conjunction with the risk model, to construct a portfolio of listed stock options and stock index options that behaves as nearly as possible like the hypothetical option.[22]

Both approaches have advantages and disadvantages. The dynamic trading strategy is elegant but somewhat difficult to implement efficiently and inexpensively.[23] The second approach requires more sophisticated technology, but the trading requirements are typically less severe than in the first approach.

Portfolio insurance was slow to be adopted by the investment management and sponsor community. However, after 1985, its acceptance grew rapidly.

The performance of insured strategies during the October 1987 crash was quite mixed. The majority performed close to their advertised benchmarks. A few, however, were quite disastrous, with the returns on the insured portfolios being less than if they had not been insured at all. By October 1988, portfolio insurance was largely out of favor, with realistic estimates of insured funds in the United States comprising less than $10 billion. Since this time, insured funds have decreased even further. However, in other countries, notably Japan, portfolio insurance is still somewhat popular.

9.07 OPTION RISK ANALYSIS: A CASE STUDY

An example of a risk analysis of an optioned portfolio follows. The portfolio is an actively managed institutional Australian portfolio. It is the active component of a larger portfolio that, in addition to this aggressive satellite subportfolio, also comprises a passively managed core subportfolio. The underlying equity component is worth

---

[22] This approach is developed further in J. Evnine and A. Rudd. "Option Portfolio Risk Analysis." *Journal of Portfolio Management* (Winter 1983).

[23] Some simple portfolio insurance strategies have been developed. See e.g., Andre Perold, "Constant Proportion Portfolio Insurance" (Harvard Business School, Aug. 1986).

FIGURE 9-20

Underlying Equity Portfolio

Ident	Name	Shares	Price	% Wgt	Beta	% Ytd	Ind
1 ANZ	Aust & NZ Bank Grp	4685721	4.82	5.04	0.85	4.72	BANFIN
2 ARN	Arnotts Limited	1817920	5.24	2.13	0.78	3.72	FOOD
3 BHP	The Brokn. Hill Pty	10635533	8.36	19.84	1.03	3.83	DIVRES
4 BHS	Brash Hldgs	181900	5.34	0.22	0.62	3.75	RETAIL
5 CCB	C-C Bottlers	2953930	3.15	2.08	0.69	2.54	FOOD
6 CLG	Challenge Bank	448300	3.35	0.34	0.79	3.87	BANFIN
7 CRA	CRA Ltd	4174157	9.46	8.81	1.29	2.01	OTHMTL
8 DOM	Dominion Min. Ltd	1400000	1.74	0.54	1.46	0.00	GOLD
9 EXI	Exicom Ltd.	440000	3.00	0.29	0.99	0.00	MSIND
10 EXL	Elders IXL Ltd.	10724533	3.26	7.80	1.11	5.37	ENTINV
11 FAI	FAI Insurances	306200	4.25	0.29	0.92	1.65	INSURE
12 GMF	Goodman Fieldr. Wat	4203239	2.55	2.39	0.89	3.84	FOOD
13 MAY	Mayne Nickless Ltd	878267	6.50	1.27	1.05	3.15	TRANSP
14 MIM	M. I. M. Holdings	5786946	2.10	2.71	1.38	1.90	OTHMTL
15 NAB	Natl Australia Bk	3990632	6.22	5.54	0.84	4.36	BANFIN
16 NCP	News Corp	2640050	10.60	6.25	1.03	0.75	MEDIA
17 PDP	Pacific Dunlop Ltd	5185604	4.43	5.13	0.97	4.63	DIVIND
18 PNC	Pioneer Concrete	4521972	3.30	3.33	0.94	3.85	BLDMAT
19 QAL	Qintex Australia	2185877	1.96	0.96	0.65	7.65	MEDIA
20 SGB	S. A Brewing Hldgs	5449612	2.20	2.68	0.88	2.92	ALCTOB
21 SPS	Spotless Serv.	1553000	0.70	0.24	0.61	7.14	MSSERV
22 STO	Santos	2981497	4.38	2.91	0.99	4.15	OILGAS
23 TNT	TNT	3134600	4.65	3.25	1.18	3.12	TRANSP
24 WBC	Westpac Bank Coop	4641024	6.48	6.71	0.88	4.37	BANFIN
25 WMC	Westn Mining Cp	6529600	6.34	9.24	1.40	2.53	GOLD

approximately $A450 million (or about $360 million (U.S.)), with the total option value comprising about 5 percent of the equities.

Figure 9-20 shows the portfolio of underlying equity holdings. The portfolio, named AUSEQTY, contains 25 Australian stocks and, as can be seen, is actively managed. The figure shows the asset name, shareholding, price at month-end, percentage holding, beta, yield, and industry group of the asset. The betas are computed relative to the standard benchmark in Australia, the All Ordinaries Share Index (Allord), and range from 0.62 to 1.46. This is almost as large a range of betas as is possible to find in Australia. The portfolio beta is 1.05, and its annual residual standard deviation is 5.34 percent. This level of risk indicates that with 2/3 probability, the return on the portfolio will fall in the range between −5.34 percent and 5.34 percent centered about the performance of the market portfolio levered to a beta of 1.05. With 1/6 probability, the excess annual returns will be greater than 5.34 percent or less than −5.34 percent.

The portfolio is heavily concentrated among the large capitalization stocks and, indeed, this exposure is the greatest source of residual risk. The portfolio also has

FIGURE 9-21

Underlying Equity Industry Holdings

Factors	AUSEQTY Weights	Allord Weights	Difference
Gold	9.78	10.83	(1.05)
Other metals	11.53	9.05	2.47
Solid fuels	0	1.12	(1.12)
Oil and gas	2.91	3.52	(0.60)
Diversified resources	19.84	9.81	10.03
Developers and contractors	0	2.95	(2.95)
Building materials	3.33	5.35	(2.02)
Alcohol and tobacco	2.68	1.84	0.83
Food and household goods	6.59	3.08	3.52
Chemicals	0	2.10	(2.10)
Engineering	0	1.65	(1.65)
Paper and packaging	0	1.96	(1.96)
Retail	0.22	4.00	(3.79)
Transport	4.53	3.27	1.26
Media	7.20	3.02	4.19
Banks and finance	17.63	9.07	8.56
Insurance	0.29	1.22	(0.93)
Entrepreneurial investor	7.80	7.27	0.53
Invest and finance service	0	1.86	(1.86)
Property trusts	0	3.19	(3.19)
Miscellaneous services	0.24	2.01	(1.77)
Miscellaneous industrial	0.29	1.67	(1.37)
Diversified industrials	5.13	10.14	(5.02)

some very significant industry exposures relative to Allord. Figure 9-21 shows the industry exposures of this portfolio. It is most overweighted in the diversified resource and banks and finance industries. The most underweighted industry is diversified industries:

The major bets in the portfolio can be classified along the following four dimensions:

1. *Market timing.* At this time, the equity portfolio has a beta of 1.05, so there is little evidence of market judgment.

2. *Types of company.* The manager may bet on certain types of companies' outperforming the market. There is substantial evidence of this style; the portfolio is highly concentrated in large capitalization companies and, to a much lesser extent, in illiquid companies and companies with low price volatility.

3. *Industry.* There are some significant industry exposures, although the bigger bets are in the lower-risk industries.

4. *Stock selection.* There are some significant individual stock selection bets. For example, BHP is overweighted by some 10 percent of the portfolio.

These elements of style can be quantitatively ranked by estimating the magnitude of risk associated with each dimension. Market timing can only be properly analyzed through a time series, but the remaining elements, which give rise to residual risk, can be determined from a risk analysis of the portfolio at a single point in time. These are given below:

Types of company	50.0%
Industry	9.3
Stock selection	40.7
Total	100.0%

The actual portfolio, called AUSPORT and including the option component, is shown in Figure 9-22. Most of the options are call options, but two puts also appear.

Each option entry contains information similar to that in the stock entries. The yield of each option is, of course, zero and is shown, as with the beta, by convention as if the option is held long. For simplicity, the options are shown in share equivalents rather than the number of contracts. Note that the betas of the calls are much larger than for the individual stocks, since they reflect the large elasticity of the options. Call betas are typically in the range of 5 to 10, although for some options that are deep out of the money, such as the News Corp./August/14 call, the beta is in excess of 25. The two put betas are negative, one at approximately -10 and the other at almost -17. This confirms the earlier notion that options are highly risky when viewed in isolation.

The asset holdings are grouped together. Thus, all of the options on a stock are listed before the stock holding itself. Each option is implicitly decomposed into an underlying stock exposure and a cash holding. There could also be other exposures. In addition, the option certainly has a small specific return (and hence risk) component as a result of possible mispricing relative to the underlying asset at the beginning and end of the period (basis risk).

Following each group of linked assets (i.e., assets related to the same underlying stock), the effective holding in each stock is shown. The effective holding is the sum of the equivalent underlying stock positions of each option plus the direct stock position itself. For the first optionable stock, the Australia and New Zealand Banking Group (ANZ), 3 million shares have written calls against them. This comprises an actual holding of -0.19 percent of the portfolio (i.e., 3 million times $0.28 = \$84,000$, or 0.19 percent of \$448 million). The effective holding in ANZ is higher than 0.19 percent because of the leverage of the option (that is, the elasticity of the option is not unity). ANZ has a beta of 0.85, while the call has a beta of 7.48; in other words, the call has an elasticity of about 8.8 relative to the underlying stock, so that a 1 percent holding in the call is equivalent (in terms of exposure to the underlying asset) to approximately 8.8 percent of ANZ itself. The total effective holding of ANZ is therefore computed as 5.2 percent in the stock itself less 1.69 percent (8.8 times 0.19 percent), or 3.51 percent.

Each option has exposures to factors other than the underlying stock. Principal among these factors is the exposure to cash. The accumulated cash from all of the options is shown as the first asset and corresponds to almost 15 percent of the portfolio. In other words, the total impact in terms of levering the underlying stock positions is to reduce the equity exposure and implicitly add almost 15 percent of the portfolio.

The overall impact of the option position is to produce a portfolio that has a beta

FIGURE 9-22
Optioned Portfolio

Ident	Name	Shares	Price	% Wgt	Beta	% Yld	Ind
**0001	Option Related Cash	90180136	1.00	20.78	0.00	12.10	
1 ARZC3	Anz Oct 5.00 Call	−3000000	0.28	−0.19	7.48	0.00	BANFIN
2 ANZ	Aust & NZ Bank Grp	4685721	4.81	5.20	0.85	4.72	BANFIN
*ANZ	*ANZ Effectv Hldg.	3159182	4.82	3.51	0.85	4.72	BANFIN
3 ARN	Arnotts Limited	1817920	5.24	2.19	0.78	3.72	FOOD
4 BHPC4	BHP Oct 9.00 Call	−8000000	0.34	−0.63	9.56	0.00	DIVRES
5 BHPP4	BHP Oct 7.50 Put	100000	0.19	0.00	−9.89	0.00	DIVRES
6 BHP	The Brokn. Hill Pty	10635533	8.36	20.49	1.03	3.83	DIVRES
*BHP	*BHP Effectv Hldg.	7549555	8.36	14.54	1.03	3.83	DIVRES
7 BSH	Brash Hldgs	181900	5.34	0.22	0.62	3.75	RETAIL
8 CCB	C-C Bottlers	2953930	3.15	2.14	0.69	2.54	FOOD
9 CLG	Challenge Bank	448300	3.35	0.35	0.79	3.87	BANFIN
10 CRAC4	CRA Sep 8.0 Call	−550000	1.74	−0.22	6.09	0.00	OTHMTL
11 CRAC6	CRA Sep 10.0 Call	−3500000	0.55	−0.44	10.28	0.00	OTHMTL
12 CRA	CRA Ltd	4174157	9.46	9.10	1.29	2.01	OTHMTL
*CRA	*CRA Effectv Hldg.	2093359	9.46	4.56	1.29	2.01	OTHMTL
13 DOM	Dominion Min. Ltd	1400000	1.74	0.56	1.46	0.00	GOLD
148 EXI	Exicom Ltd.	440000	3.00	0.30	0.99	0.00	MSIND
15 EXLC4	Exl Oct 3.60 Call	−9750000	0.15	−0.33	9.41	0.00	ENTINV
16 EXL	Elders IXL Ltd	10724533	2.26	8.06	1.11	5.35	ENTINV
*EXL	*EXL Effectv Hldg.	6955996	3.26	5.23	1.11	5.37	ENTINV
17 FAI	FAI Insurances	306200	4.25	0.30	0.92	1.65	INSURE
18 GMF	Goodman Fieldr. Wat	4203239	2.55	2.47	0.89	3.84	FOOD
19 MAY	Mayne Nickless Ltd	878267	6.50	1.32	1.05	3.15	TRANSP
20 MIMC3	MIM Oct 2.50 Call	−4000000	0.09	−0.08	9.87	0.00	OTHMTL
21 MIM	M. I. M. Holdings	5786946	2.10	2.80	1.38	1.90	OTHMTL
*MIM	*MIM Effectv Hldg.	4553091	2.10	2.20	1.38	1.90	OTHMTL
22 NABC4	NAB Oct 6.70 Call	−3500000	0.26	−0.21	8.31	0.00	BANFIN
23 NAB	Natl Australia Bk	3990632	6.22	5.72	0.84	4.36	BANFIN
*NAB	*NAB Effectv Hldg	2551088	6.22	3.66	0.84	4.36	BANFIN
24 NCPC4	NCP Aug 14.00 Call	−2000000	0.01	−0.00	26.29	0.00	MEDIA
25 NCP	News Corp	2640050	10.60	6.45	1.03	0.75	MEDIA
*NCP	*NCP Effectv Hldg.	2615127	10.60	6.39	1.03	0.75	MEDIA
26 PDP	Pacific Dunlop Ltd	5185604	4.43	5.29	0.97	4.63	DIVIND
27 PNC	Pioneer Concrete	4521972	3.30	3.44	0.94	3.85	BLDMAT
28 QAL	Qintex Australia	2185877	1.96	0.99	0.65	7.65	MEDIA
29 SBG	S. A. Brewing Hldgs	5449612	2.20	2.76	0.88	2.92	ALCTOB
30 SPS	Spotless Serv.	1553000	0.70	0.25	0.61	7.14	MSSERV
31 STOC2	STO Aug 4.55 Call	−840000	0.13	−0.03	13.54	0.00	OILGAS
32 STOC5	STO Nov 4.55 Call	−1925000	0.34	−0.15	6.44	0.00	OILGAS
33 STO	Santos	2981497	4.38	3.01	0.99	4.15	OILGAS
*STO	*STO Effectv Hldg.	1668785	4.38	1.68	0.99	4.15	OILGAS
34 TNT	TNT	3134600	4.65	3.36	1.18	3.12	TRANSP
35 WBCP2	WBC Sep 4.93 Put	330000	0.00	0.00	−18.93	0.00	BANFIN

(continued)

FIGURE 9-22   (*continued*)

Ident	Name	Shares	Price	% Wgt	Beta	% Yld	Ind
36 WBC	Westpac Bank Corp	4641024	6.48	6.93	0.88	4.37	BANFIN
*WBC	*WBC Effectv Hldg.	4637544	6.48	6.92	0.88	4.37	BANFIN
37 WMCC1	WMC Sep 7.00 Call	−1500000	0.34	−0.12	10.46	0.00	GOLD
38 WMCC7	WMC Sep 6.50 Call	−2000000	0.52	−0.24	9.08	0.00	GOLD
39 WMCC9	WMC Dec 6.50 Call	−3000000	0.87	−0.60	5.97	0.00	GOLD
40 WMC	Westn Mining Cp	6529600	6.34	9.54	1.40	2.53	GOLD
*WMC	*WMC Effectv Hldg.	4292989	6.34	6.27	1.40	2.53	GOLD

FIGURE 9-23

Optioned Portfolio Industry Holdings

Factors	AUSPORT Weights	Allord Weights	Difference
Gold	5.14	10.83	(5.69)
Other metals	6.77	9.05	(2.29)
Solid fuels	0	1.12	(1.12)
Oil and gas	1.68	3.52	(1.83)
Diversified resources	14.54	9.81	4.73
Developers and contractors	0	2.95	(2.95)
Building materials	3.44	5.35	(1.92)
Alcohol and tobacco	2.76	1.84	0.92
Food and household goods	6.81	3.08	3.73
Chemicals	0	2.10	(2.10)
Engineering	0	1.65	(1.65)
Paper and packaging	0	1.96	(1.96)
Retail	0.22	4.00	(3.78)
Transport	4.67	3.27	1.41
Media	7.37	3.02	4.36
Banks and finance	14.44	9.07	5.37
Insurance	0.30	1.22	(0.92)
Entrepreneurial investor	5.23	7.27	(2.05)
Invest and finance service	0	1.86	(1.86)
Property trusts	0	3.19	(3.19)
Miscellaneous services	0.25	2.01	(1.76)
Miscellaneous industrial	0.30	1.67	(1.36)
Diversified industrials	5.29	10.14	(4.85)

of 0.81 and a residual standard deviation of 4.26 percent. In other words, the options by themselves are individually risky, but the impact of the options collectively on the portfolio is to reduce both the systematic risk and the residual risk. It may also be noted in Figures 9-21 and 9-23, the industry holdings of the optioned portfolio, that the industry differences are in general smaller in the optioned portfolio than in the unoptioned stock portfolio.

The sources of risk in the optioned portfolio (relative to a smaller base risk level) are as follows:

Types of company	47%
Industry	16
Stock selection	37
Total	100%

One result of the option strategy is accentuation of the industry bets relative to the other sources of risk. More pronounced is the reduction of stock selection risk (risk attributable to types of company and industries) relative to common factor risk.

	AUSEQTY	*AUSPORT*	*Change*
Common factor	16.91	11.34	(33)%
Stock selection	11.57	6.84	(41)
Total (variance)	28.48	18.18	(36)%
Total (standard deviation)	5.34%	4.26%	

The option portfolio is therefore more diversified with respect to stock selection while retaining a significant strategy toward common factors. In this case, it would appear that the manager is taking advantage of the option market to design an integrated stock-option portfolio management strategy.

Suggested Reading

Black, F., and M. Scholes. "The Pricing of Options and Corporate Liabilities." *Journal of Political Economy* (May–June 1973), pp. 637–654.

Brennan, M.J., and E.S. Schwartz. "Evaluating Natural Resource Investments." *Journal of Business* (Apr. 1985), pp. 135–157.

Cox, John C., and Mark Rubinstein. *Options Markets*. Englewood Cliffs, N.J.: Prentice-Hall, Inc. 1985.

Jarrow, Robert A., and Andrew Rudd. *Option Pricing*. Homewood, Ill.: Richard D. Irwin, Inc., 1983.

Kester, W.C. "Today's Options for Tomorrow's Growth." *Harvard Business Review*, (Mar.–Apr. 1984), pp. 153–160.

Merton, R.C. "Theory of Rational Option Pricing." *Bell Journal of Economics and Management Science* (Spring 1973), pp. 141–183.

Ross, S. "Options and Efficiency." *Quarterly Journal of Economics* (Feb. 1976), pp. 75–89.

Rubinstein, M. "Displaced Diffusion Option Pricing." *Journal of Finance* (Mar. 1983), pp. 213–265.

————. "Nonparametric Tests of Alternative Option Pricing Models." *Journal of Finance* (June 1985), pp. 455–480.

————. "The Valuation of Uncertain Income Streams and the Pricing of Options." *Bell Journal of Economics* (Autumn 1976), pp. 407–425.

Schmalensee, R., and R. Trippi. "Common Stock Volatility Expectations Implied by Option Premia." *Journal of Finance* (Mar. 1978), pp. 129–147.

Smith, C. "Option Pricing Review." *Journal of Financial Economics* (Jan.–Mar. 1976), pp. 1–51.

Chapter 10
Financial Futures Markets

Thomas Schneeweis

Jot Yau

10.01 INTRODUCTION

The trading of futures contracts on financial instruments (fixed-income securities, stock indexes, and foreign currencies) began about 100 years after the development of futures trading on commodities. A financial futures contract creates an obligation to buy or sell a given amount of a specified financial instrument (or in certain financial futures markets its cash equivalent) at some future date at a price determined today. The financial futures markets thus provide a mechanism for removing the risk of unexpected price moves. The financial futures markets also enhance price discovery and trading in spot, forward, and option markets. In so doing, financial futures markets improve asset allocation over time and lower the cost of conducting financial transactions. Developments in U.S. capital markets (e.g., floating exchange rates, volatile interest rates, increased U.S. government borrowing, and institutional investment) have produced conditions that facilitate the creation and success of financial futures contracts. The financial futures markets, however, base their futures trading on commodities. An understanding of the evolution of commodity futures trading clarifies the reasons for the acceptance and rapid growth of the financial futures markets.

10.02 DEVELOPMENT OF COMMODITY FUTURES

During the 1840s, Chicago became the hub for marketing agriculture products from the Midwest. By 1850, the Board of Trade of the City of Chicago was established to provide an organized central marketplace to encourage the sale and purchase of specified farm commodities. In the 1850s, products were often bought and sold by means of "to arrive" contracts. This process became known as forward contracting. With a forward contract a producer would make an agreement to sell a commodity to a buyer at a price set today for delivery on a date following the harvest. At first, the forward contracts were not transferable, and prices would be established privately. By the 1870s, however, printed documents were developed to specify the grade, quantity, and time of delivery. These alterations created a forward contract that could be traded actively according to the rules of the Chicago Board of Trade (CBT).

In times of changing demand and supply conditions and corresponding low or high prices, defaults, however, became common. In order to protect the buyer and the seller, money was deposited with a third party as a performance bond. As trading volume increased, the mechanisms of delivery required change. A contract was often traded through a chain of buyers and sellers with the last buyer taking delivery from the first seller.

To simplify the trading process, a central clearinghouse practice was developed in the 1880s. Soon after, in 1891, the Minneapolis Grain Exchange organized the first "complete clearinghouse system" that established the clearinghouse as the third party to all transactions on the exchange. The principal purpose of the clearinghouse was to facilitate the offsetting of trades between trading houses. Firms with customer accounts were required to maintain the bookkeeping for those accounts internally. Each day, the firm settled its net position with all other firms with the payment of price differences through the clearinghouse. The daily settlement of price differences on contract purchases and sales permitted traders to enter and exit the market without having to wait until delivery to settle their trading accounts.

The operation of the clearinghouse was designed to ensure contract integrity. Buyers and sellers alike were required to post margins with the clearinghouse directly. Technically, clearing member firms were required to post necessary margins for their own accounts or those of firms clearing through them.

In addition, the clearinghouse insisted on daily settlement of all open positions, which later became known as the mark-to-market system. Losses on open positions are paid to the clearinghouse each day. The day's settlement price at the close of trading is used to value these positions. The losses paid into the clearinghouse are paid out to firms with gains on open positions. As the clearinghouse has no market position, these daily dollar flows always balance. In case of default on a daily payment, margin can be used for the payment. The clearinghouse then closes the positions in default the next day.

The clearinghouse offset combined with the public price determination system on the exchange floor were the final steps in the evolution of forward contract trading into futures market trading. The development of the clearinghouse and public price auction system increased the ease by which buyers and sellers could minimize their price risk and conduct trade. For futures markets participants, price risk is reduced by taking an opposite position in the futures market relative to the actual or anticipated spot position. With the exchanges acting as a third party in every trade, the buyer or seller of a future contract need not be concerned with contract performance. Before delivery, the seller or buyer can simply close out the futures position and complete the transaction in the spot market. Since the cash and futures prices of like commodities often rise and fall together in response to similar sets of information, any gain or loss in the spot market would be partially offset by a gain or loss in the futures market. For those individuals who have not offset their futures position prior to delivery, the clearinghouse matches buyer and seller.

Thus, commodity futures markets developed in response to an economic need by suppliers and users of various agricultural and nonagricultural goods. In offering an alternative to risk reduction and market strategies available in the spot and forward markets, commodity futures further facilitated transfer of goods. Moreover, the commodity futures market also improved the functioning of the spot and forward markets. For instance, by reducing the risk of holding spot inventories, commodity futures permit greater commodity production and trade. By providing necessary risk reduction and trading opportunities commodity futures have grown to be an essential part of the production and marketing of agricultural and nonagricultural goods.

10.03 DEVELOPMENT OF FINANCIAL FUTURES

The evolution of financial futures follows that of commodity futures. As with commodity futures, the establishment and growth of fixed-income, stock index, and currency futures markets in the 1970s and 1980s were the result of a need by both managers and investors for a means to improve the merchandizing of financial instruments and to reduce the risk of price uncertainty in financial markets.[1] A summary of the actively

---

[1] The CBT and the Chicago Mercantile Exchange and Futures Industry Institute provide information booklets describing various futures contracts and hedging strategies. The *Journal of Futures Markets, Review of Futures Markets,* and *Futures* magazine all contain articles of current interest on the development of risk and return management techniques in futures markets.

traded currency, fixed-income, and equity contracts is given in Figure 10-1. If spot, forward, or option markets provided complete trading, pricing, and risk reduction opportunities, futures markets may never have come into existence. The financial futures market, however, has grown to become a significant part of the financial markets. The financial futures markets were initated in 1972 with the establishment of foreign exchange futures on the International Money Market (IMM). By 1988, financial futures had grown to include contracts on government and nongovernment fixed-income securities as well as equity indexes. Moreover, financial futures contracts on U.S. and foreign domestic debt are now traded on foreign exchanges. For example, the London International Financial Futures Exchange (LIFFE) trades contracts on British and U.S. government bonds. Foreign exchanges also trade foreign domestic stock indexes, such as the Japanese Nikkei 225 at the Singapore International Monetary Exchange (SIMEX) and the Hang Seng Index at the Hong Kong Futures Exchange. In addition, foreign currency contracts have become available for trading in London, Canada, and other countries. The internationalization of the futures markets has provided new opportunities as well as competitive challenges. For instance, responding to foreign demand for U.S. financial future contracts, the CBT has expanded its trading on certain contracts to include evening hours. With trading across various international exchanges, it is now possible to trade certain financial future contracts almost 24 hours a day.

10.04 TYPES OF FUTURES CONTRACTS

The following sections discuss the contract characteristics of the principal financial instrument futures as well as the markets in which they are traded. A summary of contract characteristics, contract months, trading hours, contract size, and price limits is given in Figure 10-2. For each active trade financial futures contract, a sample of futures price quotations is shown in Figure 10-3. For each delivery date the opening, high, low, and settle prices are listed, as well as open interest (number of contracts outstanding) and daily volume figures.

[1] Fixed-Income Futures: Short-Term Instruments

[a] Ninety-Day Treasury Bill Futures Contract. The 90-day Treasury bill (T-bill) futures contract opened on January 2, 1976, on the IMM. Any individual who is exposed to short-term interest rate risk or who wishes to profit from correct forecasts of short-term rates may participate in the T-bill market.

The T-bill market comprises institutions or individuals that are experienced in short-term lending or borrowing, such as banks, brokerage houses, and securities dealers with positions in short-term securities. In addition, large corporations that have positions in cash equivalent securities or are issuers of commercial paper have use for short-term futures instruments. The T-bill futures contract calls for delivery of $1 million in face value of 90-day T-bills. Delivery months for up to two years in the future are March, June, September, and December. The last day of trading is the second business day, usually a Wednesday, following the T-bill auction in the third week of the delivery month.

While yields are the basic unit of the T-bill cash market, T-bill futures trading is

FIGURE 10-1

Actively Traded Financial Futures

Source: Annual Report 1991, Commodity Futures Trading Commission

Contracts	Exchange	Contract Size	Average/Month-End Open Interest (Contracts)		12-Month Volume of Trading (Contracts)		12-Month Total Contracts Settled by Delivery or Cash Settlement (Contracts)	
			1989–1990[a]	1990–1991[b]	1989–1990[b]	1990–1991[b]	1989–1990[a]	1990–1991[b]
NYSE composite stock/index	NYFE	Index × $500	5,557	5,226	1,620,595	1,539,710	7,532	6,423
Dollar index	FINEX	Index × $500	6,749	7,018	590,574	690,102	9,861	7,695
One-month LIBOR rate	CME/IMM	$3,000,000	1,978	12,546	32,389	360,941	3,673	49,172
Nikkei stock average	CME/IMM	Index × $5.00	965	6,866	2,000	222,352	0	18,071
U.S. T-bills	CME/IMM	$1,000,000	32,669	50,898	1,678,412	2,214,093	11,831	11,159
Canadian dollars	CME/IMM	100,000	30,214	27,212	1,322,274	1,172,715	24,419	31,871
Swiss francs	CME/IMM	125,000	39,694	36,431	6,193,611	6,366,179	51,506	61,673
Deutsche marks	CME/IMM	125,000	70,021	66,258	9,188,765	10,224,204	102,814	133,311
U.K. pounds	CME/IMM	25,000	29,072	28,519	2,998,446	3,916,499	29,332	51,316
Japanese yen	CME/IMM	12,500,000	65,082	56,706	7,147,497	6,734,501	73,537	100,644
Eurodollars	CME/IMM	1,000,000	658,838	733,113	35,063,000	35,798,130	489,268	516,684
S&P 500 stock index	CME/IMM	Index × $500	125,012	151,549	11,450,172	12,404,758	130,496	122,415
U.S. T-bonds	MCE	$50,000	9,877	10,331	1,464,841	1,391,710	4,506	124
U.S. T-bonds	CBT	$100,000	298,788	273,571	73,040,841	68,415,209	63,671	30,066
U.S. T-notes (6.5–10-year)	CBT	$100,000	77,634	81,126	5,987,097	35,984,553	21,978	29,481
MAXI major market stock index	CBT	Index × $250	5,793	6,741	979,631	842,418	40,830	45,043
Municipal bond index	CBT	Index × $1000	11,082	9,005	815,029	528,641	7,496	5,865

Note: FINEX = Financial Instrument Exchange, division of New York Cotton Exchange; NYFE = New York Futures Exchange; CME/IMM = Chicago Mercantile Exchange/International Monetary Market; MCE = Mid-America Commodity Exchange; CBT = Chicago Board of Trade.

[a] For fiscal year ending September 30, 1990.
[b] For fiscal year ending September 30, 1991.

FIGURE 10-2

Summary of Contract Specifications of Actively Traded Financial Futures

Source: Futures Magazine 1992 Reference Guide to Futures/Options Markets, *pp. 73–98*

Contracts	Contract Months	Trading Hours (Local Time)	Contract Size	Minimum Price Fluctuation	Daily Limit
NYSE composite stock index	3/6/9/12	9:30–4:15	$500 × index	0.05 pt. = $25 pc	18 pt.
Dollar index	3/6/9/12	8:20–3:00	$500 × index	0.01 pt. = $5 pc	Varies
One-month LIBOR rate	All months	7:20–2:00	$3,000,000	1 pt. = $25 pc	None
Nikkei stock average	3/6/9/12	8:00–3:15	$5 × index	5 pt. = $25 pc	Varies[a]
U.S. T-bills	3/6/9/12	7:20–2:00	$1,000,000	1 pt. = $25 pc	None
Canadian dollars	1/3/4/6/7 9/10/12/spot month	7:20–2:00	CD 100,000	$0.0001/CD = $10 pc	100 pt.[b]
Swiss francs	1/3/4/6/7 9/10/12/spot month	7:20–2:00	SF 125,000	$0.0001/SF = $12.50 pc	150 pt.[b]
Deutsche marks	1/3/4/6/7 9/10/12/spot month	7:20–2:00	DM 125,000	$0.0001/DM = $12.50 pc	150 pt.[b]
U.K. pounds	1/3/4/6/7 9/10/12/spot month	7:20–2:00	BP 62,500	$0.0002/BP = $12.50 pc	400 pt.[b]
Japanese yen	9/10/12/spot month	7:20–2:00	JY 12,500,000	$0.000001/JY = 12.50 pc	150 pt.[b]

Contract	Contract months	Trading hours	Contract size	Minimum price fluctuation	Daily price limit
Eurodollars	3/6/9/12/spot month	7:20–2:00	$1,000,000	1 pt. = $25 pc	None
S&P 500 stock index	3/6/9/12	8:30–3:15	$500 × index	5 pt. = $25 pc	Varies[c] 96/32 pt.
U.S. T-bonds (MCE)	3/6/9/12	7:20–3:15	$50,000	1/32 pt. = $15.62 pc	3 pt. = $1,500
U.S. T-bonds (CBT)	3/6/9/12	7:20–2:00 (Mon.–Fri.) 5:00–8:30 P.M. CST (Sun.–Thur.)	$100,000 8% coupon	1/32 pt. = $31.25 pc	3 pt. = $3,000
U.S. T-notes (CBT)	3/6/9/12	7:20–2:00 (Mon.–Fri.) 5:00–8:30 P.M. CST (Sun.–Thur.)	$100,000 8% coupon	1/32 pt. = $31.25 pc	3 pt. = $3,000
MAXI major market stock index	Next 3 months in 3/6/9/12 and next 3 consecutive months	8:15–3:15	$250 × index	1/20 pt. = $12.50 pc	None
Municipal bond index	3/6/9/12	7:20–2:00	$1,000 × index	1/32 pt. = $31.25 pc	3 pt. = $3,000

Note: MCE = Mid-America Commodity Exchange; CBT = Chicago Board of Trade.

[a] 600 below 20,000; 900 between 20,000 and 30,000; 1,200 between 30,000 and 40,000; 1,500 above 40,000.

[b] Opening limit between 7:20–7:35 A.M.; no limit after 7:35 A.M.

[c] 5 pt. first 10 minutes; 12 pt. for 30 minutes; 20 pt. for one hour; if 30 pt. hit, in effect until closing.

FIGURE 10-3

Financial Instrument Futures Prices

INTEREST RATE

TREASURY BONDS (CBT)—$100,000; pts. 32nds of 100%

	Open	High	Low	Settle	Chg	Yield Settle	Chg	Open Interest
Dec	102-08	102-17	101-14	101-15	− 27	7.853	+ .083	307,305
Mr93	101-03	101-09	100-09	100-09	− 27	7.872	+ .085	37,832
June	99-20	99-29	99-01	99-01	− 27	8.099	+ .086	5,301
Sept	98-18	98-20	97-27	97-27	− 27	8.221	+ .087	1,150
Dec	97-10	97-15	96-23	96-23	− 26	8.349	+ .086	1,314
Mr94	....	....	....	95-21	− 25	8.454	+ .084	1,884
Sept	....	....	....	93-24	− 23	8.663	+ .082	31

Est vol 400,000; vol Thur 232,991; op int 354,121, +2,164.

TREASURY NOTES (CBT)—$100,000; pts. 32nds of 100%

	Open	High	Low	Settle	Chg	Yield Settle	Chg	Open Interest
Dec	106-13	106-25	105-22	105-23	− 22	7.188	+ .093	188,154
Mr93	105-03	105-08	104-12	104-12	− 22	7.274	+ .095	14,526
June	103-22	103-22	103-00	103-09	− 23	7.567	+ .101	318

Est vol 69.666; vol Thur 49.808; open int 202,998, −3,372.

TREASURY BILLS (IMM)—$1 mil.; pts. of 100%

	Open	High	Low	Settle	Chg	Discount Settle	Chg	Open Interest
Dec	96.93	97.02	96.83	96.84	− .09	3.16	+ .09	17,418
Mr93	96.83	96.91	96.73	96.74	− .09	3.26	+ .09	14,694
June	96.45	96.46	96.35	96.35	− .11	3.65	+ .11	1,771
Sept	....	....	....	95.91	− .11	4.09	+ .11	131

Est vol 6,589; vol Thur 4,850; open int 34,098, −230.

LIBOR-1 MO. (IMM)—$3,000,000; points of 100%

	Open	High	Low	Settle	Chg	Settle	Chg	Open Interest
Nov	96.77	96.79	96.73	96.73	− .04	3.27	+ .04	21,897
Dec	96.11	96.18	95.99	95.99	− .11	4.01	+ .11	10,249
Ja93	96.67	96.67	96.60	96.60	− .07	3.40	+ .07	8,266
Feb	96.60	96.60	96.53	96.53	− .08	3.47	+ .08	1,772
Mar	96.51	96.51	96.39	96.38	− .11	3.62	+ .11	848
Apr	96.35	96.35	96.34	96.28	− .12	3.72	+ .12	286

Est vol 3,977; vol Thur 3,885; open int 43,318, +347.

MUNI BOND INDEX (CBT)-$1,000; times Bond Buyer MBI

	Open	High	Low	Settle	Chg	Open High	Low	Interest
Dec	95-03	95-12	94-24	94-25	− 9	99-18	92-31	25,135
Mr93	94-15	94-19	93-27	93-28	− 16	97-30	92-02	2,223

Est vol 5,000; vol Thur 8,735; open int 27,371, −404.
The index: Close 95-11; Yield 6.71.

EURODOLLAR (IMM)—$1 million; pts of 100%

	Open	High	Low	Settle	Chg	Yield Settle	Chg	Open Interest
Dec	96.38	96.49	96.27	96.28	− .10	3.72	+ .10	317,712
Mr93	96.40	96.49	96.27	96.28	− .12	3.72	+ .12	311,934
June	95.93	96.03	95.79	95.80	− .14	4.20	+ .14	214,303
Sept	95.46	95.52	95.33	95.33	− .15	4.67	+ .15	143,793
Dec	94.75	94.89	94.64	94.65	− .13	5.35	+ .13	97,695
Mr94	94.49	94.57	94.38	94.39	− .13	5.61	+ .13	82,438
June	94.09	94.17	93.99	93.99	− .13	6.01	+ .13	62,442
Sept	93.75	93.85	93.66	93.67	− .13	6.33	+ .13	50,308
Dec	93.31	93.38	93.24	93.24	− .12	6.76	+ .12	44,111
Mr95	93.20	93.28	93.13	93.13	− .12	6.87	+ .12	43,459
June	92.96	93.04	92.90	92.89	− .12	7.11	+ .12	32,450
Sept	92.80	92.88	92.74	92.73	− .12	7.27	+ .12	25,779
Dec	92.54	92.59	92.44	92.44	− .12	7.56	+ .12	25,399
Mr96	92.51	92.56	92.43	92.41	− .12	7.59	+ .12	22,945
June	92.34	92.39	92.26	92.24	− .12	7.76	+ .12	14,308
Sept	92.22	92.27	92.14	92.13	− .11	7.87	+ .11	9,733
Dec	92.03	92.06	91.93	91.93	− .10	8.07	+ .10	6,482
Mr97	92.06	92.09	91.97	91.96	− .10	8.04	+ .10	6,271
June	91.93	91.96	91.84	91.83	− .10	8.17	+ .10	7,410
Sept	91.83	91.86	91.74	91.73	− .10	8.27	+ .10	4,435

Est vol 373,052; vol Thur 195,259; open int 1,523,305, −8,792.

CURRENCY

	Open	High	Low	Settle	Change	Lifetime High	Low	Open Interest
JAPAN YEN (IMM)—12.5 million yen; $ per yen (.00)								
Dec	.8126	.8145	.8090	.8094	− .0043	.8419	.7410	39,729
Mr93	.8123	.8131	.8093	.8097	− .0042	.8372	.7445	2,321
June	....	....	....	.8106	− .0040	.8340	.7745	343
Est vol 13,264; vol Thur 10,761; open int 42,668, +1,832.								
DEUTSCHEMARK (IMM)—125,000 marks; $ per mark								
Dec	.6293	.6298	.6224	.6227	− .0054	.7117	.5645	108,773
Mr93	.6196	.6200	.6150	.6152	− .0054	.7025	.5724	5,884
June	.6105	.6120	.6090	.6093	− .0051	.6920	.6204	1,650
Sept	....	....	....	.6050	− .0049	.6720	.6320	302
Est vol 49,863; vol Thur 50,201; open int 116,019, +2,999.								
CANADIAN DOLLAR (IMM)—100,000 dlrs.; $ per Can $								
Dec	.7979	.7983	.7938	.7943	− .0026	.8740	.7866	20,335
Mr93	.7936	.7936	.7893	.7896	− .0031	.8712	.7780	1,230
June	.7904	.7904	.7860	.7853	− .0036	.8360	.7735	1,691
Sept	....	....	....	.7817	− .0039	.8335	.7715	503
Dec	.7810	.7810	.7810	.7782	− .0042	.8310	.7640	357
Est vol 5,491; vol Thur 3,800; open int 24,117, −85.								
BRITISH POUND (IMM)—62,500 pds.; $ per pound								
Dec	1.5324	1.5398	1.5224	1.5234	− .0052	1.9746	1.5182	31,964
Mr93	1.5190	1.5290	1.5110	1.5128	− .0048	1.9400	1.5070	1,323
June	....	....	1.5044	− .0042	1.9100	1.5000		146
Est vol 11,106; vol Thur 9,830; open int 33,433, −157.								
SWISS FRANC (IMM)—125,000 francs; $ per franc								
Dec	.7035	.7038	.6933	.6949	− .0068	.8209	.6280	39,093
Mr93	.6945	.6955	.6885	.6900	− .0067	.8140	.6790	2,802
June	....	....	.6864	− .0067	.8070	.7005		773
Est vol 21,800; vol Thur 24,512; open int 42,668, +1,832.								
AUSTRALIAN DOLLAR (IMM)—100,000 dlrs.; $ per A.$								
Dec	.6958	.7000	.6940	.6996	+ .0038	.7462	.6870	4,049
Est vol 529; vol Thur 216; open int 4,077, −21.								
U.S. DOLLAR INDEX (FINEX)—1,000 times USDX								
Dec	89.90	90.60	89.80	90.56	+ .56	94.93	79.85	6,221
Mr93	91.30	91.70	91.25	91.71	+ .56	91.70	81.45	752
Est vol 2,380; vol Thur 1,785; open int 6,976, +923.								
The index: High 89.89; Low 89.13; Close 89.88 +.64								

INDEX

S&P 500 INDEX (CME) 500 times index

	Open	High	Low	Settle	Chg	High	Low	Open Interest
Dec	417.30	418.45	416.60	417.10	− 1.20	427.25	390.00	159,506
Mr93	417.75	418.85	417.20	417.60	− 1.25	426.20	390.50	10,295
June	....	....	418.10	− 1.15	427.10	391.00		1,483
Sept	....	....	418.35	− 1.15	424.50	391.00		161

Est vol 41,447; vol Thur 41,572; open int 171,355, −467.
Indx prelim High 418.35; Low 417.01; Close 417.57 −.77

NIKKEI 225 Stock Average (CME)—$5 times index

	Open	High	Low	Settle	Chg	High	Low	Open Interest
Dec	16875.	16905.	16810.	16820.	− 290.0	21100.	14270.	14,195

Est vol 800; vol Thur 630; open int 14,278, −151.
The index: High 17022.57; Low 16818.46; Close 16869.8 − 161.78

NYSE COMPOSITE INDEX (NYFE) 500 times index

	Open	High	Low	Settle	Chg	High	Low	Open Interest
Dec	229.90	230.40	229.45	229.75	− .60	234.05	214.70	5,174
Mr93	230.00	230.00	229.80	229.90	− .60	233.70	221.60	781
June	....	....	230.05	− .55	232.40	223.10		267

Est vol 3,132; vol Thur 3,618; open int 6,226, +135.
The index: High 230.37; Low 229.78; Close 230.09 −.28

MAJOR MKT INDEX (CBT) $500 times index

	Open	High	Low	Settle	Chg	High	Low	Open Interest
Nov	341.00	341.80	340.00	341.80	− .30	356.00	326.20	2,997
Dec	340.35	343.50	340.00	340.85	− .35	358.90	326.15	657
Mr93	....	....	340.80	− .35	359.50	340.75		137

Est vol 1,000; vol Thur 915; open int 3,824, +221.
The index: High 342.34; Low 340.39; Close 341.19 −.67

Note: CBT = Chicago Board of Trade; CME = Chicago Mercantile Exchange; FINEX = Financial Instrument Exchange, division of New York Cotton Exchange; IMM = International Monetary Market at CME; NYFE = New York Futures Exchange, unit of New York Stock Exchange.

done in terms of prices. The use of prices for T-bill futures allows the T-bill futures to be put on the same price basis as futures on other deliverable instruments. The minimum price index change (or discount rate change) is 0.01. This corresponds to a $25 change in the actual value of the futures contract.

On the business day following the last day of trading, individuals who have long or short positions in the contract have delivery obligations. The buyer informs the exchange clearinghouse that a commitment exists to deliver the securities by noon of the last trading day. On the next trading day, the buyer must have provided a wire transfer of federal funds in the amount of the price to the seller's account. The clearinghouse ensures that the commitments are matched and that the delivery occurs as specified.

[b] Eurodollar Futures. Eurodollar deposit contracts began trading on the IMM in December 1981. Contracts call for delivery in March, June, September, and December of each year. Prices are quoted on an index basis as 100 minus the annualized Eurodollar futures rate. The delivery value of the Eurodollar future, like the certificate of deposit and T-bill futures, is $1 million.

The final settlement is made in cash directly through the IMM Clearinghouse based on the London interbank offered rate (LIBOR) on the last trading day. The LIBOR rate on which settlement for the IMM contract is based is the average three month time deposit rate quote on a random selection of 12 banks from the top 20 banks in the London Eurodollar market. Quotes at the termination of trading on this day and a quote collected at a randomly selected time in the last 80 minutes of trading are averaged to determine the settlement rate.

[2] Fixed-Income Futures: Long-Term Instruments—Treasury Bonds and Treasury Notes

Individuals exposed to the risk of short-term fluctuations in interest rates who look to profit from shifts in long-term rates may use long-term futures contracts. These contracts may be used to hedge exposure to government bond auctions, government and corporate bond portfolios, and mortgage commitments.

Treasury bond (T-bond) futures call for delivery of T-bonds with $100,000 face value during the delivery period. Deliverable bonds must have a maturity date and a call date no sooner than 15 years from the delivery date. Treasury note (T-note) futures are also based on $100,000 face value per contract. Deliverable notes are those maturing in no less than 6.5 years.

Price quotations in the T-bond (T-note) futures market are based on a bond (note) with an 8 percent coupon rate and a 15-year (10-year) maturity. However, various bonds (notes) may be delivered. As of October 1, 1992, any of the long-term T-bonds (T-notes) listed in Figure 10-4 may be delivered against expiring bond (note) futures contracts. However, each eligible coupon and maturity has a different value and, for delivery, this value must be adjusted to reflect the contract standard at the established settlement price. Thus the CBT relates the futures price to coupons other than 8 percent via conversion factors that represent the relative values of these deliverable bonds. As shown in Figures 10-4 and 10-5, for any delivery month all deliverable issues have a specific conversion factor reflecting their value and maturity at the particular time.

FIGURE 10-4

T-Bond Conversion Factor Table

Coupon (%)	Maturity	Dec. 1992	Mar. 1993	June 1993	Sept. 1993	Dec. 1993	Mar. 1994
7¼	May 15, 2016	0.9212	0.9217	0.9218	0.9223	0.9224	0.9229
7¼	Aug. 15, 2022	0.9155	0.9155	0.9159	0.9159	0.9163	0.9163
7½	Nov. 15, 2016	0.9470	0.9474	0.9474	0.9478	0.9478	0.9482
7⅞	Feb. 15, 2021	0.9861	0.9860	0.9862	0.9860	0.9863	0.9861
8	Nov. 15, 2021	0.9998	1.0000	0.9998	1.0000	0.9998	1.0000
8⅛	May 15, 2021	1.0137	1.0139	1.0137	1.0138	1.0136	1.0137
8⅛	Aug. 15, 2021	1.0140	1.0137	1.0139	1.0137	1.0138	1.0136
8⅛	Aug. 15, 2019	1.0137	1.0134	1.0136	1.0134	1.0135	1.0133
8½	Feb. 15, 2020	1.0550	1.0546	1.0547	1.0534	1.0544	1.0540
8¾	May 15, 2017	1.0795	1.0795	1.0790	1.0789	1.0784	1.0783
8¾	May 15, 2020	1.0825	1.0825	1.0820	1.0820	1.0816	1.0816
8¾	Aug. 15, 2020	1.0829	1.0825	1.0825	1.0820	1.0820	1.0816
8⅞	Aug. 15, 2017	1.0934	1.0928	1.0927	1.0922	1.0921	1.0915
8⅞	Feb. 15, 2019	1.0951	1.0946	1.1946	1.0941	1.0940	1.0935
9	Nov. 15, 2018	1.1082	1.1081	1.1075	1.1074	1.1068	1.1067
9⅛	May 15, 2018	1.1210	1.1208	1.1202	1.1200	1.1194	1.1192
9¼	Feb. 15, 2016	1.1305	1.1298	1.1295	1.1287	1.1284	1.1277
9⅞	Nov. 15, 2015	1.1948	1.1943	1.1932	1.1926	1.1916	1.1910
10⅝	Aug. 15, 2015	1.2720	1.2706	—	—	—	—
11¼	Feb. 15, 2015	1.3339	1.3322	—	—	—	—
11¾	Nov. 15, 2009–14	1.3425	1.3403	1.3374	1.3351	1.3322	1.3298
12	Aug. 15, 2008–13	1.3518	1.3485	1.3458	—	—	—
12½	Aug. 15, 2009–14	1.4083	1.4050	1.4022	1.3987	1.3957	1.3921
13¼	May 15, 2009–14	1.4725	1.4692	1.4652	1.4617	1.4575	1.4539

Note: All U.S. T-bonds eligible for delivery into the CBT's T-bond futures contract.

As new issues come into supply before or during the delivery month, they are added to the list. As a bond's time to maturity decreases below the eligible limit, it is dropped from the deliverable supply. A seller delivering any one of the eligible bonds calculates the invoice amount for a particular issue by multiplying the futures settlement price by the appropriate conversion factor and adding the accrued interest. The buyer then holds an investment with a yield equal to the yield he would have received had he paid the settlement price and received an 8 percent coupon. For example, if a seller delivers 12 percent bonds against one bond futures contract in December 1992 at a settlement price of 106.00, he invoices the buyer $1.0600 \times 1.3518 \times \$100,000 = \$143,290$ plus accrued interest. The same procedure is used for invoicing T-note contracts, with an 8 percent, 10-year note used as the standard note.

All active interest rate futures contracts traded on the CBT (T-bond and T-note) have similar delivery sequences. Timing and quality of delivery are at the option of the seller of futures (the "short") during the delivery month. This includes the possibility of delivery after the futures cease trading seven business days prior to the end of

FIGURE 10-5

T-Note Conversion Factor Table

Coupon (%)	Maturity	Mar. 1987	June 1987	Sept. 1987	Dec. 1987	Mar. 1988	June 1988	Sept. 1988
7⅛	Oct. 15, 1993	.9563	—	—	—	—	—	—
7¼	Nov. 15, 1996	.9507	.9515	.9525	.9533	.9544	.9552	.9563
7⅜	May 15, 1996	.9604	.9610	.9620	.9626	.9636	.9642	.9653
8⅞	Feb. 15, 1996	1.0541	1.0532	1.0519	1.0510	1.0496	1.0486	1.0472
9½	Nov. 15, 1995	1.0912	1.0891	1.0874	1.0852	1.0834	1.0811	1.0792
10½	Aug. 15, 1995	1.1486	1.1457	1.1421	1.1390	1.1353	1.1320	1.1282
11¼	Feb. 15, 1995	1.1848	1.1807	1.1759	1.1717	1.1667	1.1623	—
11¼	May 15, 1995	1.1893	1.1848	1.1807	1.1759	1.1717	1.1667	1.1623
11⅝	Nov. 15, 1994	1.2015	1.1963	1.1915	1.1860	1.1810	—	—
11¾	Nov. 15, 1993	1.1872	—	—	—	—	—	—
12⅝	Aug. 15, 1994	1.2504	1.2443	1.2374	1.2309	—	—	—
13⅛	May 15, 1994	1.2707	1.2630	1.2559	—	—	—	—

Note: All U.S. T-notes eligible for delivery into the CBT's long-term T-note futures contract.

the month. Buyers (or "longs") holding these futures contracts over the delivery period face the risk of untimely delivery of the securities either by selling in the spot market or by redelivering them in the futures market. There is risk, however, associated with changes in the value of the spot securities over the period the buyer must hold them before they are sold or redelivered.

The delivery process takes three days. This allows the buyer, seller, and clearinghouse sufficient time to notify the appropriate parties, deliver the bonds, and transfer the funds. The activities that take place on each of the three days are covered in Figure 10-6.

[3] Stock Index Futures Contracts

In addition to interest rate futures, the Chicago Mercantile Exchange (CME), the New York Stock Exchange (NYSE), and the CBT have futures contacts based on the Standard & Poor's (S&P) 500, NYSE indexes, and Major Market Index (MMI), respectively. The Kansas City Futures Exchange opened the first stock index futures on the Value Line index in February 1982. The first foreign stock index futures, the Nikkei Stock Average futures, began trading on the CME in June 1987.

Stock index futures provide a means of adjusting spot exposure to the overall stock market. These futures permit an individual to increase risk (reduce risk) exposure in anticipation of a bull (bear) market. Stock index futures can also serve as substitute for spot position in the stock index. Futures on stock indexes represent a contract to buy or sell in the index at a predetermined price. This price is the price or value of the futures contract at the time of initiation. Unlike most other futures contracts, stock index futures settle in cash rather than in delivery of the stock in the index underlying

FIGURE 10-6
Funds Delivery Process

Source: Chicago Board of Trade

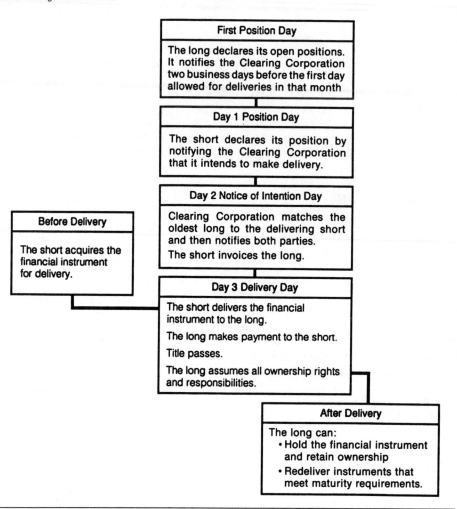

the futures contract. Cash settlement is used because of the cost and logistical problems of buying the stocks in the right amounts to carry out physical delivery.

Stock index futures have a specific termination time and date at which the final settlement price is set and the futures cease trading. For MMI, NYSE, and Value Line stock index futures contracts the time is 4 P.M., Eastern standard time, of the last trading day of the contract. Thus the final settlement price is tied to the closing value of the index on the last trading day. Cash settlement is carried out after adjustment for losses or gains marked to market daily. If the settlement price is above the price at which the futures contract was established, funds that have been marked to market by the futures sellers are credited to those with long futures positions. To reduce the effect of the quarterly cash settlement of stock index futures on the securities markets, the CME and the NYSE instituted new settlement procedures for the S&P 500 effective with the June 1987 expiration. Instead of settlement on the expiration date of the futures contract, cash settlement is now based on the opening of stock prices on that Friday, while trading in the expiring futures terminates on the prior day.

[4] Municipal Bond Index Futures

The municipal bond contract opened for trading in June 1985. Previous to that date, municipal bond cash market users were forced to hedge their positions with a futures contract such as T-bonds. Since price movements in the muni-market and the U.S. government market were often affected by different events, a futures contract that permitted a better hedge against unexpected price movements in the municipal market was required. The muni-bond contract was established to enable its users to use futures contracts to hedge inventory of municipal bonds, hedge exposure to municipal bond offerings, and manage municipal bond portfolios.

Price quotations for municipal bond contracts are also shown in Figure 10-3. The trading unit for the municipal bond contract is $1,000 times the Bond Buyers municipal bond index; that is, the muni contract does not track a specific bond but an index of 40 actively traded general obligation and revenue tax-exempt bonds. In addition, since the futures contract is based on an index (similar to equity futures), delivery must be in cash as for equity futures.

[5] Currency Futures

With the change from fixed to floating rates in the early 1970s, variability in foreign currency values increased dramatically. The possibilities of the currency futures markets for hedging, speculation, and arbitrage are countless. Companies borrowing or investing abroad; companies manufacturing, exporting, or importing goods or raw materials; and investors selling or purchasing foreign securities are some of the currency futures market users. In short, for any condition under which the uncertainty of the future value of the currency is of concern, the currency markets provide a means of hedging the risk. Foreign currency futures were established at the IMM in 1972. The IMM quotes currencies in terms of the U.S. dollar. All quotations, therefore, are prices per unit of the foreign currency. Delivery procedures follow those prescribed for other financial futures traded on the IMM. Currency index futures contracts such as the U.S. Dollar Index (USDX) provide alternatives to individual or multiple currency futures contracts to hedge currency positions. The USDX is a weighted geometric average of the foreign exchange rates of 10 currencies, and the USDX contract began trading on the Financial Instrument Exchange (FINEX) in late 1985.

10.05 MARKET ORGANIZATION

A general knowledge of the regulations, trading rules, terminology, and risk is important for an understanding of financial futures markets. As mentioned before, a number of U.S. and foreign exchanges trade financial futures. For each exchange, rules and regulations clearly define the size of a contract, what is eligible for delivery, where delivery must take place, how a contract is priced and invoiced, and when trading begins and stops. While each of these exchanges (U.S. and foreign) may have minor differences in organizational structure, they are more similar than different.

[1] Exchange Members

Members who trade on the floor of an exchange can be classified into two major categories: commission brokers and locals. Commission brokers, or floor brokers, make trades on an independent basis as well as for other dealers holding seats on the exchange. When not trading for their own accounts, floor brokers receive instructions through the firms with which they are associated or for which they are acting. Orders are normally received by telephone and recorded and time stamped before they are executed. The floor broker might be instructed to execute the order at the current market price, at a specific price or price range, or at a specific time. A floor broker who trades for his personal account must ensure that customer orders are filled before executing his personal order at an equal or better price.

In contrast to commission brokers, locals trade for themselves. Locals can be position traders, day traders, scalpers, or spreaders. The scalper provides instant market liquidity for orders by buying from or selling to a broker wishing to execute a public order. During the day scalpers trade off the minimum fluctuations that occur during trading. At the end of the day, they hope to have a zero net position. Day traders are similar to scalpers in that they hold market position only during the day and wish to have a zero (flat) position at market close. Day traders hold their positions longer than scalpers. Position traders generally initiate and hold a position longer than one day. In contrast to day traders or scalpers, they have open positions at market close. The spreader trades futures across contract months or various futures within a single contract month. The spreader may hold a position over a day or close it at the end of the day.

[2] The Clearing Corporation

The integrity of futures is maintained through the clearing corporation. Clearing corporation membership is determined by financial and professional criteria established by the board of directors of an exchange. The clearinghouses have daily responsibilities to reconcile, clear, and issue all trades. In addition to determining margin requirements for all marked-to-market contracts, the corporation also adjusts open positions to settlement prices. Daily margin calls are made to clearing members whose balances reflect a debit. If a member fails to meet a margin call by 9:15 A.M. the following day, all open positions of the firm are assigned to other clearing members in a predetermined manner. If a member's position reflects a net gain, the additional credit balance is available for withdrawal that morning.

By acting as the intermediary for all trades and providing daily collection of profit and losses, the corporation ensures that a buyer (seller) who wishes to sell (purchase) his futures contract after purchasing (selling) it does not have to worry if the original seller (buyer) wishes to purchase it back. If a seller of a contract wishes to make delivery, the clearing corporation notifies the member with the oldest outstanding long position in that particular contract. The invoicing and payment procedures are conducted between the buyer and seller under the rules of the clearing corporation.

[3] Orders Frequently Used

For most individuals, trades are conducted through their representative futures commission merchants (FCMs). FCMs are individuals or entities engaged in soliciting and accepting orders from customers for the purchase or sale of futures contracts, and accepting money or property to purchase the contracts. An associated person is an FCM or his agent who acts in the capacity of soliciting and accepting customer orders.

A commodity trading adviser (CTA) is a person who advises (for profit) as to the value and trading of financial futures. Commodity pool operators are persons engaged in a business, such as an investment trust, that receives funds for the purpose of trading financial futures. For a futures order to be executed, the order must be processed through a floor broker or his offices.

[a] **Market Order.** The most frequently used order is market order, which instructs a floor broker to promptly execute an order at the most favorable price available.

[b] **Limit Order.** A buy limit order stipulates that the floor broker executes the order within the limit set by the customer. If it is a sell limit order, the broker cannot sell for an amount less than that stipulated. If the price is touched, it is not guaranteed that the order is executed. Commodity trading price moves are rapid and numerous brokers may have orders to fill at an identical level. The limit order, however, assures a client that he will not pay more or sell for less than a specified price.

[c] **Stop Orders.** Stop orders are executed differently than limit orders. A buy stop order is placed above the current market price and becomes a market order if the price is touched. A sell stop order is placed below the current market price.

[d] **Open Orders: Good Until Canceled.** Open orders—good until canceled—will continue to be placed in the pit until the order is executed or canceled by the customer.

[e] **Order Fulfillment.** Once a commodity futures order is entered by a customer, the broker must get the order to the trading floor of the appropriate exchange. In some cases a customer may be allowed to call directly to an order desk to ensure expeditious executions. When an order is received on the floor of an exchange, it is recorded and time stamped. A copy of the order is rushed into the pit and given to a floor broker for execution. A market order is filled immediately. Other orders are held by the pit broker for the appropriate execution. Until an order is canceled, the broker assumes responsibility for its proper execution. When the order has a price limit, the phone clerk or floor broker files it in his deck. Limit orders are filed by price. If the broker holds more than one order at the same price, the orders must be executed in the sequence received.

[4] Trading Activity

Efficient pricing in the futures markets is enhanced through the trading activities and competition of different buyers and sellers. Two principal measures of the ability of a market to accept orders are trading volume and open interest. Trading volume is the number of unit contract transactions during a period of time. The trading volume is given for only one side of the trade: A volume of 20,000 translates to 20,000 contracts bought and 20,000 contracts sold. Since for every buyer there must be a seller, the number of contracts bought must always equal the number of contracts sold. Open interest is the number of open contracts at a point in time.

An individual's gain or loss in the futures contract is not determined when the position is closed out but is settled daily. To ensure that an individual will meet any daily losses on futures positions, a customer must post margin before being allowed to trade. Margins on futures transactions can be thought of as security deposits or performance bonds. Futures margin requirements are set by the exchange at a level high enough to ensure the financial integrity of the clearing members and the market. Because either buyer or seller could lose money on any given day, both sides post margin. As the price changes, each side's account is marked to the market, that is, debited or credited to reflect the most recent settlement price. When the account goes below a prescribed maintenance level, additional margin must be deposited to maintain the position.

Additional margin (variation margin) can also be called for when the price volatility of a commodity warrants it. If gains on the spot position are costly to liquidate or if the value of the position being hedged is not highly correlated with the futures, the need to mark to market will be considered an important component of hedge management. Also, when an anticipated spot position is being hedged, the profits on the spot will not be available for margin requirements during the hedge period. In these circumstances, a "hedging reserve" is needed to cover losses that may or may not be accompanied by realized gains on the spot portfolio or asset. The size of this hedging reserve depends on the size of the futures position (which should be based on the correlations between the spot and futures prices), on the volatility of daily futures prices, and on the amount of liquid assets available to the hedgers as part of the normal operations.

10.06 REGULATION OF FUTURES TRADING

Financial futures contracts traded on U.S. commodity exchanges are regulated by exchange rules that have been approved by the Commodity Futures Trading Commission (CFTC).[2] Regulation of commodity futures was originally based on self-policing by the exchanges. The first federal oversight of commodity futures trading was initiated in 1922 with the Grain Futures Act. In 1936, the Commodity Exchange Act replaced the Grain Futures Act. The Commodity Exchange Act was subsequently amended as newly discovered needs arose. The increasing use of commodity markets and the problems surfacing in the 1972 Russian grain purchase led Congress in 1974 to drastically amend the 1936 Commodity Exchange Act. The 1974 amendments authorized the CFTC, which is responsible to Congress for the functions previously assigned to

---

[2] The CFTC *Annual Report* reviews current and anticipated regulatory procedures.

the Department of Agriculture in the Commodity Exchange Act. The Futures Trading Act of 1978 renewed the CFTC's regulatory authority for three years, and subsequent legislations passed in 1982 and 1986 renewed its authority for four years each. As of the end of fiscal year 1991, reauthorization bills were approved by the U.S. House of Representatives and the Senate for two years and five years, respectively.

The CFTC has regulatory authority over almost anything that is or can be the subject of a futures contract. As new product areas developed, a further distinction was necessary between the Securities and Exchange Commission (SEC) and the CFTC on areas of regulation. Under a 1981 agreement the CFTC regulates (1) all futures contracts; (2) broadly based stock and bond index futures; (3) options on futures contracts (including financial futures); and (4) options on foreign currencies trading on commodity markets. The SEC regulates (1) all options directly on securities (stock as well as bonds, bills, and stock indexes) and (2) options on foreign currencies trading on stock exchanges.

The principal concerns of the CFTC are the safeguarding of funds, the control of monopoly, and the prevention of price manipulation. A cursory view of the structure of the CFTC permits a better view of its regulatory directions and remedies. The CFTC's organizational chart is shown in Figure 10-7. The principal regulatory divisions of the CFTC include the Division of Enforcement, the Division of Economics and Education, the Division of Trading and Marketing, and the Office of the General Counsel.

The CFTC's Division of Enforcement is responsible for investigation and prosecution of violations of the Commodity Exchange Act and CFTC regulations. This division is divided into two sections, customer protection and market integrity. The customer protection section investigates and litigates alleged violations of the sale of regulated instruments to the investing public. The market integrity section investigates possible violations directly in the exchanges.

The Division of Economics and Education is responsible for the daily analysis of market conditions to ensure against price manipulation and exchange disruptions. This division is also in charge of review of new futures contracts as well as the periodic review of current contracts. In addition to the CFTC's own surveillance programs, the exchanges themselves are responsible for self-monitoring. The CFTC's Division of Trading and Markets determines how the exchanges themselves are meeting their market surveillance and enforcement responsibilities. In addition, this division is in charge of screening applicants and reviewing exchange applications for contract market designation. Also, the Division of Trading and Markets considers exchange requests to implement new or revised rules and drafts regulations governing the operations of contract months and the registration, surveillance, and auditing entities regulated by the CFTC.

Lastly, the Office of the General Counsel is the CFTC's chief legal adviser and litigation counsel. The Counsel's office acts as reviewer of all major regulatory, legislative, and administrative matters. The Counsel also acts as advocate for the CFTC with the cooperation of the Solicitor General before the U.S. Supreme Court and the U.S. Court of Appeals, and defends the CFTC against actions brought against it.

Among the CFTC's principal regulatory responsibilities are the following:

1. Designation of (licensing) exchanges as "contract markets."

2. Conduct of periodic rule enforcement reviews of exchanges.

FIGURE 10-7

Commodity Futures Trading Commission Organizational Chart

Source: Commodity Futures Trading Commission, Annual Report 1991

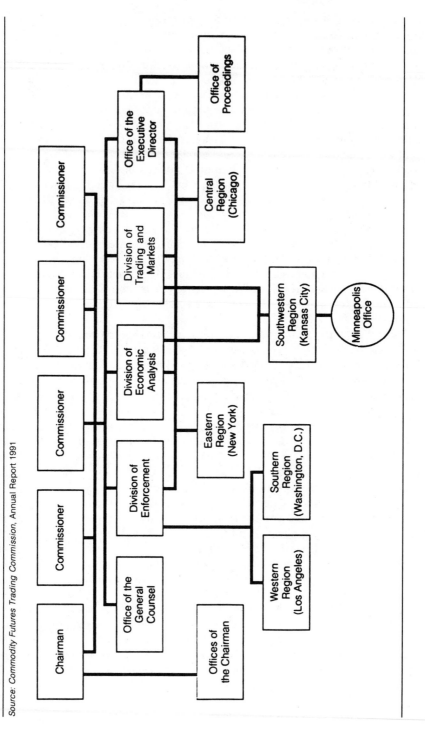

3. Review and approval of all significant exchange rules except those related to the level of futures margins.

4. Surveillance of all contracts to prevent price manipulation and market congestion.

5. Registration and regulation of commodity professionals (e.g., FCMs).

6. Enforcement of statutory prohibitions in administrative and civil judicial forums and referral of criminal violations to Department of Justice.

7. Review and application of antifraud initiatives.

This description of division directives covers only a few of the CFTC's major responsibilities. In addition to monitoring and correcting past grievances, the CFTC acts in concert with exchanges to prevent future problems from occurring. The CFTC is a regulator only in the last resort. The CFTC avoids direct government intervention as long as the exchanges themselves are attempting to deal effectively with a problem. Only when self-regulatory activities are incapable of solving the problem does the CFTC use its various powers such as suspending trading, imposing margins, or forcing a contract's liquidation.

To further enhance self-regulatory efforts, in September 1981 the CFTC registered the National Futures Association (NFA) as a self-regulatory organization. NFA activities should complement the CFTC's efforts to protect market participants with specific responsibility for registration, testing programs, and financial auditing. While governmental action has not drastically changed the present market structure, the futures industry is a dynamic one and subject to possible change in structure as well as new products.

10.07 PRICE DISCOVERY: FINANCIAL FUTURES

The two principal roles of financial futures are price discovery and risk management An understanding of these two roles, however, requires a brief review of financial futures pricing models upon which price discovery and risk management are based.

While for interest rate, equity futures, and exchange rates various models of price determination exist, the most common method is to link futures prices to current cash prices by the cost of "carrying" a deliverable security until delivery.

The cost-of-carry model can be stated as

$$FP_t = CP(1 + r)^t \tag{10.1}$$

or

Futures price $=$ cash price $+$ carrying costs

  where:

  FP_t = current price of a futures (currency) contract calling for delivery in t days

  CP = current price of a security deliverable into the futures contract

  r = rate of interest per day

  t = number of days until delivery

The futures price (FP) will equal the price of the deliverable security (CP) plus the cost of financing the purchase of that security for the t days until delivery at interest rate r. If the current price of the deliverable T-bill is 95.20, the daily interest rate is

0.8 percent, and there are three days to delivery, the T-bill's futures price should be no higher than 97.503 or

$$97.503 = 95.20 (1 + 0.008)^3$$

The FP_t will equal the price of the deliverable security CP plus the cost of financing the purchase of that security for t days until delivery at the daily interest rate r. From another perspective, the futures price equals the amount that would be accumulated if one delayed purchase of the T-bills until the delivery of the futures and deposited the price of the deliverable security (CP) in the bank to earn r interest for t days. (Both of these statements are true as long as the cost of financing equals the interest earned.)

Equation 10.1 should hold, since market participants with easy and cheap market access will quickly arbitrage away any significant deviations. Equation 10.1, however, may only be an approximation of the pricing relationship owing to various forms of risk. First, some traders are unable to lock in a carrying cost very cheaply for periods greater than a month. This means that whenever a futures contract is more than, say, a month from delivery, the trader cannot be sure exactly what the cash-carrying costs will be. A second risk of cash/futures arbitrage is the need to post immediately any losses on the futures position, mark-to-market. The interest rate component of the carrying cost reflected in futures prices is really a multiperiod rate that can vary on a day-to-day basis until the futures delivery date. The implied rate is related to the current actual overnight rate and a series of daily forward rates for each day until futures delivery. Traders can take long or short positions depending on their assessment of the forward daily repo rate structure as distinct from that implied by the "multiday" rate in the futures prices.

The futures valuation model in Equation 10.1 assumes that one is not required to account for the fact that the holder of the futures contract gives up any interest or dividend income or the cash security. If the link between futures and cash prices depends on the relative cost/benefit of holding futures as opposed to cash market instruments, a consideration of the relevant cash flows that would accrue to holders of a cash market position becomes essential. If the deliverable securities are expected to produce income (e.g., dividends or coupon interest) between the time of price determination and delivery, this income amount must be netted against any financing or other carrying charges to determine the theoretical futures price. Futures prices on T-notes, T-bonds, and stock indexes are influenced by the amount and timing of any coupon income or dividend receipts during the life of the future that would be received if one held the deliverable instruments. For futures on securities that have income cash flows, Equation 10.1 representing the pure carrying cost model of futures prices can be rewritten as

$$FP_t = CP(1 + r)^t - \sum_t \frac{I_t}{(1 + r)^t} \tag{10.2}$$

where:

I_t = the cash flows accruing to holders of the deliverable security

Thus, relative to Equation 10.1, the difference between the futures and cash price will be smaller than it would be in the absence of income.

If the underlying security pays a stream of income that is evenly distributed over the time remaining to futures delivery at constant monthly rate i, Equation 10.2 can be further simplified to

$$FP_t = CP(1 + r - i)^t \tag{10.3a}$$

$$FP_t \approx CP + [CP \times t \times (r - i)] \tag{10.3b}$$

Consider the situation in which the hedger buys the securities one month before delivery at the cash price and sells (delivers) them the following month at the futures price to earn a rate of return $f = [(FP - CP)/CP] + i$. In this case, the futures price should be such that the rate of return on the hedge (f) should equal the one-month rate of interest or carrying cost. Dividing Equation 10.3b by CP:

$$FP - CP = CP(r) - CP(i)$$

$$\frac{FP - CP}{CP} + i = r \tag{10.3c}$$

$$f = r$$

This is the expected result, because the fully hedged (risk-free) position would be expected to return the risk-free rate of interest r. Another way of looking at this same relationship is to see that the percentage difference between the future and the cash price will be equal to the difference between the carrying cost r and the income rate i, or

$$\frac{FP - CP}{CP} = r - i \tag{10.4}$$

From Equation 10.4, when repo rate or carrying cost exceeds the income return, futures prices will be above cash prices. Cash prices will be higher than futures prices when the repo rate is below the income rate. For foreign exchange rates this means when carrying costs (e.g., U.S. rates) exceed income return (foreign investment), futures prices are above today's cash price. For futures in intermediate and long-term bonds this means that when the yield curve is downward sloping, cash prices will be below futures prices and futures prices of near-term futures will be below those of long-term delivery futures. When the yield curve is upward sloping futures prices will be lower than cash prices and decrease as a function of the number of months to delivery for stock index futures. This means that cash price will be higher than futures price when the repo rate is below the dividend rate. When dividends yields are below these interest rates, as is normally the case, stock index futures tend to trade at a premium. Further modifications need to be made, however, before we have a complete model of financial futures pricing.[3] The reasons for apparent mispricing relate to special features of various contracts. For stock index futures these include the risk of uncertain dividends or delivery, cash settlement, and the transaction costs associated with arbi-

---

[3] As for other futures contracts, the general model given in Equation 10.4 does not offer an exact procedure for foreign currency futures prices. For foreign exchange futures the percentage difference between the futures (FC) and the spot price (SC) will be equal to the difference between the carry cost and the income rate only as an approximation. While the foreign exchange futures pricing model can be presented in various forms, it is most often presented as a variant of interest rate parity:

$$FC = [(1 + r_{us})/(1 + r_f)] \times SC$$

where r_{us} and r_f are U.S. and foreign interests rates respectively.

$$(FC - SC)/SC = [(1 + r_{us}) - (1 + r_f)]/(1 + r_f)$$

$$(FC - SC)/SC = (r_{us} - r_f)/(1 + r_f)$$

Since $(1 + r_f)$ approximates 1 for a small increment of time, $(FC - SC)/SC \approx r_{us} - r_f$. This is similar information to Equation 10.4.

trage. For T-bond and T-note futures contracts, significant differences between the actual futures prices and the theoretical futures prices can be in part attributed to various option contracts embedded in the futures contract. These have been identified as the quality option, or the option to choose the "cheapest" of a number of deliverable commodities and three timing options involving the choice of when to deliver (Gay and Manaster (1986)). Others have extended these theoretical and empirical studies further by addressing the impact of the quality and timing option when there are several deliverable assets (Boyle (1989)).[4]

[1] Quality Option

This option arises because any U.S. T-bond with at least 15 years remaining to call as of the first delivery date may be delivered into the T-bond contract. Correspondingly, any U.S. T-note with between 6.5 and 10 years to maturity as of first delivery date may be delivered into the T-note contract. As in other financial and nonfinancial futures contracts, the short will generally deliver the cheapest qualifying instrument based on the contract specifications. Whatever the basis for a particular holder of short position to deliver a particular cheapest-to-deliver (CTD), the ability to choose the deliverable bond is a valuable right. As such one would expect the short to be penalized based upon the perceived worth of this option. Therefore one would expect the Treasury futures to trade below the theoretical value obtained from the pricing model.

[2] Cost-Of-Carry Option

As noted previously, the short may deliver the CTD bond or note at any time during the delivery month. The ability to pick the delivery day gives rise to the right to earn positive carry ($i > r$) in a positively sloped yield curve scenario and to avoid a negative carry in a negatively sloped environment. While the value of this choice if exercised removes the opportunity of exercising other timing options (e.g., wild card and end-of-the-month), it may affect T-bond and T-note pricing.

[3] Wild-Card Option

This option arises out of the provision in the T-bond and T-note contracts that allow the short to announce his intention to deliver until 8:00 P.M. (central time) on any delivery day, even though futures stop trading at 2:00 P.M. Since the cash government markets continue to trade until at least after the close of the futures markets, the short may benefit from price movements in the spot market during this time period. The

---

[4] While it seems apparent that the value of these various options to the short position on an interest rate futures contract will result in the price being less than given in Equation 10.2, attempts to exactly model the value of these options have only begun. Estimates indicate the impact of the quality and timing options have been in the range of 2 percent to 6 percent (Kane and Marcus (1986), Boyle (1989)). However, estimates are based on assumptions as to the nature of the option model best describing the pricing process (Boyle (1989)), and other tests (Kane and Marcus (1986)) have been based primarily on simulation tests. The simulations that have been conducted have assumed basic interrelationships between futures contracts, the underlying deliverables, and option pricing theory.

value of this option depends on several factors (e.g., price risk) that affect the possible price changes in the spot market.

[4] End-Of-The-Month Option

Delivery may be made any business day during the delivery month, but the contract ceases trading at noon on the eighth-to-last business day of the delivery month. Deliveries based on a price fixed on one business day may be used to establish the delivery invoice priced up to seven business days later. Depending on the portfolio of bonds that the short has to deliver, value plays may exist.

10.08 INTRODUCTION TO HEDGING

Financial futures provide financial market risk reduction opportunities. Since financial futures markets permit individuals to buy or sell financial assets for future delivery at a price set today, financial futures contracts offer a means to hedge the risk of unexpected price changes. Individuals can hedge a foreign currency, equity, or fixed-income position by buying (selling) a futures contract to initiate a futures position. The futures position can be later closed out (offset) by selling (buying) the contract in the futures market rather than by taking delivery. The hedger benefits to the extent that the gain in the futures position offsets the loss in the existing or anticipated spot position.

For instance, a foreign currency, equity, or fixed-income hedge is usually caused by buying (selling) a futures contract to initiate a futures position and closing out (offsetting) the position at a later date by selling (buying) the contract in the futures market rather than taking delivery. The hedger benefits to the extent that a gain in the futures position offsets a loss in the spot position. An investor purchasing long-term bonds in March may wish to reduce the risk of interest rate variability by simultaneously selling a June T-bond futures contract. As shown in Figure 10-8, if interest rates rise during the holding period, the losses in the spot market are reduced by gains in the futures market.

Likewise, as shown in Figure 10-8, the foreign currency futures market offers similar protection against unanticipated currency price changes. An exporter selling goods to a German customer on March 1 but not expecting delivery (payment) until June may wish to sell a June deutsche mark futures contract. If the value of the market falls in the interim, the loss in the spot market is balanced by the gain in the futures position. It is important to note that opposite price movements result in similar final values. A fall in interest rates results in spot gains but losses in the futures market. A rise in foreign currency values results in gains on the spot market but losses in the futures market. Figure 10-8 also shows that the stock index futures market offers protection against anticipated equity portfolio price changes. In March a portfolio manager expecting to liquidate his portfolio later in the year may wish to reduce the risk of equity price variability by selling a specified number of June equity futures contracts. As illustrated in Figure 10-8, if equity prices fall during the holding period, the losses in the spot market are reduced by the gains in the futures market.

There is, of course, no guarantee that the spot market gain or loss will be offset by the futures trade. In practice, hedging does not insure against losses or assure

FIGURE 10-8

Sample Futures Transactions

	Date	Cash	Futures
Bond futures	March 1	Hold $1 million (face value) of T-bond 8.00%	Sell 10 June T-bond futures Face value of deliverable: 10 × $100,000 = $1 million
		Price 101.00	Price 95.16
		Total market value: $1,010,000	Total market value: $9,550,000
	June 1	Hold same T-bond Price 99.00 Market value: $990,000	Buy 10 June T-bond futures Price 93.16
			Total market value: $9,350,000
		Loss in value: $201,000	Gain: $120,000
		Net loss: 0	
Currency futures	March 1	Hold commitment to receive in June $5 million in deutsche marks at exchange rate DM0.5200/$ (DM9,615,384)	Sell 75 June deutsche mark futures (contract size DM 125,000) at price DM0.5210/$ Total value: $4,884,375
	June 1	Receive deutsche marks per commitment. Convert to dollar at exchange rate DM0.5160/$	Buy 95 June deutsche mark futures at price DM0.5164/$
		Total receipts: $4,961,732	Total value: $4,841,250
		Currency loss: $38,267	Gain: $43,125
		Net gain: $4,858	
Stock futures	March 1	Hold $10 million in equity portfolio	Sell 80 June (S&P) contracts Face value of futures position: 80 × $125,000 = $10,000,000 (S&P index value = 250)
		Total market value: $10 million	Total market value: $10 million
	June 1	Sell equity portfolio for $9 million	Buy 80 June S&P futures contracts at $115,000 (S&P index value = 230)
		Total market value: $9 million	Total market value: $9,200,000
		Loss in value: $1 million	Gain: $800,000
		Net loss: $200,000	

gains. The success of a hedge for risk reduction purposes depends on the degree to which the cash price follows the futures price. The difference between the cash and futures price is called the basis. As shown in Equation 10.4, basis (the difference between cash and futures price) should approximate cost of carry. When the cost of carry is positive (income on deliverable security exceeds financing cost), one can quote lower prices on futures contracts, and the basis is positive. In contrast, if financing costs are greater than income on deliverable security, one may quote higher prices on futures contracts to compensate for holding inventory, and the basis is negative. In fact, at delivery, the basis should approach zero, as arbitragers equate the price of the futures contract with the deliverable cash security and carry cost approaches zero.

FIGURES 10-9
Hedge Positions

		Cash		Futures			Basis	
Short hedge	Buy:	100	Sell:	97		+3	
	Sell:	93	Buy:	89		+4	(basis gets more positive)
		−7		+8	Change:	+1	
	Net:	+1					
Long hedge	Market price	100	Buy:	97		+3	
	Buy:	105	Sell:	103		+2	(basis gets less positive)
		−5		+6	Change:	−1	
	Net:	+1					

Understanding the basis is important because the purpose of hedging is often to create a futures position that offsets a cash market position so that the dollar price change is identical on each side of the hedge. If a hedger sells the futures short to protect against an unexpected decrease in prices, the hedge is referred to as a "short" hedge. If a hedger buys the futures to protect against an unexpected increase in prices, the hedge is referred to as a "long" hedge. The effect of basis changes on profitability can be seen more easily when the basis is viewed as either "strengthening" or "weakening."

When the basis is increasingly positive (or decreasingly negative), the basis is said to be strengthening. The futures price is falling more (rising less) than the cash price as illustrated in Figure 10-9, a short hedge is profitable if the basis strengthens. When the basis is increasingly negative (or decreasingly positive), the basis is said to be weakening. The futures price rises more (falls less) than the cash price. As illustrated in Figure 10-9, a long hedge is profitable if the basis weakens.

Changes in basis, therefore, can have either a desirable or an undesirable impact on a hedge. If the fluctuation in the basis is less than the price movement of cash, however, the variability of the change in value of the hedged position will be less than the variability of the unhedged cash position. The fluctuation in the basis is known as basis risk; that is, the risk that the futures and cash markets will not move in the same direction or magnitude.[5]

For hedging purposes, variation in the basis should be less than the price variation of the cash instrument. A hedge should reduce risk by substituting the smaller basis risk for the larger security price movement. Thus, for the hedge to be successful, the characteristics of the cash and futures instruments must be sufficiently similar to result in a high degree of positive correlation in the respective price changes.

Since price changes of the cash security and futures contract are often not of the same magnitude, the success of hedging strategy depends on determining the proper hedge ratio. The hedge ratio represents the face value of the futures contracts held relative to the face value of the cash position. The success of financial futures hedging also depends on the purpose for which the hedge is conducted. In the following sec-

---

[5] Basis risk is generally defined as change in direction or magnitude of the basis. Since both the cash price and futures contract price are expected to change, a better definition may be unexpected change in magnitude or direction of basis.

tions, various categories of hedging applications are reviewed, the hedging decision process is outlined, alternative models of hedge ratio determination and performance evaluation are illustrated, and problems in hedge ratio determination and performance are discussed.

10.09 HEDGING APPLICATIONS

Financial futures' hedging applications are almost unlimited. Financial futures enable financial institutions to hedge their interest rate exposure by bringing the interest rate sensitivity of their assets and liabilities into closer balance. Investment bankers use financial futures to hedge against the possibility of both an increase in prices on investments they plan to make and a decrease in prices on securities they plan to sell. Money managers and dealers use futures to hedge the value of the assets they hold. Futures markets permit nonfinancial firms to hedge against unexpected price rises on planned investments and against price declines on future borrowings.

Illustrating all the uses of financial futures is beyond the scope of this chapter. In the futures literature, however, hedging applications have been classified into several broad categories: (1) carrying charge hedging; (2) operational hedging; (3) anticipatory hedging; and (4) selective hedging.[6]

[1] Carrying Charge Hedge

A carrying charge hedge is used to obtain a return equal to the cost of carrying a cash position to delivery. As shown in the previous section on pricing in futures contracts for financial futures, financing costs and investment income are the principal determinants of carrying costs. Since the price of today's interest rate futures contract should equal the price of today's deliverable cash security plus any difference between the cost of borrowing and income on the deliverable security, as delivery approaches, spot and futures prices should tend to converge as cost-of-carry effects become insignificant, and arbitrage keeps prices of like financial assets in line. The profit of a perfectly hedged financial position held to delivery should thus cover the difference in financing or opportunity costs and investment income. For investors whose cost of financing is less than the rate implied in the carrying charge, an arbitrage profit may be possible.

[2] Operational Hedge

Operational hedges involve the use of futures to better manage the operational aspects of a firm's daily business transactions. For instance, a bank manager may wish to

---

[6] Many applications for financial futures, however, do not fit neatly into any of the previous hedging categories. For instance, operational and anticipatory hedges can be a selective form. In either case, a portion of the hedged cash position can be exposed as an alternative, the different types of hedging categories may more generally be classified as (1) cash hedge and (2) the anticipatory hedge. The cash hedge involves the hedge of an existing position in the cash market. In contrast, the anticipatory hedge entails the hedge of a cash position that has not been taken but is expected to be taken in the future.

liquidate a loan portfolio within a day. The size of the loan portfolio, however, may prevent the bank manager from entering the spot market without immediate liquidity effect; market prices might be driven down. The manager may wish to manage this loan sale by selling interest rate futures and later, as conditions permit, selling off the spot loan position. The short futures position would be closed out as cash market trades are successfully implemented. If spot prices fall unexpectedly before spot market sales, the spot market loss could be offset by gains in the futures market.

[3] Anticipatory Hedge

An anticipatory hedge is the purchase or sale of a futures contract as a substitute for a transaction that is expected to be made in the future. The purpose of the anticipatory hedge is to take advantage of prices reflected in current spot and futures market prices. For instance, a bank officer plans to buy a bond in the near future but wishes to obtain the price reflected in today's spot market and futures market contract prices. The bank officer could buy a futures contract today. If the price of the bond rises unexpectedly in the interim, the opportunity loss of not purchasing the bond immediately in the spot market would be balanced by a gain in selling the futures contract. Of course, a rise in interest rates would result in spot market gains but losses in the futures market.

[4] Selective Hedge

In a selective hedge, the extent to which the spot position is hedged depends on the hedger's forecast of future spot prices and the desired risk position. Financial theory holds that most security market participants trade off expected return for risk reduction. The financial future is just another asset available to produce a desired portfolio position with particular risk characteristics. The problem for the selective hedger does not differ drastically from a traditional portfolio choice problem. The hedge position held depends on expected hedging profits and risk. For instance, given a fixed or anticipated position in the spot market, a minimum risk hedge is seen as taking a position in the futures market with the object of minimizing the subjective price risk of holding the hedge position over a certain period. However, while a minimum risk hedge may not be desired, futures may still be used to obtain a maximum return/risk position.

In a selective hedge, it is not necessary that the hedge policy involves taking a continuous futures position. Stulz (1984) has shown that hedging positions are affected by various considerations. Stulz emphasizes the effect of agency theory, price uncertainty, and hedging costs on active hedging management. Stulz points out that alternative management compensation plans and capital structure formations will all affect a firm's hedging policy. It is also not necessary that a hedger attempt to minimize the risk of an established or anticipated spot position. Divergent expectations and alternative tradeable and nontradeable assets all affect a hedger's financial futures position (see Hill and Schneeweis (1982)). Howard and D'Antonio (1984) and others (Chang and Shanker (1986)) have also shown that given individual preferences, the optimal level of futures contracts held can vary greatly, depending on the individual's expectations and desired risk/return position.

10.10 HEDGE DECISION PROCESS AND HEDGE RATIO DETERMINATION

The decision to hedge requires a thorough understanding of the opportunities and risks involved in hedging with financial futures, as well as consideration of other risk reduction alternatives available; the hedger should carefully evaluate nonhedging strategies (e.g., interest rate swaps) before proceeding. Given all the alternative hedging applications, successful financial futures hedging requires a general framework and process for analyzing, implementing, and monitoring financial futures strategies. This process first requires that the objectives of the futures' strategy be set. For instance, the hedger must decide if the goal of the hedge is to minimize the total risk of a cash position or only a portion of a cash position's expected price variability.

Once the decision to hedge has been made, the hedger must decide on the type of futures contract purchased or sold to hedge the cash position. The type of futures contract used depends on the security being hedged, as well as the liquidity of the futures contract specified. The amount of futures purchased depends on various factors affecting the relative price movement of the cash position and the futures contract. The process of deciding on the face value of futures contracts to be held relative to the face value of the cash position is known as hedge ratio determination. Various methods of determining a proper hedge ratio have been suggested and are discussed in the next section. It is important to keep in mind, however, that even after a hedge position has been implemented, procedures must be established for monitoring the position. Decisions may have to be made about whether or not to continue the hedge or to change a trading strategy; thus, the hedging decision does not occur in a static environment. The dynamics of the financial markets require an established decision-making framework for reviewing and, if necessary, changing past decisions (see Figure 10-10).

As previously noted, once the decision to use futures markets to hedge an existing or anticipated asset position has been made, it is necessary to determine the required number of futures contracts to be purchased or sold to produce the desired hedged position. The principal (face) value of the futures contracts held relative to that of the principal value of fixed income, stock, or currency position is referred to as a hedge ratio. A particular hedge ratio that results in the maximum possible reduction in variability of the value of the hedged position is called the minimum-risk hedge ratio. Various methods exist for determining the number of futures contracts necessary to minimize the variability of a particular hedged position (see Figure 10-11). Since the principal value of the cash position is not always equal to the principal value of the futures contract, each hedge ratio model in Figure 10-11 must be adjusted by the relative face value of the cash position and the futures contract used to hedge the cash position. The number of futures contracts to be purchased or sold can be determined as follows:

$$\text{Number of contracts} = \frac{\text{face value of cash position}}{\text{face value of futures contract}} \times \text{hedge ratio} \qquad (10.5)$$

[1] Naive Hedging Model

In the naive model, the principal (face) value of the futures market position equals the principal value of cash market position. The hedge ratio is therefore equal to one. For instance, assume that in October an investor holds $1 million of 20-year 8.75

FIGURE 10-10

Models of Hedge Ratio Determination

Model	Hedge Ratio
Naive model	$HR = 1$
Conversion factor model/ Equivalent principal balance	$HR = $ conversion factor $HR = [1/(\text{equivalent principal balance} \div 100{,}000)]$
Basis point model	$HR = \dfrac{DVC_c}{(DVC_{cd}/CF_{cd})} \times B$

where: DVC_c = dollar value change per basis point for cash security

DVC_{cd} = dollar value change per basis point in cheapest-to-deliver security

CF_{cd} = conversion factor of cheapest-to-deliver security

B = regression of yield change of cash security on yield change of cheapest-to-deliver security

Regression model $\qquad HR = \text{cov}(\Delta P_c, \Delta P_f)/\text{var } \Delta P_f$

where: ΔP_c = change in price of cash security

ΔP_f = change in price of futures contract

Duration model $\qquad HR = \dfrac{R_i P_i D_i}{R_f P_f D_f}$

where: R_f = expected change in yield on the instrument underlying futures contracts f

R_i = expected change in yield on bond i

P_f = price agreed upon the futures contract f to be paid upon maturity of the futures contract for title to the instrument underlying f

P_i = price of bond i expected to prevail on
- the planned termination date of the hedge for an anticipatory hedge and
- today's date for a cash hedge

D_i = duration of bond i expected to prevail on
- the planned termination date of the hedge for an anticipatory hedge and
- today's date for a cash hedge

D_f = duration of the instrument underlying futures contract f expected to prevail at the delivery date

FIGURE 10-11

Example Using Naive Model

Date	Cash	Futures[a]
October 1	Hold $1 million 20-year 8.75% T-bonds priced at 94.8125 Yield: 9.25%	Sell 10 T-bond futures contracts at 86.875
October 31	Prices for bonds fall to 86.50 Yield: 10.29% Loss: $83,125	Buy 10 T-bond futures at 79.8125 Gain: $70,625

[a] Based on 8 percent 20-year bonds.

percent T-bonds priced at 94.8125 (yielding 9.25 percent). Since each T-bond futures contract has a face value of $100,000, the investor would hedge this position by selling 10 T-bond futures contracts (e.g., $1 million ÷ 100,000 = 10) at 86.875. If interest rates rise, the price of the futures contract and cash bonds will fall. As shown in Figure 10-12, by the end of October, cash bond prices have fallen to 86.50 (yielding 10.29 percent), producing a loss on inventory of $83,125. If the hedger offsets the short futures position, the cash market loss is covered by the $70,625 gain in the futures market.

However, the naive model may perform poorly, since it assumes a futures contract whose per-dollar price changes match those of the hedged cash instrument. The naive model ignores differences in the cash security and futures contract that may cause unequal price movements of the cash and futures prices. Interest rate futures, maturity, default risk, and nonparallel yield shifts may all result in differing cash security and futures contract price movements. For stock index futures, any differences in weighing between the cash position and the index underlying the futures contract may also result in unequal per-dollar price changes in the cash security and futures contract.

[2] Conversion Factor Model

To compensate for differences in the relative price movement of the cash security and futures contract, the hedge position can be weighted. One method of weighting is to adjust the futures position by the relative values of the cash security and futures contract. For T-bonds and T-notes, the hedge ratio can be derived from the "conversion factor of the deliverable security." For instance, for T-bonds, the conversion factor is the price at which (assuming a par value of one dollar) the delivered bond will yield 8 percent at its current time to maturity or, if callable, at its current time to call. Bonds with coupon rates higher (lower) than 8 percent will have a conversion factor greater (less) than one. The conversion factor for a $10\frac{3}{8}$ percent bond is 1.24 (see Figures 10-4 and 10-5 for a list of conversion factors). The conversion factor of 1.24 implies that for equal yield changes, the $10\frac{3}{8}$ percent bond is 1.24 percent as volatile as the 8 percent bond. To properly weight a futures position, the conversion factor is multiplied by the face value of the cash security or portfolio divided by the contract size of the futures contract. In Figure 10-12, the number of contracts was rounded to 12 (e.g., $1 million ÷ $100,000 × 1.24 = 12.40).

FIGURE 10-12

Example Using Conversion Factor Model

Date	Cash	Futures[a]
May 30	Hold $1 million 10⅜% T-bonds at 100.3125 Market value: $1,003,125	Sell 12 December T-bond contracts at 79.718 Market value: $956,625
September 30	Sell $1 million 10⅜% T-bonds at 87.50 Market value: $875,000 Loss: $128,125	Buy 12 December T-bond contracts at 68.906 Market value: $826,875 Gain: $129,750

[a] Based on 8 percent 20-year bonds.

The conversion factor hedging model is designed for hedging corporate bonds, T-bonds, and T-notes. The conversion model assumes the spot and futures positions are equally sensitive to yield curve shifts despite any differences in coupons or maturities. The conversion factor model thus works best when hedging the cheapest-to-deliver security. For T-bonds and T-notes, the futures may tend to track an instrument different from that of the cash security. For T-bonds and T-notes, futures prices are based on a variable cheapest-to-deliver security.

Alternatives to the conversion factor method include techniques that attempt to more closely equalize the expected dollar change between the futures contract and the cash security being hedged for a given change in yield (e.g., basis point model, regression model, duration model, and yield forecast model).

[3] Basis Point Model

When the cash security and cheapest-to-deliver security differ (e.g., maturity, coupon, default risk), the minimum risk hedge ratio must perfectly adjust for relative price movement of the cash instrument to be hedged and the futures contract. In order to obtain estimates of relative price change to an equal change in yields, a hedger may simply use relative basis point value. A basis point value represents the dollar change in the value of a $100,000 face value security in response to a one basis point or 0.01 percent change in yield. However, in response to a change in economic information, the change in yield of the cash security may be greater or less than that implied by the futures contract. To match per-dollar price changes in the cash and futures market position, the relative basis point values are multiplied by the relative yield change volatility of the cash position and the futures contract. The hedge ratio is derived as follows:

$$HR = \frac{DVC_c}{DVC_f} \times B \tag{10.6}$$

> *where:*
> DVC_c = dollar value change per basis point of the cash item to be hedged
> DVC_f = dollar value change per basis point of the futures contract
> B = relative yield change volatility of cash to futures

where B is derived by regressing the changes in the yield of the cash security (ΔY_c) against changes in the yield implied in the futures contract (ΔY_f).

$$\Delta Y_c = \alpha + B\Delta Y_f \tag{10.7}$$

Changes in yields are used, since a hedge is intended to protect against changes in the value of a security.[7]

However, changes in the price of the futures contract reflect changes in the price of the cheapest-to-deliver security (DVC_{cd}) and the conversion factor (CF_{cd}) such that $DVC_f = DVC_{cd}/CF_{cd}$. In several basis point models, the dollar value change per basis point is therefore presented in terms of the cheapest-to-deliver security and its conversion factor:

$$HR = DVC_c \div \frac{DVC_{cd}}{CF_{cd}} \times B \tag{10.8}$$

where B is derived by regressing the changes in the yield of the cash security against changes in the yield of the cheapest to deliver.

For example, assume the basis point value of the cheapest-to-deliver T-bond is $61.35. The conversion value of the cheapest-to-deliver bond is 1.13. The basis point value of the T-bond cash security if $40.85. If the volatility of changes in the yield of the cash security against changes in the yield of the cheapest-to-deliver is 1.2, the estimated hedge ratio is 0.90 (40.85 ÷ (61.351/1.13) × 1.2). If the face value of the T-bond position is $1 million the number of futures contracts purchased is 9 ($1 million ÷ $100,000 × 0.90 = 9).

The basis point model assumes that the yield change volatility of the cash security is stable with regard to the futures contract or the cheapest-to-deliver. The basis point value of a security, however, changes in response to changes in maturity and yield level. For instance, as yields increase (decrease), basis point values fall (rise). The hedger, therefore, must be willing to constantly adjust the hedge. To the degree that proper estimates of basis point sensitivity and yield sensitivity are made, the change in the dollar value of the futures position should offset the change in the dollar value of the cash position.

[4] Regression Model

In contrast to the basis point model, the regression hedging model attempts to provide directly an estimate of the change in the dollar value in relation to the cash security for a change in the dollar value of the futures contract. Using the basic principles of portfolio theory, if hedgers are concerned with expected return maximization at the minimum risk level, the optimal hedge would be the solution X_f^* to the problem below:

$$\min \text{var}(R_h) = \text{var}(R_{ct}) + X_f^2 \text{var}(R_{ft}) + 2X_f \text{cov}(R_{ct}, R_{ft}) \tag{10.9}$$

$$\text{Subject to} \quad E(R_{ht}) = E(R_{ct}) + X_f E(R_{ft}) \tag{10.10}$$

---

[7] The use of yield levels instead of yield changes to obtain an estimate of yield volatility is susceptible to methodological problems. Two securities may have a high correlation using yield levels but a low correlation using yield changes.

where:

R_{ct}, R_{ft} = price change during period t of the cash security and futures contracts

R_{ht} = change in the value during period t of a portfolio invested in a fixed level of spot commodity and a futures contract in proportion X_f

$E(R_{ht})$ = target expected return on hedged portfolio h

X_f = the proportion of the portfolio held in futures contracts: X_f^* would equal the optimal hedge ratio with $X_f^* < 0$ representing a short position and $X_f^* > 0$ a long position in futures

In Equation 10.9, the proportion or position in the cash commodity X_c is fixed at 1.0 and, therefore, does not appear explicitly in the expression. For this portfolio, X_f^* can be found by setting the partial derivative of the portfolio variance with respect to X_f equal to 0 and solving for X_f^*.

$$\frac{\partial \, \text{var} \, (R_{ht})}{\partial X_f} = 2X_f \, \text{var}(R_f) + 2 \, \text{cov}(R_c, R_f) = 0 \tag{10.11}$$

$$X_f^* = -\frac{\text{cov}(R_c, R_f)}{\text{var}(R_f)} \tag{10.12}$$

The minimum risk hedge ratio (X_f^*) is equivalent to the negative of the slope coefficient of regression of cash price changes on futures contract price changes. The higher the correlation between cash and futures price changes the higher the expected effectiveness of the futures market for hedging purposes.

The implementation of this model requires a portfolio manager to regress time series data of historical price changes of the cash instrument to be hedged (ΔP_c) against the price changes of the futures contract (ΔP_f). The optimal hedge ratio (HR) is simply the slope coefficient:

$$\Delta P_{ct} = a + \text{HR}^* \, (\Delta P_{ft}) \tag{10.13}$$

For an HR = 0.90, a \$1 change in the value of the futures position results in a \$0.90 change in the cash security. If an individual holds a \$1 million face value position the AAA bonds, a \$900,000 principal position would be taken in the T-bond futures market. Since each T-bond futures contract has \$100,000 par value, this translates into nine T-bond contracts (e.g., \$1 million ÷ 100,000 × 0.9 = 9).

Likewise, if an individual holds a \$1 million position in a stock index futures market, for an HR = 0.90, a \$900,000 principal position (0.9 × \$1 million) would be taken in the stock index futures market. For stock index futures, the contract value depends on the level of the index. For example, if the S&P futures price is 166.90, the face value of the futures contract is \$83,400 (166.90 × \$500). This would translate into 11 S&P futures contracts (e.g., \$1 million ÷ \$83,400 × 0.9 = 11). The regression-based model, however, assumes that historical relationships between price changes of the cash security and price changes in the futures contract are stable. However, for fixed-income securities, price changes are a function of duration that changes through time. The following duration model attempts to explicitly account for these duration estimates.

[5] Duration Model

As in the previous hedge models, the goal of minimum risk hedge strategy is to choose a number of futures contracts such that the value changes in the futures position will offset the value changes in the cash position.

$$\Delta P_i + \Delta P_f HR = 0 \tag{10.14}$$

$$HR = \Delta P_i / \Delta P_f \tag{10.15}$$

Here ΔP_i and ΔP_f are, respectively, the change in value of the bond to be hedged and the futures contract. If interest rates change, the size of ΔP_i and ΔP_f depends on the sensitivity of the bond and the futures contracting elation to the change in interest rates. The challenge is to select the number of futures contracts to trade (HR) to balance out the different interest rate sensitivities of the two instruments. Duration provides a measure of the percentage change in the price of a security for a given change in yield to maturity.

$$\Delta P_i / P_i = - D_i R_i \tag{10.16}$$

where:

P = change in price of bond i
P_i = price of bond i
R_i = change in yield to maturity
D_i = duration of bond i

$$P_i = D_i (R_i) \times P_i \tag{10.17}$$
$$P_f = D_f (R_f) \times P_f$$

Such that $HR = \dfrac{D_i R_i P_i}{D_f R_f P_f}$ \hfill (10.18)

where:

R_f = expected change in yield on the instrument underlying futures contract f
R_i = expected change in yield on bond i
P_f = price agreed upon the futures contract f to be paid upon maturity of the futures contract for title to the instrument underlying P_f
P_i = price of bond i expected to prevail on (1) the planned termination date of the hedge for an anticipatory hedge and (2) today's date for cash hedge
D_i = duration of bond i expected to prevail on (1) the planned termination date of the hedge for an anticipatory hedge and (2) today's date for cash hedge
D_f = duration of the instrument underlying futures contract f at the delivery date

The duration of a 10 percent coupon T-bond with a 26-year maturity and 21 years to call yielding 12.6 percent (price = 79.93) is 8.247 years. The duration of the 8 percent coupon, 20-year T-bond yielding 12.9 percent (price = 67.00) underlying the futures contract is 8.31 years. Assume that the relative yield volatility of the two bonds is the same (e.g., $R_i = R_f$). Using this information, the HR for a cash hedge is

$$HR = \frac{(\$79.93)\,(9.24)}{(\$67.00)\,(8.31)} = 1.17$$

This means that 1.17 T-bond contracts should be traded for each $100,000 face value of the cash bond held. If the manager holds $1 million in bonds, he should sell approximately 11 T-bond futures contracts ($1 million ÷ 100,000 × 1.17).

The duration model makes some assumptions about the kind of interest rate changes that will occur. Different models exist for alternative forecasts of yield shifts. The model therefore requires certain assumptions on relative yield curve shifts. Moreover, duration theory itself has been criticized as not adequately measuring bond price movement. The duration model also requires certain forecasts of expected relative yield volatilities. Historical estimates may be used; however, the stability of past yield relationships is often questionable.[8]

[6] Yield Forecast Model

Since a minimum risk hedge ratio is one for which a spot price movement is matched with a corresponding equal futures price movement, a successful model must define the differential price movement between the hedged security and the specified futures contract. As an alternative to the conversion factor, basis point, regression, or duration-based models for obtaining a single minimum risk hedge ratio, a yield forecast model may be used to illustrate minimum risk hedge ratios at various possible yield levels for various yield changes (see Schneeweis, Hill, and Phillip (1983)). For a cheapest-to-deliver security and a given cost of financing, a forecasted futures price can be determined for each yield level of the cheapest-to-deliver security. In order to determine the proper hedge ratio, the yield change with the greatest probability is chosen, which determines the expected price change for the cash security and futures contract, and the expected cash spot price change is divided by the expected change in the price of the futures contract. This approach also permits the hedger to analyze the effect of alternative assumed interest rate movements. A similar model based on forecasted interest rates and expected dividend payments can be derived for stock index figures.

10.11 PERFORMANCE EFFECTIVENESS

Various models exist for the determination of futures performance. The proper model depends in part on the goal of the hedge, such as minimum risk or optimal return for a predefined level of risk. In a minimum risk hedge, the variability of the combined cash-futures position is substituted for the variability in the price of the cash security. Risk exposure is reduced to the extent that the variability of the combined cash-futures position is less than the variability of the cash position. For instance, the R^2 from Equation 10.13 measures the reduction in an existing portfolio's return variance that results from the use of the minimum risk hedge ratio over the period used to estimate the hedge ratio. In measuring hedging performance, it is also important to distinguish between expected and ex post hedging performance (see Bell and Krasker (1986)). Ex post data may be used to establish the actual percentage reduction in the variance of the cash security. However, at the time the hedge is constructed, cash and futures prices are already expected to change. An individual may wish to hedge only the

---

[8] Other definitions of duration exist besides the one described in this chapter. These alternative formulas differ in their assumptions as to the form of interest rate changes. More advanced interest rate models attempt to take into consideration not only the duration but the change in duration. (See Nawalkha et al. (1990).)

unexpected change in the cash price. In this case, the variance of the price change should be based not on the variability around today's actual price but on today's expected cash price at hedge termination. Finally, performance effectiveness has often concentrated solely on risk reduction. Since the equilibrium return of a minimum risk hedge is the risk-free rate, hedging effectiveness may be measured by both risk reduction and a hedged return equal to the risk-free rate (Lindahl (1991)).

In contrast to the minimum risk optimization, whose objective is to create a minimum risk position for the existing portfolio, the portfolio optimization framework focuses on obtaining the optimal number of futures contracts to be combined with either a fixed or variable cash position to create the portfolio with a risk/return trade-off superior to that of the existing fixed or variable cash position. The optimal futures position is the number of contracts that maximizes the return/risk trade-off for tangency portfolio given a risk-free rate (Chang and Shanker (1986) and Yau et al. (1992)).

10.12 PROBLEMS IN HEDGE RATIO DETERMINATION AND HEDGING EFFECTIVENESS MEASUREMENT

While the derivations of hedging models are fairly straightforward, any hedging plan must be concerned with the everyday process of determining the hedge ratio. Unfortunately, there are some practical problems with determining hedge ratios and performance measurements. The problem in hedge measurement, however, should not restrict a hedger from using financial futures. With an understanding of the problems involved in determining proper hedge ratios, a more successful hedging system may be established.

Several methodological problems exist in all the hedge ratio techniques. Hedge ratios are often given in odd-lot form. Adjustments to full contracts are necessary. Risk analysis often does not reflect the variation margin that must be posted during the hedge (see Hill, Schneeweis, and Mayerson (1983)). Variation margin is a unique characteristic of futures based on the fact that changes in contract values must be settled in cash. This means that losses resulting from a drop in a futures contract's value must be posted in cash to a variation margin account. The hedger must have the cash available to meet this requirement before engaging in hedging activity.

Estimates of hedging effectiveness are also affected by other factors. Hedging effectiveness has been found to be positively related to the liquidity of the futures market, the time to delivery, and the similarity of the asset being hedged and the asset underlying the futures contract. For instance, Figlewski (1984) shows that while stock index futures may provide excellent hedging opportunities for stock portfolios, investors must be careful in hedging individual stock. Likewise, Hill and Schneeweis (1985) have shown that for corporate bonds, a closer correlation exists between high-rated corporate bonds and government-based interest rates futures. Time to delivery will also affect hedging effectiveness. For most financial futures, contract months extend for two years. Futures contracts do not exist for hedgers who wish to offset a position for greater than two years. One solution to this may be to purchase a distant contract and roll over the futures contract as the new delivery month occurs.

In addition, the price variability of the futures contract may be affected by the time to maturity. As maturity approaches, the variability of price changes of the futures contract may increase. This increase in variability may be due to the greater volume of trade as a contract maturity approaches or to the effect of an increasing amount of new information (Anderson and Danthine (1983)). The hedger may wish to make adjustments to hedge ratio estimates to account for increases in variability. For instance, if price variability of futures increases as maturity approaches, the hedge ratio may be reduced to reflect the greater anticipated movement in the price of the futures contract.

The actual performance of a minimum-risk hedge depends in part on the model of hedge ratio determination. For instance, the conventional approach for stock futures is to regress historical cash market returns on futures market returns. The resulting slope coefficient is then used as the estimated optimal hedge ratio. Three problems exist with such an approach. First, additional information is available to hedgers (e.g., barrier effects) that may affect expected relevant price movements. For instance, the covariance matrix of cash and futures prices and therefore minimum-risk hedge ratio may not be constant over time. Alternative methods for adjusting the hedge ratio for changing volatility patterns (e.g., ARCH and GARCH models) may be considered (Meyers (1991); Cecchetti et al. (1988)). Even if the covariance matrix remains stable over the estimation and hedge period, the simplified minimum-risk hedge ratio format may misestimate the required number of futures contracts required over time if they fail to tail the hedge. "Tailing the hedge" refers to reducing the size of the futures hedge to take into account the impact of mark-to-market settlements and thereby require financing of cash outflows or reinvestment of cash inflows. Full discussion of the impact of tailing the hedge is beyond this chapter; readers are directed to Figlewski et al. (1991). Lastly, Castelino (1990) also shows that in determining the optimal minimum-risk hedge ratio, consideration must also be given to the expected timing of the uplift of the futures hedge.

Hedging involves other practical considerations. First, the cost and regulatory constraints in the use of futures market must be considered. Second, when in-house firm personnel are used, the cost of acquiring, training, and supervising a staff to allow an effective hedging operation must be recognized. Regulatory decision on the accounting reports may also affect hedging policy. Individual asset hedging (micro hedging) also may hide the fact that for an investor holding many assets, an individual asset may already be hedged. In those cases, hedging the overall risk position rather than an individual asset position may be required.

10.13 ARBITRAGE, SPECULATION, PROGRAM TRADING, AND PORTFOLIO INSURANCE

[1] Arbitrage and Speculation

Efficient pricing in the futures market is enhanced through the competitive trading activities of the different buyers and sellers in the market. Speculators are motivated by the potential profit from their correct forecasts of unanticipated price changes. Arbitragers are motivated by the profit potential resulting from immediate price distortions existing between the cash and futures markets as well as within the futures market.

The activities of speculators and arbitragers are considered necessary for the orderly functioning of the market. Investors and corporate managers who use the futures markets to transfer risk required individuals capable of taking risk. Speculators are willing to buy and sell futures based on their forecast of future spot prices. Speculation can be achieved by taking open positions or spreading. Spreading in financial futures relates to purchasing the same financial futures in different contract months, or different financial futures in the same or different contract months. Arbitrage involves the simultaneous buying and selling of the same asset or types of assets at different prices to assure a profit. Therefore, pure arbitrage is defined as a riskless position that requires zero net investment and generates positive profits. Arbitrage should ensure that similar assets in competing markets (e.g., cash-futures, cash-cash, or futures-futures) produce similar returns. Investors must be aware that like a perfect hedge, pure arbitrage opportunities are very rare. In pure arbitrage, prices must be available simultaneously in the two markets. In practice, arbitrage often refers to a low-risk trade rather than a riskless position. Given the zero net investment available to some market participants, arbitrage possibilities are quickly removed.

Both arbitrage and speculation are important to the fulfillment of the economic role of futures markets. The process of arbitrage between cash and futures markets and markets of different futures contracts ensures the price of futures converge to their economic value. Without efficient pricing, the futures markets would not serve the very important function of price discovery and information transfer.

Both arbitrage and speculation contribute to the market liquidity that is one of the major means through which futures markets fulfill the economic function of risk transfer. The demands for hedging are sporadic rather than continuous. In order for a hedging transaction of some size to be executed efficiently, a liquid futures market must stand ready continuously to absorb such a trade. Markets cannot rely on hedging volume for their viability because the chance that hedges on two opposite sides of the market will meet in the trading floor at the same time is extremely small. Speculators and arbitrageurs help keep the market functioning continuously with prices that do not depart significantly from their economic value and that give correct signals to those using the market as a continuous source of economic information.

[2] Program Trading

In order to trade lists of stocks simultaneously (often representing a stock index), program trading was introduced. Program trades are often, but not always, executed by means of electronic systems. Many pension funds and money managers use program trading techniques and stock index futures markets for execution cost savings and flexibility. Applications of stock index futures in program trading include managing index funds, moving funds across asset classes or among managers, handling the investment of large cash flows, and conducting stock index arbitrage.

[3] Portfolio Insurance

Portfolio insurance refers to an investment strategy that attempts to alter the payoff pattern of a portfolio of risky assets, such as stocks or bonds. Portfolio insurance helps to reduce or eliminate downside returns while still allowing for the potential for significant upside returns. The cost of a portfolio insurance strategy refers to the expected or realized underperformance of the strategy relative to the portfolio that is being protected.

Portfolio insurance strategies can be implemented by trading in the equity or index futures markets with the goal of creating a payoff pattern that mimics the changes in value of a put-protected portfolio often referred to as dynamic hedging. In dynamic hedging, as the market value of the portfolio rises in a rising stock market, the relative size of the portion held in cash is effectively reduced by buying stock index futures (or stocks in a program trade). As the market value falls, the relative size of the amount held in cash is effectively increased by selling stock index futures (or stocks in a program trade). All three of these futures related trading approaches, program trading, stock index arbitrage, and portfolio insurance, have been accused of causing or encouraging the crash of 1987.

10.14 MANAGED FUTURES IN ASSET MANAGEMENT

Investment managers have witnessed a rapid increase in investment alternatives. Given the cost and skills necessary to invest successfully in asset markets, many investors have opted to invest through various professionally managed investment products. The rise in managed futures (professionally managed investments in commodity and financial futures markets) has been especially dramatic. In 1991, over $20 billion was under management in managed futures in contrast to less than $500 million in 1980. Investment management is generally through CTAs who are registered with and regulated by the CFTC. Currently, there are over 2,500 registered CTAs registered with the CFTC and members of the NFA.

There are three primary methods of investment in professionally managed futures products: publicly traded commodity funds, private commodity pools, and individually managed commodity trading accounts. Publicly traded commodity funds and private commodity pools are organized as vehicles for pooling investments and involve the allocation of investment funds to at least one and, often, two to five CTAs. In addition, CTAs (professional traders who trade in one or a variety of commodity markets following technical, fundamental, or hybrid trading strategies) take individually managed accounts from investors. While initial minimum investments in public funds and commodity pools are often as small as $5,000, initial investment minimums for individually managed accounts are frequently $1 million or more. While some previous research (Elton et al. (1987)) has questioned the use of individual publicly traded commodity funds as stand-alone investments, recent research (Schneeweis et al. (1991)) has shown that managed futures may provide investment alternatives as stand-alone investments or as additions to stock and bond portfolios. In addition, research (Schneeweis et al. (1992)) has recently indicated that simple trading rules may further enhance managed futures return performance with little or no increase in risk.

10.15 INTERNATIONAL DIMENSIONS

[1] International Markets and Contracts

The list of international financial futures exchanges that trade financial futures outside the United States, presented in Figure 10-13, is indicative of the widening interest in futures contracts as a means of managing financial risk in different countries. The majority of these listed exchanges were established or started trading financial futures during the 1980s. While some of these futures exchanges and contracts have not been

FIGURE 10-13

Years of Establishment of Futures Exchanges Outside of the United States and Years Started Financial Futures

Exchange	Year Founded	Year Started Financial Futures
Belgian Futures and Options Exchange	1990	1990
Bolsa Mercadorias & Futuros (BM&F)	1991	1986[a]
DTB Deutsche Terminboerse (DTB)	1988	1990
Financiele Terminmarkt Amsterdam N.V. (FTA)	1987	1987
Finnish Options Market (FOM)	1987	1988
Guarantee Fund for Danish Options and Futures (FUTOP)	1987	1988
Hong Kong Futures Exchange (HKFE)	1976	1986
Irish Futures and Options Exchange (IFOE)	1989	1989
London International Financial Futures Exchange (LIFFE)	1982	1982
Manila International Futures Exchange (MIFE)	1984	1990
Marche a Terme International de France (MATIF)	1986	1986
Mercado de Opciones Financieros Espanol S.A. (MOFEX)	1989	1991
Mercado Espanol de Futuros Financieros S.A. (MEFF)	1989	1990
Montreal Exchange (ME)	1975	1984
New Zealand Futures and Options Exchange (NZFOE)	1985	1985
Osaka Securities Exchange (OSE)	1878	1987
Singapore International Monetary Exchange (SIMEX)	1983	1984
South African Futures Exchange (SAFEX)	1988	1991
Stockholm Options Market (SOM)	1985	1985
Swiss Options and Financial Futures Exchange (SOFFEX)	1986	1990
Sydney Futures Exchange (SFE)	1960	1979
Tokyo International Financial Futures Exchange (TIFFE)	1989	1989
Tokyo Stock Exchange (TSE)	1878	1985
Toronto Futures Exchange (TFE)	1984	1980[b]

[a] Trading under Bolsa de Mercadorias de Sao Paulo and Bolsa Mercantil & de Futuros before merger.
[b] Trading under Toronto Stock Exchange.

active, many are liquid enough to provide a viable means of hedging and risk management.

[2] Globalization of Futures Trading

Some of the contracts listed on the exchanges relate primarily to the country in which they are traded. Other contracts form part of a 24-hour trading cycle for certain financial futures contracts. For example, Figure 10-14 shows that Eurodollar futures are traded in three exchanges in three different time zones.

Investors and traders can trade essentially the same Eurodollar futures in Chicago (CME) from 7:20 A.M. to 2:00 P.M., in Singapore (SIMEX) from 6:30 P.M. to 2:20 A.M., and in London (LIFFE) from 2:30 A.M. to 10:00 A.M. the next day, all central daylight

FIGURE 10-14

Trading Hours of Eurodollar Futures Markets

Source: Hill, Schneeweis, and Yau, "International Trading/Non-Trading Time Effects on Risk Estimation in Futures Markets," Journal of Futures Markets. Copyright 1990. Reprinted by permission of John Wiley & Sons, Inc.

CME		SIMEX		LIFFE		
7:20 A.M.–2 P.M.		6:30 P.M.–2:20 A.M.		2:30 A.M.–10 A.M.		
Open CME	Close CME	Open SIMEX	Close SIMEX	Open LIFFE	Open U.S.	Close LIFFE
7:20 A.M.	2 P.M.	6:30 P.M.	2:20 A.M.	2:30 A.M.	7:20 A.M.	10 A.M.
Day T					Day T + 1	

savings time. Because of the competition from the Far East (SIMEX and Tokyo Stock Exchange), the CBT in April 1987 extended its trading hours of U.S. T-bond futures to include evenings from 6:00 to 9:30 P.M. central daylight savings time in order to bring the trading up during the daytime trading hours in the Pacific Rim countries. The extension of the CBT's trading hours was meant to increase trading from Japan when the Japanese financial institutions were allowed to trade futures on overseas exchanges. On September 17, 1987, CBT extended the trading hours to include Sunday nights.

Because of the extension of the trading session into evening hours, exchanges began trying to find efficient and technologically advanced systems to handle the after-hours trading. In September 1987, the CME announced the development of the Globex Exchange (GLOBEX) system with Reuters and was later joined by the CBT. The GLOBEX system is a worldwide order-matching system that began operation in 1992 and presently provides computerized matching of futures trades on U.S. T-note and bond futures, deutsche mark, yen, and deutsche mark–yen cross-currency futures when the CME and CBT themselves are not in session. In the future it is anticipated that additional contracts will be traded and additional exchanges will participate in GLOBEX.

[3] Studies of International Financial Futures Markets

While most financial research in the area of futures and options has focused on the U.S. markets, there is an increasing interest in the ability to transfer research results in U.S. markets to those existing in foreign markets. In general, research has shown that futures contracts for foreign countries provide similar risk/return management opportunities as U.S.-based financial futures contracts. For instance, for futures contracts based in Pacific Rim countries, Bailey (1989), Brenner et al. (1989), and Yau et al. (1990a) have studied SIMEX's Nikkei Stock Average futures, and Yau et al. (1990b) have examined the price relationship between the futures and cash on the Hang Seng Index traded on the Hong Kong Futures Exchange. For European futures markets, studies include Geman and Schneeweis' (1992) analysis of the French CAC40 futures contract, Geman et al.'s (1991) study of the French notional bond futures contract, and Stulz et al.'s (1990) examination of over-the-counter futures market for the Swiss Market Index. These studies showed that, as for U.S. futures contracts, foreign futures markets provide similar hedging and risk/return opportunities.

[4] Twenty-Four-Hour Trading

Researchers (Hill et al. (1990) and Geman et al. (1991)) have studied the impact of 24-hour trading and information transfer on financial futures contracts. Hill et al. (1990) tested the effect of trading and nontrading time on risk estimation on two of the most actively traded futures contracts in the international financial futures markets: U.S. T-bonds and Eurodollars. The results showed significantly different return variance for U.S. T-bond and Eurodollar contracts depending on the time and day and in which markets the futures contracts were traded. Moreover, the variance is greater during the U.S. trading hours, when information is released more often than in the nontrading hours. Savanayana et al. (1992) have documented that the U.S. T-bond futures return variance differs between days of information arrival and days with no information releases. Geman et al. (1991) have studied the trading and nontrading time variance of French government bond futures. The results of their study show a surprisingly different pattern of trading/nontrading variance than that of the U.S. securities documented by Hill et al. (1990). Geman et al. found that on average the reported variances of the French notional government bond futures contract during the French nontrading periods were often significantly greater than reported variances during trading time periods.

Geman et al. suggest that news released during the French nontrading time for the French notional bond futures contract (e.g., U.S. and Japan trading time) may be more volatile and have greater impact on the opening price of the French notional bond futures than news released during the trading time in the French futures markets. However, they also show that on days of French public information releases (money supply and trade balance figures), the variances of price changes for the French notional bond futures contract are similar in magnitude over trading time and nontrading time periods. Therefore, even when the local futures market is closed, the futures contract value in these markets is not protected against any adverse information from other markets. Simply put, previous studies have shown that the impact of 24-hour trading cannot be ignored by investors or researchers. Moreover, results from studies on the U.S. markets may not reflect situations in other international financial futures markets.

[5] Currency Futures in Risk Management

The introduction of exchange rate risk adds a different dimension to asset allocation in international asset management. Evaluation of the performance of international assets requires an analysis of the impact of currency exchange risk and return. In recent years, various studies have explored the use of foreign currency futures and forward rates in forecasting future spot exchange rates, in determining the time pattern of currency returns, and in measuring the performance of currency-hedged and unhedged international portfolios.

In measurement of exchange rate risk, previous studies have emphasized the importance of currency futures and forwards in obtaining minimum-risk positions (Hill and Schneeweis (1982), Solnik (1990)), in improving the risk/return characteristics of an established spot portfolio (Chang and Shanker (1986)), and in forming optimal portfolios in which the futures contract and the spot assets are considered simultaneously (Levy (1987)). Each of these studies is sound given its own perspective; however, each deals with risk and return trade-offs that are specific to a particular objective.

For instance, Hill and Schneeweis (1982) analyze the ability of futures contracts to minimize potential price risk associated with a given currency position devoid of expected return considerations. Solnik (1990) focuses on the use of currency forwards (futures) in reducing the total risk of the portfolio, incorporating risk of both domestic assets and currencies and their cross-correlations. Chang and Shanker (1986) take into account both return and risk characteristics of the futures contract in testing for the incremental improvement that a futures contract adds to the risk/return performance of a fixed-currency portfolio. In contrast, Levy (1981) views the use of currency futures as an alternative to spot assets in a multi-asset portfolio framework with variable futures and spot positions.

The minimum-risk hedge ratio can be adjusted to consider an objective other than minimizing the pure foreign-currency-denominated investment. Black (1989, 1990) has developed a universal hedging formula, consistent with the equilibrium capital asset pricing model, which indicates that the proportion of currency exposure that should be hedged depends on the expected excess (above risk-free) return on the world market portfolio and exchange rate volatility averaged across all investors and all countries. Based on recent historical data, Black's model indicates that the proportion hedged will range from 30 percent to 77 percent, depending on expected returns to the world market portfolio. In contrast, Adler and Prasad (1990) contend that there exists almost no possibility that a universal hedge ratio exists. Adler and Prasad maintain that optimal positions in foreign currencies depend on a careful assessment of each client's performance. For instance, investors may determine unique optimal currency positions during periods when short-term, conditional forward-risk premiums are not zero. For most circumstances, however, Perold and Shulman (1989) have concluded that currency hedging reduces exposure to exchange risk with no reduction in expected returns (e.g., expected changes in exchange rates are already built into the existing currency rate structure). They conclude that when currency hedging provides equal expected return with lower risk, there is a "free lunch." The evidence, however, is not conclusive. Other studies (Kritzman (1989); Froot and Thaler (1990)) have shown that the return/risk dominance of a currency hedge portfolio is time and transactions dependent. In short, the free lunch may have hidden costs.

Suggested Reading

Adler, M., and B. Prasad. "On Universal Currency Hedges." Working Paper, Center for the Study of Futures Markets, # 209 (Aug. 1990).

Anderson, R., and J. Danthine. "Time Pattern Hedging and the Volatility of Futures Prices." *Review of Economic Studies* (Apr. 1983), pp. 249–266.

Bell, D.E., and W.S. Krasker. "Estimating Hedge Ratios." *Financial Management* (Summer 1986), pp. 34–49.

Black, F. "The Pricing of Commodity Contracts." *Journal of Financial Economics* (Jan. 1976), pp. 167–179.

———. "Equilibrium Exchange Rate Hedging." *Journal of Finance* (July 1990), pp. 899–907.

Boyle, P. "The Quality Option and the Timing Option in Futures Contracts." *Journal of Finance* (Jan. 1989), pp. 101–114.

Brenner, M., M.G. Subrahmanyam, and J. Uno. "Arbitrage Opportunities in the Nikkei Spot and Futures Markets." *Journal of Financial Economics*, Vol. 23 (1989), pp. 363–383.

Castelino, M. "Minimum-Variance Hedging With Futures Revisted." *Journal of Portfolio Management*, Vol. 16(3) (1990), pp. 74–80.

Cecchetti, S.G., R.E. Cumby, and S. Figlewski. "Estimation of Optimal Futures Hedge." *Review of Economics and Statistics*, Vol. 70 (1988), pp. 623–630.

Chang, J., and L. Shanker. "Hedging Effectiveness of Currency Options and Currency Futures." *Journal of Futures Markets* (Summer 1986), pp. 289–305.

Commodity Futures Trading Commission, *Annual Report 1991*.

Elton, E.J., M.J. Gruber, and J.C. Rentzler. "Professionally Managed, Publicly Traded Commodity Funds." *Journal of Business*, (Apr. 1987), pp. 177–199.

Figlewski, S. "Hedging Performance and Basis Risk in Stock Index Futures." *Journal of Finance* (July 1984), pp. 657–669.

Figlewski, S., Y. Landskroner, and W. Silber. "Tailing the Hedge: Why and How." *Journal of Futures Markets* (Apr. 1991), pp. 201–212.

Froot, K., and R. Thaler. "Anomalies: Foreign Exchange." *Journal of Economic Perspectives*, Vol. 4 (Summer 1990), pp. 179–192.

Futures Magazine. *1992 Reference Guide to Futures and Options Markets* (Jan. 1992).

Gay, G.D., and S. Manaster. "Implicit Delivery Options and Optimal Delivery Strategies for Financial Futures Contracts." *Journal of Financial Economics* (May 1986).

Geman, H., and T. Schneeweis. "The French CAC40 Futures Contract in Risk/Return Management." Working paper, University of Massachusetts (1992).

Geman, H., U. Savanayana, and T. Schneeweis. "Trading/Non-trading Time Effect in French Futures Markets." In J. Ronin (ed.), *Accounting and Financial Globalization*. New York: Quorum, 1991.

Hill, J., and T. Schneeweis. "On the Estimation of Hedge Ratio for Corporate Bond Positions." In C.F. Lee (ed.), *Advances in Financial Planning and Forecasting*. Greenwich, Conn.: JAI Press, 1985.

———. "The Hedging Effectiveness of Foreign Currency Futures." *Journal of Financial Research* (Spring 1982), pp. 95–104.

Hill, J., T. Schneeweis, and B. Mayerson. "An Analysis of the Impact of Variation Margins in Hedging Fixed Income Securities." *Review of Research in Futures Markets*, Vol. 2 (1983), pp. 136–159.

Hill, J., T. Schneeweis, and J. Yau. "International Trading/Non-trading Time Effect on Risk Estimation in Futures Markets." *Journal of Futures Markets* (Aug. 1990), pp. 407–423.

Howard, C.T., and L.J. D'Antonio. "A Risk Return Measure of Hedging Effectiveness." *Journal of Financial and Quantitative Analysis* (Mar. 1984), pp. 101–112.

Kamara, A. "Issues in Futures Markets: A Survey." Center for the Study of Futures Markets, #30 (Mar. 1982).

Kane, A., and A. Marcus. "The Quality Option in the Treasury Bond Futures Market: An Empirical Assessment." *Journal of Futures Markets*, Vol. 6 (1986), pp. 115–119.

Kritzman, M. "Serial Dependence in Currency Returns: Investment Implications." *Journal of Portfolio Management* (Fall 1989), pp. 96–102.

Levy, H. "Optimal Portfolio of Foreign Currencies with Borrowing and Lending." *Journal of Money, Credit and Banking*, Vol. 13 (1981), pp. 325–341.

———. "Futures, Spots, Stocks and Bonds: Multi-Asset Portfolio Analysis." *Journal of Futures Markets* (Aug. 1987), pp. 383–395.

Lindahl, M. "Risk-Return Hedging Effectiveness for Stock Index Futures." *Journal of Futures Markets* (Aug. 1991), pp. 399–410.

Meyers, R. "Estimating Time-Varying Optimal Hedge Ratios on Futures Markets." *Journal of Futures Markets* (Feb. 1991), pp. 39–54.

Nawalkha, S., N. Lacey, and T. Schneeweis. "Closed-Form Solutions of Convexity and M-square." *Financial Analysts Journal* (Jan./Feb. 1990), pp. 75–77.

Perold, A.F., and E.C. Schulman. "The Free Lunch in Currency Hedging: Implications for Investment Policy and Performance Standards." *Financial Analysts Journal* (May/June 1988), pp. 45–50.

Savanayana, U., T. Schneeweis, and J. Yau. "Trading/Non-trading Time and Information Effects in US Treasury Bond Futures Markets." In S. Khoury (ed.), *Recent Developments in International Banking and Finance*. Oxford, U.K.: Blackwell, 1992.

Schwarz, E., J. Hill, and T. Schneeweis. *Financial Futures: Fundamentals, Strategies, and Applications*. Homewood, Ill.: Dow Jones-Irwin, 1986.

Schneeweis, T., J. Hill, and M. Philipp. "Hedge Ratio Determination Based on Bond Yield Forecasts." *Review of Research in Futures Markets*, Vol. 2, No. 3 (1983), pp. 338–349.

Schneeweis, T., U. Savayanana, and D. McCarthy. "Alternative Commodity Trading Vehicles: A Performance Analysis." *Journal of Futures Markets* (Aug. 1991), pp. 475–490.

———. "Multi-Manager Commodity Portfolios: A Risk/Return Analysis." In C. Epstein (ed.), *Managed Futures*. New York: John Wiley & Sons, Inc., 1992.

Solnik, B. "Optimal Currency Hedge Ratios: The Influence of the Interest Rate Differential." In S.G. Rhee and R.P. Chang (eds.), *Pacific-Basin Capital Markets Research*, Vol. I. Amsterdam, Netherlands: Elsevier Science Publishers B.V. (North-Holland), 1990.

Stulz, R.M. "Optimal Hedging Policies." *Journal of Financial and Quantitative Analysis* (June 1984), pp. 127–140.

Stulz, R., W. Wasserfallen, and T. Stocki. "Stock Index Futures in Switzerland: Pricing and Hedging Performance." *Review of Futures Markets*, Vol. 9 (1990), pp. 576–592.

Yau, J., J. Hill, and T. Schneeweis. "An Analysis of the Effectiveness of the Nikkei 225 Futures Contract in Risk-Return Management." *Global Finance Journal*, Vol. 1 (1990a), pp. 255–276.

Yau, J., U. Savanayana, and T. Schneeweis. "Alternative Performance Models in Interest Rate Futures." In B. Goss (ed.), *Rational Expectations and Efficiency in Futures Markets*. London and New York: Rutledge, 1992.

Yau, J., T. Schneeweis, and K. Yung. "The Behavior of Stock Index Futures Prices in Hong Kong: Before and After the Crash." In S.G. Rhee and R.P. Chang (eds.), *Pacific-Basin Capital Markets Research*, Vol. I. Amsterdam, Netherlands: Elsevier Science Publishers B.V. (North-Holland), 1990b.

Chapter 11

Auctions in Finance

Robert Hansen

11.01 INTRODUCTION

Many transactions in the financial world are accomplished via an auction process. Among the important financial auctions are the following:

- U.S. Treasury auctions of securities
- Auctions of companies, both through tender offers and through private sales
- Secondary market auctions for equity, debt, and other financial instruments and for commodities
- Dutch auctions for share repurchases and dividend and interest rate resets
- Letting of underwriting contracts
- Real estate transactions

Current events and economic trends are making the study of some of these auctions even more interesting and relevant. After the U.S. Department of the Treasury discovered that a major U.S. investment bank had violated certain bidding rules for the Treasury auctions, the debate over the efficiency of the entire Treasury auction process was rekindled. Also, auctions for companies are now very prevalent, and U.S. courts have come close to mandating auctions in certain hostile takeover situations. Questions have arisen in this area about the performance of auctions versus negotiated sales and about the overall way in which an auction of a company should be conducted. In addition, the distressed nature of real estate in the United States has made the auction the preferred method of sale for many transactions, thereby raising a whole host of questions: Will the auction method, once started, remain the dominant method of sale? Should real estate be sold in single pieces or in pools? What kind of auction (oral, sealed-bid, electronic, and so forth) should be used? The final current event driving the interest in auctions is the emergence of securities markets in many developing (or newly capitalistic) countries. All major existing securities markets use some auction variant as the trading mechanism, so questions of structure for the emerging markets must involve auctions.

This chapter introduces the theory of auctions and competitive bidding, surveys the major findings of this theory and its empirical tests, and discusses several specific applications in finance. As far as possible the discussion is nontechnical, but it should be noted at the outset that analysis of auctions and bidding is inherently very difficult. Anybody who has had to put in a sealed bid will probably agree that it is not an easy task to choose a bid (much less an optimal bid). The difficulty exists for at least two reasons. First, auctions have a strategic characteristic: What one bidder should do often depends on what other bidders are believed to be doing. Second, auctions are fraught with uncertainty; bidders usually do not know what other bidders are doing or even who else is bidding, and bidders sometimes do not even know for sure the value of the thing for which they are bidding. Auctions are therefore natural candidates for the application of game theory, and this can mean the use of some heavy mathematics.

It should also be noted that most auction research has been done on generic auctions by economists. Applications in finance are but a small part of a large and rapidly growing body of literature on auctions in economics. Much of what follows in this chapter will apply to a wide range of financial as well as nonfinancial auctions. Specific applications in finance will be taken up last.

11.02 BIDDING AND AUCTION THEORY

To analyze auctions, one best begins by addressing very simple questions, such as: Is something being bought or sold by the auction? What are the characteristics of the thing being sold? What are the rules of the auction being considered? These simple questions will naturally lead to more complex ones concerning valuations by bidders and the nature of bidders' information. These questions in turn lead into analysis of bidding strategy and auction performance (in terms of price), and finally full circle back to questions on the design of auction rules (from the point of view of the seller).

[1] Buying, Selling, or Both? One Item or Many?

Is the auction being considered one in which an item (or items) is being sold by one seller to many buyers or being purchased by one purchaser from many sellers, or is the auction two-sided in that items can be both bought and sold? The most common auction is probably the standard "seller's" auction, in which one seller offers one item for sale to several potential buyers. This is certainly the institution that has been studied the most and is the basis for much of the discussion that follows. It is easy, however, to use any results from analyzing the standard auction for the reverse auction, i.e., where a buyer solicits bids from sellers in order to make a purchase. In the standard auction, bids are positive amounts of money offered for the purchase of the item, and the auctioneer will sell the item to the bidder offering the highest bid. In the reverse auction, purchase auction bids represent amounts for which sellers are willing to sell an item or service; the auctioneer will purchase the item or service from the seller offering the lowest bid.[1] The analytical equivalence of these auctions can be seen by considering bids in a purchase auction to be negative amounts; the auctioneer therefore selects the highest bid just as in a selling auction (the highest bid is the lowest bid in absolute value terms), and the winning bidder purchases the right to sell something for the amount of the bid (which is negative, so it means that the bidder receives payment).

Multiple items for sale and two-sided auctions are also common in practice and in theory. The U.S. government, for example, frequently auctions large numbers of oil leases at a single point in time. Obvious questions for a multiple-object auction such as this concern the bundling of items into pools and the sequential or simultaneous nature of bidding. Government auctions of Treasury bills and notes represent another type of multiple-object auction. Open outcry securities markets represent yet another multiple-object auction, this time with the further twist of having both buying and selling occurring.

[2] Auction Rules

There are a variety of rules employed in any auction. The most important of the rules are those concerning actual price determination: How is the winning bidder chosen

---

[1] A common example for this reverse auction is the solicitation of bids from contractors by a municipal government for the building of a highway. In finance, a reverse auction occurs when a company solicits bids from underwriters for the distribution of the company's securities. In both cases, bids represent the amount that the "auctioneer" will have to pay, so the auctioneer will choose the lowest bid.

and what price will he or she pay? For convenience, the discussion will assume a standard selling auction with only one item.

One common set of price determination rules are those of the open outcry auction, also known as an oral or English auction. This is the common auction for antiques in the New England countryside and for artworks sold by Christie's or Sotheby's. The auctioneer solicits a first bid for the item; competing bidders are then free to offer higher amounts. The item is awarded to the highest bidder when nobody wants to top the current bid. The highest bidder then purchases the item for the amount of the bid plus any fees associated with the auction.

An interesting variant on the open outcry auction is the introduction of uncertainty over when the auction will end. In olden times, this was accomplished using a candle with a pin stuck into it; bidding stopped when the candle burned down far enough to allow the pin to drop.[2] Today, some corporate auctions seem almost like candle auctions in that it is not always clear that the auctioneer (a board of directors or its advisors) will allow additional bids after the bidding has gone on for some time.

Sealed-bid auctions, another common type of auction, can involve either first-price or second-price rules. In a first-price sealed-bid auction (sometimes also called a discriminatory auction), bidders submit sealed bids; the highest bidder wins the auction and pays the amount of the bid. In a second-price sealed-bid auction, bidders submit sealed bids and the highest bidder still wins, but now the high bidder pays the amount of the second-highest bid. Such second-price auctions are sometimes called Vickrey auctions or nondiscriminatory auctions. Variants of second-price auctions are used in finance.

Dutch auctions are the third common form of auction. Formal Dutch auctions are used primarily for flowers in Holland and tobacco in Canada, but Wall Street has adopted a variant of the Dutch method for certain applications. In the formal Dutch auction, a clock-like mechanism is used to take increments off an initially high price. That is, the price starts high and then begins to drop mechanically, as a clock's hand points to successively lower prices. Each bidder has the ability to stop the clock at any time; the first one to do so wins the auction and pays the price that stopped the bidding.

Dutch auctions on Wall Street are not formal Dutch auctions but are instead more akin to second-price sealed-bid auctions for multiple objects. Generically, these auctions can be viewed as offers for sale of a number of securities.[3] Bidders submit bids specifying a price (or a yield) and a quantity of securities they are willing to buy at that price. The bids are ranked, and, using the bid quantities, a demand curve is constructed: The quantity demanded at the highest bid is the quantity associated with that bid only; the quantity demanded at the second-highest bid would be the quantity associated with that bid plus the quantity associated with the highest bid, and so on. The intersection of this demand curve with a vertical supply curve determines the market price. Any bidder who bid at least that much would get the securities sought and pay the clearing price. Figure 11-1 illustrates this process. The Treasury puts an additional twist on this type of auction by having bidders pay not the clearing price but the actual amount of their bids. The Treasury, in short, follows a price discrimina-

---

[2] Hence the phrase "to hear a pin drop."

[3] F.S. Fabozzi and I.M. Pollack, eds., *The Handbook of Fixed Income Securities* (Dow Jones-Irwin, 1983).

FIGURE 11-1

A Financial Dutch Auction

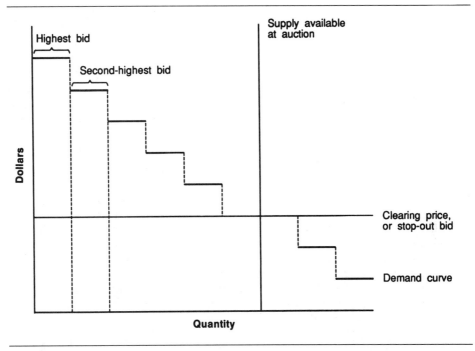

tory rule. The Treasury auctions, therefore, are more first-price auctions than second-price auctions.

Other rules of an auction that are important concern reserve prices, entry fees, means of payment, formation of bidding consortia, and disclosure of information to bidders. Reserve prices are often set by sellers; sometimes they are disclosed, and sometimes they are kept secret.[4] Entry fees may be set to limit the number of bidders viewing proprietory information or simply to collect revenue. Means of payment other than cash are often used; examples include royalty payments and the acceptance of securities issued by the purchaser.[5] Formation of bidding consortia occurs in oil lease auctions and securities auctions. Disclosure of information is an extremely important element of auction performance.[6] Sotheby's and Christie's typically provide experts'

---

[4] For an analysis of optimal entry fees in auctions, see J. Riley and W. Samuelson, "Optimal Auctions," *American Economic Review,* Vol. 71 (June 1981), pp. 381–392.

[5] For a discussion of why sellers can benefit from using royalties and other contingent payment schemes, see R.G. Hansen, "Auctions With Contingent Payments," *American Economic Review,* Vol. 75 (Sept. 1985a), pp. 862–865; R.G. Hansen, "Empirical Testing of Auction Theory," *American Economic Review,* Vol. 75 (May 1985b), pp. 156–159; R.G. Hansen, "A Theory for the Choice of Exchange Medium in Mergers and Acquisitions," *Journal of Business,* Vol. 60 (Jan. 1987), pp. 75–97.

[6] Information issues abound in auction theory. For a discussion of the key role of disclosure in auctions of companies, see R.G. Hansen, "Auctions of Companies," Tuck School Working Paper, 1991.

evaluations of items they offer for sale, as well as allowing bidders to view the items presale. When companies are auctioned, there is an extensive process of disclosing information to potential bidders, including allowing bidders to visit plants and speak to management.

One last issue worth considering under auction rules concerns the ability of a seller or auctioneer to commit to any of the stated rules. In the auction of RJR Nabisco, for example, there were several rounds of "best and final" bids.[7] There is obvious incentive for an auctioneer to say that sealed bids will be best and final and then to go to the second-highest bidder and see if that bidder is willing to bid above the highest bid. Just as obviously, if bidders fear opportunistic behavior like this, they will change their behavior accordingly (bidding lower in anticipation of later rounds). Since, under certain conditions, sealed bids do have better performance than oral auctions, it is in the interest of auctioneers to build reputations for honest dealing or in some other way establish auction rules that will not change during the auction.

[3] Valuations and Information

How do different bidders value the item for sale, and what do the bidders know about one another's values? These are critical characteristics that must be considered by both bidders (in figuring out their own bid) and the seller (in structuring the auction rules). Two polar cases have been analyzed in the literature and one synthesizing case has recently been introduced. The first polar case is known as the independent private values model, and the second is known as the common value model.[8]

With independent private values, each bidder is assumed to have an intrinsic, personal value that is placed on the item being sold and is known with certainty. Bidders generally have different private values, however, and bidders usually do not know one another's values. It is this uncertainty over others' values that makes bidding (at least with sealed bids) in such an auction a difficult task. How much can one bid below one's own value and still stand a good chance of winning the auction?

Independent private values assumptions probably characterize quite well certain auctions, e.g., those of antiques or famous paintings.[9] The assumptions do not work well in auctions where the item for sale has a similar value for whoever owns it. A Treasury note, for instance, will have the same value one month from now for all investors. Similarly, an oil lease will either have oil beneath it or not, and, at least in the first approximation, the value of that oil in the ground will be very similar to different oil companies.[10] Auctions like this are known as common value auctions. In

---

[7] Bryan Burrough and John Helyar, *Barbarians at the Gate: The Fall of RJR Nabisco* (New York: Harper & Row, 1990).

[8] The classic treatment of the independent private values models is Riley and Samuelson, *op. cit.,* while D.K. Reece, "Competitive Bidding for Off-Shore Petroleum Leases," *Bell Journal of Economics,* Vol. 9 (Autumn 1978), pp. 369–384, gives an excellent view of a classic common value auction. P.R. Milgrom and R.J. Weber, "A Theory of Auctions and Competitive Bidding," *Econometrica,* Vol. 50 (Sept. 1982), pp. 1089–1122, summarize both before generalizing to a combination model.

[9] This is because, in such auctions, it is safe to assume that the item's worth to someone is whatever that person feels it is worth. The possibility of resale imparts some degree of common value characteristics even to art auctions.

[10] Permitting oil companies to have different cost structures for extracting oil imparts some independent private values characteristics even to oil lease auctions.

such an auction, the item for sale is worth the same amount to all bidders (the common value). What makes the auction interesting is if bidders do not know what the true value is before they submit their bids. This uncertainty causes strategic problems in choosing a bid, just as in the independent private values auction.[11] It also introduces a new problem, that of the "winner's curse," discussed later.

One can easily see that the independent private values model and the common value model represent rather strong polar sets of assumptions. Many auctions would seem to involve both private values and common value aspects. For example, bidders for a company would probably have individual characteristics that make them value the same company differently, yet there are certainly some components of a company that create common value aspects as well. It is possible to analyze auctions under such conditions, but the model gets quite complex.[12]

[4] Analysis of Optimal Bidding

In formulating an optimal bid strategy, the first step is to select an objective. Typically, one assumes that bidders want to maximize expected profit; this is calculated as the probability of winning (Pr(win)) times the value of the item bought (v) minus the price paid (p):

$$\text{Expected profit} = \text{Pr(win)}(v - p) \tag{11.1}$$

Rather than expected profit, considerations of risk might make one maximize instead a utility function that incorporates risk aversion. Risk associated with winning or losing a bid, however, is probably diversifiable risk, so maximizing expected profit is likely to be the proper objective. In maximizing expected profit, of course, it is taken for granted that bidders do not care about winning per se.[13]

Bidding to maximize expected profit in either oral or second-price sealed-bid auctions is quite straightforward, at least for independent private values cases. For now, the analysis is restricted to independent private values auctions. The key differences from common value auctions are brought out later. In an oral auction, the best strategy is to stay in the auction—i.e., to remain an active bidder—until either the bidder wins the auction or the bid surpasses his or her private value. There is no reason to bid more than the minimum bid increment above the last-highest bid. Leaving the auction before the bid surpasses one's private value would be irrational, since the item might be bought at a price that could still yield a profit; similarly, it would be irrational to bid above one's private value, since that would only mean losing money if the auction was won. In the oral auction, then, the item will be sold to the bidder with the highest value, but the price will essentially be the amount of the second-highest value. From the seller's point of view, then, the oral auction yields an expected price equal to the

---

[11] That is, one bidder will not know what another bidder thinks the item is worth—i.e., what the other bidder's information is.

[12] For an example, refer to Milgrom and Weber, *op. cit.*

[13] This point often causes trouble for practitioners, who feel that occasionally an auction must be won. The proper treatment of such a situation is to include the cost of losing in v, the value of the item. Thus, if an oil refinery would be shut down without an auction's being won, the value for the lease being sold should reflect the cost savings if the refinery need not be shut down.

FIGURE 11-2

The Simple Analytics of an Optimal Bid

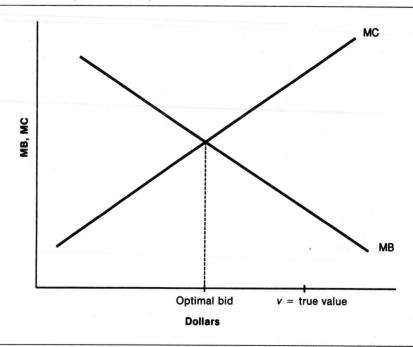

Optimal bid v = true value

Dollars

expected value of the second-highest private value. As it turns out, this is the same expected price the seller will receive under any auction form.

Turning to the second-price sealed-bid auction, one can see that Equation 11.1 is maximized by submitting a bid equal to one's private value. Bidding less than value would not increase profit because in a second-price auction one's own bid does not determine the price one pays. Bidding greater than value would also not pay because the additional auctions thereby won would have to entail a price paid in excess of value. In the second-price auction, therefore, the item is again won by the bidder with the highest value, who then will pay an amount equal to the second-highest value. In theory, then, the second-price sealed-bid auction's performance is identical to that of the oral auction.

Choosing a bid to maximize expected profit in a first-price sealed-bid auction is more difficult, as it involves a trade-off. A higher bid increases the probability of winning but decreases the profit if the auction is won. Similarly, bidding lower will reduce the chance of winning, but if the auction is won, the profit will be greater. Clearly then, an optimal bid weighs the marginal benefit of bidding higher (as reflected in the change of winning) against the marginal cost (as reflected in a higher price paid if the auction is won). Figure 11-2 illustrates the general determination of an optimal bid. The marginal benefit curve (MB) will probably be declining, since at higher bid levels a given increase in the bid is less likely to result in a significant increase in the win probability. Likewise, the marginal cost curve (MC) will be rising, since at higher bid levels the probability of winning is higher, so an increase in the bid makes it more likely that the bidder will end up paying more.[14]

The information needed to solve for an optimal bid is the probability of winning at different bid levels. This involves the other bidders in the auction. The bidder must first know or be reasonably able to guess who his or her competitors are. Then the bidder needs estimates of how those competitors will be bidding. Such estimates could be based on an evaluation of how the competitors will value the item for sale (putting oneself in the competitors' shoes, so to speak) and then estimating the competitors' bids based on the estimates of value (historical information on competitors' bids is useful here). An alternative approach can be followed when information is lacking: A bidder can simulate various values for competitors as well as their bid policies and choose the best response (in a statistical sense, of course). A last approach is to bid according to the equilibrium theory. This is optimal if all competitors use it as well, but it can also be quite robust in that it is near-optimal in many situations.

[5] Equilibrium in the First-Price Auction

Equilibrium is a concept that is commonly used in economic models to denote a situation in which no change should be expected. In auctions, equilibrium bidding strategies are bidding policies that, when followed by all bidders, would lead to each bidder's wanting to continue using his or her current bid policy. Thus, there is in an auction equilibrium no incentive for any bidder to adopt a different bid strategy.

In the oral auction it was argued that a bidder should remain in the auction until the price goes above his or her own value. This argument did not depend on what other bidders were doing. In terms of game theory, the strategy is a dominant strategy: No matter what other bidders do, the best strategy is to bid up to one's value or until the auction is won. All bidders will see the logic of this, and therefore the common strategy of bidding one's value is also an equilibrium strategy.

In a first-price sealed-bid auction, finding an equilibrium is not so easy. If all other bidders are bidding low, it would pay the remaining bidder to also bid low. Optimal bidding therefore depends on what others are doing.

An example of an equilibrium derivation should help to clarify the nature of equilibrium bidding in sealed-bid auctions, as well as giving some qualitative guidance on the size of an optimal bid. The example is kept as simple as possible. Suppose there are only two bidders and one item for sale. There is no reserve price. Each bidder's private value can be viewed as a draw from a uniform probability distribution over the interval [0, 100].[15] That is, bidder 1 knows his value and believes that bidder 2's value is something between 0 and 100, with all values in that range being equally

---

[14] Mathematically, this can be seen by taking the first derivative of Equation 11.1 with respect to the bid:

$$\frac{d\Pr(\text{win})}{db}(v - b) - \Pr(\text{win}) = 0 \tag{11.2}$$

Equation 11.2 is the first-order condition for an optimal bid. The first term is positive and represents the marginal benefit of bidding higher: the change in win probability times the profit upon winning. The second term is negative and represents the marginal cost of bidding one dollar higher: simply, the win probability.

[15] See Chapter 4 for a review of the uniform probability distribution.

likely. Bidder 2 similarly believes the same about bidder 1's value. These probabilistic assumptions define the uncertainty that each bidder has about his opponent's value.[16]

It would seem reasonable under the conditions described to believe that the winning bidder will be the one with the higher value. (This will be true if the two bidders use the same bid strategy, since then the bidder with the higher value will bid higher and win.) In this case, a bidder can view the probability of winning as being equal to the probability that his or her value is the higher of the two. Using the uniform probability distribution, Equation 11.1 then becomes

$$\text{Expected profit} = \frac{v}{100}(v - b) \tag{11.3}$$

Now comes the trick that is often used in solving auction equilibria. View b as a fixed function $b(v)$, and instead of thinking of the bidder as choosing a bid, think of the bidder as choosing a v to "report" and thereby implicitly defining his bid via $b(v)$. Denoting this "reported v" as v', Equation 11.3 becomes

$$\text{Expected profit} = \frac{v'}{100}(v - b(v')) \tag{11.4}$$

Now, we differentiate Equation 11.3 with respect to v' and solve for $b(v)$, the equilibrium bid function:

$$b(v) = \frac{v}{2} \tag{11.5}$$

In this auction, the equilibrium bid strategy is to bid one half of one's own private value. Of course, this explicit solution depends on the assumptions used, particularly that there are only two bidders. As the number of competing bidders increases, $b(v)$ gradually approaches v.

The most important observation from Equation 11.4, however, is that the expression $v/2$ gives the expected value of the other bidder's value, assuming that the other bidder's value is less than one's own. Generalizing this provides a general rule for equilibrium bidding in a sealed-bid auction: Bid an amount equal to the expected value of the second-highest value, assuming that your value is the highest. This rule has a certain intuitive appeal, as it simply tells a bidder to submit a bid that will just beat the (expected) competition.

One last note on this equilibrium is called for. If each bidder bids according to the rule given, it follows that the price in any auction is in essence the expected value of the second-highest private value. But this is exactly what the price in either the oral or second-price sealed-bid auction yields! This result is known as the revenue equivalence theorem: Under a fairly broad set of conditions, any auction mechanism yields the same expected price to the seller, and this price is simply the expected value of the second-highest private value.[17]

---

[16] Note this is a symmetric auction in that each bidder believes the same about one another. Asymmetric auctions have been studied; asymmetry could be relevant where one bidder is generally thought to have an advantage or a disadvantage. See P.R. McAfee and J. McMillan, "Auctions and Bidding," *Journal of Economic Literature,* Vol. XXV (June 1987), pp. 699–738.

[17] W. Vickrey, "Counterspeculation, Auctions, and Competitive Sealed Tenders," *Journal of Finance,* Vol. 16 (March. 1961), pp. 8–37, first developed the revenue equivalence theory. It was generalized by Riley and Samuelson, *op. cit.*

[6] Bidding in Common Value Auctions

Uncertainty over the item's value in common value auctions creates a very interesting bidding problem. Consider an auction where common value characteristics predominate, e.g., for the sale of an oil lease. Who is likely to be the highest bidder in such an auction? Common sense as well as statistical theory suggest that the highest bidder will be the one who has most overestimated the value of the item being sold! If this is the case, the winning bidder may suffer the "winner's curse" of paying more than the item is truly worth. The winner's curse—or, more accurately, bidders insufficiently recognizing the winner's curse—has been blamed for poor economic returns to bidders in oil lease, construction contract and corporate auctions.[18]

What does recognition of the winner's curse imply for optimal bidding? Qualitatively, it generally means that bids should be lowered beyond what they otherwise would be. More formally, bidders can still use some of the rules developed for independent private values if they make one very important substitution. Instead of basing bids on a known private value, bids must be based on a bidder's estimate of the item's common value. Most important, this estimate must be adjusted downward for the winner's curse problem: A bidder's estimate value must be an expected value conditional on his or her original estimate's being the highest of all of the bidder's estimates. This last adjustment can be quite significant. For example, if bidders' estimates are normally distributed, the highest of two estimates is expected to be 0.56 standard deviations above the true value of the item. With four bidders, the highest estimate will on average be one standard deviation above true value, and with eight bidders, 1.4 standard deviations above. With eight competitors, a bidder must reduce his initial value estimate by 1.4 standard deviations just to make the resulting conditional value estimate an unbiased estimate of true value if the bidder in fact wins the auction! This concept of the winner's curse and the qualitative advice it implies—bid low to make money—is one of the most important and practical revelations of auction theory.[19]

11.03 BIDDING AND AUCTIONS: RESULTS AND EXTENSIONS

[1] Information Disclosure

The preceding discussion suggests that auction prices will be lowered by uncertainty over the item's common, true value. This is true; the winner's curse phenomenon causes low bidding (if bidders are rational), and greater uncertainty exacerbates the

---

[18] See R. Roll, "The Hubris Hypothesis of Corporate Takeovers," *Journal of Business,* Vol. 59 (Apr. 1986), pp. 197–216, for an explanation of acquiring firms' poor share price performance that relies on the winner's curse. The classic article on winner's curse in oil lease auctions is E.C. Capen, R.V. Clapp, and W.M. Campbell, "Competitive Bidding in High-Risk Situations," *Journal of Petroleum Technology,* Vol. 23 (June 1971), pp. 641–653.

[19] The natural objection to this advice is that low bids never win auctions. This is somewhat true, so a rational bidder in an auction sometimes faces a dilemma: Bid low and do not win, or bid high enough to win but then suffer a winner's curse. This dilemma is strongest when competitors do not recognize the winner's curse phenomenon and therefore overbid. In such a case, publishing an article on optimal bidding in a practitioner's journal (as Capen, Clapp, and Campbell did) might be the best strategy.

winner's curse.[20] To offset the price-reducing effect of uncertainty, sellers should therefore have a policy of disclosing information on the item being sold. The large auction houses of Sotheby's and Christie's do this by providing expert appraisals; the U.S. government provides some data on oil leases and allows bidders to do further limited testing; and auctions of mortgages often allow bidders access to information on the mortgages' histories. All of these practices are consistent with the theoretical finding on information disclosure.

[2] Contingent Pricing

Another way for a seller to alleviate the effect of uncertainty in a common value context is to move away from all-cash bidding to some form of ex post or contingent payment scheme. The motivation for this idea arises from the observation that the winner's curse really arises because bidders must pay for all of the item up front, before they know its true value. If payment could both be delayed and made contingent on true value, some of the risk associated with the transaction could be eliminated. Payments' being contingent on value simply means that if value turns out to be low, total payments will be low, and vice versa. Methods for making price contingent on value include, among others, royalty payments, guarantees, future payments conditional on a company's earnings, or the acceptance of securities such as equity (whose value depends on the true value of the item being sold).

[3] First-Price Versus Second-Price Auctions Revisited

Previously, it was argued that a revenue equivalence theorem exists, so that the expected price under any form of auction is the same. This is strictly true only under conditions of independent private values. In a common value auction setting, or more generally in auctions that combine private and common value aspects, it turns out that second-price auctions produce a higher average price. Intuitively, the reason for this can be seen as follows: Common value aspects create a "linkage" between bidders' value estimates, so that when one bidder receives a high estimate it is likely that others do so too. With a first-price auction, this linkage does not have an impact on the price the winning bidder pays, but in the second-price auctions it does: If the winning bidder in a common value, second-price auction has a high value estimate, it is likely that the second-highest value estimate will also be high, and that means a higher price will be paid.

Thus, when the item for sale is suspected of having common value characteristics, the seller should adopt a second-price auction format.

[4] Reserve Prices

A common thread running through much of auction analysis is that a seller is hard put to get a price greater than the second-highest value, no matter what the auction

---

[20] Milgrom and Weber, *op. cit.*, prove that a policy of disclosing information raises the expected auction price. Of course, in any auction the price can rise or fall, depending on whether the specific information in that sale is positive or negative. It is the reduction of uncertainty overall, however, that induces bidders to bid higher on average.

form. Reserve prices can improve somewhat on this. Consider the case of an oral auction. By instituting a reserve price, a price below which the seller will refuse to sell, the seller creates the chance that it will be the reserve price that sets the price for the highest bidder, rather than the second-highest value. In this case, the seller will get a higher price than if it set a zero reserve. The cost, of course, is that there will be times when the seller's reserve exceeds any bidder's value, and therefore the seller retains the item. In balancing the benefits and costs, however, it is found that an optimal reserve price is always above the seller's own value for the item.

[5] Collusion in Auctions

Collusion by bidders is frequently a worry and sometimes a fact. Collusion has been suspected or proved in timber auctions, highway contracts, and, of course, the famous bid-rigging case involving electric turbines.[21]

There are several possible responses for a seller who suspects collusion among the bidders. First, it was pointed out long ago by Stigler[22] that a policy of announcing each bidder's bid after an auction aids a cartel, since it gives the cartel information on defection by any of its members. Thus, if a seller is to hold a sealed-bid auction, it should announce the winner but not the successful bid. Second, there is probably an advantage to a first-price sealed-bid auction if a cartel is present. One reason cartels fail is that their members might have incentive to defect and bid a price higher than they were supposed to. With an oral auction, such a defection will not pay, since other cartel members can detect the defection and bid the price high enough to eliminate any profits for the defector. With first-price sealed bids, however, a defector will not be detected until after he or she wins the auction (and if the seller does not disclose the winning bid, the defector may claim that the bid was low but won anyway). A first-price, sealed-bid auction can therefore strengthen the internal contradictions inherent in any cartel. Third, sellers should increase reserve prices above what they would otherwise set if they suspect a bidder's cartel.

[6] Multiple Objects for Sale

Often, an auction involves multiple objects for sale. Examples include Treasury securities, mortgages and real estate, and oil leases. Many of the previous results concerning single-object auctions continue to hold with multiple objects. Perhaps most important, in a multiple-object auction where bidders submit both a bid and a quantity desired at that price, if the independent private values framework applies, the revenue equivalence result still holds. If a common value framework holds, a winner's curse problem still exists and the second-price auctions still yield a higher average price than the first-price auctions.

Multiple-object auctions, however, introduce the question of bundling. A seller with

---

[21] The electrical equipment conspiracy of the 1950s involved 29 companies selling a variety of generators, transformers, and so forth. Markets were allocated among the conspirators, and complex bid-rigging schemes (some relying on phases of the moon!) were used to determine who would win each auction.

[22] See G.J. Stigler, "A Theory of Oligopoly," *Journal of Political Economics,* Vol. 72 (Feb. 1964), pp. 44–61.

n pieces of real estate to sell must decide whether to sell the *n* pieces as a package or to sell them one at a time. The answer depends on the number of bidders: With many bidders, the seller should unbundle, but with few bidders, the seller should bundle.

[7] Double Auctions

Many secondary securities markets are double auctions, with both buyers and sellers able to make bids for transactions. Double auctions are extremely difficult to model analytically; most of what is known about their performance, therefore, has arisen from experimental studies. Experimental work suggests that double oral auctions are very effective in quickly finding a true underlying equilibrium price (the underlying equilibrium price is determined by giving buyers and sellers demand and supply curves for the goods being traded). More work is progressing in the area of double auctions as the field known as market microstructure continues to develop.[23]

11.04 EMPIRICAL AND EXPERIMENTAL EVIDENCE

There is already a large body of experimental evidence on auction performance and a growing body of empirical auction evidence.[24] On the empirical side, U.S. Forest Service timber auctions have been extensively studied because of the Forest Service's experimentation with both oral and sealed-bid auctions. The statistical work on these auctions supports the revenue equivalence theorem: that the Forest Service received identical average prices from oral and sealed-bid auctions.[25]

A number of studies have documented effects associated with the winner's curse phenomenon. In one study, it was shown that individual bids on oil leases fell as more bidders entered the auction; this is consistent with bidders adjusting for a more severe winner's curse as more competitors appear.[26] Another study documents additional effects of a more severe winner's curse that occurs when one bidder has better information than the others. Data for this study came from bidding for drainage tracts in oil lease auctions.[27] A drainage tract is a piece of land that borders another tract that is currently producing oil. The owner of the producing tract can be expected to have superior information on the value of the tract currently for sale. This situation of asymmetric information should exacerbate the winner's curse problem for less-informed bidders and thereby result in a low expected price for the auction and low

---

[23] R.A. Schwartz, *Equity Markets: Structure, Trading, and Performance* (New York: Harper & Row, 1988), provides a good introduction and many references.

[24] C. Plott, "Industrial Organization Theory and Experimental Economics," *Journal of Economic Literature*, Vol. 20 (Dec. 1982), pp. 1485–1527; V.L. Smith, "Microeconomic Systems as an Experimental Science," *American Economic Review*, Vol. 72 (Dec. 1982), pp. 923–955, for general surveys on experimental auctions.

[25] See R.G. Hansen, "Sealed-Bid Versus Open Auctions: The Evidence," *Economic Inquiry*, Vol. 24 (Jan. 1986), pp. 125–142.

[26] O.W. Gilley and G.V. Karels, "The Competitive Effect in Bonus Bidding: New Evidence," *Bell Journal of Economics*, Vol. 12 (Autumn 1981), pp. 637–648.

[27] K. Hendricks and R.H. Porter, "An Empirical Study of an Auction With Asymmetric Information," *American Economic Review*, Vol. 78 (Dec. 1988), pp. 865–883.

expected profits for the less-informed bidders. The evidence on drainage tract sales confirms at least some of these predictions.

Much experimental (laboratory) work has been conducted on auctions. The most intriguing result from this work is that the winner's curse seems alive and well in common value auctions. That is, bidders in experimental common value auctions very often—indeed, on average—bid more than theory says they should and/or more than the item is worth. Although there are always problems inherent in laboratory economics experiments, these findings suggest very strongly that the winner's curse is a real phenomenon to which bidders have trouble adjusting.[28]

11.05 FURTHER DISCUSSION OF SPECIFIC FINANCE APPLICATIONS

[1] Treasury Auctions

The Treasury sells billions of dollars of bills and notes on a weekly basis.[29] The most significant characteristic of these auctions is that they are discriminatory, first-price sealed-bid auctions. Bidders submit sealed bids specifying both a bid (in yield terms) and a quantity of bills desired at that bid. This is a so-called competitive bid; noncompetitive bids can also be submitted. A noncompetitive bid specifies only a quantity; the price paid by noncompetitive bidders is a weighted average of the successful competitive bids. Using the competitive bids, the Treasury constructs a demand curve for the bills, as described previously. The highest successful bid (the highest since bids are in yield terms) is the bid for which the cumulative quantity desired at that bid or below equals the number of bills available for competitive bidders. Unlike a nondiscriminatory, second-price auction, however, each successful competitive bidder will pay the amount of his or her own bid (rather than the market-clearing bid).

Does the first-price nature of Treasury auctions increase the revenues of the Treasury? That is, are average prices higher with first-price bidding than they would be with a system of second-price bidding? This issue has been much debated.[30] The first and by now obvious point is that the answer is not clear-cut. If bids remained the same under the two systems, then clearly making each bidder pay his or her own bid would yield the Treasury more revenue. But bid strategy is not the same under the two systems. If second-price bidding were initiated, bids would probably increase, since every bidder could now expect that the price paid would be set not by his or her own bid but by someone else's. If bids increased enough, the second-price system could in fact increase revenues.

---

[28] See J.H. Kagel and D. Levin, "The Winner's Curse and Public Information in Common Value Auctions," *American Economic Review,* Vol. 76 (Dec. 1986), pp. 894–920, and R.G. Hansen and J.R. Lott Jr., "The Winner's Curse and Public Information in Common Value Auctions: Comment," *American Economic Review,* Vol. 81 (Mar. 1991), pp. 347–361.

[29] Stigum and Fabozzi, "U.S. Treasury Obligations," in Fabozzi and Pollack, *op. cit.,* provide an overview of Treasury auctions.

[30] See, e.g., M. Friedman, *A Program for Monetary Stability* (New York, 1960); A. Brimmer, "Price Determination in the United States Treasury Bill Market," *Review of Economics and Statistics* (May 1962); C.C. Baker, "Auctioning Coupon-Bearing Securities: A Review of Treasury Experience," in Yakov Amihud, ed., *Bidding and Auctioning for Procurement and Allocation* (New York: New York University Press, 1976), pp. 146–151.

This analysis of common value auctions suggests that second-price bidding would perform better. Treasury bill auctions certainly have a common value aspect to them, so that assumption does apply and bidders have to fear a winner's curse. In this case, making the price paid a function of all bids, as a second-price auction really does, increases the average price paid. The Treasury did experiment with different auction forms at one time, and the limited data available suggest that the second-price auction does perform marginally better.[31]

The more recent controversy over Treasury auctions concerns an ancillary rule that the Treasury applies concerning the maximum quantity of any one auction that a single bidder can win. The rule was violated in several auctions during the early 1990s.[32] The rule is ostensibly meant to prevent a monopoly in the secondary (resale) market from ensuing if one investment dealer were to purchase a large number of securities from any one auction. The cost of the rule is an obvious one: The only way one dealer can get a large quantity is by bidding high; if auction rules prohibit such activity, the average price must be lower. There is currently research going on to resolve whether the quantity-restriction rule is, on balance, beneficial.

[2] Auctions of Companies

Auctions are frequently involved in the sale of companies. In the discussion of auctions of companies, it is useful to distinguish between the sale of public companies through tender offers and the sale of private companies or divisions of public companies through controlled auctions.

There are several active areas of research concerning tender offers and the association bidding process, and some interesting findings have been presented. First, in looking at profits to bidding (acquiring) firms, it has been found that the stock price reaction of successful bidders is lower (indicating a lower profit associated with the acquisition) the more bidders there are.[33] This simply verifies the most basic characteristic of auction performance, that the price should increase with competition.

Perhaps a more interesting finding is that bidders' stock prices often react negatively to news of a successful acquisition bid (coupling this with the previous result, it follows that acquirers have strongly negative stock price reactions to acquisitions when many bidders were present).[34] Although there are several reasons why an acquiring firm's stock price might fall with an acquisition, there is a compelling explanation based on auction theory: Acquiring firms simply have not learned to adjust their valuations and bids for the winner's curse.

Another question on auctions in the takeover context concerns whether an auction should be required whenever a public company gets "in play." In *Revlon, Inc. v. MacAndrews & Forbes Holdings, Inc.*,[35] the court ruled that when it is inevitable that a public company will be sold, the board of directors' sale obligation is to obtain the highest possible price for the shareholders. This decision has led some lawyers and

---

[31] Baker, *op. cit.*

[32] B.J. Feder, "Salomon Violations Detailed," *New York Times* (Aug. 15, 1991), p. D1, col. 3.

[33] See G.A. Jarrell, J.A. Brickley, and J.M. Netter, "The Market for Corporate Control: The Empirical Evidence Since 1980," *Journal of Economic Perspectives*, Vol. 2 (Winter 1988), pp. 49–69.

[34] *Ibid.*

[35] Revlon, Inc. v. MacAndrews & Forbes Holdings, 506 A2d 173 (Del. 1986).

corporate advisers to believe that an auction must be held whenever a company is in play. Applying auction theory, Macey[36] argues that forcing auctions in all cases would likely be inefficient. His argument is basically as follows: Any auction process will necessitate considerable information collection and analysis by the bidders. This activity is necessary because of the uncertainty in value of the selling company and the bidders' desire to avoid a winner's curse. These costs, however, must be reflected in lower bids for the company. Furthermore, to the extent that all uncertainty is now removed by preauction analysis, bidders will keep their bids low, again to avoid a winner's curse (assuming that they behave rationally). Both of these effects, therefore, imply a cost to holding an auction. Some of this cost could be avoided if a negotiated sale were held, where the idea of a negotiated sale involves one-on-one discussions between the selling company and one acquiror. Such a negotiation could be more efficient because it avoids having several bidders go through information collection and analysis activities.[37] Also, in a negotiation with one acquiror, a target may be more amenable to releasing proprietary, competitive information on itself (e.g., information on costs, market shares, and prices). This additional information disclosure should reduce the sole bidder's uncertainty, thereby allowing a higher bid to be made for the company. Overall, then, negotiation might be better than an open auction for the selling shareholders.

A last line of research in tender offer auctions concerns bidder strategy. In contrast to the oral auction strategy discussed here, there might be a reason for a bidder in a takeover contest to make a large initial preemptive bid. (This contrasts with the typical oral auction strategy of bidding just a little above the last bid.) The reason for a preemptive bid is to signal to other potential bidders how much one is willing to pay for the selling company and thereby discourage others from even beginning to think about making a competing bid.[38] There may also be an advantage to bidders in making offers that involve some form of contingent pricing (e.g., offering stock instead of cash). Intuition for this result relies on the ability of contingent pricing to alleviate the effects of uncertainty and thereby increase the effective price offered.

Auctions of private companies are in some ways more intricate than tender offer auctions for public companies. The reason for this is that the owners of a private company are in a much better position to control an auction process and therefore do some things that would simply not be feasible in a tender offer context. As one example, auctions of private companies are frequently first-price, sealed-bid auctions. Sealed-bid auctions are difficult to implement in public company auctions because directors may have to consider a bid made after announcement of the highest sealed bid (shareholders would be sure to sue for breach of fiduciary duty if such a bid were turned down). More interesting yet, auctions of private companies often involve a two-stage process. In the first stage, bidders submit nonbinding "indications of interest" that qualify them for admission into a second round.[39] Although admission into the second

---

[36] J.R. Macey, "Auction Theory, MBOs and Property Rights in Corporate Assets," *Wake Forest Law Review,* Vol. 85 (1990).

[37] K.R. French and R.E. McCormick, "Sealed-Bids, Sunk Costs, and the Process of Competition," *Journal of Business,* Vol. 57 (Oct. 1984), pp. 417–441, show that the seller in effect bears the cost of information collection of all the bidders.

[38] M. Fishman, "A Theory of Preemptive Takeover Bidding," *Rand Journal of Economics,* Vol. 19 (Spring 1988), pp. 88–101, provides this explanation.

[39] R.G. Hansen, "Auctions of Companies," Tuck School Working Paper, 1991, describes the auction of private companies and provides a rationale for the process.

round is not solely on the basis of these initial bids, there is a strong belief that a higher bid is more likely to qualify for second-round admission. What keeps bidders in the first round from bidding very high, just to get into the second round (where additional sensitive information is disclosed)? One mechanism that could ensure good faith first-round bidding would be a policy of setting a second-round reserve price on the basis of the first-round prices. The higher the first-round bids, the higher would be the second-round reserve price. This effectively creates a cost to bidding higher in the first round, so first-round bidders have to balance the benefits of a higher bid (greater chance of second-round admission) with the costs (higher reserve price and, therefore, lower expected profits in the second round).

[3] Dutch Auction Share Repurchases

One way for a corporation to distribute cash to its shareholders is via a share repurchase, and one way to conduct a share repurchase is to use a Dutch auction.[40] A Dutch auction here is again the Wall Street version, which really means a second-price, sealed-bid auction. Shareholders are asked to submit bids for the price at which they would be willing to sell shares and the number of shares they are willing to sell. The company then constructs a supply curve and sets the purchase price at that bid for which the cumulative quantity supplied at that bid or below equals the amount the company wants to buy. All tenderers pay this price.

Auction theory suggests that Dutch auctions are an efficient means of buying back shares from stockholders, since the auction should select shareholders that value the shares the least. Empirical evidence on this matter is somewhat ambiguous. Although the share price of companies using a Dutch auction share repurchase increases upon announcement of the event, the share price increase associated with a fixed-price share repurchase is somewhat larger still.[41] This should probably not be interpreted as evidence against the relative efficiency of the Dutch auction method, since it is likely that share repurchases generally convey information to investors about the company's prospects, and this signal might vary with the repurchase method used.

[4] Competitive Bidding for Underwriting Contracts

There has been a long-standing controversy over the best method for a company to use in selecting an underwriter to distribute a public offering of securities.[42] The two most common methods of selection are competitive bidding (a first-price sealed-bid auction) or one-on-one negotiations with a single investment bank. A tremendous amount of effort has gone into comparing the net interest costs for these two methods. The best empirical research, as discussed in this chapter, presumes that competitive bidding will be a low-cost transaction method only under appropriate conditions. More specifically, competitive bidding is probably not the low-cost method when underwriters face relatively high uncertainty over the value of the securities they will be pur-

---

[40] D.B. Hausch, D.E. Logue, and J.K. Seward, "Dutch Auction Share Repurchases," Tuck School Working Paper, 1991, give a description and theoretical analysis of Dutch auction share repurchases.

[41] *Ibid.* Hausch, Logue, and Seward review the empirical evidence on this matter.

[42] The title of a paper by Fabozzi and West suggests the length of the controversy: "Negotiated Versus Competitive Underwritings of Utility Bonds: Just One More Time" (1981).

chasing. Negotiation with one underwriter is better under these circumstances, for the same reasons discussed previously. Empirical work done using this theory as a framework has found that issuing companies seem to select competitive bidding or negotiation on the basis of which method should yield lower cost given current conditions. The research has also found that competitive bidding is less likely to be chosen when financial markets are volatile.[43] This is understandable, since volatility probably implies significant uncertainty to underwriters over the value of the securities being purchased.

[5] Design of Secondary Trading Markets

As has already been noted, auctions are the basic method of exchange in most securities markets around the world. The exact forms of the different markets vary considerably, however. Some securities markets are periodic call markets, for which trading (an auction) occurs only at certain times during the day (and maybe only once per day). Other securities markets are continuous markets, with traders free to bid to buy or sell securities at any time. Some securities markets allow for monopolistic provision of dealer services (e.g., the New York Stock Exchange's specialist system) while others allow dealers to compete with one another in some open bidding format (e.g., the National Association of Securities Dealers Automated Quotation over-the-counter market in the United States). The degree of automation also differs greatly across markets, with some using electronic auction systems while others are still oral auctions.[44]

Although there has been a tremendous amount of research into these different market designs, there is uncertainty about their relative performance. At best, the research has pointed out certain trade-offs that are inherent in choosing one design over another. Such a trade-off can be illustrated by considering the question of monopoly versus competitive dealers. This application also fits nicely in the discussion here, since it uses ideas based on common value auctions and a resulting winner's curse.[45]

One cost of a monopoly dealer system is obvious: There will always be temptation for the monopolist to raise the price. Price, in this case, is the bid-ask spread for the security being traded. The bid-ask spread measures the cost of an immediate round-trip transaction and therefore the cost of what the dealer is providing: immediacy or liquidity.

What might be the offsetting benefit to this cost? To understand the potential benefit, recognize that securities are perfect examples of common value assets: The value of a financial asset is almost identical no matter who holds it. Of course, value is something that only becomes known with time; at any point in time, individuals only have estimates of value. Securities dealers operate under the same conditions, so dealers must set their bid and ask prices in the face of significant uncertainty. This uncertainty could be alleviated if a dealer could see the orders of final investors. That is, by seeing

---

[43] See R.L. Smith, "The Choice of Issuance Procedure and the Cost of Competitive and Negotiated Underwriting: An Examination of the Impact of Rule 50," *Journal of Finance*, Vol. XLII (July 1987), pp. 703–720.

[44] K.J. Cohen, S.F. Maier, R.A. Schwartz, and D.K. Whitcomb, *The Microstructure of Securities Markets* (Prentice-Hall, 1986), ch. 2, provide an excellent review of the organization of all the world's major securities exchanges.

[45] *Ibid.* See Chapters 5 and 8 for an elaboration of this discussion.

the demand and supply of final investors, especially in terms of customers' limit orders, a dealer can get a better idea of a security's market value and therefore set bid and ask prices more accurately. A more accurate setting of bid and ask prices will in turn reduce dealers' losses from mistakes and therefore permit a smaller bid-ask spread on average. The last link in this chain of analysis is to note that giving one dealer a monopoly franchise will force all of the orders to that dealer. Seeing the entire order flow in this way should, along the lines discussed previously, give dealers lower costs and therefore induce them to price their services lower.

As can be seen in this example, some of the concepts arising out of auction and bidding theory are quite general, so that they can be applied in a variety of market settings.

11.06 SUMMARY

Auctions have been used in a variety of cultures for thousands of years as a method of exchanging property. The popularity and longevity of the auction method demonstrate more strongly than anything else its relative transactional efficiency. Because there are transaction costs associated with using auctions, however, they should not always be the institution of choice. The theory and evidence discussed in this chapter show that it is possible for sellers to make a knowledgeable choice about when to use an auction and what kind of auction to use. Such information also serves as an important guide to bidders in selecting a rational bid strategy.

Suggested Reading

Cassady, Ralph, Jr. *Auctions and Auctioneering.* Berkeley, Cal.: University of California Press, 1967.

McAffee, P.R., and J. McMillan. "Auctions and Bidding." *Journal of Economic Literature,* Vol. XXV (June 1987), pp. 699–738.

Milgrom, P.R., and R.J. Weber. "A Theory of Auctions and Competitive Bidding." *Econometrica,* Vol. 50 (Sept. 1982), pp. 1089–1122.

Vickrey, W. "Counterspeculation, Auctions, and Competitive Sealed Tenders." *Journal of Finance,* Vol. 16 (Mar. 1961), pp. 8–37.

Index